ON THE CREATION OF THE COSMOS
ACCORDING TO MOSES

Philo of Alexandria
Commentary Series

General Editor
Gregory E. Sterling
Associate Editor
David T. Runia

Editorial Board
Harold W. Attridge
Ellen Birnbaum
John Dillon
David Hay
Annewies van den Hoek
Alan Mendelson
Thomas Tobin, S.J.
David Winston

Number 1

ON THE CREATION OF THE COSMOS
ACCORDING TO MOSES

David T. Runia

ON THE CREATION OF THE COSMOS ACCORDING TO MOSES

Introduction, Translation, and
Commentary by
David T. Runia

Society of Biblical Literature
Atlanta

ON THE CREATION OF THE COSMOS ACCORDING TO MOSES

Copyright © 2001 by Koninklijke Brill NV, Leiden,
The Netherlands

This edition published under license from Koninklijke Brill NV, Leiden, The Netherlands by the Society of Biblical Literature.

All rights reserved. No part of this work may be reproduced or transmitted in any form or by any means, electronic or mechanical, including photocopying and recording, or by any means of any information storage or retrieval system, except as may be expressly permitted by the 1976 Copyright Act or in writing from the Publisher. Requests for permission should be addressed in writing to the Rights and Permissions Department, Koninklijke Brill NV, Leiden, The Netherlands.

Library of Congress Cataloging-in-Publication Data

Philo, of Alexandria.
  [De opificio mundi. English]
  On the creation of the cosmos according to Moses / Philo of Alexandria ; introduction, translation and commentary by David T. Runia.
    p. cm. — (Philo of Alexandria commentary series ; v. 1)
  Includes bibliographical references and index.
  ISBN 1-58983-160-8 (paper bdg. : alk. paper)
  1. Creation—Early works to 1800. 2. Bible. O.T. Genesis I–III—Criticism, interpretation, etc.—Early works to 1800. I. Runia, David T. II. Title. III. Series.

BS651.P4712 2005
222'.1106—dc22

2005000234

Printed in the United States of America
on acid-free paper

This book is dedicated to

J. C. M. (BERTRAM) VAN WINDEN
MENTOR AND FRIEND

CONTENTS

General Introduction to the Philo of Alexandria Commentary Series
   by Gregory E. Sterling, General editor ix

Preface xv

Abbreviations xvii

Introduction 1
  1. The place of the treatise in the Philonic corpus 1
  2. The genre of the treatise 5
  3. Analysis of the treatise's contents 8
  4. The use of the Bible and the role of exegesis and exegetical
     traditions 10
  5. The main themes of the treatise 21
  6. Special theme: number symbolism and the arithmological
     tradition 25
  7. The intellectual *Sitz im Leben* (including sources) 29
  8. The *Nachleben* of the treatise 36
  9. The text of the treatise 38
  10. *Status quaestionis*: previous scholarship on the treatise 40
  11. Some notes on the method used in the translation 44
  12. Some notes on the method used in the commentary 45

Translation
   Philo of Alexandria, *On the creation of the cosmos according to Moses* 47
   Notes to the text and translation 94

Commentary 96
   Title of the Work 96
   Chapter 1: Introduction (§§1–6) 98
     Excursus 1: Law, cosmos and nature 106
     Excursus 2: An alterative interpretation of the seal image (§6) ... 108
   Chapter 2: A preliminary comment on God and the Cosmos
     (§§7-12) 110
     Excursus: Recent interpretations of Philo's argument 121
   Chapter 3: The scheme of six days (§§13-15a) 124
   Chapter 4: Day one: creation of the intelligible cosmos (§§15b–25) 132
     Excursus 1: Philo and the doctrine of ideas as God's thoughts 151
     Excursus 2: Philo on the origin of matter 152

Chapter 5: *In the beginning* does not mean creation in time
(§§26–28) 156
Chapter 6: The chief contents of the intelligible cosmos
(§§29–35) 163
  Excursus: Wolfson's and Winston's interpretation of §29 171
Chapter 7: Second day: creation of the firmament (§§36–37) 174
Chapter 8: Third day: creation of the earth (§§38–44) 179
Chapter 9: Fourth day: a puzzle and the significance of its number
(§§45–52) 187
Chapter 10: Fourth day: creation of the heavenly bodies (§§53–61) 197
  Excursus: The Hellenistic cosmic religion 207
Chapter 11: Fifth day: creation of the animal world (§§62–68) 211
Chapter 12: Why is the human being created "after God's image"?
(§§69–71) 222
Chapter 13: Why was the human being not created by God alone?
(§§72–76) 236
Chapter 14: Why was the human being created last of all?
(§§77–88) 245
Chapter 15: The seventh day: excursus on the Hebdomad
(§§89–128) 260
  Excursus 1: On John Lydus and the interpretation of §100 298
  Excursus 2: Further discussion of Philo's use of sources 301
  Excursus 3: A translation of Anatolius' chapter on the Hebdomad 304
Chapter 16: A summarizing reflection (§§129–130) 309
Chapter 17: The separation of the fresh from the salt water
(§§131–133) 314
Chapter 18: Creation of the first human being from the earth
(§§134–135) 321
Chapter 19: The excellence of the first human being (§§136–147) . 330
Chapter 20: The giving of names (§§148–150) 348
Chapter 21: Woman appears on the scene (§§151–152) 354
  Excursus: Philo's attitude towards women and sexuality 359
Chapter 22: Events in the garden of delights and their interpretation
(§§153–156) 362
Chapter 23: Interpretation of the snake (§§157–166) 373
Chapter 24: The consequences of wickedness (§§167–170a) 385
Chapter 25: Moses teaches five vital lessons (§§170b–172) 391

Bibliography 404
  1. Philo of Alexandria 404
  2. Other ancient texts 405
  3. Modern scholarly literature 407

Indices 424
  1. Index of biblical passages cited 424
  2. Index of Philonic texts cited 424
  3. Index of ancient texts cited 427
  4. Index of subjects and names 430
  5. Index of Greek terms 440

THE PHILO OF ALEXANDRIA COMMENTARY SERIES
GENERAL INTRODUCTION

GREGORY E. STERLING
GENERAL EDITOR

Philo of Alexandria (c. 20 B.C.E.– c. 50 C.E.) was a member of one of the most prominent families of the large and influential Jewish community in Alexandria. We know more about his brother and his family than we do about Philo. His brother, Julius Gaius Alexander, held a responsible governmental position (Josephus, *AJ* 18.159, 259; 19.276–77; 20.100) and became known to the emperor's family through Herodian intermediaries (Josephus, *AJ* 19.276–77). His *praenomen* and *nomen* suggest that the family was associated in some way with Julius Gaius Caesar. It may be that Caesar granted Roman citizenship to Alexander's grandfather for assistance during the Alexandrian War (48–47 B.C.E.). Alexander made the most of his position and became exceptionally wealthy (Josephus, *AJ* 20.100). Josephus reported that he covered nine of the temple doors in Jerusalem with gold and silver (*BJ* 5.201–05), an act of patronage that attests his immense resources as well as his commitment to Judaism. Alexander's standing is confirmed by the roles of his two sons. The archive of Nicanor suggests that Marcus Julius Alexander was active in the import-export business that moved goods from India and Arabia through Egypt to the West. He married Berenice, the daughter of Herod Agrippa I and later partner of the emperor Titus, but died prematurely c. 43 C.E. (Josephus, *AJ* 19.276–77). His brother had one of the most remarkable careers of any provincial in the first two centuries of the Roman Empire. Tiberius Julius Alexander moved through a series of lower posts until he held governorships in Judea, Syria, and Egypt. When he backed Vespasian in the Flavian's bid for the throne, his career quickly rose to its apex: he served as Titus' chief of staff during the First Jewish revolt in 66–70 C.E. (Josephus, *BJ* 5.45–46; 6.237) and as prefect of the praetrorian guard in Rome after the war (*CPJ* 418b). While his career strained his relationship with his native Judaism to the breaking point (Josephus, *AJ* 20.100; Philo, *Prov.* and *Anim.*), it attests the high standing of the family.

The most famous member of this remarkable family was paradoxically probably the least known in wider circles during his life. This is undoubtedly due to the contemplative nature of the life that he chose. His choice was not total. He may have had some civic function in the Jewish community. At least this would help to explain why the Alexandrian Jewish community selected him to lead the first Jewish delegation to Rome after the pogrom in Alexandria in 38 C.E., a delegation that probably included his brother and nephew of later fame (*Legat.* 182, 370; *Anim.* 54). The political arena was not, however, where his heart lay; he gave his heart to the life of the intellect (*Spec.* 3.1–6). He undoubtedly received a full education that included training in the gymnasium, the ephebate, and advanced lectures in philosophy. The final training was of enormous importance to his intellectual formation. While he knew and made use of different philosophical traditions such as Stoicism and Pythagorean arithmology, his basic orientation was Platonic. Middle Platonism (c. 80 B.C.E.– c. 220 C.E.) had become a vibrant intellectual movement in Alexandria in the first century B.C.E., especially in the work of Eudorus (*fl.* 25 B.C.E.). Philo became convinced that Plato and Moses understood reality in similar ways, although he was unequivocal about who saw it most clearly. His commitment to Judaism is evident in his training in the LXX: he knew it with the intimacy of one who lived with it from the cradle onwards. He also knew the works of some of his Jewish literary predecessors such as Aristobulus, Pseudo-Aristeas, and Ezekiel the tragedian. He was aware of a significant number of other Jewish exegetes to whom he alluded, but always anonymously (*Opif.* 26, 77, and *Migr.* 89–93). The most probable social setting for his literary work is a private school in which he offered instruction in much the same way that philosophers and physicians did.

One of the ways that he taught was through writing. His treatises constitute one of the largest corpora that has come down to us from antiquity. We know that he wrote more than seventy treatises: thirty-seven of these survive in Greek manuscripts and nine (as counted in the tradition) in a rather literal sixth century Armenian translation. We also have excerpts of another work in Greek and fragments of two more in Armenian. The lost treatises are known from references to them in the extant treatises, gaps in his analyses of the biblical texts in the commentary series, and *testimonia*.

The treatises fall into five major groups: three separate commentary series, the philosophical writings, and the apologetic writings.

The three commentary series are Philo's own literary creations; the philosophical and apologetic series are modern constructs that group conceptually similar but literarily independent treatises. Philo also wrote an introduction to the Torah in the form of a biography in the two volume *Life of Moses*. The work is similar in function to Porphyry's *Life of Plotinus* which introduces readers to the *Enneads*. Philo's biographical introduction was probably intended for any interested reader, whether Jewish or pagan.

The heart of the Philonic enterprise lay in the three commentary series. Each of these was an independent work with a distinct rationale and form. The most elementary of the three is the twelve book *Questions and Answers on Genesis and Exodus* that cover Gen 2:4–28:9 and Exod 6:2–30:10. As the title suggests, Philo used a question and answer format to write a running commentary on the biblical text. The questions are often formulaic, but demonstrate a close reading of the text. The answers typically introduce both literal and allegorical interpretations. Although earlier Jewish authors such as Demetrius (FF 2 and 5) and Aristobulus (F 2) used the question and answer device, they did not write zetematic works. The closest literary parallel to Philo's commentary series is the series of zetematic works which Plutarch composed. The pedagogical character of the format and the listing of multiple interpretations suggest that Philo's *Questions and Answers* were written for beginning students in his school who needed to learn the range of possible readings.

The Allegorical Commentary shares some features in common with the *Questions and Answers*, but is profoundly different. Like the *Questions and Answers* these treatises use the question and answer technique in a running commentary. Unlike the *Questions and Answers*, the format is no longer explicit but is incorporated in a more complex form of exegesis. Literal readings are largely ignored; instead the focus is on allegorical interpretations which are expanded through the introduction of secondary biblical texts (lemmata). The scope is also different: the Allegorical Commentary is confined to Genesis 2:1–41:24. While these expansions give the treatises a meandering feel, there is almost always a thematic unity that makes the treatise coherent. Philo was by no means the first Jewish author to use allegory: earlier Jewish writers such as Aristobulus and Pseudo-Aristeas had used allegorical interpretation; however, they did not write allegorical commentaries. Philo's allegorical commentaries are closer in form to commentaries in the philosophical tradition, e.g., the Platonic *Anonymous Theaetetus Commentary*, Plutarch's *On the Generation of the Soul in the Timaeus*, and Porphyry's *On the Cave of Nymphs*. Yet even here there are considerable differences; for example, Philo's treatises have more thematic unity than his pagan counterparts. If the *Questions and Answers* were for beginning students, the Allegorical Commentary was most likely composed for advanced students or other exegetes in the Jewish community. It certainly places much greater demands on the reader, as any modern reader who has worked through them can attest.

The third series, the Exposition of the Law, is different yet. It is not a running commentary, but a systematic exposition of the law of Moses. It focuses on literal readings and largely ignores allegorical possibilities. Its scope extends beyond Genesis and Exodus to include the entire Torah. Philo organized his understanding of the law in three parts (*Praem.* 1–3). The first part deals with creation, demonstrating the harmony between the cosmos and the law. The second part is the historical or biographical section that consists of biographies that show how the ancestors embodied the law before it was given to Moses. The third and most complex part is the legislative. Just as some later rabbis, Philo worked through the decalogue and then used each of the ten commandments as a heading to subsume the remaining legislation in the Torah. Unlike the later rabbis, he added a series of appendices under the headings of virtues. He brought the series to a conclusion in a treatise *On Rewards and Punishments* in direct imitation of the end of Deuteronomy. The series was probably intended for a Jewish audience that included but was not limited to the school.

If the three commentary series accentuate Philo's role within the Jewish community, the last two groups of his treatises reflect his efforts to relate to the larger world. The philosophical works use Greek sources and philosophical genres to address some of the major philosophical issues Philo and his students confronted. The apologetic works were probably written — for the most part — in connection with the events of 38–41 C.E. They were designed to assist Philo in his efforts to represent the Jewish community to the authorities.

This expansive corpus is the single most important source for our understanding of Second Temple Judaism in the diaspora. While some of the esoteric and philosophical aspects of his writings reflect a highly refined circle in Alexandria, the corpus as a whole preserves a wide range of exegetical and social traditions which enable us to reconstruct a number of beliefs and practices of Jews in the Roman empire. The difficulty that we face is the limited evidence from other Jewish communities.

This can be partially solved by expanding the comparisons to early Christian writings which were heavily indebted to Jewish traditions. As is the case with virtually all Second Temple Jewish texts composed in Greek, Philo's corpus was not preserved by Jews but by Christians who found his writings so irresistibly attractive that they gave him a *post mortem* conversion. In some *Catenae* he is actually called "Philo the bishop." A number of important early Christian authors are deeply indebted to him: Clement of Alexandria, Origen, Didymus, Gregory of Nyssa, and Ambrose in particular. While there is no solid evidence to show that New Testament authors knew his writings, they certainly knew some of the same exegetical traditions that he attests. His writings therefore serve both as a witness to some exegetical traditions of first century Christians and as a source for some second century and later Christians.

One of the factors that made Philo so attractive to Christians was the way that he combined Greek philosophy, especially Middle Platonism, with exegesis. The eclectic nature of his thought and the size of his corpus make his writings a particularly important source for our understanding of several Hellenistic philosophical traditions. The combination of Middle Platonism and Jewish exegesis also makes Philo important for the study of Gnosticism, especially for those scholars who argue that the second century Christian Gnostic systems had significant antecedents in Jewish circles.

It is remarkable that in spite of the obvious importance of these writings and their complexity, no series of commentaries has been devoted to them. The present series is designed to fill that void. Each commentary will offer an introduction, a fresh English translation, and a commentary proper. The commentary proper is organized into units/chapters on the basis of an analysis of the structure of each treatise. Each unit/chapter of the commentary will address the following concerns: the context and basic argument of the relevant section, detailed comments on the most important and difficult phrases, passages where Philo treats the same biblical text, the *Nachleben* of Philo's treatment, and suggestions for further reading. There will be some variation within the series to account for the differences in the genres of Philo's works; however, readers should be able to move from one part of the corpus to another with ease. We hope that in this way these commentaries will serve the needs of both Philonists who lack sustained analyses of individual treatises and those who work in other areas but consult Philo's works.

Most of the volumes in this series will concentrate on Philo's commentaries. It may seem strange to write and read a commentary on a commentary; however, it is possible to understand the second commentary to be an extended form of commentary on the biblical text as well. While Philo's understanding of the biblical text is quite different from our own, it was based on a careful reading of the text and a solid grasp of Greek philosophy. His commentaries permit us to understand how one of the most influential interpreters of the biblical text in antiquity read the text. The fact that his reading is so different from ours is in part the fascination of reading him. He challenges us to enter into a different world and to see the text from another perspective.

University of Notre Dame

PREFACE

The writing of a commentary on an ancient text in conformity with the exacting standards of modern scholarship is a not task to be undertaken lightly. The present work could not have been written without the indispensable assistance of a number of institutions and a larger number of persons.

My greatest debt has been to Greg Sterling (Notre Dame). Not only was it his idea to launch the Philo of Alexandria Commentary Series, but he has also carried out his duties as General Editor of the series with the utmost seriousness. Throughout a period of four years we had many conversations on how the task should be tackled and what the general method of the commentary should be. When the manuscript was finished he read it through entirely and made many valuable suggestions. At an earlier stage, in November 1998, parts of the commentary were read at the Annual meeting of the Philo of Alexandria Seminar in the somewhat surreal venue of Disneyworld, Orlando, Florida. I would like to thank all the members of the group for their constructive comments. In this context I would like to make special mention of Adam Kamesar (Hebrew Union College, Cincinnati) for the stimulating conversations we had on Philo and the problems associated with writing commentaries on his works.

In 1998 I was privileged to spend five months at the Netherlands Institute for Advanced Study in Wassenaar, as a member of a research group under the leadership of Michael Stone (Jerusalem) and Jos Weitenberg (Leiden). I would like to thank the Rector and the staff for providing me with ideal working conditions. My stay at the NIAS was additionally supported by a teaching replacement grant from the Netherlands Organization for Scientific Research (N.W.O.). In 1990 I spent an additional six months doing research in the Institut für Altertumswissenschaft at the University of Münster with the support of a stipendium from the Alexander von Humboldt Foundation. I would like express my warmest thanks to my host Matthias Baltes, who together with his research team helped me in every possible way. I am also grateful to Folker Siegert, Director of the Institutum Judaicum Delitzschianum of the same University, for his encouragement and assistance. None of this research would have been possible without the continuing support of my own home institution, the University of Leiden, which rewarded my long stint as Dean of the Faculty of Philosophy with two periods of research leave. I also thank the C. J. de Vogel Foundation for giving me leave from my teaching duties at the University of Utrecht during the spring of 1998.

In the final stages of preparing the book Hans van der Meij and Pim Rietbroek of the publishing house E.J. Brill in Leiden gave valuable advice on questions of style and layout. Two doctoral students at the University of Notre Dame, Lesley Baines and Brad Milunski, read through the manuscript and spotted numerous errors and inconsistencies. For the final appearance of the book, and for so many other forms of support, I am deeply indebted to my wife, Gonni Runia-Deenick of Philomatheis Desktop Publishing.

As early as 1980 my dear mentor and friend J. C. M. (Bertram) van Winden, then Professor of Later Greek literature at the University of Leiden, wanted me to write this book, though at the time he proposed I should go no further in my commentary than §35. Throughout the years we continued to discuss the work in all its various aspects. My translation and commentary have benefited enormously from his enviable knowledge of Philonic and Patristic Greek. His Dutch version of the work was constantly on my desk while I was working on both the translation and the commentary. In deep gratitude and with great affection I dedicate this book to him.

Leiden
September 1st 2001

ABBREVIATIONS

In general the abbreviations used for biblical and ancient texts and for modern scholarly literature follow the guidelines set out in *The SBL Handbook of Style*, Peabody Mass.: Hendrickson, 1999, and in *The Studia Philonica Annual*, volume XII, 2000, pages 235–241.

Abbreviations of Philonic treatises

Abr.	*De Abrahamo*
Aet.	*De aeternitate mundi*
Agr.	*De agricultura*
Anim.	*De animalibus*
Cher.	*De Cherubim*
Contempl.	*De vita contemplativa*
Conf.	*De confusione linguarum*
Congr.	*De congressu eruditionis gratia*
Decal.	*De Decalogo*
Deo	*De Deo*
Det.	*Quod deterius potiori insidiari soleat*
Deus	*Quod Deus sit immutabilis*
Ebr.	*De ebrietate*
Flacc.	*In Flaccum*
Fug.	*De fuga et inventione*
Gig.	*De gigantibus*
Her.	*Quis rerum divinarum heres sit*
Hypoth.	*Hypothetica*
Ios.	*De Iosepho*
Leg.	*Legum allegoriae*
Legat.	*Legatio ad Gaium*
Migr.	*De migratione Abrahami*
Mos.	*De vita Moysis*
Mut.	*De mutatione nominum*
Opif.	*De opificio mundi*
Plant.	*De plantatione*
Post.	*De posteritate Caini*
Praem.	*De praemiis et poenis, De exsecrationibus*
Prob.	*Quod omnis probus liber sit*
Prov.	*De Providentia*
QE	*Quaestiones et solutiones in Exodum*
QG	*Quaestiones et solutiones in Genesim*
Sacr.	*De sacrificiis Abelis et Caini*
Sobr.	*De sobrietate*
Somn.	*De somniis*
Spec.	*De specialibus legibus*
Virt.	*De virtutibus*

Other abbreviations

BAGD	*A Greek-English Lexicon of the New Testament and other Early Christian Literature*, edited by W. Bauer, W. F. Arndt, F. W. Gingrich, F. W. Danker, 1979².
BPS	*Biblia Patristica Supplément: Philon d'Alexandrie*. 1982.
CLG	M. Alexandre, *Le commencement du livre Genèse I-V: la version grecque de la Septante et sa réception*, 1988.
CM	T. H. Tobin, *The Creation of Man: Philo and the History of Interpretation*, 1983.
DG	H. Diels, *Doxographi Graeci*, 1879.
D-K	H. Diels and W. Kranz, *Die Fragmente der Vorsokratiker*, 1951⁶.
DPA	H. Dörrie and M. Baltes, *Der Platonismus in der Antike*, 1987– .
FM	R. Radice, "Commentario a *La creazione del mondo*", in C. Kraus Reggiani et al., *La filosofia mosaica*, 1987, 231-313.
G-G	H. L. Goodhart and E. R. Goodenough, "A General Bibliography of Philo Judaeus", in E. R. Goodenough, *The Politics of Philo Judaeus: Practice and Theory*, 1938, 125–321.
GLAJJ	M. Stern, *Greek and Latin Authors on Jews and Judaism*, 1974–84.
HWPh	*Historische Wörterbuch der Philosophie*, Darmstadt, 1974– .
L&S	A. A. Long and D. N. Sedley, *The Hellenistic Philosophers*, 1987.
LSJ	H. G. Liddell, R. Scott, H. S. Jones, edd. *A Greek-English Lexicon*, with Revised Supplement. Oxford 1996.
OTP	J. H. Charlesworth, ed. *The Old Testament Pseudepigrapha*, 1983–85.
PA	D. Winston, *Philo of Alexandria: The Contemplative Life, The Giants and Selections*, 1981.
PEC	D. T. Runia, *Philo in Early Christian Literature: a Survey*, 1993.
PAPM	R. Arnaldez, J. Pouilloux, C. Mondésert, edd., *Les œuvres de Philon d'Alexandrie*, 1961–92.
PCH	L. Cohn, I. Heinemann et al., *Philo von Alexandria: die Werke in deutscher Übersetzung*, 1909–64.
PCW	L. Cohn, P. Wendland, and S. Reiter, edd., *Philonis Alexandrini opera quae supersunt*, 1896-1915.
PG	Patrologia Graeca
PL	Patrologia Latina
PLCL	F. H. Colson, G. H. Whitaker (and R. Marcus), *Philo in Ten Volumes (and Two Supplementary Volumes)*, Loeb Classical Library, 1929–62.
PT	D. T. Runia, *Philo of Alexandria and the* Timaeus *of Plato*, 1986².
RAC	Reallexikon für Antike und Christentum
R-R	R. Radice and D. T. Runia, *Philo of Alexandria: an Annotated Bibliography 1937–1986*, 1988, 1992².
RRS	D. T. Runia, *Philo of Alexandria: an Annotated Bibliography 1987–1996*, 2000.
SC	Sources Chrétiennes
SPh	*Studia Philonica*
SPhA	*The Studia Philonica Annual*
SVF	J. von Arnim, ed. *Stoicorum veterum fragmenta*, 1905–24.
TB	J. Kugel, *Traditions of the Bible*, 1998.
TLG	Thesaurus Linguae Graecae

For fuller details on works thus abbreviated see the Bibliography.

INTRODUCTION

1. *The place of the treatise in the Philonic corpus*

The work which this translation and commentary seeks to elucidate, Philo of Alexandria's treatise *On the creation of the cosmos according to Moses*,[1] has the privilege of standing first in all editions and translations of Philo's works, with only a single recent exception. This practice was commenced in the *editio princeps* of A. Turnebus (1552) and has continued until the French edition of Arnaldez, Pouilloux and Mondésert (1961–92). Only in the Hebrew translation commenced in 1986 has it been discontinued.[2] Moreover, in all editions and translations except two it is followed by the writings of the so-called Allegorical Commentary, commencing with *Allegories of the Laws* and proceeding through to the two surviving books of *On dreams*. The exceptions here are the German translation commenced by L. Cohn in 1909 and the new Hebrew translation mentioned above.

On both accounts this privileged position of our treatise is incorrect. As the very title indicates, it is an exposition of the creation account of Moses. But who is Moses? Could Philo assume that all his readers would be sufficiently informed about the author of the work he is expounding? It is plain that from the outset of his treatise he assumes knowledge of the life and work of Moses. This he himself had provided in a special treatise devoted to this subject, *On the life of Moses* in two books. This work should be the first treatise in our editions and translations.[3] Thereafter *Opif.* could follow.

More important, however, is the relation of *Opif.* to the other exegetical works of Philo. Why, we may well ask, did L. Cohn, the

---

[1] On the title in its Greek and Latin versions see below Commentary, §0 Title of the Work. In what follows I use the conventional abbreviation *Opif.* In the Introduction I will refer to treatises in full by their (translated) English titles, but in abbreviated form to the customary abbreviations based on the Latin titles. Section numbers without further specification refer to passages in *Opif.*

[2] This work follows the order recommended by Goodenough 1962, 30–51, starting with the historical and apologetic treatises, followed by *Mos.*, and then *Opif.* and the Exposition of the Law. See Daniel-Nataf 1986 & 1991, and summaries at R–R 2601 & RRS 2602.

[3] This is demonstrated in Geljon 2000, 11–46, who gives a thorough review of the scholarly literature on the status of the work.

editor of the critical edition of Philo, place *Opif.* with the Allegorical commentary in the edition, but offer a different arrangement in the translation produced under his guidance? This apparent anomaly has to do with the structure and organization of the *corpus Philonicum*. It has long been recognized that all of Philo's numerous exegetical works except *Mos.* belong to three great series of works, each of which constitutes a commentary on the Pentateuch of Moses.[4] These have received the names Exposition of the Law, Allegorical Commentary, and *Questions and Answers on Genesis and Exodus* (only the third name is explicitly Philonic). There can be no doubt that *Opif.* is the opening treatise of the first-named series. Three kinds of evidence support this conclusion.[5]

(a) *Internal evidence.* In the introduction of the treatise *On Abraham* Philo writes (§2):

> The manner in which the creation account has been ordered we elucidated as best we could in the previous treatise (σύνταξις). But since it is necessary to examine the laws in the right sequence, let us postpone the treatment of the particular laws, which are like copies, and first examine those which are more general ...

A few pages later (§13), when discussing the number four, he says that the reason Moses honours it "has been stated in the previous treatise," i.e. at *Opif.* 47–52. There cannot be the slightest doubt, therefore, that *Opif.* and *Abr.* belong together in the sequence of a series of writings on the laws of Moses. That *Opif.* is the opening work of the series might be inferred from its opening words (§§1–3), which commence by speaking of Moses as a lawgiver and (by implication) of the importance of observing the Law. Confirmation of the sequence can be found in Philo's retrospective glance at *On rewards* 1–3. There he speaks of the division of the Mosaic oracles, which he relates to the treatises he has already written. The first kind is the creation account, and it is described as "taking its beginning from the genesis of heaven

---

[4] See Cohn's detailed study of 1899, which built on the results of 19th century German and French scholarship. The most recent overview is the excellent survey of Morris, 1987, 819–870, with exhaustive references to scholarly literature; on *Opif.* see 844–845.

[5] See the excellent treatment of the question in Terian 1997. I agree with all his arguments, with one important exception. I do not think it is possible to make a direct connection between the stylistic features of Philo's treatises and their chronology. See also the arguments of Kraus Reggiani 1979, who follows her translation of *Opif.* with *Abr.* and *Jos.* But this order was not retained in the later publication of the same translation in Kraus Reggiani, Radice and Reale 1987.

and ending with the construction of humankind" (§1). This is an excellent summary of the contents of *Opif*.[6]

(b) *Manuscript evidence.* The order of the treatises in the manuscripts is for the most part a total jumble. Nevertheless, as Terian has shown, *Opif.* is always linked with treatises from the Exposition (with one exception).[7] This is also the case in the two mss. where *Opif.* is the opening treatise.[8] It is never linked together with *Leg.* or any other treatise of the Allegorical Commentary.

(c) *Evidence of the indirect tradition.* In their lists of Philo's writings Eusebius and Jerome do not mention *Opif.* But we may be sure that a copy was present in the Episcopal library of Caesarea, because Eusebius cites it four times.[9] Of great interest are his introductory words when citing §§7–12 at *Praep. Ev.* 8.12.22: "We should again cite Philo from the first book of his commentary on the law (ἀπὸ τοῦ πρώτου τῶν εἰς τὸν νόμον)." The translation and interpretation of Eusebius' reference here is controversial.[10] On its own it cannot definitely prove which group of writings *Opif.* belonged to, especially since it is far from clear that the church father had a clear view of Philo's three different series. I agree with Terian, however, that the series of writings most likely referred to is the series that has the express purpose of expounding the law, i.e. the Exposition of the Law.[11]

The arguments that can be used to link *Opif.* to the Allegorical Commentary are not strong enough to controvert the above evidence.[12] Cohn was well aware of this. It is clear from remarks in both his edition and translation that he placed *Opif.* at the beginning of his edition, not because he believed this was the right position, but because he did not want to change the traditional order any more

---

[6] On this passage see further our comments on §82.

[7] See Terian 1997, 28–30. The exception is ms. V, in the *Vorlage* of which it was linked with *QG*; see the pinax cited in Runia *PEC* 21.

[8] The mss. H (Venetus gr. 40 = G-G no. 84) and P (Petripolitanus XX A a1 = G-G no. 104). In ms. G (Vaticano-Palatinus gr. 248 = G-G no. 83) *Opif.* follows as second treatise straight after *Mos.*

[9] See *Nachleben* in Commentary Chs 2, 5–8, and also the list at Runia 1993, 223; on Philo, Eusebius and the library of Caesarea, see Runia *PEC* 16–21 and 1996a.

[10] I agree with Morris 1987, 845 against Terian 1997, 25 that the reference is to a commentary (the usual meaning of the phrase τὰ εἰς ...).

[11] Terian 1997, 26. Cohn 1899, 407, however, is confident that Eusebius knew the title of the entire series.

[12] Some cogent arguments, based on content, can be given. See for example Nikiprowetzky 1977, 197–200. Because I was impressed by these arguments, I included *Opif.* in both series at *PT* 64–65 (n. 20 shows that this was not done inadvertently, as Terian 1997, 22 n. 12, thinks). I now think this was a mistake.

than he had to.¹³ In the translation his hands were freer and he allowed *Opif.* to be followed by *Abr.*, just as Philo intended. The order in the edition, however, was taken over by Colson and Whitaker in their English translation.¹⁴ In retrospect Cohn's decision was a mistake. The two most influential text editions in use today both separate *Opif.* from the rest of the commentary to which it belongs. This has all kinds of unexpected repercussions. For example, in the two word indices of Philo's writings preserved in Greek and the electronic TLG CD-ROM references to *Opif.* are followed by the Allegorical Commentary.¹⁵

In this Commentary *Opif.* will be rigorously treated as belonging the Exposition of the Law. This has important consequences for its interpretation. The main themes of the work will be viewed primarily in the light of the remainder of the larger work. Also when we give parallel passages, we will usually give references first to the Exposition of the Law, then the Allegorical Commentary, the *Quaestiones* and other Philonic works. This is contrary to the usual practice in Philonic studies.

Finally a brief word on chronology. If we take the reference to "an ocean of political troubles" in the preface of *On the Special Laws* III to refer to the events of 37–40 C.E., as is generally assumed in Philonic studies, and we further assume that Philo did not take too long to write the seven intervening treatises in the Exposition, then we may conclude that *Opif.* was written in the decade 30–40 C.E., when Philo was probably in his fifties. It is thus a mature work. I agree with Terian that the reference to the work *On numbers* in §52 should not be taken to imply that this work had not yet been written. This means that there is no justification for concluding that *Opif.* was written earlier than *Mos.* or the *Quaestiones*, in which Philo refers to *On Numbers* as an already existing work.¹⁶ Unlike Terian, however, I do not think it is possible to determine the chronological relation of the Exposition of the Law to *Mos.* and the other two major commentaries.¹⁷

---

[13] See PCW 1.lxxxii, PCH 1.vi.
[14] See Colson's justification at PLCL 6.ix.
[15] Cf. Mayer 1974; Borgen, Fulgseth and Skarsten 2000.
[16] See Terian 1991, 41–44, against Nikiprowetzky 1977, 217, 232.
[17] In 1997, 35 he argues there is a progression in Philo's style from "midrashic type exegetical commentaries ... to thematic expositions with ever-increasing apologetics, on the basis of which the chronological order of the three major commentaries would be: *Quaestiones*, Allegorical Commentary, Exposition of the Law." Too many assumptions are made here.

2. The genre of the treatise

Three times in retrospective cross-references Philo calls *Opif.* a σύνταξις (*Abr.* 2 [cited above], 13, *Praem.* 3 [in the plural referring all the books of the Exposition of the Law up to *Virt.*]). This term literally means something like "ordered composition," and can be taken as a general term for a didactic or systematic prose work — so not a speech or a dialogue —, written for publication in the ancient sense of the term.[18] Philo uses the term 12 times: 7 times for the Exposition of the Law (also at *Decal.* 1, *Spec.* 1.1, 2.1, *Virt.* 201), twice for *Mos.* (2.1, cross-reference at *Virt.* 52), twice for parts of the Allegorical commentary (*Her.* 1, *Mut.* 53),[19] and once in general for treatises on inebriation at *Plant.* 174.[20] We cannot take the term, then, to refer specifically to the genre of treatises contained in the Exposition of the Law, though it seems to be particularly suitable for them.

Scholars agree that all three series of exegetical treatises can be called commentaries on the books of Moses in the loose sense of the word, but that in formal terms they differ quite markedly from each other. The *Quaestiones* have a quite distinctive method: questions are posed concerning the biblical text and answers are given, without any further structuring outside the individual *quaestio* (e.g. in the form of an introduction). The separate books of this work are no more than collections of questions and answers on stretches of biblical text. The Allegorical Commentary is a running commentary on Genesis divided into separate sections of book length, each with its own title.[21] The biblical text is cited at regular intervals (and almost always at the beginning of the treatise). The complex structure of the treatises is

---

[18] See LSJ s.v. I 3, with references to authors from Aristotle to Galen. Philo is unusual in using the term for a treatise and not a book in several parts; see Nikiprowetzky 1997, 221 n.179 and now Royse 2001, 69–70. On how treatises were written and prepared for publication in the ancient world, see Dorandi 2000.

[19] Curiously, both these texts refer to the lost *On covenants*. Though Morris 1987, 838, is undoubtedly correct in arguing that the subject of this work was called forth by the rewards mentioned in Gen 15:1, it is possible that formally it resembled *Somn.*, i.e. an exegetical treatise focusing on a particular theme, and not a running commentary in the manner of *Her.* etc. This would mean that the term σύνταξις was not used of the treatises in the Allegorical Commentary as we have them.

[20] Other terms for treatises in Philo are: book (βιβλίον, βίβλος) at *Plant.* 1, *Ebr.* 1; writing (γραφή) at *Somn.* 1.1, account (λόγος) at *Prob.* 1. He does not use σύγγραμμα (prose writing) to refer to his own works, but uses it in a general sense at *Abr.* 23, *Mos.* 1.3, to refer to works of Ocellus and Plato at *Aet.* 12, 15, and to exegetical treatises possessed by the Therapeutae at *Contempl.* 29.

[21] It is likely, but not wholly certain that the titles go back to Philo himself; cf. Alexandre 1997, 256–257.

based on the biblical text being commented upon and the themes it contains, linked together with other biblical texts. There are sometimes brief introductory sections (e.g. *Ebr.* 1–10), but the contents of individual treatises are never systematically structured.

The Exposition of the Law is the most systematic and thematically unified of the three commentaries. As we read in *Praem.* 1–3, the fundamental division of the work is based on a tripartition of the Pentateuch into a part on creation, a part on history, and a part on legislation. In its original form the entire work contained 12 treatises in the following sequence:

I   a treatise on the creation account (*Opif.*);
II   (a) lives of the three patriarchs (*Abr.*, the other two lost);
     (b) life of Joseph as the statesman (*Ios.*)
III   (a) exposition of the Decalogue (*Decal.*)
     (b) exposition of the Special Laws that fall under the Decalogue (*Spec.* I, II, III, IV)
IV   (a) additional systematic treatment of the excellences or virtues described and illustrated by Moses (*Virt.*)[22]
     (b) rewards and punishments received and promised or threatened (*Praem.*)

Throughout the entire series Philo is careful to compose his treatises with introductory, transitional and concluding sections, corresponding to the internal systematics of his treatment. No reader could possibly lose track of the general structure.[23] It is true, as Peder Borgen has pointed out, that Philo through this method basically covers the entire contents of the Pentateuch.[24] But the work differs from what we find in Jewish works such as *The Book of Jubilees*, Ps.-Philo *Biblical Antiquities*, and even the first four books of Josephus' *Jewish Antiquities*, in that it is much more systematic in its treatment.[25] This applies

---

[22] The distinction between *Spec.* and *Virt.* is in fact less tidy than this. Philo already begins with justice at *Spec.* 4.135. Presumably he wanted his books to be not too dissimilar in length.
[23] This was of course particularly important in the absence of instruments such as tables of contents or indices.
[24] See Borgen 1996 and 1997, 63–79. The former article is the best recent treatment of the Exposition in its entirety. Borgen approaches the subject primarily from the viewpoint of exegesis rather than from literary structure. At 1997, 79 he claims that on the whole the Exposition belongs to the Jewish genre of "rewritten Bible" (as formulated by P. Alexander). I am entirely in agreement with the critique of Kamesar 1999 that he fails to take the influence of Greek modes of composition sufficiently into account.
[25] I disagree with Borgen 1996, 118 and 1997, 79 on this point. Josephus in all likelihood knew Philo's work. It is possible that the work on the laws which he

especially to the sections on the Special laws and the Virtues, but also in the lives of the patriarchs there is a perceptible tension between narrative and systematization. This means that many historical incidents in the Pentateuch are not covered, and conversely biblical figures are often treated from more than one viewpoint (e.g. the first man and woman are not only introduced in the final chapters of *Opif.*, but they are also used as examples of noble birth in *On the Virtues* 203–205).

From the formal viewpoint *Opif.* too contains various features of the structured treatise in the Greek style. There is an introduction (§§1–6), a further preliminary section (§§7–12), various transitional and organizational passages (e.g. §§15, 52, 65, 77, 87, 89–90, 157 etc.), and a conclusion (170b–172). It is also true, however, that the treatise is very clearly tied to the narrative structure of the biblical text of Gen 1–3. It is certainly not a *running* commentary. As we shall see below (§4), the biblical text is only cited sporadically and not very systematically. Yet its narrative progression has a strong influence on the way the treatise proceeds. From §13 to §128 the scheme of the seven days of creation is dominant and determines the treatise's structure. From §129 the narrative of the "second creation" of humankind and the events in the garden forms the basis, though Philo's handling is far from complete and reorganizes the sequence of the narrative at various points.[26] Because it is linked to the biblical text which describes a series of events, *Opif.* is less systematic than the later treatises on the Laws proper. From this perspective it is closer to *On Abraham* and *On Joseph*, which also combine narrative with systematizing features.

There is a final feature which links *Opif.* to the other kinds of exegetical treatises written by Philo. At regular intervals the thematics and structure of the account are determined by questions that Philo poses at the biblical account or in relation to it. The method is used explicitly at §72 and §77. But elsewhere implicit use of questions to structure the exegesis is also quite common; cf. §§46, 69, 131, 133, 157, 160, 163, and 165. This not only recalls the method of the *Quaestiones*, but, as Nikiprowetzky and Borgen have shown, the same method is very often practised in the Allegorical Commentary as well.[27]

---

announces at *Ant.* 3.223 might have shown a greater resemblance to Philo's approach.
[26] E.g. in discussing the naming of the animals before introducing the garden; cf. our comments at Commentary Ch. 20.
[27] See the detailed comments on §72.

We shall return to Philo's method of biblical commentary in *Opif.* in § 4 of the Introduction below.

3. *Analysis of the treatise's contents*

The treatise can be divided relatively easily into a sequence of twenty-five chapters, each dealing with a discrete part of the biblical narrative or a separate theme.[28] These chapters are indicated by the headings in the translation and at the same time form the divisions of our Commentary.

1. §§1–6. *Introduction.* The subject of the treatise is the Law of Moses, which starts with a marvellous account of creation. As interpreter Philo is daunted by the task, but he will do his best.

2. §§7–12. *A preliminary comment on God and the cosmos.* First it is necessary to say something about the relationship between the cosmos and its Maker.

3. §§13–15a. *The scheme of six days.* The six days of creation should not be taken literally, but are an indication of order.

4. §§15b–25. *Day one: creation of the intelligible cosmos.* On "day one" God above all creates the intelligible cosmos, which is located in and can be identified with the divine Logos.

5. §§26–28. *In the beginning does not mean creation in time.* The words "in the beginning" (Gen 1:1) should not be taken in a temporal sense, but indicate what God did first.

6. §§29–35. *The chief contents of the intelligible cosmos.* There are seven chief components of the noetic cosmos, as indicated in Gen 1:1–3.

7. §§36–37. *Second day: creation of the firmament.* The second day involves a transition to the corporeal realm, the best part of which is the heaven.

8. §§38–44. *Third day: creation of the earth.* Next dry land is ordered to emerge and the earth is adorned with the botanical world.

9. §§45–52. *Fourth day: a puzzle and the significance of its number.* The earth is adorned before the heaven in order to teach humans a lesson. A brief excursus on the number four demonstrates its suitability for what is created on this day.

---

[28] Compare the analyses of Cohn PCH 1.25–27, Arnaldez PAPM 1.141–142, Radice *FM* 574–575. The discrepancies of the various analyses are due to the fact that Philo, particularly when he is following the biblical narrative, sometimes uses shorter units of text which are best grouped together. This can be done in different ways.

10. §§53–61. *Fourth day: creation of the heavenly bodies.* The heavenly bodies cause great benefits for humankind: light and sight, time, number, signs.

11. §§62–68. *Fifth day: creation of the animal world.* Various kinds of animals are created in a sequence which needs to be carefully explained.

12. §§69–71. *Why is the human being created after God's image?* The human being is created "after God's image" (Gen 1:26–27) because he resembles God through his mind, which allows him to soar in contemplation of the cosmos and what lies beyond.

13. §§72–76. *Why was the human being not created by God alone?* The troublesome plural in Gen 1:26 indicates that God had helpers in the creative task, so that he could not be held responsible for wrongdoing.

14. §§77–88. *Why was the human being created last of all?* Four different answers are given, each assuming that humankind has a very special place in the creational order.

15. §§89–128. *The seventh day: excursus on the hebdomad.* The institution of the Sabbath is consistent with the special importance of the number seven, as is proven by an exceptionally long excursus (which should be regarded as a single unit).

16. §§129–130. *A summarizing reflection.* Gen 2:4–5a indicates that the ideas preceded the sense-perceptible particulars.

17. §§131–133. *The separation of the fresh from the salt water.* Moses separates the fresh from the salt water because it is necessary for the growth of plants.

18. §§134–135. *Creation of the first human being from the earth.* There is a vast difference between the human being "after the image" on the one hand and the human being fashioned from clay and inbreathed by the divine spirit on the other.

19. §§136–147. *The excellence of the first human being.* Both in body and soul the first human being was truly superior, and we his descendants are related to him.

20. §§148–150. *The giving of names.* The task could be carried out well because the first human being was wise and possessed an innate authority.

21. §§151–152. *Woman appears on the scene.* Excellence and well-being turn into wickedness and ill-fortune because the appearance of woman gives rise to the quest for bodily pleasure.

22. §§153–156. *Events in the garden of delights and their interpretation.* The trees in paradise represent boundaries in the soul. God saw that the first humans inclined to wickedness and expelled them.

23. §§157–166. *Interpretation of the snake.* The snake symbolizes pleasure, as can be shown by examining the characteristics of the lover of pleasure.

24. §§167–170a. *The consequences of wickedness.* The punishments incurred by the first man and woman receive further explanation.

25. §§170b–172. *Moses teaches five vital lessons.* Philo concludes by summarizing the treatise's contents in five doctrines. If understood and memorized, they will bring about a life of well-being.

4. *The use of the Bible and the role of exegesis and exegetical traditions*

(a) Philo's references to the biblical text

As we saw in §2 above, *Opif.* is an exposition of the contents of the first three chapters of Genesis, consisting partly of narrative rewriting and partly of thematic treatment. Not only is the sequence of subjects determined by the biblical account, but Philo also frequently refers to it verbally in his exposition. This has been made visible through the markings in and footnotes to the translation of the treatise. It will be useful to gain an additional overview of Philo's usage of the biblical text if we take the Septuagintal text and indicate those places where he directly refers to it. The text on which the following translation is based is virtually identical with the biblical text which Philo read and probably knew by heart.[29] Two kinds of markings have been included in it: **bold** indicates direct allusion — sometimes in running quotation — or appropriation of terms or phrases; ***bold italics*** indicate paraphrase and substitution of close synonyms. At the end of each verse the sections where Philo refers to the text are added in square brackets. The markings correspond to the highlighting of the biblical text in the translation of *Opif.* and can be further checked there.[30]

---

[29] My translation, based the Göttingen text of J. W. Wevers, is deliberately rather literal in order to give the flavour of the LXX text. Phrases which sound somewhat strange in English will have also done so in the Greek for an educated person such as Philo. I have tried to be rigorously consistent in my rendering of terms, but one crucial word defies such treatment: *kalos* must be translated sometimes as "beautiful" (and God saw that it was beautiful), and sometimes as "good" (the tree of knowing good and evil). The word *agathos* scarcely occurs in Genesis. On possible text variants see (b) below.

[30] On this highlighting see further below Introduction §11.

Genesis [12]

1:1. **In the beginning God created the heaven and the earth.** [§§26, 27, 29, 170] 2. Now **the earth** was **invisible** and unstructured, and **darkness** was above the **abyss**, and the **spirit of God** was borne above the **water**. [§§29, 30, 32]. 3. And God said: *Let there be* **light.** And there was light. [§§29, 30, 31]. 4. And God saw the light that it was **beautiful**, and God separated in between the light and in between the darkness. [§30] 5. And God **called** the **light day** and the **darkness** he called **night**. And it was evening and it was morning, **day one**. [§§15, 34, 35]

6. And God said: Let there be a firmament in the middle of the water, and let it be dividing in between water and water. And it happened thus. 7. And God **made** the **firmament,** and God divided in between the water which was under the firmament, and in between the water above the firmament. [§36] 8. And God *called* the **firmament heaven.** And God saw that it was beautiful. And it became evening and it became morning, a **second day.** [§37]

9. And God said: Let the **water** under the heaven *be gathered together* in a single collection, and let the **dry land** be seen. And it happened thus. And the water under the heaven was gathered together into their collections, and the dry land was seen. [§38] 10. And God called the dry land earth and the composites of waters he called *seas.* And God saw that it was beautiful. [§§39, 136] 11. And God said: Let the earth sprout forth *pasture of grass*, sowing seed after its kind and after its similarity, and fruit trees bearing *fruit*, whose seed is in it after its kind on the earth. And it happened thus. [§40] 12. And the earth brought forth pasture of grass, sowing seed after its *kind* and after its *similarity*, and fruit trees bearing **fruit**, whose **seed** is in it after its *kind* on the earth. And God saw that it was beautiful. [§§43, 44] 13. And it became evening and it became morning, a third day.

14. And God said: Let there be luminaries in the firmament of the heaven for lighting of the earth in order to divide in between the day and in between the night, and let them be **for signs** and **for right times** and for **days** and for **years**, [§§55, 58–60] 15. and let them be for lighting in the firmament of the heaven so as to shine on the earth. And it happened thus. 16. And God made the two great luminaries, the **great** luminary for *rule* of the **day** and the lesser luminary for *rule* of the **night**, and the **stars**. [§§56–57] 17. And God placed them in the firmament of the heaven so as to shine on the earth, 18. and to rule over the day and the night and to divide in between the light and in between the darkness. And God saw that it was beautiful. 19. And it became evening and it became morning, a **fourth day**. [§45]

20. And God said: Let the waters bring forth reptiles with living souls, and flying creatures flying over the earth along the firmament of the heaven. And it happened thus. 21. And God made the large **sea-creatures** and every soul of reptile creatures, which the waters brought forth after their **kinds**, and every *flying creature* with wings after its *kind*. And God saw that they were beautiful. [§63] 22. And God blessed them, saying: Increase and multiply and fill the waters in the seas, and let the flying creatures multiply on the earth. 23. And it became evening and it became morning, a fifth day.

24. And God said: **Let the earth bring forth** every soul **after** its **kind**, four-footed creatures and **reptiles and wild beasts** of the earth after their kind. And it

happened thus. [§64] 25. And God made the wild beasts of the earth after their kind and the **livestock** after their kind and all the reptiles of the earth after their kind. And God saw that they were beautiful. [§64] 26. And God said: **Let us make a human being after our image and likeness,** and let them rule over the fishes of the sea and the flying creatures of the heaven and the livestock and all the earth and all the reptiles creeping over the earth. [§§69, 71, 72, 75] 27. And God **made the human being, after God's image** he made him, **male and female** he made them. [§§25, 65, 69, 76, 134] 28. And God blessed them, saying [§84]: Increase and multiply and fill the earth and exercise command over it and rule the fishes of the sea and the flying creatures of the heaven and all the livestock and all the earth and all the reptiles creeping over the earth. 29. And God said: Behold, I have given you every seed-bearing grass sowing seed, which is above all the earth, and every tree which has in it fruit with seed fit for sowing — let them be yours for eating — 30. and for all the wild beasts of the earth and all the flying creatures of the heaven and every reptile creeping over the earth, which has in it the soul of life, and every green grass for eating. And it happened thus. 31. And God saw all that he had made, and behold they were exceedingly beautiful. And it became evening and it became morning, a sixth day.

2:1. And the heaven and the earth and *all their adornment* were *completed.* [§89] 2. And God completed on the sixth day his works which he had made and he rested on **the seventh day** from all his works which he had made. [§89] 3. And God blessed the seventh day and made it *holy,* because on it he rested from all his works which he had begun to make. [§89]

4. **This is the book of the genesis of heaven and earth when they came into being, on the day that God made the heaven and the earth,** [§129] 5. **and all the green of the field before it came into being on the earth and all the grass of the field before it rose up** [§129]; for God had not caused rain on the earth, and there was no human being to work the earth. 6. **Now a spring went up from the earth and watered all the face of the earth.** [§§131, 133] 7. **And God moulded the human being, clay from the earth, and inbreathed onto his face the breath of life**, and the human being became a living soul. [§§134–135, 139]

8. And the Lord *God planted* **a garden of delights** in Eden on the East and he *placed* there the human being which he had moulded. [§§153, 155] 9. And God also made to rise from the earth every tree fair for seeing and beautiful for eating, and the tree *of life* in the middle of the garden of delights, and the tree *of the making known of good and evil.* [§§153–154, 156] 10. Now a river goes forth from Eden to water the garden of delights. From there it is divided into four beginnings. 11. The name of one is Phison; this is the river that encircles the entire land of Evilat, there where the gold is. 12. And the gold of that land is beautiful; and there is the ruby and the green stone. 13. And the name of the second river is Geon; this is the river that encircles the land of Ethiopia. 14. And the third river is the Tigris; this is the river that goes along the Assyrians. And there is the fourth river; this is the Euphrates.

15. And the Lord God took the human being which he had moulded, and *placed* him in the garden of delights to work it and guard it. [§155] 16. And the Lord God gave instructions to Adam, saying: From every tree in the garden of delights you may eat for food. 17. But from the tree of knowing good and evil you will not eat from it; and on the day that you eat from it, you will die in death.

18. And the Lord God said: It is not good that the human being is alone; let us make for him a helper after himself. 19. And God **also moulded** from the earth all the wild beasts of the field and all the flying creatures of the heaven, and he **led** them **towards** Adam **to see** *what* he would call them, and everything which Adam called the living soul, this was its name. [§149] 20. And Adam called **names** for all the livestock and all the flying creatures of heaven and all the wild beasts of the field, but for Adam no helper similar to him was found. [§148] 21. And God cast upon Adam a trance and he slept; and he took one of his ribs and filled in flesh in its place. 22. And the Lord God *constructed* the rib which he took from Adam into a *woman*, and he led her towards Adam. [§151] 23. And he said to Adam: This is now bone from your bones and flesh from your flesh; she will be called **woman**, because she was taken from her husband. [§151] 24. And on account of this a human being will leave his father and his mother and will cleave unto his wife, and the two will be one flesh. 25. And they were both naked, Adam and his wife, and they were not ashamed.

3:1. And the two were naked, Adam and his wife, and they were not ashamed. Now the **snake** was the most cunning of all the wild beasts on the earth which the Lord God had made; and the snake said **to the woman**: Why did God say: Do not ever eat of any tree in the garden of delights? [§§156, 165] 2. And the woman said to the snake: From the fruit of the wood of the garden of delights we eat, 3. but of the fruit of the tree which is in the middle of the garden of delights God said: You shall not eat from it, nor shall you touch it, lest you die. 4. And the snake said to the woman: You will not die in death; 5. for God knew that on the day that you ate from it, your eyes would be opened, and you would be as gods *knowing good and evil*. [§156] 6. And the woman saw that the tree was *beautiful* for eating, and that it was pleasing for the eyes *to see* and fair to understand, and taking from its **fruit** *she ate*; and *she gave* also **to** her **husband** with her, and they ate. [§§156, 165] 7. And the eyes of the two were opened, and they knew that they were naked, and they stitched fig-leaves and they made loin-cloths for themselves.

8. And they heard the voice of the Lord God walking in the garden of delights in the evening, and Adam and his wife hid from the face of the Lord God in the middle of the wood of the garden of delights. 9. And the Lord God called Adam and said to him: Adam, where are you? 10. And he said to him: I heard your voice as you were walking in the garden of delights and I was afraid, because I am naked, and I hid. 11. And he said to him: Who reported to you that you are naked, unless you ate from the tree, of which alone I instructed you not to eat from it? 12. And Adam said: The woman, whom you gave me to be with me, she gave me from the tree, and I ate. 13. And God said to the woman: Why did you do this? And she said: The snake *deceived* me, and I ate. [§155] 14. And the Lord God said to the snake: Because you did this, you will be accursed among all the livestock and among all the wild beasts of the earth; you will go on your breast and on your belly and you will eat earth all the days of your life. [§157] 15. And I will place hatred in between you and in between the woman and in between your seed and in between her seed; it will watch out for your head, and you will watch out for its heel. 16. And to the woman he said: I will multiply and multiply your **griefs** and your groaning, *in sufferings* you will bear **children**; and your turning will be towards your **husband**, and he *will lord it* over you. [§167] 17. And to Adam he said: Because you listened to the voice of

your wife and you ate from the tree, of which alone I instructed you not to eat from it, accursed will be the earth in your labours; in sufferings you will eat it all the days of your life; 18. it will cause thorns and prickly plants to rise up for you, and you will eat the grass of the field. 19. In the **sweat** of your face you will eat your bread until you return to the earth, from which you were taken; because you are earth, and to earth you will go back. 20. And Adam called the name of his wife Life, because she was the mother of all those who live.

21. And the Lord God made for Adam and his wife garments of leather and he clothed them. 22. And God said: Behold Adam has become as one of us in knowing good and evil, and now he should never extend his hand and take from the tree of life and eat and have everlasting life. 23. And the Lord God sent him away **from** the luxurious **garden of delights** to work the land, from which he had been taken (when he was created). [§155] 24. And *he expelled* Adam and caused him to dwell opposite the luxurious garden of delights, and he established the cherubim and the flaming sword which turns in order to guard the path to the tree of life. [§155]

The only other biblical text to which Philo refers directly in the entire work is Lev 11:21–22 at §163:

21. And these you will eat from the flying **reptiles** which walk on four feet: those **which have legs above its feet to jump** with them *on* **the earth**. 22. And these you will eat from them: the locust and its similars and the cricket and its similars and the grass-hopper and its similars and **the snake-fighter** and its similars.

For the sake of completeness we should also include Ps 8:7–9, to which Philo clearly alludes in §84:

7. And you *appointed* him over the works of your hands,
 you subjected all things under *his* feet,
8. sheep and all cattle,
 and also the beasts of the field,
9. the flying beings of the heaven and the fishes of the sea ...

The fact that, apart from these two exceptions, *Opif.* never refers to secondary biblical texts is a feature that distinguishes it sharply from the treatises in the Allegorical Commentary, which continually alternate between the primary biblical text and other Pentateuchal verses.[31]

It can be ascertained on the basis of the marked translations of Philo's text and the Genesis text that Philo shows a great variation in the way he refers to the biblical text. Three levels can be distinguished:
(a) The text is seldom quoted directly at any length. Brief quotes of Gen 1:1 and 1:2 are found in §26 and §32 respectively, and of Gen 1:26 in §72. Three longer quotes, all from Gen 2:4–7, are found in

---

[31] On this fundamental difference see Runia 1984, 1987.

§129 to §134. In these quotes the text is cited word for word, with only a minimal number of changes.

(b) Very occasionally Philo briefly paraphrases the biblical text, substituting words, changing the grammatical construction, and so on. See for example §§39, 64 (almost a quote), 69, 89, 149, 153, 155, 156, 163 (Leviticus).

(c) Philo's most frequent method, however, is to pick out key terms from phrases in the Genesis account and weave them into his exegesis. This can be very clearly seen, for example, in §55 and §§59–60, where the main functions of the heavenly bodies as given in Gen 1:16 are used to structure the discussion. Compare also the account of the events of the garden in §§153–156. Terms that are too exotic, however, are not selected. Philo will cite, for example, the abyss in Gen 1:2 because he can explain it and indeed needs it for his cosmology. But unusual terms or expressions such as φωστῆρες (luminaries) in 1:14, εἰς ψυχὴν ζῶσαν (to a living soul) in 2:7, and ξύλον (wood meaning tree) in the paradise account are set aside.

It is also illuminating to see how the references to the biblical account are distributed through the work. If we take the number of biblical words cited or referred to per chapter, taking into account how many sections are contained in the chapter, a significant amount of variation can be discerned, as becomes clear in the following graph:[32]

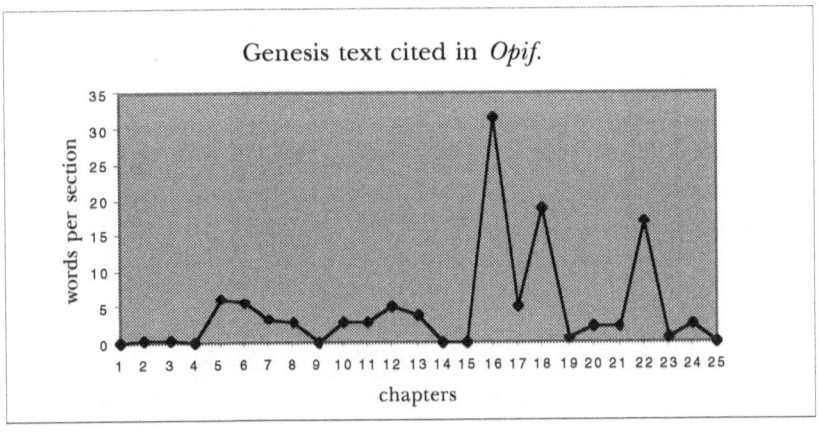

[32] Only the use of the Genesis text is included in this text, not the references to Leviticus 11 or Psalm 8.

In a number of chapters Philo makes detailed reference to the biblical text: see Ch. 5, 6, 12, 16–18, 22. These chapters either quote significant sections of text (esp. Ch. 16, 18) or give rather detailed exegesis, in which they cite a considerable number of biblical terms (esp. Ch. 22). At the opposite extreme is another group of chapters, which contain virtually no reference to scripture at all. These include the introductory and concluding sections (Ch. 1–4, 25), but also Ch. 9, 14–15 and 19. Particularly striking is Ch. 14, which asks why the human being was created last of all. It contains no references to the biblical text whatsoever, couching the entire discussion in rather high-flown Greek literary style (Ch. 23 is rather similar if the references to Leviticus are set aside). Other chapters falling outside these groups tend to contain limited references to key terms, but these do play an important role in the exegesis. Examples are the narrative chapters 7–8, 10–11, 20–21, and 24.

From these results it is clear that Philo has combined a number of different exegetical styles in his work. Philosophical and literary passages are alternated with sections of reasonably dense exegesis. The result is an attractive, variegated composition.

Finally, it will be worthwhile taking a closer look at the markings in the text of Genesis 1–3 above in order to see on which parts Philo focuses his attention. We see that the hexaemeral account in Genesis 1 is fairly well covered in the exegesis, with a certain concentration on days one and four. Since Philo wants to relate the Mosaic text to current thinking, all features relating to the archaic Hebraic or Near-Eastern cosmology and zoology of the account are passed over in silence, except in day one, where they are radically reinterpreted. Noteworthy omissions are the blessings of the animals and humankind on the fifth and sixth day,[33] and any reference to God's resting on the seventh day. As we noted above, the so-called second creation account of the Yahwist, Gen 2:4–7, is cited in great detail, though the explanations given are rather brief. The remaining part of the creation account is treated in less detail. Many features of the passage are noted briefly (e.g. the creation of woman) or not at all (e.g. the rivers of Eden, the first couple's nakedness, the hiding from God). Nevertheless, when we consider that Philo devotes only about a fifth of the treatise to this part, it is in fact surprising how many themes are

---

[33] As becomes apparent in Ch. 14, Philo does allude to the theme of human dominion over the earth, but he does not refer to the biblical text in expounding it (except to Ps. 8).

referred to at least briefly. There is, however, a vast difference when a comparison is made with the much more detailed treatment of these chapters in *Leg.* (some of which has been lost) and in *QG* 1.1–57.

(b) Philo's method of exegesis in *Opif.*

At first sight it might seem that the method of exegesis used in the treatise is quite straightforward. The biblical narrative is followed. The actions of the creator are linked to brief explanations of the cosmological features of what he creates and the significance these have for humankind. Here and there an exegetical *quaestio* or an excursus is thrown in. Is this not a form of literal exegesis, not very different from recounting the life of Abraham as an exemplar of the living law in *On Abraham*? But appearances can deceive.

In the first place, a creation account is not straight history.[34] We read in §13 that the narrative of six days is a structural and didactic device, and this view is repeated in §28 and §67. Moses has cast the account of creation into the narrative of six (or seven) days in order to illustrate the ordered nature of noetic and visible reality. His deepest intent is philosophical, wishing to convey to his readers that there is both a metaphysical/cosmological and a moral order, both of which are of the greatest importance for human life. In response Philo makes use of symbolic exegesis, where one thing stands as a symbol for another, and appeals especially to the symbolism of number, which in his view is directly related to order. This explains the extraordinary role of arithmology in the treatise (on this aspect see further below §6). Admittedly it often seems as if Philo gets carried away with his narrative, and that we are reading a Hellenistic-Jewish recasting of familiar Greek cosmogonies such as we find in Plato's *Timaeus* or Book I of Diodorus Siculus' *Universal History*. Yet we should not overlook that the *Timaeus* too has a complex attitude to protological narrative. Plato, as later exegetes convincingly argued, meant his cosmogony to be read "for the sake of instruction."[35]

In the case of *Opif.* it is crucial that the reader keep this deeper symbolical exegesis in mind at all times, since without it many features of the treatise remain obscure or even confused.[36] It becomes

---

[34] As Philo warns when giving exegesis of Gen 2:4 in *Leg.* 1.20; *QG* 1.1.
[35] See further Runia *PT* 96–103, 412–420, both on the *Timaeus* and Philo's application of it to his own exegesis.
[36] This was first pointed out in the seminal article of Nikiprowetzky 1965, on which see Introduction §10.

all the more important when we reach the anthropology of the final part and have to interpret the difficult matter of Philo's interpretation of the double creation of the human being. The climax of the non-literal interpretation comes almost at the end, when Philo sets aside the narrative approach altogether and allegorizes the events of the garden in terms of full-blown moral allegory (§§157–166), wholly parallel to the method in *Legum Allegoriae*. Philo continues to reserve an important role for symbolic exegesis throughout the remaining treatises of the Exposition of the Law.[37]

Another way to make this clear is to point out that Philo is in fact much less interested in a quasi-historical narrative of creation than might at first seem. In his account of the third day we already start to notice that the exegesis takes on a particular slant. Philo is above all interested in what the creation account means for human beings. From the time the first human being is created on the sixth day, this emphasis takes over more and more. In the exegesis a tension develops between what we might call a quasi-historical exposition and interpretation of creation in terms of what is typical for or generally applicable to humankind as a whole. Adam is thus not only the first human being, but he typifies what human life can be like at its best, i.e. before the fall from grace, and what it is very often like now, i.e. a descent into passion and sin. This tension reaches its climax in the full-blown allegory of the story of the first woman and the snake.

Finally it should be pointed out that the combination of four exegetical factors — the basis in the cosmogonic narrative of Genesis, the regular use of the method of the *quaestio*, the importance of symbolic exegesis, and the prominence of arithmology —, give the treatise a somewhat episodic or even atomistic nature, which can be discouraging for the reader who tries to interpret the work as presenting a coherent theory. Although Philo usually tries to link the chapters together, the connections are sometimes not clear enough. For example, at §134 Philo indicates that the second creation of humankind follows upon but differs from the first explained in §§69–71. But what the precise relation between the two presentations is does not receive explanation, and is in fact very difficult, if not impossible, to determine. On crucial occasions, as for example in §§134–135, the

---

[37] See for example the exegesis of the migrations of Abraham at *Abr.* 60–88, which combines literal and allegorical exegesis (expressly stated at §88), the explanation of circumcision at *Spec.* 1.8–10, the division of the sacrificial animal at *Spec.* 1.209–211, etc.

exegesis is simply too brief.[38] These features, when taken together, have given the treatise a reputation for difficulty which is not really deserved, and which I am sure was not its author's intention.[39] It is best, I believe, to take the exegesis as it comes, though at all times bearing in mind the larger themes that Philo wishes to expound (to be outlined in the following section). This is what we have tried to do in our Commentary.

(c) traditions of exegesis

During the past three decades Philonic scholarship has expended much energy in critically re-examining the thesis of W. Bousset that the Philonic corpus is a kind of melting-pot of pre-existing Alexandrian exegetical traditions reworked, not always very smoothly, by their compiler.[40] Exponents of this theory are R. Goulet, who argues that Philo's religious Platonism has been superimposed on an earlier allegorical tradition developed by a group of radical allegorists who had written a rigorously philosophical allegorical commentary on the Pentateuch,[41] and T. Tobin, who on the basis of apparent inconsistencies in Philo's account of the creation of humankind postulates that he has combined differing kinds of interpretations which were developed during a long period of Alexandrian exegesis.[42] In my view there can be no doubt that Philo was dependent on and records anterior exegetical traditions. D. Hay has collected an impressive list of references to such traditions in Philo's own works.[43] An excellent example is found in §77, where Philo gives an answer to an exegetical *quaestio* by appealing to "those who have made a profounder study of the laws and have elucidated its contents to the best of their ability with much attention to detail." In §154 an interpretation of the tree of life is given, which in *QG* 1.10 is presented as traditional ("and some have said..."). The link between the creation account, the

---

[38] This habit of becoming too brief in the exegesis when the going gets rough is an exegetical equivalent of what we find in Aristotle at a philosophical level, notoriously in *An. Post.* 2.19 and *An.* 3.5.

[39] Famously stated by Goodenough in 1962, 35: "The cosmological introduction [of the Exposition of the Law] is presented in what I consider Philo's most difficult treatise, entitled *On the Creation of the World*. It is the treatise printed first in all editions of Philo, and its difficulty has only too often made it the last as well as the first for a reader to attempt."

[40] Bousset 1915.
[41] Goulet 1987. For critiques see Runia 1989; Dillon 1995, 110.
[42] Tobin 1983. For critiques see Winston 1985b; Runia *PT* 556–558.
[43] Hay 1979–80. For the social and educational setting see below §7 and n. 64.

sabbath and the number seven is already found in Philo's predecessor Aristobulus.[44] It must be accepted, therefore, that much of the material that Philo presents in *Opif.* has a background in the traditions of Alexandrian exegesis.[45]

But what does this background mean for our interpretation? Philo is a keen proponent of multiple exegesis.[46] Not only are the powers of the individual exegete limited when confronted with the riches of scripture (cf. §§4–6) and his explanations tentative and provisional (cf. §72), but the biblical text can also be legitimately understood at various levels and in various differing and compatible ways. Philo is thus happy to record and preserve, but that does not necessarily make him into a compiler, let alone an exegetical photocopier. This is basically the assumption of Tobin, who thinks it is possible to reconstruct anterior traditions from the way Philo has preserved them. I am sceptical about such textual "archaeology,"[47] and especially the claim that it is possible to locate very early anti-anthropological traditions in passages such as §§69–71 and §§72–75. Methodologically this is suspect because it stands to reason that Philo has reworked his material to fit in with his general conception of the creation account. In practice, moreover, this approach tends to exaggerate differences between passages which can be, if not made fully consistent with each other, at least read quite comfortably in parallel. Various examples will be discussed in the course of our commentary; see the comments on §§69–71, 129, 134–135, 153–154. It may be concluded, therefore, that, although we do not necessarily have to know the background of Alexandrian exegesis in order to understand Philo (which is just as well, given how little we can be certain about), we will understand him better if we take its presence into account.

(d) Philo's text of the Pentateuch

When citing the Pentateuchal text, Philo's readings often diverge from the LXX as transmitted in later manuscripts. The reasons for

---

[44] See our General Comments at Ch. 15.
[45] It is also possible that there is a link to Jewish exegetical traditions outside Alexandria. Attempts have been made to reconstruct earlier Jewish traditions in Philo on the basis of parallels in rabbinic literature; cf. Borgen 1965, 1997; Cohen 1995.
[46] Cf. Nikiprowetzky 1996 (1965), 48.
[47] The same applies to the results of Goulet, but these are less crucial for an understanding of *Opif.* See already the wise words of Nikiprowetzky 1977, 174. But Dillon 1983, 83–86, goes too far in suggesting that Philo is "inventing" predecessors (esp. opponents).

this lie both in his method of quotation and in the vagaries of the manuscript transmission of the Philonic corpus. Much research has been carried out on this subject, particularly by P. Katz and D. Barthélemy.[48] For our treatise this subject is of minor significance. There is only one passage in which Philo's quotation differs from the received LXX text. See the comments on §134.

5. *The main themes of the treatise*

Although the contents of *Opif.*, as we saw above in our discussion of Philo's exegesis, adhere rather closely to the biblical text and, as a result, often have a somewhat episodic character, they do contain a large number of recurrent philosophical and theological themes which, when assembled together, form an impressive body of thought. In the following overview these themes will be outlined. Numbers in square brackets refer to the *chapters* of our commentary (i.e. *not* sections of the text), where in all cases further discussion will be found (including references to the scholarly literature, on which see also the *status quaestionis* below).

(a) the pre-eminence of Moses
The Jewish lawgiver Moses is superior to all other lawgivers and philosophers, not only because he commences his legislation with a creation account [1], but also because that account itself is superior, the result both of divine inspiration and superior philosophical insight [2, 17]. Moses is the teacher *par excellence*, teaching in the treatise five fundamental lessons [25]. In the case of the theme of naming the various parts of creation, it is sometimes difficult to tell who is doing the naming, God the creator (as in Genesis) or his prophet Moses [6, 7].

(b) law and nature
But why does Moses first begin with a creation account? Law involves the prescriptive ordering of reality in all its diversity, as seen in the laws of nature, but especially in the ordering of human life, which can so easily decline into disorder and anarchy. The creation account is meant to demonstrate the indissoluble link between the law of nature for the entire cosmos and the law of Moses for human beings [1]. The first human being was able to live entirely in accordance with the law of nature, but we, his distant descendants, have declined from

---

[48] Katz 1950; Barthélemy 1967; cf. also Gooding and Nikiprowetzky 1983.

those original heights (and so need the law of Moses) [19]. This background of prescriptive law must be borne in mind at all times when reading the treatise. The creation account lays a foundation for the entire Exposition of the Law (cf. Introduction §1), portraying the cosmos and human life as it was meant to be, but also how it fell away from the intended perfection.

(c) God and creation

The most fundamental divide of all is between God, transcendent eternal Being and sole first principle, and that which receives the benefit of his creative activity, belonging to the realm of genesis (hence the title of Moses' book) [2]. God is, to use the famous Platonic phrase, "father and maker" of this universe. "Maker" expresses the dominant demiurgic or technical metaphor: God gives form to unformed matter [4].[49] The biological metaphor "Father" connotes above all the doctrine of Providence: God looks after what he has made [2, 25]. The cosmos is good because God is good. It is the beneficence of divine grace that allows the great divide between God and passive matter to be overcome [4]. At the same time, however, Philo strongly emphasizes divine transcendence, both in his account of the creative act [2, 4] and in his account of the ascent of the human mind [12].

(d) the cosmic order

But why does Moses employ his striking schema of the seven days of creation? It is a mistake to think that God needed time for his creative labours [3, 5]. The sequence of days symbolize order and proper succession [3, 5, 11]. An insightful reading of the creation narrative reveals that there are two orders or realms of creation, one that is the object of the mind only and is created on "day one," the other accessible to sense-perception and created on the second to sixth days [3, 4, 7, 16]. The noetic cosmos, identified with the Logos of God in the act of creation, serves as model or blueprint for the physical world [4, 17]. It is superior and thus created first. The relation between the two realms is especially indicated by the metaphor of the seal or marking, which imposes intelligibility and order on brute physicality [4, 6, 12, 13, 16, 18, 19, 25]. The role of number as indicating order and hierarchy is pervasive in the account of the seven days [3, 4, 7, 9,

---

[49] But we are not told where the matter comes from; see the Excursus in Ch. 4.

11, 15; see also Introduction §6]. A correspondence can be seen with the role of the Logos in "measuring out" the divine goodness in such a way that creation can absorb it [4]. A special place is reserved for the number seven, closely related to the monad and so universally prominent in both realms of reality [15].

In his creation account Moses does not offer anything like a systematic cosmology. Only certain basic features are described, e.g. separation of the waters [8, 17], the brilliance and purposefulness of the heavenly bodies [10], and the correlation between living beings and the diverse cosmic elements or regions [11]. The creational order is astoundingly beautiful. It is marked by variation and variegation, as Philo loves to convey in his rich prose [8, 9, 14, 19]. At the same time it is also profoundly teleological. Everything has a purpose: plants provide food [8], the heavenly bodies indicate time and furnish signs [10], and so on. And for the most part this finality points in a single direction, towards the jewel in the creational crown.

(e) the human being in the cosmos

The special place of humankind in the creational order can be gauged from the fact that its creation on the sixth day forms the climax of the entire account [11, 12, 14]. Humankind is created "after the image of God." But in which respect does the human being resemble God? It is in respect of his incorporeal intellect, which enables him above all to explore and contemplate reality and even aspire to knowledge of God [12]. It also equips him with the authority to dominate the animal and plant world as God's viceroy on earth [14]. But Mosaic anthropology is more complex. A second creation of the human being ensues, in which the body is fashioned from the elements and the soul is inbreathed with the divine spirit. This represents the individual human being who stands squarely in physical reality, but with a borderline status, immortal with regard to his soul, mortal with regard to his body [18]. Moses' view of the cosmos is plainly anthropocentric. But is it also androcentric? In principle perhaps not. Humankind created as intellect is pre-sexual [13]. But in the second creation the man is created first, followed by the woman, with disastrous consequences [21].

(f) goodness and evil

Moses agrees with Plato that the reason for the creation of the cosmos is God's inexhaustible goodness [4]. It is axiomatic that God cannot be held responsible for any evil [13]. Yet it seems that he deliberately created a world with a moral order, whose protagonist is the human being. He is created with a mixed nature, able to perform both good and evil deeds. In order to avoid any responsibility for later wrongdoing, God has helpers to assist him in the creative task [13]. When the first humans are placed in paradise, they are put to the test and found wanting [22]. Woman is seduced first, but the man too fails to obey. Both succumb to the pleasure resulting from sexual passion as symbolized by the snake [21, 22, 23]. Rightful punishment must ensue, yet God is also merciful [24]. In fact punishment can be seen as educational, and thus as not really an evil [24]. Real evil is moral failure. But the treatise does not reflect on broader questions of theodicy not connected with human action. We should note also that Moses is negative about sexual passion, but not about sexuality itself. It is required for the continuation of the species [21]. (Philo's thought is thus not proto-gnostic [13].)

(g) protology and typology[50]

The creation account undoubtedly reports on the nature and fortunes of the first human beings. The first man was a paragon of perfection, far outstripping his later descendants in excellence of mind and body. This allowed him to emulate God in admirable fashion [19]. His excellence was apparent in the way he named the animals in his charge [20]. The first couple's disobedience brought about a drastic change in their living conditions [24]. But Philo is only moderately interested in matters of proto-history. We, the remote descendants of the first man and woman, still have a kinship to them, and through them, to God [19]. The first humans are above all *types*, and that constitutes their chief relevance. The goal should be to regain the perfection of the first human being, who, we recall, lived in total accord with the law of nature [19]. The radical reversal of their lives, from immortality and bliss to mortality and toil, is not primarily a historical event, i.e. "the fall," but rather elucidates a fundamental structural aspect of human existence [22]. The story of the snake, however, requires an even more radical form of interpretation, namely the allegory of the soul: pleasure makes use of the senses to seduce the mind into ruinous passion [23].

---

[50] I use the term here in the general sense, and not, of course, to refer to specifically Christian typology.

(h) excellence, devotion to God and the good life

The goal of human life is to emulate God's blessed and blissful nature, i.e. to achieve well-being (*eudaimonia*) [18, 19]. This will occur through the practice of the excellences or virtues (*aretai*), chief among which is devotion to God [15, 22, 25], which in turn presupposes recognition of his existence and his beneficent activity [4, 25]. As reward the human being will receive the immortality that is available to him [13, 18, 20]. The opposite will occur if we emulate the failure of the first human couple, succumbing to passion [21, 23], or if we choose to ignore Moses' lessons altogether, for example by denying God's existence or the efficacy of his providential activity [25]. This leads to punishment and mortality [24]. But just as in the case of the first human beings, there are still always grounds for hope.

The message of *Opif.* is not subtle. The cosmos as ordered created reality, symbolized by the six days of divine creative activity, is fundamentally good. The moral order which it embraces, when applied to human existence, entails an entire list of polarities: good and evil, virtue and vice, life and death, reward and punishment. It is up to the human being to chose, aided by divine grace, just as Israel was offered the choice between life and death in Deut 30:15–20. Moses' five chief lessons are significant, but in the broader perspective of Philo's exegetical *œuvre* they form no more than prolegomena to the further lessons that are provided through the lives of the patriarchs and the study of the Law. *Opif.* contains fascinating theological, cosmological and anthropological themes, but in the end its ethical and religious purpose prevails, as indicated by the final words of the treatise.[51]

6. *Special theme: number symbolism and the arithmological tradition*

A special feature of *Opif.* that will soon catch the attention of every reader is the prominence of number symbolism in the work, attached exclusively to the schema of the seven days in Moses' creation account. More than a quarter of the entire work is taken up with this material. It is unevenly distributed over the following numbers:

the unit	§15, 35
the two	not mentioned[52]

---

[51] Cf. the judicious remarks of Radice *FM* 312, who in turn concurs with the judgment of Baer 1970, 6–8.
[52] See the General comments on Ch. 7 and the comments on §37.

the three	not mentioned, but cf. §62
the four	§§47–52
the five	§62
the six	§§13–14, cf. 89
the seven	§§89–128

Fully 49 sections of the work deal with numbers, predominantly of course in the long excursus devoted to the seven.

The reason that such an extraordinary amount of space is devoted to the theory of numbers is explained in §13, where we read: τάξει δὲ ἀριθμὸς οἰκεῖον, "number is inherent in order." Moses uses the schema of the seven days to indicate and illustrate the order and structure of creation. This interpretation of biblical numbers patently draws on a Pythagorean background. Having discovered the arithmetic basis of musical harmony, Pythagoras and his followers posited that all things are informed by or even consist of numbers. Numbers can also be connected with incorporeal things such as gods (e.g. Apollo and the monad) or concepts (e.g. justice and the four). Plato was strongly influenced by these theories in the *Timaeus* and other dialogues. As the result of trenchant criticisms by Aristotle and others, these number speculations fell out of favour during the Hellenistic period, because they were not considered sufficiently scientific. In the 1st cent. B.C.E., however, they enjoyed a strong revival and their popularity lasted until the end of antiquity. As H. Moehring stated in his excellent study devoted to Philo's arithmology, such use of numbers takes the place of science:[53]

> ... what we have in Philo is a serious attempt to relate the cosmic order to a rational system — expressed in numbers — and thereby to reach an understanding of the universe within thought categories that are available to any and all. It was exactly the mathematically universal character of arithmology which Philo found so attractive for his exegetical work: it could help him to explain the sacred texts of the books of the law in terms that were universally understood, even though not universally accepted.

Differing from Moehring, however, I would wish to distinguish between arithmology and number symbolism.[54] Arithmology is the body

---

[53] Moehring 1995 (1978), 146. Though concentrating primarily on the hebdomad, this article is the best introduction to Philo's use of arithmology in his writings. Moehring also gives a valuable overview of the philosophical background; see 146–154.

[54] Cf. Moehring 1995 (1978), 143–146. I fully agree with his rejection of terms such as "numerology" and "number mysticism."

of lore connected with numbers, e.g. that six is a perfect number because it consists of all its factors added together or multiplied together (cf. §13). Number symbolism is the method whereby such lore is used to explain the appearance of a particular number in a particular context, whether textual or otherwise. The six thus symbolizes the creation of the cosmos, because both it and the cosmos are perfect and complete (i.e. perfection is the common element, the so-called *tertium comparationis*). What is rather surprising in our treatise is that in the case of the unit, the five and the six, Philo explains what the relevance of the number is for the day concerned, but in the case of both the four and the seven he fails to do so. Yet for these latter two numbers he gives a lengthy account of arithmological lore, as if that were enough to explain the importance of the number. Whatever the reason for this may be, it is clear that in *Opif.* number symbolism takes over the role of allegory as the form of symbolism most suited to physical reality.[55]

As we already noted in §1 above, in §52 Philo most likely alludes to another work *On numbers* (Περὶ ἀριθμῶν), to which he refers explicitly at *Mos.* 2.115, *QG* 4.110, *QE* 2.87, and implicitly also at *Spec.* 2.200. This work, which is not mentioned by Eusebius in his catalogue, is now lost, but fragments have been tentatively identified among the Armenian and Latin translations of Philo's works.[56] The nature and contents of this work have given rise to much speculation. Most likely it was a collection of arithmological material compiled as a kind of source book for exegetical application.[57] For this reason it departed from the Greek arithmological tradition in proceeding beyond the decad. In an important Tübingen dissertation published in 1931, K. Staehle attempted to reconstruct this missing work on the basis of all the references to arithmology found in Philo's exegetical writings. Staehle's method was totally flawed. It is quite impossible to reconstruct Philo's lost work. But the overview of Philo's arithmological passages which he furnishes is extremely valuable.[58]

---

[55] Cf. the valuable comments on the role of numbers in *Opif.* in Nikiprowetzky 1996 (1965) 74–78. He compares them with the role of the idea-numbers in the late Plato, but goes too far when he says that numbers are the true ideas or measures in the creation account. The link between the numbers of the days and the divine measuring (of the Logos) in §23 is speculative.

[56] See Petit 1973, 2.89, Terian 1984.

[57] Cf. Robbins 1931, 359–361; Staehle 1931, 9–11; Dillon 1977, 159; Nikiprowetzky 1977, 214. I agree with Nikiprowetzky that the work probably had an exegetical purpose, but not that its contents focused on biblical numbers.

[58] See also the useful list at Bréhier 1908, 43–44.

From Staehle's collection it is overwhelmingly apparent that Philo's material has been taken over from already existing arithmological collections. Important research in this area was carried out by F. E. Robbins, who concluded that parallels in various writings dating from Posidonius and Varro in the 1st cent. B.C.E. to Isidore of Seville in the 7th century C.E. strongly suggested a unified tradition that went back to a single source in the 2nd cent. B.C.E., probably to be identified with an unknown Neopythagorean thinker.[59] Philo occupies an early position in this tradition. In his analysis Robbins makes excessive use of the method of the *Einquellenhypothese*, but his results have not been superseded.[60] A definitive monograph on the history of ancient arithmology is badly needed.

The most important arithmological texts which we shall use to illustrate Philo's passages are, in chronological order (additional texts only relevant for the hebdomad are listed below in the Commentary, Ch. 15, General comments):

Nicomachus of Gerasa, much used by Ps.-Iamblichus (see below);
Theon of Smyrna, *Exposition of mathematical matters useful for reading Plato*, ed. E. Hiller, Leipzig: Teubner, 1878;
Alexander of Aphrodisias, *Commentary on Aristotle's Metaphysics*, ed. M. Hayduck, Berlin: Reimer 1891;
Censorinus, *On the Birthday*, ed. N. Sallmann, Leipzig: Teubner, 1983; French translation with notes by G. Rocca-Serra, Paris: Vrin, 1980;
Anatolius, *On the first ten numbers* (also partly cited by Ps.-Iamblichus *Theology of Arithmetic*), ed. J. Heiberg, Annales Internationales d'histoire, Paris 1901, including a French translation by P. Tannery;
Calcidius, *Commentary on the Timaeus*, ed. J. H. Waszink, Leiden: Brill 1962;
Ps.-Iamblichus, *Theology of arithmetic*, ed. V. de Falco, Leipzig: Teubner, 1922; English translation by R. Waterfield, Grand Rapids: Phanes Press, 1988;
Macrobius, *Commentary on the Dream of Scipio*, ed. J. Willis, Leipzig: Teubner, 1963, English translation by W. H. Stahl, New York: Columbia University Press, 1952;

---

[59] Robbins 1921; see esp. the stemma on p. 123. Robbins reacts against earlier research which on the basis of the most slender evidence identified the origin of the arithmological tradition with the figure of Posidonius; see Robbins 1920.

[60] See also the valuable comments of Boyancé 1963, 83–95.

Martianus Capella, *On arithmetic*, ed. J. Willis, Leipzig: Teubner, 1983; English translation by W. H. Stahl, New York: Columbia University Press, 1977;

John Lydus, *On the months*, ed. R. Wuensch, Leipzig: Teubner, 1898;

Isidore of Seville, *Book of scriptural numbers*, PL 83.179–199.

Detailed references to treatment of individual numbers in these sources can be found in Staehle's monograph. A fine impression of this kind of literature can be gained from Waterfield's translation of Ps.-Iamblichus, with a brief but informative introduction on the nature of arithmology. The practice of number symbolism is by no means extinct. For purposes of comparison I quote from time to time from the study of a modern successor to Philo, the Islamic scholar A. Schimmel, *The Mystery of Numbers*.[61]

Although the arithmological material exploited by Philo is derived from Greek sources, the exegetical use to which it is put is Jewish. Comparative material can be found in an excellent survey of the use of number symbolism in contemporary Jewish and early Christian apocalyptic literature by A. Yarbro Collins.[62] We note that most of these sources make creative use of numbers, continuing biblical practice rather than explaining it. For our purposes the most significant example Yarbro Collins cites is Philo's Alexandrian predecessor Aristobulus, who in a fragment on the sabbath dwells on the special characteristics of the seven in a manner highly reminiscent of Philo.[63]

7. *The intellectual* Sitz im Leben

In this section my aim is to introduce the intellectual milieu which forms the backdrop for the treatise and its contents. Naturally an intellectual milieu presupposes a social and educational setting, Basic knowledge of this will be assumed.[64] The intellectual *Sitz im Leben* is particularly important because it supplies us with much of the comparative material which will enable us to understand Philo's treatise better. We will regularly call upon the sources mentioned in this section in our Commentary.

---

[61] Schimmel 1993.
[62] Yarbro Collins 1984.
[63] See further the Commentary, Ch. 15, General comments.
[64] For Philo's social and historical setting see accounts in Borgen 1997, 14–45; Haas 1997, 91–103; Sly 1995; Tcherikover 1957, 55–78; for his educational setting Sterling 1999.

(a) Judaism

Philo's treatise is a product of Alexandrian Judaism. This kind of Judaism is so distinct, and Philo is so distinctive a representative of its tendency, that it is no exaggeration to say that the treatise could not have been written anywhere else. Philo stands in a long tradition of Hellenistic-Jewish literature, which commenced with the translation into Greek of the Pentateuch and reached full flower in the two centuries preceding Philo's death. Regrettably the remains of this rich body of literature are scanty.[65] Most of it will have focused on the biblical themes, even when Greek literary forms were adopted. A striking example is the drama in Iambic trimeters on the life of Moses by Ezechiel.[66] As noted above in our discussion of Philo's exegesis, §4(c), it is as good as certain that a long tradition of biblical exegesis existed in Alexandria and that Philo drew on it when writing his own exegetical treatises. The chief texts that we can now use for comparative purposes are the fragments of Aristobulus (frg. 5 on the Sabbath refers to the creation account) and the Wisdom of Solomon. The latter work, now included in the Septuagint, must have been written in a milieu very similar to that of Philo.[67] It does not, however, dwell at great length on the creation account, but is more concerned with God's salvific action in history. Both of these texts show the undoubted influence of Greek philosophy. Other Jewish-Hellenistic texts, such as the *Letter of Aristeas* and *Jewish Synagogal prayers* do so to a much lesser degree.

It is implausible to think that Alexandrian Judaism pursued its study of the Bible in complete isolation from the rest of Judaism. New Testament texts and for example the exegesis of Genesis 1–11 found in Theophilus of Antioch *Ad Autolycum* Book 2 bear witness to other streams of Jewish exegesis in Greek.[68] Because Josephus made use of Philo we reckon his evidence as belonging primarily to Philo's

---

[65] Most of the remains have been collected and presented in English translation with copious annotation in Charlesworth 1983–85, *passim* and esp. 2.775–919; for more detailed treatment see the full commentary in four volumes by Holladay 1983–96.

[66] See the full commentary by Jacobson 1983.

[67] See the full commentary by Winston 1979, who goes so far as to claim that it may have been written during the troubles of 37–41 C.E., i.e. contemporary with Philo and perhaps within a few years of when *Opif.* was written.

[68] On the New Testament see the survey at Runia *PEC* 63–86 (esp. the Logos texts are relevant for our treatise). On Theophilus see Grant 1988, 157–164, who compares it with both Philo and Rabbinic texts; see also Introduction §8 on Philo's *Nachleben*.

Nachleben.⁶⁹ A more vexing question is the relation of Philonic biblical interpretation to Jewish exegesis in Hebrew or Aramaic. Recently scholars such as P. Borgen and N. Cohen have argued that Philo should not be read in isolation from rabbinic writings. Although chronologically these writings are posterior to Philo, they are thought to contain traditions that in some cases could well be contemporary with him.⁷⁰ Although rabbinic literature is not the area of my expertise, I have tried to take this material into account to some degree in the Commentary, despite some misgivings about the severe chronological problems involved.⁷¹ Of particular interest is the collection of material distilled in *Genesis Rabbah*.⁷² It cannot have been compiled until the 5th century at the earliest, and most of its material must post-date Philo by centuries.⁷³ Not only are we limited by constraints of space, but we should also be ever cognizant of the danger of "parallelomania." It is advisable to respect the judgment of an eminent expert on the entire field of ancient Jewish exegesis, J. Kugel, who, when confronted with a particular Philonic answer to a particular exegetical problem (the plural in Gen 1:26) states laconically that "it is, as usual, somewhat *sui generis*."⁷⁴

This impression of Philo as an exceptional figure even in his Jewish-Alexandrian milieu is confirmed by the brief testimonies that we have concerning him. According to Josephus he "had an excellent reputation in all matters ... and was not unskilled in philosophy," while Eusebius states that "he was distinguished for his learning not only of our writings but also of those that had an external origin."⁷⁵ Both refer — in Josephus' case implicitly — to the double nature of Philo's culture, with which all readers of his writings are familiar and which are often summarized under his twin names Philo Judaeus and Philo Alexandrinus, namely his Judaism and his Hellenism. It is crucial to bear in mind at all times that his first loyalty was to Judaism and his prime intellectual commitment to the exposition of the thought of Moses. This meant in practice that, no matter how much

---

⁶⁹ See below, following section.
⁷⁰ See Borgen 1965, 1997; Cohen 1995.
⁷¹ Valuable collections of material, digested to a greater or lesser extent, are found in Ginzberg 1909–38; Urbach 1987 (1975); Kugel *TB*.
⁷² English translations by Freedman in Freedman and Simon 1939; Neusner 1985.
⁷³ See on these issues Strack and Stemberger 1991, 303–305.
⁷⁴ Kugel *TB* 79; on this question see Commentary Ch. 13.
⁷⁵ Josephus *Ant.* 18.8.257; Eusebius *Hist. Eccl.* 2.4.2.

his thought was influenced by streams of Greek philosophy, his relationship to Hellenism could not be the same as that of a Greek intellectual. In other words, Philo could not be a committed member of a Greek *hairesis* (school of philosophy), because he was already a member of the *hairesis* of Moses.[76]

(b) Hellenism

The contents of *Opif.* bear witness to the wealth of Greek learning, particularly in the area of philosophy, which Philo could draw upon when writing his works. This learning must have been the result of a lengthy and thorough training, but the exact manner in which he obtained it remains elusive.[77] All we can do is deduce it from the evidence in the writings themselves. On this basis J. Dillon has concluded that Philo was a man who had studied the important philosophical texts at first hand, and was not dependent for his knowledge on handbooks and compendia.[78]

By far the most important philosophical background for our treatise is the Platonic tradition, and in particular, the exegesis of one dialogue, the *Timaeus*. It is apparent as early as Ch. 2 (with its clear allusions in §§9, 10 and 12) that Philo perceives a far-reaching parallelism between the Mosaic creation account and Plato's famous mythic cosmogony. In §21 we even encounter an anonymous reference to Plato in the words "what one of the ancients also said."[79] This complex *rapprochement* was already studied by J. Horovitz in his excellent 1900 dissertation, and it was also the main theme in my own dissertation, in which it is analysed in comprehensive depth.[80] In my study I could build on excellent research carried out by P. Boyancé, W. Theiler and Dillon on the more specific background of Philo's exegesis.[81] It is plain that many features of his reading of the dialogue stand in a specific early Middle Platonist tradition of exegesis. Theiler suspected an influential commentary on the *Timaeus*, tentatively ascribed to the Alexandrian Neopythagorean philosopher Eudorus,

---

[76] See further Runia 1999 on Philo and the Greek *hairesis* model.
[77] He may well have had the benefit of private tutors, as well as extensive contact with Alexandrian intellectuals; see my discussion at *PT* 35–37.
[78] Dillon 1977, 140.
[79] Note the little word "also," i.e. in addition to Moses. The direct reference to Plato in §119 is much less important, since it is no more than a literary embellishment.
[80] Horovitz 1900; Runia *PT*.
[81] Boyancé 1963; Theiler 1965, 1971; Dillon 1977, 139–181; see further *PT* 485–519.

who lived about a generation before Philo. Though this suggestion must remain speculative, it is clear that Philo learnt to read the *Timaeus* in a particular way, as can be seen from the way he views the ideas as thoughts of God. Such interpretations were then adapted to the specific requirements of the Mosaic creation account, where, for example, there is no room for the World-soul, that entity which is so central in Middle Platonist cosmology. Most Middle Platonist literature has been lost. The best we can do is cite a considerable number of authors in order to illustrate the background to Philo's exegesis (notably Plutarch, Atticus and the handbook of Alcinous).[82] Apart from the use of arithmology the specific influence of Pythagorean ideas, other than the themes found in the *Timaeus*, is not particularly strong. More important is Philo's use of other Platonic dialogues, notably the *Republic*, the *Symposium*, and above all the *Phaedrus* with its celebrated myth of the flight of the soul. This theme has been exhaustively studied by A. Méasson, who draws extensively on the research of Boyancé mentioned above.[83] Both scholars remind us that Philo is earlier than the majority of Middle Platonists, and that his thought can be illumined by Platonic themes already found in the late writings of Cicero. It is most unlikely that Philo read works such as *On the nature of the gods* and *Tusculan disputations*, but the two thinkers share a common late Hellenistic background,[84] as well as similar attitudes towards the dominance of Hellenic thought from the perspective of a differing religious tradition.

The next most important philosophical background for *Opif.* is the thought of the Stoic school. On frequent occasions Philo exploits terms and doctrines of the Stoa, particularly in the areas of epistemology, psychology and ethics. The strong anthropocentric emphasis of the cosmology in *Opif.* is also in sympathy with the Stoic school. Remarkably no less than ten passages of the work have been included in Von Arnim's standard collection of Stoic fragments.[85] We may indeed be certain that Philo had a thorough knowledge of the basic doctrines of the school.[86] But the presence of the Stoa is much more

---

[82] A superb overview of the tradition is given in the volumes of Dörrie and Baltes *DPA*.

[83] Méasson 1986.

[84] Associated esp. with the philosophers Panaetius, Posidonius and Antiochus, all of whom combine Stoicism with a predilection for Plato.

[85] §§3, 8, 26, 36, 43, 66, 67, 73, 142–143, 166. Usually this is on questionable grounds; see the Commentary ad locc.

[86] Philo's life overlaps with that of Arius the Stoic who was court philosopher to

diffuse than in the case of Platonism. Partly this may have to do with our ignorance of Philo's exact sources. It is also caused, however, by the fact that many Stoic doctrines had entered the philosophical *koine* of Philo's day and were no longer exclusively tied to the rigorous systematics of the school.[87] It is not possible to tie Stoic themes in *Opif.* down to the specific influence of important later Stoics such as Posidonius and Antiochus (if we may regard him as such).[88]

In the first century B.C.E. a revival of Aristotelianism took place. Philo is acquainted with the central doctrines of Aristotle, based on reading of both school treatises and exoteric works now lost.[89] The influence of Aristotle's thought on *Opif.* is modest, confined to some basic theological, psychological and biological doctrines.[90] On this issue I disagree with the interpretation of the Dutch scholar A. P. Bos, who sees a stronger influence of Aristotelian ideas in the opening chapters of the work.[91] I would argue that these ideas are present, but that they have been largely absorbed into a Platonizing framework.

The basic tenets of the Epicurean school are anathema to the religious thinker and moralist Philo. But once again it emerges that he was surprisingly well acquainted with the main doctrines of the school and was prepared to use them when relevant for the understanding of the biblical text. In his allegorical interpretation of the snake as pleasure Philo gives an account of the Epicurean doctrine of *oikeiôsis* which supplies details unknown elsewhere.[92]

The final philosophical school of thought that is relevant for the treatise is scepticism. In his understanding of the task of the exegete and his approach to certain philosophical and scientific subjects Philo is prepared to take over terms and even doctrines from this school,

---

the Emperor Augustus, after having persuaded him not to destroy the city of Alexandria after the battle of Actium in 30 B.C.E. The identification with Arius Didymus must, after the monograph of Göransson 1995, be regarded as questionable.

[87] There is no recent all-round treatment of Philo's appropriation of Stoic thought. For ethical doctrines see Winston 1984. Reydams-Schils has recently shown that Philo's Platonism has also undergone the influence of the Stoic school; cf. 1995, 1999, 135–165. See also Runia *PT* 480–485.

[88] In particular Theiler's inclusion of passages from *Opif.* as fragments of Posidonius is highly dubious; see on §38 and §133.

[89] On Philo's knowledge of Aristotle see Boyancé 1974; Runia *PT* 477–479; Martín 1996.

[90] This corresponds to the general contours of Aristotelian influence in Philo's day, with the exception of his logical works. See Barnes 1997 on the Roman Aristotle.

[91] See Bos 1998.

[92] Analysed by Lévy 2000.

even though his basic temperament is far from sceptical.[93] In *Opif.* these borrowings reflect the Academic school of Carneades and Philo of Larissa rather than the Neopyrrhonist movement of Aenesidemus, which he draws on elsewhere.[94]

Philo's treatise contains remarkably little scientific doctrine, as distinguished from the science practised by philosophers.[95] This is worth noting when one considers how much cosmology could be used to explain the Genesis account. This bias undoubtedly reflects the preferences and limitations of Philo's own education. The knowledge of botany and biology revealed in the treatise is fairly superficial, though adequate for the task at hand. The one exception worth mentioning is Philo's treatment of the watery chaos on the third day, which is repeated at Gen 2:6. Here he appears to draw on quasi-evolutionary accounts of the origin of the cosmos and the earth which we find elsewhere in authors such as Lucretius, Diodorus Siculus, Pliny the Elder and Ovid.[96]

The final aspect of the treatise's *Sitz im Leben* that should be mentioned is the language and literary style of the work itself. In spite of its exegetical content, Philo writes as much as possible like an educated Greek.[97] Undoubtedly he had contact with contemporary rhetors in Alexandria and these will have exerted influence on his style.[98] Moreover, close analysis of his writings reveals intimate knowledge of the conventions of Greek rhetoric.[99] Literary allusions and other poetical embellishments are less frequent in *Opif.*, however, than in many of the remaining treatises in the corpus.[100]

Philo's Hellenic erudition is thus broad and often genuinely profound. In *Opif.* it is actively applied to a task which has little to do

---

[93] See on Philo's scepticism Nikiprowetzky 1977, 186–191; Mansfeld 1988.

[94] Famously in *Plant.* 166–202, the earliest of the three main sources for the tropes of Aenesidemus.

[95] The arithmology discussed above in Introduction §6 can also scarcely be regarded as science.

[96] The standard monograph on this material is still Spoerri 1959.

[97] On the language and style of *Opif.* see also the discussion of Cohn's first edition below in Introduction §10.

[98] See now Winter 1997, 60–112.

[99] As demonstrated by Conley 1987, 1997; Alexandre 1999.

[100] Apart from the material included in the arithmological excursus §§89–128. Outside this section the best example is found in §133. A good overview of Philo's knowledge and use of Greek literature is still a desideratum. But see the collected references in the indices of Leisegang PCW 7.3–26 and of Earp PLCL vol. 10. For Philo's knowledge of Homer and Homeric exegesis (important as background for his allegorical method) see Boyancé 1963, 73–79, Siegert 1996, 165.

with Hellenism, but is rather grounded in Philo's *Sitz im Leben* as an Alexandrian Jew.

8. *The* Nachleben *of the treatise*

One of the aims of the Commentary series is to take account of the influence which Philo's treatises exercised on later authors. This subject is not only of great intrinsic interest. In recent years there has also been increasing recognition that the *Rezeptionsgeschichte* of a text or an author should not be separated from the study of that text or author. In the case of Philo this is particularly obvious. Without the great interest that the Church fathers showed in his writings and thought, the corpus would certainly not have survived. Until fairly recently the study of Philo's reception was a neglected subject.[101] Fortunately this is no longer the case. Two recent projects have shed a flood of light on the subject. First we mention the project *La Bible d'Alexandrie* initiated by M. Harl. Her annotated translation of the Septuagint Genesis gives a valuable overview of Hellenistic-Jewish and Christian exegesis.[102] But for the first chapters the sheer amount of material is overwhelming. Harl's treatment has been greatly expanded in a more detailed study dedicated to the first five chapters of the Greek Genesis by Monique Alexandre. This truly magnificent work, which discusses the biblical text and its early interpretation verse by verse and phrase by phrase, has been of inestimable value in the difficult task of hunting down Philonic themes in the vast repository of Patristic exegesis.[103] Secondly I should mention my own two studies, in which I attempted to trace Philo's presence in early Christian literature up to the year 400 C.E.[104] These results are at present being deepened (and sometimes corrected) by the research of other scholars.[105] This research has provided the basic framework for the sections on *Nachleben* in the present Commentary.

The only ancient writer who mentions *Opif.* by name is, as we already saw (Introduction §1), Eusebius.[106] There can be little doubt,

---

[101] Note, however, the important references to the church fathers in the *apparatus testimoniorum* of PCW; see the index at Runia 1995, 240–249.
[102] Harl 1986.
[103] Alexandre *CLG*; the absence of comprehensive indices is regrettable.
[104] Runia *PEC*, 1995.
[105] Notably by the research of A. van den Hoek on Origen, 2000a. Her earlier study on Clement's use of Philo, 1988, has also been a valuable resource. See also Geljon 2000.
[106] There are also direct references to the work in the *Sacra Parallela*; see the

however, that the treatise circulated widely. This can be deduced from the considerable number of writings in which subsequent use of the work can be demonstrated. On the Jewish side the harvest is small. The similarities between the opening chapters of Josephus' *Antiquities* and *Opif.* are too great to be coincidental, but the usage remains fairly superficial.[107] The rabbis neglected Philo because they were not interested in his kind of exegesis. We have found only two exceptions, Rabbi Hoshai'a of Caesarea in the 3rd century and the very late *Midrash Tadsche*.

On the Christian side the situation is very different.[108] The backbone of the transmission of Philo's thought in early Christian literature is formed by the Alexandrian tradition, commencing with Clement, reaching its apogee in Origen, and finding a 4th century continuation in Didymus the blind. The remarkable discovery of a papyrus copy of Didymus' *Commentary on Genesis* compensates a little for the calamitous loss of Origen's commentary on the same work, which covered only the first four chapters in 13 books and undoubtedly contained a wealth of Philonic material. The only 2nd century author outside Alexandria of importance for our research is Theophilus of Alexandria,[109] whose exegesis of Genesis 1–11 has already been mentioned in the previous section.[110] From Origen the torch passes on to Eusebius, and from him to the Cappadocian fathers Basil and Gregory of Nyssa. Basil's *Hexaemeron*, despite the similarities of subject matter, uses Philo relatively little. Gregory is more sympathetic to Philo's approach and draws on him for various anthropological themes, as does Nemesius in his little work on the nature of humankind. The greatest 4th century use of Philo is found, however, in the writings of the bishop of Milan, Ambrose, and *Opif.* is

---

apparatus testimoniorum in PCW.

[107] Josephus' treatment of the account of creation and the events in paradise is brief in the extreme. At §25 and §29 he says he is postponing a deeper treatment of the subject involving discussion of causes to a subsequent work. But this intention was apparently not carried out. The detailed monograph on Josephus' treatment, Franxmann 1979, recognizes Philo's influence but does not study it systematically. Feldman's extensive commentary on *Ant.* 1–4, 2000, is also very cursory in its attention to Philonic indebtedness.

[108] For an overview of the transmission of Philo's writings, which runs largely parallel to the usage of his writings, see the chart at Runia *PEC* 18.

[109] On this author the research of J. P. Martín and R. M. Grant has been particularly valuable; see esp. Martín 1986, 1989; Grant 1988.

[110] Note that the *Cohortatio* of Ps.-Justin is to be dated to the 3rd or even 4th century (to the latter if the attribution to Marcellus of Ancyra put forward as an hypothesis by Riedweg 1994 is correct).

no exception, being drawn upon extensively in a number of his letters. Traces of material from *Opif.* can be discerned in Calcidius, Augustine and Jerome, but thereafter its direct influence seems to diminish in both the East and the West. Whether the considerable overlap between *Opif.* and the book *On the months* by the Byzantine writer John Lydus (490–565) is due to direct appropriation is still an unresolved question.[111] The Armenian translators working in 6th century Byzantium did not, as far as we know, translate *Opif.* Extracts from the work were, however, taken up in the *Sacra Parallela* of John of Damascus and its tradition.[112]

Finally it should be noted that the exact manner in which Philonic material is appropriated is not always easy to determine.[113] Sometimes direct usage is absolutely clear, as for example in Ambrose. At other times, however, the parallelism between texts can also be explained in a different manner, e.g. through an indirect transmission. For later authors the strong influence of Origen's Genesis commentary may often be suspected. In the context of our Commentary we have thought it legitimate to include as much material as we could. Our aim has been to focus as much as possible on direct usage, but it is highly probable that some of the examples we have cited rest on indirect transmission. After all, these examples too belong to the *Nachleben* of Philo's treatise.

9. *The text of the treatise*

Our translation is based on the Greek text edited by L. Cohn in the monumental critical edition of Philo's works which he published together with P. Wendland.[114] The preparation of the edition of *Opif.* was undertaken with more than usual care due to circumstances that are worth briefly mentioning. During the course of the 19th century it became increasingly clear that T. Mangey's edition of Philo's writings extant in Greek (1742), for all its virtues, was not a truly critical text and had to be replaced. But various efforts to achieve this goal failed. In 1887, at the instigation of the famous classicist H. Diels, the Prussian Academy of Sciences offered a prize for a new edition of *Opif.*

---

[111] See our discussion in Ch. 15, Excursus II.
[112] We have not pursued these references on account of the confused and largely unedited state of the texts.
[113] On these methodological problems in the study of Philo's reception see the conclusions reached in *PEC* 335–342 and esp. the diagram on 341.
[114] PCW 1.1–60, published in 1896.

Two scholars submitted entries. Cohn (1856–1915) presented an edition based on a thorough study of the manuscript tradition. This study was subsequently published in 1889.[115] The other scholar, P. Wendland (1864–1915), lacked the opportunity to study the manuscripts and so submitted an edition based on a knowledge of Philo and other relevant authors only.[116] But Wendland's philological brilliance was such that this study too made a substantial contribution. Both scholars obtained the full prize. They decided to work together on the new critical edition, for which the prize money provided valuable resources. In 1890 Wendland published a detailed review of Cohn's edition.[117] Many of the changes he proposed were incorporated in the new edition which Cohn published as volume 1 of the *editio maior* in 1896. Translated into contemporary terms, the prize can be regarded as offering a subsidy for the promising research of two young scholars, while Cohn's first edition amounts to a kind of pilot version of the final product of the promised research.

A study of the two editions and their prolegomena reveal that the text we have translated is based on a solid transmission of the work.[118] The treatise is included in most of the major manuscripts of Philo's writings. It has the added great advantage of being present (though only for §§1–91) in the oldest of all Philonic manuscripts, the famous Vienna codex, the text of which closely resembles the excerpts found in Eusebius, and goes back to the original archetype of our ms. tradition.[119] *Opif.* is also found in M, the quality of which is second to V. The text can be further checked through excerpts in the indirect tradition of the *Sacra Parallela*.[120] There are, however, no papyri or ancient translations of the work that can be used for purposes of comparison. To my knowledge no major new manuscripts containing *Opif.* have come to light since the publication of Cohn's edition.[121] The text published in the Loeb Classical Library edition of Philo is identical with that of Cohn and mentions only a single textual emendation.[122] The French edition prepared by Arnaldez is also

---

[115] Cohn 1889. See further §10 on the *status quaestionis*.
[116] For an account of the *Preisfrage* see Pohlenz 1916, 60.
[117] Wendland 1890.
[118] See Cohn 1889, i–xli; PCW 1.i–xliii.
[119] On this codex see Runia *PEC* 21.
[120] PCW 1.lxiii–lxvii.
[121] The palimpsest containing a very ancient text of Philo (probably 10th cent.), reported by Alexander 1977, apparently did not include *Opif.*
[122] At §71. Colson paid much more attention to the textual basis in subsequent volumes.

based on Cohn, but it makes a number of useful remarks on the text which we have been able to use to our profit.

Our method has been to take Cohn's text, with its very detailed critical apparatus, as our starting point, but to take all manuscript variants into account when preparing our translation. This has led to about twenty departures from his text, all of which are noted in the Notes to the translation, and are usually further discussed in the Commentary. The erudition and philological acumen of Cohn and Wendland deserves the highest admiration. Fashions in the editing of texts are subject to change, and modern editors are usually less inclined to emend texts than their 19th century counterparts. Cohn was, in the context of his times, a careful and fairly conservative editor. Nevertheless on a number of occasions he alters the text on the basis of subjective judgments which now seem dubious. From time to time the influence of Wendland, who was a more speculative editor, can be felt.[123] In one respect the modern editor has a distinct advantage over his predecessors. Through the advent of electronic searching the entire Philonic corpus can be checked in a matter of seconds. This helps us to determine that at least on occasion Cohn chose the wrong textual variant.[124]

10. Status quaestionis: *previous scholarship on the treatise*

The translation and commentary offered in this study is able to build on a long tradition of Philonic scholarship. This research can be divided into two parts, the former consisting of those studies which focus directly on the text of our treatise, the latter consisting of those which study Philo's writings and thought in a more general fashion.

(a) scholarly literature specifically focused on *Opif.*
Editions of Philo's text have already been discussed above in the previous section on the text of the treatise (§9). A little more, however, should be said about Cohn's first, separate edition, because, in addition to the critical text, it offered four more aids to the reader with a good knowledge of Latin and Greek. Firstly, in a separate apparatus under the text a limited selection of relevant Philonic passages was

---

[123] An example is found at §158, where the words καὶ ἀνδραποδίζουσαι, though still present in the 1889 edition, are bracketed on Wendland's advice. Cohn and Wendland's text is criticized for its speculative alterations by Harl 1962, 328.

[124] E.g. at §139; see the Commentary ad loc.

printed. Secondly, Cohn added an appendix to the text containing a more extensive collection of "selected passages suitable for illustrating the doctrine of Philo's little book" drawn from Greek and Latin authors (68–85). This collection has been of great value for the preparation of our Commentary. Thirdly, the introduction contains a valuable section entitled "observations on Philo's language," as exemplified by the contents of *Opif.* (xli–lviii). This section is an invaluable resource for questions of language, syntax and style. Finally, we should mention the full *index verborum*, which contains all but the most common words in the treatise (86–108).

Two earlier commentaries have been written on *Opif.* The first was published as long ago as 1841 by the German theologian J. G. Müller.[125] Based on a faulty text[126] and difficult to use on account of its outdated references, it is now mainly of antiquarian interest. But it does contain many useful parallels from Greek and Latin literature (often exploited by Cohn), as well as many pertinent observations on the details of Philo's language and style. The second is of much more recent origin, published in 1987 by the Italian scholar R. Radice.[127] It is based on a translation by C. Kraus Reggiani.[128] Radice's commentary differs markedly in style and method from our own. Though paying a certain amount of attention to the exegetical context, its primary focus is analytic and philosophical. The mastery of the relevant scholarly literature is remarkable.[129] Though it divides the text into units similar to ours, it does not follow the argument sentence by sentence and does not comment on individual passages. This means that it pays little attention to ideas and problems in the text itself and seldom identifies its literary and philosophical allusions.[130] The amount of overlap with the present commentary is thus surprisingly limited.

Four modern translations of *Opif.* have been regularly consulted:[131] in German by J. Cohn (1909);[132] in English by G. H. Whitaker, with

---

[125] Berlin 1841.
[126] See the severe criticisms of Cohn 1889, xxxiv.
[127] Milan 1987, accompanied by a commentary on the *Legum Allegoriae*.
[128] Substantially the same as that published earlier in Kraus Reggiani 1979.
[129] As befits the chief author of R–R! See the extensive bibliography in Kraus Reggiani, Radice and Reale 1987, 5–32.
[130] The commentary was criticized on this score by Dillon 1990, 181.
[131] I have not been able to consult those of Triviño 1976 (in Castilian), Calvetti 1978 (in Italian), Montserrat I Torrents 1983 (in Catalan), Daniel-Nataf 1991 (in Hebrew). On these see R–R 2301, 2401, 2353, RRS 2602 and *SPhA* 7 1995, 225–226.
[132] Not to be confused with L. Cohn. He was, as A. Kamesar has informed me, the editor's older brother.

notes by F. H. Colson (1929);[133] in French by R. Arnaldez (1961); and the above-mentioned Italian version by Kraus Reggiani (1987). The first three are all accompanied by useful annotations.[134] The notes of J. Cohn are particularly strong in the area of rabbinic studies. Whitaker's translation suffers from being the first in the famous Loeb Classical Library edition of Philo's works. Its language is now in many cases archaic. Though generally accurate, it does contain some egregious mistakes.[135] Also deserving of mention is the splendid anthology of Philonic texts accompanied by learned notes by D. Winston, which includes nearly a third of the work.[136] I have also been greatly assisted by an unpublished Dutch translation by J. C. M. van Winden. Finally mention should be made of other volumes in the French edition which have supplied much valuable comparative material for the commentary.[137]

(b) general studies

Despite the truly copious secondary literature on the writings and thought of Philo,[138] very little is specifically directed at the study of *Opif.* on its own.[139] The contents of our treatise are almost invariably discussed in connection with other texts from the vast *corpus Philonicum*. The following overview is meant to introduce the more important scholarly works on Philo which we have used in the preparation of our Commentary.[140]

The centrality of exegesis for the understanding of Philo's writings and the importance of his role as commentator of scripture was demonstrated by V. Nikiprowetzky in his famous monograph and a host of articles (among which special mention should be made of his flawed but seminal article on the Mosaic creation account as under-

---

[133] I have also occasionally consulted the fluent translation of Yonge 1854, recently republished 1993; its accuracy is necessarily limited, however, because it is based on a defective text.

[134] Arnaldez' introduction and notes cannot, however, compare with some of the later volumes of the series under his editorship, Les œuvres de Philon d'Alexandrie. It too suffered from being the first in the series. The review article of Boyancé 1963a is rightly critical.

[135] Notably the translation at §12 of ἀιδιότητα as "the infinite and undefinable"!

[136] Winston 1981; unfortunately inadequately indexed, but see the list on p. 422.

[137] Notably those by Méasson (*Sacr.*), Harl (*Her.*), Alexandre (*Congr.*), Petit (*Prob.*), and Hadas-Lebel (*Prov.*).

[138] See the standard Philonic bibliographies, G-G, R-R, and now RRS.

[139] Some rare examples are Grumach 1939; Van Winden 1983; Belletti 1987; Runia 1989; Gilaberti Barberà 1990.

[140] For recent overviews of Philonic scholarship in general see Runia *PT* 3–31; Borgen 1997, 1–13.

stood by Philo).¹⁴¹ This emphasis on exegesis has been carried further by P. Borgen, who, as we saw earlier,¹⁴² has strongly emphasized the place of the treatise in the Exposition of the Law and the Jewish context of much of its exegesis.

For the study of Philo's theological and cosmological thought the celebrated (but deeply flawed) study of H. A. Wolfson is still indispensable.¹⁴³ A better picture will be gained, however, from the more compact studies of J. Dillon and D. Winston, and the synoptic section of my own monograph on Philo's Platonism.¹⁴⁴ Older studies using the method of the History of Religions school no longer stand at the forefront of Philonic research.¹⁴⁵ On the role of humankind in the cosmos valuable studies have been contributed by D. Jobling and P. Borgen.¹⁴⁶ As we have already noted, the study of Philo's anthropology, which is closely connected to his exegesis of Gen 1:26–27 and Gen 2:7, is fraught with difficulties. The monographs of R. A. Baer and Tobin survey the texts and provide valuable insights on their interpretation, even if one cannot always agree with their methodology.¹⁴⁷ Baer's study of Philo's views on sexuality and the body have been deepened by further studies by D. Sly and Winston.¹⁴⁸ Synoptic studies in the area of Philonic ethics are still scarce, and in certain respects the monograph of W. Völker is still unsurpassed.¹⁴⁹ It can be supplemented by general studies cited above,¹⁵⁰ as well as by additional articles by Winston and C. Lévy.¹⁵¹ Scholarly literature specially devoted to Philo's arithmology has already been discussed above.¹⁵²

---

¹⁴¹ Nikiprowetzky 1977, and the collection of articles in 1996, including the article on "La récit de la création," 1965, also cited above at n. 36.

¹⁴² See above n. 25.

¹⁴³ Wolfson 1947; the penetrating critique of Bormann 1955 is still worth studying.

¹⁴⁴ Dillon 1977; Winston 1985a; Runia *PT*. The study of Radice 1989 is largely consistent with his commentary. His views on Philo's role in the history of philosophy, on which see the English article 1991, are controversial, because he concludes that Philo acted as a catalyst in the Greek philosophical tradition.

¹⁴⁵ E.g. Bréhier 1908 (though valuable on philosophical questions); Goodenough 1935; Früchtel 1968.

¹⁴⁶ Jobling 1977; Borgen 1995.

¹⁴⁷ Baer 1970; Tobin 1983. See on the question of exegetical traditions above Introduction §3.

¹⁴⁸ Sly 1990; Winston 1998.

¹⁴⁹ Völker 1938.

¹⁵⁰ See esp. Wolfson 1947; Dillon 1977; Runia *PT*.

¹⁵¹ See esp. Winston 1984, 1986, 1990; Lévy 1998. We eagerly await Winston's comprehensive monograph on the whole of Philo's thought.

¹⁵² Introduction §6.

11. *Some notes on the method used in the translation*

Translating is a treacherous and dissatisfying business. When languages are as far apart as Philo's ancient Greek and modern English, it is well-nigh impossible to render the meaning of a text both accurately and fluently, and still capture something of the style and flavour of the original. In the trade-off between accuracy and fluency we have chosen to give preference to accuracy, in the knowledge that many modern readers rely on the translator for access to the original Greek. A further consideration is that a relatively literal translation facilitates the task of the commentary based on it.[153] This means, for example, that we will occasionally use a participial construction which in modern English seems rather bookish. Philo's style is ornate and tends to the verbose, with periods which on average are at least twice as long as a sentence in English. Frequently we have had no choice but to break these periods up into shorter sentences, a move which detracts from the reproduction of Philo's style. Having been trained in the school of philosophical and expositional writing, he also likes to use connective particles and phrases more than is customary in English. For the sake of accuracy we have retained more of these than is preferable from the stylistic point of view. Another area of difficulty is the rendering of important philosophical terms. We have tried where possible to render terms consistently, for example always translating νοῦς by "intellect" and διάνοια by "understanding", but in some cases (notoriously in the case of ἀρχή and λόγος), this kind of correspondence is quite impossible to maintain. For some further comments on particular difficulties in rendering Philo into English see the notes to the translation. It is important to note that words added in brackets have been added to the translation for the sake of clarity or fluency, but are not present in the original Greek.

It should further be noted that there is an exact parallelism between the divisions of the translation and the structure discerned and implemented in the Commentary. Chapter divisions of the Commentary are given in square brackets in the headings of the translation. The headings themselves, which are the work of the translator, form the titles of the chapters of the Commentary. Paragraph divisions in the translation correspond exactly to the numbered subdivisions of the analysis of the relevant chapter in the Commentary.

---

[153] Similar views are now voiced by S. Mason in the Preface to the first volume of the Brill Josephus project, Feldman 2000, x–xii.

Mindful of the importance of the exegetical basis of the treatise, we have attempted to indicate Philo's references to the biblical text as accurately as possible by means of markings in the translation itself. Words and phrases highlighted in **bold type** correspond verbally to the biblical text. Those highlighted in ***bold italics*** are based on the biblical text or even refer to it directly, without sharing the same lexical or grammatical form. For example the phrase φῶς ... γέγονε in §29 is clearly based on καὶ ἐγένετο φῶς in Gen 1:3, but the use of the perfect tense in this case is sufficiently different to warrant the placement in bold italics rather than in the bold type used for direct citation.

12. *Some notes on the method used in the commentary*

The commentary on *Opif.* that we present in this study does not aim to be exhaustive. It is clear that, when the central place of the treatise in Philo's thought is added to the vast extent of the Philonic corpus and its pervasive relations to contemporary Jewish and Hellenistic thought, it would not have been difficult to write a commentary double the length, provided of course that one had the time and the energy. Such a commentary could not be written within the confines of the present series. We have had to be selective.

As we saw above in §3, the treatise is divided up into 25 chapters, each of which corresponds to a chapter of the Commentary. Each chapter consists of at least five sections. In the first, entitled *Analysis/ General comments*, we first indicate the place of the chapter in the work as a whole and give a structural analysis of its contents. This is followed by some general comments on the major themes of the chapter, together with their background in Greek philosophy or Jewish thought. Brief comments are also sometimes made on the relevant scholarly literature. The main body of each chapter consists of the *Detailed comments*. These are linked to short sections of the translation printed in bold italic type. The detailed comments undertake to explain major terms and concepts in Philo's text,[154] as well as dealing with problems raised by the text and illuminating its background through comparison with other Philonic texts and detailed references to Greek and Jewish sources outside the corpus. Within

---

[154] In the detailed comments I have generally presented Greek terms in the original Greek script. Some very common words have been transliterated into Roman letters (*ê* corresponding to η and *ô* to ω).

this section the divisions of the analysis of the chapter given earlier are indicated at the appropriate points. If a particular detailed theme is too complex to be dealt with adequately within the confines of a single comment, it is discussed in a separate *Excursus* at the end of this section. These excursuses have been kept to a minimum. Three shorter sections conclude each chapter. Firstly in the *Exegetical parallels* we briefly indicate other Philonic texts where the same biblical passage and/or problems are dealt with. Next the *Nachleben* of the chapter's themes is outlined. Finally some guidance is offered for *Further reading* on the contents of the chapter.

The length of the commentary has been kept down through the following three measures. (1) I have been rather selective in my citation of Philonic parallels, concentrating on the texts which are found in the Exposition of the Law or which are particularly relevant to the subject at hand. Philo is a highly repetitive writer and it is often not difficult to give parallel passages virtually *ad libitum*. (2) Philological and stylistic matters have generally only been discussed when they are important for the subject under discussion. (3) The references to scholarly literature have also been selective, with a concentration on the more recent literature. This is not because I believe that the research of earlier scholars was inferior, but because very often the best results of a generation of scholars are absorbed by the following one, and also because by reading recent studies one can generally find one's way back to important earlier research. A bias towards literature in the English language cannot be denied, but I also have tried, where possible, to point out the most important contributions in other languages used by Philonic scholars.

TRANSLATION

Philo of Alexandria
On the creation of the cosmos according to Moses

[Chapter 1] *Introduction*[1]*

(§1) If you consider the other lawgivers,[2] you will find that some drew up the regulations that they regarded as just in an unadorned and naked fashion, while others enclothed their thoughts with a mass of verbiage and so deceived the masses by concealing the truth with mythical fictions. (§2) Moses surpassed both groups, regarding the former as lacking reflection, indolent and unphilosophical, the latter as mendacious and full of trickery. Instead he made a splendid and awe-inspiring start to his laws. He did not immediately state what should be done and what not, nor did he, since it was necessary to form in advance the minds of those who were to make use of the laws, invent myths or express approval of those composed by others. (§3) The beginning is, as I just said,[3] quite marvellous. It contains an account of the making of the cosmos, the reasoning for this being that the cosmos is in harmony with the law and the law with the cosmos, and the man who observes the law is at once a citizen of the cosmos, directing his actions in relation to the rational purpose of nature, in accordance with which the entire cosmos also is administered.

(§4) In celebrating the beauty of the thoughts contained in this creation account, no one, whether writing poetry or prose, can do them true justice. They transcend both speech and hearing, for they are greater and more august than what can be adapted to the instruments of a mortal being. (§5) This does not mean, however, that we must keep our peace. No, on behalf of the God-beloved (author)[4] we must dare to speak, even if this goes beyond our ability, presenting nothing from our own supply and stating only a few things instead of many, namely those to which the human mind can reasonably attain when it is possessed by a love and desire for wisdom. (§6) For just as even the tiniest seal when it has been engraved is able

---

* For the notes on the text and translation see below p. 94.

to contain the representations of things with colossal dimensions, so it may be that the overwhelming beauties of the making of the cosmos as they have been written in the laws, even if they bedazzle the souls of the readers with their brightness, can be elucidated with delineations on a smaller scale. But first a preliminary remark needs to be made, which should not be passed over in silence.

[Chapter 2] *A preliminary comment on God and the cosmos*

(§7) There are some people who, having more admiration for the cosmos than for its maker, declared the former both ungenerated and eternal, while falsely and impurely attributing to God much idleness. What they should have done was the opposite, namely be astounded at God's powers as Maker and Father, and not show more reverence for the cosmos than is its due.

(§8) Moses, however, had not only reached the very summit of philosophy, but had also been instructed in the many and most essential doctrines of nature by means of oracles. He recognized that it is absolutely necessary that among existing things there is an activating cause on the one hand and a passive object on the other, and that the activating cause is the absolutely pure and unadulterated intellect of the universe, superior to excellence and superior to knowledge and even superior to the good and the beautiful itself. (§9) But the passive object, which of itself was without soul and unmoved, when set in motion and shaped and ensouled by the intellect, changed into the most perfect piece of work, this cosmos. Those who declare that it is ungenerated are unaware that they are eliminating the most useful and indispensable of the contributions to piety, the (doctrine of) providence. (§10) Reason demands that the Father and Maker exercise care for that which has come into being. After all,[5] both a father aims at the safety of his children and a craftsman aims at the preservation of what has been constructed, using every means at their disposal to repel all that is injurious and harmful, while desiring to provide in every way that which is advantageous and profitable. But there is no affinity between that which did not come into being and the one who did not make it. (§11) It is a worthless and unhelpful doctrine, bringing about a power-vacuum in this cosmos, just like (what happens) in a city, because it does not then have a ruler or magistrate or judge, by whom everything is lawfully administered and regulated.

(§12) But the great Moses considered that what is ungenerated was of a totally different order from that which was visible, for the entire sense-perceptible realm is in a process of becoming and change and never remains in the same state. So to what is invisible and intelligible he assigned eternity as being akin and related to it, whereas on what is sense-perceptible he ascribed the appropriate name **becoming** (**genesis**) [a][6]. Since, therefore, this cosmos is both visible and sense-perceptible, it must necessarily also be generated. Hence he was not off the mark in also giving a description of its **becoming**, thereby speaking about God in a truly reverent manner.

[Chapter 3] *The scheme of six days*

(§13) He says that the cosmos was fashioned in six days, not because the maker was in need of a length of time—for God surely did everything at the same time, not only in giving commands but also in his thinking—, but because things that come into existence required order. Number is inherent in order, and by the laws of nature the most generative of numbers is the six.[7]

Of the numbers (proceeding) from the unit, six is the first perfect number. It is equal to (the product of) its parts and is also formed by their sum, namely the three as its half and the two as its third and the unit as its sixth. It is also, so to speak, both male and female by nature, forming a harmonic union out of the product of each of them, for among existing things the odd is male and the female is even. The first of the odd numbers is the three, of the even numbers it is the two, and the product of both is the six. (§14) So it was right that the cosmos, as the most perfect[8] of the things that have come into existence, be built in accordance with the perfect number six, and, because births resulting from coupling would take place in it, also be formed in relation to a mixed number, the first even-odd number which contains both the form of the male who sows the seed and the form of the female who receives it.

(§15) To each of the days he assigned some of the parts of the universe, making an exception for the first, which he himself does not actually call first, in case it be counted together with the others. Instead he gives it the accurate name[9] **one** [b], because he perceived the nature and the appellation of the unit in it, and so gave it that title.

---

[a] Title of the book Genesis. [b] Gen 1:5.

[Chapter 4] *Day one: creation of the intelligible cosmos*

We must now state as many as we can of the things that are contained in it, since it is impossible to state them all. It contains as pre-eminent item the intelligible cosmos, as the account concerning it (day one) reveals. (§16) For God, because he is God, understood in advance that a beautiful copy would not come into existence apart from a beautiful model, and that none of the objects of sense-perception would be without fault, unless it was modelled on the archetypal and intelligible idea. Therefore, when he had decided to construct this visible cosmos, he first marked out the intelligible cosmos, so that he could use it as a incorporeal and most god-like paradigm and so produce the corporeal cosmos, a younger likeness of an older model, which would contain as many sense-perceptible kinds as there were intelligible kinds in that other one.

(§17) To state or think that the cosmos composed of the ideas exists in some place is not permissible. How it has been constituted we will understand if we pay careful attention to an image drawn from our own world. When a city is founded, in accordance with the high ambition of a king or a ruler who has laid claim to supreme power and, outstanding in his conception, adds further adornment to his good fortune, it may happen that a trained architect comes forward. Having observed both the favourable climate and location of the site, he first designs within himself a plan of virtually all the parts of the city that is to be completed—temples, gymnasia, public offices, market-places, harbours, shipyards, streets, constructions of walls, the establishment of other buildings both private and public. (§18) Then, taking up the imprints of each object in his own soul like in wax, he carries around the intelligible city as an image in his head. Summoning up the representations by means of his innate power of memory and engraving their features even more distinctly (on his mind), he begins, as a good builder, to construct the city out of stones and timber, looking at the model and ensuring that the corporeal objects correspond to each of the incorporeal ideas. (§19) The conception we have concerning God must be similar to this, namely that when he had decided to found the great cosmic city, he first conceived its outlines. Out of these he composed the intelligible cosmos, which served him as a model when he completed the sense-perceptible cosmos as well. (§20) Just as the city that was marked out beforehand in the architect had no location outside, but had been engraved in the soul of the craftsman, in the same way the cosmos composed of the ideas would have no other place than the divine Logos who gives these (ideas) their ordered disposition. After all, what other place would there be for his powers, sufficient to receive and contain, I do not speak about all of them, but just any single one in its unmixed state?

(§21) Among these is also his cosmos-producing power, which has as its source that which is truly good. For if anyone should wish to examine the reason why this universe was constructed, I think he would not miss the mark if he affirmed, what one of the ancients also said, that the Father and Maker was good. For this reason he did not begrudge a share of his own excellent nature to a material which did not possess any beauty of its own but was able to become all things. (§22) Of itself it was unordered, devoid of quality, lacking life, dissimilar, full of inconsistency and maladjustment and disharmony; but it received a turning and change to the opposite and most excellent state, order, quality, ensoulment, similarity, homogeneity, sound adjustment, harmony, indeed all the characteristics possessed by the superior idea. (§23) With no one to assist him—indeed who else was there?—, but relying solely on his own resources, God recognized that he had to confer the unstinting riches of his beneficence on the nature which of itself without divine grace could not sustain any good whatsoever. But he does not confer his blessings in proportion to the size of his own powers of beneficence—for these are indeed without limit and infinitely great—but rather in proportion to the capacities of those who receive them. The fact is that what comes into existence is unable to accommodate those benefits to the extent that God is able to confer them, since God's powers are overwhelming, whereas the recipient is too weak to sustain the size of them and would collapse, were it not that he measured them accordingly, dispensing with fine tuning to each thing its allotted portion.

(§24) If you would wish to use a formulation that has been stripped down to essentials, you might say that the intelligible cosmos is nothing else than the Logos of God as he is actually engaged in making the cosmos. For the intelligible city too is nothing else than the reasoning of the architect as he is actually engaged in the planning of the foundation of the city. (§25) This is the doctrine of Moses, not my own. When describing the genesis of the human being in what follows, he explicitly declares that the human being was in fact formed **after God's image** ᶜ. Now¹⁰ if the part is image of an image, it is plain that this is also the case for the whole. But if this entire sense-perceptible cosmos, which is greater than the human image, is a representation of the divine image, it is plain that the archetypal seal, which we affirm to be the intelligible cosmos, would itself be the model and archetypal idea of the ideas, the Logos of God.

[Chapter 5] *"In the beginning" does not mean creation in time*

(§26) When he says that **in (the) beginning God made the heaven and the earth** ᵈ, he does not take the (term) **beginning**, as some people think, in a temporal sense. For there was no time before the cosmos, but rather it either came into existence together with the cosmos or after it. When we consider that time is the extension of the cosmos' movement, and that there could not be any movement earlier than the thing that moves but must necessarily be established either later or at the same time, then we must necessarily conclude that time too is either the same age as the cosmos or younger than it. To venture to affirm that it is older is unphilosophical.

(§27) If **beginning** ᵉ in the present context is not taken in the temporal sense, it is likely that its use indicates beginning in the numerical sense, so that the expression **in (the) beginning he made** ᶠ is equivalent to **he** first **made the heaven**. It is indeed reasonable that heaven should in fact be the first thing to enter into becoming. It is the most excellent of the things that have come into existence and is also composed of the purest substance, because it was to be the holiest dwelling-place for the gods whose appearance is perceived by the senses. (§28) Even if the maker proceeded¹¹ to make all things simultaneously, it is nonetheless true that what comes into a beautiful existence did possess order, for there is no beauty in disorder. Order is a sequence and series of things that precede and follow, if not in the completed products, then certainly in the conceptions of the builders. Only in this way could they be precisely arranged, and not deviate from their path or be full of confusion.

ᶜ Gen 1:27.   ᵈ Gen 1:1.   ᵉ Gen 1:1.   ᶠ Gen 1:1.

[Chapter 6] *The chief contents of the intelligible cosmos*

(§29) First, therefore, the maker made an incorporeal **heaven and an invisible earth** [g] and a form of air and of the void. To the former he assigned the name **darkness** [h], since the air is black by nature, to the latter the name **abyss** [i], because the void is indeed full of depths and gaping. He then made the incorporeal being of **water** [j] and of **spirit** [k], and as seventh and last of all of **light** [l], which once again was incorporeal and was also the intelligible model of the sun and all the other light-bearing stars which were to be established in heaven.

(§30) Both **spirit** and **light** were considered deserving of a special privilege. The former he named **of God** [m], because **spirit** is highly important for life and God is the cause of life. Light he describes as exceedingly **beautiful** [n], for the intelligible surpasses the visible in brilliance and brightness just as much, I believe, as sun surpasses darkness, day surpasses night, and intellect, which gives leadership to the entire soul, surpasses its sensible sources of information,[12] the eyes of the body. (§31) That invisible and intelligible **light** *has come into being* [o] as image of the divine Logos which communicated its genesis. It is a star that transcends the heavenly realm, source of the visible stars, and you would not be off the mark to call it "all-brightness." From it the sun and moon and other planets and fixed stars draw the illumination that is fitting for them in accordance with the capacity they each have. But that unmixed and pure gleam has its brightness dimmed when it begins to undergo a change from the intelligible to the sense-perceptible, for none of the objects in the sense-perceptible realm is absolutely pure. (§32) Well said too is the statement that *there was* **darkness above the abyss** [p], for in a way the air is over the void, since it is mounted on and has filled up the entire gaping, empty and void space that extends from the region of the moon to us.

(§33) As soon as the intelligible **light**, which existed before the sun, was ignited, its rival **darkness** [q] proceeded to withdraw. God built a wall between them and *kept* them *separate* [r], for he well knew their oppositions and the conflict resulting from their natures. Therefore, in order to ensure that they would not continually interact and be in strife with each other, and that war would not gain the upper hand over peace and bring about disorder (*akosmia*) in the cosmos

---

[g] Gen 1:1–2. [h] Gen 1:2. [i] Gen 1:2. [j] Gen 1:2. [k] Gen 1:2. [l] Gen 1:3.
[m] Gen 1:2. [n] Gen 1:4. [o] Gen 1:3. [p] Gen 1:2. [q] Gen 1:4. [r] Cf. Gen 1:4.

(*kosmos*), he not only separated light and darkness, but also placed boundaries in the extended space between them, by means of which he kept the two extremes apart. For if they were neighbours, they would produce confusion in the struggle for dominance and would strip in readiness for a great and unceasing rivalry, unless boundaries were fixed in between them to restrain and resolve their confrontation. (§34) These (boundaries) are **evening** and **morning**[s], of which the latter announces in advance that the sun is about to rise and gradually forces back the darkness, while the evening follows on the setting sun and gently admits the massive onset of the darkness. Mark well, however, that these two, I mean **morning** and **evening**, must be placed in the order of incorporeal and intelligible reality. For in that realm there is nothing at all that is sense-perceptible, but everything there is ideas and measures and marks and seals, incorporeal entities required for the genesis of the other bodily realm. (§35) So when **light** came into being, **darkness**[t] retired and withdrew, while **evening** and **morning** were fixed as boundaries in the extended space in between, this necessarily entailed that a measure of time was produced forthwith. The maker **called** this measure **day**[u], and not the first day, but **day one**[v]. It was named in this way because of the aloneness of the intelligible cosmos which has the nature of the unit.

[Chapter 7] *Second day: creation of the firmament*

(§36) Now that the incorporeal cosmos had been completed and established in the divine Logos, the sense-perceptible cosmos began to be formed as a perfect offspring, with the incorporeal serving as model. As first of its parts, which indeed was also the very best of all, the creator proceeded to **make** the heaven, which he correctly named **firmament**[w] (*stereôma*), inasmuch as it is a bodily object; for the body is by nature solid (*stereon*), because it is extended in three directions. What other conception of what is solid and bodily is there than that which has been extended in all directions? Suitably, therefore, he opposed the sense-perceptible and corporeal heaven to its intelligible and incorporeal counterpart and called it **firmament**. (§37) Then he immediately *named* it **heaven**[x] (*ouranos*), an apposite and highly appropriate title, either because it is the boundary (*horos*) of all things, or because it came into existence as first of the visible

---

[s] Gen 1:5.   [t] Gen 1:4.   [u] Gen 1:5.   [v] Gen 1:5.   [w] Gen 1:7.   [x] Gen 1:8.

things (*horatôn*). After its genesis he also names the **day second**[y], devoting the entire extension and measure of a day to heaven on account of its high value and honour in sense-perceptible reality.

[Chapter 8] *Third day: creation of the earth*

(§38) Now the entire body of water had been poured out over all the earth and had penetrated throughout all its parts like a sponge which has absorbed moisture. This meant that there were swamps and deep mud, the result of both elements having been mixed and confounded, in the manner of a paste, into a single indistinct and shapeless nature. God next commands **the water** that is salty and would be cause of infertility to plants and trees to flow together and *assemble* from the pores of the entire earth, and **the dry land**[z] to emerge. The moisture of the sweet water was left behind in it for the sake of preservation—for the sweet moisture when measured out acts as a kind of glue for binding together opposed elements—, both so that the earth would not be completely parched and so become childless and sterile, and so that like a mother it would offer not just one kind of nourishment, namely food, but would furnish, as if to its offspring, both food and drink. For this reason he proceeded to flood its veins in the manner of breasts, and these, when they had obtained a mouth, would pour forth as rivers and springs. (§39) Similarly he also extended invisible moisture-bearing capillaries throughout the rich and fertile soil, so that it would yield a most copious supply of crops. Having given these (parts) their ordered disposition, he proceeded to impose names on them, *calling* **the dry land earth** and *the* separated *water sea* [a].

(§40) Then he starts giving the **earth** its adornment. He commands it to bear green shoots and crops, and to bring forth all kinds of *plants* and well-*grassed* [b] plains and everything which would serve as forage for animals and as food for humans. In addition he also caused all kinds of trees to grow, not omitting any of the wild or any of the so-called domesticated timber. Immediately on their first creation these trees were all heavily laden with *fruit*[c], contrary to the manner in which this now takes place. (§41) For now plants develop in succession at different times, and not all together at a single opportune time. Everyone knows that first sowing and planting

---

[y] Gen 1:8.   [z] Gen 1:9.   [a] Gen 1:10.   [b] Cf. Gen 1:11.   [c] Cf. Gen 1:11.

occur, and second the growth of what has been sown and planted. This growth partly extends downwards, establishing roots like foundations and partly extends upwards, whereby the plants lift themselves to a height and develop stems. Next come shoots and the growth of leaves, and finally the production of fruit takes place. And in this case too the fruit is not (immediately) full-grown, but undergoes all manner of changes, both quantitatively in terms of size and qualitatively in many different forms and shapes. When the fruit is first given birth, it resembles tiny specks so small as to be hardly visible. You would not be off the mark in calling them the first perceptibles. After this, in a gradual process, it grows in size and attains a bulk that is fully complete. This occurs both through the channelled nourishment which waters the tree, and through the fine mixture of winds which warm it and nurse it in a combination of cool and milder breezes. And together with its size it also alters its qualitative characteristics, offering varieties of colour as if produced with a painter's art. (§42) But in the case of the first genesis of the universe, as I just said,[13] God caused all the timber of the plants to rise from the earth complete with fruit which was not imperfect but at its peak, fully ready for the immediate use and enjoyment of the living beings that were very soon to come into existence. (§43) He thus gives orders to the earth to generate all these things. The earth, like a woman who has been pregnant for a long time and is now in travail, gives birth to every kind of sown plant, every kind of tree, and also countless kinds of fruit. But the fruit was not only ready to serve as food for living beings. It was also equipped for the perpetual genesis of **what is similar** in kind, containing as it does **spermatic**[d] substances in which the indistinct and invisible patterns of the entire organisms are found. These patterns become distinct and visible as the cycles of the seasons proceed. (§44) For God had decided that nature should run a cyclical race, thereby immortalizing the **kinds**[e] and giving them a share of eternity. On this account he not only guided and urged the beginning on towards the end, but also caused the end to turn back towards the beginning. Out of the plants emerges the fruit, as an end out of a beginning, while out of the **fruit** that encloses the **seed**[f] within itself the plant emerges again, as a beginning out of an end.

---

[d] Cf. Gen 1:12.   [e] Cf. Gen 1:11–12.   [f] Gen 1:12.

[Chapter 9] *Fourth day: a puzzle and the significance of its number*

(§45) On the **fourth day** [g], now that the earth was finished, God proceeded to order the heaven with variegated adornment, not because he placed it behind the earth in rank, thereby giving a privileged position to the inferior nature and considering the superior and more divine deserving of the second position only, but rather in order to give a very clear demonstration of the might of his sovereignty. He understood in advance what the humans who had not yet come into existence would be like in their thinking. They would focus their aim on what is likely and convincing and contains much that is reasonable, but not on the unadulterated truth, and they would put their trust in appearances rather than on God, thereby showing admiration for sophistry rather than wisdom. Moreover, when they observe the revolutions of the sun and moon, by means of which summer and winter and the solstices of spring and autumn occur, they would suppose that it was the circuits of the heavenly bodies which were responsible for the emergence and growth of things out of the earth each year. Not wishing that some people, either out of shameless insolence or through overwhelming ignorance, would dare to attribute the first causes to any created being, he says: (§46) Let them turn back in their minds to the first coming into existence of the universe, when, before the sun and moon even existed, the earth bore all manner of plants and all manner of fruits. Reflecting on these matters in their minds, let them expect that the earth will once again bring forth such produce at the command of the Father, whenever it seems appropriate to him. He does not stand in need of his heavenly offspring. He has given them powers, but these certainly do not mean full autonomy. Just like a charioteer who takes hold of the reins or a pilot who grasps the rudder, he guides each process according to law and just desert in whichever direction he wishes, not needing anyone else's help. After all, for God all things are possible. (§47) This is the reason why the earth sprouted and brought forth verdure earlier (than the heaven).

But the heaven in its turn was ordered with a perfect number, the four. You would not go astray in affirming that it is the principle and source of the all-perfect number ten; for what the ten is in actuality, the four, it would seem, is potentially. If the numbers from the unit

---

[g] Gen 1:19.

to the four are added up, they will produce the ten. It forms the boundary for the infinitude of numbers, which wind around it like a turning post and turn back. (§48) The four also contains the ratios that produce the musical accords, namely the quart, the quint, the octave and the double octave. Out of these the most perfect system (of music) is generated. For the quart the ratio is one plus a third, for the quint one plus a half, for the octave double, for the double octave quadruple. The four contains all of these: one plus a third in the ratio four to three, one plus a half in the ratio three to two, double in the ratio two to one, quadruple in the ratio four to one. (§49) There is also another capacity of the four which is really marvellous to describe and understand. It is the first number that has revealed the nature of the solid, the numbers before it being devoted to the incorporeal realm. Under the one is aligned what in geometry is called the point; under the two the line, because the two is constituted through extension of the one and the line through extension of the point. A line is length without breadth. When breadth is added, surface arises, which is aligned under the three. For surface to attain to the nature of the solid it requires just one thing (more), depth; if this is added to the three, the four arises. Hence this number in fact has great significance: it has led us from the incorporeal and intelligible substance to a conception of three-dimensional body, which is by nature the first object to be perceived by the senses. (§50) If someone does not grasp what has been said, he will understand by taking notice of a very common game. People playing with nuts are in the habit of laying out three nuts on a plane and placing one more on top, thereby producing a pyramidal figure. The triangle in a plane thus stops at the three, while the unit placed on top produces the four in the realm of numbers and the pyramid in the realm of shapes, and then you already have a solid body. (§51) In addition another fact must be not ignored, namely that four is the first of the numbers that is square, the product of two equal factors, and so is a measure of fairness and equality. Moreover it alone has the ability to be produced from the same factors by both addition and multiplication, by addition from two plus two, by multiplication in turn from two times two. It thus demonstrates a splendid form of concord, which in fact is not possessed by any other number. For example, six is produced by adding together two threes, but if these are multiplied not six but another number results, namely the nine. (§52) The four possesses many other capacities, which should be further demonstrated in more detail in the account specially devoted to it. It will suffice to add the following. It was also a principle for the genesis of the entire heaven and cosmos. The four elements, out of which this universe was constructed, flowed forth, as from a source, from the four in the realm of numbers. Moreover the annual seasons which are responsible for the birth of animals and plants are four, the year having received a fourfold division into winter and spring and summer and autumn.

[Chapter 10] *Fourth day: creation of the heavenly bodies*

(§53) Since the above-mentioned number had been considered worthy of such a privileged position in the nature of reality, it was inevitable that the Maker would proceed to order the heaven with the four, decorating it with a splendid and most god-like adornment, the light-bearing heavenly bodies. Knowing that light was the most excellent of things that exist, he produced it as an instrument for the most excellent of the senses, sight; for what the intellect is in the soul, this is what the eye is in the body; each of them sees, in the one case the objects of thought, in the other the objects of perception. The intellect requires science in order to gain knowledge of the incorporeal realities; the eye has need of light in order to gain apprehension of bodies. For humans it is the cause of many other benefits, but especially of the greatest of them, love of wisdom. (§54) Through light sight had its attention drawn upwards. It observed the nature of the heavenly bodies and their harmonious motion, the well-ordered circuits of fixed stars and planets, the former circling in the one and same manner, the latter following a double revolution, each differently and in the opposed direction. When sight observed the concordant choral dances of all these, ordered in accordance with the laws of perfect musicality, it instilled in the soul unspeakable delight and pleasure. Feasting on a succession of spectacles, the one following after the other, the soul was filled with an insatiable desire for contemplation. Then, as is its inclination, it started to busy itself with further enquiries: what is the substance of these objects of sight? are they by nature uncreated or did they obtain a beginning of genesis? what is the manner of their movement, and what are the causes by means of which each thing is administered? From enquiry into these matters the pursuit of philosophy arose. No more perfect good than this has entered into human life.

(§55) Using as his model that form of intelligible light which was discussed in connection with the incorporeal cosmos,[14] he proceeded to create the sense-perceptible heavenly bodies, divine images of exceeding beauty. These he established in heaven, as in a temple made of the purest part of bodily substance, for many reasons: firstly to **give light**[h], secondly for **signs**, then to give the **right times** for the annual seasons, and finally for **days** and months and **years**[i], which indeed have come into existence as the measures of time and also have generated the nature of number. (§56) The value and usefulness of each of the above-mentioned tasks is quite self-evident, but for a more accurate understanding it is perhaps not out of place to track down the truth in a reasoned account as well. Since the whole of time has been divided into two sections, day and night, the Father proceeded to give authority over the **day** to the sun, like to a **great** king, while authority over the **night** was given to the moon and the multitude of the remaining **stars**.[j] (§57) The greatness of the power and *sovereignty*[k] possessed by the sun is most clearly proven by what was just said: though a single entity and quite alone all by itself, it has nevertheless been allotted the **day**, which constitutes half of the whole of time, whereas all the other heavenly bodies, together with the moon, received the other part, which was called **night**[l]. And when the sun rises, the appearances of all those heavenly bodies not only become dim, but even disappear completely through the outpouring of bright light, but when it sets, they all begin together to disclose their own qualities. (§58) They have come into existence, as he himself said, not only for the purpose of sending forth light onto the earth, but also in order to reveal in advance **signs**[m] of future events. By observing their risings or settings, or eclipses, or their appearances or occultations, or other variations in their movements, humans make predictions about what will happen, the supply or lack of crops, the births and deaths of animals, clear weather and cloudiness, wind still weather and violent winds, river torrents and dried-up riverbeds, calm and stormy seas, alterations in the annual seasons, whether in the form of a wintry summer or a scorching winter, a spring that feels like autumn or an autumn that feels like spring. (§59) There are also people who have based conjectures on heavenly movements and have given indications in advance that tremors and earthquakes would occur, as well as numerous other

---

[h] Cf. Gen 1:14. [i] Gen 1:14. [j] Gen 1:16. [k] Cf. Gen 1:16, 18. [l] Gen 1:16, 18; cf. 1:5. [m] Gen 1:14.

more unusual phenomena, so that it was most truly said that the heavenly bodies have come into existence **for** (serving as) **signs**[n]. Moreover (the phrase) **for** (indicating) **right times**[o] was also added. By **right times** he understood the annual seasons, and this is surely reasonable. For what else is the notion of *right time* than the time when a right result is achieved? The seasons bring everything to fruition and achieve a right result, whether it be sowing and planting of crops or births and growth of livestock. (§60) They have also come into existence to serve as measures of time, for by the ordered revolutions of the sun and moon and other heavenly bodies **days** and **months** and **years**[p] have been constituted. And immediately that most useful thing, the nature of number, was revealed because time makes it manifest. For from a single day the number one is derived, from two days two, from three days three, and from a month thirty, from a year the number equivalent to the days produced by twelve months, and from infinite time the number that is infinite.

(§61) This is how great and how indispensable the benefits are which the natures of the heavenly bodies and their movements supply. I am sure that there are many others which are unclear to us—for not everything is known to the human race—, but contribute to the preservation of the whole. These are fully and invariably achieved in accordance with the ordinances and laws which have been immutably established in the universe by God.

[Chapter 11] *Fifth day: creation of the animal world*

(§62) Now that the earth and the heaven had been ordered with the adornment appropriate to them, the one by means of the three, the other, as has been explained,[15] by means of the four, he proceeded to undertake the formation of the kinds of mortal living beings. He started with the aquatic creatures on the fifth day, considering that nothing bears such a family-resemblance to anything else as the five does to living beings. The chief difference between living beings with and without soul is the possession of sense-perception. Sense-perception is divided five-fold, into sight, into hearing, into taste, into smell, into touch. To each of these the maker distributed special materials and its own criterion by which it would judge what falls under its notice. For sight there were colours, for

---

[n] Gen 1:14. [o] Gen 1:14. [p] Gen 1:14.

hearing sounds, for taste flavours, for smell aromas, while for touch there were things soft and hard, hot and cold, smooth and rough. (§63) He therefore commands all manner of **kinds** of fishes and **sea-creatures** q to be constituted, differing in both size and characteristics according to (their) location, for in the various seas various types are found, but sometimes also the same ones. But he did not proceed to form all the kinds in every location, and this was surely reasonable. Some feel at home in shallow water and not in the very deep sea; others love bays and harbours, being able neither to creep on land nor to swim far from it; yet others spend their time right out in the depths of the sea, avoiding headlands which jut out or islands or rocks. Some thrive in a clear and calm sea, others are fond of storms and huge waves, for they are conditioned by the continual buffeting, and the strong effort involved in moving around makes them more powerful and sleek. Immediately thereafter he proceeded to create the *kinds of birds* r, because these are related to the creatures in the water—both sorts are in fact floaters—, not leaving any form of airborne creatures unachieved.

(§64) Now that the water and air had received the kinds of living beings that were appropriate to them as a kind of native allotment, he once again called on the earth to produce the part (of its task) that remained—after the plants, the land-animals had still been left to do— and says: **let the earth bring forth** *livestock* **and wild beasts and reptiles after** each **kind** s. The earth then immediately releases what it had been commanded, animals varying in build and strength and the possession of powers that which can harm or give benefit.

(§65) To crown all he proceeded to *make* **the human being** t. How he did this I shall say a little later.[16] But first I want to show that he (Moses) employed a truly excellent sequence of succession in describing the birth of the animal realm. The most sluggish and least delineated type of soul has been allotted to the kind of the fishes, the most developed and in every respect best type has been assigned to the kind of the human beings. The type of soul bordering on these both is found in the living beings which inhabit the land and the air, for it is more sensitive than the soul found in fishes, but feebler than that found in humans. (§66) For this reason, as the first of all ensouled beings, he produced fishes, which share in more of the substance of body than of soul. In a sense they both are and are not

---

q Gen 1:21.   r Cf. Gen 1:21.   s Gen 1:24 (and 25).   t Cf. Gen 1:27.

living beings. They move, yet do not really have soul. The soul-principle has been sown in them in order to preserve their bodies, just like they say salt is added to meat, so that it will not easily go bad. After the fish come the birds and land-animals. These are already more sensitive and in their make-up they reveal more clearly the characteristics of being ensouled. To crown all, as was said,[17] he produced the human being, whom he endowed with intellect as special gift, a kind of soul of (the) soul just like the pupil in the eye. Indeed those who carry out more accurate research into the nature of reality call this eye of (the) eye. (§67) At that time everything was constituted simultaneously. But even though everything was constituted together, it was still necessary that the ordered sequence should be outlined in an account, because in the future beings would originate from each other. When individual beings come into existence, the following ordered sequence takes place: nature begins with what is most insignificant and ends with what is best of all. What this sequence is I should now show. It is a fact that for living beings seed is the starting-point of the process of genesis. It is common knowledge that seed is something very insignificant, similar to foam. But when it has been deposited in the womb and has established itself there, it immediately obtains movement and is turned into natural growth. Natural growth is superior to seed, since movement is superior to quiescence in the realm of becoming. Like a craftsman, or to put it more accurately, like an irreproachable art, nature moulds living beings by distributing the moist substance to the limbs and organs of the body, and the life-giving substance to the faculties of the soul, namely nourishment and sense-perception. The faculty of reasoning should be set aside for the moment on account of those who affirm that, as something divine and eternal, it enters the living being from the outside. (§68) Therefore nature began from seed, something of little value, and ended with what is most precious, the structure of an animal and of a human being. The same was also the case when the universe came into existence. When the creator decided to form the living beings, the first in the ordered sequence were pretty insignificant, namely the fishes, while the last were the best, human beings. The other (kinds) are situated in between the extremes, being superior to the first group but inferior to the other, namely land-animals and birds.

[Chapter 12] *Why is the human being created after God's image?*

(§69) After all these other creatures, as has been stated,[18] he says that the **human being** has come into existence **after** *God's* **image and after his likeness** [u]. This is most excellently said, for nothing earth-born bears a closer resemblance to God than the human being. But no one should infer this likeness from the characteristics of the body, for God does not have a human shape and the human body is not God-like. The term **image** [v] has been used here with regard to the director of the soul, the intellect.

On that single intellect of the universe, as on an archetype, the intellect in each individual human being was modelled. In a sense it is a god of the person who carries it and bears it around as a divine image. For it would seem that the same position that the Great director holds in the entire cosmos is held by the human intellect in the human being. It is itself invisible, yet it sees all things. Its own nature is unclear, yet it comprehends the natures of other things. By means of the arts and sciences it opens up a vast network of paths, all of them highways, and passes through land and sea, investigating what is present in both realms. (§70) Next it is lifted on high and, after exploring the air and the phenomena that occur in it, it is borne further upwards towards the ether and the revolutions of heaven. Then, after being carried around in the dances of the planets and fixed stars in accordance with the laws of perfect music, and following the guidance of its love of wisdom, it peers beyond the whole of sense-perceptible reality and desires to attain the intelligible realm. (§71) And when the intellect has observed in that realm the models and forms of the sense-perceptible things which it had seen here, objects of overwhelming beauty, it then, possessed by a sober drunkenness, becomes enthused like the Corybants. Filled with another longing and a higher form of desire, which has propelled it to the utmost vault of the intelligibles, it thinks it is heading towards the Great King himself. But as it strains to see, pure and unmixed beams of concentrated light pour forth like a torrent, so that the eye of the mind, overwhelmed by the brightness, suffers from vertigo.

Since, however, not every single image resembles its archetypal model, but many are dissimilar, he added to the words **after the**

---

[u] Gen 1:27 (and 26).   [v] Gen 1:26–27.

image as an extra indication the words **after his likeness**[w], in order to emphasize that it is an accurate and clearly marked casting.

[Chapter 13] *Why was the human being not created by God alone?*

(§72) It would not be off the mark to raise the difficulty as to why only in the case of the human being he attributed his coming into existence not to a single creator as in the case of the other creatures, but as if to a plurality. For he introduces the Father of the universe as saying these words: **let us make a human being after our image and likeness**[x]. Surely, I would say, he to whom all things are subject would not be in need of anyone whatsoever. Or is it likely that when he made heaven and earth and sea, he did not need any collaborator, but that in the case of such a tiny and perishable creature as the human being, he was unable to fashion it all by himself without the assistance of others? Of necessity only God knows the truest reason for this, but we should not conceal the answer that seems to be convincing and reasonable, based on a likely conjecture. It is the following.

(§73) Of the creatures that exist, some share neither in goodness or in evil, such as plants and animals without reason, the former because they do not possess soul and are regulated by a nature without imagination, the latter because they have been excluded from intellect and reason. Intellect and reason may be regarded as the home where goodness and evil naturally reside. Other beings have taken part in goodness only and are without share in any form of wickedness, such as the heavenly beings. These are said not only to be living beings, but living beings with intelligence, or rather each of them *is* an intellect, excellent through and through and not susceptible to any kind of wickedness. But there are also creatures of a mixed nature, such as the human being, who admits opposite characteristics, wisdom and foolishness, self-control and lack of restraint, courage and cowardice, justice and injustice, and— to summarize— good deeds and evil deeds, fine behaviour and foul, goodness and wickedness.

(§74) Now for God the universal Father it was highly appropriate to make the virtuous beings on his own because of their family relationship with him, and in the case of the indifferent beings it was

---

[w] Gen 1:26.   [x] Gen 1:26.

not alien to him to do so, since these too have no part in the wickedness that is hateful to him. In the case of the mixed natures, however, it was partly appropriate and partly inappropriate, appropriate on account of the better kind mixed in with them, inappropriate on account of the kind that was opposite and inferior. (§75) For this reason it is only in the case of the genesis of the human being that he states that God said **let us make** [y], which reveals the enlistment of others as collaborators, so that whenever the human being acts rightly in decisions and actions that are beyond reproach, these can be assigned to God's account as universal Director, whereas in the case of their opposite they can be attributed to others who are subordinate to him. After all, it must be the case that the Father is blameless of evil in his offspring, and both wickedness and wicked activities are certainly something evil.

(§76) Most excellently, after he had called the genus **human being**, he separated its species and stated that it was created **male and female** [z], even though the individuals had not yet taken shape. This is because the most proximate of the species are present in the genus and become apparent as if in a mirror to observers with sharp vision.

[Chapter 14] *Why was the human being created last of all?*

(§77) You might inquire for what reason the human being was the final item in the creation of the cosmos, for, as the holy scriptures indicate, the Maker and Father produced him after all the others.

Now those who have made a profounder study of the laws and have elucidated its contents to the best of their ability with much attention to detail assert that, when God granted to the human being kinship to himself through the possession of reason, which is the best of all gifts, he also did not begrudge him other benefits. So for the living being which was dearest and closest to him in nature he made everything ready in advance, it being his will that once the human being had come into existence, he would lack nothing that was required both for life and for the good life, the former furnished by the abundant supply of things that give enjoyment, the latter by contemplation of the heavenly realm, which strikes the intellect with wonder and engenders in it the passionate desire to gain knowledge of what it observes. This is what caused the pursuit of philosophy to

---

[y] Gen 1:26.   [z] Gen 1:27.

spring up, enabling humankind, though mortal, to achieve immortality. (§78) Just as those who give a banquet do not invite their guests to the meal until all the preparations for the feast have been completed, and those who organize athletic or dramatic contests, before they assemble the spectators in the theatres and the stadiums, first have a vast number of competitors and spectacles and sound effects to get ready, in the same way the Director of the universe too, like an organizer of games and a holder of a banquet, when he was about to invite the human being to a lavish feast and a spectacle, first brought into readiness what was required for both kinds of entertainment, so that, when the human being entered into the cosmos, he would immediately encounter both a festive meal and a most sacred theatre, the former replete with all the things that earth and rivers and sea and air supply for his use and enjoyment, the latter filled with all manner of things to see, absolutely stunning in their essential natures, absolutely stunning in their features, revealing the most wonderful motions and rhythmic dances performed in harmonic sequences by means of numerical proportions and concordant revolutions. You would not be mistaken if you said that in all these movements the original and true and paradigmatic science of music was embodied. The human beings who came later inscribed the images of this music on their souls, and so handed down to human life a most indispensable and useful art.

(§79) This was the first reason, it appears, why the human being was created after all the other creatures. It will not be off the mark to mention a second. When the human being first came into existence, he found all the equipment required for living. This was meant to teach those humans who would be born later a lesson. Nature was all but shouting aloud that, if they follow the example of the original ancestor of their race, they will lead a life without toil or trouble amidst a most lavish supply of the necessary goods. This will take place when unreasoning pleasures fail to gain the upper hand by constructing gluttony and lust as battle stations in the soul, when the desire for fame and money and power fails to gain control over life, when grief does not constrict and distract the mind, when that bad advisor fear does not upset the impulses towards virtuous deeds, when foolishness and cowardice and injustice and the enormous number of other vices do not mount their assault. (§80) At the present time, however, when all these vices that have just been mentioned flourish and human beings have unconditionally surrendered themselves to the passions and to uncontrolled and blameworthy desires which it is unlawful even to mention, they are confronted with punishment as rightful retribution for their unholy practices. This punishment is that the necessities of life are difficult to obtain. With difficulty humans plough the plains and channel the streams of springs and rivers. They sow and plant, and continually by day and by night they take upon themselves the labour of working on the land. So throughout the year they gather together the supplies which they need, but these are often meagre and quite insufficient because for various reasons they are damaged. The produce has either been swept away by continuous torrents of rain or been crushed by the accumulated weight of hailstorms or become frozen by snowfall or been torn up roots and all by the violence of the winds; for water and air have many violent means to bring about the improductivity of crops. (§81) If, however, self-control were to alleviate the immoderate impulses of the passions, a sense of justice were to do the same for the ambitions and inclinations to injustice, and in short the virtues and deeds in accordance with these virtues were to put an end to the vices and the never-ending evil deeds they bring about, and if then the war in the soul, which is truly the harshest and most burdensome of wars, were to cease and peace would gain the upper hand, calmly and gently bringing the powers within us to good order, then we might entertain the hope that God, who is a lover of virtue and fine behaviour and is moreover well-disposed to humankind, will cause the good things of life to be supplied to the race spontaneously and ready for consumption. After all, it is obviously easier to lavishly bestow a good supply of produce from what already exists without the intervention of the farmer's art than to bring what does not yet exist at all into existence.

(§82) Let this be said as the second reason. A third is as follows. God, having reasoned that the beginning and end of creation should be harmonized together in a necessary and loving relationship, proceeded to make heaven as its beginning and the human being as its end, the former as the most perfect of immortal beings in the sense-perceptible realm, the latter as the best of earth-born and mortal creatures. Indeed, if the truth be said, he is a miniature heaven who carries around in himself numerous star-like beings as divine images, taking the form of arts and sciences and noble theories corresponding to each excellence. Since the mortal and the immortal are by nature opposite, he assigned the finest example of each kind to the beginning and the end respectively, to the beginning heaven, as has been said, to the end the human being.

(§83) Last of all, however, the following is also stated as a necessary reason. The human being had to emerge as last of all creation so that, when he finally came and all of a sudden appeared before the other living beings, he would instil astonishment in them. On first seeing him, they would be amazed and would worship him as their natural director and master. For this reason, when they saw him, they became thoroughly tame, and those who had the wildest natures on the first glance in his direction immediately became manageable. They still demonstrated their savage aggression against each other, but towards the human being alone their behaviour was compliant. (§84) For this reason the Father, when he brought him into existence as the living being who was by nature dominant, not only in fact but also by means of a pronouncement [za] *appointed*[zb] him king of all the creatures in the sub-lunary realm, those on land and in the sea and borne on the air. *All* the mortal creatures in the three elements earth, water and air *he subjected to his rule*[zc], excluding the creatures in heaven because they have obtained a portion that is more divine. Of this sovereignty our experience furnishes the clearest proof. It can happen that vast flocks of animals are led by a single ordinary human being, who does not wear armour or carry a weapon of iron or bear any other kind of defensive instrument, but only has a leather jacket for protection and a staff for pointing the direction and for leaning on if he grows weary during his wanderings. (§85) Thus flocks consisting of numerous sheep, goats and cattle are lead by a shepherd, a goatherd or a cowherd, men who are not so physically robust and energetic that through their bodily condition they instil astonishment in those who look at them. The combined strength and power of so many well-armed creatures—for they are endowed by nature with equipment to defend themselves—stand in awe of him like slaves before their master and carry out his commands. Oxen are yoked for ploughing the earth. Cutting deep furrows during the day and sometimes also at night, they make a long track under the direction of a single farmer. Rams, weighed down in springtime by their thick coats of wool, at the command of a shepherd remain quietly standing or even calmly lie down, allowing their fleece to be shorn. Like cities they are accustomed to presenting their annual

---

[za] Cf. Gen 1:28. [zb] Cf. Ps 8:7. [zc] Cf. Ps 8.7.

tribute to him who is by nature their king. (§86) Another example is the most spirited of animals, the horse, who is easily harnessed and led along[19] so that he does not refuse the reins and jump away. He hollows his back and so offers an excellent seat to his rider. Lifting him on high, he moves at a swift pace, doing his best to bring and convey his charge to the places where his mount would have him go. The latter sits up there quite peacefully without getting tired, and by making use of another's body and limbs completes his ride. (§87) Much more could be said if anyone wishes to extend this account and offer more examples in order to demonstrate that no creature has gained its freedom and been exempted from the rulership of humankind. Let what has been said suffice by way of example.

It is important, however, to be aware that the human being was not created last of all as an indication of inferior rank. (§88) As witnesses we can call on charioteers and pilots. The former come after their team and have their place behind it. They guide it wherever they wish with the reins in their hands, sometimes loosening them for a fast trot, at other times restraining it if it races along faster than is required. Pilots in turn take up their position on the stern at the very end of the ship, but they are, so to speak, the best of all those sailing, because they hold in their hands the safety of the ship and the people on it. The Maker thus proceeded to fashion the human being after all the others as a kind of charioteer and pilot, so that he could guide and steer earthly affairs, taking on the care of animals and plants like a governor acting on behalf of the first and great King.

[Chapter 15] *The seventh day: excursus on the hebdomad*

(§89) When **the entire cosmos** had been **completed**[a] in accordance with the nature of the perfect number ***six***[b], the Father proceeded to **honour** the **seventh day** which followed by praising it and calling it ***holy***[c]. For this day is a festival, not of a single city or country, but of the universe, the only day which rightly deserves to be called universal and the birthday of the cosmos.

(§90) I do not know whether anyone can give sufficient praise to the nature of the seven. It is superior to every form of speech. Nevertheless, even though it is more wonderful than the words used to describe it, this does not mean that we should keep our peace.

---

[a] Gen 2:1.   [b] Cf. Gen 2:2.   [c] Gen 2:3.

Even if we are unable to tell everything or even the most important aspects, we should still be bold enough to elucidate at least those features that are accessible to our minds.

(§91) The seven is spoken of in two ways. In the former case it is confined within the ten. It is measured by taking the unit on its own seven times and consists of seven units. In the latter case it falls outside the ten, a number whose starting-point in each case is the unit in accordance with the double or the triple or with numbers generally corresponding to these, such as 64 and 729, the former attained by doubling (seven times) from the unit, the latter by tripling.

(§92) Each kind should not be just incidentally investigated. The second kind possesses a distinction which is very apparent. Every time that a number, beginning from the unit, is doubled or tripled or generally multiplied analogously, the resultant seventh number is both a cube and a square. This number contains the kinds of both incorporeal and corporeal being, the former through the surface produced by squares, the latter through the solidity produced by cubes. (§93) A very clear proof of this is given by the numbers just mentioned. To start with, the seventh number attained from the unit by doubling, the 64, is a square if eight is multiplied eight times, and is a cube if four times four is multiplied four times. And in the other case the seventh number attained from the unit in the triple relation, the 729, is a square if the 27 is multiplied by itself and a cube if nine times itself is multiplied nine times. (§94) And invariably if you take the seventh number as starting-point instead of the unit and you increase it according to the same procedure until you reach the seven, you will find that the number attained in each case is both a cube and a square. So if you multiply from 64 by doubling you will generate the seventh number 4096, which is at the same time a square and a cube, a square which has a side of 64, and a cube with a side of 16.

(§95) We should now move on to the other kind of the seven which is contained within the ten. It reveals a marvellous nature not inferior to the kind just dealt with. To start with, the seven consists of one, two and four, and so possesses two most harmonious ratios, the double and the quadruple, the former producing the chord of the octave, the quadruple the chord of the double octave. The seven also contains other divisions which as it were form yoked pairs when taken together, for it is divided first into the one and the six, then into the two and the five, and finally into the three and the four. (§96) The relationship between these numbers is also highly musical. Six to one has a six-fold ratio, and the six-fold ratio produces the greatest distance among things that exist, the distance which separates the highest from the lowest sound, as we shall demonstrate when we move on from numbers to harmonic theory. The ratio five to two demonstrates considerable harmonic power, almost rivalling that of the octave, as is shown very clearly in the mathematical theory of music. The ratio four to three produces the prime harmony of one plus a third, which is the quart. (§97) The seven also demonstrates another of its beauties, a most sacred object of knowledge. Consisting as it does of the three and the four, it supplies that which among existents is by nature perpendicular and straight. How this happens should be made clear. The right-angle triangle, which is the starting-point of the qualities, consists of the numbers three, four and five. The three and the four, which make up the substance of the seven, produce the right angle. The obtuse and the acute angles reveal irregularity, disorder and inequality, because there are various degrees of acuteness and obtuseness. The right angle, however, does not admit comparison, nor can the one be more upright than the other, but it remains unaltered and never changes the nature it possesses. If the right-angled triangle is indeed the starting point of shapes and qualities, and its most indispensable feature, the right-angle, is furnished by the nature of the seven as formed by the three and the four together, the seven may be reasonably considered to be the source of every shape and every quality. (§98) In addition to what has been said, another aspect needs to be mentioned. Three is the number of the surface's shape—since the point is ordered under the one, the line under the two, the surface under the three—, while four is the number of solid shape through the addition of the one, depth being added to surface. From this it is apparent that the being of the seven is the starting-point of geometry and stereometry and—to summarize—of both incorporeal and bodily reality.

(§99) So sacred is the nature inherent in the seven that it possesses a special feature not shared by all the other numbers in the ten. Of these numbers the first group generate but are not generated themselves, a second group are generated but do not themselves generate, while a third group do both, generating and being generated. Only the seven is not observed in any of these categories. This assertion should be confirmed by a demonstration. Now the one generates the entire succession of numbers, and is not generated by any of them at all. Eight is generated by twice four, but generates none of the numbers in the ten. Four in turn falls under the categories of both parents and offspring: it generates the eight by being doubled, while it is generated by twice two. (§100) Only the seven, as I said, has the nature neither to generate or be generated. For this reason the rest of the philosophers liken this number to motherless Victory and to the Maiden, who according to the account appeared out of the head of Zeus, but the Pythagoreans liken it to the Director of the universe. For that which neither generates nor is generated remains unchanged. Generation[20] involves change, since <both that which generates> and that which is generated cannot do without change, in the one case so that it can generate, in the other case so that it can be generated. The only being who neither changes or is changed is the very ancient Ruler and Director, of whom the seven would fittingly be called an image. As a witness for this account I can call on Philolaus when he says: "There exists the Director and Ruler of all things, God who is one, always existent, abiding, unchanged, himself identical to himself and differing from all others."

(§101) In the realm of intellect, therefore, the seven demonstrates what is unchanging and not subject to action, but in the realm of sense-perception it demonstrates a great and most essential power, <in the seven planets and the Great Bear and the choir of the Pleiades>,[21] by which all things on earth are able to make progress, and also in the revolutions of the moon. How this occurs should be investigated. If the numbers in succession starting from the unit are added up, the seventh number generates the 28, a perfect number which is equal to its own parts. The generated number restores the moon back to its original shape, from which it began visibly to increase and to which it returns through diminution. From the first appearance of the crescent-shape it waxes to the half-moon in seven days, then in another such period it becomes full-moon. From here it turns back again and follows the same route along the back part of the track, from the full moon to the half-moon in another seven days, and then from this stage to the crescent-shape in the same number. Out of these four (periods) the above-mentioned number is completed.

(§102) The seven is also called by those who are in the habit of using names correctly "the completion-bringer," since by means of this number all things are brought to completion. Evidence for this may be gained from the fact that all bodies with instrumental force possesses three dimensions, length, breadth and depth, as well as four limits, point, line, surface and solid body. When these are added together the seven is produced. It would have been impossible to measure bodies with the seven in accordance with the addition of the three dimensions and four limits, were it not the case that the ideas of the first numbers, one, two, three and four, which form the foundation of the ten, contain the nature of the seven; for the numbers just mentioned have four boundaries, the first, the second, the third and the fourth, as well as three intervals, the first from one to two, the second from two to three, the third from three to four. (§103) Aside from what has already been said, the clearest manifestation of the completion-bringing power of the seven is also furnished by the stages of life of human beings from infancy to old age. These stages are measured by the number seven. During the first period of seven years the growth of the teeth takes place. During the second the right time occurs for being able to emit fertile seed. In the third the beard develops and in the fourth the progress to full strength occurs. In the fifth it is the right season for marriage, in the sixth the peak of intelligence is attained. In the seventh improvement and increase in both the powers of intellect and speech take place, while in the eighth perfection in both departments is reached. During the ninth there is a time of mildness and serenity, as the passions are considerably moderated. In the tenth the end of life that one has prayed for occurs, when the bodily parts are still in working condition; for advanced age has the habit to tripping each of them up and removing their force. (§104) These stages of life have been described by Solon, the lawgiver of the Athenians, when he composed the following elegaic verses:[22]

> The young child, still an infant, grows a line of teeth,
>   and expels them in the first seven years.
> But when God has made complete another set of seven years,
>   the signs of advancing youth become manifest.
> In the third period, while the limbs still lengthen,
>   the chin grows downy and the complexion loses its bloom.
> In the fourth period of seven each person is at the very peak[23]
>   of strength, which men possess as marks of excellence.
> In the fifth it is time for a man to be mindful of marriage,
>   and to seek a family of children for hereafter.
> In the sixth a man's intellect gains mastery in all things,
>   and no longer wishes to perform reckless deeds.

In the seventh seven he is best in intellect and speech,
   and the eighth too, fourteen years for both periods.
In the ninth he is still capable, but for great achievement
   his speech and wisdom have less power.
If he reach the tenth in completion of due measure,
   he would obtain his allotment of death not unseasonably.

(§105) Solon thus enumerates human life by means of the ten sevens just outlined. But the doctor Hippocrates says that there are seven stages of life: child, boy, youth, young man, man, older man, old man. These are measured by sevens, he says, but not in direct succession. He writes as follows: "In human nature there are seven seasons, which are called stages of life: child, boy, youth, young man, man, older man, old man. A human being is a child up to the age of seven and the expulsion of teeth; a boy up to the growth of seed, until twice seven; a youth up to the growth of down on the chin, until three times seven; a young man up to the maturity of the entire body, until four times seven; a man up to one short of fifty years, until seven times seven; a older man up to fifty-six, until seven times eight; from then on he is an old man." (§106) Another feature of the seven that is mentioned in order to introduce it as having a wonderful position in nature depends on the fact that it consists of three and four. If you start doubling, you will find that the third number from the one is a square, the fourth number a cube, while the seventh number formed from both is both a cube and a square. Thus the third number from the one in the double ratio, four, is a square, the fourth number, eight, is a cube, and the seventh number, 64, is both a cube and a square. It may be concluded that the seventh number is truly a completion-bringer, because it proclaims both kinds of equality, of the surface by means of the square, based on the affinity with the three, and of the solid by means of the cube, based on the close connection with the four. From the three and the four the seven results.

(§107) The seven is not only a "completion-bringer," but is also so to speak harmonious in the highest degree and in a sense source of the most beautiful table, which contains all the accords—the quart, the quint, the octave—, as well as all the proportions—arithmetical, geometrical, and also harmonic. This "brick" consists of the following numbers: six, eight, nine, twelve. Eight to six is in a ratio of a one plus a third , which is the accord of the quart; nine to six is in a ratio of a one plus a half , which is the accord of the quint; twelve to six is a double ratio, which is the accord of the octave. (§108) It also contains, as I said, all the proportions. The arithmetical consists of six and nine and twelve; by the same number that the middle term exceeds the first term, namely three, the final term exceeds the middle term. The geometrical consists of four numbers; the same ratio that eight has to six, also occurs in the case of twelve to nine; this is the ratio of one plus a third. The harmonic consists of three numbers, six, eight and twelve. (§109) There are two ways of determining whether you have a harmonic proportion. The first is whenever the ratio of the final term to the first term is the same as the ratio which the excess by which the final term exceeds the middle term has to the excess by which the first term is exceeded by the middle term. You may obtain a very clear proof of this from the numbers set out before us, six, eight and twelve. The final number is double the first, while the excess is also double: twelve exceeds eight by four, eight exceeds six by two; four is the double of two. (§110) The other test for determining whether you have a harmonic proportion is whenever the middle term both exceeds and is exceeded by the same fraction of the end-terms. Eight is the middle term and exceeds the first by the fraction of a third; for if you subtract six from it, two remains, which is a third of the first term. It is exceeded by the final term by the same fraction; for if eight is subtracted from twelve, four remains, which is a third of the final term.

(§111) Let these remarks suffice as explanation of the august nature possessed by the table or "brick" or however it should be called. All these features and still more the seven demonstrates in the incorporeal realm which is the object of intellect. But its nature also extends to the whole of visible reality, reaching as far as heaven and earth, the limits of the universe.[24] After all, what section of the cosmos is not philhebdomadic, overpowered by love and desire for the seven?

(§112) To start with, they say the heaven is girdled by seven circles, the names of which are: arctic, antarctic, summer solstice, winter solstice, equator, zodiac, and in addition the milky way. The horizon should be excluded because it is a matter of our own experience, depending on whether we have clear vision or not, the sense of sight sometimes marking off a smaller and sometimes a larger circumference. (§113) As for the planets, that army which forms a counterweight to the sphere of the fixed stars, they are ordered in seven ranks, which display a very close affinity with the air and the earth. The air they convert and change into the annual seasons, as they are called, bringing about numerous changes for each: wind still weather, clear skies, clouds, extremely violent storms. In addition they cause rivers to swell and to diminish, and plains to become marshy and—the opposite—to become parched. They also bring about the alternation of low and high tides. It can happen that broad bays, when the sea recedes in the ebb-tide, quite suddenly form an extended beach, yet a little later, when the sea flows back, they become very deep stretches of water, navigable not only for small craft but even for large cargo ships. Moreover, they cause all things on earth to grow, both living beings and fruit-bearing plants, and bring them to completion, enabling the nature in each of them to run the full cycle, so that new fruits bloom and reach maturity on old plants, furnishing a lavish supply of necessary goods. (§114) The Great bear, which they call the sailors' escort, consists of seven stars. By keeping their gaze directed towards it, skippers have opened up countless routes, applying themselves to an incredible task which goes beyond human nature, for by targeting the above-mentioned stars they discover hitherto undisclosed lands, those who live on the mainland discovering islands, islanders in their turn finding continents. It was indeed fitting that the living being that is most God-beloved, the race of human beings, be shown the distant parts of both land and sea by the purest form of being, the heaven. (§115) In addition to what has been said, the starry choir of the Pleiades is also made complete by the seven. The risings and settings of these stars are the cause of great boons for everyone. When they set, the furrows are cut open for sowing. When they are about to rise, they announce the harvest-time, and when they have risen, they wake up the farmers who are glad to gather in the necessities of life. Joyfully they store away the supplies of food for daily use. (§116) The great ruler over the day, the sun, in completing two equinoxes each year, in the spring and autumn—the spring equinox in the Ram, the autumn equinox in the Balance—, gives the clearest proof of the majesty of the seven. For each of these equinoxes occurs in the seventh month, and in both cases it is prescribed by law that the largest and most popular public festivals be celebrated, because at both times the products of the earth reach full growth, in spring the produce of corn and all the other things that are sown, in the autumn the produce of the vine and most other fruit-bearing trees.

(§117) Since things on earth are dependent on the heavenly realm through a natural affinity, the principle of the seven, which began on high, has also come down to us and made its presence felt among the mortal kinds. To start with, the part of our soul separate from the directive part is divided sevenfold, into the five senses, the organ of speech, and finally the reproductive part. Just like in puppet shows, all these are manipulated by the ruling element through the nerves. Sometimes they are at rest, at other times they move, each producing its own appropriate disposition and movement. (§118) Similarly, if you were to undertake to examine the external and internal parts of the body, you will find seven in each case. Those that are visible are: head, chest, abdomen, two hands, two supports. The parts within, called internal organs, are: stomach, heart, lungs, spleen, liver, two kidneys. (§119) Moreover the most directive part of the living being, the head, has seven highly essential parts: two eyes, the same number of ears, two nostrils, and as seventh the mouth, through which, as Plato has said, mortal things have their entry and immortal things have their exit. Food and drink enter inside by way of the mouth, perishable foods for a perishable body. But what goes out is speech, immortal laws of an immortal soul, by means of which the life of reason is guided. (§120) The objects discriminated by the best of the senses, sight, share in this number according to kind, for there are seven sorts of things we see: body, extension, shape, size, colour, movement, rest, and no others besides these. (§121) It is certainly the case that the modulations of the voice too are seven in all: acute, grave, circumflex, as fourth the aspirated sound, the unaspirated as fifth, the long as sixth and the short as seventh. (§122) But it is also the case that there are seven motions: upwards, downwards, to the right, to the left, forwards, backwards, circular. These are demonstrated above all by people who make a display of dancing. (§123) It is also said that the secretions of the body are restricted to the above-mentioned number. Through the eyes tears flow forth, through the nostrils the filtrations of the head, through the mouth the saliva that is spat out. There are also two discharges for drawing off what remains after the digestion of food and drink, one at the front and one at the back. The sixth occurs all over the body, a profusion in the form of sweat, while the seventh is the emission of seed through the reproductive parts, which is very much a part of nature. (§124) Hippocrates too, the authority on what happens in nature, states that in seven days the fixing of the seed and the formation of flesh is secured. Moreover in the case of women the menstrual flow continues for at most seven days. It is natural for the foetus in the womb to reach full development in seven months, which results in a highly paradoxical fact: seven-month old foetuses are viable, whereas those of eight months are generally unable to survive. (§125) Serious illnesses of the body, especially when we are racked by unremitting fevers resulting from the bad mixing of our powers, are mostly resolved on the seventh day. This day adjudicates the struggle for life, allotting recovery to some and death to others.

(§126) The power of the seven has not only made its presence felt in the areas just mentioned, but also in the best of the sciences, grammar and music. The seven-stringed lyre produces renowned harmonies, similar to what occurs in the choral dance of the planets, giving it virtually the leading position in the entire instrumental production of music. As far as the elements in grammar are concerned, the vowels (or "vocals") are seven in number. These are named in conformity with their nature, because they plainly sound of their own accord, and when aligned with the others (the consonants) they produce articulated sounds. In the case of the semi-vowels, they fill in what is lacking and bring about complete tones, while in the case of the voiceless consonants they change and convert their nature by breathing in some of their own power, so that what was unspeakable can now be spoken.

(§127) It seems to me, therefore, that those who in the beginning conferred names on things, because they were wise, called this number seven (*hepta*), on account of its venerability (*sebasmos*) and the august nature (*semnotês*) that it possesses. The Romans indicate this even more clearly by adding the letter S, which the Greeks leave out. They call the number *septem* and this name, which, as was just said, comes from *semnos* (august) and *sebasmos* (venerable), conforms more closely to its true nature.

(§128) All this and even more has been stated and philosophized about the seven. For these reasons it has obtained the highest honours in nature, and is also honoured by Greeks and foreigners of the highest reputation who practise the science of mathematics. But it has been especially honoured by that lover of excellence, Moses, who recorded its beauty in the most holy tables of the law and also imprinted it on the minds of his followers. He commanded them after every period of six days to keep the seventh day holy, refraining from all the work required for the pursuit and provision of a livelihood, and keeping themselves free to concentrate on one thing only, practising philosophy for the improvement of their character and the examination of their conscience, which has been established in the soul and like a judge is not at all bashful about administering rebukes, making use both of threats that are rather forceful and of warnings that are more moderate. The former it applies to those unjust deeds which appear to be deliberate, whereas it uses the latter for involuntary acts done through lack of foresight, in order that a similar lapse will not happen again.

[Chapter 16] *A summarizing reflection*

(§129) Reflecting on his account of the creation (so far) with a summarizing statement, Moses says: **This is the book of the genesis of heaven and earth when it occurred, on the day that God made the heaven and the earth, and all the green of the field before it came into being on the earth and all the grass of the field before it rose up** [d]. Does he not clearly present here the incorporeal and intelligible ideas, which are in fact the seals of the completed products perceived by the senses? For **before the earth became green**, this green itself was present in the nature of things, he says, and **before grass rose up**, there was **grass** [e] that was not visible.

(§130) It should be understood that for each of the other things which the senses judge, anterior forms and measures also pre-existed, by means of which the things that come into being are given form and measured. For even if he has not gone through the partial things all together,[25] being as concerned as anyone ever was to attain brevity of speech, nevertheless the few things mentioned are indications of the nature of the whole of reality, which brings none of the things that are sense-perceptible to completion without an incorporeal model.

[Chapter 17] *The separation of the fresh from the salt water*

(§131) Holding on to the sequence of thought and preserving the series of what follows in relation to what precedes, he next states: **a spring went up from the earth and watered all the face of the earth** [f]. Other philosophers say that the entirety of water is one element of the four from which the cosmos was fashioned. Moses, accustomed as he is to sharply observing and understanding even distant things with

---

[d] Gen 2:4–5a.   [e] Gen 2:5.   [f] Gen 2:6.

a more penetrating gaze, regards the great sea as an element, a fourth part of the entirety of things, which those who came after him called the Ocean, considering the seas that we traverse as having the size of harbours. The sweet and drinkable water, however, he proceeded to separate off from the sea-water. He assigned it to the earth and understood it to be part of it and not of the (element) water for the reason mentioned earlier,[26] namely so that the earth would be held together by a sweet quality as if by a bond in the manner of a unifying glue. For if it had been left behind as dry earth and the moisture had not sunk in and penetrated through its pores by multiple division , it would have fallen apart. But now its contents are held together and continue to exist partly through the force of the unificatory spirit, and partly through the moisture that does not allow it to dry out and be broken into small and large clumps.

(§132) This was one explanation, but we should also state another which aims at the truth like a target. Nothing of what grows on earth can gain its structure without moist substance. This is shown by the deposition of seed. Either it is moist itself, as in the case of animals, or it does not grow without moisture, as in the case of plants. From this it is clear that the above-mentioned moist substance has to be part of the earth which gives birth to all things, just as in the case of women there has to be the menstrual flow. For it is said by men of science that this is the bodily substance of foetuses.

(§133) What I now shall state is also in harmony with what has been said so far. Nature has equipped every mother with a highly essential (bodily) part in the form of breasts like *fountains*[g], and so has prepared food in advance for the child that will be born. It seems that the earth too is a mother. For this reason the first humans decided to call her Demeter, combining the words for mother (*mêtêr*) and earth (*gê*). For, as Plato has said, it is not earth who has imitated woman, but rather woman who has imitated earth. The race of poets are quite correct in calling it "mother of all" and "crop-bearer" and "giver of all" (Pandora), since for all living beings and plants alike it is the cause of birth and continuing existence. It was quite reasonable, therefore, that nature equipped the earth, as oldest and most fertile of mothers, with flowing rivers and springs like breasts, so that it could both water the plants and provide a generous supply of drink for all living beings.

---

[g] Cf. Gen 2:6.

[Chapter 18] *Creation of the first human being from the earth*

(§134) After this he says that **God moulded the human being,** taking **clay from the earth, and he inbreathed onto his face the breath of life** [h]. By means of this text too he shows us in the clearest fashion that there is a vast difference between the **human being** *who has been moulded now* and the one who previously came into being after the **image of God** [i]. For the **human being** *who has been moulded* as sense-perceptible object already participates in quality, consists of body and soul, is either man or woman, and is by nature mortal. The human being **after** the **image** is a kind of idea or genus or seal, is perceived by the intellect, incorporeal, neither **male** nor **female** [j], and is immortal by nature.

(§135) He says that the sense-perceptible and individual **human being** has a structure which is composed of earthly substance and divine spirit, for the body came into being when the Craftsman took **clay** and *moulded* [k] a human shape out of it, whereas the soul obtained its origin from nothing which has come into existence at all, but from the Father and Director of all things. What **he breathed in** was nothing else than the divine *spirit* [l] which has emigrated here from that blessed and flourishing nature for the assistance of our kind, in order that, even if it is mortal with regard to its visible part, at least with regard to its invisible part it would be immortalized. For this reason it would be correct to say that the human being stands on the borderline between mortal and immortal nature. Sharing in both to the extent necessary, he has come into existence as a creature which is mortal and at the same time immortal, mortal in respect of the body, immortal in respect of the mind.

[Chapter 19] *The excellence of the first human being*

(§136) That first human being who was born from the earth, the original ancestor of our entire kind, seems to me to have come into existence as most excellent in both body and soul, superior by far in both respects to those who came later. He was indeed truly a noble person. Evidence for the excellent form of his body can be gained from three considerations, of which the first is this. Since the **earth** [m]

---

[h] Gen 2:7. [i] Gen 1:27. [j] Gen 1:27. [k] Gen 2:7. [l] Gen 2:7. [m] Gen 1:10, 2:5, 2:7.

was newly established, having just appeared when the great body of water which was named **sea**[n] was separated out, it was the case that the material for those things that came into being was unmixed and undefiled and pure, as well as receptive and easy to work with. Products made from it would surely be beyond reproach. (§137) Secondly, it is not likely that God took clay from any part of the earth which he happened to come across when he wished to mould this statue in the form of a human being with the utmost care, but rather that he separated out the best part from the entire mass, taking from pure matter the purest and utmost refined part which was especially suited for the construction. For it was built as a home or holy temple for the rational soul, which it was to carry around as the most god-like of images. (§138) The third argument, which bears no comparison with what has been said so far, is the following. As in other things, the creator also excelled in knowledge, so that each of the parts of the body received individually the proportions it required and was carefully fashioned to fit in harmoniously with the whole. And, in addition to this symmetry, he proceeded to model it with a beauty of flesh and embellish it with a beauty of colour, because he decided that the first human being should possess the most beautiful appearance possible. (§139) That he was also excellent in respect of his soul, is obvious. For it is fitting that for his construction God used no other model belonging to the realm of becoming, but only, as I said,[27] his own Logos. For this reason he says that the human being has come into existence as its likeness and representation by *being inbreathed* **into the face**[o], which is the location of the senses. By means of these the creator gave soul to the body, but as for reason, having established it as king in the directive part, he arranged for it to be flanked with bodyguards for the apprehension of colours and sounds and tastes and smells and related sensations, which on its own without sense-perception it was unable to grasp. The representation of a splendid model must be splendid itself. The Logos of God is even superior to the beauty[28] which is beauty as it occurs in nature. It is not adorned with beauty, but, if the truth be told, is itself beauty's[29] pre-eminent[30] adornment.

(§140) Such was the nature, it seems to me, of the first human being in body and soul, surpassing all those living now and all our predecessors as well, for our origin is from other human beings,

---

[n] Gen 1:10.   [o] Gen 2:7.

whereas he was created by God. The greater the superiority of the maker, the greater is the excellence of what comes into being. For just as that which is at its peak is always better than that which is past its prime, whether it concerns a living being or a plant or a fruit or whatever else might be found in nature, so it is likely that the first moulded human being was the acme of our entire species, while those who came later were no longer at the same peak, since generation by generation they obtained both outward appearance and capabilities which were ever inferior. (§141) I have seen this happen in the arts of sculpture and painting. Copies are deficient when compared to the originals, while those (products) that are painted and sculpted on the basis of the copies are even more so, because they stand at a great remove from the origin. A similar phenomenon is demonstrated by the magnetic stone. The iron ring that touches the stone itself is most powerfully affected, the ring next to the one touching is affected less, while the third hangs from the second, the fourth from the third, the fifth from the fourth, and so forth in a long series. They are held together by a single attractive force, but not to the same degree, for the rings which are suspended further away from the origin are held less and less tightly,[31] the reason being that the attractive force weakens and is no longer able to constrain them in equal measure. Something similar also appears to have happened to the race of human beings. In each generation they receive capabilities and qualities of both body and soul that are fainter and fainter.

(§142) If we describe that original ancestor not only as the first human being, but also as the only real citizen of the cosmos, we shall be telling the absolute truth. The cosmos was his home and city, since no hand-made constructions built out of materials of stone and wood were yet present. He resided in the cosmos with complete safety like in his native land, wholly without fear, because he had been found worthy to exercise dominion over earthly affairs and all mortal creatures stood in awe of him, having either been trained or compelled to obey him as master. And so he lived in the enjoyment of peace without conflict. (§143) But since every well-governed city has a constitution, it was the case that the citizen of the world necessarily made use of the constitution which belonged to the entire cosmos. This is the right reason of nature, which is named with a more appropriate title "ordinance" (*thesmos*), a divine law, according to which obligations and rights have been distributed to each creature. This city and its constitution must have had citizens before the human being. These might justly be called citizens of the great city, since they have obtained the greatest precinct to dwell in and have been enrolled in the community which is greatest and most complete. (§144) Who else would these be than the rational and divine natures, some of whom are incorporeal and intelligible beings, while others have bodies of the kind that the stars in fact possess? Consorting and having fellowship with these beings, the first man surely passed the time in undiluted well-being. He was closely related and akin to the Director, because the divine spirit had flowed into him in ample measure, and so all his words and actions were undertaken in order to please the Father and King, in whose footsteps he followed along the highways that the virtues mark out, because only those souls are permitted to approach him who consider the goal of their existence to be assimilation to the God who brought them forth.

(§145) Our description of the beauty, both in soul and in body, of the first-born human being has been given to the best of our ability, even if it falls far short of the truth. His descendants, who partake of his form, necessarily still manage to preserve the marks of the family relationship with their ancestor, even if these have become rather faint. (§146) What does this family relationship consist of? Every human being, as far as his mind is concerned, is akin to the divine Logos and has come into being as a casting or fragment or effulgence of the blessed nature, but in the structure of his body he is related to the entire cosmos. For it is a compound made from the same things, earth and water and air and fire, each of the elements making the required contribution for the completion of an entirely sufficient material, which the creator had to take to hand in order to fabricate this visible image. (§147) In addition he resides in all the above-mentioned elements as locations that are most congenial and familiar to him, alternating and spending time in different places, so that the human being can most justifiably be said to be everything at once, a being of the earth, of the water, of the air, and of the heavens. For inasmuch as he dwells and walks on the earth, he is a land-animal. Inasmuch as he frequently dives and swims and sails, he is a water-creature—merchants and sailors and divers and those who hunt after oysters and fish are the clearest proof of what has been said. Inasmuch as his body moves around lifted up and raised from the earth, he might rightly be called an airborne creature. Finally he is also heavenly, because through sight, the most directive of the senses, he draws near to the sun and moon and each of the other planets and fixed stars.

[Chapter 20] *The giving of names*

(§148) Most excellently he also ascribed the imposition of **names** [p] to the first human being. This is a task involving wisdom and kingship. That person was wise with a self-taught and self-instructed wisdom, having come into existence through divine beneficence.[32] Moreover he was king, and it is fitting for a ruler to address each of his subjects by name. The power of the authority attached to that first human being was surely exceedingly strong. God had moulded him with care and considered him worthy of the second rank, establishing him subordinate to himself but as ruler over all other creatures. Even those who are born so many generations later, when the race has become feeble through the long revolutions of time, still manage to rule over the creatures without reason, preserving a torch—as it were—of rule and authority handed down from the first human being.

(§149) He says therefore that God **led all** the living beings **to** the human being,[33] wishing **to see *which*** [q] titles he would impose on each of them, not because he was in any doubt—for nothing is unknown to God—, but because he knew that he had fashioned the rational nature in the mortal being with freedom of movement, so that he himself would have no share in wickedness. He proceeded to test him, as a teacher tests a pupil, inciting his innate disposition and inviting him to demonstrate the appropriate actions, so that he would of his own accord produce epithets that were not inappropriate or unfitting, but would reveal in an excellent fashion the individual characteristics of their subjects. (§150) After all, the rational nature in his soul was still uncorrupted, and not a single weakness or disease or passion had found its way in. So he took in wholly unblemished impressions of things material and immaterial, and made appellations that were accurate, taking aim in excellent fashion at what was revealed, so that their natures were pronounced and understood at the very same time.

In this way he distinguished himself with every fine attribute, attaining the very limit of human well-being.

---

[p] Gen 2:20. [q] Gen 2:20.

[Chapter 21] *Woman appears on the scene*

(§151) But, since nothing is stable in the world of becoming and mortal beings necessarily undergo reverses and changes, the first human being too had to enjoy some ill fortune. The starting-point of a blameworthy life becomes for him **woman**ʳ. As long as he was single, he resembled God and the cosmos in his solitariness, receiving the delineations of both natures in his soul, not all of them but as many as a mortal constitution could contain. But when **woman** too *was moulded*ˢ, he observed a sisterly form and a kindred figure. Rejoicing at the sight, he came up to her and gave her a greeting. (§152) She, seeing no other living creature that looked more like herself than he, was glad and modestly responded to his greeting. The love that ensues brings together the two separate halves of a single living being as it were, and joins them into unity, thereby establishing in both a desire for union with the other in order to produce a being similar to themselves. But this desire also gave rise to bodily pleasure, which is the starting-point of wicked and law-breaking deeds, and on its account they exchange the life of immortality and well-being for the life of mortality and misfortune.

[Chapter 22] *Events in the garden of delights and their interpretation*

(§153) While the man was still leading his solitary life and the woman had not yet been moulded, it is related that **a garden of delights** *was planted by God*ᵗ which bears no resemblance to those in our experience. For these have timber without soul, filled with all manner of trees. Some bloom all the time and give continuous visual pleasure, others blossom and grow leaves in the spring season; some bear domesticated fruit for human beings, not only supplying the necessary nourishment but also the additional enjoyment of luxurious living, while others bear a different sort, which of necessity has been apportioned to wild animals. But in the case of the divine **garden of delights** all the plants in fact possess soul and reason, bearing fruit in the form of the virtues and in addition neutral[34] understanding and keenness of mind—by which *what is good and what is evil is recognized*ᵘ—, as well as life without disease and indestructibility and whatever is of a similar kind to these. (§154)

ʳ Gen 2:23. ˢ Cf. Gen 2:19, 22. ᵗ Gen 2:8. ᵘ Cf. Gen 2:9, 17.

These themes, it seems to me, are philosophized symbolically rather than in the proper sense of the words. No trees **of life** [v] or understanding have ever appeared on earth in the past or are ever likely to appear in the future. Rather, it would seem that with the **garden of delights** he hints at the ruling part of the soul, which is filled with countless opinions just like plants, while with the tree **of life** he hints at the most important of the virtues, reverence for God, through which the soul is immortalized, and with the tree which ***makes known***[35] ***good and evil things*** [w] at intermediate practical insight, through which things which are opposite by nature are discriminated.

(§155) Once he had ***placed*** [y] these boundaries in the soul, he proceeded like a judge to observe in which direction it would incline. When he saw it leaning towards cunning and having little regard for piety and holiness, from which immortal life results, he ***expelled*** it [z], as might be expected, and banished it **from the garden of delights** [a]. He did not offer any hope of future return to a soul which was going incurably and irremediably astray, since the reason for the ***deception*** [b] too was in no small measure blameworthy. This is a subject that deserves not to be passed over in silence.

(§156) It is said that in ancient times the venomous and earth-born ***reptile*** [c], **the snake** [d],[36] could project a human voice, and that one day he approached the first man's wife and reproached her for being slow and excessively cautious, because she delays and postpones picking a **fruit** which is highly **attractive** ***to behold*** [e] and most pleasant to taste, and moreover is extremely advantageous for enabling one ***to discern what is good and what is evil*** [f]. Without further reflection, as the result of an unstable and unsettled conviction, she consented to the idea, ***ate*** **of the fruit and** ***shared it with*** **her husband** [g]. This was the event which suddenly changed them both from innocence and simplicity of character to cunning. The Father was outraged by this act, for it was a deed deserving to give rise to anger. They had passed by the tree **of immortal life** [h], perfection of excellence, though which they could have enjoyed the fruits of an age-long life of well-being, and made the choice for that ephemeral and mortal existence, not a life but a time span full of misfortune. So he determined the punishments against them which they deserved.

---

[v] Gen 2:9. [w] Gen 2:9. [y] Cf. Gen 2:8, 15. [z] Gen 3:24. [a] Gen. 3:23. [b] Cf. Gen 3:13. [c] Cf. Gen 1:24, 30 etc. [d] Gen 3:1. [e] Gen 3:6. [f] Cf. Gen 3:5. [g] Gen 3:6. [h] Gen 2:9.

[Chapter 23] *Interpretation of the snake*

(§157) These are not the fabrications of myth, in which the race of poets and sophists rejoice, but indications of character types which invite allegorical interpretation through the explanation of hidden meanings. You will follow a reasonable conjecture if you say that the above-mentioned snake is suitable as a symbol for pleasure, firstly because it is a legless creature which lies face-forward on its **stomach**, secondly because it takes clumps of **earth** [i] as food, and thirdly because it carries poison in its teeth, by which it able to kill those whom it bites. (§158) None of the above-mentioned traits are missing in the lover of pleasure. Only with difficulty can he raise his head, burdened and dragged downwards as he is by the lack of self-control which throws him forward and trips him up. He does not feed on the heavenly food which wisdom extends to lovers of contemplation by means of words and doctrines, but rather on what is provided from the earth according to the annual seasons, from which arise indulgence in wine and love of delicacies and gluttony. These stimulate the appetites of the stomach to break loose and become inflamed and enslaved[37] to excessive eating, as well as making the lusts of the lower parts burst forth. Greedily he desires after the labours of caterers and chefs de cuisine. Moving his ugly head in a circle,[38] he longs to partake of the smells of the delicious food. Whenever he sees a well-supplied table, he hurls himself and spreads out full-length onto what has been laid out, hastening to fill himself with everything all at once and making his aim not to reach satiety but to make sure that nothing of what has been laid out is left behind. (§159) Hence this person, no less than a snake, carries poison in his teeth. Teeth are the servants and assistants of insatiable appetite. Everything to do with food they chop up and grind, first handing it over to the tongue which examines the flavours for approval, then to the throat. A lack of moderation in food is deadly by nature and poisonous, because it does not allow digestion on account of the influx of new food which occurs before the previous lot has been absorbed.

(§160) The snake is said to project a human voice because pleasure makes use of countless defenders and champions, who have taken its care and advocacy upon themselves and go so far as to teach that the power of pleasure attaches itself to all things great and small,

---

[i] Gen 3:15.

without any exception whatsoever. (§161) Certainly the first intercourse of the male with the female has pleasure as its guide. Impregnation and birth take place through its agency. The offspring naturally first feel an affinity to nothing else but it, rejoicing in pleasure and disliking its opposite pain. For this reason babies cry when they are born, feeling pain, it would seem, because of the chill around them. After spending a long time in the extremely warm and fiery location of the womb, they all of a sudden emerge into the air, a chilly and unaccustomed place. It gives them a fright and their cries are the clearest evidence of their distress and the fact that they dislike pain. (§162) Every living being, they say, strives after pleasure as its most necessary and essential goal, but this applies especially to the human being. Other living beings seek it through taste and the genital organs only, but the human being does so through the other senses as well, pursuing all the sights and sounds that give delight to ears and eyes. (§163) A vast number of other assertions are made in praise of this passion, arguing that it is something highly native and akin to living beings. But what has been said so far is sufficient to demonstrate the reason why the snake appeared to project a human voice. For this reason, it seems to me, in the detailed laws too, when he wrote about which animals should be offered as food and which not, he gave special praise to the animal named **the snake-fighter**[j]. This is a **reptile which has legs above his feet**[k], enabling it **to jump from the earth** and be lifted in the air just like the species of **the grasshoppers**[l]. (§164) The snake-fighter, it seems to me, is nothing but a symbol of self-control, which engages in an unrelenting battle and unremitting war against lack of self-control and pleasure. Self-control especially welcomes simplicity and frugality and whatever is required for an austere and holy life, whereas pleasure loves luxury and extravagance, which cause soul and body to grow soft and decadent, and result in a life which in the view of sensible people is in fact blameworthy and harsher than death.

(§165) Pleasure does not dare to offer her tricks and ***deceits***[m] **to the man**[n], but rather **to the woman**[o] and through her to him. This is said quite suitably and appropriately, for in us the intellect has the role of man, while sense-perception has that of woman. Pleasure encounters and consorts with the senses first, and through them she deceives the ruling intellect as well. Each of the senses is seduced by

---

[j] Lev 11:22. [k] Lev 11:21. [l] Lev 11:22. [m] Cf. Gen 3:13. [n] Gen 3:6. [o] Gen 3:1.

her charms. They rejoice in what is set before them, sight responding to varieties of colour and shape, hearing to melodious sounds, taste to the sweetness of flavours, and smell to the fragrances of exhaled vapours. On receiving these gifts, in the manner of female servants, they offer them to reason as their master, taking persuasion along as their advocate so that none of the offerings whatsoever would be rejected. He is immediately ensnared. Instead of being a ruler he becomes a subject, a slave instead of a lord, an exile instead of a citizen, a mortal instead of an immortal being. (§166) In short, one should not be unaware that, like a shameless prostitute, pleasure desires to get hold of a lover and seeks out pimps that can help her lure him. It is the senses that act as pimps for her and solicit the lover. Once she has ensnared them, she will easily bring the intellect under her sway. They convey the external appearances inside, announce and display them, imprinting the characteristics of each thing on it and activating the passion that corresponds to them. For, just like in wax, the intellect receives the impressions via the senses. It needs them in order to comprehend bodily reality, not being able on its own to do this, as I have said already.[39]

[Chapter 24] *The consequences of wickedness*

(§167) The consequences of pleasure were immediately discovered by those who first became slaves of a passion that is harsh and difficult to heal. **The woman** obtained the strong **labour-pains** and the **griefs** that occurred successively during the rest of her life, especially those to do with the birth of **children**[p] and their upbringing and sickness and health and good fortune and misfortune, to which was added the loss of freedom and the ***absolute mastery*** of the **husband**[q] at her side, whose commands she had to obey. The man in turn obtained toil and hardships and the ***sweat***[r] of continual hard labour in order to obtain a supply of the necessities of life. He was deprived of the spontaneous good things which the earth had been taught to bear without the mediation of agricultural science, but had to take part in unremitting labours in order to find the means of living and food and not perish through starvation. (§168) I believe in fact that, just as the sun and the moon always shine forth after they had once been commanded to do so at the first genesis of the universe and

---

p Gen 3:16.   q Gen 3:16.   r Cf. Gen 3:19.

continue to keep the divine command for no other reason than that wickedness has been exiled far away from the borders of heaven, in the same way the fertile and crop-bearing soil of the earth would have continued to bear a lavish supply (of goods) in accordance with the annual seasons without the art and assistance of farmers. But now that wickedness has begun to abound at the expense of the virtues, the ever-flowing fountains of God's grace have been blocked, lest they be lavished on those who do not deserve to receive them. (§169) Indeed, if the human race had undergone the punishment that was appropriate, it would have been wiped out on account of the ingratitude that it showed towards God its benefactor and saviour. But he, being merciful by nature, took compassion and moderated the punishment. He allowed the race to survive, but no longer provided food ready to hand in the same way as before, lest they, by indulging in two forms of wickedness, laziness and over-indulgence, go astray and become insolent in their behaviour. (§170) Such was the life of those who **in the beginning**[s] enjoyed innocence and simplicity, but then preferred evil deeds, from which one should abstain, to virtue.[40]

[Chapter 25] *Moses teaches five vital lessons*

By means of the creation account which we have discussed he (Moses) teaches us among many other things five lessons that are the most beautiful and excellent of all. The first of these is that the divinity is and exists, on account of the godless, some of whom are in doubt and incline in two directions concerning his existence, while others are more reckless and brazenly assert that he does not exist at all, but is only said to exist by people who overshadow the truth with mythical fictions. (§171) The second lesson is that God is one, on account of those who introduce the polytheistic opinion, feeling no shame when they transfer the worst of political systems, rule by the mob, from earth to heaven. The third lesson is, as has already been said,[41] that the cosmos has come into existence, on account of those who think it is ungenerated and eternal, attributing no superiority to God.[42] The fourth lesson is that the cosmos too is one, since the creator is one as well and he has made his product similar to himself in respect of its unicity, expending all the available material[43] for the

---

[s] Cf. Gen. 1:1.

genesis of the whole. After all, it would not have been a complete whole if it had not been put together and constituted of parts that were themselves whole. There are those who suppose there to be multiple cosmoi, and there are others who think their number is boundless, whereas they themselves are the ones who are really boundlessly ignorant of what it is fine to know. The fifth lesson is that God also takes thought for the cosmos, for that the maker always takes care of what has come into existence is a necessity by the laws and ordinances of nature, in accordance with which parents too take care of their children.

(§172) He, then, who first has learnt these things not so much with his hearing as with his understanding, and has imprinted their marvellous and priceless forms on his own soul, namely that God is and exists, and that he who truly exists is one, and that he made the cosmos and made it unique, making it, as was said,[44] similar to himself in respect of its being one, and that he always takes thought for what has come into being, this person will lead a blessed life of well-being, marked as he is by the doctrines of piety and holiness.

NOTES TO THE TEXT AND TRANSLATION

[1] Both chapter numbers (corresponding to chapters of the Commentary) and titles are added by the translator. Section numbers correspond to the editions of PCW and PLCL. On the method of translation see the introductory remarks in the Introduction §11.

[2] Literally "Of other lawgivers, some ... others ..."

[3] In §2.

[4] Words placed in brackets indicate that they are not present in the Greek, but are added for the sake of fluency in English.

[5] I use this expression from time to time to render causal γάρ. Philo uses this little word no less than 166 times in our treatise. Often it can be rendered with "for," but it is not good English style to start too many sentences with this conjunction. Many times it has to be left untranslated, even though it does have a function in Philo's argument.

[6] The very common Greek word γένεσις is difficult to translate into English. The best translations "coming into existence" or "coming into being" are a bit cumbersome. But the usual translation "creation" has unwelcome extra connotations. We shall usually translate "coming into being (or existence)," but also sometimes simply "genesis."

[7] The translation of Greek numbers poses some problems for the translator. Greek uses the collective term (monad, dyad, triad etc.) and sometimes also the cardinal with the article, both of which are quite rare in English. On the whole I shall render the cardinal with "x," and both the cardinal with article and the collective with "the x." An exception is the term monad, which I shall translate with "unit."

[8] The word τέλειος can also mean "complete."

[9] Here the translated text differs from PCW: μίαν δ' ὀνομάσας εὐθυβόλως προσαγορεύει. See the Commentary.

[10] For the remainder of the section the translated text differs from PCW: εἰ δὲ τὸ μέρος εἰκὼν εἰκόνος, δῆλον ὅτι καὶ τὸ ὅλον· εἰ δ' ὁ σύμπας οὗτος ὁ αἰσθητὸς κόσμος, ὃς μείζων τῆς ἀνθρωπίνης ἐστίν, μίμημα θείας εἰκόνος, δῆλον ὅτι καὶ ἡ ἀρχέτυπος σφραγίς, ὅν φαμεν νοητὸν εἶναι κόσμον, αὐτὸς ἂν εἴη τὸ παράδειγμα, ἀρχέτυπος ἰδέα τῶν ἰδεῶν ὁ θεοῦ λόγος.

[11] This is the first example in the treatise of the use of the inceptive imperfect, which Philo regularly uses for God's actions in the creative process. We shall often translate it as here with "proceeded to." See the Commentary on §28.

[12] Reading, contrary to PCW, τῶν αἰσθητικῶν κριτηρίων νοῦς; see the Commentary.

[13] In §40 and §41.

[14] In §30–31.

[15] In §§47–52.

[16] In §69.

[17] In §65.

[18] In §65.

[19] Reading against PCW ἄγεται χαλινωθείς. Philo often puts a preliminary general verb first, and then works the idea out further.

20 Reading γέννησις instead of γένεσις as in PCW; see the Commentary.
21 For the lacuna in the text at this point we suggest ⟨πλάνησι ἑπτά τε ἄρκτῳ καὶ πλείαδι⟩; see the Commentary.
22 In my translation of Solon's poem I have been indebted for some phrases to a verse translation by West 1993, 80.
23 Reading, with West and Gentili & Prato, ἐν ἑβδομάδι μέγ' ἄριστος.
24 Or perhaps "the limits of everything." What is meant is that in the geocentric universe you cannot go higher than the heaven or lower than the earth.
25 Reading with a good number of manuscripts εἰ μὴ τὰ κατὰ μέρος ἀθρόα πάντα, and thus rejecting the conjecture of Cohn, εἰ μὴ κατὰ μέρος ⟨ἀλλ'⟩ ἀθρόα πάντα. Tobin *CM* 123 prefers the reading of ms. M, εἰ μὴ κατὰ γένος ἀθρόα πάντα. See the Commentary.
26 In §38.
27 In §§24–25.
28 Reading [αὐ]τοῦ κάλλους. Cf. §8 αὐτὸ τὸ καλόν, and see the Commentary.
29 Or perhaps "the former's," i.e. God's. See further the Commentary.
30 Reading ἐκπρεπέστατος against PCW εὐπρεπέστατος.
31 Reading χαλῶνται (ἧττον).
32 Reading χάρισι with the majority of the mss. and not χέρσι with ms. M and PCW.
33 Reading τὸν ἄνθρωπον with the majority of the mss. and not τὸν Ἀδαμ with ms. M and PCW.
34 Reading ἀδιάφορος with some of the mss.; PCW prefers ἀδιάφθορος. See further the Commentary.
35 Reading γνωστικοῦ with the majority of the mss. (PCW γνωριστικοῦ). See the Commentary.
36 We retain the words ὁ ὄφις, because the noun is included in all the manuscripts (the article is found only in M), and because the snake is described in §157 as having already been mentioned. This means that the reading προσελθών of most mss. should also be retained (it has been emended to προσελθόν by PCW).
37 Retaining καὶ ἀνδραποδίζουσαι, bracketed by Cohn on the advice of Wendland.
38 The text is difficult, but something should be done with τῆς εἰδεχθείας found in all mss. I suggest τὴν κεφαλὴν περιάγων μεταλαμβάνειν τὴν εἰδεχθέα ὀρέγεται (or perhaps better τὴν εἰδεχθέα μεταλαμβάνειν).
39 In §139.
40 PCW reads κακίαν ἀντ' ἀρετῆς προτιμώντων [ὧν ἄξιον ἀπέχεσθαι]. There seem no good grounds for bracketing the final three words, which are found in all the mss. But if they are retained, then the reading of three mss. κακίας should be preferred. See the Commentary.
41 In §7.
42 Or "and so ascribe no further activity to God" (literally the text merely says "and attributing to God nothing more").
43 Reading οὐσίᾳ with all mss. except M, which has the reading adopted by PCW, ὕλῃ.
44 In §171.

COMMENTARY

Title of the Work

Living just a generation or two before the transition to the codex started to take place, Philo wrote his treatise on a papyrus roll. This is clear from the length of his book. The writing materials which he used to a large degree determined the length of the book. The 1310 lines of the treatise (in PCW) would have occupied a moderately long roll, about five metres in length. (This is based on comparison with the surviving roll of Plato's *Symposium* (*P.Oxy.* 843), one of the longest still extant, which is almost seven metres in length. Our treatise is about three-quarters of that dialogue's length; (on rolls and book length see Reynolds and Wilson 1974, 2.) It was customary in Philo's time to place the title of the treatise at the end of the roll. This meant that it was better protected, since the book was rolled up from end to beginning. It is possible, but not so likely, that the title was also given at the beginning of the treatise. In the case of the two Philonic treatises completely preserved in the Coptos codex, the titles are still given at the end; see Scheil 1891, 187, 215; Runia *PEC* 23. On book titles in general see the overview in Schubart 1962, 88–93.

In his critical editions, 1889, 1 and PCW 1.1, Cohn settles for the title Φίλωνος Περὶ τῆς κατὰ Μωυσέα κοσμοποιίας. Literally translated it reads *Of Philo Concerning the cosmos-making according to Moses*. It is very likely that this title goes back to Philo himself. It corresponds exactly to the way he introduces his subject-matter in the introductory passage (Moses in §2, κοσμοποιία in §4). Unfortunately we cannot confirm the title in our earliest evidence. Eusebius of Caesarea does not refer to our treatise in the catalogue of Philonic works found in his *Ecclesiastical History* (2.18). In his *Preparation of the Gospel* he cites from the work four times (8.13.1, 11.24.1-12), but only refers to it by name once (8.12.22) when he says he is quoting "from the first of the books *On the Law*." On this ambiguous reference see above Introduction §1. But Cohn's title *is* found in the famous *pinax* (table of contents) of the Vienna codex. The manuscript is 11th century, but its *pinax* goes back to the 4th century, as indicated by the famous cross of bishop Euzoius; see further Runia *PEC* 20–22; 1996, 478–481 (both with photos). Moreover this title is confirmed by references in the *Sacra Parallela*, to be dated to about the 6th century (cf. apparatus testimoniorum in PCW, indexed at Royse 1993, 157). As Cohn's apparatus criticus shows, the later mss. contain titles that are similar, but somewhat different: many have *of Moses* instead of *according to Moses*, some have *Of Philo the Jew* instead of just *Of Philo*. The weight of the earlier evidence makes the title chosen by Cohn almost certainly correct.

The Latin title now in common use, *De opificio mundi* (*On the manufacture of the cosmos*), did not become standard in this precise form until Cohn's two editions (for previous Latin titles from the 16th to 19th centuries see Alexandre 1997, 259, 279, 282 & n. 201). It has the disadvantage that it fails to draw attention to the fact that it concerns the creation account of Moses. Philo adds the words "according to Moses" because in Greek authors the term κοσμοποιία, literally "cosmos-making," was also used for other accounts of the origins of the universe. Aristotle, for example, uses it to describe works of Empedocles (*Phys.* 2.4, 196a22) and Anaxagoras (*Metaphys.* A 4, 985a19). In the Christian tradition, from Clement and Origen onwards, the term on its own is the standard way to refer to the creation account. It is also found in this sense at 4 Macc. 14:7. This suggests that it must have also been standard in Hellenistic Judaism.

A phrase almost identical to the title of our work is found at *Plant.* 86. Philo observes that the name God (*theos*) is used τῇ κατὰ ἱερώτατον Μωυσῆν κοσμοποιίᾳ πάσῃ (in the entire creation account according to the most holy Moses). Since the name Lord (*kyrios*) first occurs in Gen 2:8, it could be concluded that Philo confines the κοσμοποιία to the account of the seven days and the epilogue in Gen 2:4. This seems to be the implication of the phrase "reflecting on the κοσμοποιία" in §129. Cf. also *Fug.* 178, when he quotes Gen 2:6 and states that this text is found "after the κοσμοποιία." On the other hand, there are two passages, both referring to Gen 2:7, which say that this text occurs in the κοσμοποιία: *Abr.* 258, *Spec.* 4.123. It would seem, therefore, that Philo is not consistent in his usage. He uses the term both to refer to the work of seven days (Gen 1:1–2:4), and for the entire creation account up to the expulsion of the first human pair from paradise (Gen 1–3). Given the contents of our treatise, it is apparent that the title must be read in the second way. For further remarks on the exact meaning of the term κοσμοποιία see Ch. 1 on §3.

Chapter One
Introduction (§§1–6)

Analysis/General comments

Philo begins his treatise with an introduction which occupies about a page of text. The function of this introduction is best understood if one reflects on how in Philo's day a prose treatise was presented to its readership. Such a work did not have a table of contents or a separate preface as we find in modern books. It was thus necessary for the author at the outset of the treatise to tell the reader what he needed to know before starting to read. From the beginning of Greek prose literature it was the standard practice to preface the actual contents of the work with an introduction or preface, often called the προοίμιον (literally "prelude") or πρόλογος ("preliminary account"), in which the author stated his intentions and made other pronouncements that he considered relevant for his readership. Themes that were commonly included were:

(a) the subject matter and main themes of the treatise;
(b) the specific addressee of the work or, in more general terms, the audience that the author has in mind;
(c) the method that the author is going to use in order to treat his subject;
(d) the qualifications that the author has for dealing with the subject (and why he is better equipped than others for the task);
(e) the sources of information on the subject which the author has consulted or has at his disposal;
(f) the qualifications required by the reader in order to be able to read the book.

In the present introduction the first, third and fourth of these topics are addressed. We observe that the treatise is not dedicated to a specific addressee, and that Philo also does not indicate what his projected audience is except in the vaguest terms when he speaks of "readers" of scripture in §6. This is in fact the case in almost all his writings (in the *prooimion* at *Mos.* 1.1 he states that he is writing his account "for those who are worthy not to remain in ignorance of it", but this is also extremely vague; only *Prob.* is dedicated to a specific person). It would seem that Philo simply assumed the social and educational setting of his writings, but this makes it very difficult for us now precisely to determine what that setting was; see further Introduction §7(a). Philo also does not tell us what his sources were. Here too we may assume important exegetical traditions on which he draws (as hinted at in his statement in *Mos.* 1.4); see once again our discussion in Introduction §7(a).

Fine examples of introductory passages in Philo's treatises are found at *Mos.* 1.1–4, *Aet.* 1–2, *Prov.* 1.1. Many of Philo's treatises do not have an elaborate introduction because they are linked to previous treatises in the same sequence, e.g. at *Abr.* 1, *Ios.* 1, *Decal.* 1 etc. The *prooimion* at *Contempl.* 1 is in the same category (the previous treatise is no longer extant), but nevertheless shows a number of marked resemblances to *Opif.* 4–6. For analysis of Philo's introductory passages see Alexander 1993, 157–160. She argues that *Opif.* differs from the treatises mentioned above because it does not begin with a "separate personal preface". In my view Philo's preface, despite its impersonal formulation, does constitute a conventional preface because it emphasizes the role of the exegete which Philo is about to undertake. It is thus a fitting preface for a commentary.

The introductory section can be divided into two parts.

(1) The *subject* of the treatise is introduced in combination with an apologetic motif. It is a striking fact that Moses commences his laws with a creation account, in contrast to the practice of other legislators. They either just state their laws, or they preface their laws with preambles involving the use of myths and falsehoods. Moses' practice is thus superior. There is a direct relation between legislation for human life and the rational structure of the cosmos. The person who observes the Law of Moses will feel at home in the cosmos as totality. The guiding thought behind this idea is the concept of the law of nature. The apologetic emphasis on the superiority of Moses as thinker and author is pervasive throughout the treatise (and Philo's entire *œuvre*), but is particularly strong in the opening chapters (see also especially §8) (§§1–3).

(2) The *method* that Philo will adopt in his work is that of the interpreter, who rigorously subordinates himself to the text on which he is commenting. The superiority of the Mosaic text is expressed in terms that are quite hyperbolic. The thoughts that it contains are so superior that they cannot be adequately expressed with the resources of human language and literature (yet, we might observe, Moses did manage to put them in writing). Philo's self-presentation is suitably modest. He is hardly qualified for such a task, he claims, yet he must do what he can. The necessary qualification, it is implied, is a love and desire for wisdom, and this at least (it is implied) he possesses in adequate measure. The gulf between the greatness of the contents of the text and the paltriness of the commentary is expressed by the vivid image of a seal, which depicts huge objects in a tiny compass (§§4–6).

In a sense this image might seem to be the reverse of what actually happens in the treatise. After all, the brief words of Moses (cf. §131) give rise to a mountain of commentary, and this procedure is continued in the rich legacy of the subsequent hexaemeral tradition. Philo assumes that a text which can inspire so much detailed explanation must be immensely rich and profound. We might compare the exclamation of Augustine at *Conf.* 12.17 when expounding the same creation account: "What wonderful profundity there is in your [God's] utterances! The surface meaning lies open before us and charms beginners. Yet the depth is amazing, my God, the depth is amazing (transl. Chadwick)." Augustine concludes that a single interpretation cannot do justice to the depth of the text's meaning (12.35).

We note, finally, that Philo does not tell his reader in the introduction that he will be giving an exposition of the entire Mosaic legislation. This only becomes plain in his introduction at *Praem.* 1–3, where he looks back at the entire sequence of treatises. Perhaps he made up his plan as he went along. But he does make clear at the outset that his commentary on the creation account is motivated by its place in the Mosaic *Law*. On the place of the treatise in Philo's *œuvre* and its relation to the other treatises of the Exposition of the Law see further Introduction §1.

Detailed comments

(1) §1 **the other legislators.** In the ancient world the legislator (νομοθέτης) has an honoured position because he is the author of the law that gives the community its constitution. Philo is presumably thinking mainly of Greek examples here, e.g. the mythical King Minos of Crete or archaic statesmen such as Lycugus, the lawgiver of the Spartans, and Solon, the lawgiver of the Athenians (cf. §104). Early philosophers too were famous for having written laws for their communities, e.g. Pythagoras in Croton and Parmenides in Elea. In later times philosophers have less direct influence, but instead write idealized constitutions, e.g. Plato in the *Republic* and the *Laws*, the founder of the Stoa Zeno in his lost *Republic*, Cicero in the *De re publica* and *De legibus*. An excellent parallel for the esteem in which lawgivers were held is found in a passage in Philo's younger contemporary Plutarch:

> There has come down from theologians and lawgivers to poets and philosophers this very ancient opinion, which cannot be traced back to any source, but which has gained a strong and almost indelible conviction, and is found among Greeks and barbarians, not only in reports and traditions, but also in rites and sacrifices, namely ... (*Is. Os.* 369B)

For "theologians" we can compare the description of Moses in §8 and §12. Plutarch implies here that lawgivers are an earlier and therefore more august source of knowledge than poets (e.g. Homer) and philosophers (e.g. Plato).

some ... others. Whether legislation should be preceded by explanatory and exhortatory preambles was a controversial point in philosophical discussions on the ideal legislation. At *Leg.* 722c Plato criticizes existing laws for merely using compulsion rather than a mixture of persuasion and force. Laws should have two elements, the law itself and the prelude to the law (723e). Cicero agrees with him (*Leg.* 2.14). The 1st cent. B.C.E. philosopher Posidonius, however, disagrees:

> I disapprove of Plato's practice of adding preambles to his laws. A law should be brief, so that the unskilled may grasp it more easily. Let it be like a voice sent from heaven; let it order, not argue. Nothing seems to be more pedantic, more pointless than a law with a preamble. Advise me, tell me what you want me to do; I am not learning, I am obeying (frg. F178 E.-K., cited at Seneca, *Ep.* 94.38, transl. Kidd).

This position might seem suitable for the Decalogue and some of the injunctions of the Law, but the Pentateuch contains much more. The apologist Philo sees a third course which represents a mean between two extremes.

deceived. A variant reading deserving consideration is ἐξετύφλωσαν ("blinded") instead of ἐξετύφωσαν. But the very similar passage at *Spec.* 1.28, which also contains polemic against myths, supports Cohn's choice. This text is cited below on §2.

concealing the truth with mythical fictions. See on the second group in §2, and see also further on §170.

§2. ***Moses surpassed both groups.*** In *De vita Moysis* Moses is presented as king, legislator, priest, and prophet. It is apparent that his role as lawgiver, expounded in 2.3–65, fitted in excellently with Greek ideas on the founder of a community. Both Aristobulus (frg. 2–4) and Josephus *C. Ap.* 2.154–286 exploit this situation. In Greco-Roman texts on Judaism Moses is also frequently presented as a lawgiver; cf. Stern *GLAJJ* nos. 11, 58, 115, 301, 331. The same contrast between Moses and two groups of other lawgivers is worked out in more detail in *Mos.* 2.48–51. As is noted in the Introduction §1, Philo expects his readers already to be acquainted with this work before reading *Opif.*

the former ... If the lawgiver states: "Thou shalt honour thy father and thy mother," then some indication should be given why this is a good thing to do. Otherwise people have to accept the law purely on the basis of authority and might be inclined to rebel and disobey. At *Mos.* 2.50–51 Philo gives a fuller explanation:

> But Moses thought that the former approach was tyrannical and despotic, issuing commands without words of encouragement as though to slaves rather than free persons, as indeed it was ... For in his commands and prohibitions Moses suggests and encourages rather than commands, attempting to give the most copious and necessary instructions by means of prologues and epilogues, with a view to exhortation rather than force.

In the *Let. Arist.* 131 Moses is also praised for giving more than just prohibitions. Philo sometimes refers to the book Deuteronomy as "The Exhortations" (τὰ προτρεπτικά, e.g. *Fug.* 142, *Mut.* 236), presumably because he thought the element of admonition and exhortation was so strong in that book. In Greek philosophy protreptic literature is a special genre which encourages people to become philosophers, e.g. Plato's *Euthydemus*. Through study and observance of the Law the Jewish people too become "philosophers" (cf. *Mos.* 2.216, *Contempl.* 28), the term now being used in the broader sense of "studying and practising one's ancestral religion". See further on §54.

the latter ... What does this second group do that Philo disagrees with? They are long-winded, apparently, but more importantly, they resort to myth. Philo shares with other Hellenistic-Jewish writers an abhorrence for the use of myth when speaking about God (cf. Aristobulus frg. 2 [10.2], Josephus *Ant.* 1.14 etc.). Some common ground here is shared with Plato in his polemics against myths about the gods found in Homer (*Resp.* 378–381). But Hellenistic Judaism is far more radical because all polytheism is rejected. See for example the passage at *Spec.* 1.28–31 where Philo first rejects "all those (gods) whom the makers of myth have invented and deceived people with, building up false doctrines against the truth and introducing new gods *ex machina* in order that the eternal and truly existent God would be consigned to oblivion," and then continues with a fierce polemic against all cultural expression of polytheism through literature and art. On Moses and the use of myth, see further below on §157.

But here the concern is with lawgivers. When did they use myth? Philo knows of course that the early lawgivers of Greeks operated in a polytheistic religious context. He may, however, be thinking more specifically of Greek philosophers such as Plato, who begins his legislation (*Leg.* 715e–717b) by first furnishing it with a religious basis (and also prefaces it with a quasi-historical account containing numerous mythical elements, cf. 677–703). Cicero adopts the same approach, *Leg.* 2.16: "From the beginning let the citizens be persuaded of this, that the gods are lords and rulers of all things, and that what should be done is done with their authority and will ..." Such a polytheistic basis for law is unacceptable to the Jew Philo.

The phrase "concealing the truth with mythical fictions" in §1, which is further explained in §2, is found in an almost identical form in the concluding summary of *Opif.* at §170, where Philo speaks of people who "overshadow the truth with mythical fictions". As will emerge in our comments on §170, Philo is thinking there of the radical atheist Critias, who regards religion as an *invention* of lawgivers who wish their laws to be obeyed even when no one is looking. I do not think that Philo can be thinking of this rationalist view of the religious foundation of law here. See further on §170.

form in advance. The verb προτυπῶσαι is the first example of the language of "marking" or "moulding" that will be so prominent in the treatise. See further on §§6, 16–19.

§3. *The beginning.* The term ἀρχή here refers to the beginning of Moses' legislation, but that beginning itself contains a "beginning", namely that of the cosmos, as will be explained in §26. Such a beginning was not found in existing Greek legislations, and so can be exploited for apologetic purposes. The author of *De sublimitate* was impressed by the inspired beginning of Moses' legislation; see 9.9 = Stern *GLAJJ* no. 148.

the making of the cosmos. The same term κοσμοποιία is used in the title of the treatise; see our remarks on the Title above. The term itself emphasizes the demiurgic metaphor of creation (on which see the Introduction §5c), which the first sentence of Genesis legitimates. If the approximately 20 passages in which Philo uses the word are examined, it emerges that the term is slightly ambiguous: it can mean "act or process of cosmos-making" or the *account* of that act or process (i.e. by Moses). The latter meaning certainly predominates in our treatise (§§3, 4, 129, 170), but in §6 the former may be meant. In the case of the title both are possible, but the former meaning is the more likely.

the cosmos is in harmony with the law. The context indicates that "law" (*nomos*) here means primarily the Law of Moses. But at the same time Philo connects this law with the universal law of nature propounded in Greek philosophy. See further Excursus 1 below. Josephus, who is surely dependent on Philo (see *Nachleben*), writes at *Ant.* 1.24: "for if they [his readers] will look at it [his work] in this way nothing will appear to them unreasonable or incongruous with the majesty and benevolence (φιλανθρωπία) of God, for all things have their arrangement in harmony with the nature of the universe."

the man who observes the law. Philo uses here the term for "man" (ἀνήρ) and not "human being" (ἄνθρωπος). This is consistent with the strong tendency towards androcentrism that will emerge later in the treatise; see further below Chs. 19, 21–24.

citizen of the cosmos. The term is κοσμοπολίτης, where our word "cosmopolitan" comes from. Before Philo it is found in a "one-liner" attributed to the 4th cent. Cynic philosopher Diogenes (Diogenes Laertius 6.63): when asked where he came from, he replied "I am a citizen of the world." Note, however, that Diogenes uses the term negatively to express alienation from his community (cf. Schofield 1991, 144), whereas Philo means it positively. On the kind of universalism Philo has in mind see further Excursus 1 below. The word is scarcely found outside Philo and the later Church fathers dependent on him. Philo appears to have had a great love for compound words of this kind, and often he is the first recorded author to use them. For this reason I have named such words *verba Philonica*; cf. further Runia 1992b, 314–317. The term recurs in §§142 and 143.

actions. The Law is concerned with what people should and should not *do*. In this treatise cosmology is in the final analysis subordinated to ethics. Cf. further on §172 and the Introduction §5(g).

rational purpose of nature. With this phrase Philo makes it clear that he is linking the Law of Moses with the way nature operates in the cosmos, as postulated by philosophers. For further discussion see Excursus 1 below.

(2) §4. ***In celebrating the beauty*** ... As Dillon 1990, 181 has observed, Philo's choice of language deliberately echoes Plato, *Phdr.* 247c3–4: "The place beyond the heaven none of the poets here has or ever will celebrate as it deserves." This allusion is surely more than a literary reminiscence. For Plato the *hyperouranios topos* is the metaphorical location of the ideas (cf. below on §17); contemplation of its beauty is the goal of the soul's journey (cf. 250b5). Philo is hinting that the thoughts contained in the creation account are similarly transcendent and beautiful.

poetry or prose. Most biblical exegesis is of course written in prose, but in Hellenistic Judaism poets also tried their hand, e.g. Philo's namesake the Epic poet and Ezechiel the tragic dramatist; see Charlesworth *OTP* 2.781–784, 803–819.

to the instruments of a mortal being. That is to say, the power of language as expressed through sound and word. In my view Philo is referring to the capacities of the exegete, namely himself. This does raise the question of how Moses himself was able to use these instruments to formulate the text that Philo is commenting on. An implicit answer to this question is given in §8. But see also Excursus 2.

§5. ***on behalf of the God-beloved (author)***. The phrase ἕνεκα τοῦ θεοφιλοῦς can be interpreted in two ways, either as in our translation or as "in order to please God." I agree with Whitaker against all the other translators that the former is to be preferred. Three reasons may be given. (1) It fits the context better, because Philo is discussing his exegesis of the *Mosaic* account of creation. (2) Moses is very often called the God-beloved, based on the text in Exod 33:11; see the list at PLCL 10.388. (3) The term θεοφιλής in Philo almost always means "beloved by God," whereas his usual term for "loving God" is φιλόθεος; cf. the two terms together at *Abr.* 50; *Virt.* 184; *QG* frg. 10 Petit. Moreover the alternative translation seems to double up with the subsequent claim that "love of wisdom" is required for the exegete's task.

we must keep our peace. Both here and in the next sentence Philo uses an impersonal construction involving the verbal adjective (ἡσυχαστέον, ἐπιτολμητέον). As Alexander 1993, 159 has noted, Philo shows a great preference for impersonal constructions, and many will be found in the present treatise; see further on §§52 and 92. Despite the impersonal tone, however, Philo *is* speaking as author in this passage.

beyond our ability. The qualifications of the writer is a standard theme of ancient introductory passages. Ideally there should be a correspondence between the subject-matter and the author's ability to deal with it. But this is out of the question when the author has to confront such a majestic theme. Compare similar statements at §90 when Philo embarks on the theme of the wonders of the hebdomad, and at §145 when he describes the beauty of the first human being. Another text that should be compared is *Aet.* 1–2, where the theme of the cosmos' indestructibility is similarly grand, but Philo invokes divine aid and hopes that he can reach a semblance of the truth. On the modesty that befits the exegete see further on §72.

nothing from our own supply. Philo will expound to the best of his ability the thoughts contained in the Mosaic account, adding no additional material of his own that might compromise its truth. Compare the very similar statement at *Contempl.* 1 when he undertakes to describe the Therapeutae. Philo's claim here is all the more remarkable when we consider how much Greek philosophy he invokes when explaining Moses' meaning. Is this not taken from his own knowledge? Philo would argue that he is merely explaining what is present in the biblical text.

possessed by a love and desire for wisdom. A classic Greek theme, above all associated with Platonism. Love (ἔρως) and desire (πόθος) should not be focused on bodily or earthly matters, but rather on the quest for wisdom. This will result in the practice of philosophy. The theme is further developed with appropriate passion at §§69–71. It is important to note that Philo practises philosophy by being an exegete.

§6. **just as even the tiniest seal.** The interpretation of Philo's image depends on what is being compared. In my view Philo compares the wonderful thoughts of the creation account with his own paltry efforts as exegete. The *tertium comparationis* is the reduction in scale involved: Philo can only state a little of all the riches contained in the original text. For a discussion of an alternative interpretation of this image see Excursus 2.

The image of seal and impression was used in Greek philosophy for the reception and storage of information; see further our detailed comments on §§16–19. Here the emphasis lies on the reduction of size, which is necessarily accompanied by a reduction in precision. A fine example of what Philo might have had in mind is the coin containing a representation of the famous Alexandrian Pharos (lighthouse), one of the seven wonders of the ancient world, which is depicted on the cover of the French translation series (on the coin itself see PAPM 1.10). The relation between a mould and a coin is the same as between a seal and the impression it makes in wax.

colossal dimensions. The adjective κολοσσιαῖος is derived from another of the seven wonders of the ancient world, the Colossus of Rhodes. Elsewhere Philo uses it only of enormous statues; see *Ios.* 39; *Legat.* 188, 203, 306, 337.

with their brightness. Another Platonic theme, as indicated by the term μαρμαρυγαί (dazzling beams of light). Plato uses the term for the person who leaves the cave and is overwhelmed by sunlight (*Resp.* 515c9, 518a8).

By writing his commentary Philo comes to the aid of the reader who might be dazzled by the brilliance of its contents. This is consistent with the allusion from the *Phaedrus* above in §4. Understanding scripture is comparable with contemplation of the ideas. The term returns in §71.

a preliminary remark. See further Ch. 2 below.

not be passed over in silence. Exactly the same phrase is also found at §155.

EXCURSUS ONE
Law, cosmos and nature

The Law of Moses is meant as the norm and guide for human society (and in particular for the Jewish people in their various communities), but it is in Philo's view also related to the structure of cosmic reality. Of central importance here is the translation of the Hebrew word *torah* (instruction, guidance) with the Greek term *nomos* (usage, convention, law, statute), which goes back to the translation of the LXX and the beginnings of Hellenistic Judaism. This rendering enormously facilitated the link to Greek political and philosophical thought which partly underlies Philo's usage. See the important discussion in Dodd 1935, 25–41. But Bickerman 1988, 114 is right to point out that there is a shift from the plural to the singular in Hellenistic Jewish thought. Greek texts always speak of "the laws" and not "the law", also when they speak about the Mosaic legislation. With the singular the Jews wish to indicate that "for them the Torah was not just another code, but the revealed, fundamental order within which man, all other creatures, and all the elements of the cosmos as well ought to live" (*ibid.*). Philo would largely agree with this statement, but would add the distinction between Law of Moses and law of nature. On this theme see the further discussion in Segal 1987.

In earlier Greek thought the cosmic dimension of law is often implicit (e.g. in Anaximander's famous fragment, 12B1 DK, and in Heraclitus, cf. esp. 22B114 DK). Plato explores the intrinsic relation between cosmic reality, society and the individual person in his dialogues *Republic, Timaeus*, and *Laws*. Nature obtains a normative loading as being responsible for the order which is the cosmos, to which humans must respond. Unquestionably the school which develops this line of thought the furthest is the Stoa. The law of the cosmos is identified with the logos, the divine principle which pervades and structures the whole of physical reality, including human beings, and is to be identified with Zeus, Nature, Providence, Fate (cf. Diogenes Laertius 7.135–136, L&S ch. 54). The goal of human life is "to live by following nature, i.e. in accordance with our own human nature and the nature of the universe, carrying out no actions that the common law (ὁ νόμος ὁ κοινός) forbids, which is the right reason (ὁ ὀρθὸς λόγος) pervading all things, identical with Zeus the director of the universal order" (Diogenes Laertius 7.88). Philo's formulation in §3 is clearly influenced by such ideas (but it is an exaggeration to regard it as a Stoic fragment, as Von Arnim does by incorporating it in *SVF* 2.336–337, together with §§142–143). In another Hellenistic work, Ps.-Aristotle *De mundo*, the law of the city and the law of the cosmos are seen as analogous: God *is* the cosmic law (§6, 400b14–28).

The question remains: what is the relation between cosmic law and the laws laid down for human communities? The early Stoics undoubtedly emphasized that reason constituted a higher law than any local regulations (cf. L&S §67, esp. 1.435). By Philo's time, under the influence of the spread of Hellenistic culture, this view had been developed into a kind of universalist ideology. As an example we may cite Arius Didymus (1st–2nd cent. C.E.), who formulates Stoic thought as follows (Eusebius *Praep. Ev.* 15.15.4–5): "... the universe is like a city consisting of gods and humans, the gods exercising leadership, the humans subordinate. Community exists between them because they share in reason, which is natural law (νόμος φύσει) ..." Philo, however, is above all concerned to demonstrate the superiority of the Law of Moses. As Cohen 1987, 164 rightly points out, his use of the term *nomos* in §3 is deliberately equivocal. He clearly means the Law of Moses, but also wants to exploit the associations with natural or cosmic law. The Law of Moses is not identical with the cosmic or natural law, but a far-reaching harmony exists between them. In terms of their deeper intentions they may be regarded as amounting to the same (or, in a more Platonic perspective, as model and faithful copy), but the Mosaic law has been adapted to the requirements of human society. At *Mos.* 2.44 Philo makes the bold claim that, if the prosperity of the Jewish nation would increase, all peoples would abandon their ancestral ways and honour the Jewish laws alone (cf. also Josephus *C. Ap.* 2.281–286). A comparable tension is found in the Roman statesman Cicero: at *Leg.* 1.18–19 he describes law in terms of nature and reason, existing before any states had been established; at 2.23–24 he affirms that the ideal state should have laws approximating the laws and customs of early Roman society.

There has been considerable controversy about the conception of the "law of nature" (νόμος φύσεως, not found in our passage, but cf. §171) ever since H. Koester pointed out in 1968 that the phrase is rarely found prior to Philo and argued that he was responsible for its later popularity. This claim is not convincing because it fails to take into account important parallels in Cicero. See further Horsley 1978 and my comments at *PT* 466 n.333.

The most detailed analysis of the relation between the Law of Moses and the law of nature in Philo is found at Nikiprowetzky 1977, 117-155, whose conclusions I largely follow above. On the historical background of Philo's views and comparisons with Cicero and Augustine, see now Lévy 1992, 509–521, Girardet 1995, 292–298. Grumach 1939 points out interesting Platonic parallels, but his suggestions on Stoic sources are outdated.

EXCURSUS TWO
An alternative interpretation of the seal image (§6)

Recently in an article on Philo's philosophy of language, Maren Niehoff, 1995, 245–247, has presented an interpretation of the seal metaphor which differs markedly from mine. In her translation she renders κοσμοποιία in §4 as "the creation of the world," i.e. not Moses' account thereof. Moreover she sees in the expression "smaller markings" (§6) a reference to written characters or letters (n. 72). According to Niehoff the text refers to Moses' literary activity when writing the Torah, and the comparison is between unwritten thoughts and written language. Scripture contains thoughts that are too great for human apprehension and adaptation to human instruments. As remedy Moses resorts to written language. Because of this gift of written language embodied in the Torah, humankind has a measure of access to divine truth. "Philo suggests a new alternative to the Platonic vision of the Forms: reading Scripture" (247).

The difficulty that I have with this reading is that it does not allow for a distinction to be made between the writer Moses and the exegete Philo. In writing his commentary, Philo will go beyond his own powers. This is not what happens to the divinely inspired prophet. Note the use of the future tense when the image is explained. The beauties of the creation (account) *will be* elucidated ... This surely refers to the commentary that Philo is about to write, not the scriptural text that Moses has already produced. Of course we are left with the problem of the origin and status of the Mosaic text, but this will be explained to us a few lines later in §8. The comparison with Platonic contemplation is apt and is indicated by Philo's language, as we have seen above (see above on §5). But scriptural interpretation is only the first stage. Through scripture access is gained to the intelligible realm and to God himself (cf. §§69–71). We can compare Platonists in Philo's day who philosophize by studying Plato.

Parallel exegesis

Not relevant for this introductory section. A parallel treatment of introductory matters is found in *Mos.*; for §§1–3 compare *Mos.* 2.47–52, for §§4–6 compare *Mos.* 1.1–4

Nachleben

In the introductory section of his account of Jewish customs and history at *Ant.* 1.18–27 Josephus introduces Moses as author of the Law. The lawgiver does not commence with contracts and rights, but first leads the thoughts of his readers to God and the structure of the universe (§21). Everything in the law is presented in harmony with the nature of the universe (§24). The entire passage betrays acquaintance with *Opif.*; see Thackeray's notes at LCL ad loc., Feldman 2000, 9, and the analysis of

Sterling 1999a, 27–29. In *C. Ap.* 2.172–178 his strategy is similar to that of Philo here, showing how Moses avoided the two opposite methods of Greek legislators. The details, however, differ.

Theophilus of Antioch introduces his exegesis of the Hexaemeron (*Autol.* 2.12) with a reflection on the grandeur of the Mosaic text which, to judge by similarity of theme and parallels of language, is directly indebted to a reading of §§4–6. See the parallel columns at Runia *PEC* 115, and also Martín 1986, 155. Note also the prologue at Basil *Hex.* 1.1, 2A, where a contrast is made between the weakness of the interpreter and the profundity of the author. If "these small words" is a reminiscence of Philo's "smaller markings," then Basil must have understood the text similarly to Niehoff (see above Excursus 2).

Further reading: Radice *FM* 233–234 (rather brief); Winston *PA* 167 and notes; see also the references given in the Excursuses above.

Chapter Two
A preliminary comment on God and the cosmos (§§7-12)

Analysis/General comments

As announced in the final words of the Introduction (§6), before Philo starts on the commentary proper, he finds it necessary to make a preliminary comment. Its purpose is to inform the reader on a major philosophical and religious issue that forms the background to the entire creation account, namely the nature of the cosmos and its relation to God as first principle. Following common practice in philosophical treatises, Philo approaches the subject by presenting and arguing against the view that he disagrees with (see §7). The entire passage can be analysed into three parts.

(1) First Philo states both the false view and its opposite which he himself defends. Those who declare the cosmos to be ungenerated and eternal go astray by giving it too much honour and God its creator not enough. This view attributes idleness to God. Instead they should be astonished at God's creative powers (§7).

(2) The argument in favour of Philo's position involves two steps, the former positive and representing his own view, the latter negative and directed against his opponents.
(a) Moses recognized that there was a vast ontological divide between God the creator, who is wholly active and transcendent mind, and physical reality founded on matter, which is wholly passive and needs the creative power of the active cause in order for it to be converted into the cosmos (§§8–9).
(b) If it is held that the cosmos has not come into existence, then God cannot have acted as its maker. But this would mean that we have to abandon the conviction that God exercises providence over the cosmos. Using an analogical argument, Philo states that there can be no providential relation between that which has not been created and a being who did not create. But such divine lack of involvement (compare the idleness in §7) is contrary to our conception of God as first cause (§§9–11).

(3) In the final paragraph Philo summarizes how he understands the Mosaic conception of the relation between God and the world. This amounts to a Platonizing division of reality into two spheres. God is intelligible (i.e. known to the intellect only) and eternal, whereas the cosmos, as sense-perceptible reality, is the sphere of becoming and has obtained the appropriate name Genesis. This is the expression of a sound theology (§12).

These six short paragraphs are extremely rich both in the philosophical background that they assume and in the points of contact that they reveal with other Philonic writings. Our detailed comments will have to be selective. There has been much scholarly discussion about the identity of the opponents whom Philo has in mind and the basic philosophical position he attributes to Moses. My position in brief is the following. The opponents come closest to the views that he attributes elsewhere to the Chaldeans. These thinkers represent a mentality rather than any particular Greek philosophy, i.e. the opinion that rejects God as creator and ruler of the cosmos. Aristotle cannot be the main opponent that he has in mind, since Aristotle does recognize a *nous* as ultimate and transcendent cause. The doctrine attributed to Moses in §8 and §12 is not so easy to pin down. It is certainly not Aristotelian or Stoic, but is an adaptation of fundamental Platonic views, as evidenced by the paraphrase of the *Timaeus* in §12. For further discussion see the Excursus below.

Philo also makes use of the opportunity in this section to tell us more about the sources of Moses' authority. He was both extremely well trained in philosophy and instructed through divine inspiration (§8). We should note, however, that, in spite of this emphasis on the divinely inspired nature of Moses' doctrine (§8) and the recurring insistence on the need for pious and reverential thought about God (§§7, 9, 12), Philo does not want us to accept his views merely on the basis of religious authority. Within limits theology can be supported by philosophical argumentation.

The background material, both religious and philosophical, that Philo introduces in this section is fundamental for the treatise as a whole. It is striking how many of its themes return in the concluding summary of the "five fundamental doctrines" in §§170–172. Both introduction (§§1–6) and preliminary comment (§§7–12) have been carefully planned and well written.

Detailed comments

(1) **§7. *There are some people who* ...** From Aristotle onwards it was standard practice for philosophical treatises to start with a doxographical section in which the views of other thinkers on the question being discussed are briefly outlined and critiqued. An excellent example is found in *Aet.* (see below). One of the lessons that can be drawn from such views is how *not* to approach the question. Philo adopts this procedure here.

admiration for the cosmos. For Plato and Aristotle admiration and wonder are the starting-point for philosophy (cf. *Theat.* 155d, *Metaph.* A 2, 982b11). Philo agrees that wonder can lead humankind to the rational conclusion that God has created the cosmos (*Praem.* 42). But in the present passage admiration clearly has religious overtones. If one is impressed by something, one naturally regards it as important, and this applies *a fortiori* if one concludes that it is the highest principle of all that exists. As has recently been pointed out by Bos 1998, 68–70, there are a number of passages in which Philo associates the doctrine of the excessive admiration of the cosmos with the creed of the Chaldeans:

> They [the Chaldeans] glorified visible existence and had no conception of what was invisible and intelligible, but in exploring the order in numbers ... and the sympathy between heaven and earth, they supposed that the cosmos itself was god, thereby unlawfully likening what has come into existence to the one who had made it (*Abr.* 69).
> He [Nahor] does not emigrate from the land of Chaldea, that is he does not sever himself from the study of astrology, but instead honours what has come into existence instead of the maker and the cosmos instead of God, and regards the cosmos itself as an autonomous god and not as a work of God who is absolute in power (*Congr.* 49).
> The Chaldean doctrine ... persuades men to honour and worship the works of the world instead of the creator of the world (*QG* 3.1, transl. Marcus LCL).

The background to Philo's doctrine of Chaldeanism is twofold: (a) what he attacks refers implicitly to the Hellenistic "religion cosmique," on which see further the Excursus to Ch. 10; (b) the method of his attack is indebted to the Hellenistic-Jewish tradition of polemic against the worship of created things, e.g. heavenly bodies or idols, e.g. at Deut 4:19 (cited at *Spec.* 1.15); Wis 13:1–9; Paul at Rom 1:20–25; on this tradition see further Pépin 1964, 278–284; Winston 1979, 248–249. The chief texts on the Chaldeans are listed at Earp PLCL 10.298, Runia *PT* 460. See also below on §45.

than for its maker. Too much admiration for the cosmos leads to the false view that it has not been created by God. None of the passages on the Chaldeans specifically attribute to them the view that the cosmos is uncreated. Their mistake is to think that the cosmos is the first god and not the *work* of the first God; cf. *Abr.* 75; *Migr.* 193–194; *Her.* 97; *Congr.* 49 (cited above). The implication could be that the cosmos has always been there, but it is also compatible with an evolutionist point of view. At *Migr.* 180, Philo affirms that the Mosaic doctrine that the cosmos is created and one (cf. *Opif.* 171) is consistent with the Chaldean doctrine of cosmic sympathy.

both ungenerated and eternal. The Greek terms are ἀγένητος and ἀίδιος. The former is the opposite to γενητός, the adjective derived from the noun *genesis* introduced in §12. The latter term is perhaps better translated as "everlasting", because it does not imply any kind of timelessness, but because Philo uses the noun of God in §12, the translation "eternal" has to be retained. According to the view introduced here the universe has always existed and will never cease to exist. In modern cosmology this is called the "steady-state" view of the universe, in contrast to the "big-bang theory" which holds that the ever-expanding universe originated in a

primal event. In the ancient world the question of whether the universe has always existed or not was one of the most hotly debated issues in philosophy and a standard example in doxographical surveys (cf. *Abr.* 162; *Her.* 246; Pépin 1964, 79; Mansfeld 1988, 90). Philo gives a very clear account of the views held on the question in the doxographical passage *Aet.* 7–19:
   1a. many *kosmoi* generated and destructible, held by Democritus and Epicurus (§8);
   1b. one cosmos generated and destructible, held by the Stoics (§§8–9);
   2. cosmos ungenerated and indestructible, maintained by Aristotle and before him Ocellus the Pythagorean (§§10–12);
   3. cosmos generated and not to be destroyed, the view of Plato, Hesiod and Moses (§§13–19).

The view imputed to Philo's opponents in our text thus comes closest to the position of Aristotle as presented in *Aet.* Philo also recognized, however, that certain Platonists interpreted the Platonic position in such a way that it did not entail a temporal beginning of the cosmos' existence. So they also effectively fall under the Aristotelian position (see *Aet.* 14). It should not be concluded, however, that Aristotle and these Aristotelianizing Platonists are the primary figures behind Philo's anonymous opponents. See further the Excursus at the end of the Chapter.

impurely. Cohn reads ἀνάγνως on the basis of Eusebius and our oldest ms. V. As an adverb, however, it is a *hapax* in the corpus. Other mss. read οὐκ εὐάγως (not without guilt). This expression is found three times elsewhere, including the very similar passage *Abr.* 69 cited above. In terms of meaning, however, there is very little difference. On Eusebius see below *Nachleben*.

idleness. God is idle because, if he does not create the cosmos, he can have nothing to do with it (this will emerge below in §§9–11). The term is reminiscent of the famous argument which Aristotle appears to have directed against Plato's presentation of demiurgic creation in the *Timaeus*: what did the god do before he proceeded to create? was he simply idle? see *Aet.* 83; Aëtius 1.7 at Ps.-Plutarch 881B-C; Effe 1970, 27–31. The argument was taken over in the Epicurean tradition; cf. Cicero *Nat. d.* 1.21 and Pease's comments ad loc., who follows the tradition right through to Augustine's celebrated use of the motif at *Conf.* 11.14. For Aristotle the unmoved mover is pure actuality, thus always active and never idle. At the same time he is not directly involved in administering the cosmos, since that burdensome task would interfere with his felicity (cf. *Metaph.* Λ 7, *Nic. Eth.* 10.8). For Philo too God's resting, e.g. on the Sabbath, most emphatically does not mean any kind of ἀπραξία: God is always active; cf. *Cher.* 87 and further remarks on §8 and §§9–11.

God's powers as Maker and Father. There *may* be a reference to the doctrine of the divine powers here, which will be further set out at §21; cf. Bos 1998, 68, 75. It is more likely in my view that Philo, anticipating his argument in §§8–11, wants to emphasize what God as active cause is capable of doing (cf. *Congr.* 49 cited above; the same emphasis in Atticus frg. 4.9, 4.13, 37, in the argument for providence cited below on §9).

The expression "Maker and Father" is taken over from Plato *Tim.* 28c3: the sequence here is the same as in Plato; at §10 and §21 the order is reversed. See further *PT* 107-111, where I note that the words also have biblical resonances, though the epithet "father" is less common in the Hebrew Bible than in the New Testament; see also below on §10. We capitalize the terms when they are used as titles (this is not the case in §13, for example, where the text reads ὁ ποιῶν).

(2a) §8. ***Moses ... had not only reached ...*** As above in §2, Moses shows superiority in insight compared with his rivals. This passage is important because Philo states in the space of a few words what the basis of this superiority is. It has a double origin, as given in the two clauses placed side by side (καί ... καί indicating a mild disjunction, cf. *PT* 73).
(a) In *Mos.* 1.21-24 Moses is anachronistically portrayed as receiving an excellent training in Greek, Egyptian and Chaldean science (cf. also Acts 7:22). In this text, however, Philo is probably thinking in more general terms. "Philosophy," in line with the presentation later at §§53-54 and §§69-71, represents the sum total of *human* efforts to reach the truth on the nature of the cosmos and God.
(b) In addition Moses has been initiated in the higher mysteries of theology and what we might call metaphysics. Philo is no doubt thinking of his experiences on the mountain as recorded in Exodus 3, 20, and 33; cf. esp. *Spec.* 1.32-50. The initiation into the mysteries through oracles is part of Moses' role as prophet. In a seminal article Winston has argued that in the case of Moses Philo recognizes two kinds of prophecy, ecstatic and hermeneutical (or noetic); see 1989, based esp. on an analysis of *Mos.* 2.188; summary of Winston's position at 1990, 12-17. The former kind of prophecy is required to predict the future. As for the latter, "in the light of the general thrust of Philo's philosophical thought, it is very likely that he understands 'noetic' prophecy to refer to the activation of his higher mind or his intuitive intellect, by means of which he grasps the fundamental principles of universal being viewed as a unified whole" (1990, 16). This interpretation would seem to cohere well with the present passage. Moses' knowledge has in part a divine origin, but does not involve the elimination of the human intellect. See also Burkhardt's monograph, 1988, which reaches a comparable position (on our text 189-190).

most essential doctrines of nature. The phrase introduces the pronouncement on first principles that is to follow. It is reinforced by the term "most necessary" in the following line. The superlative συνεκτικώτατος is very common in Philo. On its meaning see further below the comment on §101.

among existing things. This phrase (ἐν τοῖς οὖσι) is used by Philo elsewhere on a number of occasions where it includes God: cf. *Cher.* 87 (an important parallel, see next note); *Sacr.* 41; *Migr.* 179 (the Chaldeans);

Mut. 17. On the basis of Ex. 3:14 God is the Existent (τὸ ὄν) *par excellence.*

an activating cause on the one hand. Philo now proceeds to present a brief doctrine of the first principles of reality (or at least so it seems). There are two such principles, the δραστήριον αἴτιον and the παθητόν (passive object). There has been much discussion about the origin of these terms and the basic philosophical orientation of the doctrine. The possibilities are the following:
(a) Although Stoicism has a well-known doctrine of two principles (cf. L&S §44, taken over by Antiochus of Ascalon, Cic. *Acad.* 1.24), it is hardly relevant to what Philo intends here, because its theology is both materialist and immanentist, a view that Philo is clearly trying to surmount. Von Arnim was not justified in including this text at *SVF* 2.302.
(b) "If anyone emphasized the distinction between an active and a passive principle it was Aristotle," writes Bos 1998, 71, pointing to texts such as *De an.* 3.5 430a10-12; *Mot. An.* 8, 702a11–16; *De gen.* 1.7, 323b29; cf. Wolfson 1947, 1.296 and Winston 1981, 303, who add *Phys.* 8.4, 255a12-15; *De gen.* 2.9, 335b29. None of these texts, however, is really cogent for explaining Philo's text, because they either refer to two aspects of the same substance or to the distinction between efficient and material cause for a particular thing.
(c) There are a few texts which interpret Plato's *Timaeus* in terms of a doctrine of two principles, notably Theophrastus *Phys. dox.* frg. 9; Diog. Laert. 3.69; Aëtius at Stobaeus *Ecl.* 1.29, 37.8 Wachsmuth; see discussions at Runia *PT* 143-144; Dörrie and Baltes *DPA* vol. 4, §119. The difficulty here is that none of these texts translate the principles in terms of the distinction between active and passive (though the report at Aëtius comes close).

It is a mistake, in my view, to consider this passage in isolation from the rest of the context. Both in this section and in §12 and §§16–25 Philo strongly emphasizes the transcendence of the active cause. When this is combined with his emphasis on creation and his allusions to the *Timaeus*, it must be concluded that the basic thought here is Platonist, but formulated with some reference to Stoic and Aristotelian terminology. For other Philonic texts which emphasize the active nature of the first cause in opposition to the passivity of matter and the toil material things, cf. *Spec.* 3.178–180; *Cher.* 87 (note the denial of divine ἀπραξία, the same term as in §7); *Det.* 161; *Fug.* 8–13 (note here the Anaxagorean *nous* and cf. below on §24). As the last text shows, Philo assumes as a matter of course that what is active is superior to what is passive, just as the male is superior to the female (cf. also *QE* 1.7!). On this passage and its relation to Greek philosophical theology see further Runia 2001a, 281–316.

a passive object on the other. Philo does not repeat the word αἴτιον with παθητόν, and I am convinced that this is deliberate. We should not follow Arnaldez PAPM 1.147 in supplying the term and translating "passive cause." The Greek syntax does not assume that αἴτιον necessarily goes with both expressions. In contrast to contemporary Greek philosophers, Philo does not wish to speak about *two* principles or causes. Only the former is the cause, the latter is merely passive. The formulation betrays the influence of the Judaic strain in Philo's thought. The lack of clarity would be completely resolved if we follow some of the mss. and read δραστήριον ὡς αἴτιον, "an activating (principle) as cause".

the absolutely pure and unadulterated intellect of the universe. Philo's language could be understood in a immanentist and materialist manner, but this is certainly not his intention. The *nous* could be "of the universe" as *part* of it or as *superior* to it (i.e. as its maker). Compare the difference between the captain and the coach of a football team. The former is part of the team, the latter is not (but should be superior in insight!). Cf. also *Migr.* 192–193, where Philo emphasizes that the *nous* of the universe stands outside material nature and compares the relationship between the cosmos and God with that of a son who comes to maturity under his father's care.

The two superlatives indicating purity emphasize that the mind is totally unmixed with anything else. Mixture involves plurality, whereas God is single and simple (cf. *Mut.* 184). The same words can also be used of the human mind which approaches God; cf. *Spec.* 1.46 and Harl PAPM 15.110. Strictly speaking the terms could also be used of a very pure and fine material. In fact Philo has difficulty ridding himself of material terms when speaking of God. It illustrates how difficult the process of emancipation from the materialism of Hellenistic philosophy was.

Philo seldom refers to God as *nous*, despite its popularity in Aristotelianism and Platonism; Leisegang's Index, PCW 7.563b, collects about a dozen passages, many with the expression ὁ νοῦς τῶν ὅλων. Its position here is very deliberate. The relation between mind and the ordered nature of created reality will be further explored in §§16–25; cf. Ch. 4. It cannot be denied that in this depiction of the relationship between God and cosmos Philo has made great concessions to Greek philosophical conceptuality. The Bible does not speak of God as intellect in the philosophical sense (a text such as Isa 40:13, "who has known the mind (νοῦς) of the Lord" is quite different).

superior to excellence ... Why is God superior to ἀρετή and ἐπιστήμη? Either because he is not involved in such activities (as argued by Aristotle, cf. *Nic. Eth.* 10.8, 1178b7–22, *Metaph.* Λ 7), or because he is the source of the goodness and knowledge on which they are based. The following words suggest the latter answer. That God should be superior to the ideas of the good and the beautiful (the Platonizing formulation with "itself" can mean nothing else) can only mean that God is also the origin of the ideas. Similar hyperbolic language is found at *Praem.* 40; *Contempl.* 3; *Legat.* 5. Philo is going to have to explain further how this super-transcendence is to be understood. This occurs at least partially in §§16–25; see esp. the comments on §19.

§9. *But the passive (object) ...* To be understood as matter (ὕλη), the underlying foundation of physical reality. Its passivity means that it is unable to undertake any kind of action of itself, but always has to rely on some other cause in order to receive form and structure. The ultimate source of such form and structure is God the creator. Philo in fact does not use the term ὕλη in a cosmological context until §171. At §21, as we shall see, he speaks of οὐσία.

without soul and unmoved. Two adjectives with an alpha-privative, indicating lack, are balanced by three participles (in a reverse order) which convey that the lack has been overcome:

without soul (ἄψυχον)   ensouled (ψυχωθέν)
                         shaped (σχηματισθέν)
without motion (ἀκίνητον)   set in motion (κινηθέν).

We might suspect that an adjective "without shape" (ἀσχημάτιστον) has fallen out here, but no editor has suggested its inclusion. On many occasions in his writings Philo gives similar lists of opposite terms indicating the difference before and after creative activity. Such lists go back to Plato's description of the moment of creation in *Tim.* 30a and find many parallels in Middle Platonist texts. See *PT* 140–148 and below on §§21–22 for further details. In contrast to §§21–22, matter is here presented as being without any kind of motion. This is because Philo wants to emphasize its total passivity.

changed. The past tense is deliberate. The cosmos is the result of a creational event, but its consequences continue right through to the present, as will become clear during the course of the treatise.

the most perfect piece of work. For the first time in the treatise Philo uses the "language of excellence" to describe the cosmos. This language involves the frequent use of superlatives. It is derived primarily from Plato's *Timaeus* (cf. esp. 29a, 92c). Because God is good (§21), the cosmos is as good as it can be. See *PT* 118 and detailed treatment in Runia 1992a. The adjective τέλειος, used here in its superlative form, means both "perfect" and "complete." Here the former meaning predominates, in §14 the latter.

(2b) *that it is ungenerated.* Philo now returns to the original assertion of the people he disagreed with in §7. If God makes and matter undergoes (the premiss established so far), how can it be said that the cosmos never came into existence? On the other hand, if the cosmos was always simply there, as Philo's opponents seems to assume, then there is no need to postulate a creator.

most useful ... of the contributions to piety, ... providence. The argument proceeds by now assuming the consequences of the *denial* of the doctrine of creation. This means that the conviction of God's providential concern with the cosmos must also be abandoned. The doctrine of providence has to be seen as the obverse of the doctrine of creation. The order and structure of the created cosmos needs to be maintained. Otherwise it will perish, as happens to so many things that come into existence in our experience. But the doctrine of providence extends beyond cosmology. God is concerned not only with the macrocosm, but also with the microcosm, humankind. The cosmos is constructed in such a way that humans can live well in it. But if they live badly, then punishment will ensue.

The doctrine of providence was one of the most characteristic doctrines of Stoicism. See for example the frontal attack of the Epicurean Velleius in Cicero *Nat.d.* 1.18–20 and the lengthy reply by Balbus in Book 2. But the Stoic system is cyclical: the cosmos came into existence and will pass away in a never-ending cycle. Very interesting in the context of Philo's argument is the polemic of the Platonist Atticus (2nd cent. C.E.), who writes in a fragment preserved by Eusebius:

> When Plato deals with the question of the genesis of the cosmos, he also thinks it necessary to thoroughly examine the great and very helpful doctrine of providence and concludes that for something that did not come into existence there is no need for a maker or protector to guarantee a fine existence, so, lest he deprived the cosmos of providence, he removed from it the characteristic of being ungenerated (*Praep. Ev.* 15.6.1, = frg. 4 Des Places).

The argument reminds us of Philo and there are even a few verbal similarities. Both authors are making use of the same tradition. Unlike Philo, however, Atticus continues with a fierce attack on Aristotle and those Platonists who follow him in affirming the uncreatedness of the cosmos. On Atticus and his Platonic "fundamentalism" see Dillon 1977, 252; Baltes 1976–1978, 1.51–53.

On numerous occasions in his works Philo emphasizes how important he finds the doctrine of providence. He even dedicated one of his philosophical treatises to this question, the *De providentia* in two books. See 1.6–8 for a further discussion of the question of the eternity of the cosmos. The passage is extremely difficult to interpret, because it is only preserved in an Armenian translation. See further the translation and commentary in Hadas-Lebel, PAPM 35.133–135; also *PT* 148–155. The coupling of creation and providence is already found in Philo's Jewish-Hellenistic predecessor Aristobulus, frg. 4 (= Eusebius. *Praep. Ev.* 13.12.4), frg. 5 (=13.12.12).

The doctrine of providence returns in the summary of chief doctrines at §171, where Philo looks back to the argument here. It "contributes to piety" because it lays the foundation for God's concern with the fate of humankind, which will become the chief theme of the treatise from §69 onwards (and in the entire Exposition of Law, cf. *Praem.* 1–3).

§10. **Reason demands**. The argument proceeds analogically *e minore ad maius*. Parents produce children, craftsmen create works of art. In both cases they look after what they have produced. It has been shown (§§8–9) that the cosmos is ontologically dependent on God the active cause. Therefore he too will look after what he has made (providence). But this means that the cosmos too must have come into being (for otherwise it would not be looked after). Compare the very similar formulation at *Praem.* 42, where it is regarded as a law of nature that a maker should exercise care over what has been made, and also the summary statement at §171.

a father ... and a craftsman. The two analogies illustrate perfectly the two metaphors, biological and technical, which are constantly used, from Plato onwards, in creationist explanations of the order and structure of the cosmos. The former includes the giving of life and the possibility of growth which the latter cannot achieve. Compare the interesting reflections of Plutarch, *Quaest. plat.* 2, 1000E, on the phrase "maker and father" at *Tim.* 28c4 (on which see above §7), which also involves both metaphors. The term craftsman here translates δημιουργός, the most striking of the metaphors used by Plato to describe the creating god in the *Timaeus* (first found at 28a6). It can also mean "builder." See further below on §18, and on the term itself also the comment on §36.

no affinity. We might paraphrase the term οἰκείωσις with "proprietary relationship," i.e. referring to what belongs to you, what is your own. A child belongs to a parent, and so the parent feels the need to look after it. On this term see further §§146, 161.

§11. *a worthless and unhelpful doctrine.* I.e. the doctrine of Philo's opponents set out in §7. For "unhelpful" contrast the "very helpful doctrine of providence" in the quote from Atticus cited above on §9.

a power-vacuum ... just like in a city. Philo returns to the comparison between the cosmos and a city or community, which was already implicit in §3 (and is explicit in the parallel passage at *Praem.* 41–42). I have not translated Philo's term ἀναρχία with "anarchy," because that rendering obscures the meaning of a lack of legitimate authority. But of course when that is missing, anarchy in the modern sense ensues. As a Jewish inhabitant of Alexandria, Philo knew at first hand what civil anarchy could mean. Witness the dreadful pogrom of 38 C.E. Implicit here is the apologetic theme of the monarchic rule of the God of Israel. God is the first cause and highest principle of the cosmos. All other causes are subordinate to him. Cf. similar statements in *Decal.* 155; *Conf.* 170. In the latter text Philo cites the famous Homeric lines (*Il.* 2.204–205), "It is not good that many lords should rule, let there be one lord, one king", also cited in a theological context by Aristotle in *Metaph.* Λ 10, 1076a4.

(3) §12. *But the great Moses.* Moses is again introduced in opposition to the false view set out in §7.

what did not come into existence. The doctrine of Moses is couched in terms that every educated reader would recognize as derived from Plato. The argument is a succinct summary of *Tim.* 27e–28b, the classic text for the Platonist doctrine of the two worlds of being and becoming. Becoming (γένεσις) is precisely the title given by Moses to the first book of the Law. The assumption on Philo's part must be that Plato is somehow indebted to Moses. After all, the central doctrine of God as Being (ὁ ὤν) is Mosaic doctrine, Exod 3:14. The implication of dependence is made explicit by Ps.-Justin, *Coh. Gr.* 20–22 (*Tim.* 27d–28a is cited in 22.2); see the comments of Riedweg 1994 ad loc.

for the entire sense-perceptible realm ... Philo gives a compact paraphrase of *Tim.* 27d6–28a4:

> What is that which always is and has no becoming, and that which is becoming, but never is? The former is grasped by intellection together with reason, and is always the same. The latter is opined by opinion together with unreasoning sense-perception, becoming and perishing and never staying in the same state.

Philo emphasizes the ontological terms and leaves out most of the epistemology (except the contrasting pair αἰσθητός/νοητός). Being (τὸ ὄν) in Plato refers here to the intelligible realm of the ideas. Philo replaces it with the expression τὸ ἀγένητον (that which is ungenerated). Does it too refer to the noetic realm of ideas? This is unlikely, because they are not introduced until §16 and belong to "day one" of creation. In the light of §8 it is more likely that the term refers to God (in spite of what I argued at *PT* 94 n. 4). For further details of Philo's adaptation and references to similar texts see *PT* 92–94.

what is invisible. The term ἀόρατος is not found in the part of the *Timaeus* that Philo is drawing on. I am less confident than I was at *PT* 93 n.1 that its use here is inspired by its occurrence in Gen 1:2, which Philo — as we shall see at §29 — interprets as referring to the intelligible world. Here it is more likely, in the light of §§7–8, that God is being referred to. There are plenty of texts where God as highest cause and king is described as ἀόρατος: cf. *Abr.* 74; *Decal.* 59–60; *Spec.* 1.46 (τοῦ ἀοράτου καὶ νοητοῦ, exactly parallel to the phrase here).

eternity. The term is ἀιδιότης, equivalent to the adjective used falsely of the cosmos in §7. On the term see further our note on §7. Whitaker's translation at PLCL 1.11, "the infinite and undefinable," is *very* wide of the mark.

the appropriate name becoming. This *must* refer to the title of the first book of the Pentateuch. Unlike the Hebrew Bible, which refers to the books of the Torah by their initial words, the LXX translation gives thematic titles to the five books which are still in use in the Christian Old Testament. There are two other texts in which Philo refers to this title: *Abr.* 1 (immediately following *Opif.*), the first of the five books of the Law is called Genesis "from the genesis of the cosmos, which it contains at its beginning;" *Aet.* 19, where Gen 1:1–2 is quoted from the LXX and an allusion is made to Gen 8:22 in order to prove that Moses espoused the doctrine that the cosmos had come into existence and will remain indestructible (part of the doxography discussed above on §7). On these titles see further Cohen 1997, 55–57 (but she does not mention our text).

Philo exploits the fact that the term *genesis* can mean both "coming into existence" and "(the process of) becoming." For Platonic philosophy the latter is more important, and Philo often uses it in this sense, especially in his allegories. But here in the context of the creation account the first meaning is also highly relevant. Philo will explain how he understands the coming into existence of the cosmos in Ch. 5.

this cosmos is both visible and sense-perceptible. The second part of the argument again follows Plato. At *Tim.* 28b2-c2 he applies the earlier division cited above to the particular case of the cosmos:

> Now as to the entire cosmos ... we must first enquire ... whether it always existed and had no beginning of genesis, or whether it came into existence, taking its beginning from some origin (or principle). Well, it came into being. For it is visible and tangible and has a body, and all such things are sense-perceptible ...

This text is the chief witness in the huge controversy on whether Plato meant his cosmogony literally or not. Literalists appealed to the pronouncement γέγονεν (it came into being). Opponents said that philology was not enough; one had also to look at what Plato intended. The entire controversy has been thoroughly examined by Baltes 1976–1978; Dörrie and Baltes *DPA* vol. 5, §§136–145. Philo betrays acquaintance with the controversy at *Aet.* 14, where he argues against the non-literalist interpretation. But here it is not yet clear what the "generated" nature of the cosmos entails and in which way it is opposed to what the opponents think in §7. This will be explained in Ch. 5.

speaking about God in a truly reverent manner. Philo rounds off his preliminary remark with an elegant piece of ring-composition. The Mosaic creation account, which describes how the cosmos came into being and recognizes God's creatorship, stands in marked contrast to the false views which were outlined at the beginning of the chapter. Many translators do not recognize that θεολογέω simply means "speak about God;" cf. LSJ s.v. and Lampe *PGL sub* I. This is the only extant text in which Philo uses the verb. The noun θεολόγος is used of Moses in *Mos.* 2.115; *Praem.* 53; *QG* 2.59; 3.21.

EXCURSUS
Recent interpretations of Philo's argument

In my study on Philo and Plato's *Timaeus* (*PT* 100) I followed the view of Wolfson 1947, 1.295; Arnaldez PAPM 1.146; Dillon 1977, 157 (cf. also Radice *FM* 235), that Philo had primarily the philosophy of Aristotle in mind when describing his opponents in §7, to whom might also be added Xenocrates and the Platonists who did not wish to read the *Timaeus* literally. One of the chief reasons for this interpretation was the link that was laid with the doxography in *Aet.*, in which Aristotle's view is rejected. Moreover the reference to idleness in §7 and the denial of providence in §9 also seemed to point to Aristotle. I still believe it is possible to read Philo's argument in this way. This would mean that in §9 he assumes that certain philosophers accept the distinction between *nous* and matter, but nevertheless hold that the cosmos did not come into existence. This applies both to Aristotle and to the Platonists, the former with his theory of the first principle as final cause, the latter with their theory of *creatio aeterna*. It has to be admitted that this interpretation involves an extra premiss which is not present in the text, namely that Philo's opponents do accept the distinction between transcendent *nous* and the material realm introduced in §8.

In a recent article Bos 1998 has argued that Philo does not direct his argument against Aristotle at all, but is in fact strongly indebted to him. He points out that Philo's description of his opponents' views in §7 and §§9–11 is closer to his descriptions of the Chaldeans than to an outline of Aristotle's philosophy. Bos' interpretation fits the argument in §9 better because no extra unstated premiss is required: a mentality like that of the Chaldeans rejects the existence of a creative, transcendent *nous*. I am persuaded that this interpretation is to be preferred, and have incorporated it in my analysis and comments above.

On the other hand I do not agree with Bos that the positive doctrine that Philo attributes to Moses is strongly indebted to Aristotle. I persist in regarding its philosophical roots as Platonic. So I would direct the following critical comments towards his thesis.

(a) When Philo describes Aristotle in *Aet.* 10 as reacting "piously and religiously," this must be read dialectically, i.e. as describing his reaction against the atomist and Stoic views (in the case of the latter *avant la lettre*). It cannot be disputed that Philo supports the Platonic view, which is also the Mosaic position (cf. *Aet.* 19). On the difficulties of interpreting this treatise, see Runia 1981 and more briefly *PT* 394–396, on the relation to *Opif. PT* 96-101.

(b) The doctrine of the active cause and the passive object in §8 is not Aristotelian but closer to Platonism, as Philo makes quite clear in §12. See my comments on both passages above. Bos argues that it is not Platonic, which is no doubt correct, but that does not mean that it is not Platonist, or at least strongly influenced by Platonists.

(c) Aristotle's theology is still vulnerable to the charge that he leaves no room for divine providence, as put forward with great vehemence by the later Platonist Atticus. It should be noted that Aristotle's views on divine providence are somewhat controversial. The view in the *Metaphysics* that the unmoved mover is the ultimate *archê* of the cosmos only as final and not as efficient cause excludes the possibility of divine providence altogether. In later reports of Aristotelian doctrine we read that he admitted providence, but only in the supra-lunary realm (see for example Aëtius at Ps.-Plutarch 2.4). Although Philo never explicitly condemns Aristotle, it is clear that both versions of his view clearly fall short of what is required. He would have been in full agreement with the position of Atticus quoted above at §9.

(d) It is possible that Philo knew the Ps.-Aristotelian treatise *De mundo* and thought that it was genuinely Aristotelian (cf. also Radice 1994). As Bos points out, there are many themes in this work which find parallels and perhaps even echoes in Philo's theology. But it must have surely struck Philo that this work is totally silent on the creation of the cosmos. On the question of providence he may have also found it rather unsatisfactory, because God's providence is not exercised directly, but rather via his power as exercised by the heavenly bodies (cf. the image of the Great king and his satraps at §6, 398a20) On the *De mundo* and Philo's doctrine of the Powers see also on §21.

Parallel exegesis

On references to the title of the book Genesis see above on §12.

Nachleben

At *Praep.Ev.* 8.13 Eusebius quotes this entire chapter *verbatim* in order to illustrate the wisdom of the Jews in matters of theology and their excellence in the use of argument (*logoi*). The chapter is given the heading "Of Philo on God and on the createdness of the cosmos." It is striking how many divergences there are from the text established by Cohn, including some bad mistakes. In eight cases (including the case mentioned above on §7) Eusebius agrees with ms. V, the archetype of which came from Caesarea (on this ms. see Introduction §9 and the comments above on the Title), against all other mss.

On similar views on the relation between Moses and Plato in Ps.-Justin *Coh. Gr.* see the note above on §12. There is also a remarkable verbal parallel between §10 and *Coh.* 23.2, to which I drew attention in 1991, 402. Riedweg 1994, 405, thinks it indicates common use of a Middle Platonist tradition.

At the beginning of *Ep.* 44 PL (= *Ep.* 31 Faller), written to a certain Orontianus on the subject of the creation of the world, Ambrose gives a quite lengthy paraphrase of §§8–9 and 11–12, without mentioning Philo explicitly; the text is cited at PCW 1.xc, full text at Faller 1968, 215–216. Less certainly the opening words of *Hex.* (1.1.2), where the eternity attributed to the cosmos is connected with divine honours paid to its parts, may reflect §7, perhaps via Basil *Hex.* 1.7 17B (on which see Runia *PEC* 238).

A particularly interesting passage is found at Basil *Hex.* 2.3 33B, where the Church father, against the background of the Christian doctrine of *creatio ex nihilo*, appears to criticize Philo's doctrine of active cause and passive object in §8: "Let them explain to us how the activating power of God and passive nature of matter happen to complement each other so snugly, the one offering a substrate without form, the other having knowledge of shapes without matter to apply it to, so that what each lacks is supplied by the other." Cf. Giet 1968 ad loc.; Pépin 1964, 362 n.2.

Further reading: Radice *FM* 234–237; Runia *PT* 100-101 (but see the Excursus above), 143-145; Winston *PA* 96, 175; Bos 1998; Runia 2001a.

Chapter Three
The scheme of six days (§§13-15a)

Analysis/General comments

One of the most striking aspects of the biblical creation account is its organization in terms of a sequence of seven days. No other ancient cosmogony possesses this particular feature (Westermann 1984, 89). Modern interpreters regard the scheme as an extrapolation from history (seven days in the week, humankind's relation to God) to cosmology (ibid. 90). For Philo the movement is the other way around. The creation account lays a foundation for how humankind should live.

Throughout the centuries exegetes have been concerned to explain how the seven days should be interpreted. Philo is no exception. This passage can be seen as another preliminary comment. After all, there is no mention of days until Gen 1:5. It also serves as a transition to the works of "day one," which is introduced in §15. At the same time it allows Philo to say something about the role of numbers in his interpretation of the Genesis account. Because of the scheme of the seven days arithmology is going to be very prominent in the treatise up to §127. See further the Introduction §5(d) and §6, where we emphasize the link that Philo sees between the scheme and the role of order and structure in his cosmology

The chapter can be analysed in terms of three short sections.

(1) Philo is convinced that the scheme of the six days (he is now only concerned with the six days on which parts of the cosmos are made) should not be read literally. It is philosophically quite improbable that God should need time in which to create. So another explanation for the striking scheme needs to be given. The solution is to tie the aspect of number to order, which in turn involves hierarchy and structure. This is not further explained in the present context. His meaning will become clearer in §§27-28, §§67-68. The application of this solution to the actual six days involves two steps.

(2a) Firstly, three relevant features of the six are outlined: (i) it is the most generative of numbers; (ii) it is the first perfect number; (iii) it is the first odd-even number, and thus possesses the characteristics of both male and female.

(2b) These three features prove highly apposite for the cosmos because (α) it is the most perfect of things that come into existence (cf. ii), and (β) the coupling of male and female will occupy an important place in it because this is necessary for the perpetuation of life (cf. i & iii).

(3) Philo next applies the scheme of six days to the actual creation of the cosmos. On each day some of the parts are made, with the exception of the first day, which Moses in fact calls "day one." The reason for this separate status will become clear when the contents of that day are explained in the following chapters (Ch. 4–6, see esp. §§15b, 35), but Philo already gives a hint that this has to do with the special features of the number one.

Philo was certainly not the first Jewish exegete to ponder on the scheme of the six days and interpret it in terms of order. His Alexandrian predecessor Aristobulus had already done so; see the text cited in the comments on §13. He may well, however, have coined the word ἑξαήμερος to describe the account of the six days, as suggested by Alexandre *CLG* 47 (cf. *Leg.* 2.12; *Decal.* 100, but not used in *Opif.*). It was to become the standard term for both the biblical account and the commentaries written on it (on this tradition see Alexandre *CLG* 215–216; Van Winden 1988, Robbins 1912). There can be no doubt that Philo was encouraged in developing his exegesis by the controversies surrounding the interpretation of Plato's *Timaeus* (see the comments on §12). If the cosmogony was not meant literally, then the author must have had a didactic purpose involving structure and order. See further Ch. 5 and *PT* 416–420.

Detailed comments

(1) §13. *in need of a length of time.* In the Allegorical commentary Philo often stresses that God is in no way in need of anything. The relationship between God and his creation is not reciprocal. See, e.g., *Cher.* 44: "God sows, but what is engendered ... is his gift; for God engenders nothing for himself, since he is need of nothing, but everything for the one who needs to receive it;" also *Leg.* 3.181; *Post.* 4 etc. Here, however, we have the additional aspect of God's relationship to time, that intrinsic aspect of physical reality and the process of becoming. If God could not do without time, it would place him on a level with what he creates. Philo explores the relationship between creation and time further in §§26–28.

everything at the same time. Creation is envisaged as an instantaneous process. It is Moses' *account* of what took place that separates and organizes its various aspects. Philo repeats this assertion at §28 and §67. See the comments ad loc. It should be noted that the argument against a literal reading of the six days is not strong. If God is almighty, as Philo assumes, he could just as easily create the cosmos in a period of six days as he could instantaneously. In fact Philo is subjecting God's act to the restrictions of reason. "Surely" translates εἰκός, i.e. what is likely or probable in terms of reason. From the viewpoint of reason a length of six days is arbitrary, unless a fitting reason can be found for it. Philo's primary interest, however, is in what motivates the writer and from a cosmological point of view the scheme is quite plausible.

not only in giving commands but also in his thinking. The "giving commands" here refers to the characteristic commands given by God during the creation account. Philo sometimes draws attention to these (e.g. below at §43), though they are not as prominent in his explanation as in the original text. The "thinking" refers to the planning activity further explored in §§16–25. Another formulation is found at *Sacr.* 65:

> The divine teacher anticipates time, which, even when he produced the universe, did not co-operate with Him, since time itself was only established together with the cosmos when it came into existence (cf. §26). God spoke and acted together, placing no interval between the two. Indeed, if one were to urge a truer doctrine, his speech (*logos*) was his deed (*ergon*).

In this text God's commands are related to his *logos* as speech (not thought as in §24). As philosophical background the Platonist doctrine of the coincidence of thought and action in the realm of *nous* may be assumed; cf. Baltes 1976–78, 1.91. Philo appears to allude to this doctrine in the difficult text *Prov.* 1.7 (cf. *PT* 150 and our note above on §9). The text here, however, is primarily interested in the particular features of the creation account.

Number is inherent in order. Philo's meaning is made clear if we adduce the further explanation in §28 (and the example he gives — heaven as first — in §27). Order involves sequence and hierarchy, which cannot do without number. If one thing is later or lower than another, then this is expressed by the ordinal numbers first, second, and so on. Here is the first indication that arithmology is going to play an important part in the Commentary.

A similar idea (without explicit reference to number) is found in Aristobulus frg. 5 (= Eusebius *Praep. Ev.* 13.13.12): "For the legislation signifies that *in six days* he *made heaven and earth and all things which are in them* in order that he might make manifest the times and foreordain what precedes what with respect to order (transl. Yarbro Collins)." Note that Aristobulus here quotes not Gen 1 but Exod 20:11.

by the laws of nature. Number is intrinsic to the way things are, i.e. "the nature of things." Numbers also have their own nature, which is reflected in the way they appear in reality. In our treatise Philo constantly speaks of the "nature of numbers" or what they are "by nature;" see the comment on §90. I would not wish to read a reference to the background of Pythagoreanizing Academic metaphysics in this particular phrase, as done by Radice (*FM* 238), although Philo is acquainted with this tradition.

the most generative of numbers is the six. Without further ado Philo begins to introduce the relevant aspects of the number six. In Pythagorean number speculation the six is above all associated with the coupling of male and female for reasons that Philo will make quite clear. Elsewhere he refers to the Pythagorean names for the six, "marriage" and "harmony" (*QG* 3.38). On arithmological traditions associated with the number six see esp. Theon of Smyrna *Expos.* 102, Anatolius 34–35, Ps.-Iamblichus *Theol. Arith.* 42–54, and other sources listed at Staehle 1931, 32. At 32–34 Staehle gives an analysis of Philonic passages dealing with the six, to which can be added *QG* 2.45 and 3.49. Philo also calls six γεννητικώτατος at *QG* 3.38 (Greek text at Petit PAPM 33.141). The only other text to use this epithet is John Lydus *Mens.* 2.11, 32.4; see further *Nachleben.* Elsewhere Philo calls six γονιμώτατος (most fertile), *Decal.* 159; *Spec.* 2.177; the same epithet at Anatolius 40.9, Ps.-Iamblichus 86.24. Both epithets are based on the male-female aspect of the number explained in the next section.

A modern book on number symbolism, Schimmel 1993, 122, describes the six as "the perfect number of the created world." The tradition initiated by Philo, directly related to the Judaeo-Christian creation account, has thus supplanted the earlier Pythagorean tradition. Note, however, that Ps.-Iamblichus' account of the six perceives many links with the Platonic cosmogony in the *Timaeus,* e.g. *Theol. Arith.* 50.8–10: "Because the perfection of the cosmos falls under the six, the excellence of the demiurgic god is rightly thought to be hexadic." Greek and Judaeo-Christian approaches thus run parallel. If the tradition recorded by Ps.-Iamblichus goes back to Philo's time or earlier, it may have inspired him in his interpretation of the Mosaic six days.

(2a) *the first perfect number.* The most striking arithmological feature of the six, is given pride of place by all sources: 6 = 1 + 2 + 3 and 1 x 2 x 3. On "product of its parts" see below on §14.

both male and female. The association of male with odd and female with even is implicit in the Pythagorean table of *systoichiai* (coupled opposites) given by Aristotle at *Metaph.* A 5, 986a25. According to Plutarch *Mor.* 288D one of the reasons is anatomical. If you regard numbers as stripes and these are removed from left and right at the same time, in the case of odd numbers a stripe will always be left, whereas in the case of even numbers only an empty space remains, i.e. | | | | | ⇒ |, | | | | | | ⇒ | |. On the basis of such considerations Philo concludes at *QE* 1.7: "Therefore it is said by men of science that the female is nothing else than an incomplete male." This arithmological/metaphysical aspect of male/female relations is ignored by the monographs of Baer 1970 and Sly 1990.

harmonic union. A clear reference to the Pythagorean name "harmony" mentioned above.

(2b) §14. *So it was right* ... With Arnaldez PAPM and Van Winden I take γάρ here as explanatory, i.e. explaining why the six with the features outlined was most suitable to be used in the account of the cosmos' creation.

as the most perfect. As noted above on §9, τέλειος means both "perfect" and "complete." Here the latter meaning predominates, but the translation "perfect" has to be maintained on account of the link with the "perfect" number six. The analogy is obvious. Just like the six, the cosmos consists of the totality of its parts and thus is most perfect. Interestingly the verb used in §13 for consisting of the sum of its parts, συμπληρόω, is the same term used by both Plato and Philo for the plenitude of the cosmos; cf. *Tim.* 92c6, *Prov.* 2.110 and *PT* 230. In both cases what fills the cosmos is its living beings, which supplies a link to the following application.

mixed number. Mixed or even–odd (ἀρτιοπέριττος) numbers are those which can be separated into two factors, of which one is even and the other odd: e.g. 6, 10, 14, 18 etc. In a celebrated passage *Resp.* 546b Plato associates procreation in his ideal state with a perfect number, which is agreed to be $1,296,000 = (6 \times 10)^4$. Six is not explicitly mentioned, but it is understood to be the area of the right-angled triangle 3–4–5. Cf. also Plutarch *Procr. an.* 1018C. A parallel passage is found at *Spec.* 2.58 on the Sabbath:

> But Moses, starting from a more august subject, called it (the seventh day) perfection (συντέλεια) and all-completion (παντέλεια), assigning to the six the generation (γένεσις) of the parts of the cosmos, but to the seven their completion. For the six is the even–odd number, formed from twice three, having the odd as male component, the even as female, and these are the sources of generation (γενέσεις) by the unchanging ordinances of nature ...

On this text, which doubtless has Gen. 2:1 in mind as well as the schema of six days, see further Ch. 15 Parallel exegesis.

sows the seed. Philo describes the process of generation at length in §67. It is necessary for the continuation of the species. But when the first man and woman engage in sex (§§151-152), problems ensue!

(3) §15. *To each of the days* ... As Philo will explain in his commentary on the successive days in §§36–88. The text should not be taken to mean that to each of the days some of the features of the parts created on other days are assigned, as done by Carmichael (1996, 62, 94, 97, 115). Such "interrelatedness" (97) is nowhere emphasized by Philo.

first ... one ... appellation of the unit. The LXX in Gen 1:5 reads ἡμέρα μία, "day one." This is a literal translation of the Hebrew original, which uses the cardinal and not the ordinal number which is used for the remaining six days. In Greek the expression is striking, and Philo takes it as an indication that he must look for a deeper meaning. As it happens, it also fits in perfectly with an important doctrine of Greek arithmology.

Philo thus now turns to a consideration of the arithmological features of the unit or monad. It should not be reckoned on a par with other numbers. It is the starting-point or principle (ἀρχή) of numbers and so is separate from them (for this reason three is the first odd number, as we just saw in §13). Philo's brief remarks here should be combined with his statement at the end of his treatment of "day one" at §35 where he notes the solitary nature of the unit (μόνωσις) and associates it with the intelligible cosmos introduced in §16. For this reason the monad is often associated with God, (cf. *Leg.* 2.3; *Spec.* 3.180 etc). The association with God and the intelligible world is also found in arithmological sources. Note esp. Theon of Smyrna *Expos.* 99.24–100.8:

> The monad is starting-point (ἀρχή) of all things and the most dominant of all ... (lacuna) And from it all things arise, yet it does not arise from anything: it is indivisible and all things potentially, unchangeable, never standing outside its own nature through multiplication. It is the mode of existence for all that is intelligible and ungenerated, and also for the realm of the ideas and God and mind and beauty and goodness and each of the intelligible substances, such as beauty itself, justice itself, equality itself; for each of these is thought as a unity and by itself.

On the one in Greek arithmological sources see further Theon 18–19; Anatolius 29–30; Ps.-Iamblichus *Theol. arith.* 1–7. For further Greek sources and Philonic texts see Staehle 1931, 19–22 (to which §35 should be added). A modern writer on number symbolism, Schimmel 1992, 42, says of the One that it "became the symbol of the primordial One, the divine without a second, the non-polarized existence. It comprises relation, entirety, and unity and rests in itself but stands behind all created existence." The first etymology of the monad given by Theon in the passage quoted above is not explicitly mentioned by Philo, but it should be noted that it is perfectly congruent with the exegesis of "day one" as embracing the noetic cosmos which he is about to give in the following chapter. For the relation between the monad and the intelligible cosmos in Greek arithmology see below on §35.

gives it the accurate name. I cannot believe that Philo wrote μίαν δ' ὀνομάσας ὀνόματι εὐθυβόλῳ προσαγορεύει, as conjectured by Cohn on the basis of ms. V. The expression is simply too awkward and no parallels can be given. The more straightforward reading of the majority of the mss., μίαν δ' ὀνομάσας εὐθυβόλως προσαγορεύει, is to be preferred.

Philo has already mentioned that Genesis is a very appropriate name for the account of creation (see §12). Now he says the same for the expression "day one," and many more instances will follow throughout the work. See also Ch. 7 on §§36–37. The theme of naming is of course strongly present in the Genesis creation account. On five occasions God names parts of the cosmos (vv. 5, 8, 10), and Adam later receives the task of naming the animals (2:19). But here of course the subject has to be Moses.

Parallel exegesis

There are many passages in which Philo connects the number six with the days of creation. These are especially found in the *Quaestiones*, which contain much more number symbolism than Philo's other works. See *QG* 1.91; 2.17; 3.38, 49; 4.164; *QE* 2.46.

In the Allegorical Commentary, at *Leg.* 1.2–6, Philo gives exegesis of Gen 2:2, which speaks of God completing his works on the *sixth* day (the text of the LXX, see further on §89). He gives a list of features of the six which is fuller than what is given in *Opif.* He is also constrained by the context to indicate the relation between the six days and the seventh. The solution is that God makes mortal things on the sixth day and divine and blessed things on the seventh. Somewhat similar is *Spec.* 2.58, where the six is associated with the genesis of the parts of the cosmos and the seven with their completion.

Similar arguments against a literal reading of the account of six days are found at *Leg.* 1.2, 20; *QG* 1.1. But the passage on "day one" and its special status is unique in Philo's writings.

Nachleben

Philo's brief reflections on the six and the one gave rise to a vast number of patristic explanations. Especially his followers in the Alexandrian tradition appear to draw on him directly. We note Clement of Alexandria *Strom.* 5.93.4–5 (six as γόνιμος ἀριθμός, creation "in the monad"; see also Ch. 4); 6.142.2 (creation together with thought). In a fragment giving exegesis on Gen. 2:1 Origen states (*Sel. Gen.* 27, PG 12.97C) "Some ... think that it is for the sake of order that the account of the days and what is created in them has been made," which is clearly an anonymous reference to Philo; cf. Runia *PEC* 161, Van den Hoek 2000a, 61 (who thinks that Origen disagrees with this view, but there is no evidence for this in the passage itself). Further texts in Origen are cited in Alexandre *CLG* 99. Didymus the blind also draws on Philo directly at *Comm. Gen.* 34.25–27: "So God, since he was making a perfect piece of work, ought to bring it into existence in the first perfect number ...," preceded by a long disquisition on perfect numbers (note the same construction ἔδει plus infinitive that we find in §14); also 35.6, "since all things came into existence together, this number (six) was taken for the sake of order and harmony ..." Basil (?), *Hom. gen. h.* 2.8 (*SC* 160.247) cites specialists in arithmology who state that there is a connection between the six and the creation of the cosmos, but a few lines later the author finds this kind of exegesis too speculative for the needs of the Church (see on this text also Ch. 15 *Nachleben*). Theodoret of Mopsuestia too is critical of Philo's use of arithmology to explain the creation account, which he thinks exerted a bad influence on Origen; see the preface to his Commentary on Ps 118, cited at Runia *PEC* 267. Ambrose paraphrases §13 at *Ep.* 44.2 (text at PCW 1.lxxxx). Augustine connects the completion of the work of the creation on the sixth day (cf. §89) with the six as perfect number at *Gen. litt.* 4.2.6, but this need not have been drawn directly from Philo.

Josephus, *Ant.* 1.29, observes that Moses speaks not of the "first day" but "day one," and promises an explanation in a separate work on causes, but this promise was apparently not fulfilled. Origen, *Hom. Gen* 1.1 (*SC* 7^b.27), makes the same observation and gives as the reason that time did not exist before the world, but commenced to exist from the days that follow. The second and third and fourth and all the other days begin to designate time. If we take this to mean that time is excluded from day one, then there is some resemblance to Philo, though for Origen the works of the first day are not incorporeal. See further *Nachleben* in Ch. 5. Exactly the same tradition is found at Gen. Rab. 3.9 (Rabbi Samuel b. Ammi); other rabbinic texts at Feldman 2000, 11. Origen and the rabbis may go back to a tradition shared with Philo. Unfortunately the papyrus text of Didymus' commentary is too damaged at this point.

The Byzantine author John Lydus notes at *Mens.* 2.4, 21.3–5 that the first day of the week is called "one" because it is "alone and not in communion with the others." This may draw on Philo, as suggested by Staehle 1931, 20 (cf. also §35). At *Mens.* 2.11, 32.4–14 he may have §13 on the six in mind, but *QG* 3.38 is a more likely source. It is controversial whether Lydus made use of *Opif.* directly. See our discussion in Excursus 2 in Ch. 15.

Further reading: Radice *FM* 237–239; Runia *PT* 101; Winston *PA* 106; Alexandre *CLG* 47, 97–100 (on *Nachleben*).

Chapter Four
Day one: creation of the intelligible cosmos (§§15b–25)

Analysis/General comments

Philo now continues with an explanation of what is created on "day one." Before citing Gen 1:1 (in §26) he first treats the day as a whole (i.e. the entire description Gen 1:1–5). Its chief component is the intelligible cosmos (κόσμος νοητός), which serves as the model for the rest of the creation process. This interpretation is rather surprising, to say the least. Who would have thought, when reading "In the beginning God made the heaven and the earth," that this refers to the creation of the *ideas* of heaven and earth? Apart from the arithmological reasons already given in §15a (see above Ch. 3), Philo does not give internal exegetical reasons for this interpretation (the "proof" in §25 refers to a later text, Gen 1:27). They can, however, be easily furnished: various parts of the cosmos, but notably heaven and earth are mentioned twice (e.g. heaven again in 1:8, earth again in 1:10); moreover the earth in 1:2 is called "invisible" (ἀόρατος), a common epithet of the ideal realm (see the comment below on §29).

The explanation of the intelligible cosmos as a whole is given in considerable detail, with elaborate reference to theological and philosophical aspects of the interpretation. In §§16–20 Philo concentrates on the intelligible cosmos, and then turns to the theme of divine beneficence as an answer to the reason why God created the cosmos at all. In contrast to Radice's commentary, I have preferred to treat the passage §§15b–25 as a whole, because at §§24–25 Philo returns to the theme of the intelligible cosmos and attempts to situate it theologically (and also gives a proof that it is not his doctrine, but is based on the thought of Moses, as he had promised in §5). The passage as a whole, therefore, can be analysed into four parts.

(1) The most striking content of "day one" is the intelligible cosmos, and it needs to be explained first. It is the model for the sense-perceptible cosmos, which God had to mark out first, so that the latter would be without fault. There is a correspondence in their contents. The model and the copy both contain the same kinds (*genera*). In the former case these are intelligible, i.e. objects of thought, in the latter case they are the objects of sense-perception. Noteworthy here is the first mention of the metaphor of the seal and impression (but recall §6), which Philo uses to explain the relation between the non-physical reality of the ideas and the physical reality of the world as we experience it (§§15b–16).

DAY ONE: CREATION OF THE INTELLIGIBLE COSMOS

(2a) But Philo's proposed exegesis gives rise to a question: where is this intelligible cosmos located? In order to give an answer Philo uses an extended image drawn from the world of our own experience. I interpret this image as not only giving an answer to the question posed (given in §20), but also formulated in such a way that it sheds further light on the way we should envisage the relationship between God and the whole of created reality, both intelligible and sense-perceptible (§17a).

(2b) The comparison is with the founding of a city, an event which frequently took place in the Hellenistic world, most famously in the case of Philo's own city Alexandria. There are two protagonists involved. Firstly, there is a king who has supreme power and celebrates his success by having a city built. Secondly, there is an architect who comes along, examines a suitable site and makes a complete plan of the city that is to be built. The location of the plan is nowhere else than in his mind. So when he sets about actually building his city, he first gets the plan completely fresh and clear in his mind, and then uses it to construct all the various parts of the city. We note that there are three functions involved in the entire process, corresponding to three stages of execution. The king takes the initiative and supplies the opportunity. The architect designs the plan and then executes. In this final stage of building he is actually no longer architect but builder, as Philo's text emphasizes (§§17b–18).

(2c) The extended image is now given its application to the act of creation. When God decides to found the cosmos, he first forms the intelligible cosmos as plan and then executes it, using the plan as model. Where, then, is the plan located? Where else than in the divine Logos. That is the only place where God's powers in their fullness can be located. The location is thus not spatial but transcends space (and time). What is striking in the application is the fact that the king and the architect appear to be no longer separated. I interpret the discrepancy as a deliberate attempt on Philo's part to preserve God's absolute transcendence. He cannot accept any hierarchy of creative deities such as is found in Middle Platonism. Therefore he distinguishes between God (as Being) and his Logos (and powers). The final sentence, which introduces the divine powers, serves as a transition to the second half of the chapter, in which the implications of the theology outlined so far are worked out for the relation between God and the cosmos (§§19–20).

(3a) The activity of God's creative power results from God's essential goodness, as already affirmed by "one of the ancients," i.e. Plato. The antithesis between the active cause and the passive object

(§8) is now bridged. The divine creative and beneficent activity enables the unformed material to participate in divine excellence and be converted from disorder and disharmony into an ordered and harmonious whole, in conformity with the model. Creation is thus a matter of pure grace (§§21–22).

(3b) But are there not constraints on the way that the gap between God and physical reality can be bridged? Indeed divine beneficence cannot be applied without mediation, for otherwise physical reality would collapse under the weight of goodness. It must be measured out in proportion to the capacity of the recipient. This measuring too, we may infer, is the task of the divine Logos. What Philo does not disclose is the exact process whereby the formation of the cosmos takes place. We must surmise that this too is the task of the powers, which penetrate and give form to matter. One might compare the famous account of the *Logos tomeus* in *Her.* 133–236, in which it is the divine Logos who pervades the material realm and orders it through rational division (§23).

(4a) Finally Philo returns to his earlier explanation of the intelligible cosmos in relation to the divine Logos (§20). There is in fact no need to speak of a location for the ideas at all. The intelligible world and the Logos — as object and subject of thought respectively — may be identified because they are both intrinsically tied to God's creative activity (§24).

(4b) It should not be thought, however, that this interpretation rests on philosophical speculation that has no basis in the biblical text. At Gen 1:26–27 Moses himself uses the relation of model and imitation when describing the creation of humankind. But Philo goes a step further. As Van Winden has shown, in this passage Philo attempts to furnish a kind of proof that the intelligible cosmos is to be identified with the Logos. This interpretation, though not without its difficulties, has the virtue of adhering more closely to the text as found in the manuscripts and rendering Cohn's emendations unnecessary (§25).

As in the case of §§7–12, this chapter is extremely rich in philosophical themes. The basic concept used to explain "day one," the noetic cosmos, is actually found here for the first time in Greek philosophy, but certainly is taken over from earlier philosophical writings. The predominant kind of thought exploited by Philo is clearly Platonist, and derived primarily from exegesis of the *Timaeus*. This is seen not only in the distinction made between the intelligible world as model and visible world as copy, but also in the veiled reference to Plato in §21 and the paraphrase of *Tim.* 29e–30a in

§§21-22. But Philo's formulations are not just directly drawn from Plato's great dialogue. Various terminological and conceptual clues show that he is drawing on interpretative traditions which have benefited from developments in Hellenistic philosophy. See further Introduction §7(b). This entire background was extensively studied in Runia *PT*, to which we shall make frequent references in our detailed comments

At the same time, however, the passage reveals how solidly Philo's thought is rooted in Hellenistic Judaism, especially in the area of theology. We note especially the themes of God as creator, divine transcendence, the divine Logos, and the divine powers. These themes can be paralleled elsewhere, but Philo works them out with greater philosophical sophistication. In fact, it is quite difficult to disentangle the Greek philosophical and Hellenistic-Jewish roots of his thought. It is as if they have been fused together. It is also worth noting that, although the interpretation of "day one" in terms of the noetic cosmos is unique to Philo, the considerations that led him to this interpretation are also found in other Jewish authors. As Kugel (*TB*, 72) has noted: "The book of Jubilees and some later texts seek to resolve the apparent contradiction between the creation of light on the first day and the creation of the sun and moon on the fourth day by suggesting the first day's creation of light was more theoretical than actual." Indeed, when *Jubilees* 2:2 writes: "And [he created] the abysses and darkness — both evening and night — and light — both dawn and daylight — which he prepared in the knowledge of his heart," this comes strikingly close to what Philo intends with his "intelligible cosmos," though it is not explained in philosophical terms.

Detailed comments

(1) §15b. *the things that are contained in it.* In §§16-25 Philo sets out the chief feature of "day one," the intelligible cosmos. In §§29-35 he discusses individual contents of that cosmos as indicated by the text of Gen 1:1-5 (see below Ch. 6).

It contains as pre-eminent item ... This sentence is difficult to translate because it contains two ambiguous phrases, resulting in a large amount of variation among the various translations. The first ambiguity is the adjective ἐξαίρετος, used to describe the intelligible cosmos. It may mean something extraordinary or exceptional (e.g. Cohn, Van Winden) or perhaps pre-eminent (Whitaker, Kraus Reggiani), i.e. the outstanding feature of the day. It is also possible to relate the term to the separate or special status of the monad, as emphasized in §15a (the verb ὑπεξαιρέω used there is directly related to the adjective here). This interpretation is followed by Arnaldez, who translates it by "séparé." A clue to Philo's meaning may be provided by a text at Proclus *El. theol.* 134, where we read that 'it is ἐξαίρετον of the intelligence to know the real existents and to have perfection in its knowledge'. This parallel suggests that Philo means that the intelligible cosmos is that which makes "day one" distinctive and to be distinguished from what is created on other days. In the concluding passage on "day one" at §35 the intelligible cosmos is described as unique. A somewhat parallel usage is found in §99, where the hebdomad is said to possess a special feature because it is neither factor nor product. See further the commentary ad loc. In a little-known study published in Hebrew in 1925, Schwabe suggested that the word ἐξαίρετος might be a corruption of καὶ ἀόρατον (and unseen), based on the text at Gen 1:2. The suggestion is intriguing but too audacious. See further Schwabe 1999, an English translation of the article with valuable comments by A. Kamesar.

the intelligible cosmos. Philo introduces this term to comprise the contents of the day as a totality, in contrast to the individual contents outlined in §§29–35. It is in fact the first time that the term νοητὸς κόσμος occurs in extant Greek literature. A similar phrase ὁ ἰδανικὸς κόσμος (the ideal cosmos) occurs in Timaeus Locrus §30 (often dated to about 25 B.C.E.). The same phrase is found in the doxographer Aëtius (50–100 C.E.) at Ps.-Plutarch *Plac.* 1.7 and 2.6, when reporting the views of Plato. Though it is not found in Plato himself, various Platonic passages will have stimulated its formulation, e.g. the reference to the "noetic place" at *Resp.* 508c1, to the "things outside the cosmos" and the "place beyond the cosmos" in the *Phaedrus* myth at 247c1–2, and the "intelligible living being" in *Tim.* 30c–31c (on which see below). On the term see further Runia 1999b. Clearly Philo will have to explain what he means by the concept. This happens in §§16–20.

as the account concerning it reveals. The second ambiguous phrase of the sentence, ὡς ὁ περὶ αὐτῆς λόγος μηνύει, gives rise to two difficulties. (a) The word *logos* which it contains is notoriously polyvalent. (b) The word "it," because of the feminine gender in the Greek, must refer to a feminine noun. Most likely it refers to "day one" (note the last word of the previous sentence is the pronoun αὐτῇ which certainly refers to this noun), but it could also refer to the "monad." The phrase has been interpreted in three different ways:

(a) "as is shown in the treatise dealing with the "One"" (Whitaker LCL). This must then be taken as a reference to the treatise of numbers also mentioned by Philo at §52. In both cases, however, *logos* more naturally means simply "account" (contrast *Mos.* 2.115, where Philo uses the term πραγματεία, "treatise"). This interpretation is accepted by Terian (1991, 42), which is somewhat surprising in the light of his earlier statements on p. 32 that "very rarely does Philo use λόγος or λόγοι in the sense of σύνταξις, the usual word for treatise ..." and "a more common meaning of λόγος or λόγοι in contexts such as the above [i.e. *QG* 2.4, on which see below] is "subject," "discourse," "discussion," "an account," or "a passage," that is, as part of a treatise."

(b) "as the biblical account says concerning it" (Cohn, probably followed by Arnaldez and Kraus Reggiani), i.e. the hints in the biblical text that point to a separate status for "day one."

(c) "as the account concerning it (which I shall give) reveals" (Yonge, already suggested by Müller 1841, 148, cf. also Van Winden). Both translators still read the future μηνύσει with Mangey (good parallel at *Fug.* 7), but the majority of mss. read the present μηνύει, which is printed by Cohn.

At *PT* 171-172 I still opted for the second alternative, but I have now changed my mind and think the third alternative more likely. As Paramelle argues in relation to a similar phrase at *QG* 2.4 (see 1984, 147 n. 23), the present tense often has a future connotation in such phrases. Moreover we should note that the following sentence begins with γάρ. This is best taken as explanatory after an announcement in the previous sentence, i.e. supporting alternative (c).

§16. **For God, because he is God.** Much can be read into the brief words ὁ θεὸς ἅτε θεός. Firstly, they pick up God the creator as subject of the first sentence of the creation account. Secondly, they suggest that God is acting *qualitate qua*, i.e. in his capacity as God. In Philonic theology *theos* is the divine name referring to God's creative activity (this is the reason, according to Philo, that it is used throughout the creation account, as is observed at *Plant.* 86, *QG* 2.16). Thirdly, they may also suggest that God, being the supreme creator, knows exactly what he is doing, and for this reason makes the model first.

understood in advance. The participle προλαβών, and the verb προεξ-ετύπου (first marked out) a few lines later, both start with the prefix *pro-*, indicating precedence. Here is a case (cf. §§13, 27) where what seems to be temporal precedence actually indicates ontological precedence. See also our comment on §129. The intelligible cosmos is superior. The same is indicated by the contrast "older" and "younger" a few lines later. On this contrast see *PT* 201, and cf. also Ch. 9 on §45.

a beautiful copy ... a beautiful model. The relationship between the two worlds, ideal and sense-perceptible, is explained primarily in terms of the relationship between model and copy (or imitation, μίμημα). At this point Philo — no doubt deliberately — gives away the philosophical inspiration of his interpretation, namely the Platonic theory of the two worlds in conjunction with the mythical account of the *genesis* of the cosmos in the *Timaeus*. The divine demiurge first looks to an intelligible model before making the various components of the cosmos. The two terms used here occur in a summary given at *Tim.* 48e4-49a1: "The earlier two kinds sufficed for the previous account: one kind was proposed as a model, intelligible and always staying the same; the second as an imitation of the model, something that possesses *genesis* and is visible." Philo in fact takes over here Plato's dialectical argument at 28a5-b2 that there is a correspondence between model and product: if the demiurge looks to an immutable model, the result will be beautiful (καλόν), if to a changing model, the result will not be beautiful (there has been much discussion about what this inferior model could be; perhaps Plato is thinking of the primal disorderly situation described in 30a).

The intelligible cosmos, therefore, is based on Plato's conception of a model for the creative process. It is an integral part of the demiurgic metaphor (on which see Ch. 2 on §10): a craftsman such as a sculptor looks towards a model when he sculpts his statue. There are, however, two highly significant developments which distinguish Philo's account from the Platonic source of inspiration.

(a) As noted above on §15b, Philo is the first extant source to speak of a κόσμος νοητός. Plato's model is described as a νοητὸν ζῷον, intelligible living being (the term is found at 39e1, cf. also 30c–31b). It is generally agreed (cf. esp. 39e) that this model does not represent the ideal world in its totality, but rather the ideas of the genera and species of living beings that make up the cosmos (note, however, that this covers a great deal, since the heavenly beings and the earth and even the cosmos in its totality are all living beings). On the contents of the two respective models see the comment further below. Philo's description in this section clearly works with a set of opposed terms:

intelligible cosmos	sense-perceptible cosmos
incorporeal	corporeal
model	copy/imitation
older	younger
containing intelligible kinds	containing sense-perceptible kinds.

Two characteristics cut across the list, namely that both worlds form a totality (as cosmos) and both are "beautiful" (καλόν). From the transcendent and creational perspective used here the noetic cosmos serves as model, a kind of plan or blueprint for creation. From a perspective within the cosmos itself it is perceived as a higher duplicate of the experienced world which can only be attained through the activity of the mind. At *Somn.* 1.188 Philo calls the visible cosmos a gate into the intelligible cosmos. This "down-up perspective" is found in our treatise in the ascent of the soul at §§70–71. Philo in fact refers to the intelligible cosmos (or equivalent expressions such as the "incorporeal cosmos" in §36) on numerous occasions in his works, most often in exegetical contexts. The ark of the covenant, for example, is consistently interpreted as a symbol of this higher world; cf. *Mos.* 2.127, *QG* 2.4, *QE* 2.68.

(b) The second crucial difference is that Philo's intelligible cosmos is created by God. It is the work of "day one" of creation. In Plato's *Timaeus* the demiurge looks to the model (as here), but no indication is given of where that model came from. It was simply there, as transcendent idea. Plato's demiurge, it would seem, is ontologically either inferior to or perhaps on the same level as the ideas, but certainly not superior to them. Elsewhere Philo is also very clear on the relation between God and the intelligible world, e.g. in the treatise following *Opif.*, *Abr.* 88, he states that

DAY ONE: CREATION OF THE INTELLIGIBLE COSMOS   139

God is both maker and ruler of both sense-perceptible and intelligible reality (also *Virt.* 214; *Praem.* 37; *QG* 4.188). Plato's ideas thus become the thoughts of God. They remain transcendent in relation to this world, but can no longer be regarded as first principles. Most scholars agree that Philo reflects a development in Platonist interpretation that probably took place in the century before Philo. It has, however, been argued by Radice (1989 and 1991), that Philo may have made an original contribution and acted as a catalyst for the philosophical tradition. On this question see further Excursus 1 below.

would be without fault. It is part of the demiurgic conception of the creation process that a "design" is first required for a thing before it can be properly made. The two alternatives are unacceptable: (a) that design or order occurs spontaneously or automatically (the atomist view, cf. *Ebr.* 199); (b) that design or order is an internal characteristic of nature that has always existed (unacceptable for Philo because it denies the doctrine of creation, cf. §§7–11).

modelled on the archetypal and intelligible idea. Interesting here is the preposition πρός ("on" or "in relation to"), taken over from Plato (e.g. *Tim.* 28a6) and part of the so-called "prepositional metaphysics" developed by Platonists in order to indicate the various causal explanations intended by Plato; cf. *PT* 171–174, Sterling 1997. On "archetypal" see the following note.

he first marked out. It is striking how Philo both here and in the complex image in §§17–20 uses the imagery of the seal and impression to describe the formation of the model and its relation to the created product. The seal or mould (σφραγίς, §§25, 34, 129) first has to be engraved or marked out with markings (τύποι, §§18, 19, 34; χαρακτῆρες, §18) before it can be used to imprint form on receptive material. Because it is the prime source of the transferred design, it is also called the ἀρχέτυπον (literally "first or chief marking," §25), where the modern terms "archetype" and "archetypal" come from. The origin of this imagery is Platonic (cf. *Tim.* 39e7, 50c–d), but it is strongly developed in Middle Platonism under the influence of the Stoa; cf. Dillon 1977, 200; De Vogel 1985, 13; *PT* 163; Popa 1999, and further below on §18.

as many sense-perceptible kinds ... The direct relation that Philo envisages between Moses and Plato can be gauged from his description of the Platonic doctrine, in a passage where he argues that Plato propounds a real beginning to the cosmos and not a *creatio aeterna, Aet.* 15:

> ... throughout the entire treatise he describes that moulder of divinity (θεοπλάστης) as the father and maker and demiurge, and this cosmos as his product and offspring, a visible imitation of the archetypal and intelligible model, containing in itself all the objects of sense-perception which the model contains as objects of intelligence, a wholly perfect imprint for sense-perception of a wholly perfect model for mind.

The language is virtually identical with what we find in *Opif.* A difference between the two texts is that in *Opif.* Philo specifies that the contents are γένη (kinds). He may be influenced by the fact that the Genesis text speaks so frequently of kinds (cf. also §§76, 129). These kinds replace the "living beings" in Plato's model (for γένη cf. 31c6). On the contents of the intelligible cosmos as envisaged by Philo see further our comment on §24.

(2a) §17. *exists in some place.* Place (τόπος) can be used in two senses. If it is taken physically, then it is not applicable to the ideas, since they do not have a material aspect. The solution is to take location figuratively, i.e. in God's mind. Philo's question makes good sense in a Platonic context. As we noted above on §16, Plato had spoken of a "place beyond the heavens" (*Phdr.* 247c) glimpsed by gods and disembodied souls, and also of the intelligible place (*Resp.* 508e1) for the location of the idea of the good in the image of the sun. But at *Tim.* 52b he states that it is a misconception to think that Being has to be "in some place" (cf. also Aristotle *Cael.* 1.9, 279a18–22, though there not ideas but divine minds are meant).

How it has been constituted. Philo jumps from "where" to "how," because he has just disqualified the question as to the (physical) location of the intelligible cosmos. But if we know *how* it has been put together (a kind of non-physical *genesis*), we may also know where it is (figuratively) located.

to an image drawn from our own world. Philo's extended image is much more elaborate than is usually the case in philosophical writings. Formally it can be compared with Plato's image of the cave and also the elaborate image of the Great king and his servants in Ps.-Aristotle *Mund.* 6, 398a10–b8. Not only the *tertium comparationis* is important (in this case the mind of the architect and the Logos of God), but other aspects are also worked out in detail.

In a detailed analysis of the contents of the image (Runia 1989), I argue that Philo has above all the founding of his own city, Alexandria, in mind. In our sources various accounts are given of this event: some emphasize that Alexander himself took the initiative and made the original plan (e.g. Arrian, *Anab.* 3.1.4–2.2), others mention that he made use of architects, and esp. the famous architect Dinocrates of Rhodes (e.g. Vitruvius, *Arch.* Pref. to book 2). Further details will be mentioned at the relevant parts of the text.

(2b) ***a king or a ruler who has laid claim to supreme power.*** Both epithets suit Alexander the Great perfectly, especially since the second (ἡγεμών) is often used of a military leader. We recall, of course, God's *monarchia* already argued for in §§7–11; cf. esp. God as "absolute in power" in *Congr.* 49 cited in our comments on §7. In the Platonic tradition the "king" is the chief image for the highest principle; cf. *Resp.* 509d2; *Ep.* 2, 312e; Atticus frg. 4.12; Numenius frg. 12; Dörrie 1970.

it may happen that a trained architect. The syntax is such that it markedly dissociates the architect from the king. No causal link between them is indicated. The image of the architect is a kind of upgrading of the demiurgic metaphor pioneered by Plato in the *Timaeus*. It is more suitable

DAY ONE: CREATION OF THE INTELLIGIBLE COSMOS   141

to compare the creation of the cosmos with the building of a city than the making of a pot. Aristotle may have contributed; cf. esp. *Metaph.* A 1, 981a30–b6. Cicero's Epicurean spokesman does his best at *Nat. d.* 1.19 to make the image look ridiculous: "What power of mental vision allowed your master Plato to envisage the vast and elaborate architectural processes adopted by God in constructing the world? What method of engineering was employed? What iron tools and levers and cranes?" (transl. LCL, modified). See further parallels at *PT* 168.

both the favourable climate and location. Alexandria was famed for its advantageous location on a thin strip of land between the Mediterranean sea and Lake Mareotis. The same terms are used of its site in the accounts of its foundation in Diodorus Siculus 17.52.2, Strabo 17.1.7.

within himself. This must mean in his mind or rational soul (cf. §18). The point is that the plan has no external manifestation. Contrast Rabbi Hoshai'a's revisionist image discussed below in the *Nachleben*.

harbours, shipyards ... Only possible for a city that is to be built on the coast, such as Alexandria.

§18. in his own soul like in wax. Here, most interestingly, the imagery of seal and impression is not used for the relation between model and copy, but is given an epistemological application. The image was pioneered by Plato at *Theat.* 191c (text cited by Philo, *Her.* 191) and thereafter exploited by Aristotle and the Stoics (it is the origin of the empiricist notion of the *tabula rasa*, which is of course quite unplatonic). It is possible that the combination of this epistemology with the ontological presentation in the *Timaeus* is a development in early Middle Platonist exegesis, though parallels are scarce; cf. our earlier discussion on §16.

he carries around ... as an image. The verb ἀγαλαμταφορέω recurs at §§69, 82, 137. It is perhaps the most remarkable of all the so-called *verba Philonica* (see above on §3). The image involved is that of statues (ἀγάλματα) located in a temple or being carried in a procession. Socrates is said to carry divine statues inside himself at Plato *Symp.* 215b. Philo uses it for humanbeings or the body carrying the intellect around in the head (cf. §§69, 137) or the intellect itself carrying around thoughts (as here and §82). Further discussion of the term and its origins at Boyancé 1963a, 109; *PT* 333; Graffigna 1991; Runia 1992b, 317–320.

Summoning up ... engraving their features ... We may conclude from these elaborate formulations that Philo wants to retain a distinction between the mind as subject and the plan as object.

as a good builder. Here the stage of construction comes in view and the architect becomes the δημιουργός. It remains, however, the same person, carrying out the work (presumably not without the help of others, but they are not mentioned). The description "good" anticipates §21.

out of stones and timber. I.e. the material required for creation. Note that we are not told where these come from.

looking at the model. Cf. above on §16. The preposition here is εἰς, used by Plato at *Tim.* 28b1.

(2c) §19. *concerning God.* The application to the creation of the cosmos now follows. A striking aspect, to which no explicit attention is drawn, occurs at the outset. The distinction between the king and the architect is dropped, and their two functions are coalesced in the single role of God as creator. This was first noted by Wolfson 1947 1.243, who drew valid and important conclusions from it, namely that God does need any kind of helper and that the cosmos is not the result of any ambition or desire, but rather an expression of pure goodness. We may, however, ask ourselves why the dissociation is so pronounced. The king is given no direct participation in the founding of the city (unlike Alexander's involvement according to one line of the tradition). He does not even issue the architect an invitation. This could be read in terms of a super-transcendence, but this is not, to my mind, a Philonic line of thinking. I prefer to suggest (cf. *PT* 167) that Philo wishes to indicate that God's creative activity does not exhaust the fullness of his Being (just as *theos*, i.e. God, is just one of his names). This interpretation, if correct, has important consequences for our interpretation of the divine Logos and the contents of the intelligible cosmos.

the great cosmic city. A single term, μεγαλόπολις, yet another *verbum Philonicum* (cf. also μεγαλοπολίτης at §143). Outside Philo (and excluding patristic imitators) it is only attested for large cities, not for the cosmos. At *Flacc.* 163 it is used to describe Alexandria.

its outlines ... the intelligible cosmos. Here Philo makes quite clear that he distinguishes between the making of individual marks, i.e. the ideas, and the formation of the totality of the intelligible cosmos. For this reason he keeps on speaking about the *composition* of the latter (§§17, 19) and its being *ordered* (§20). Exegetically the distinction has to be related to the individual ideas located in Gen 1:1-5 and explained in §§29-35.

§20. **no location outside.** More specifically now the application of the extended image is directed to the question posed at the outset in §17.

the soul of the craftsman. This picks up the earlier reference in §18. It is perhaps a little surprising that Philo in both cases speaks of "soul" rather than "mind." He means of course the rational (part of the) soul. See the next note. "Craftsman" here translates τεχνίτης, a person who is skilled, possesses τέχνη. This more general term covers both architect and builder.

the divine Logos. The first reference to Philo's celebrated theory of the Logos in our treatise. In general we can say that the name covers that aspect of God that is directed towards creation, whether conceptually (e.g. in the formation of the intelligible cosmos) or in terms of active participation in the ordering of physical reality and its administration (in conjunction with God's powers). Here we might translate with "God's Reason." At §8 God was presented in general terms as intellect and active principle. Now this Intellect is directed towards creation and so focuses its thought towards the production of physical and corporeal reality. The Logos thus bridges the gulf between transcendent and physical reality. It is possible to systematize Philo's conception by distinguishing between a transcendent

DAY ONE: CREATION OF THE INTELLIGIBLE COSMOS

and an immanent Logos (cf. Wolfson 1947, 1.226–239), of which the former is dominant in our treatise. But Philo is not interested in systematic theology here. In fact he appears to assume a certain familiarity of his reader with the main lines of his theology. The chief background of the doctrine is clearly philosophical, but it is not easy to locate exactly. The Stoic *logos* only suits the immanent aspect (Dillon's appeal to *logoi spermatikoi*, 1977, 159, in our context is unconvincing). There is some evidence to suggest that Middle Platonists employed the theological concept of the *logos*, e.g. by Plutarch at *Is. Or.* 373A–B, but the relation to the transcendental world is far from clear. On Philo's doctrine of the Logos see further Winston 1985a; Runia *PT* 446–451, 1995; Tobin 1992. All three scholars emphasize that the doctrine has important antecedents in Hellenistic Judaism, but that the biblical background should also not be ignored. The prominence of the Logos in our treatise cannot be separated from the repeated "and God said" of Gen 1, but the verbal and dynamic aspects of the biblical *dabar* have to a large extent given way to a conceptual emphasis.

no other place. In §17 Philo denied that the intelligible world could be contained in a place. Now it receives a place in the divine Logos. This is an equivocation, to be sure, but one that can easily be understood. In Philo's platonizing worldview there is physical place and supra-physical place. Numerous texts in Philo reflect on the relation between God and place. Particularly relevant to our context is *Somn.* 1.62: "Now place is understood in three ways: firstly a space filled by a body; secondly the divine Logos, which God himself has completely filled with incorporeal powers; thirdly God himself is called a place in that he contains whole things and is not contained by anything whatsoever." Note that this analysis is not purely philosophical, but also takes biblical usage into account. More texts listed at Theiler 1964, 398.

who gives these (ideas) their ordered disposition. Whitaker LCL (modified by Dillon 1977, 160) translates "who was the author of this ordered frame," i.e. taking ταῦτα to refer to the physical cosmos. I follow Wolfson 1947, 1.230 in taking the word to refer to the ideas which the Logos forms into an ordered world. The Logos in Philo is himself/itself never regarded as the Creator, but as God's instrument in various capacities.

for his powers. Straight after the Logos, God's powers are introduced as well. Their role is explained in §§21–23. Implicit here is the view that the intelligible cosmos itself is a divine power. At *Spec.* 1.48 Philo equates the divine powers with the ideas which bring form to what is unordered; cf. also *Deo* 6. But at *Conf.* 172 the intelligible cosmos is constructed through the agency of the powers.

in its unmixed state. I.e. not adapted to the person or thing receiving it. The necessity of this adaptation is shown in §23. On the distinction between God's unmixed and humankind's mixed state see *Deus* 77, *Mut.* 184.

(3a) §21. **Among these is also his cosmos-producing power.** Now that Philo has finished explaining the role and location of the noetic cosmos, he can turn to the role of God as creator, which is expressed in terms of the doctrine of the divine powers. The part of Philo's elaborate doctrine that is most relevant here is his presentation of two chief powers, each associated with a divine name: the creative power as indicated by the name *theos*, the kingly or sovereign power by the name *kurios*; see the standard accounts at *Abr.* 121, *Mut.* 28–29. More than once Philo points out that in the creation account the former title is used until Gen 2:8, when humankind is ready to respond to God's call; cf. *Plant.* 86, *QG* 2.16. So where we read about God, already in the very first verse, Philo sees an allusion to God's creative power. Philo also often emphasizes that the creative power is associated with God's goodness, the kingly power with his justice.

As in the case of the divine Logos, Philo appears to assign both a transcendent and an immanent role to the powers. In our text the former is dominant, but the latter too must be assumed. For systematic accounts of the doctrine see Wolfson 1947, 233–239, 261–282; Bormann 1955, 45–75; on its biblical and philosophical background Winston 1985a, 19–22; Bos, 1998, 75–79, sees as dominant influence the distinction between God's essence (οὐσία) and power (δύναμις) also found in Ps.-Aristotle *Mund.* 6, 397b19–28 (but it should be noted that this is not in the context of a doctrine of creation).

that which is truly good. Earlier God the activating cause was said to be beyond the good itself; see our comments on §8 above. Now presumably the idea of goodness is to be localized on the level of the Logos, and *may* be localized in the intelligible world, depending on how broadly we interpret that entity. See also further below.

the reason why. Not a question that the biblical account poses. The very question itself might seem to detract from acceptance of the pure contingency of created reality. But the answer that Philo gives in terms of unconditional divine grace is clearly in line with the biblical tradition.

what one of the ancients also said. Plato, at *Tim.* 29d7–e3: "Let us state the reason why he who constructed becoming (γένεσις) and this universe did construct it. He was good, and in a good person there can never be present any begrudging of anything whatsoever. So, being free of envy, he decided that everything should be as much like himself as possible." Philo loosely paraphrases Plato's famous text, combining it with 28c3 (cf. comments above on §7). For an analysis of the citation see Runia 1997a, 265. The immediate context also contains other allusions to Plato's text: "the reason why" is based on 29d7, "did not begrudge" on 29e2.

It seems to me that the veiled reference to Plato is deliberate: Philo wants us to know that much of his exegesis of the Mosaic creation account is inspired by similarities that he has perceived in the most celebrated cosmogony in Greek philosophy. There are several other passages where Philo has this seminal Platonic text in mind, notably *Leg.* 3.78; *Cher.* 127; *Deus* 108; *Plant.* 91; see the detailed analysis in *PT* 132–136 (with many references to parallels in Middle Platonist authors).

He did not begrudge. The theme of God's lack of envy is taken over from Plato *Tim.* 29e2, who reacts strongly against notions of divine vengeance and nemesis in pre-philosophical theology. Cf. esp. *QG* 1.55 (exeg. Gen 3:22): "The Deity is without part in any evil and is not envious of immortality or the good of anyone else. And here is a certain proof. Without being urged by anyone, he created the cosmos as a benefactor ..." (translation Marcus LCL modified); further texts and discussion at *PT* 136.

a share of his own excellent nature. Philo's adaptation of Plato's words (cited above), "as much like himself as possible." The emphasis differs somewhat. Plato stresses that the demiurge is constrained by necessity and the disorder he confronts (cf. also 48a). Philo does not want to draw attention to possible restrictions on God's omnipotence, but argues that there are limits to the amount of goodness created reality can absorb (§23). If this were not the case, the difference between the activating principle and the passive object (§8) would be effaced.

a material. The term is οὐσία. It represents neither Platonic "being" or Aristotelian "substance," but is functionally equivalent to "matter" (*ousia* can meaning "property" or even "stuff"). It is commonly found in Philo (e.g. *Spec.* 1.328, *QG* 1.55 etc.). On the Stoic and Platonist background see Cherniss' note to Plutarch *Mor.* 1014B (LCL), *PT* 141.

§22. ***Of itself it was unordered ...*** Similarly too in §§8–9 we find a list of negative attributes applied to the material which are one by one opposed to the positive attributes which result from the divine act of creation. One of the negative attributes, "dissimilar," has been supplied by an emendation suggested by the 18th century scholar Jeremiah Markland. If it were missing, there would be an imbalance between the two lists.

There is a significant difference between this text and §§8–9: Philo does not state that the material is without movement. Indeed we get the strong impression that it possesses some kind of disorderly motion. How otherwise would its lack of order and harmony be explained? Much more than in the other passage, Philo is influenced by Plato's account of the moment of creation at *Tim.* 30a2–6, just after the passage cited in §21, where the demiurge confronts a situation of disorderly and disharmonious movement and "led it from disorder to order." We observe that these are the two epithets that head the respective lists in Philo. Cosmos is above all order, as the word itself signifies. As I note at *PT* 141, the antithesis between order and disorder corresponds to deep-seated metaphysical, psychological and political convictions in Philo's thought. He knew from experience what disorder in the metropolis of Alexandria was like.

The description of the material that is to receive divine beneficence emphasizes its *negativity* (Platonic, note the many alpha-privatives), and also its *potentiality* ("able to become all things"; this is more Aristotelian and Stoic). But its *passivity* is reduced compared with the description at §§8–9. The discrepancy is a puzzle. Where does the disorderliness come from? Has Philo been influenced by a tradition which exploited the *tohu wa bohu* of Gen 1:2, even though it would be totally incompatible with this exegesis of "day one"? But there is an even more pressing question: Philo does not tell us where this disordered material comes from. For a discussion of this problem, see Excursus 2 at the end of this chapter.

harmony. The resultant cosmic harmony is above all perceptible in the ordered motions of the heavens. See further Commentary on §§53–54.

the superior idea. Referring to the model. We recall the use of the singular at §16; similarly at Alcinous *Did.* 12.1 and the table at *PT* 160.

§23. With no one to assist Him. A clear indication that Philo's theological scheme of God, Logos and powers (and also the implications of his extended image) in no way imperils God's unity. He alone is creator. In §§72–75 Philo will modify this position somewhat. In Middle Platonism a distinction is regularly made between the highest transcendent god and the second god who orders the cosmos by being turned towards him; see for example Alcinous *Did.* 10.2–3, Numenius frg. 12–13.

divine grace. Creation is an act of grace, as Philo emphasizes in numerous texts, e.g. *Deus* 108 (exeg. Gen 6:8): "he has given good things in abundance to the whole and its parts, not because he judged anything worthy of grace, but because he looked to his eternal goodness and considered it incumbent on his blessed and felicitous nature to be beneficent ... (followed by a further allusion to Plato *Tim.* 29e)." We should note that Philo's formulations in both texts ("must confer," "incumbent on") seem to hint at the later scholastic doctrine *bonum diffusivum sui*. "Goodness is self-distributing" in the sense that it is intrinsic to the nature of goodness that it not be cooped up but rather be distributed to that which is able to receive it. In other words: God, being good, cannot but be beneficent. The doctrine of grace naturally extends from this cosmic perspective to the relation between God and humankind. For a full treatment of Philo's doctrine of grace, see Zeller 1990 (on this text 41).

powers of beneficence. Translating χάριτες, which could also be translated as "favours," i.e. the acts of grace that God can confer.

(3b) without limit and infinitely great. This is one of the texts in Philo that suggests that he is prepared to ascribe infinity to God, even though in Greek philosophy so far (e.g. Plato and Aristotle) this view was rigorously denied. A fully fledged doctrine of divine infinitude is first found in Gregory of Nyssa, who was clearly influenced by Philo as well as developments in Neoplatonism. On this issue I side with Armstrong in Armstrong and Markus 1960, 10–15 against Mühlenberg 1966, 58–64; see now Geljon 2000, 152–173.

in proportion to the capacities of those who receive them. Here another scholastic adage springs to mind: *quidquid recipitur, recipitur ad modum recipientis* (whatever is received, is received according to the mode of the one receiving). The material world cannot receive God's beneficence without mediation. Such mediation occurs by means of measurement and is effectuated by the Logos and the intelligible cosmos (whose relations are further discussed in the following section, §24). The principle has

DAY ONE: CREATION OF THE INTELLIGIBLE COSMOS   147

both an ontological (as here) and an epistemological application. When Moses asks God to reveal himself to him, the answer is (*Spec.* 1.43–44):

> I graciously bestow what is in accordance with the recipient. For not everything that I can give with ease is within humankind's power to accept. Hence I extend to the person worthy of grace all that he is capable of receiving. But the understanding of me (i.e. the essence) neither the nature of the human being nor the entire heaven or cosmos is able to sustain.

Cf. *Abr.* 203; *Praem.* 39; *QE* 2.13; *Post.* 145; further texts and discussion at *PT* 137-138. See also the comments below on §151.

accommodate ... confer. The Greek verbs ποιεῖν and πάσχειν, to which has been added the adverb εὖ (well), recall the distinction between activating cause and passive object first introduced in §8.

would collapse. Philo's emphasis on the superiority of the divine power is extremely graphic. Creation would suffer from an "overdose of being," unless the overwhelming nature of the divine beneficence is moderated. Despite the metaphysical language we gain a sense of the majesty and power of the biblical Creator. On the Greek philosophical side, as I point out in a discussion in Runia 2001a, 298, it is not easy to find good parallels before Proclus. But see the next note.

He measured them accordingly. Many texts in Philo indicate that it is the task of the divine Logos (and the powers) to measure out the divine beneficence; cf. *QG* 1.4; 4.23; *Sacr.* 59; and see further *PT* 138. As is stated in §130, the ideas (or the noetic cosmos) can also play a role in this process; see the Commentary in Ch. 16. Philo's formulation must remind us of the famous statement in Wisdom 11.20, "but you [God] ordered all things by measure and number and weight," which via Augustine became a central text in medieval philosophy. The participle which I have translated "dispensing" can also mean "weighing out (as on a balance)". See further Winston 1979, 234, who cites many Philonic and Greek philosophical parallels. Later in Neoplatonism the concept of mediated goodness lies at the very heart of the doctrine of emanation.

For the connection between the intelligible world of ideas and measurement compare the lapidary formulation at Alcinous *Did.* 9.1: "The idea is considered in relation to God as his thinking, in relation to us as the primary object of thought, in relation to matter as measure, in relation to the sense-perceptible cosmos as the model, and in relation to itself as the essence." In Seneca *Ep.* 65.7 (an account of the Platonic doctrine of causes) a link is made between the ideas as patterns or models and the measures and harmonies required in the process of creation. These texts are also relevant to Philo's formulation in §24.

(4a) **§24, *formulation that has been stripped down to essentials.*** Literally "with more naked words." I take this to mean not so much simplicity of wording, or the expression of the "naked truth," as rather a formulation which does not resort to any kind of imagery or figurative speech. Perhaps Philo was concerned about the discrepancy between his denial of a "place" for the ideas in §17 and his phrases "no other place" and "what other place" used in §20, as we noted above in our comments.

you might say. It is striking that Philo three times (§§12, 20 and here) uses the optative when drawing a philosophical conclusion on the basis of argument. This is not meant, I believe, to indicate that his conclusion is tentative, but is rather a urbane expression of modesty. A similar practice is often found in Aristotle, cf. *Eth. eud.* 2.1, 1219a38; *Eth. nic.* 10.7, 1177b16.

the Logos of God as He is actually engaged in making the cosmos. The effect of the formula is to bring God as creator, the intelligible cosmos as plan for creation and the Logos (i.e. Reason) as conceiver and executor of the plan into a tight unity. This is reinforced by the inclusion of the particle ἤδη, translated "actually," which has the effect of confining the intelligible cosmos to God's creative activity. Once again Philo may be hinting that creation by no means exhausts the fullness of God's being (cf. the comments above on §17). In the act of creation the creating cause and his thought can only be analytically separated. The influence of Aristotelian psychology may be suspected, (cf. *Metaph.* Z 7, 1032b13, Λ 3, 1070a14, Theiler 1971, 31), but here raised to a cosmic and transcendent level.

A illuminating parallel to our passage is found at *Fug.* 12 (exegesis of Gen 31). Laban, who keeps the unmarked sheep, represents a materialist philosophy which recognizes no immaterial activating cause. Jacob, the supporter of true monarchy (cf. *Opif.* 7–11), receives the marked sheep and shows up Laban's mistaken ideology:

> For the cosmos has come into existence and assuredly through some cause [cf. Plato *Tim.* 28a-b]. The Logos of the one making it is itself the seal, by which each of the existents is shaped. For this reason from the beginning perfect form accompanies the things that come into existence, since it is the impression and image of the perfect Logos.

Here the seal replaces the intelligible cosmos because Philo is not speaking about the cosmos as a whole, but rather about individual creatures within it. A difference in emphasis between the two passages is that in *Fug.* Philo dwells on the role of immanent form in the cosmos, i.e. when the Logos has stamped the intelligible idea on matter (hence the marked sheep). This aspect is ignored (or perhaps rather simply assumed) in *Opif.*

reasoning of the architect. Philo's choice of terms is noteworthy. In Platonism λογισμός is generally used for discursive reasoning in contrast to the contemplation of the ideas. This suggests that there is an element of construction in the *genesis* of the intelligible cosmos, just as there patently is in the designing of the city by the architect. The conception of *logismos* and foresight (πρόορασις) involved in the genesis of the cosmos which Plotinus argues against at *Enn.* 3.2.1.18, seems very close to what Philo has in mind here. Horovitz 1900, 84–89, who does not think Philo wishes to argue the identification of the intelligible cosmos and the Logos, concludes from the comparison with the architect that the intelligible cosmos

DAY ONE: CREATION OF THE INTELLIGIBLE COSMOS   149

is not to be taken as the sum total of the ideas. He is reacting here against the earlier distinction suggested by Drummond (1886, 176): "An architect is capable of planning many cities; and therefore any particular city as conceived in his thought is only one out of many modes which that thought might assume. But there is only one cosmos, and its ideal is exhaustive of the divine Thought." This interpretation certainly misreads Philo's thought, for it ignores the distinction introduced between the king and the architect. The Logos, as we saw above at §19, represents (only) that aspect of God turned towards creation, and so the reasoning of the Logos *cannot* exhaust the divine thought. The conceptual world of the ideas is fundamentally linked to the world as we experience it, since it is its model. It must contain, therefore, everything in intelligible form that is required to understand the nature of the world, and perhaps more. This, we may surmise, would mean that it also contains ideas of abstract concepts such as goodness, beauty etc., as well as the mathematical concepts that Philo discusses in his arithmological passages. So I would be inclined to disagree with Horovitz's restricted interpretation of the contents of the intelligible cosmos. Such speculative discussions, however, distract us from what Philo is trying to convey in his exegesis. Central to that exegesis is the notion that the intelligible world belongs somehow to the *genesis* of the cosmos, but in a manner quite different to the rest of created reality. It is required so that the cosmos can be as excellent and beautiful as possible. The conception flows from Philo's use of the demiurgic model in which thought and planning play a central role. See further Radice *FM* 242, who argues that God's intellect, intelligible cosmos and Logos are identical in essence, but not in extension.

(4b) §25. *This is the doctrine of Moses.* Philo promised in §5 that he would adhere to the biblical text and only explain what was present there. His interpretation of "day one" in terms of an ideal world located in the divine Logos is here claimed not to be the result of pure philosophical speculation. But how does Philo attempt to show this? The passage has been interpreted in two ways. According to Horovitz 1900, 85 and Radice *FM* 244 Philo wants to demonstrate that the relation between model and copy is already found in Moses. Undoubtedly this is at least part of his intention. In a thorough analysis of the entire passage, however, Van Winden (1983) argues that Philo wants to do more, namely prove the *identification* of the intelligible cosmos and Logos which he has postulated in §20 and §24. His analysis (partly anticipated by Colson at PLCL 1.20) is able to do justice to the text of the passage, and has been followed in my comments below.

after God's image. As the argument that follows shows, Philo reads the biblical expression in Gen 1:27 as involving a double image (and double paradigm) relation. The Logos is God's image, so humankind is created as an image of the image. Cf. esp. *Spec.* 1.81; 3.83; *Leg.* 3.96; *Her.* 231 etc.; full discussion at Tobin *CM* 58–65. Philo returns to this text when he expounds the creation of humankind at §69 and §134, but there he does not dwell on the double relation. Rösel 1994, 49, in a discussion of the terminology of the LXX translation, argues not very plausibly that the Platonic cosmological background of the term may have contributed to its use in Gen 1:26–27. See also further the comments on §31.

it is plain that ... These words were bracketed by Cohn in his editions, but he failed to see that Philo intends two premises in his argument, each involving a protasis with "if" (printed in bold below) and an apodosis. Following Van Winden we accept the following changes compared with Cohn's text:

our text	*Cohn*
δῆλον ὅτι	bracketed
καὶ τὸ ὅλον· εἰ δ' ὁ	καὶ τὸ ὅλον εἶδος
ὃς μείζων (Van Winden ἣ, see below)	εἰ μείζων
τὸ παράδειγμα, ἀρχέτυπος ἰδέα τῶν ἰδεῶν	bracketed

Our readings largely coincide with the reading of our oldest manuscript V, on which see Introduction §9.

On the basis of this text, the full argument can be reconstructed as follows (for detailed explanation the reader is referred to Van Winden's analysis):

(1) According to Moses humankind is created according to God's image, i.e. as an image of an image.
(2) Humankind is part of the created cosmos.
(3) *If* humankind as part is created as an image of the image, then this must apply *a fortiori* to the whole, i.e. the sense-perceptible cosmos.
(4) But the image of God is the Logos.
(5) And it was earlier determined that the sense-perceptible cosmos must be an imitation or copy of the intelligible cosmos (cf. §16).
(6) Therefore, *if* the entire cosmos is an image of the Logos (= 4) and it is a copy of the intelligible cosmos (= 5), then the intelligible cosmos is to be identified with the Logos (for if A = B and A = C, then B = C).

There are two difficulties in the argument. Firstly, the premiss in (4) appears to come out of thin air. Philo has so far not explained that the Logos is God's image and in what sense this doctrine is to be understood. Secondly (and more seriously), in §69 Philo argues humankind is God's image because of the intellect and not in respect of the body. If the move from part to whole in (3) is to be taken at face value, then the whole must refer to the intellect of the cosmos. But such an intellect is nowhere mentioned in the exegesis and seems to be deliberately avoided. Philo assumes instead that the cosmos is a physical system endowed with life and thus with soul. Van Winden (1983, 215) suggests that a microcosm/macrocosm relation is assumed, even though this is not strictly speaking a part-whole relation. Plainly full exegetical consistency and philosophical coherence prove elusive here.

which is greater. Van Winden opts for the reading of V, ἣ μείζων, taking the relative pronoun as feminine by attraction to the noun εἰκών which

DAY ONE: CREATION OF THE INTELLIGIBLE COSMOS   151

follows. He is right that the corruption to εἰ can more easily be explained. But the masculine ὅς agreeing with κόσμος, which is found in the most manuscripts, is easier to construe.

archetypal idea of the ideas. Philo piles up four phrases to describe the intelligible world which is identified with the Logos, of which only the final one, "idea of ideas," is entirely new. The same expression is used of the Logos at *Migr.* 103; *QE* 2.124 (both exegesis of the high-priestly vestments). This expression is a strong indication that the intelligible cosmos should be regarded as a complex of the entire realm of ideas, and not just a limited construct comparable to Plato's "intelligible living being" (cf. above on §24). We may compare two contemporary Middle Platonist documents for this conception. Arius Didymus at Eusebius *Praep. Ev.* 11.23.6 writes:

> As the particular archetypes (ἀρχέτυπα) so to speak precede the bodies which are perceived by sense, so the Idea which includes in itself all ideas, being the most beautiful and most perfect, exists as model (παράδειγμα) for this cosmos; for it (the cosmos) has been made similar to that idea by the demiurge and produced in accordance with providence out of the whole material (οὐσία).

The passage is adapted by Alcinous *Did.* 12.1, who states that God created the cosmos by "looking towards an idea of the cosmos." For further discussions of these passages see Tobin *CM* 65–66; Dillon 1993, 114–117.

The double use of the term "archetypal" in this sentence is a bit awkward, and perhaps one of them should be removed. But I disagree with Van Winden 1983, 217 that it cannot go with "idea of the ideas." I take this genetival expression not to indicate greatness (as in "king of kings"), but as indicating that the model consists of all the ideas taken together (note that there is no definite article in the text).

EXCURSUS ONE
Philo and the doctrine of the ideas as God's thoughts

As noted above, Philo's explanation of "day one" can be brought in connection with an important development in the Middle Platonist interpretation of Plato, namely the doctrine of the ideas as God's thoughts. Whereas in Plato's dialogues the Ideas are always regarded as fully independent of the existence or contents of any mind, both in Philo and Middle Platonism they are regarded as the object or the contents of the divine mind. The first evidence of the doctrine is found in an unusual text, an allegorical interpretation of the Samothracian mysteries by Varro recorded in Augustine *Civ.* 7.28: Jupiter represents the heaven *by which*, Juno the earth *out of which*, Minerva the model *according to which* something comes to be. The prepositional metaphysics clearly assumes the three principles of standard Middle Platonism. Compare for example Alcinous *Did.* 9.1 (cited above on §23) and the doxographical formulation at Hippolytus *Ref.* 1.19.1–2, "Plato affirms the principles of the universe to be god and matter and model ...; the model is the thought (διάνοια) of the god, which he also calls idea, like an image (εἰκόνισμα), to which the god directed attention in his soul and created the universe." As the Varronian quote already shows, the doctrine of three principles is a kind of compromise. The ideas are the objects of God's thought, but they are not fully independent of him (after all, in the original Greek myth *Athena* springs forth fully clad from the head of Zeus). In §8, however, we saw that Philo adapts for himself the doctrine of two principles, which resolves the issue by making the ideas fully dependent on the creator. The exegesis of "day one" in terms of a created *kosmos noêtos* is an even more radical affirmation of the dependence of the ideas as model on God. For an overview of literature on the doctrine of the ideas as thoughts of God see *PT* 53 & n. 102, 163–164, Dillon 1993, 93–100 (commentary on Alcinous *Did.* 9), and the survey of the Middle Platonist doctrines of two and three principles in Dörrie–Baltes *DPA* vol. 4, §§111–122 (esp. §§113, 119).

Radice (1989, 281–306) has argued that Philo's original presentation of the doctrine of the ideas as thoughts of God in his exegesis of the Mosaic Genesis account may have interacted with the Middle Platonist development of the doctrine. Philo should not be regarded as the originator of the doctrine, but rather as its catalyst. See the English summary of his thesis in Radice 1991. The evidence he adduces is that earlier documents such as Timaeus Locrus and the *Timaeus* interpretation in *Aet.* 15 do not refer to the doctrine, and that Philo may have influenced Seneca's presentation in *Ep.* 65. These arguments are in my view not strong enough to support his radical thesis.

EXCURSUS TWO
Philo on the origin of matter

In both §§8–9 and §§21–22 Philo appears to speak about the material basis of physical reality, in the former text emphasizing its passivity, in the latter its disordered state. In both cases he describes how the cosmos came into existence when that material was brought to order and life. But he does not tell us where it comes from. The point at issue is whether Philo subscribes to the doctrine of *creatio ex nihilo*, thereby anticipating the development of this doctrine in Christian systematic theology. This is one of the most controversial topics in Philonic studies, on which so far no consensus has emerged. Broadly speaking three positions can be taken on this issue in relation to the text of *Opif.*

(a) Philo espouses the doctrine of *creatio ex nihilo*, even though it clashes with the fundamental Greek philosophical axiom *ex nihilo nihil fit*, but does not state this explicitly. It can, however, be deduced from his text. This is the solution of Wolfson and Winston, both of whom reach their divergent conclusions on the basis of an analysis of §§29–32. See the Excursus below in Ch. 6.

(b) Philo never gives an answer to the fundamental theological and philosophical problem at issue, because his primary aim is exegetical and ethical. This view is put forward by Radice *FM* 236.

(c) Philo does not give a clear answer to the question of the origin of matter because, unlike later Christian thinkers challenged by Gnosticism, he is not constrained to take a radical position against any form of dualism with regard to the question of the origin of evil. This is the view I defended at *PT* 453–455, in agreement with Weiss 1966, 59–74, and May 1994, 9–21. Note, however, that this view does not mean that Philo accepts matter as a principle next to God: §8 is quite clear on this issue.

The second and third views agree that this question can in any case not be resolved on the basis of the text of *Opif.* It may seem thoroughly logical that, if the intelligible cosmos is "created" by God in his Logos, he should also create the material on which the archetypal model is stamped. But this is simply not said (cf. also §171). Philo is in fact discouraged to do so by his interpretation that the whole of Gen 1:1–5 refers to the intelligible world. Compare the solution of Augustine who interprets the earth in Gen 1:1 as referring to unformed matter created by God as the substrate for the subsequent creation of the physical cosmos (*Conf.* 12.5–9).

Parallel exegesis

To my knowledge the interpretation that Philo gives here of Gen 1:1–5 as describing the *genesis* of the intelligible cosmos is unique in his *œuvre*. For further references to individual parts of the intelligible cosmos (e.g. heaven and light) see Parallel exegesis in Ch. 5 and Ch. 6. Philo often refers to the intelligible cosmos elsewhere, but not in relation to the first day of creation.

Nachleben

The only patristic author who fully takes over Philo's exegesis of "day one" is Clement of Alexandria, *Strom.* 5.93.5–94.2. He first states that "barbarian philosophy" (i.e. Moses) knows the distinction between the intelligible and sense-perceptible world, being model and image respectively, associates them with the monad and the six respectively (cf. *Nachleben* in Ch. 3) and then outlines some of its contents, mentioning heaven, earth and light only and citing Gen 1:1–2 and 1:5. He then suggests that Plato drew his conception of the ideas of living beings in the intelligible cosmos from this source (which is equivalent to the recognition that Philo's exegesis must be read against the background of Platonist philosophy). On this passage see further Lilla 1971, 191.

Other Christian exegetes interpret the first mention of "heaven" in Gen 1:1 (in distinction to the heaven created on the second day) as referring to an invisible or intelligible heaven. Cf. Theophilus *Aut.* 2.13 and famously Augustine *Conf.* 12.1, 12.9. On this tradition, which is only partially parallel to Philo's interpretation, see the detailed analysis of

Pépin *Ad* 1977 (1953), esp. 104–107 on the relation to Philo, Alexandre *CLG* 75–76, and also *Nachleben* in Ch. 6. A somewhat different interpretation of the relation between ideal and sense-perceptible cosmos is found in Ps.-Justin *Coh.* 30. As Riedweg (1994, 147, 456) notes, without Philo in the background Ps.-Justin's exegesis of Gen 1:1–6 as ascribed to Plato (!) — and also the double creation of the human being in Gen 1:26, 2:7 —, would be unthinkable, yet the differences of interpretation (Gen 1:1 physical world, Gen 1:2 ideal world) are so great that direct usage of Philo is not so likely; see further also Runia *PEC* 187. On the author of this work see Introduction §9.

Philo's image of the architect proved popular among later exegetes. Origen *Comm. Joh.* 1.114 applies the image to the role of the Logos (or Wisdom) which he discerns in the words "in the beginning" in Gen 1:1:

> I think that, just as a house is built and a ship is constructed in accordance with the architectonic markings (τύποι), the house and the ship having their origin in the marks and reasonings in the craftsman, so all things came into existence according to the reasonings of the future things outlined in advance by God in (his) wisdom.

At *Sel. Gen.* 12.97, however, Origen states, just before the text cited in Ch. 3 *Nachleben*, that God is *unlike* an architect who needs several days to complete his work. The same image is found at Didymus *Comm. Gen.* 2A.7 (text unfortunately damaged, but a reference to architect and city is certain); cf. also *Comm. Eccl.* 89.24. Note also the example in the Christian Gnostic Basilides cited by Hippolytus *Haer.* 7.23.5 (combined with 1 Cor. 3:10). On use and adaptation of the same image in Athanasius see De Vogel 1985, 12–13, Runia *PEC* 195–196.

On the first page of Genesis Rabbah the following image is attributed to Rabbi Hoshai'a of Caesarea (translation Freedman and Simon 1951) 1.1:

> The Torah declares: "I was the working tool of the Holy One, blessed be He." In human practice, when a mortal king builds a palace, he builds it not with his own skill but with the skill of an architect. The architect moreover does not build it out of his head, but employs plans and diagrams to know how to arrange the chambers and the wicket doors. Thus God consulted the Torah and created the world, while the Torah declares, "in the beginning God created (1:1)," "beginning" referring to the Torah ...

Since the rabbi was a contemporary and friend of Origen, who had taken Philo's works with him to Caesarea, it seems highly likely that the image is inspired by §§17–20 and in fact tries to correct its model by emphasizing that the architect uses *written* plans, i.e. the pre-existent Torah, and not the mental design placed by Philo in the divine Logos. Particularly striking is the fact that he takes over the distinction between king and architect. For discussions of this passage see Wächter 1962; Urbach 1987 198–201; Runia 1989, 410–412; 1993, 14. In the Midrash there are numerous other examples of similar images; e.g. Rab at *Gen. Rab.* 1.5, another example closer to Philo cited by Urbach 1987, 777. For the possible use of an architectural metaphor to explain the passage from the invisible to the visible creation in the apocalypse 2 *Enoch* 24.5, see Sterling 1999a, 8.

Further reading: Radice *FM* 239–244; Runia *PT* 158–174; Winston *PA* 96–100; 1984, 23–24; Dillon 1977, 158–160; Horovitz 1900 (on the noetic cosmos); Van Winden 1983 (on the text and interpretation of §§24–25).

Chapter Five
In the beginning does not mean creation in time (§§26–28)

Analysis/General comments

Having explained the special status of "day one", Philo now commences his commentary of the text of the creation account. He cites its famous opening words, and immediately focuses on the initial phrase "in (the) beginning" (ἐν ἀρχῇ). These words can easily be misunderstood, and so he feels constrained to return to the question of the relation between genesis and time which had already been broached in §§13–14. There is some overlap between the two passages, but here the emphasis is less on number and more on order. The text can be analysed into two parts, the first arguing against a wrong interpretation, the second putting forward a better alternative.

(1) It is philosophically impossible, Philo argues, that we take "in (the) beginning" in a temporal sense, as some people think. Time cannot be separated from the cosmos itself, since it is a product of the cosmos' movement. It must, therefore, either be equally as old as the cosmos itself, or it came into existence after the cosmos. Of the two alternatives the former must surely represent Philo's own view. We recall that in §13 he argued that in God's creative act everything occurred simultaneously — this is repeated in §28 —, because it cannot be that God needs time in which to achieve his end. The latter is perhaps mentioned because it is suggested by a literal exegesis of the six days (§26).

(2) If "in (the) beginning" is not meant temporally, how should it then be interpreted? The answer is similar to that already given in §§13–14. The expression should be taken numerically, since there is a close relation between number and order. "In (the) beginning" thus means "first," and this interpretation makes excellent sense, for the first part of the cosmos to be made, heaven, is its most excellent and beautiful part. But here too care is required. Even when we say that "the heaven is the first part to be made," we should not make the mistake of taking this in a temporary sense. It is first in order and value. Philo, consistent with his interpretation of "day one" in §§15–25, refers such ordering to the conceptuality in the minds of the producers (we recall especially the architect in §18). But in actual fact the same approach can also be used for the sense-perceptible cosmos, if it is also produced in a *creatio simultanea* (see the further reflections on order and hierarchy in §§65–68) (§§27–28).

As in §§7–12 Philo here draws on the doctrines of Greek philosophy in order to explain Moses' meaning. As has already been observed in our comments on §12 and the General comments on Ch. 3, Philo's interpretation of the nature of the creative act and the purpose of a narrative of sequential creation has benefited from the extensive discussions on what Plato meant by his account of creation in the *Timaeus*. As early as Aristotle (see *Cael.* 1.10) this involved discussions on the nature of time. The conception of time put forward by Philo here is strongly objectivistic, emphasizing the connection with cosmic movement and ignoring the psychological considerations to which Aristotle and later Augustine drew attention. It should be noted, however, that his argument only serves to refute those who take an unsophisticated literal view of creation, assuming that time is somehow unrelated to the cosmos itself, so that it can be created "in time". Strictly speaking Philo's argument here is compatible with two different views of creation, *creatio simultanea* and *creatio aeterna*. In the former case creation took place as a temporal *event*, but it involved a beginning, not *in time*, but *of time*. In the latter case there was never a first creation of time, but creation expresses an everlasting ontological dependence of the cosmos on God. There are two arguments in favour of the former view. Firstly, it seems to me that the argument of §§7–12 makes better sense in terms of a real beginning of time. Secondly, in *Aet.* 14 Philo polemicizes against the non-literal interpretation of the *Timaeus*, and then aligns Plato with Moses (§19). This implies that he does not interpret the Mosaic cosmogony in a non-literal sense either (provided of course that one understand literal creation in a philosophically sophisticated sense). It has to be admitted, however, that Philo's notion of creation of time, in contrast to the view of Augustine with which he is sometimes associated (see *Nachleben*), remains somewhat problematic in the absence of a fully-articulated doctrine of *creatio ex nihilo* (see Excursus 2 in Ch. 4). For further discussion of Philo's views on time see Runia *PT* 215–222. For the problem of *creatio simultanea* and *creatio aeterna*, see *ibid.* 426–433 and the detailed analysis of Sterling 1992, who after a lengthy examination of differing views, supports the interpretation of *creatio aeterna*. See also the Excursus to Ch. 6.

Detailed comments

(1) §26. **When he says that in (the) beginning** ... Gen 1:1 is quoted with complete accuracy. Word for word citation is rather infrequent in our treatise; see the overview in Introduction §4(a). In translating the phrase ἐν ἀρχῇ, I follow the traditional rendering (but see next note). Although the LXX leaves out the article in the phrase, this is not important for

Philo's interpretation. In Greek the article is often omitted in prepositional expressions of time; see Smyth 1956, §1127.

The words *bereshit* (Hebrew Bible), ἐν ἀρχῇ (LXX) and *in principio* (Latin Bible) in Gen 1:1 were the subject of endless discussion and speculation. In the Jewish tradition they were often taken to refer to Wisdom and later to the Torah. In the Christian tradition a favourite explanation was "in the principle," i.e. the Logos or the pre-existent Christ. On the interpretation of Gen 1:1 in Jewish and patristic literature see Kugel *TB* 44–47, 54; Alexandre *CLG* 65–71; and esp. the important studies of Van Winden collected in 1997.

the (term) beginning. The term ἀρχή is one of the most fundamental in Greek philosophy. The semantic field of the term is indicated by the fact that it can mean "beginning", "principle," and "rule". The basic meaning is something like "starting-point," which can then be taken temporally (beginning), ontologically (principle), or in terms of authority and power (rule). The word occurs 36 times in our treatise, usually in the first sense, but for an example of the meaning of principle see §52, and for the meaning of rule see §45.

as some people think. Implicit criticism of literalists. Compare similar polemical statements at *QG* 1.1 and *Leg.* 1.20 on the words "when they came into existence" in Gen 2:4.

it came into existence either together with the cosmos or after it. A rather similar argument is found at *Leg.* 1.2, where Philo concludes that time is "more recent" than the heaven, because it is produced by its movements. Two other texts have a different perspective. In *Aet.* 52–53 it is argued that time itself is without beginning or end. This is the Aristotelian position, which Philo presents dialectically, i.e. it is not his own considered view (cf. Runia *PT* 218). At *Decal.* 58, on the other hand, he writes that "there was a time when the cosmos did not exist," precisely what he here disallows. It is best to take this as a piece of carelessness, or to conclude that it should not be taken at face value (cf. Winston *PA* 17). Elsewhere, using a theological formulation Philo can say: "before the cosmos was, God is;" cf. *Mut.* 11–12, 27–28; and less satisfactorily *Sacr.* 76.

time is the extension of the cosmos' movement. Cf. *Aet.* 52: "Those who make it their habit to give definitions of things have accurately explained time as the extension of the movement of the cosmos." At *Aet.* 4 Philo attributes the definition directly to the Stoic philosophers. According to later reports Zeno defined time simply as the extension of movement (as opposed to Aristotle for whom it was the number of movement), but a century later Chrysippus added the further specification that it was the movement of the cosmos; see texts at *SVF* 1.93; 2.509–519; L&S §51 (Von Arnim includes our text at *SVF* 2.511). The same definition was attributed to Plato by Aëtius at Ps.-Plutarch *Plac.* 1.21 and Alcinous *Did.* 14.6, the assumption being that the later definition corresponded to Plato's intentions in *Tim.* 37c–38e (note esp. 38b6 "time came into existence together with the heaven ...," cited by Philo at *Prov.* 1.20). The conception of time presented here is strongly objectivistic, postulating a direct connection with ordered cosmic movement and ignoring the psychological considerations to which Aristotle and later Augustine drew attention. It is sufficient for Philo's straightforward requirements in this passage.

any movement earlier than the thing that moves. As the more detailed passage in *Leg.* 1.2 makes clear, Philo means here the ordered movement of the heavenly bodies, which give the measures of time (see further below §60). We might be inclined to ask Philo about his description of disorder in §§21–22. Does this not involve some kind of disharmonious motion, and therefore assume some kind of duration, if not time? This is the same question that was directed at Plato by Aristotle and others in relation to the pre-cosmic chaos in *Tim.* 30a. Philo's account is too vague to allow any but the most speculative kind of answer. What is clear is that his position is more coherent if coupled with the doctrine of *creatio ex nihilo*, as was to be the case in Augustine's famous account in *Conf.* 11.15–16. For a discussion adducing all the relevant texts see Sorabji 1983, 203–209. On the option of *creatio aeterna* see the General comments above.

we must necessarily conclude. As in §12, Philo uses the method of philosophical argumentation. Here we have a classic Aristotelian syllogism in barbara, which can be set out as:

Premiss 1: B (motion) is predicated of A (time)
Premiss 2: C (of equal age or younger than cosmos) is predicated of B (motion)
Conclusion: C (of equal age or younger than cosmos) is predicated of A (time).

unphilosophical. Philosophy here is understood in a narrower sense than in §2 and §8, i.e. in accordance with the canons of Greek philosophical argumentation. See also the comments on §128.

(2) §27. *beginning in the numerical sense.* The same emphasis on number as in §§13–14, but now with a different application. There Philo was concerned with the separate status of "day one," so he drew attention to the separate nature of the unit. Here it is a matter of the order within the creations of "day one" (as emerges in §29), so the ordinal number "first" is appropriate.

It is indeed reasonable. For the term εὔλογον see the comments on §45.

most excellent ... composed of the purest substance. Philo might give the impression here that he is talking about the visible and corporeal heaven, but this is not the case, as he makes quite clear in §29. Of course the idea of heaven exhibits all the essential features that characterize the physical heaven, but cannot itself be composed of any kind of material. On the composition of the heaven see further §55. The physical heaven (i.e. the firmament) is also created first on the second day (cf. §36), but it is not ordered until the fourth day, for reasons that are explained in §§45–46.

the holiest dwelling-place. Philo is no doubt thinking of the comparison of the heaven with a temple; see further §55. It is the basis for the symbolism of the tabernacle in the Pentateuch and the temple in Jerusalem. See esp. *Spec.* 1.66: "The highest and in the true sense holy temple of God must be thought to be the entire cosmos, which has as its sanctuary the holiest part of the substance of existing things, the heaven, as its dedicatory objects the stars, as its priests the angels ... But there is also the temple made by hands ..."

for the gods whose appearance is perceived by the senses. Here Philo appears to make a concession to pagan tastes by describing the heavenly bodies as "visible gods." Though very severe in condemning any kind of polytheistic worship of the stars and also any concessions to astral fatalism (cf. esp. *Spec.* 1.13–20; *Prov.* 1.77–88; and see §§45–46), Philo does recognize how important the heavenly bodies are for life on earth. And he is also surprisingly unpuritanical in the way he describes them. Even at *Spec.* 1.19, in the very passage in which he condemns worship of the heavenly bodies, he describes them as "all the gods in heaven whom sense-perception observes." Perhaps Philo is influenced by the fact that the Septuagint does speak of "gods" from time to time, most notoriously at Exod 22:27, where the text reads "You shall not revile the gods"; on the interpretation of this text in Philo, Josephus and Christian authors, see Van der Horst 1993.

§28. *proceeded to make.* This is the first example of Philo's striking use of the inceptive imperfect to describe God's actions during the process of creation. At least ten more instances will follow during the course of the treatise. Although the English translation with "proceed" is a little too heavy, I have decided to use it in order to draw attention to Philo's usage. The inceptive imperfect is used especially for the beginning of an action or a series of actions; cf. Smyth 1956, §1900. Philo wants to emphasize the process of creation, as it takes place in a sequence of creative acts (even though everything in fact happened together).

simultaneously ... possess order. This is simply a repetition of what has already been said in §13.

Order is a sequence and series of things that precede and follow. The terms used to define order here are ἀκολουθία and εἱρμός. Exactly the same terms are used later in §65 and §131. Order, according to Philo, involves everything happening in the right sequence. This can be understood hierarchically or developmentally. In the former case (cf. §65) it is applied to various separate objects whose creation needs to take place in such a way that their different places and functions in the whole are taken into account. For example, when building a house, you do not start constructing the walls before the foundations, and the roof has to come last. If taken developmentally (cf. §67) it means that processes of growth have to take place in the right order, as happens in the development of natural things. In both cases the sequence of creation or development can tell us about the rational structure of the things concerned. See further my analysis at *PT* 416–420. For a different approach, interpreting order in terms of the sequence of events within the cosmos once it has been created, see *QE* 2.58.

if not in the completed products ... If we take our illustration of a house again, it can only be built in a particular sequence, e.g. first foundations, then walls, then roof. But the analogy cannot be applied directly to the cosmos, for Philo has stated that, for theological reasons, all things were created simultaneously. Therefore the structural sequence can only be located in the mind of the builder, which brings us back to the comparison with the architect in §18, applied in §20 to the divine Logos.

not deviate from their path. The term ἀπλανεῖς, literally "not wandering," suggests that Philo is thinking especially of the heavenly bodies in heaven itself, which must move in such a way that no collisions occur. This is presumably taken care of in the design of the intelligible heaven. Compare Plato *Tim.* 36d, where the heavenly bodies are placed within the bands of the world-soul, which were designed in accordance with the laws and numbers of musical harmony. At *Decal.* 104 Philo vigorously denies that there is any wandering motion in the heavens, despite the fact that we speak of planets (a theme taken over from Plato, *Leg.* 821c–d).

confusion. The opposite of order. Confusion is the chief theme of *Conf.*, where it is applied allegorically to the soul.

Parallel exegesis

Both at §82 and *Praem.* 1 Philo repeats that God began his creative work with the creation of the heaven (cf. also *QG* 2.18; 4.215), no indication being given that an intelligible heaven preceded the sense-perceptible one. At *Leg.* 1.43 Philo appears to preserve a tradition which interprets ἀρχή in terms of wisdom; cf. Kugel *TB* 46. *QG* 2.18 perhaps alludes obliquely to an allegorical interpretation of heaven and earth in terms of mind and sense-perception and body respectively.

Nachleben

Five aspects may be briefly mentioned.
(1) Origen agrees with Philo that ἐν ἀρχῇ should not be taken as referring to time. In *Hom. Gen.* 1.1 he says only that it is not meant in a temporal sense, but "in the saviour." But the remarks at Calcidius *Comm. in Tim.* 276 are fuller (cited by PCW 1.8): "Origen asserts that he was persuaded by the Hebrews ... that beginning is not meant in a temporal sense, for neither was there any time before the ordering of the world nor were there the alternations of night and day by which intervals of time are measured." I agree with Van den Hoek 2000a 65 that Philo is being indirectly referred to here. See also Ch. 3 *Nachleben* on *Sel. Gen.* 27. His rejection of the temporal interpretation is followed by Didymus *Comm. Gen.* 1B12.
(2) Eusebius *Praep. Ev.* 11.24.4–7 quotes §26 and the first part of §27 (up to "heaven") as a continuation of §§24–25 in order to illustrate the Mosaic theory of ideas.
(3) The specific interpretation of ἐν ἀρχῇ as "first" reappears in Ambrose at *Hex.* 1.8.28, and as one of the multiple exegeses suggested by Augustine at *Conf.* 12.39; *Gen. litt.* 1.2 (where it is distinguished from a temporal reading).

(4) The definition of order in terms of sequence and series, and its application to the order of creation (and also to other themes) is frequently found in Gregory of Nyssa (cf. Runia *PEC* 252), who has taken it over from Philo. See for example *An. res.* PG 46.105A, 129A, 133B. In the lexicon of the Alexandrian lexicographer Hesychius (5th–6th cent. C.E.) τάξις is described s.v. as "the deposit of money owed (cf. our word tax) or sequence and series." The second phrase ἀκολουθία καὶ εἱρμός is identical to what we find in Philo and may be drawn from him (Hesychius also records the *verbum Philonicum* ἀγαλματοφορέω, on which see the comments on §18).

(5) As a curiosity we record a long-distance reflection of our text. The English physicist Barrow writes in a book on modern cosmology (1991, 55):

> There is a long-standing philosophical puzzle regarding the nature of time ... It reduces to the question of whether time is an absolute background stage on which events are played out but yet remains unaffected by them, or whether it is a secondary concept wholly derivable from physical processes and hence affected by them ... The alternative, an idea that emerges in Aristotle's writings and more memorably in those of Augustine and Philo of Alexandria, before being elaborated by some of the early Islamic natural philosophers, is that time is something that comes into being with the Universe. Before the Universe was, there was no time, no concept of "before."

Further reading: Radice *FM* 245–247; Runia *PT* 101–102; Winston *PA* 106–107; Alexandre *CLG* 68 (on the *Nachleben*); Sterling 1992.

Chapter Six
The chief contents of the intelligible cosmos (§§29–35)

Analysis/General comments

In §§16–25 Philo had introduced his reader to the concept of an intelligible cosmos. He now embarks on a discussion of its contents, basing his account closely on the Mosaic text in Gen 1:1–5, as can be seen by the many highlighted words in the translation. We may assume that he thinks detailed exegesis of these contents will reinforce the persuasiveness of his rather radical interpretation of "day one" in terms of intelligible rather than physical reality. This passage may be divided into three parts.

(1) Firstly, an outline is given of the main contents of the intelligible cosmos, amounting to seven components, a significant number encountered here for the first time in the treatise (see further §§89–127). These seven are all derived from vv. 1–3. Two of the identifications made by Philo, air and the void, are already very briefly explained in the course of this outline (§29).

(2a) But more explanatory remarks are required. Firstly, why does Moses speak not of "spirit" (*pneuma*) alone, but of "spirit of God"? The answer is given in terms of a connection of spirit with life which is caused by God (§30).

(2b) Philo then dwells at some length on the role of light. Just as light has a special place in the world of physical reality and is especially connected with the heavenly bodies, so this must be the case in the intelligible cosmos, and since the latter world is at a higher ontological level than the world of our experience (where light can be so dazzling), this can give us some idea of how brilliant that intelligible light must be (§§30–31).

(2c) Finally a brief comment is made on the statement in Gen 1:2 that "there was darkness above the abyss." In Philo's interpretation this involves the relationship between air and the void (§32).

(3) Philo then turns to the contents of Gen 1:4–5, which were excluded from the earlier summary of the seven items. The creation of light as seventh item meant the emergence of a pair of opposites, i.e. light and darkness. These two have to be kept apart, otherwise there would be disorder in the intelligible realm and it would cease to be a cosmos. So "evening" and "morning" are interpreted as forming boundaries between the opposing forces. But once morning and evening exist, then a measure of time is produced and a day

ensues. This allows Philo to round off his exegesis by returning to the theme of "day one" already introduced in §15 and reminding his reader of the connection between the intelligible cosmos and the monad (§§33–35).

Taken in its entirety, there can be no doubt that a philosophically schooled reader would have, at a first reading, found this passage rather bizarre. The concept of the intelligible cosmos, as introduced in §§16–25, was clear enough. As we saw, it was inspired by the Platonist interpretation of the *Timaeus*. Although Plato did not use the concept of the intelligible cosmos as such, he was certainly preoccupied with the question of the relations between the ideas in the intelligible realm. A famous passage at *Sophist* 254–256 discusses the five "greatest kinds" — being, same, different, movement, rest — and the relations that necessarily have to be postulated between them. Four of these five kinds are opposites, which yields a similar problem to the relation between light and darkness noted in §33. It is plain, however, Philo is not interested in abstract philosophical problems. He sticks closely to the contents of the biblical text and tries to make the most of them. His chief difficulty is that the text appears to deal with aspects of the sense-perceptible world. Indeed Philo's own descriptions of light and darkness and the boundaries of morning and evening between them are so concrete that the reader could easily make the mistake of forgetting about their intelligible status altogether. For this reason Philo feels the need to remind his reader of their incorporeal nature in §34. The reader might, however, draw a quite different conclusion, i.e. that Philo's interpretation of the whole of Gen 1:1–5 in terms of an intelligible cosmos is rather contrived.

A similar problem occurs when we examine what Philo means by heaven, earth, water and air. Some interpreters think he has the ideas of the four elements in mind. His descriptions, however, indicate that he is thinking more of the regions of the cosmos. The entire chapter reveals a palpable tension between the contents of the biblical text being explained and the philosophical doctrines being used for that explanation.

Detailed comments

(1) §29. ***First, therefore***. Based on the conclusion of the discussion of "in the beginning" in §27.

invisible earth. Philo combines the "earth" in Gen 1:1 with the adjective used to describe it in Gen 1:2. The LXX translation of *tohu wa bohu* as ἀόρατος καὶ ἀκατασκεύαστος (literally "unseen and unconstructed") is striking, but can be explained. "Unseen" probably refers to the fact that it was as yet covered by water (it becomes visible in v.9), while "unconstructed" refers to the fact that it had not yet received its (dry) form. (Dodd 1935, 111, however, takes the translation to refer to Hellenistic-Jewish speculation on the creation of the cosmos out of pre-existent invisible elements.) Philo ignores the second epithet and takes the former in the sense of "invisible," i.e. as referring to the realm of the ideas (cf. Plato *Resp.* 529b5; *Soph.* 246b7; *Tim.* 52a3; Alcinous *Did.* 7.4 etc.). It is therefore, an important textual support for his interpretation of "day one," even if this is not explicitly stated. Rösel (1994, 82) has recently revived the idea that the LXX translators of Genesis themselves were influenced by Plato's *Timaeus*, but in this case the hypothesis lacks all plausibility. It is Philo who sees the connection.

he assigned the name. Who is the subject here? If Moses is meant, we have an awkward change of subject, since two lines later more objects are given to the same verb ἐποίησεν with which the sentence begins. The passage ὧν τὸ μὲν ... ἀχανές is then best taken as parenthetical. But perhaps the subject is God, who, as we noted above on §12, does quite a lot of naming in Genesis 1. Moses is under divine inspiration (§8), so the distinction is moot.

the air is black by nature. This explanation may seem odd, since air seems to be transparent rather than black, but it finds support in many ancient texts. Cf. Plutarch on the Stoics at *Mor.* 948D; 952C; 1053F; Ps.-Aristotle *Mund.* 2, 392b7. At Plato *Tim.* 58d2–3 one of the varieties of air is called "murkiest mist and darkness (σκότος, as in Philo)." See further Radice *FM* 249 and Winston's learned note on Wisdom 17:10 at 1979, 306–307. Most ancient explanations emphasize that air also includes all kinds of haze, mist and fog, and for this reason is murky, dark, or even black (this goes back to Homer). At *QE* 2.85 (exeg. of the curtains of the tabernacle), however, Philo gives another explanation: "for the air is black and has no illumination in itself, wherefore it is illuminated by another light." Identification of darkness and air is attributed to the Stoics by Alexander of Aphrodisias, *De an.* 139.1 (= *SVF* 2.432).

the void is indeed full of depths and gaping. For Philo the void is simply empty space, i.e. where nothing corporeal exists. He generally follows the Platonic and Aristotelian view that the cosmos occupies the whole of physical reality, so that no void actually exists (cf. *Plant.* 6–8, *QE* 2.68, with in both cases a special task for the Logos). The Stoic view that there must be a void outside the cosmos to accommodate its increase and decrease in size is rejected at *Her.* 228, but apparently tolerated at *Prov.* 2.55–56. See further below on §32.

"Gaping (ἀχανές)" recalls chaos (χάος), often etymologized as "gaping." In Hesiod's *Theog.* 116 it is the first of all things to come into existence, followed by Earth (cf. *Aet.* 17–18). It was often interpreted as referring to the void or empty space (e.g. Aristotle *Phys.* 4.1, 208b31). Epicurus resolved to become a philosopher when his school-teacher could not tell him what preceded chaos in Hesiod's account (Diogenes Laertius 10.2; Sextus Empiricus *Adv. Phys.* 2.19).

as seventh. It cannot be without significance that the chief contents of the intelligible cosmos amount to seven items (my comment at *PT* 288 n. 8 was, I now think, too literalistic). On the link between the unit and the seven see below on §100 and *Deus* 11–13. It is strange that Philo does not make more of this. He may be allusively referring to an already existing exegetical theme. Compare two other texts:

> *Spec.* 2.59: The seven is completely unmixed, and if the truth be told, is the light of the six. For what the six generates, the seven has revealed as completed;
> *Leg.* 1.18 (exeg. Gen 2:3): the reason why the person who guides himself according to the seventh and perfect light is blessed and holy is that the formation of mortal things ceases in that nature [i.e. of the seventh day]. For the matter stands as follows. When that most brilliant beam of excellence has risen, the coming into existence of the opposite nature stops ...

Clearly an interpretative link is laid between the first six creations on the first day and the seventh, and the first six days of creation and the seventh. A similar theme is already present in Aristobulus frg. 5a (= Clement, *Strom.* 6.138); see further Walter 1964, 65–66, Holladay 1983–1996, 3.179. A further parallel, noted by Nikiprowetzky 1996 (1965) 66, is found at *Jubilees* 2:2–3, where a connection is made between the Sabbath and the first day and God is said to receive praise because he made seven great works on that day. Two differences, however, meet the eye: (a) the philosophical concept of an intelligible cosmos is absent (but note our remarks above in Ch. 4 General comments); (b) "spirit" is interpreted in terms of the angels that minister before God. See also *Nachleben* below.

last of all. The first of ten occasions that Philo uses the phrase ἐπὶ πᾶσι (or ἐφ' ἅπασι). See the comment on §65.

(2a) §30. *spirit is highly important for life*. The term πνεῦμα (literally "life-breath") poses special problems for Philo. On the one hand, when identified with the "divine inbreathing" of Gen 2:7 (where the actual term is πνοή), it must be given a high status, as we shall see below at §135. On the other hand, the term had various materialistic associations which he needs to handle with care. In Stoic philosophy (from Chrysippus onwards) it represents the bodily substance which is instrumental in giving form and structure to the entire universe, and especially to living organisms (cf. L&S §47). In Aristotelian biology it is the instrument which allows psychic action to affect the body (cf. *Mot. an.* 10, 703a10, Freudenthal 1995). Here too, since Gen. 1:2 speaks of "the spirit *of God*," Philo must give the concept a positive evaluation, but the explanation is put forward very briefly and in the most general terms. The word θεοῦ is clearly taken as a objective genitive, i.e. the spirit that is created by God for the benefit of living beings in creation. See further the comments at §67 on πνευματική as "the life-giving substance, " and in Ch. 18 on the exegesis of Gen. 2:7. On Wolfson's interpretation in terms of the idea of life in general see the Excursus. A useful survey of Philo's use of *pneuma* is given by Bormann 1955, 106–111. For a quite different exegesis of Gen 1:2 see Parallel exegesis below.

(2b) *exceedingly beautiful.* The biblical text which Philo comments on says no more than "and God saw the light that (it was) beautiful (καλόν)." Why then does he add the adverb? Horovitz (1900, 66) agrees with Müller (1841, 178) that it is used because it is only said of light among the creations of "day one" that it is beautiful. Compare *Abr.* 156, where Philo states that light is "the most beautiful of things that exist and the first to be named 'beautiful' in the holy scriptures" (but note that no indication is given here that intelligible light is meant in Gen 1:4)." This interpretation is not, however, supported by the explanatory statement that follows (introduced by "for"), which contrasts the intelligible and the sense-perceptible worlds. The adverb itself suggests transcendence (it contains the preposition ὑπέρ, "beyond"). I suggest that Philo inserts the adverb because of the pre-eminent importance he attaches to light as a symbol of God and wisdom. The theme is exceedingly rich in his writings, combining central biblical and philosophical themes. On the one hand we have the glory of God radiating on Moses' face when he descends from the mountain (Exod 34:29, cf. *Mos.* 2.70): God is known through God, just as light is seen by means of light (*Praem.* 46, inspiring the title of Goodenough's famous monograph, 1935; note also the quotation of Ps. 26:1, cited at *Somn.* 1.75, discussed below on §31). On the other hand there is the famous Platonic use of the theme in the images of the sun and the cave, exploiting the double aspect of light, namely that it can both illuminate and bedazzle (cf. comments above on §6). Light is used in both traditions as an important analogical metaphor. Physical light illuminates the world around us so that it can be seen. Light thus becomes a symbol of knowledge gained through mental or spiritual illumination. Light can be so dazzling that it overwhelms our sense of sight. It is then a symbol of the ontological superiority of God, or, as Plato prefers, of the Good. Philo gets another chance to expatiate on the virtues of light in his exegesis of the fourth day; see below on §§53–54.

The great French Philonist Valentin Nikiprowetzky conceived the plan to write a comprehensive study on the themes and traditions of light in the thought of Philo, taking into account the Septuagintal and Platonic background and analysing the great number of subjects in relation to which Philo speaks about light. Unfortunately this work remained unfinished at his death in 1983. See, however, a kind of summary that was published in 1989, which gives a wonderful overview of the subject (references unfortunately are scanty, but on *Opif.* see esp. 10–15). For earlier treatments of the theme of light see Goodenough 1935 and Klein 1962, both of whom are strongly influenced by the History of Religions approach to the theme.

intellect ... surpasses its sources of information. The epistemological application of the theme of light, implicit in the concepts of intelligible and sense-perceptible reality, is here made explicit. Cohn's bracketing of the words τὰ κριτήρια in his text is to me quite inexplicable. All mss. (and Eusebius) contain some reference to the senses as κριτήρια (i.e. conveyors and arbiters of external impressions). I translate the reading of three mss. τῶν αἰσθητικῶν κριτηρίων, which Cohn read in his 1889 edition ad loc. If the reading of Eusebius and V, τὰ κριτήρια, is retained, we would have to take this as an accusative of respect ("and with regard to the sources of information ..."). On the other hand I prefer, with PCW but against Cohn 1889, 9, the reading ὀφθαλμῶν of Eusebius and V to the καὶ ὀφθαλμοί of the other mss., taking it in apposition to κριτηρίων (the objection to saying that the eyes are superior to the body is that they, unlike the *nous*, are part of it). On the senses as κριτήρια see also §62 and the note of Alexandre PAPM 16.119 on *Congr.* 21.

§31. ***as image of the divine Logos which communicated its genesis.*** It would seem that Philo is alluding here to the formulation of "and God said" which occurs for the first time in Gen 1:3 and is repeated at the beginning of the remaining five days. The verb is based on the noun ἑρμηνεύς, and might also be translated "acted as interpreter in its genesis." God's Logos now does not plan, as in §§16–25, but pronounces. In order to understand this difficult text, we may compare *Somn.* 1.75 (I accept the reading of the text by Colson PLCL 5.336, including his conjecture):

> God is light, for it is sung in the Psalms, "the Lord is my illumination (φωτισμός) and my Saviour (Ps. 26:1)." And he is not only light, but also the archetype of every other light, rather he is anterior and superior to every archetype, having the relationship of a model <of a model>. For the model is his Logos in its plenitude, light in fact, for as he (Moses) says, "God said: let light come into existence," whereas he himself is similar to none of the things that have come into existence.

Here a distinction is made between God and his Logos, and the intelligible light created on day one is equated with the Logos (though light is not called intelligible in this text, it may be assumed). The difficulty of our present passage is that the intelligible light is called "image" (εἰκών) of the divine Logos. This is not easy to rhyme with the identification of the intelligible cosmos and the Logos as affirmed and proven in §§24–25. It might be argued that light is but one part of the intelligible cosmos as a whole, but a part-whole relation, even at the intelligible level, is not the same as a model-image relation. Perhaps the text is corrupt. The text as read by PCW is the shorter version found in Eusebius, V and the *Sacra Parallela*. The other mss. have a longer version which reads (with some variation): "but the invisible and intelligible divine Logos and Logos of God he says (to be) image of God. And of this image that intelligible light came into being as image ..." This alternative text unfortunately does not offer a solution to our problem.

a star that transcends the heavenly realm. Philo has already told us that the intelligible light surpasses what is experienced in the physical realm (§30). He now calls it a transcendent star, because it is the model and source for the light of the heavenly bodies. On the relation between the stars and the intelligible heaven see also *QE* 2.37 (exeg. Exod 24:11). On the special light of creation in Second temple Jewish sources see Kugel *TB*, 72–74.

source of the visible stars. Boyancé (1963a, 102) finds the image of source odd for the participation of the sensible in the intelligible, but it is the same image of emanation so favoured by Plotinus, which is particularly suited to light, heat and other forms of physical power (or energy, as we would say).

'all-brightness'. As a TLG search shows, the word παναύγεια is only found here (and in Eusebius who cites this passage) in the whole of Greek literature. Boyancé's hypothesis, loc. cit., that Philo must have drawn it from a philosophical source is quite unnecessary. We have already seen (above §16) that he likes coining unusual compound words. There are frequent examples of compounds with παν- (= all) in his works, some of which are quite rare: see, for example παμμήτωρ at §133, παμπρύτανις at *Somn.* 1.142 (unique according to the TLG), πανάρχοντες at *Prob.* 42 (only one other example).

in accordance with the capacity they each have. Compare the capacity to receive goodness outlined in §23. Presumably the sun is brighter than the other heavenly bodies because it is able to draw a greater amount of light. At *Spec.* 1.279 God is called the "sun of sun, being in the intelligible realm what it is in the sense-perceptible, supplying from invisible fountains the visible beams to the person who sees." In this passage "God" is used as a form of theological short-hand. There is no need for Philo to go into details on the Logos and the intelligible cosmos in every case. Hovering in the background is Plato's comparison of the sun with the idea of the Good in *Resp.* 508–509.

unmixed and pure gleam has its brightness dimmed. The same term αὐγή that forms the basis of παναύγεια used above. At *Aet.* 86 Philo describes αὐγή as one of the three forms of fire: live coal, flame, and fire as light. The last-named is "what co-operates with the eyes to enable apprehension of visible things." When Plato at *Phdr.* 250c4 describes the contemplation of the incorporeal souls which have ascended to the *hyperouranios topos*, he says it occurs "in pure brightness (ἐν αὐγῇ καθαρᾷ)." The same phrase is quite common in Philo, e.g. *Deus* 3, 29, 135.

absolutely pure. Light is not absolutely pure because it has an admixture of the corporeal, i.e. in terms of ancient physics, fire. But if the dazzling light of the sun is impure, imagine how overwhelming the absolutely pure intelligible light must be!

(2c) §32. **Well said too** ... The third of Philo's explanatory comments on the seven chief ideas in Gen 1:1–3. Philo regularly makes encomiastic remarks about Moses as thinker and writer; cf. also §§65, 131. The implication here is that he adapts his presentation to the level of his readers.

it is mounted on and has filled up the entire gaping, empty and void space. The void as (conceptual) empty space (cf. above on §29) forms a kind of substrate for the whole of physical reality, including earth and heaven. But it is best visualized in the case of air, which is emptier than the other regions of the cosmos. In the four-tiered universe of the Platonic-Aristotelian worldview the region of the air stretches from the earth to the moon; cf. the place of air in the "phytological cosmology" at *Plant.* 3. Once again we might be excused for thinking that Philo is talking about the physical rather than the intelligible world. On whether he is thinking about the idea of air here, or rather the idea of the region of the cosmos, and whether we learn anything about primordial matter, see the Excursus below.

(3) §33. *He not only separated light and darkness.* Compare Philo's excursus on the Logos as divider in *Her.* 133–236, where Gen 1:4–5 is cited at §163, but with an added emphasis on equality. Horovitz (1900, 68) makes two pertinent comments. He notes that Philo appears to have forgotten here that in §29 and §32 darkness is taken to represent the air. The inconsistency is perhaps surmountable if we recall that the darkness of the air is caused by the absence of light (cf. above on §29), i.e. darkness makes itself manifest above all in the air. He also observes that Philo's exegesis contains some similarities to what we find in the Midrash. Cf. Gen. Rab. 3.7:

> Imagine a king who had two chiefs of the guards, one in command by day and the other in command at night, who used to quarrel with one another ... Thereupon the king summoned the first and said to him, "So-and-so, the day shall be your province;" summoning the second he addressed him, "So-and-so, the night shall be your province."

Philo is rather plastic and concrete here, but even so he is more philosophically minded than the rabbis. Light and darkness conflict because they are opposites. Both, however, are firmly under the control of the creator, unlike in the Manichean cosmogony that Augustine found so difficult to surmount; cf. *Conf.* 5.19–21.

would strip in readiness. A metaphor from athletics and esp. wrestling. On such metaphors see the comments on §44. For the term ἐπαποδύομαι see Harris 1976, 112; it is also used at *Abr.* 256, *Det.* 32. V has the correct reading here, in contrast to the other mss. which did not understand the metaphor.

§34. *evening and morning.* The same order as in the biblical text of Gen 1:5.

Mark well, however. Philo is thus aware that his descriptions could lead the reader to forget that the whole of "day one" refers to the intelligible cosmos.

ideas and measures and marks and seals. The list summarizes the terms used to explain the relation between the two worlds in §§16–25. See esp. our comments on §§16, 18, 24.

§35. *necessarily entailed.* If you have an evening and a morning, then you must necessarily also obtain a day, since a day can be defined as the space of time between one evening (or morning) and the next. Philo ignores the fact that in Gen 1:5a day is equated with light and night with darkness.

a measure of time. Once again the relation between the two worlds becomes problematic. In §13 days were not temporal in any way, but symbolic and arithmological. Moreover, as we read in *Deus* 32 (cf. *Mut.* 267), there is no time in the intelligible cosmos, but its life is time's archetypal model, αἰών (usually translated "eternity"), in which there is no past and future, but only the present. At *Mut.* 267 Philo interprets "another year" (Gen 17:21) not as an ordinary interval of time, but as something mysterious and strange and new, belonging to the incorporeal realm. Perhaps this is similar to what Philo intends here, not a day in any literal sense, but a symbolic day, not to be compared with other days, as shown in the phrase "day one." On the theme of *aiôn* in Philo see now Keizer 1999, 205–246, who argues that it always relates to created reality, not to God himself, and that it links up the themes of time, life and wholeness.

aloneness ... the nature of the unit. The association of the intelligible world with the aloneness (μόνωσις) of the unit — it is a number that cannot be counted with any other, being neither odd nor even — was not yet stated above in §15, when Philo first explains the significance of "day one." Compare Theon of Smyrna *Expos.* 19.12: "It is called monad either from remaining (μένειν) unchanged and not stepping outside its nature ... or from having been separated and *become alone* (μεμονῶσθαι) in relation to the remaining multitude of numbers." Philo thus neatly rounds off his treatment of "day one" by emphasizing the most striking aspect of his interpretation.

EXCURSUS
Wolfson's and Winston's interpretation of §29

In a controversial section of his great study on Philo's thought, Wolfson (1947 1.306–310) contended that an interpretation of §§29–32 can shed light on the vexed question of *creatio ex nihilo* and the origin of matter in Philo. In a somewhat simplified form the argument is as follows. The seven chief items of the intelligible cosmos in §29 refer to the ideas of the four elements (heaven = fire, air, water, earth), the void, life and light. The creation of the idea of the void is a deliberate rewriting of Plato's account in the *Timaeus*, where the receptacle, the place in which the cosmos is created, is postulated as the third genus, but Plato does not make clear where it comes from, and whether it is eternal or not. Philo introduces clarity on this point. Since the ideas of the elements, and also the idea of the void, are created by God, it must follow that the void and the copies of the elements which appear in the void must also be created by him (Wolfson also appeals to *Conf.* 136 for this). This means that the matter of the cosmos must be created, i.e. Philo indirectly indicates in this passage that he holds the doctrine of *creatio ex nihilo*.

Winston (*PA* 10–12) comments on this interpretation. He appears to accept the interpretation of §29 in terms of ideas of the four elements and the void, but notes that two further modifications on Philo's part were overlooked by Wolfson. Plato does not conceive of an idea of space (i.e. the void) and he never calls his receptacle the void. He goes on to argue that analysis of the implicit argument in the passage leads to the conclusion that Philo espoused a doctrine of *creatio aeterna*.

Although I am in agreement with both scholars that the influence of Plato's *Timaeus* is very strong in the opening chapters of *Opif.*, I am persuaded that they read more into the text than it can bear. It seems to me that even the conclusion that Philo introduces here the forms of the four elements is doubtful. There is no mention of fire in §29, but only of heaven. Air is described as extending from the earth to the moon in §32. It seems to me likely that Philo is thinking more of the regions of the cosmos in their intelligible form (which of course are related to the elements, but are not identical). As we noted throughout our commentary, Philo, taking the Platonist two-worlds theory as his point of departure, is rather concrete in his descriptions of the intelligible cosmos, even though he does warn his reader to bear in mind the difference between intelligible and sense-perceptible things (§§31, 34). The contents of the intelligible cosmos are not used as the basis of an argument on the first principles of physical reality. For references to other discussions of Wolfson's argument (mainly critical — it is only accepted in full by Reale 1979 only) see Radice *FM* 248.

Parallel exegesis

The most important parallel texts have already been mentioned in our commentary above: *Spec.* 2.59 and *Leg.* 1.18, implicitly referring to Gen. 1:3, above on §29; *Somn.* 1.75, in which Gen 1:3 is cited (cf. also *Abr.* 156), above on §31; *Her.* 163, in which Gen 1:4 is cited, above on §33. In *Somn.* 1.75 it can be assumed that Philo has the creation of intelligible entities in mind. This is not the case for the other texts. Alternative exegeses where the "spirit of God" in Gen 1:2 is interpreted with reference to the physical world are found in *Gig.* 22 and *QG* 4.5.

Nachleben

For the rare patristic interpretations of the contents of "day one" in terms of the intelligible cosmos see Ch. 4. Note especially the reference to

Clement *Strom.* 5.93.5, where a very brief summary of §29 is given in which only three items of the seven are taken over. Eusebius *Praep. Ev.* 11.24.7–12 cites §§29–31 and §§35–36 as additional evidence of the Mosaic theory of ideas. Apart from these two texts, Philo's exegesis in §§29–35 appears to have exerted little influence. Martín (1986, 156–160) points to Theophilus *Ad Aut.* 2.13 and his portrayal of the creation of the four elements, but the relation seems to me tenuous (note that for Theophilus only the first heaven is invisible, and so possibly intelligible). At *Comm. Matt.* frg. on 25:30 Origen states that "we read one of our predecessors who gave an exposition on the darkness of the abyss (Gen 1:2) and said that the abyss and the darkness were outside the cosmos." This *could* refer to Philo, though it does not fit in too well with Philo's interpretation in terms of an intelligible world; see further the discussion at Van den Hoek 2000a, 95.

Interesting too are possible links with Jewish exegesis. The text in *Jubilees* 2:2–3 has been mentioned above in connection with §29, but it is a parallel rather than a case of influence (*Jubilees* is dated to the 2nd cent. B.C.E. and considered to be of Palestinian provenance). This is not the case for the very late *Midrash Tadsche* 6, where it is stated that seven kinds are created on the first day, exactly those seven found in Philo on the basis of Gen 1:1–3. In the light of other Philonic borrowings in this document (on which see further Ch. 15 *Nachleben*), I agree with Epstein (1890, 85) and J. Cohn (PCH 1.36 n.) against Wolfson (1947, 1.306 n.) that the author has taken his cue from Philo. Other rabbinic texts recounting seven things created by God before creation (Torah, tabernacle etc.) are not directly relevant to our text, *pace* Cohn ibid., as rightly argued by Wolfson ibid.

Further reading: Radice *FM* 247–250; Runia *PT* 287–289; Winston *PA* 10–13, 100; 1984, 24; Wolfson 1947, 1.300–310 (see Excursus above); Bormann 1955, 42–44 (on Wolfson).

Chapter Seven
Second day: creation of the firmament (§§36–37)

Analysis/General comments

Philo now turns to the second day of creation described in Gen 1:6–8. His treatment is remarkably brief, covering no more than a dozen lines of text, and proceeds in four brief steps.

(a) He first recalls that the transition from "day one" to the second day is the transition from the intelligible to the sense-perceptible cosmos. The formulation of the difference between the two worlds deliberately picks up the terminology that he had set out with much care in §§16–25 (§36).

(b) God is then described as creating the heaven and naming it "firmament." The Greek term used is quite unusual, but it can be exploited because it is related to the Greek word for "solid." Moses thus indicates, in Philo's view, that the second day involves the transition to corporeal reality, which has as its chief feature that it is three-dimensional and solid. Philo surprisingly decides not to devote any attention to the number two in this context, although there were excellent possibilities he might have exploited (§36).

(c) Moses also describes God as calling the firmament "heaven." Here too the etymology is not without significance, because it indicates either that heaven is a "limit" or the first of "visible things" (§37).

(d) Finally Philo notes that after the creation of the heaven Moses names the day the "second." The heaven — but not the heavenly beings located in it — is the only thing created on the day, it seems. On no other day does the creator do so little. This accords, Philo argues, with the high rank and value that the heaven enjoys in the realm of physical reality (§37).

In fact more happens in the Genesis text than Philo wants to explain. His final remarks are a bit of a cover-up. Moses also speaks of the division of firmament into the waters above and below it. But there is simply no way that Philo can fit the cosmology presupposed in the biblical text into his strongly hellenized cosmology, in which the contents of heaven are the heavenly bodies consisting of ensouled fire or ether. These heavenly creatures will be formed on the fourth day. So what we have here is the creation of the whole without its parts. We note too that, although heaven is mentioned for the second time in the biblical text (also earlier at Gen 1:1), Philo does not draw attention to this double mention explicitly. The exegetical problem involved is dealt with implicitly, by means of his explanation in terms of the relation between the intelligible and the corporeal cosmos as wholes.

For discussion of the specific cosmological features of the biblical creation account and their religious and philosophical significance, see — in addition to the Genesis Commentary of Westermann 1984 — Knight 1985 and Oden 1992. Knight rightly draws attention to the strong emphasis on order, which Philo translates and "modernizes" in terms of the Platonic-Aristotelian worldview dominant in his time.

Detailed comments

(a) §36. *the incorporeal cosmos*. Philo deliberately picks up the terminology which he had introduced and used extensively in §§16–25: for ἀσώματος, cf. §§16, 18; θεῖος λόγος §20; αἰσθητὸς κόσμος §§19, 25; παράδειγμα §§16, 18, 19, 25. The phrase ἀσώματος κόσμος, however, is new. It also occurs in §55; *Spec.* 1.302; *Conf.* 172; *QG* 4.8 (Greek frg. at Petit PAPM 33.148). See further our Commentary in Ch. 4.

had been completed. The Greek πέρας εἶχε means literally "had (or held) a limit (or completion)." The term *peras* in this context is intriguing. Philo may be wishing to indicate that the formation of the intelligible cosmos in the divine Logos is a delimitation of God's infinite (and inscrutable) wisdom. See further the Analysis in Ch. 4 and our comments on §23.

(b) *creator*. The Platonic term δημιουργός is now for the first time in the treatise specifically applied to God. See the comments on §§10 and 18. From now on it is applied to God and will be translated as "creator;" see also §§68, 72, 138, 139, 146, 171.

correctly. The term ἐτύμως indicates that there is a true and valid etymology involved. For Philo the importance of the naming carried out both by Moses as author and by God in the biblical narrative lies in the fact that the terms used yield vital information about the nature of the things created. In the Genesis text God is not explicitly said to name the firmament (v. 6), as is the case for the heaven in v. 8 given exegesis in §37, but it should be assumed that he is the subject of both verbs. On etymologies see further the comments on §127, on the importance of naming in the treatise see the comments on §148.

firmament. The Greek word στερέωμα in the LXX renders *râqî'a* in the Hebrew Bible and has its roots in Hebrew cosmological conceptions (cf. Westermann 1984, 117–118). The subsequent popularity of this term in the Judaeo-Christian tradition should not blind us to the fact that in Philo's time it must have been a rare and unusual word. As noted by Alexandre (*CLG* 102), there is no precedent for its application to the heaven in earlier Greek literature. In a report of the doctrine of Anaxagoras and Democritus it is used to show that the moon is a fiery *mass* or *lump of earth* (Aëtius at Ps.-Plutarch *Plac.* 2.25, Stobaeus *Ecl.* 1.26.1). This shows that the link that Philo makes, via the etymology, with materiality is plausible enough. But it should be noted that Philo does nothing with the cosmological purport of the term and gives it a philosophical and symbolic meaning. The fact that he only uses the word here and at *Conf.* 96 (when citing Exod 24:10) may be an indication of his embarrassment with a rare and unconventional term.

solid, because ... extended in three directions. A link is plausibly laid between στερέωμα and the word στερεός, meaning solid, massive. In the text of the Latin Bible the same connection was made between *firmus* and *firmamentum*, from where our word "firmament" derives. Solidity as characteristic of the body of the cosmos consisting of the four elements is emphasized by Plato at *Tim.* 31b4–8, where he uses the term στερεός at 31b6 and associates it above all with earth; See further Runia *PT* 178. The connection between the three-dimensionality of body and solidity is found in the Stoic definition attributed to Apollodorus at Diogenes Laertius 7.135 (= L&S §45E): "Body is what has threefold extension (τὸ τριχῇ διαστατόν) — length, breadth and depth; this is also called solid body (στερεὸν σῶμα)." The wording corresponds exactly to our text (which Von Arnim includes as *SVF* 2.358). Philo does not include, however, the aspect of resistance (ἀντιτυπία), which the standard Stoic definition includes (cf. L&S §45F). Philo returns to the subject of three-dimensionality in his exposition of the tetrad at §49.

Suitably. This is the first time that Philo uses the adverb εἰκότως, one of his favourite terms for expressing the inherent plausibility and conformity to rational expectation of scripture as expounded in the exegete's interpretation. Such explanation, however, is *not* to be equated with the absolute truth, as is made very clear below in §45. Further examples at §§59, 63, 133.

(c) §37. **he named it heaven**. In this chapter, as in the previous ones, there are problems with regard to the question who names what. None of the three verbs of naming have an explicit subject. Here the subject must be God, because he is explicitly mentioned as naming the firmament "heaven" in Gen 1:8. In the other two cases the subject should be Moses. See also comments on §29.

boundary ... first of the visible things. Again the etymology is considered to be instructive (see notes on §36). Etymology here consists not so much in finding and explaining the root of the word, but rather in making a link with similar sounding words. This practice is parodied by Plato in the *Cratylus*, but he uses it extensively himself, and is followed therein by Aristotle and notoriously by the Stoa. In this case οὐρανός is connected with ὅρος (boundary) and ὁρατός (visible). Heaven is the boundary of the cosmos because in the Platonic-Aristotelian world-view there is no void outside it; see our comments above on §29. This contrasts above all with the atomistic world-view in which there is an infinite number of *kosmoi* separated by empty space (briefly alluded too below on §171; see our comments ad loc.). For this first etymology cf. Ps.-Aristotle *Mund.* 6, 400a7 (combined with ἄνω, upwards); Cornutus 1, 1.4 Lang; Achilles *Isagoge* 5,

36.13 Maass (perhaps from Eudorus); etc. Philo also alludes to it at *Plant.* 3; *Her.* 227–229. A different parallel is found at Timaeus Locrus 8 and 11, where the model is regarded as the absolute boundary of the noetic realm, the cosmos (not the heaven) as that of the sense-perceptible realm. The Platonist two-worlds representation is very close to what we find in our Philonic text, but the etymology is not exploited.

The second etymology is Platonic; cf. *Resp.* 509d3, implicit in *Tim.* 32a6–7. The former text is a *locus classicus* for the Platonist two-worlds doctrine (division into ὁρατόν and νοητόν, mention of the νοητὸς τόπος). Philo adapts it by interpreting it as indicating what is visible *par excellence*. "First" is meant in terms of the narrative, but from §13 we know that ontological precedence is the truer meaning. On *QG* 1.64 see Parallel exegesis below.

second. The Mosaic narrative shifts from the cardinal to the ordinal number (contrast §15), but Philo does not draw attention to the fact. The arithmological sources emphasize that the dyad, resulting from the doubling of the monad, symbolizes the emergence of matter, visibility and genesis; cf. Theon of Smyrna *Expos.* 109.9–12, other texts given by Staehle 1931, 22. Philo alludes to this doctrine in *Spec.* 3.180; *Praem.* 46; *Leg.* 1.3; *Somn.* 2.70. It would have suited his interpretation of the transition to the visible world well. The reason he omits it probably has to do with his adherence to the biblical text. As we observed above on §36, the theme of solidity is connected arithmologically with the tetrad and is explained in §49.

its high value and honour. In the geocentric and hierarchical Platonic-Aristotelian cosmology the further an object is from the centre, the higher its ontological status. The stars, as highest beings of all, have perfectly regular and unchanging movements. Moreover the heaven as realm of immortality is regarded as having no part whatsoever in evil. Two Philonic texts which illustrate these views are:

> *Mos.* 2.194: For in the universe heaven is a most holy palace, whereas earth is an outer region, in itself worthy enough, but in comparison with the ether as inferior as darkness is compared with light, night with day, destruction with indestructibility, mortal with God.
> *QG* 4.57: ... for who does not know that heaven has no share or mixture or part of evil, nor do whatever sense-perceptible gods (cf. §28) are borne in a circle around it, for they are all good and altogether most perfect in virtue (trans. Marcus LCL)?

For lengthier passages which indicate the place of heaven in the cosmos see *Plant.* 3–9 and the symbolism of the high-priestly robes in *Mos.* 2.117–135. On the role of heaven in Philo's cosmology and exegesis see further Harl PAPM 15.94–99.

Parallel exegeses

Philo does not refer explicitly to Gen 1:6–8 elsewhere in his writings. At *QG* 1.64 he gives an exegesis of Gen 4:7 which leads him to expatiate on the theme of cosmological division: "But he [the Creator] marked off and separated the pure nature, heaven, and surrounded and enclosed the universe by it, that it might be visible to all ..." Aucher (1826, 44) rightly conjectured "visible" for the Armenian reading "invisible" (the conjecture is taken over by Mercier PAPM 34A.135). So we have the same play on words that we found in §37. But there is no direct reference to the biblical text; this is also not the case in the better-known passage on cosmological division at *Her.* 133–136.

Nachleben

In spite of its brevity various ideas launched by Philo in this passage were taken over or adapted by the Fathers.

(1) The earliest Christian exegesis is found in Theophilus *Ad Aut.* 2.13, where a distinction is made between the heaven (in Gen 1:1) which is invisible to us (ἀόρατος), "after which this heaven visible to us (ὁρατός) is called στερέωμα." Here we have the same play on words as in Philo, but the essential distinction between intelligible and visible is missing. Other details of Theophilus' exegesis are also very different. As noted above (see Ch. 1 *Nachleben*), it has proved extremely difficult to determine whether Theophilus is directly dependent on Philo or not. On this passage see further Martín 1986, 159–160.

(2) As noted by Le Boulluec 1981, 302, at *Strom.* 5.94.1 Clement gives a brief summary of §36 (with brief allusions to §38 and §55 added). He avoids the word στερέωμα and speaks of a στερεὸς οὐρανός instead.

(3) Similarly Origen at *Hom. Gen.* 1.2 has the same idea as §36 and appears to take over some of the terminology (*corporeum caelum, corpus firmum ... et solidum*); cf. Van den Hoek 2000a, 65, who concludes that "dependence seems likely." Basil takes the exegesis over in *Hex.* 3, 25c-d, but adds the notion of resistance (ἀντιτυπία) from the Stoic definition which Philo leaves out. The rest of Basil's lengthy exegesis concentrates on the cosmological issues that Philo avoids.

(4) Eusebius paraphrases §36 at *Praep. Ev.* 11.6.19 and then quotes it verbatim in 11.24.12 as continuation of §35, illustrating the Mosaic theory of ideas. In the former passage he also makes a link with Plato's etymology of οὐρανός in the *Cratylus* (ἄνω ὁρᾶν), no doubt inspired by Philo, though the etymology differs.

(5) The firmament as limit of corporeal reality is taken over by Gregory of Nyssa, *Apol. Hex.* §§18–23 Forbes, where the terms ὅρος and πέρας are both used.

On the Jewish side Josephus *Ant.* 1.30 avoids the term στερέωμα, and links the heaven with ice (explaining its solidity) and water (the waters of the biblical text). This can be compared with a rabbinic text such *Gen. Rab.* 4.2; see further Ginzberg 1909–38, 1.13.

Further reading: Radice 1987, 250–252; Runia *PT* 174; Alexandre *CLG* 102–112 (on the *Nachleben*).

Chapter Eight
Third day: creation of the earth (§§38–44)

Analysis/General comments

The treatment of the third day is longer than that of the second day, but is still on the short side. The larger themes of the biblical text are picked up, but most details are neglected, while the specific terminology of the LXX is largely ignored. Philo divides the account into two parts, dealing first with the formation of the earth as described in Gen 1:9–10, and second with the creation of the botanical world portrayed in Gen 1:11–13.

(1a) First a description is given of the situation before the divine command is given. The elements water and earth were amorphously mixed together, forming a kind of smooth mixture of mud. Water appears to have the upper hand, because land is not visible and has to be brought forth (this is the reason that God's command is addressed to the water) (§38).

(1b) Next the separation of salt water at God's command is described, allowing the dry land to emerge. The dry land still contains water, but this water is sweet and is required not only to keep the earth from crumbling, but also to supply nourishment for living beings. Philo, by giving a division of the various kinds of water involved (see the comments on §38), supplements the biblical account (§§38–39).

(1c) A brief paraphrase is then given of the naming of earth and sea, as described in Gen 1:10 (§39).

(2a) In the second half of the passage Philo moves on to the creation of the botanical world. In terms of content he adheres reasonably close to the biblical text, although there is very little terminological overlap. Firstly, the divine command is set out, as given in v. 11. God orders plants or grasses to grow, which produce crops, and then also trees, which produce fruit (§40).

(2b) Next he reflects on the fact that all the trees that God commands to be created immediately bear fruit. For Philo the chicken definitely precedes the egg. In a rather verbose description he outlines the normal cycle of origin and growth in the botanical world, with which the process of immediately achieved creation is contrasted. This is reminiscent of the statements of creation all at once in §§13, 28 and 67. But in the final sentence there is a difference of emphasis. All has to be in readiness for the emergence of living beings. The motive is thus not theological and cosmological, but teleological and (as emerges more clearly in §§79–81) anthropocentric (§§41–42).

(2c) Finally Philo expounds the response of the earth to God's command, as described in v. 12. The earth gives birth to the kinds of plants and fruit that have already been described. But Philo also takes the opportunity to broach an additional theme, inspired by the biblical description of plants in v. 11–12, σπεῖρον σπέρμα κατὰ γένος καὶ καθ' ὁμοιότητα (sowing seed according to kind and according to similarity). The botanical world is not only created ready for use, but is also equipped for the perpetuation of the species, as observed especially in the seeds of plants, in which the patterns of the species to be reproduced are found. It should be noted finally that the last short verse on the duration of the third day, v. 13, is wholly ignored. This is the only day for which Philo makes not a single reference, whether explicit or implicit, to arithmological lore (§§43–44).

The events of the third day move the exegete's attention to the earthly realm. In drawing on philosophical and scientific literature for explanatory purposes, Philo can no longer make use of Plato's *Timaeus*, which does not explain the formation of earth and scarcely pays any attention to the plant world. In describing the primeval situation of mud and ooze, it may be suspected that he was helped more by cosmogonic than by cosmological literature, since in the latter the final (and incomplete) separation of water and earth is taken as a fact. Reminiscent of Philo's description are mechanistic-evolutionist accounts which contain descriptions of primal mud (see the comments on §38). An important difference, however, is that these accounts do not share Philo's teleological framework. Other sources of inspiration are accounts of great floods, e.g. the disaster on a cosmic scale envisaged by Seneca in *Nat.* 3.27–30. The descriptions in Philo closest to what we find here are precisely those describing the effects of the great flood of Gen 6–8; see further Parallel exegesis.

But even before Philo embarks on his description of the plant realm, his thought contains overtly teleological features. Sweet water is required for plants to grow and for living beings to be able to live. The description of the earth as mother will be further developed in §§131–133 in connection with Gen 2:6. Then, when the plants and trees are ordered to appear, they do so fully developed, thus providing food for the living beings that would be created on the fifth and sixth day. The teleology of Philo's botany of course corresponds to Aristotle's teleological view of the workings of nature, which is taken over in the Stoa. Moreover he also assumes the Aristotelian doctrine of the permanence and immortality of the species, which reproduce themselves in a never-ending cyclical process. The overt anthropological emphasis, however, is not Aristotelian and corresponds to Plato's brief remark at *Tim.* 77a-c. Implicit here is an answer to the exegetical question why the creation of the botanical world occurs at this point in the creational sequence. As is stated explicitly at §§77–81, the earth had to be brought in readiness for the animals that would be created on the fifth and sixth days. We might compare the idea found in some Second Temple Jewish and rabbinic texts that paradise was created on the third day; see *Jubilees* 2:7; *Gen. Rab.* 12.5; Kugel *TB*, 57, 111.

Detailed comments

(1) §38. **had been poured out.** The term ἀναχέω used of water is characteristic for Philo's description of the great flood; cf. *Abr.* 42; *Mos.* 2.63; and also *Aet.* 147 (flood as natural catastrophe, together with fire). As Radice (*FM* 254) rightly notes, Philo appears to see a parallel between the primal situation of the third day and the result of the great flood; see the descriptions of the latter at *Abr.* 42–44; *Mos.* 2.63; *QG* 2.18, 29. Noah is thus compared with Adam; cf. *QG* 2.66 (in which Gen 1:9 is cited; see Parallel exegesis).

swamps and deep mud. Primal ooze or mud is a common feature of many Greek cosmogonic accounts. A fine example is found at the beginning of Diodorus Siculus' *Universal History*:

> ... all that was mud-like and thick and contained an admixture of moisture sank because of its weight into one place; and as this continually turned about upon itself and became compressed, out of the wet it formed the sea and out of what was firmer, the land, which was like potter's clay and entirely soft. But as the sun's fire shone upon the land, it first of all became firm ... (*Bibl.* 1.7.1, transl Oldfather LCL)

Similar accounts are found in Lucretius 5.480–499; Ovid *Met.* 1.5–20; on such cosmogonies, which have a history going back to Presocratic natural philosophy, see further Spoerri 1959, 1–45. Philo cannot of course appeal to the role of the sun because it has not yet been created. An interesting allegorical application of the theme of flooding is found at *Her.* 32: if the torrent of God's goodness is too great, our fields will not be able to cope and will become like a swamp (τελματῶδης) instead of fruitful soil; the inflow thus has to be measured out for fertility (cf. the theme of measurement in §23).

both elements having being mixed and confounded ... This is the first time that Philo uses the term στοιχεῖον in the treatise. The negative treatment of mixture and confusion which we noted in comment on §28 is not found here. Indeed it will emerge at §136 that the mixture has some positive characteristics.

(1b) *water ... assemble.* The compound verb ἐπισυναχθῆναι is plainly derived from the LXX συναθήτω ... εἰς συναγωγὴν μίαν, but apart from the terms for water and dry land it is the only reminder of the biblical text. We note how Philo omits the description of the water as being "under the heaven," for the same reason as his omission of the division of waters in §36. But his description of the various kinds of water that ensue from God's command goes into more detail than is found in the biblical text. Implicit is the following straightforward division:

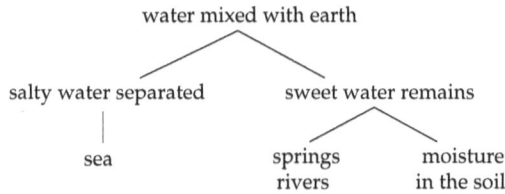

Philo wants to supplement the biblical account and make it more precise. We can compare the division into salt and sweet water at *Her.* 136; *Somn.* 1.18. But, as Radice (*FM* 253) rightly points out, the cosmological scheme of division which Philo exploits at great length in *Her.* 133–160 does not form the basis for Philo's account here. The division into salt and sweet water is repeated at §131, where it is attributed to the insightfulness of Moses

kind of glue. The idea that earth needs moisture as a binding element or glue to stop it from crumbling and falling apart is a fairly commonplace scientific idea; cf. Aristotle *Mete.* 4.4, 382b1 (citing Empedocles); Plotinus *Enn.* 2.1.6 (contrasting it with *Tim.* 31b). There seems no need to regard this passage as specifically exploiting the doctrine of the 1st cent. B.C.E. Stoic philosopher Posidonius, as postulated by Theiler 1982, F308, who goes so far as to include our §38 and §131 as fragments!; see also 1971, 33. Rather similar to Philo is a text on the earth in Pliny's *Natural History*:

> The reason for this formation [of earth and water] must be thought to be the inability of earth when absolutely dry to cohere of itself and without moisture, and of water in its turn to remain standing without being held up by earth; the intention of the artificer of nature must have been to unite earth and water in a mutual embrace, earth opening her bosom and water penetrating her entire frame by means of a network of veins radiating within and without ... (2.166, trans. Rackham LCL)

We note the same teleological approach that we find in Philo. The idea is further developed and expanded in §131 on Gen 2:6. According to Seneca *Nat.* 2.1.4 questions about the properties of earth and its relation to water belong to geology and are separated from the higher science of cosmology. Philo is thus exploiting well-known scientific ideas.

like a mother. The image of the earth as a mother giving birth to life and having springs and channels like breasts is another commonplace theme, developed at greater length in §§132–133 (on Gen 2:6), where it suits the exegetical context better than here. The same idea is developed in the cosmogonic context at *Plant.* 15. See further our comments in Ch. 17.

§39. *crops.* The Greek word καρπός causes a difficulty for the translator and interpreter because it means both the produce of plants (e.g. corn) and the fruit of trees (e.g. apples). I have translated according to the context. Here the former is primarily intended; in §40 only the latter can be meant.

(1c) *calling ... the separated water sea.* Note two differences in relation to the biblical text. In Gen 1:9 it is the collected waters that are named, for Philo it is the water that has been separated off (from the earth). The LXX speaks of "seas" plural, Philo changes to the singular (just like Josephus *Ant.* 1.31). As the parallel passage at §131 indicates, Philo is thinking of the Ocean which surrounds the entire earth. The word θάλασσα is seldom used in the plural in standard Greek. Philo thus "normalizes" the language of the LXX.

(2a) §40. *giving the earth its adornment.* Philo uses the term διακοσμέω five times for the creation of heaven and earth (also §§45, 47, 53, 62). Since Anaxagoras (frg. 59B12 DK, Plato *Phd.* 97c2) it had been a standard term (together with its noun διακόσμησις) for the ordered formation of the cosmos in Greek philosophy (e.g. Plato *Tim.* 37d5; Ps.-Aristotle *Mund.* 2, 392b12), and was especially associated with the cyclical process of Stoic cosmo-biology (cf. the doxography at *Aet.* 4). But as §62 suggests, Philo is also mindful of the summarizing words at Gen 2:1, "when the heaven and the earth and all their adornment (κόσμος) were completed," and so deliberately uses the term for the adornment of heaven and earth. In this instance, therefore, philosophical and biblical terminology converge.

plants and well-grassed plains. The terms βοτάνας and εὔχορτα are clearly based on the language of the LXX, which speaks of βοτάνην χόρτου, "pasture of grass." See further below on §43.

all kinds of trees. Alexandre (*CLG* 127) notes how Philo replaces the LXX word for tree ξυλόν (which normally means cut wood, log) with the more classical term δένδρον.

so-called domesticated timber. The noun here is ὕλη. Originally it meant wood or timber, but mainly through the agency of Aristotle and the Stoa it comes to mean more generally "material" or, even more abstractly, "matter." Here the original meaning is retained. The adjective ἥμερος can be used of both animals and plants. Not surprisingly in the light of his vast general knowledge, Philo is well aware of the process of grafting plants; at *Det.* 107 he states that he observed this being carried out, perhaps on the family estates; see also *Agr.* 6.

(2b) §41. *all together at a single opportune time.* "All together" in the sense of no temporal differentiation. The Greek term καιρός means the right or appointed time for something. It can also mean "season" (cf. below §59), but that cannot be the right meaning here, since crops and fruits reach maturity at different seasons, as Philo points out in a different context at §116.

first perceptibles. This reads like a technical term in botany. But I have not found any parallels. It is worth bearing in mind that the ancients never had the benefit of any form of magnification.

as if produced with a painter's art. The technological metaphor for creation (on which see the introduction, §5c) is now adapted to the aspect of colour. For the theme of variety see the comment on the verb ποικίλλω below at §45.

§42. ***timber.*** See the note above on §40. Here one might also translate "material."

imperfect. The word ἀτελής has the same root as in τέλειος (complete), meaning that it has not yet reached its τέλος or "end-point."

use and enjoyment. The same pair of nouns are used in the elaborate description of creation as a banquet for the benefit of humans in §78. This suggests that here too Philo primarily has human beings in mind, i.e. his approach is anthropocentric. See further Ch. 14.

(2c) §43. ***The earth, like a woman.*** The image of the earth as mother is repeated from §38; see our comments there.

spermatic substances ... invisible patterns. The biblical text, which in v. 12 speaks of grass "sowing seed" (σπεῖρον σπέρμα) and fruit containing "seed" (σπέρμα again) induces Philo to expatiate with the mention of σπερματικαὶ οὐσίαι which contain ἄδηλοι λόγοι. This recalls the well-known Stoic theory of the *spermatikoi logoi*, developed on the basis of Aristotelian biology (cf. Hahm 1977, 75–77; Von Arnim includes this text as *SVF* 2.713). With amazing intuition the Stoics deduced that the seed must contain a kind of formula which determined the ordered growth of the organism (both plant and animal). This pattern was material, but could not be seen ("indistinct," ἄδηλος, is also an Epicurean term, that which is "not evident," and so has to be determined by extrapolation on the basis of experience, cf. Diogenes Laertius 10.32). One cannot but think of the modern discovery of DNA. The Stoa gives the theme an important place in their cosmo-biological ideas (cf. L&S §46A, also *Aet.* 85; *QG* 2.16). Philo also refers to the theory at *Legat.* 55; *Anim.* 20, 96 (see the notes of Terian 1981, ad loc.). At *Her.* 115 he emphasizes that "the first beginnings of plants" start not with the sowing of the farmer, but with the "invisible deeds of invisible nature" which is in turn equated with God (cf. also *Her.* 119). This text implies that Philo does not share the Stoics' materialism. The patterns (*logoi*) can be best understood as immanent dynamic forms.

§44. ***run a cyclical race.*** Philo employs here one of his favourite images, the metaphor of an athletic race held in a stadium. The competitors run the full length of the stadium till they reach the turning point. Then they have to make a sharp 180° turn and run all the way back on the other side. In fact we have to distinguish between two kinds of races, the δίαυλος involving one circuit, and the δόλιχος consisting of several laps. As the verb δολιχεύειν indicates, in the present passage Philo exploits the latter image (also found in §§85, 113, and *QE* 1.1 cited below), while the former is used at §101.

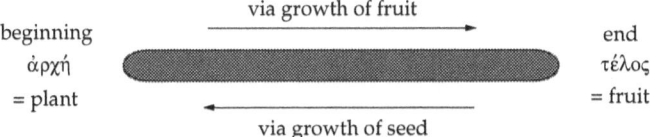

As Winston (*PA* 341) points out, the image is already used by Aristotle for the process of genesis (*Gen. An.* 2.5, 741b24). Philo uses the metaphor of the athletic race for all manner of cyclical processes (plants again in §113, phases of the moon in §101, youth and old age in *Aet.* 58, the motions of the planets in *Decal.* 104, the activity of the immanent Logos in *Plant.* 9, and so on). On Philo's love of athletic images see the monograph of Harris 1976, on the two kinds of races and this text 61–63. He rightly points out that the *dolichos* is the more suitable metaphor in the present context, because the growth and reproduction of plants is an on-going process.

immortalizing the kinds and giving them a share of eternity. The term γένη (kinds) is evidently inspired by the phrase κατὰ γένος (after its kind), which occurs twice in v. 12 of the Genesis text. There it is meant to refer to the various species of grass and fruit, but in Philo the philosophical sense of genus takes over; cf. its use in *Aet.* 69 cited below. For the term ἀιδιότης (eternity) cf. the comments above on §7.

In the Platonic-Aristotelian worldview espoused by Philo, with its strict hierarchical structure, the earth is the part of the cosmos where no real permanence is to be found. Genesis and destruction are inexorably linked. This also applies to humankind, except that it can partially extricate itself from mortality through its relationship to God and the exercise of intellectual activity (cf. §§77, 135). On the other hand, life on earth does have a permanent character in the sense that its ordered structure is fixed. There is no evolution of living things. Everything is cyclical. Philo thus firmly ascribes to the Aristotelian doctrine of the permanence of the species (cf. *An.* 2.4, 415b1–7; *Gen. An..* 2.1, 731b32). A strong statement is found at *Aet.* 69 (cited as part of the arguments of the Peripatetic Critolaus): "What each of us is unable to take for ourselves, nature gives to the genus as a whole, namely immortality. The genus (γένος) remains always, whereas the particular specimens (τὰ ἐν εἴδει) perish, a truly marvellous and divine achievement. If humankind, a tiny part of the universe, is something eternal, then the cosmos too must be without beginning, and so also indestructible." The conclusion of this passage, which runs counter to *Opif.* (cf. §7), is dialectical, i.e. put forward for the sake of argument, and will have been refuted in the missing part of *Aet.*, as argued in Runia 1981. See also *Aet.* 35–38; *QG* 2.12; Wolfson 1947, 1.342. The same theme in Wisdom 1:13, on which see the comments of Winston 1979 108–109.

end out of a beginning. Exactly the same idea is formulated in more theological terms at *QE* 1.1 (Greek fragment at Petit PAPM 33:233):

> When the fruits of plants have reached completion, the trees receive a beginning of genesis, so that the gracious gifts of God run a cyclical race forever, receiving from and connecting with each other the ends (τέλη) with the beginnings (ἀρχαί) and the beginnings with the ends.

Philo's description here is non-technical and is consistent with the Aristotelian doctrines of potentiality and actuality and the coincidence of the formal cause and the final cause in the mature organism, but also with the Stoic doctrine of the *spermatikoi logoi* explained above in our comments on §43.

Parallel exegesis

Philo seldom refers to Gen 1:9–13 elsewhere. In the "phyto-cosmological" excursus of *Plant.* 1–27 there are brief reminiscences at §§3 and 15. The most interesting text is *QG* 2.66, where Gen 1:9 is quoted in order to illustrate that in both the creation account and the account of the flood, the earth is flooded by water. As the Greek fragment shows (PAPM 33.121), Philo leaves out the words "below the heaven" in the biblical text. At *QG* 2.47 Philo argues that the text at Gen 8:14 implies by its date (beginning of spring) that when the earth recovered from the flood, God caused all the plants immediately to yield their produce, just like what happened at the creation of the cosmos: "For also in the creation of the world, in one day out of the six He completed the production of plants." The connection between the original creation and spring renewal is also made in *Spec.* 2.151, where the spring equinox is said to be an imitation of what happened at the time of creation, when "the earth was adorned (διεκοσμεῖτο) with all manner of plants, and the hills and the valleys, wherever the soil was good and deep, began to bloom and become verdant." The theme of spring is completely absent in *Opif.*

Nachleben

None of the early Christian exegetes appear to have been directly inspired by Philo's account. There are of course plenty of similarities. For example, Origen *Hom. Gen* 1.4 and Basil *Hom.* 5.2 mention the permanence of the species, but not in terms directly taken from Philo.

For Josephus *Ant.* 1.31, cf. above on §39. His description of the third day shows similarities to Philo, but it is too concise to draw firm conclusions on dependence.

Further reading: Radice *FM* 253–255; Runia *PT* 319; Winston 1981, 109.

Chapter Nine
Fourth day: a puzzle and the significance of its number (§§45–52)

Analysis/General comments

Philo's treatment of the fourth day is quite extensive, from §45 to §61, and occupies almost exactly a tenth of the entire treatise. This certainly reflects the importance that he attributes to the heavenly realm, which in the Platonic-Aristotelian world-view and in ancient thought generally has a superior status to that enjoyed by the earth. Heaven has a permanence which earthly things cannot match. Though heaven was already created on the second day, its full splendour cannot be appreciated until it is adorned with its own inhabitants, the heavenly bodies. I have divided Philo's treatment into two parts. In the first (Ch. 9) he examines two preliminary questions. In the second (Ch. 10) he expounds various themes contained in the biblical text.

(1) After an introductory statement summarizing the main event of the day, the adornment of the heaven (§45), Philo immediately proceeds to answer an implicit exegetical problem: why are the heavenly bodies, whose activity (especially of the sun) is indispensable for all life on earth, created *after* and not before the earth? An answer in terms of not taking the days literally (cf. §13) is insufficient, for even if God created all things together, there must be a didactic purpose for such a blatant reversal of the usual hierarchy in the sequence of the account.

Philo's answer is interesting because it combines an epistemological reason with a religious perspective. The passage teaches us not to rely on what seems reasonable to the mind, but to focus on sheer truth. It might seem reasonable that the heavenly bodies are the first causes of earthly growth, but the truth is that God is the supreme cause. The doctrine that Philo attacks here is a form of Chaldeanism, already introduced in §7. Exact interpretation of Philo's position is tricky because of its brief formulation. Despite appearances to the contrary, he is not defending a form of miraculous intervention coupled with knowledge based on direct revelation; see further our comments on §46. This answer was to prove very popular in the Hexaemeron literature; see below *Nachleben* (§§45–47a).

(2) It might be expected that Philo will now go on to describe the creation of the heavenly bodies. But — contrary to the biblical text, which does not mention the fourth day until the end — he first deals with another exegetical problem: why is this particular creative

task undertaken on the fourth day? So somewhat unexpectedly he launches into a fairly extensive excursus on the virtues of the number four. It can be divided into five parts:
(a) arithmetic importance of the four in relation to the ten (§47b);
(b) musicological importance of the four (§48);
(c) stereometrical importance of the four (§§49–50);
(d) a further arithmetic feature of the four (§51);
(e) cosmological importance of the four (§52).

Two comments may be made here. Firstly, the return to arithmetical considerations at §51 might seem a poor piece of composition. But, just as we shall see in the much longer excursus on the hebdomad in §§89–128, Philo is not concerned to present his arithmological material in a tightly ordered sequence. Moreover arithmetic is the common thread in all of the first four features, but in the second and third it is applied to two other mathematical sciences. Secondly, in §52 we have the same transfer from the conceptual to the physical realm that plays an important role in the section on the seven (see below on §111). Philo, however, does not draw attention to the fact here.

But the most puzzling aspect of this passage is that Philo makes no attempt whatsoever to relate the features of the number four to what actually takes place on the fourth day. A connection might be perceived between four, ten and perfection (see the comment on §47), but the relation to the heavens is not made explicit. The presentation of the chief features of the four has no other purpose than to show how significant this number is in the general scheme of things. For this reason, although the enumeration of the virtues of the four interrupts the account of creation, it should be regarded as an excursus rather than a digression. In this case, it seems, the only way to demonstrate the importance of the number is to list some of its chief characteristics. From this perspective the passage is fairly restrained, certainly when compared with the much longer passage on the seven later on (§§89–128; see the General comments below at chap. 15). On the important role of arithmology and numbers in the treatise as a whole, see further Introduction §6.

Detailed comments

(1) §45. *was ordered.* Philo again uses an inceptive imperfect, but it is awkward to translate as such when it is in the passive voice. For the verb διακοσμέω see our comment above on §40.

variegated adornment. The same verb ποικίλλω has already been used in §41 where it is connected with the image of the painter illustrating the great variety of the botanical world. The primary association of the word (and the noun ποικιλία) is with craftsmanship, and especially with the arts of weaving and embroidery, painting, and working with precious metals. Following in the footsteps of Plato and other writers (cf. *Resp.* 529d7; *Tim.* 39d2, 40a7; *Epin.* 977b4; Euripides *Helen* 1096; Critias quoted at Sextus Empiricus *Adv. Phys.* 1.54, 1.34), Philo often speaks of such variegation in relation to the heavens and the cosmos as a totality. See especially the rich passage at *Somn.* 1.203–207, where he exploits the biblical usage of the word in connection with the tabernacle (Exod 26:36 etc.) and invests it with a cosmo-theological significance (note also *Spec.* 1.84). The philosophical significance of the term has to do with complexity. The best world is one that is neither simple nor irreducibly complex, but combines order and variety (compare later the cosmological calculus of Leibniz). As Plotinus *Enn.* 3.2.11.6 says, a craftsman does not make an animal with eyes only, even if the eyes are its finest feature.

behind ... in rank. Philo uses the same term (ὕστερος) as Plato does at *Tim.* 34b10 when he states that, although his account describes the creation of the cosmos' body before its soul, it should not be concluded that the latter is ontologically inferior (see also our comment on §16). This is closer to Philo's problem than one might at first think, because for Plato the heaven is the world-soul's chief domain. Plato gives as explanation the contingency of his account, which differs from Philo's emphasis on the limitations of human reason. See further Runia *PT* 201.

might of his sovereignty. As explained in more detail in §46.

understood in advance. Exactly the same formulation is found in §16 on the creation of the intelligible world before the sense-perceptible one.

likely and convincing and contains much that is reasonable. The three terms used by Philo here (εἰκότα, πιθανά, εὔλογον) are all associated with the philosophy of the New Academy, which turned the heritage of Plato in a sceptical direction. Since the certainty of truth is unattainable for humans, we have to be content with what is reasonable (Arcesilaus) or convincing (Carneades). See further L&S §§68–69; Long 1974, 88–106; 1995, 944–946. The dogmatist reaction of Antiochus of Ascalon to this philosophy two generations before Philo's birth paved the way for the rise of Middle Platonism: cf. Dillon 1977, 52–69; Tarrant, 1985. Philo, however, is prepared to make use of these earlier doctrines when they suit his purpose. On his exploitation of sceptical epistemology see further our comments on §72 and Introduction §7. At *Sacr.* 12 the same terms are used to express the contrast between reasonableness and sheer truth: "Moses does not welcome what is likely and convincing, but pursues the truth in its purity." On "focus their aim" (στοχασταί) see further the comments on §72.

showing admiration. As above in §7, it is obvious that the theme of admiration has religious overtones. If one is impressed by something, one comes to trust it and rely on it, which leads to reverence, veneration, worship.

sophistry rather than wisdom. Following the lead of Plato, Philo associates sophistry with people who aim at persuasion and effect (like the modern advertising industry) rather than truth, i.e. not trying to find out and state the way things really are. The same negative attitude to sophists and sophistry is found in §157. At *QG* 3.33 sophists are compared with "Academics and sceptics." On sophists in Philo see further the detailed study of Winter 1997 but this passage is not commented on).

first causes. Once again, as in §7, we can detect the philosophy of Chaldeanism, which Philo frequently opposes to true theism. It is the conviction that events in the cosmos are determined by immanent causes, usually associated with the influence of the heavenly bodies (i.e. astrology), and not by God as first cause. See for example *Migr.* 181: "he [Moses] differs from their opinion on God, for he considers neither the cosmos nor the soul of the cosmos to be the primal God, and also not the stars or their elaborate motions (χορείας, cf. §§54, 70) to be the most ancient causes of what happens to humans ..." Philo describes God as the first cause (πρῶτον αἴτιον) at *Spec.* 3.180; *Conf.* 123–4, and often elsewhere by implication. It is of course standard Aristotelian and Platonic doctrine, as systematised in Middle Platonism, e.g. at Alcinous *Did.* 10.2. See further our comments on §11, and compare also the questions asked about the heavenly bodies in §54.

he says. Once again there is a problem with the implied subject of the verb. So far in the sentence the subject has been God, who must be doing the "thinking in advance." At this point, however, Philo seems to change to Moses as subject, because in the words quoted God is referred to in the third person, but it is not impossible that God is referring to himself.

§46. *heavenly offspring ... full autonomy*. Philo certainly recognizes that the heavenly realm is ontologically superior and plays a crucial role in directing natural events on earth. Here he follows Plato in describing them as God's ἔκγονοι (cf. *Tim.* 41a–42d, the title "young gods" at 42d6; the same expression as Philo at Alcinous *Did.* 16.1). An important parallel passage using similar language and conceptuality is found at *Spec.* 1.13–14 on the first commandment of the Decalogue:

> Some have supposed that the sun and moon and other stars are gods with absolute powers, to whom they ascribed the causes of all things that come into being. But Moses was of the view that the cosmos was created and is like a great city with rulers and subjects: the rulers are all the planets and fixed stars in heaven, the subjects are the natures that exist below the moon in the air and on earth. The above-mentioned rulers are not autonomous, but are subordinates of the one Father of the universe, whose government carried out over each created thing in accordance with just desert and law they emulate and so exercise rightly. But those who do not catch sight of the charioteer stationed above attribute the causes of what comes into being in the cosmos to the yoked team as though they were independent agents.

See also below §§72–75 on God's subordinates. The denial of autonomy to the heavenly bodies is all the more relevant because in Philo's times so-called "gnostic" ideas were developing, which were to attribute to them tyrannical and malevolent powers. On these various themes see further Runia *PT* 249–251, and also the Excursus to Ch. 10.

chariotteer ... or a pilot. Philo habitually uses these images from ancient transport systems for the directive and providential activity of God (cf. also §88). They are also ubiquitous in the Platonist tradition, derived primarily from the myths in the *Phaedrus* and the *Politicus*. On these images see the detailed treatment in Méasson 1986, 19–137.

according to law and just desert. Almost exactly the same phrase as in *Spec.* 1.14 cited above (the two terms are reversed).

for God all things are possible. This is one of Philo's favourite slogans; cf. *Abr.* 175; *Ios.* 244; *Mos.* 1.174; *Spec.* 1.282; *Somn.* 1.87; *QG* 2.47; 3.56; 4.17. But what does this omnipotence amount to in the present context? I agree with Winston (1981, 18, who cites this passage) against Wolfson (1947, 1.355, followed by Radice *FM* 255), that Philo does not imply here that God acts outside of or contrary to the order of nature which he has instituted (he can of course use that order in order to intervene providentially). Similarly, *pace* Radice, the sheer truth at which Philo thinks humans should aim does not necessarily depend on direct revelation (as received by Moses according to §8), but can be attained through the processes of natural theology as hinted at in §54 and §§69–71, and more fully worked out at *Spec.* 1.32–35; *Praem.* 41–43; *Leg.* 3.97–103. The appearance of fully grown fruit-bearing trees when the sun was not yet present might suggest miraculous divine powers, but this is not what Philo argues in this text.

(2a) §47. *perfect number, the four.* Philo returns to the theme of arithmology, as inspired by the scheme of the six days. The material collected here is derived from arithmological handbooks. For similar passages see Theon of Smyrna 93.17–99.23, 101.11–13; Anatolius 31–32; Ps.-Iamblichus, *Theol. arith.* 20.1–30.15; Lydus *Mens.* 2.9, 4.64, 76; fuller list at Staehle 1931, 26 n.; parallels at Cohn 1889, 73–74. For further material in Philo see Staehle 1931, 26–31, and Parallel exegesis below. A modern book on number symbolism, Schimmel 1993, 86, describes four as the number of material order: "Four is inseparably connected with the first known order in the world, and thus points to the change from nature to civilization by arranging a confusing multiplicity of manifestations into fixed forms."

The four is perfect (or complete, τέλειος) for a different reason than the six (see §13). Because the first four numbers add up to ten, it is regarded as fundamentally related to the decad, the base of the Greek numerical system and so of all arithmetic. Implicit here is the Pythagorean *tetraktys*, the most celebrated doctrine of Pythagoreanism (on this see Porphyry, *Vit. Pythag.* 20; Sextus Empiricus *Adv. Log.* 1.94–99; Critchlow in Waterfield 1988, 9–21). Surprisingly Philo never refers to it by name. Because the fundamental musical accords can be made from the numbers one to four (cf. §48) and because the movements of the heavenly bodies are characterized by perfect harmony (the so-called "music of the spheres"), the perfection of the four (and the ten) symbolizes the perfection of the heavenly realm. As noted above, it is perplexing that Philo does not make this connection explicit. Radice (*FM* 257) suspects that the connection is *implicit* on account of the fact that Philo begins his treatment of the four by immediately indicating the connection with the ten. Even if this were right, our puzzlement must remain, for the addition of a couple of words would have been enough to make things fully clear.

all-perfect number. The description παντέλεια was a standard Pythagorean epithet for the ten (see the text from Anatolius cited in the next note). We might also translate "all-completing," since the ten completes the list of real numbers (see next note). In this context it indicates that the perfection of the ten is more embracing than that of the four, which has a generative function only. Cf. *Mos.* 2.84, where the ten is παντέλεια and the four is its οὐσία (perhaps "material" rather than essence, since the ten is made "out of" the four) and also *Spec.* 2.200. At *Plant.* 123 the four is said to be called "all," but reference there is to scripture (Lev 19:24) and not arithmological lore. Other passages on the relation between four and ten are *Plant.* 123–124; *Decal.* 26. For the four as principle (ἀρχή) and source of ten, cf. also *Spec.* 2.40; *QG* 3.12.

the limit for the infinitude of numbers. In Greek number theory, inspired by Pythagoreanism (cf. Aristotle *Metaph.* A 5, 986a9), there are ten real numbers, from one to ten. The remainder are all derivative. The Greek word for eleven is "one-ten," for twelve "two-ten," for thirteen "three-and-ten" etc. The feature given here in fact belongs primarily to the doctrine on the ten, and is worked out in more detail at *Decal.* 27 and *QG* 2.32. The image of the turning post is again taken from athletics and chariot-racing (cf. the comments on §44). Harris 1976, 47 translates "turn around ten ... and come back to the start" and sees here a reference to a person using an abacus. The image is certainly not Philo's invention. Almost exactly the same language is found at Anatolius 39.6–8, also cited in Ps.-Iamblichus *Theol. arith.* 86.3–5: "It is the perimeter and limit of all number: for they run their course by winding and turning around it as if around a turning post. Moreover it is the boundary for the infinitude of numbers. It is also called "power" and "all-completing" (παντέλεια) because it limits all number ..."

(2b) §48. **musical accords.** It was the discovery of Pythagoras and his followers that musical harmony has a arithmetical basis which encouraged them to postulate the mathematical basis of reality. The first four numbers produce the three most basic accords or concords (συμφωνίαι) between two sounds (the double octave in Philo's enumeration is otiose, but in the context four accords are better than three). Similar accounts are given at *Mos.* 2.115 and *Spec.* 2.200 (and cf. §107). The doctrine is, of course, a very basic piece of musicological knowledge, found in many arithmological accounts of the tetrad (e.g. Anatolius 32.17–28; Theon of Smyrna 93.17–94.2 etc.). Philo sets the theory out as clearly as he can.

most perfect system. I take Philo to mean that on the basis of these numerical ratios an entire musical scale can be built by filling in the intervals. Plato exploits this idea in the construction of the world-soul at *Tim.* 35b–36b, on which see Cornford's exposition, 1937, 68–72.

third plus one ... half plus one. My translations for the technical musicological terms ἐπίτριτος and ἡμιόλιος (literally "third on top," "half (plus) whole"), rather than the technical English renderings sesquitertian and sesqualter. The ratios involved are of course between whole numbers, namely 4 to 3 and 3 to 2.

(2c) §49. *has revealed the nature of the solid.* In §36 the solidity of the physical world was associated with the creation of the firmament on the second day, but no connection was made with arithmological doctrine. The reason now becomes clear. Solidity is especially associated with the number four, because if you relate numbers to dimensions, you need four things in order to produce three dimensions. Philo illustrates this with the example of the nuts in §50. Strictly speaking points, lines and surfaces as defined in geometry cannot be physical, but have to be abstracted as such from physical things. There is an important philosophical background here. In the Old Academy, during and after Plato's lifetime, a metaphysical system was developed in which physical reality was derived from the realm of thought through a derivation system involving point, line, surface and solid and the numbers one to four. Aristotle protested vigorously against this attempt, declaring it to be impossible. But this background, *pace* Krämer (1964, 271), is tangential to the present passage, because its emphasis is purely arithmological.

It is noteworthy that the very phraseology of Philo's presentation of this feature is closely shared by a number of other sources: Anatolius 32.3–6, reworked by *Theol. arith.* 29.10–12; Lydus *Mens.* 115.15–17. Compare especially the opening phrase:

Philo πρώτη γὰρ αὕτη τὴν τοῦ στερεοῦ φύσιν ἔδειξε
Anatolius πρῶτος ἔδειξε τὴν στερεοῦ φύσιν
Theol. arith. πρώτη ἡ τέτρας ἔδειξε τὴν τοῦ στερεοῦ φύσιν
Lydus ἀλλὰ μὴν καὶ πρῶτος ἔδειξε τὴν στερεὰν φύσιν.

Philo is working within a common tradition, of which he is the oldest and, in this case, most detailed witness. See further our remarks in the Introduction to §6, and on the problem of Lydus' relation to Philo Excursus 1 in Ch. 15.

through extension. Literally "by flowing" (ῥύσει), which is a particularly suitable description for the production of a line from a point.

§50. *People playing with nuts.* Exactly the same illustration is found in Anatolius' treatment of the same theme. Both authors use the same rare verb καρυατίζω, the only instances of its use with this sense. Philo thus did not make up this illustration himself.

the four ... and the pyramid. Philo implies here the connection between arithmetic and stereometry. In Greek arithmetic numbers were envisaged spatially (each number represented by a round dot, cf. the nuts). The arithmetical handbook of Nicomachus of Gerasa devotes a chapter to "solid numbers" (*Intro. arith.* 2.12). The simplest of these are the pyramids with triangular base, of which the four is first after the unit (2.12.8). See further the comment on §92.

(2d) §51. *first of the numbers that is square.* Philo now reverts to arithmetic. The spatial representation of numbers invites a link with plane geometry. The four is the first "square number" after the unit. On this kind of number see Nicomachus *Intro. arith.* 2.9. The mention of the four as the first square number is regularly found in accounts of the tetrad, e.g. at Anatolius 32.1.

a measure of fairness and equality. Famously the Pythagoreans associated (or even identified) the number four with δικαιοσύνη (usually translated "justice," but in this context "fairness" is better). Aristotle briefly mentions this at *Metaph.* A 6, 985b26, giving rise to the following comment by Ps.-Alexander of Aphrodisias *Comm. Met.* 38.10–16, which explains the idea behind it well:

> They supposed that the distinguishing characteristic (ἴδιον) of δικαιοσύνη was reciprocity and equality, so they looked for this in numbers and for this reason said that δικαιοσύνη was the first number equal to the multiplication of itself ... Some said that it was four, since this was the first square number and was divided into equal parts and was equal ...

At *Plant.* 121–122 Philo explains this feature in terms of the square having four equal sides, "so that it is demonstrated that the number is a symbol of equality and fairness and all excellence in a way that other numbers are not." Anatolius gives this feature particular prominence by beginning his account of the four with it (31.22).

a splendid form of concord ... not possessed by any other number. In the case of the unit, addition is greater than multiplication, in the case of three and all subsequent numbers, addition is less than multiplication. Only in the case of two are they equal. This explanation suggests that the current feature is actually better assigned to the dyad, where in fact Anatolius 30.20 and Ps.-Iamblichus *Theol. arith.* 10.20 place it. Philo has probably made the adaptation himself. This means that the parallel passage at Lydus *Mens.* 30.8–15 is probably taken directly from *Opif.* rather than another arithmological source; see further Excursus 1 in Ch. 15.

(2e) §52. *must be further demonstrated ... in the account.* This sentence serves as a transition from the arithmetical account of the four so far to an examination of the role of the four in the physical world. The same transition is found in the longer account of the hebdomad at §111, where it is explained in terms of a distinction between the incorporeal and the visible realm. As in the case of the similar text at §15, we *may* have here a veiled allusion to Philo's separate collection of arithmological material in his treatise *On numbers.* See further our comments in the Introduction §6 and at §15, where we justify our translation of λόγος. Terian (1991, 41–44) rightly concludes that Whitaker (PLCL 1.39) is wrong in translating the impersonal construction with the verbal adjective here (προσυποδεικτέον) by a future tense instead of having it express necessity (cf. Smyth 1956, §§2149–52; Philo commonly uses this construction in introductory or transitional statements — there are 19 other examples in our treatise alone: §§5 [2x], 15, 19, 51, 67 [2x], 72, 79, 90 [2x], 92, 95, 97, 99, 101,

130, 132, 166). For a discussion of the chronological conclusions that some scholars have drawn from this reference see Introduction §1.

principle for the genesis of the entire heaven and cosmos. Philo's treatment of examples of the four in the physical realm is very short. He selects only two, the elements and the seasons. Both are also found at *Plant.* 120, and are of course ubiquitous in the arithmological literature: cf. Anatolius 32.6; Ps.-Iamblichus, *Theol. arith.* 23.19, 24.12 etc. Here too Philo makes no effort to relate these examples to the exegetical context of the commentary.

flowed forth, as from a source. An allusion to the famous verse on the Pythagorean *tetraktys*, quoted by Sextus Empiricus, *Adv. Log.* 1.94:

I swear by the person who handed down to our head the *tetraktys*,
source containing the roots of ever-flowing nature.

The term for roots could be taken as meaning "elements" (it was used as such by Empedocles, the inventor of the four-element theory, frg. 31B6).

Parallel exegesis

The only other passage where Philo refers to the works of the fourth day is *Plant.* 117, as part of a eulogy of the number four inspired by his citation of Lev 19:24, "in the fourth year all its fruit shall be holy, for giving praise to the Lord." Here we read: "In many places in the legislation, but especially in the account (κατάλογος) of the genesis of the universe, the number four is seen to be venerated by the prophetic word." Philo then goes on to mention the creation of visible light and the heavenly bodies. See further the next section of our commentary. The brief account of the virtues of the four at *Plant.* 120–125 is the best parallel for the passage §§47–52 in our text. At *Abr.* 13, when discussing Enos, the fourth generation from Adam, Philo also cites Lev 19:24 and refers back to this particular treatment in *Opif.*; see Introduction §1.

Other exegetical texts which dwell on features of the four are: *Somn.* 1.15, 33 (on Gen 21:25, 26:19, four wells); *Mos.* 2.84 (on Gen 26, colours and size of the curtains of the tabernacle); *Mos.* 2.115 (four letters of the tetragrammaton); *QG* 2.2 (on Gen 6:14, square beams of Noah's ark); *QG* 3.12 (on Gen 15:16, fourth generation); *QG* 4.195[i] (text at Petit 1973, 70–72; on Gen 26:32, fourth well); *QE* 2.27 (on Exod 24:1, four persons go up), *QE* 2.87 (on Exod 26:2, breadth of curtains of tabernacle); *QE* 2.93–94, 97 (on Exod 26:32–37, four pillars of tabernacle); *QE* 2.99 (on Exod 27:1, quadrangular altar).

Nachleben

(1) Theophilus *Ad Aut.* 2.15 repeats the main idea of §§45–46 with considerable accuracy:

On the fourth day the luminaries came into existence. Since God has foreknowledge, he understood the nonsense of the foolish philosophers (cf. Col. 2:9), who were going to say that the things produced on earth come from the elements, so that they might reject God (cf. 1 Thess. 4:8). In order, therefore, that the truth might be demonstrated, plants and seeds came into existence before the elements. For what comes into existence later cannot cause what is prior to it (translation Grant, modified).

Two features of this text, God's foreknowledge and the emphasis on truth, incline me to the view of Martín (1986, 162) that Theophilus is directly dependent on Philo. Note, however, that his language is quite different (e.g. using the term "elements" for the stars), and the polemical attitude towards the philosophers differs from Philo's usual emphasis. On Theophilus and Philo see further Introduction §§7(a), 8.

The theme is taken over by Basil *Hex.* 5.1 96B, 6.2 120C, from where it becomes a topos in the Hexaemeron tradition; see the list in Alexandre *CLG* 142 (to which now add *Catena in Gen.* 71 at Petit 1992–97, 1.45).

In the *Midrash Tadsche* 1 (Wünsche 1910, 88, noted by J. Cohn at PCH 1.41) we read: "Why did the Holy One, blessed be he, decide to allow on the third day grass and shrubs and fruit trees to spring forth out of the earth and on the fourth day he first created the luminaries? Only in order to demonstrate his power ..." The explanation is very brief. The fact, however, that the same work uses Philo more extensively justifies the conclusion that the author is indebted to him here too. See further on §§29–31 and 115–123.

(2) A remnant of Philo's arithmological concerns is found at Didymus *Comm. Gen.* 36.17–20 (repeated 36.9–10); the same text is excerpted in *Catena in Gen.* 84 (cf. also Procopius *Comm. in Gen* PG 87.85A–B). I cite the latter because the text is better:

> For this reason the luminaries too are said to come into existence on the fourth day on account of the reason that they are deserving of honour. For the four, being potentially ten, is deserving of honour, for the unit and the two and the three and the four, when added to each other, make the ten. Throughout the whole of scripture the ten is the object of praise.

This is clearly derived, directly or indirectly, from *Opif.* 47.

Further reading: On §§45–46, Radice *FM* 255–256; Runia *PT* 201, 418. On §§47–52, Radice *FM* 256–259; Cohn 1889, 72–74 (arithmological parallels).

Chapter Ten
Fourth day: creation of the heavenly bodies (§§53–61)

Analysis/General comments

Philo continues his exposition of the fourth day of creation.

(1) For the third time he recounts that God ordered the heavens (§53, cf. §§45, 47). This time he adds what God decorated the heavens with, namely the heavenly bodies. But even now he does not turn to the biblical text, but first embarks on a eulogy of the light which is produced by these heavenly beings. Light is a prerequisite for sight. Without light and sight humans would not have been able to develop the activity that is most beneficial for them, love of wisdom or philosophy. In §54 Philo expands the theme by showing how contemplation of the heavens led to the development of philosophy. The paraphrase of Plato *Tim.* 47a7-b2 at the end of the section will have indicated to the informed reader where his inspiration for this theme came from (§§53–54).

For all its eloquence, this passage seems somewhat out of place. In a sense it anticipates one of the reasons why, according to the biblical text as expounded in §55, the heavenly bodies were created, namely in order to give light (φωσφορεῖν in §55 picks up φωσφόροις in §53). But light is specifically related to the human sense of sight (which was also the main emphasis of the Platonic text), even though humankind will not be created until the sixth day (§69). Philo's reading of the fourth day of creation thus receives a strong anthropocentric emphasis. The importance of the heavenly bodies is explained in terms of what they mean for human beings. This emphasis is continued in the exposition of the text in §§55–61. At the same time the theme of contemplation gives Philo the opportunity to speak at greater length about the marvellous ordered motions of the stars, a perspective which is missing in the biblical text.

(2a) For the fourth time Philo introduces God's creative activity. A brief reference is made to the relation between the paradigmatic light created on "day one" (cf. §§30–31) and the light of the heavenly bodies. But now he turns to the biblical text. From Gen 1:14 four reasons are extracted as to why God established the heavenly bodies in the heaven. Each of the aspects is dealt with in turn in the remainder of the passage (§§55–56a).

(2b) For the first theme Philo somewhat unexpectedly does not concentrate on the light-giving function of the heavenly bodies, as emphasized in Gen 1:15. No doubt he thinks his explanation in

§§53–54 was sufficient. Instead he expounds the division of time into day and night, and the assignment of each to the sun on the one hand and moon and stars on the other, as outlined in Gen 1:16, 18. The theme of light returns at the end in order to explain why the moon and stars are not visible during the day (§§56b–57).

(2c) The heavenly bodies also have the function of giving signs of future events. By studying their movements humans can predict what will happen in the realm of nature (§§58–59a).

(2d) They also indicate "right times," which Philo, in agreement with the intention of the biblical text, relates to the coming and going of the seasons. His treatment here is very brief (§59b).

(2e) In the last place the heavenly bodies are created in order to indicate time. This is not interpreted in terms of a calendar (including religious dates such as annual festivals, as the biblical text probably implies, cf. Westermann 1984, 130). Instead he picks up another philosophical theme from Plato's *Timaeus*: their task is to teach humankind the importance of number, as derived from the counting of the regularities of celestial motions (§60).

(3) In the concluding paragraph Philo emphasizes that, though human knowledge concerning the heavenly bodies is limited, it is possible to understand the manifold benefits that they bring both humans and the cosmos as a whole. Their unchanging nature is the direct result of God's creative activity, which has not only formed them, but fixed their motions and tasks by means of permanent ordinances and laws (§61).

Taken as a whole, the passage §§53–61 has a double character which is typical of the entire treatise. For the most part Philo adheres rather closely to the biblical text, incorporating a number of its phrases in his commentary and allowing his comments to be structured by various biblical themes. But he is also keen to translate these themes into terms drawn from Greek cosmology. His chief inspiration, as he himself subtly indicates in §54, is Plato's *Timaeus*. And it must be said that the coincidences are not entirely fanciful. Let me quote my own words, *PT* 222–223 (slightly modified):

> Nowhere, it might be argued, are the points of resemblance between Plato's cosmology and the creation account of Moses so apparent as in the creation of the heavenly bodies, which according to Moses takes place on the fourth day and according to Plato after the creation of the cosmic soul. Surely no educated Greek who happened to read the words "they were established ... for days and for years" at Gen 1:14 could fail to be reminded of *Tim.* 37e1, 39c1-5. Conversely every devout Jew who was confronted with the statement that the

heavenly bodies obeyed the demiurge's command (*Tim.* 38e6) must have immediately thought of the commands that God the creator issues on the various days of the creation account, including on the fourth day.

The themes of the origin of philosophy and the discovery of number are both taken from Plato. The Mosaic terminology is modernized in order to conform to the expectations of Greek science. Various details of this adaptation will be noted in the detailed comments below. Yet here too there are interesting limits to his adaptations. Firstly, he resists all temptation to give a technical exposé of the doctrines of Greek cosmology. These are assumed and only briefly alluded to (esp. in §54). The same applies to his discussion of time and number. Secondly, Philo does not fully take over Plato's strong anthropocentric emphasis. According to Plato the heavens should be the object of contemplation and study because they so impressively embody the principle of rationality that permeates the entire cosmos. By studying the heavens, humans can give direction to their own lives (cf. esp. 47a-c, 90a-d). Philo assumes this rationality in the order of creation (cf. the last words of §61), but he does not dwell on it. He prefers to emphasize the magnificence and munificence of God as creator. Finally we note that traces can be detected, here and elsewhere in the treatise, of the veneration that intellectuals felt during the Hellenistic period for the heaven and the cosmos in its entirety as divine manifestation of order and splendour. See the Excursus at the end of the chapter on "cosmic religion." Such sentiments, however, are kept within strict bounds because of Philo's prevailing Jewish theocentrism.

Detailed comments

(1) §53. **in the nature of reality**. I translate ἐν τῇ φύσει in this way, because it is plain from §106 that *physis* here covers not only the physical realm, but also immaterial reality.

proceed to order. See the comment above on §45.

with the four. On the difficulty of translation here see our discussion on the parallel passage below at §62.

most god-like adornment. As in §16, but in contrast to §69 and §137, the adjective θεοειδής here has no special theological significance. See further the comment on "divine images" in §55 (and also on "gods" above in §27). The word for "adornment" is κόσμος, used here in its primary meaning. The relation between adornment, order, rationality, and beauty is fundamental for Greek cosmology.

heavenly bodies. The Greek term ἄστρα must cover both stars and planets here, and so should not be translated "stars" (Yonge) or "étoiles" (Arnaldez).

light ... the most excellent of things that exist. Because of its illuminating power, making knowledge and understanding possible. Philo's language is rather loose. By "things that exist" he perhaps means physical things, since one would expect God to be the ἄριστον τῶν ὄντων, as indeed we find at *Virt.* 179 and *Fug.* 91.

the most excellent of the senses, sight. Exactly the same phrase at §120. Philo often discriminates between the various senses. For example, at *QG* 3.5 he affirms that sight and hearing together are regarded as the "philosophical senses" required for good living, whereas the others are servants and have been created for living only; cf. also *Spec.* 1.174, 339–343; *Mos.* 2.211. But in the case of sight and hearing too there is a hierarchy. Sight is superior to hearing; cf. *Spec.* 4.60 (with an allusion to the famous aphorism of Heraclitus B101a cited at Herodotus 1.8); *Ebr.* 82; *Abr.* 150 etc. Sight is the portion of Israel, "he who sees God," while hearing belongs to Jacob (*Conf.* 72) or Ishmael (*Fug.* 208). As has often been remarked, by privileging sight above hearing Philo appears to stand closer to the Greek than the biblical tradition, in which the words of the Shema (Deut 6:4) summon Israel to *listen* to the word of God. See also the comments on the encomium of sight in §54.

intellect in the soul ... eye in the body. With quasi-mathematical precision Philo sets out the analogy between the perceptual role of sight and the cognitive role of mind. The analogy is a philosophical commonplace, much used from Plato (*Resp.* 518c1) and Aristotle (*Top.* 1.17, 108a11) onwards. See the long list of texts in Pease's note on Cicero *Nat. d.* 1.19 and further comments on §71 below. A fine parallel is found at *Mut.* 4:

> What the eyes of the body observe, they perceive through the co-operation of light, and light is something different from both the object seen and the person who sees. What the soul sees, it sees through itself without the assistance of anything else. For the objects of thought are a bright light to themselves. In the same way we learn the sciences. The mind applies its eye that never closes or falls asleep to the doctrines and theories which it studies and sees them not with a bastard light, but with a genuine light that shines forth from itself.

The comparison can be positive (as in our text) or negative, depending on the context. See for example similar texts at *Abr.* 57; *Virt.* 11–12; *Deus* 46. Goulet 1987, 138, considers the mention of the intellect and intelligibles somewhat gratuitous in the context, and suspects the remnants of an allegorical interpretation in terms of mind and senses. Philo's purpose, however, may simply be elucidatory. Usually sight illustrates the workings of the mind; here it is the other way around.

science. The term is ἐπιστήμη, i.e. knowledge in an organized form. It is a Platonic theme that through knowledge and dialectic the philosopher gains access to the truth of the intelligible realm.

love of wisdom. The Greek term is φιλοσοφία. See further the comment on the final lines of §54.

§54. *sight ... observed the nature of the heavenly bodies.* Our treatise contains no less than three extended passages in which Philo gives effusive and lyrical descriptions of the order of the cosmos, and especially of its heavenly regions, describing how observation of that order instils in the soul love of contemplation leading to love of wisdom. The passage at §§77–78 is quite similar to the one here and also draws on Plato, *Tim.* 47 a–c. The soul delights in the spectacle of cosmic order while remaining here on earth. The passage at §§69–71 differs somewhat in emphasis, notably in that the soul itself ascends to the heavens, even passing beyond them and attaining to the incorporeal realm. Its chief model is the famous myth in Plato's *Phaedrus.* See further below Ch. 12 and Ch. 14 respectively. In all three cases Philo draws on his considerable literary skills in order to give a description of the cosmos which does justice to its beauty and order. The essential ideological background here is what Festugière has entitled the "cosmic religion," initiated by Plato and his circle and developed in the Hellenistic period. See further the Excursus below.

In total there are about a dozen passages in Philo in which he gives an encomium of sight exploiting the thematics of *Tim.* 47a–c to a greater or lesser degree. The longest passage is *Abr.* 156–164, which contains numerous parallels to the present passage, but is too long to quote. See also *Abr.* 57–58; *Spec.* 3.184–192; *Congr.* 21; *QG* 2.34; and the detailed analysis at *PT* 270–276.

the well-ordered circuits. Philo competently and compactly outlines the chief features of the geocentric cosmological model developed by Plato, Aristotle and 4th century astronomers. The heavenly bodies move in two different directions, the circles of the same and different as Plato calls them at *Tim.* 36c–d. The fixed stars all move together in the same direction, completing a full circuit every 24 hours (we now know that this is impossible, because their speed would have to exceed that of light, but Plato's and Philo's universe was small and cosy). The seven planets, including sun and moon, have a double motion. They move along with the entire cosmos and the fixed stars in one direction, but at the same time they have their own motions which go in the opposite direction and are all dissimilar. Elsewhere, e.g. at *Cher.* 21–25 and *Spec.* 3.187–188, Philo gives more technicalities. See further Runia *PT* 208–213, 225–226. Whitaker's translation at PLCL 1.41 misunderstands the terminology completely. For a splendid account of how Plato's philosophical assumptions were decisive in the development of the Ptolemaic astronomical model that was not superseded until Copernicus, see Vlastos 1975, 22–65.

concordant choral dances. My translation follows that of Miller (1986, 60), whose monograph traces the theme of the choral dance (χορεία) of the stars from Plato, who institutes it (*Tim.* 40c3), through to Neoplatonism and the Christian Platonism of Dionysius (on Philo 56–80). Other Philonic texts that speak of the χορεῖαι of the stars are §§70, 78, 126; *Spec.* 1.34; 3.188; *Aet.* 4 etc. Implicit in the term "concordant" (ἐμμελής) is the Pythagorean doctrine of the "harmony of the spheres," which Philo endorses with enthusiasm at *Somn.* 1.35–36; *QG* 3.3 (PLCLSup 1.181). See also §126.

pleasure. Because it is the accompaniment of intellectual activity, pleasure is here positively evaluated, in contrast to the highly negative attitude later in the treatise. See the comments at §§157–158.

Feasting. Philo anticipates here the more elaborate treatment in §§77–78.

busy itself. The verb περιεργάζομαι and its cognate noun περιεργία often have a negative connotation, e.g. at *Migr.* 187, where the reader is exhorted to abandon Chaldeanism and to quit his "meddling with heavenly concerns" (cf. in other contexts *Ebr.* 167; *Fug.* 162). Later the theme would develop into the famous *curiositas* doctrine of Augustine. But here Philo's usage is positive.

further enquiries. Philo's model for this passage in Plato, *Tim.* 47a, reads as follows:

> As my account has it, our sight has indeed proved to be a source of supreme benefit to us, in that none of our present statements about the universe could ever have been made if we had never seen any stars, sun or heaven. As it is, however, our ability to see the periods of day-and-night, of months and of years, of equinoxes and solstices, has led to the invention of number, and has given us the idea of time, and opened the path to inquiry into the nature of the universe (a2–7, translation Zeyl).

Philo has substituted four specific questions belonging to physics, each concerning the subject of the heavenly bodies (substance, origin, motion, causes), in order to illustrate the kind of enquiries that led to the development of philosophy. The questions that he poses can be compared with similar lists given in the parallel passages *Abr.* 162–163; *Spec.* 3.190; cf. also *Ebr.* 199; *Her.* 246–247. In the present passage he limits them to the heavenly bodies, in the other two he casts a wider net. All three passages are of interest for historians of philosophy because they provide valuable evidence on the *Sitz im Leben* of the doxographical genre of *Placita* literature, collections of views of philosophers on the main questions of physics. Philo's questions are quite similar to the chapter-headings of book 2 of Aëtius, the chief representative of this genre, as listed in Ps.-Plutarch, *Plac.* 885E–886B. On Philo's evidence see further Mansfeld and Runia 1996, 317–318. See further the General comments on Ch. 25.

what is the substance ... The term is οὐσία, i.e. what are the heavenly bodies made of. Cf. the chapter headings of Aëtius: 2.13, What is the substance (οὐσία) of the stars; 2.20, What is the substance of the sun; 2.25, What is the substance of the moon. In a passage that contains highly important evidence for the history of doxography, *Somn.* 1.21–24, Philo presents the sceptical view that the nature of heaven and the heavenly bodies cannot be known with certainty; on this passage see Mansfeld 1990, 3117, and Mansfeld and Runia loc. cit. See also §§55 and 61.

beginning of genesis. The classic phrase ἀρχὴ γενέσεως, derived from *Tim.* 28b6, which was used as a *Leitmotiv* for the question of whether the universe did or did not come into existence. Cf. *Aet.* 14 and the comments of Baltes 1976–1978, 1.86; Runia *PT* 97. See further Ch. 6 above.

each thing. The meaning of the text is not entirely clear here. Is Philo still referring to the heavenly bodies? In that case he means the causes responsible for their motions, e.g. God (Philo) or the demiurge (Plato) or the unmoved movers (Aristotle), etc. Or does he mean the phenomena on earth influenced or determined by the celestial beings? Of the translators Cohn, Whitaker, and Arnaldez opt for the second alternative, Yonge and Kraus Reggiani for the first. Both interpretations are possible. I have sided with the latter group for two reasons: (a) the parallel at *Spec.* 3.190; (b) the fact that Philo changes gender, from ἀγένητοι (φύσεις;ⱷ) to ἕκαστα.

the pursuit of philosophy. At this point Philo's adaptation of his model Plato is so close that we may speak of a loose paraphrase. The passage cited above continues (47a7-b2): "These pursuits have supplied us with (the) kind (γένος) of philosophy. No greater good has come or ever will come to the mortal race as a gift from the gods." The original texts can be compared as follows:

Plato, *Timaeus* 47a7-b2
... περί τε τῆς τοῦ παντὸς φύσεως ζήτησιν ἔδοσαν· ἐξ ὧν ἐπορισάμεθα φιλοσοφίας γένος, οὗ μεῖζον ἀγαθὸν οὔτ' ἦλθεν οὔτε ἥξει ποτὲ τῷ θνητῷ γένει δωρηθὲν ἐκ θεῶν.

Philo §54
ἐκ δὲ τῆς τούτων ζητήσεως τὸ φιλοσοφίας συνέστη γένος, οὗ τελειότερον ἀγαθὸν οὐκ ἦλθεν εἰς τὸν ἀνθρώπινον βίον.

Philo is probably citing from memory. He substitutes "more perfect" for "better" and removes the reference to the gods. Dörrie at Dörrie–Baltes *DPA* 1.518 sees great significance in the change from γένος to τὸ γένος: Plato means just a part of philosophy, i.e. arithmetic, and Philo expands this to the whole of philosophy: "wer Platon so zitiert, ist kein Metaphysiker." It is, however, questionable whether Plato's text should be interpreted in such a restricted fashion. Experience of the natural world and study of the sciences based on it (e.g. astronomy, cf. *Resp.* 529–30) leads to the pursuit of philosophy in general.

We might be tempted to conclude that Philo is running away with himself here. Is it likely that such "contemplation of the cosmos" has furnished humankind with the greatest of benefits? Is there not the risk of admiring the cosmos rather than the creator (§7)? In fact the passage is partial, limited by its context of the heavenly bodies on the fourth day. It has to be supplemented by §§69–71. It will also later become plain that *philosophia* in Philo has a broader sense, including the quest for God and the study of the Law. See further the comment on §128.

(2) §55. **Using as his model.** A necessarily somewhat free translation of Philo's expression πρὸς τὴν ... ἰδέαν ἀπιδών (looking away towards the form), which exploits the technical jargon of Platonist descriptions of the demiurgic process. The preposition πρός indicates the formal cause. See further the comments above on §§16 and 18, with reference to the *Timaeus* and Middle Platonist parallels. The idea itself was earlier

introduced on the basis of Gen 1:3 in §§30–31, the passage to which Philo himself cross-refers.

divine images. In spite of the anthropocentric bias of the treatise, Philo consistently assumes that heaven is a higher and purer realm than earth, which also means closer to God, and thus more divine. See the similar language on the stars at *Abr.* 159; *QG* 4.87. Note the term for "image" is ἄγαλμα (not εἰκών as in the biblical text at Gen 1:26–27), which usually (though not at *Tim.* 37c7) refers to statues of gods. See also the next comment and §69.

as in a temple. The image is of a temple or sacred precinct (i.e. heaven) containing numerous images of gods and heroes (i.e. the stars). Once again Plato set the trend: at *Tim.* 37c7 the heaven is a shrine (ἄγαλμα) for the everlasting gods. He is followed by Aristotle (*De phil.* frg. 14 & 18) and numerous later authors. For a contemporary text cf. Seneca *Ep.* 90.28:

> Such are wisdom's rites of initiation, by means of which is unlocked, not a village shrine, but the vast temple of all the gods — the universe itself, whose true images and true aspects she [wisdom] offers to the gaze of our minds, for the vision of our eyes is too dull for sights so great (trans. Gummere, modified).

See also Plutarch *On tranquillity* 477c; Dio Chrysostom *Or.* 12.33–34; and the discussion in Pépin 1986, 421–430; Runia *PT* 224. For Philo the comparison has an extra dimension on account of the temple in Jerusalem. It of course housed no images whatsoever, but in Philo's eyes (cf. Wisdom 18:24) it is nevertheless a clear symbol of the universe in its totality. The comparison in *Spec.* 1.66 is particularly revealing. See the text cited above at §27; further discussion at Früchtel 1968, 69–115; Winston 1981, 279 and notes.

purest part of bodily substance. Philo does not specify what material substance this is. In the parallel passage at *Abr.* 162 he indicates that the question is controversial: "the mind proceeds to investigate ... whether the four elements make up all things, or whether heaven and the beings in it have been allotted a special nature and have received a substance that is more divine ..." (cf. also the comments on §54, and below §61). For Plato the heavenly bodies consisted mainly of fire, but later Platonists were impressed with Aristotle's doctrine of the quintessence or ether. Philo vacillates somewhat on this issue; cf. Harl PAPM 15.90, Dillon 1977, 171. The question is not relevant to his presentation here.

for many reasons. Philo now switches to direct exegesis of the Mosaic text. First a summary is given of the reasons for the creation of the heavenly bodies based on Gen 1:14. These are then worked out in more detail in §§56–61, with further reference to Gen 1:15–18.

(2b) §56. **value and usefulness.** On the fundamental anthropocentrism of Philo's approach see the General comments above.

perhaps not out of place. Once again Philo adopts the persona of the modest exegete. Cf. above §§4–6, and see further the notes on §72. The verbosity of the language reflects the Greek original.

FOURTH DAY: CREATION OF THE HEAVENLY BODIES

to the sun, like to a great king. It has been speculated that the Genesis text refuses to mention the sun and moon explicitly lest they be regarded as divinities and not as creations of God; cf. Westermann 1984, 129. Philo here seems quite impervious to this problem. Not only does he call them by their usual names, but — encouraged by the description "great luminary" in the text (1:16) — he even compares the sun to a great king, the title he usually reserves for God the creator himself, e.g. at §71. The absence of the article here is of course significant, but even so the description is surprising. As I noted at *PT* 224, Philo does not take over the vocabulary of the LXX, in which the sun and moon are called φωστῆρες (literally "beamer" or "twinkler"), but replaces it with the conventional terms of Greek cosmology.

§57. *sovereignty.* Based on the biblical phrase εἰς ἀρχάς, used for both sun and moon, but Philo changes the unusual plural (literally "for rulerships") to the more regular singular. On the preposition see the comment on §59.

a single entity and quite alone all by itself. Philo piles up no less than four phrases to emphasize the aloneness of the sun.

was called night. Perhaps also a back-reference to the naming of night in Gen 1:5.

(2c) §58. *They have come into existence.* Three times (also in §§59, 60) Philo uses the verb γεγόνασι with reference to the biblical text. He seems to be paraphrasing the two verbs γενηθήτωσαν (let them come into existence) and ἔστωσαν (let them stand) in vv. 14 and 15. The structure of divine command and creational response characteristic of the biblical narrative is again lost. The perfect tense is used to indicate that the situation in the present is the result of the creational event that took place in the past.

as he himself said. Probably Moses, but God could also be meant, since he pronounces the words on signs in Gen 1:14.

signs of future events. The term σημεῖα, which Philo found in the biblical text, is also found in *Tim.* 40c9-d2, where Plato warns that the complex movements of the planets can "bring terrors and signs of future events to those who are unable to calculate properly." Usually Philo is very critical of astrological fatalism and all forms of divination: it is part of the doctrine of Chaldeanism; cf. *Spec.* 1.59–63; *Her.* 97; *Migr.* 181; *Prov.* 1.77–88 etc. Here, however, the biblical text constrains him to be positive, so he interprets it in terms of a prediction of meteorological phenomena. Whereas the heavenly bodies show perfect regularity in their movements (§54), the effect in the sub-lunary realm can be quite irregular, and potentially catastrophic for human beings.

the supply or lack of crops. The theme of farming and the supply of food for human life will become important in the latter part of the treatise; cf. §§80, 167–168.

a wintry summer or a scorching winter. Philo's language is deliberately hyperbolic. The intent is to express highly unusual climatic circumstances.

§59. *came into existence for ... signs.* As he does very often, Philo returns to the biblical passage in order to round off his treatment. PCW 1.19 and Colson PLCL 1.44 are wrong to include γεγόνασιν in quotation marks, since Philo is paraphrasing the biblical text (see above on §58). The use of the preposition εἰς in the phrase εἰς σημεῖα to indicate purpose ("with a view to") after the verb γίγνομαι reflects Hebrew influence in the Greek of the LXX; cf. Blass and Debrunner 1961, §145; Harl 1986, 75. In an English rendering it is best to add a participle.

(2d) *right times.* As noted above at §41, καιρός in Greek can mean "season," as is meant in the LXX text, but Philo exploits the additional meaning of "right time," as he makes clear by adding the explanatory term κατόρθωσις (right result), which contains the root ὀρθός (right).

the annual seasons. The anthropocentric emphasis on agriculture is continued.

surely reasonable. On εἰκότως see the comment above on §36.

(2e) §60. *measures of time.* The Greek has the plural χρόνοι (times), but this is unidiomatic in English.

days and months and years... the nature of number. The biblical text speaks of days and years (v. 14), but not of number. This is a philosophical theme which Philo has imported from Plato's *Timaeus.* Twice, at 39b6 and 47a6, we read there that observation of the planetary movements (and especially that of the sun) teaches rational beings how to count (this aspect is left out above at §54). As I noted at *PT* 225, the phrase "days and months and years" is a compromise between Gen 1:14 and *Tim.* 37e1, 39c1–5 (where "nights" are added). An excellent parallel is found at *Spec.* 1.91, where the theme is called forth by exegesis of the High Priest's ceremonial dress at Exod 28:30 (LXX δήλωσις, "showing," Hebrew Urim), i.e. the heavens "show" or "reveal" time and number: "What else except the heavenly bodies could have revealed the nature of number in accordance with the computation of the parts of time."

the number one. Unlike Plato, Philo illustrates with some simple examples.

infinite time. This illustration cannot be used to shed light on whether Philo supports the doctrine of *creatio aeterna* (see ch. 5). Unending time can be meant *a parte ante* (into the past) or *a parte post* (into the future) or both. Because Moses anticipates Plato in arguing that the universe is indestructible (cf. *Aet.* 13–19), time is taken by Philo to stretch out infinitely into the future. Whether it also stretches back into the past depends on how we interpret his views on creation.

(3) §61. *unclear to us.* Like many ancient authors, Philo is pessimistic about what human knowledge can achieve on the nature of the heavens and its relation to events on earth (cf. also the comment above on §54). Here it is the benefits that are not fully known. Matters are "unclear" (ἄδηλος) because of a fundamental lack of empirical evidence. The ancients had no telescopes. For this reason Epicurus propounded his

notorious theory of "multiple causation": for many celestial and meteorological phenomena it is not possible to give a single cause, not because the causes are actually multiple, but because all one can do is put forward hypotheses, one of which is likely to be correct; see Diogenes Laertius 10.86. For a more optimistic view on the progress of human knowledge, cf. Seneca *Nat.* 7.25. In the larger perspective, however, Philo is optimistic, and this is above all connected with his views on providence (cf. §§9, 171). Compare the affirmation at *Prov.* 2.109: "Just as the sun and the moon came into existence through providence, so did all the heavenly beings, even if we are unable to track down the natures and capacities of each of them and therefore keep our peace."

with the ordinances and laws. Heaven is a vital part of the cosmic order which in §3 is perceived as being in harmony with the Law of Moses. When Philo says that these ordinances have been established by God and will remain unchanging, something of the command structure of Genesis 1 may shine through. But equally we sense the influence of the Greek philosophical notion of a rational order which is embodied in the cosmos as the product of a divine intelligence. As we noted above in the comments on §20, this tension is inherent in the notion of a divine Logos. The terms θέσμος and νόμος are also connected together in §143 and §171. On the difference between them see the comment on §143.

EXCURSUS
The Hellenistic cosmic religion

Philo's somewhat ambivalent attitude towards the heavenly bodies — he often praises them effusively, but also insists that they should not be worshipped — needs to be seen against the background of important developments in Greek thought from the fourth century B.C.E. onwards. When the traditional religion of the polis starts to lose its intellectual appeal for philosophers and other members of the intelligentsia, we observe an increasing tendency to admire the beauty and rationality of the cosmos, and in particular its heavenly regions. The cosmos and the heavenly bodies are regarded as the highest manifestation of the divine. The first impulses for this development are found in the writings of Plato (esp. the *Timaeus*) and Aristotle (esp. his lost *De philosophia*). A major document is the Ps.-Platonic *Epinomis*, written (probably by Philip of Opus) in the decade after Plato's death, in which the author consciously tries to introduce contemplation and reverence for the astral gods:

> Anyone who has attained felicity (ὁ εὐδαίμων) began by being struck by awe at this cosmos, and then conceived a passion for learning all that a mortal can, believing that this is the way to live the best and most fortunate life, and that when he dies he will go to places where excellence (ἀρετή) is at home. Further, once he is really and truly initiated and has achieved perfect unity and a share of true wisdom, he continues for the rest of his

days as an observer of the fairest things sight can see (cf. §53) (986c5–d4, trans. McKirahan modified).

Compare also works such as Ps.-Aristotle *De mundo*, the *Hymn to Zeus* of the Stoic Cleanthes (where Zeus stands for the rational spirit pervading the universe), the astronomical poem of Aratus, and so on. On the basis of these and many other texts Festugière in the second volume of his studies on the background of the Hermetic writings, *Le dieu cosmique* (1949), rightly concluded that we can speak of a "cosmic religion," which appealed to the religious sensibilities of intellectuals during the Hellenistic period. The link to the immanentist theology of the Stoa is particularly clear; cf. the speech of Balbus in Cicero, *De natura deorum* Book 2. Even after the revival of transcendent theology in Middle and Neoplatonism it is continued in a modified form, e.g. in the solar theology of Julian and the *Platonic Theology* of Proclus. For an excellent survey of the entire subject see Pépin's article (1986), entitled 'Cosmic Piety.' At the outset he emphasizes that the tradition of rivalry between the cosmos and humanity, and the strictures against divinization of the cosmos are rooted in the Judaeo-Christian tradition, by which we have all been influenced. For this reason the religion of the cosmos seems strange to modern eyes.

The same sentiments are certainly present in Philo. When he expounds the first commandment in *Spec.* 1.13–20, he first cites Deut 4:19, "when you see the sun and moon and the stars and the entire ordered host (*kosmos*) of the heaven, do not go astray and worship them" (§15) and then continues (§§16–19):

> Those who see the sun with its advances and retreats producing the annual seasons in which animals and plants and produce are brought from birth to maturity at appointed times, and the moon as servant and successor to the sun taking over at night the care and charge of all that the sun supervised by day, and the other heavenly bodies in accordance with their affinity (συμπάθεια) to things on earth acting and working in a thousand ways for the preservation of the all (cf. §61), have gone infinitely astray in surmising that they are gods. If they had made the effort to follow the path that does not go astray, they would have immediately recognized that, just as sense-perception is the servant of the intellect (cf. §53), in the same way all these visible gods (cf. §28) are servants of the God apprehended by the intellect, and they will be well content if they receive the second place ... All the gods observed by sense-perception in heaven should not be considered autonomous (cf. §46), but have received the rank of subordinate powers ... (trans. LCL modified).

Philo's double attitude emerges quite clearly. The heavenly bodies may be recognized as superior and even in a sense divine (to this extent he is to some degree influenced by the cosmic religion), but they should not be worshipped or regarded as autonomous (this is authentically Jewish). See also the pronouncements on the cosmos in §7 and on the heavenly bodies in §§45–46.

In Judaism, both Hellenistic and Palestinian/rabbinic, there is a tradition associating the Patriarch Enoch with the discovery of astronomy; cf.

Kugel *TB*, 177, 191. The consistent exegesis of Abraham's departure from the land of Chaldea in terms of abandonment of cosmic worship reveals a sharp awareness of the dangers of cosmic religion as it developed in the Hellenistic world; cf. Kugel *TB*, 244–267. As was noted above in the comment on §46, by Philo's time a new danger was beginning to make its presence felt. The heavenly bodies could not only be admired and worshipped, but also feared, as will occur in Gnosticism, in which they are regarded as malevolent powers (see further Rudolph 1987, 67–70). Philo perhaps has a presentiment of this development, and so makes sure that the role of the heavenly bodies as important but subordinate causes is made quite clear.

Parallel exegesis

As noted in the previous chapter, the only parallel passage where Philo specifically refers to the biblical passage Gen 1:14–19 is *Plant.* 118, where he gives a kind of summary of our present chapter. The Platonic themes of light and sight and the disclosure of number are briefly alluded to. In four other passages Philo refers more generally to the fact that the motion of the heavens reveals the nature of time (*Leg.* 1.2; *Spec.* 1.90–91; *Aet.* 19; *QG* 2.55). In the last two of these passages Gen 8:22, which mentions spring and summer, day and night in the context of the promise to Noah, also plays a role.

It should not be overlooked, however, that a number of the themes alluded to in this section (heaven, heavenly bodies, cosmic order, temple, prediction of future etc.) are very prominent in the Exposition of the Law, and esp. in the exposition of the special laws associated with the first two commandments in *Spec.* 1.13–97.

Nachleben

The Fathers follow Philo in his general interpretation of the "signs" as referring to meteorological events and the "right times" as referring to the seasons. See Alexandre *CLG* 135–138. She points out that Didymus *Comm. Gen.* 40–41, in discussing the signs, interestingly adds to Philo's meteorological examples that of a kingdom, no doubt referring to the star that guided the Magi (Matt 2:2).

Characteristic for the Philonic reading is his introduction of the philosophical themes of light, time and number. I have not discovered any significant resonances of these themes in the Patres. Origen *Hom. Gen.* 1.7 converts the theme of light into the illumination of the heart by Christ and the church; cf. also Basil *Hex.* 6.2, 121B. Not surprisingly these philosophical ideas are also not found in the rabbis. Josephus' account (*Ant.* 1.31) is reduced to a single sentence with no specifically Philonic reminiscences.

At *Praep. Ev.* 11.30.1–3 Eusebius makes a direct comparison between Gen 1:14 and *Tim.* 38c2–8, which may have been inspired by his reading of *Opif.* (of which passages are cited in 11.24).

Further reading: Radice *FM* 259–262; Runia *PT* 222–225, 271–272 (both scholars extensively discuss the relation to Plato's *Timaeus*); Alexandre *CLG* 132–142 (on the LXX and patristic exegesis).

Chapter Eleven
Fifth day: creation of the animal world (§§62–68)

Analysis/General comments

In the biblical text which Philo is commenting on, the creation of the animal world is divided between the fifth and sixth days. On the fifth day the waters bring forth fish and birds in their various sorts, and these are given a blessing by the creator (Gen 1:20–23). On the sixth the earth produces land-animals of various kinds (1:24–25). Then humankind is created and given a blessing (1:26–31).

Once again we note that Philo is rather selective and somewhat cursory in his explanation of the events of these two days. As can be seen in our overview at Introduction §4(a), his references to the biblical text are also quite limited. Indeed he appears to be in a hurry to reach the part in which human beings are introduced. Most remarkable of all is that the division between the two days is wholly ignored (which justify the biblically inaccurate title of this chapter). For Philo the six is associated with the creation of the cosmos in its entirety (§§13–14, 89), not with the creation of land-animals and human beings (for a different approach see *Leg.* 1.4, where mortal creatures are associated with the six, blessed beings, i.e. God, with the seven). The reason for Philo's sleight of hand is not far to seek. The strong anthropocentric emphasis of the treatise induces him not only to set the creation of humankind apart from the other animals (thereby blurring the boundary between the two days), but also to treat the creation of the animal world very much in the perspective of the creation of the dominant land-animal which is to follow. These two aspects will emerge clearly in our analysis of the passage.

(1a) Philo first announces that the fifth day is devoted to the creation of the mortal kinds. As in the case of the fourth day (cf. §47), he begins by explaining why the number five is appropriate: it is the fitting number for creatures endowed with sense-perception — for the obvious reason that there are five senses —, and sense-perception is what characterizes living beings that have soul. The use of arithmological symbolism is this time very restrained: no more examples are given (§62).

(1b) Most of the following section is devoted to the creation of fish. Philo retains the biblical feature that only sea-fish are spoken about, but he does not have them brought forth by the "waters" (cf. Gen 1:20), in contrast to how the earth is described in §64. The description of different kinds of fish adapted to different environments illustrates the biblical statement that they were created according to their kind (Gen 1:21). Philo exploits the zoological term "kind" or "genus" and uses it repeatedly in these sections. It allows him to relate the Mosaic account to philosophical discussions on the distribution of genera of living beings in the cosmos (§63a).

(1c) The description of the creation of the birds is dealt with in a few lines. The only comment Philo makes is to explain why the two kinds of living beings are grouped together, i.e. on the fifth day. The answer focuses on their particular kind of movement: they both float (rather than support their weight, as land-animals do) (§63b).

(2) Next a very brief description is given of the creation of the land-animals. As noted above, the fact that it takes place on the following day is totally covered in silence. Philo bases his description on his citation of a paraphrase of the biblical text in Gen 1:24. The diversity of the animals created is only briefly touched on in a single sentence (§64).

(3a) It then seems as if Philo wants immediately to expound the creation of humankind in Gen 1:26-31. But first another question arises, namely what is the rationale behind the sequence of creation that Moses presents in his account. This question is related to that which will be discussed below in §§77-83 (why was humankind created last), but is not quite the same. Philo wants to demonstrate that the creational sequence of the Mosaic account is rational and thus philosophically defensible. This encourages him to explain it with reference to the doctrines of zoology and psychology. His explanation takes up the rest of the passage and proceeds in two steps. (§65a)

(3b) The sequence of creation, fishes–birds–land-animals–humankind, is to be explained as follows. Characteristic of livings beings or animals, as distinct from plants, is the fact that they possess soul. The sequence outlined above corresponds to an increase in the powers of the soul, with fishes and humankind representing the extremes and the other two kinds in between. The claim is then further illustrated in a brief section on animal psychology, which explains the four kinds in the proper hierarchical sequence found in the text (§§65b-66).

(3c) But a problem remains. As already indicated in §§13-14 and 26-28, the creational sequence in the account of the six days is not to be taken literally. All things in fact are created simultaneously. Moses' presentation is meant structurally and indicates the order present in the created cosmos. This exegetical idea corresponds very well to the way that Platonist exegetes interpreted the creational myth in Plato's *Timaeus* (see on this subject Ch. 3 and Ch. 5). But there is, it seems, a crucial difference between Plato and Moses. The creational sequence of the former is *descending* (heavenly bodies, lesser gods, men, women, birds, land-animals, reptiles, fishes). The demiurge begins with the noblest creatures first. For Moses on the fifth and sixth days it is *ascending* (on this difference see further my discussion at *PT* 227–228, 418–420). In order to defend the Mosaic presentation Philo hits on the idea of drawing an analogy with the birth and growth of natural things. In all cases the process begins with something insignificant and undeveloped (a seed) and gradually unfolds until the final fully developed living being is achieved, i.e. the final product is ontologically superior to the initial starting-point. The conclusion is then drawn for the cosmos as a whole. Here too what is created first is ontologically inferior to what is created later and especially to what is created last of all (§§67–68).

Philo's argument is not particularly convincing, since it compares two different things, a distribution of genera and a process of birth and growth applying to all genera (*pace* Arnaldez PAPM 1.185 there can be no question of one genus evolving into another). But there is a compensation. It constrains him to draw on some fairly general zoological ideas on the role of nature in order to illustrate his idea (these have a Aristotelian rather than a Stoic background; see the comments on §67). Parallel to his exposition in §§43–44 he can show how God's creative activity, embodied in nature, initiates a process of genesis in which the genera are able to reproduce themselves in perpetuity.

Detailed comments

(1a) §62. *with the three ... with the four.* All translators except Yonge (and to some extent Arnaldez, who gives an unsatisfactory compromise) render "on the third day ... on the fourth day." But the Greek cannot mean this. Philo uses exactly the same phrase at §53. In both texts the adornment received is *identified* with number of the day involved. I try to preserve this in the translation by using the same preposition. In the case of the earth the pronouncement is surprising, because in his commentary Philo fails to explain the relevance of the three to the creation of the earth and the botanical world (as we observed above in Ch. 8).

formation. Philo uses the verb ζῳοπλαστεῖν here, meaning literally "to form or mould into a living being." It is another example of *verba Philonica*, compound words which Philo uses regularly (and are taken over by the Patres), but which are almost wholly absent in pagan literature; see also the comments on §§4, 18. The only preserved instance of this word is found in the 3rd cent. B.C.E. author Lycophron, where it means "to make statues". See further Runia 1992b, 315; similar terms are θεοπλαστεῖν, κοσμοπλαστεῖν, ἀνθρωποπλάστης, πρωτόπλαστος.

the aquatic creatures. The Greek term is ἔνυδρα, quite different from the idiosyncratic LXX language (v. 20 "creeping things having life") and most likely inspired, either directly or indirectly, by Plato *Tim.* 40a1, 92b1. On these generic terms see further §64.

the five ... to living beings. Philo illustrates the affinity of the number five to the creative work on the fifth day only with the obvious example that animals have at most five senses. The same piece of arithmological lore is found at *Mos.* 2.81; *Plant.* 133; *Migr.* 201; *QG* 4.110; *QE* 2.97. It is of course very common in Greek arithmological literature; cf. Anatolius 33.19, Ps.-Iamblichus *Theol. Arith.* 34.3–5 (who also sees a family-relationship — συγγένεια, cf. Philo — with the five elements!); further references at Staehle 1931, 31. For a modern arithmologist five is the number of life (connected with the five senses) and love (it is the indivisible union of the masculine 3 and the feminine 2); see Schimmel 1993, 105–106.

with and without soul. I.e. ἔμψυχα and ἄψυχα. The possession of sense-perception (of whatever kind) separates plants from animals. Plants cannot feel or perceive. In the Stoicizing scheme of *Deus* 35 (cited below on §131) it is the transition from *physis* (plants) to *psychê* (animals). As Alexandre (*CLG* 147) notes, the emphasis on soul as distinguishing characteristic fits in well with the biblical words ψυχῶν ζωσῶν (of living souls). In the citation of Gen 1:24 in §64, however, the equivalent expression is deleted.

divided fivefold ... We have here a typically Philonic didactic cameo. He is very good at giving brief lists of basic philosophical and scientific knowledge. The contents are not profound, but the terminology is accurate and informative. Cf. a more elaborate list at *Cher.* 62, which also includes the five senses. The simplicity of the presentation is perhaps some indication of the audience Philo has in mind for the work.

into sight, into hearing ... The five-fold epanaphora is no doubt meant to reinforce the five-fold division.

its own criterion. On the senses as κριτήρια see §30 and our comments.

for touch ... Exactly the same list of three contraries is given in the parallel arithmological passage at *Plant.* 133.

(1b) §63. *he commands*. Exactly the same use of the historic present as in §40 on the third day.

differing ... according to location. As Radice rightly observes in *FM* 264, the emphasis on ecological bio-diversity and the brief illustratory passage are meant to explain the phrase "according to their kinds" in the biblical text. Philo has noted the zoological term γένος (kind or genus) in the biblical text and uses it repeatedly in these sections. It allows him to relate the Mosaic account to philosophical discussions on the distribution of genera of living beings in the cosmos. For the creationist Philo the various sorts of animals are created in order to live in the different environments. They do not evolve into different species in response to the requirements of their ecological niches, as in modern biological theory. Rather similar to Philo is Cicero's description of the workings of divine providence at *Nat. d.*

2.100: "How great is the beauty of the sea! ... how numerous and how different the species of marine animals, some dwelling in the depths, some floating and swimming on the surface, some clinging in their own shells to the rocks (transl. Rackham LCL)." Comparison of the two passages shows how Philo has used his literary talents to make his description more vivid.

(1c) *kinds of birds.* The LXX πᾶν πετεινὸν πτερωτὸν κατὰ γένος (every winged flying thing according to kind) is converted into τὰ γένη τῶν πτηνῶν and two lines later τῶν ἀεροπόρων. These are exactly the terms used by Plato, *Tim.* 40a1 (ἄλλη [ἰδέα] δὲ πτηνὸν καὶ ἀεροπόρον). See further on §64.

floaters. Arnaldez in his note ad loc. aptly cites Aristotle's observation at *Progr. an.* 15, 713a2–15:

> Generally in birds and winged insects and creatures that swim in the water, ... it is not difficult to see that it is better that the attachments of their instrumental parts should be oblique ... For the wings in birds, the fins in fishes, and the wings in flying insects all grow obliquely. This enables them to cleave the air or water with the greatest speed and force ... (translation Peck LCL).

(2) §64. *the kinds of living beings ... as a kind of native allotment.* As noted in our comments on §63, the terminology that Philo uses for the genera of living beings appears to follow the *Timaeus*, and especially the passage 39e–40a. This impression is reinforced by the generic term used for land-animals in this section, χερσαῖα: cf. *Tim.* 40a2. Moreover the phrase "own allotment" suggests a straightforward correspondence between the four cosmic elements (fire/ether, air, water, earth) and the living beings that inhabit each region. Philo assumes this correspondence elsewhere, e.g. *Plant.* 151–154; *Her.* 139–140; *Spec.* 4.118 (in connection with the dietary laws). It is part of the rational structure of the cosmos as he sees it. For a straightforward parallel compare the cosmogony in Philo's exact contemporary, Ovid, *Metamorphoses* 1.72–75: "So that every region should have its appropriate inhabitants, stars and divine forms occupied the heavens, the waters afforded a home to gleaming fishes, earth harboured wild beasts, and the yielding air welcomed the birds."

Elsewhere, however, Philo develops more complex schemes involving the presence of demons or incorporeal souls and necessitating a correspondence with five elements: cf. *Gig.* 6–11; *Plant.* 12–14; *Somn.* 1.143–141. For a discussion of the entire question of the genera of living beings see Runia *PT* 227–231, Sterling 1998, 360–373. In this context we need only note that Philo is content in *Opif.* to assume the simplest scheme (going back to the *Timaeus*), and he does not develop the more philosophical aspects of the scheme (e.g. the principle of plenitude referred to at *Prov.* 2.110, cf. Runia *PT* 230).

let the earth bring forth. This is not in fact an exact quote but a paraphrase. The strange words (in Greek) "living soul according to kind" are deleted, "livestock" is imported from v. 25, the order of the three categories is altered, and "each" is added to the phrase "according to kind." This is the only time that Philo comes close to quoting one of the divine commands in the creation account. The reason becomes clear in the following sentence.

The earth ... releases. The genesis of living beings from the earth, whether men or lower animals, is a very common conception in Greek thought, both in mythology and in scientific literature. It is of course directly related to the conception of the earth as mother outlined in §38 and §§131–133. The first man is described as γηγενής at §136; see our comments ad loc. In the evolutionary account at Diodorus Siculus 1.7.3–4 living beings are produced spontaneously through the combination of moisture and earth. Philo, in contrast, stresses that the earth produces what the creator commands.

(3a) §65. *To crown all.* As we already noted above on §29, the expression ἐπὶ πᾶσι occurs on ten occasions in the treatise. Often it can be translated as "finally," e.g. at §§41, 55, and in a list in 117. But in this chapter and in Ch. 14 it has a greater significance. Literally it means something like "on top of all these", i.e. the emphasis falls on the fact that man is created as *climax* of the creative acts of the six days and of the sequence of living beings on the fifth and sixth days. The Mosaic creational sequence is ascending. The phrase is repeated in §66. It is difficult to find a suitable English phrase. Here and in the next section I have adopted Whitaker's translation, PLCL 1.51. In §§77–79, and also in 83 and 88, other translations are required; see the comments ad loc.

(3b) *a truly excellent sequence of succession.* In §28 Philo wrote: "Order (τάξις) is a sequence (ἀκολουθία) and series (εἰρμός) of things that precede and follow ..." Here the latter two terms are not placed in parallel, but the sequence is made dependent on the series (which means that, for the sake of English euphony, the rendering has to be slightly altered). The third term "order" is introduced in §67. These two passages, when combined, indicate in the clearest way that the present interpretation has to be related to the principles set out in §§13–14 and 26–28. See further Ch. 3 and Ch. 5.

least delineated ... most developed. Philo once again uses the metaphor of the seal or impression, this time to express complexity of design. Since it is considered suitable for the relation between ideas and copies (cf. above §16), it can also be used for the soul, whether immaterial or material. An excellent parallel is found at *Anim.* 29 (but in relation to mind rather than sense-perception).

bordering. On the term μεθόριος see the comment on §135.

more sensitive. The term is αἰσθητικώτερα, i.e. possessing a more developed sense-perception (αἴσθησις).

§66. *are and are not living beings.* Plato too (*Tim.* 92b) is rather denigrating about fish. To call fish κινητὰ ἄψυχα (literally "moving soulless (creatures)") as Philo does, when sense-perception is the defining characteristic of soul (cf. §62), goes rather far. After all, fish generally have eyes. The intermediate position between plants and animals suggested by the expression is in fact more suitable for the so-called zoophytes, such as shell-fish and oysters, which hardly seem to move and only have the sense of touch (cf. the quote from Cicero cited above on §63). Alexander attributes virtues and emotions to aquatic creatures at *Anim.* 60 (pilot-fish) and 67 (dolphin), but Philo argues against this view (93). As so often, the context determines the direction of the argument.

to preserve their bodies. Philo may be adapting a witticism on the pig attributed to the Stoic philosophers Cleanthes and Chrysippus, e.g. at Cicero *Nat. d.* 2.160: "indeed Chrysippus actually says that it was given a soul to serve as salt and keep it from rotting." Further texts are cited by Pease ad loc. and at *SVF* 1.516, 2.723 (Von Arnim includes our text as 2.722). Philo expatiates on salt as a preservative at *Spec.* 1.289, in connection with Lev 2.13. The salt analogy is used in a well-known rabbinic exchange to illustrate the status of the human fetus; cf. *Gen. Rab.* 34.10, Winston 1998, 44.

intellect as special gift. Humankind is distinguished by *nous*, the capacity for knowledge and thought. Hence its top position in the hierarchy of the sub-lunary world. This is the capacity that Philo will concentrate on in §§69–71.

a kind of soul of (the) soul just like the pupil in the eye. The analogy between soul and eye is given a different twist than in §53. Philo's intentions are well elucidated by the parallel text at *Her.* 55: "The term soul is used in two ways, both for the whole soul and for its dominant part, which properly speaking is (the) soul of (the) soul, just as the eye can mean either the whole orb or its most significant part, by which we see." The ambiguity goes back to Plato, who speaks of the soul both when he means the rational soul (which is immortal) and the soul which contains both rational and irrational faculties and propensities. The issue is further complicated when one tries to determine the relation between intellect (*nous*) and soul. See further Billings 1917, 47–49; Dillon 1977, 174–176; Runia *PT* 299–305, 330–332. In general terms, as noted by Pépin (1971, 86 n. 3), the comparison probably goes back to the famous passage at Plato, *Alc.* I, 133a-b, where the eye looks at the pupil and the soul gets to know itself by looking at its excellence and wisdom. But apart from the two passages cited, I have found no parallels for the phrase "soul of soul" (in both cases without articles). Cf. *Congr.* 97, where the *nous* is said to be properly speaking ἄνθρωπος ἐν ἀνθρώπῳ (human being within human being). On such phrases see further below on "eye of the eye." For the comparison with the pupil, cf. also *Prob.* 140: "for Athens is in Greece what the pupil is in the eye and reason is in the soul."

What Philo means by the analogy can be stated as follows: just like in the eye it is the pupil that is essential for sight, but it needs the rest of the organ so that it can carry out its function, so the essential (or highest) faculty of the human soul is thought, but it needs the other psychic faculties as instruments (especially sense-perception) so that it can perform.

carry out more accurate research. Philo often uses this kind of description to indicate scientists and philosophers, in contrast to himself, who is a kind of generalist using their knowledge to explain the Mosaic text. A similar example is found at §128.

the eye of (the) eye. I.e. ὀφθαλμοῦ ὀφθαλμόν (again without articles). Philo himself indicates that the phrase does not originate with himself, but I have found no parallels. The closest is found elsewhere in his own corpus, *Congr.* 143:

> Just as the eyes see, but the intellect sees further by means of the eyes, the ears hear, but the intellect hears better through the ears, the nostrils smell, but the soul smells more clearly through the nose, and the other senses perceive their own objects, but the understanding perceives them with more purity and clarity — for it could rightly be called eye of the eyes, hearing of hearing and purified sense of each of the senses ...

Taking *Congr.* 143, and *Opif.* 66 together, we have four examples of a noun qualified by itself in the genitive in order to indicate comparison, in each case without use of the article. The origin of this stylistic feature appears to be Greek poetry; cf. Smyth 1956, §1064.

(3c) §67. *everything was constituted simultaneously.* As in §65 Philo deliberately recalls the same terms used in §13 and §28 (in both texts ἅμα occurs). In this section the term τάξις, "order" or "ordered sequence," is added to the two already recalled in §65; see the comments ad loc.

should be outlined in an account. I.e. the narrative sequence has a didactic purpose. On the use of the word λόγῳ here and its background in interpretations of the narrative structure of the *Timaeus* see Runia *PT* 102, with reference to Baltes 1976–78, 1.211.

in the future beings would originate from each other. Here lies the problem of Philo's analogical argument. Future genesis takes place within the species, whereas the sequence in the creation account involves differing genera. See the General comments above.

seed ... similar to foam. At *QG* 1.64, in an exposé on division, a distinction is made between plants that come from dry seeds and animals that come from moist seeds (the word σπέρμα is used for both). The former have already been dealt with in connection with the third day of creation at §43. In Greek physiology semen is not just compared to foam but it is regarded as being foam, e.g. by Aristotle in *Gen an.* 2.2, 736a13–17: "The cause of the whiteness of semen is that it is foam, and foam is white ..." This view goes back to the Presocratic Diogenes of Apollonia. In the generation before Philo it was defended by the medical scientist Alexander Philalethes (cf. Ps.-Vindicianus, *Frg. de semine* 1, text at Wellmann 1901, 208). In other words, Philo is presenting up to date scientific evidence.

obtains movement ... natural growth. The Greek term is simply φύσις, which I have translated by "natural growth," because its chief feature is that it develops by means of growth (this is what κίνησις means in this context), whereas seed remains unaltered. *Pace* Radice ad loc., I do not think the famous Stoic scheme of *hexis–physis–psychê–logos*, as outlined by Philo at *Leg.* 2.22 and *Deus* 35–48, is relevant here, because in that scheme *physis* is associated especially with plants (so the inclusion at *SVF* 2.745 is dubious). It is true that for the Stoics the embryo is like a plant (cf. Aëtius *Plac.* 5.15), but Philo is not distinguishing between embryo and living being here.

in the realm of becoming. The phrase is added because this is not the case in the divine realm, where rest is superior: cf. *Cher.* 19, *Gig.* 49 etc.

like a craftsman ... like an irreproachable art. The distinction that Philo makes between τεχνίτης and τέχνη here is perhaps best explained in terms of Aristotle's conception of the φύσις δημιουργήσασα. Nature works towards its goal of the realization of form and structure not in the manner of the Platonic demiurge, who is presented as deliberating at every point, but rather immanently within the organism itself. Cf. *Part. an.* 1.5, 645a9–15, where the comparison with a τέχνη is made explicitly. A nice parallel is found at *Spec.* 3.108, where a miscarriage interferes with nature's work. Elsewhere, however, Philo rejoices in the consciously demiurgic function of nature and virtually identifies nature with God: e.g. *Spec.* 1.100; 3.184. For valuable remarks on the question of the relation between God and nature in Philo see Nikiprowetzky 1977, 150–151. Philo may have taken the distinction between craftsman and art from a source he is using. In the present context it does nothing to strengthen his already weak argument.

life-giving substance. Literally the πνευματικὴ οὐσία. The presence of *pneuma* or life-breath is responsible for the development of the psychic faculties of the organism. This sounds very Stoic. As noted above on §30, from Chrysippus onwards *pneuma* was the manifestation of the logos that accounted for structured growth in living organisms. From the context, however, it is clear that Philo is drawing on the Aristotelian-Peripatetic conception of the *pneuma* as corporeal instrument (matter) which enables the incorporeal soul (form) to carry out its faculties in conjunction with the body, i.e. the vegetative and perceptive faculties referred to in Philo's text. See further the comment on §30.

faculties ... nourishment and sense-perception. The terms θρεπτική and αἰσθητική are recognizably Aristotelian. Cf. the classic exposé in *An.* 2.2. The same tripartition (i.e. together with the faculty of reasoning) is found at *Spec.* 4.123; *QG* 2.59. Note too that Aristotle rejects Plato's notion of the parts of the soul and prefers to speak of faculties (δυνάμεις, as here); cf. *An.* 1.5, 411a27–b24. He is followed by the Stoic Posidonius, frg. F142–145 E.-K.

for the moment. The subject will return very soon, at §69, and then again at §§134–135.

divine and eternal. The capacity for thought is not something that nature can develop through the semen, as in the case for the other faculties. See the next comment.

from the outside. By using the distinctive word θύραθεν Philo gives away the source, i.e. Aristotle *Gen. an.* 2.3, 736b27–29: "It remains then that intellect alone enters in from the outside and that it alone is divine, because physical activity and its (mental) activity have nothing in common." Whether the mind enters the human being at birth is one of the unanswerable questions posed in the sceptical passage at *Somn.* 1.31. Although the external provenance of the *nous* became a standard doctrine in Middle Platonism (cf. Timaeus Locrus 45; Atticus frg. 7.13; also attributed to Xenocrates frg. 205 Isnardi Parente), Philo's language betrays his direct dependence on Aristotle (esp. θύραθεν ἐπεισιέναι θεῖον ... ὄντα). In the light of the earlier parallels on semen and *pneuma* noted earlier, we may suspect that Philo was directly acquainted with Aristotle's biological treatise, and that he was not just dependent on a secondary source (e.g. θύραθεν εἰσκρίνεσθαι τὸν νοῦν in Aëtius at Stobaeus *Ecl.* 1.48.7, though there Aristotle is not mentioned). But the addition of the adjective ἀίδιος (eternal) to the citation from Aristotle speaks against this view. It is probably an allusion to the eternal nature of the Nous as depicted in *Metaphys.* Λ 7, 1072b28. Philo does not use the term for the soul or the intellect directly, but reserves it for God, of whom the human mind is an image; cf. *Virt.* 204–205, and see further §69. Elsewhere in the treatise the term is used of the cosmos at §7 and §171, an ascription with which Philo strongly disagrees.

§68. *began ... and ended.* This scheme of beginning and end contrasts with that proposed at §82; see the comment ad loc.

the same was also the case. Here Philo draws the analogy. Note how he moves from nature to the creator (δημιουργός).

in between the extremes. Cf. §65, "bordering these both." Philo closes the argument with a form of ring-composition. There are two kinds in the middle, but the sequence "land-animals and birds" seems wrong. At *Her.* 139 we find a different scheme: the aquatic creatures are found in between the birds and land-animals. In this text native habitat takes precedence over biology and the Mosaic creational sequence.

Parallel exegesis

Philo almost never refers to the works of the fifth (and sixth) day in anything but the most general terms (the references in *BPS* 28 are very vague). In two texts, however, he follows a different line of interpretation than in the present chapter. Both texts are concerned with the fact that in Gen 2:19 the biblical text includes a second account of the creation of living beings on earth (this time only land-animals and birds). In *QG* 1.19 he poses the question why this double creation occurs and suggests (note the answer begins with "perhaps") that the earlier things created during the six days were "incorporeal and symbolically typical species (ἰδέαι) of beasts and birds" (transl. Marcus PLCL), while now the sensible likenesses were formed. We return to this question in connection with §§130 and 134.

At *Leg.* 2.11–13 Philo deals with the same text and the same problem, but this time in the context of an allegorical interpretation. Gen 1:24 is quoted literally rather than paraphrased as occurs in §64. The wild animals (θήρια) in both texts thus represent the passions (πάθη). From the physical point of view (φυσικῶς, i.e. to do with the nature of things) this means that previously in the ἑξαήμερον (period of six days) the genera and ideas of the passions were made, whereas now the species come into being. Philo goes on to say that this is Moses' procedure in all cases, including the creation of humankind. Apart from the problematics of the double creation already mentioned above, this passage is remarkable for two reasons. It is the only clear case in Philo where the contents of Gen 1 are allegorized; see further Goulet 1987, 139. As noted above in Ch. 2, this is the first recorded use of the term *hexaemeros* for the creational work of the six days; see Van Winden 1988, 1256; Alexandre *CLG* 47.

Nachleben

Amid the vast amount of exegesis on the creation of the animal world on the fifth and sixth day in patristic literature, a number of *specific* themes from *Opif.* have been taken over.
(1) The arithmological connection between the fifth day and sense-perception belonging to living beings is only found to my knowledge in Didymus *Comm. Gen.* 44.8–12, 48.8. In making the contrast between animals on the fifth day and man on the sixth, Didymus, like Philo, is forced to obfuscate the divisions between the two days.
(2) The family-relationship between fish and birds created on the fifth day (§63) is taken over by Basil *Hex.* 8.2, 72B, from where it passes on to Ambrose *Hex.* 5.14.45.
(3) The interpretation of the fifth day in terms of creatures with soul (§62) with reference to Aristotelian psychological distinctions is found in Basil *Hex.* 7.1, 63C, and Didymus *Comm. Gen.* 42.13–16.
(4) For the conception of a chain of succession in terms of functions of the soul (§§65–66) cf. Gregory of Nyssa, *An. res.* 60A–61B: the human being was created last because he possesses every form of life. Gregory does not, however, relate this sequence to the growth of the individual from the seed, as Philo does in §§67–68. A curious reflection of this latter Philonic idea appears to be present at Didymus *Comm. Gen.* 49.19–27, commenting on "and God made" in Gen 1:25: in the transmission (διαδοχή) of living beings, they deposit the seed, but God forms and perfects the living being; but in the first creation there was no lapse of time between the two processes (the papyrus is damaged at this point).
Once again Josephus' exposition of the biblical text is extremely brief; cf. *Ant.* 1.32. It is striking that he calls the fish νηκτά (an unbiblical word, also found in Wis 19:19); the term may have been taken from Philo §63, though Josephus does use it twice elsewhere, at *Ant.* 4.102; 8.44. In several rabbinic texts the close relationship between fish and birds is noted; cf. Ginzberg 1909–38, 1.28, 5.46, who adduces the Philonic parallel. But dependence is unlikely.

Further reading: Radice *FM* 262–266; Runia *PT* 102, 227–228, 418–419.

Chapter Twelve
Why is the human being created "after God's image"? (§§69–71)

Analysis/General comments

After his digression on the sequence of creation on the fifth and sixth days, Philo returns to the creation of humankind. As we noted in our introductory remarks on the previous chapter, Philo blurs over the clear distinction in the biblical text between the fifth and sixth days. The creation of human beings is certainly the climax of the divine creative act, but it is not specifically connected with the sixth day.

In this and the following chapter Philo does not give a general account of the creation of humankind, but rather focuses on three particular details of the biblical text in Gen 1:26–27: (a) the words "after God's image and after his likeness" (§§69–71); (b) the plural verb "let us make" (§§72–75); and (c) the statement that God made humankind "male and female" (§76).

(1) The first of these discussions, on which we concentrate in this chapter, unfolds in a number of quick steps (on the argument see further Tobin *CM* 37; Borgen 1997, 235). (a) Philo first sets up the discussion by presenting a rather loose paraphrase of the biblical text, in which all the emphasis is placed on the two prepositional phrases which indicate the relation between humankind and its creator. (b) Moses is then praised for his formulation and a brief introductory summary is given of what he says. (c) A warning is given not to read the text in the wrong way, namely to take the "image" relation between God and humans as including bodily features. (d) The correct view is then presented: the term εἰκών is used here with a specific point of reference: it is on account of his intellect (νοῦς) that the human being resembles God (§69a).

(2a) But the nature of the resemblance requires further explanation. What precisely are the characteristics of the human intellect that cause it to resemble God? There is an analogy between the role that God has in the universe and the place of the intellect in the human being. Just as in the case of God, the intellect cannot be seen or known, yet it sees all things and understands all things. (b) In order to illustrate the God-like nature of the human intellect, Philo launches into an eloquent description of the human quest for knowledge and wisdom, presented in terms of the "flight of the mind." The journey proceeds in five stages. (i) First the earthly region is explored by land and sea. (ii) Then turning upwards, the intellect explores the air and the meteorological phenomena found there. (iii) Travelling further, it reaches heaven and joins the heavenly bodies in their celestial motions. (iv) Guided by its love of wisdom, it has the ambition to pass beyond the physical realm and proceeds to contemplate the world of the ideas. (v) But the journey has not yet reached its goal. Propelled by a higher longing, the intellect heads for the great King himself, but is overwhelmed by the beams of light radiating from him which cause it to suffer from vertigo (§§69b–71).

(3) Somewhat anticlimactically Philo returns to the biblical text and explains that the words "after his likeness" are added to "after God's image" in order to emphasize that the image is a clear and accurate impression (§71).

This striking passage, written in an elevated style, has attracted much attention in the scholarly literature. The discussions focus chiefly on two questions. Firstly, how is one to place the exegesis here within the interpretation of the creation of humankind as a whole? What is actually created here, the human being in its entirety or only his intellect? This question becomes more acute when posed in the light of the later passage in §134, where Philo distinguishes between the two accounts in Gen 1:26–27 and 2:7, and speaks of a double creation of humankind, an exegesis that is also prominent elsewhere in his *œuvre*. Moreover, in contrast to §25, which also contains an allusion to Gen 1:27, he makes no reference in the current passage to the divine Logos. It has in fact proved very difficult to supply a systematically coherent account of the various texts, even when these are confined to the passages in *Opif.* For a thorough survey of the scholarly discussion see Radice *FM* 268–271 and further my comments below on §134 (the discussion in Giblet 1948 is also useful, though outdated in some respects).

An entirely different approach to this question is found in Tobin *CM* 36–44. A valiant attempt is made to disentangle a number of anterior exegetical traditions in the interpretation of Gen 1:26–27 and 2:7, which Philo has taken over without managing (or wanting) to integrate them into a coherent whole. Tobin argues that the text under discussion, together with a number of others (including §§72–75), represents the earliest layer of exegetical tradition on the creation of humankind found in Philo. Its focus is primarily apologetic and has a strong anti-anthropomorphic emphasis, arguing against views that tend to take too human a view of God. A prominent feature of these early traditions is that they are rather "isolated." They cannot be easily integrated into a systematic interpretation. Although we are not in agreement with Tobin's method (see Introduction §4c), we agree with him that the text makes the best sense when read on its own, without trying to integrate it fully into a coherent scheme of the creation account. Philo is answering a specific question raised by the biblical text. For this reason, perhaps, he is not concerned to give a full anthropology. His doctrine that humankind is above all characterized by its intellectual powers is significant enough.

The second focus of scholarly attention has been the philosophical and religious background of the passage. It is obvious that Platonic themes — and especially motifs from the *Phaedrus* myth — are strongly present in the description of the ascent of the mind, but claims have been made for Stoic influence as well. Moreover in a number of cases it is plain that Philo does not take these themes directly from Plato, but rather is influenced by the early Middle Platonist interpretative tradition. See especially the detailed analysis and discussion by Méasson 1986, 369–390, which elaborates and synthesizes earlier research by Boyancé 1963b and Theiler 1965, 199–203. The attempt by Borgen (1997, 236) to uncover a significant Jewish background is less successful. See our detailed comments on §69. In our view the present passage, with its marked emphasis on the role of the intellect, is one of the clearest examples of the strong influence of Greek philosophy on Philo's thought. The climax of the passage, however, where the mind falters on approaching God directly, combines Hellenic apophaticism with a strong Jewish awareness of the divine splendour and power.

Detailed comments

(1a) §69. **the human being has come into existence ...** Philo does not quote the biblical text but paraphrases it, citing those words which will occupy his attention in this section. In Gen 1:26 the text actually reads "in our image," because God himself is speaking. This is altered by taking the words from Gen 1:27, "God's image."

(1b) **This is most excellently said.** Philo very often reacts to the citation of the biblical text by explicitly praising the excellence of Moses' words. Cf. in our treatise §76 and §148. This practice is particularly common in the Allegorical Commentary, which is structured by means of citations of the biblical text. For examples see *Leg.* 3.56; *Cher.* 1; *Sacr.* 12–14; *Agr.* 2; *Migr.* 50 etc.

nothing earth-born. The epithet perhaps suits the second account of the creation of humans in Gen 2:7 better. See further the comments on §§132–133. The earth is humankind's natural environment, but humans are not confined to it in the way that other animals are, as Philo will try to make clear in the remainder of the chapter.

(1c) **God does not have a human shape.** In Hellenistic Judaism there is a strong tradition that argues against anthropomorphic representation of God. It is already found in Aristobulus (esp. frg. 2) and is continued in numerous passages in Philo. The *locus classicus* is *Deus* 50–69; see also *Conf.* 98; *Somn.* 1.235 etc. But it is important to bear in mind that the central focus of these texts is hermeneutical: why does the Pentateuch speak in a human way about God? This is not the case in our text, where the point at issue is primarily philosophical and religious. "Human shape" refers here to the physical body. From the Presocratic philosopher Xenophanes onwards, many Greek philosophers rejected the anthropomorphic representation of the gods in Homer and Greek myth. Especially influential was Plato's attack in *Resp.* 377–381. In Philo's time only the Epicurean school retained such an anthropomorphic conception; see Cicero *Nat. d.* 1.46–49. Philosophers made no objection, however, to artistic representation of the gods, in contrast to Jewish thinkers. At *Decal.* 66–75 and *Spec.* 1.21 Philo regards such images as idols.

As noted in our General comments, Tobin sees an anti-anthropomorphic tendency as characteristic of the earliest layer of interpretation of the creation account. But to my mind he greatly exaggerates the importance of this argument in his interpretation of the passages in *Opif.* In the present passage Philo uses it only as a springboard for an exposition of his own view on how the relation between God and humankind should be seen. Although I doubt whether Philo has any concrete thinkers in mind here, it is worth noting that some Jewish and early Christian interpreters did not shrink back from concluding from this text that God was a kind of "super-human" being with a body much greater than what humans have; see Kugel *TB*, 81 with further references.

(1d) **The term image.** The LXX in Gen 1:26–27 uses the term εἰκών, which is philosophically far from innocent. Philo has already exploited it in §25 above; see our comments ad loc. In contrast to §25 and numerous other Philonic texts, Philo here virtually ignores the preposition κατά and interprets humankind *as* God's image. This means that there is no intermediate figure such as the Logos between God and the human being. Tobin (*CM* 51), in line with his method, sees this as an indication of an early, less sophisticated approach. But this need not be the case. Philo could be leaving this further theological aspect out of consideration because it is not required in this particular context, which explores the general question of the relation between God and the human being. Moreover we should never forget that in Philo's theology the name God itself indicates the supreme Being in relation to the world, i.e. at the level of the Logos (cf. Winston 1985a, 19).

to the director of the soul, the intellect. As Méasson (1986, 374) rightly points out, the description of the human intellect has been deliberately formulated to be parallel to God as the "Great director" (μέγας ἡγεμών) of the cosmos (see below). Plato speaks of the ἡγεμὼν νοῦς at *Laws* 631d5 and 963a8, but not in relation to the soul (cf. also *Phdr.* 247c7 "the *nous*, pilot of the soul"). The LCL translation speaks of the "sovereign element," but that would be the (Stoic) phrase τὸ ἡγεμονικὸν τῆς ψυχῆς (cf. §§117, 154). On the relation between the soul in its totality and the intellect see my analysis at *PT* 331, where I conclude that in Philo *nous* is very often in effect equivalent to the rational part of the soul and is responsible for guiding the soul in its entirety, including its senses and passions. See also our remarks above on §§66–67. An important parallel for the present passage is found in a discussion of Mosaic anthropology in *Det.* 79–90, and especially the description of the rational faculty:

> But the faculty that flows forth from the fountain of reason has obtained the spirit (πνεῦμα), not moving air, but an impression (τύπος) and representation of the divine power, which Moses gives the appropriate name "image" (εἰκών), making clear that God is the archetype of rational nature, and that humankind is his imitation and likeness, not the living being with a double nature (i.e. body and soul), but the best form of the soul, to which has been allotted intellect and reason. (§83, accepting the reading κεκλήρωται, as argued by Whittaker 1996, 1)

For the remainder of the passage see below on "invisible," and on the role of *pneuma* in Philo's psychology the comment on §135.

(2a) **On that single intellect of the universe.** Philo now undertakes to explain what the characteristics of the human intellect are which allow it to be described as the image of God. He thus begins an enormously long period which contains a single elaborated train of thought and is not rounded off until just before the end of §71 (ending at "suffers from vertigo"). The first three sections of the period are all connected with the explanatory conjunction γάρ (= "for"); thereafter the motif of the "journey of the mind" is presented by means of three further sections each connected by καί (= "and"), which has the effect of emphasizing the continuity of the quest. Only when the mind approaches the final goal does the movement appear to falter: the final section of the period is connected with the particle δέ (= "but"). It is not practical to try to emulate Philo's style in our translation. The long period has been broken up into no less than 9 sentences.

Just as in §8, God is clearly regarded as *Nous*. The actual term is missing in the Greek. The conjecture of Wendland, ἐκεῖνον ⟨νοῦν⟩, is tempting but not necessary. See further our comment at §8.

as on an archetype. The image of the seal yet again. For the term ἀρχέτυπος see our comments at §§16 and 25.

the intellect in each individual human being. Note how this formulation speaks about the relation between God and the human being, but tells us nothing about who or what was actually created on the sixth day.

In a sense ... a god of the person. Philo's expression here is quite remarkable. In the Greek philosophical tradition it is common to describe the mind or rational soul as the divine element in the human being. For this motif see esp. Plato *Alc.* 133c: "Can we therefore say that there is any part of the soul more divine than the part with which we know and think? No, we cannot. This part of it, then, resembles the divine." See also *Tim.* 41c7, 90c8; Aristotle *Nic. Eth.* 10.7, 1177a16; full discussion of the theme in Pépin 1971. At *Tim.* 90c4 Plato calls it our δαίμων (virtually equivalent to "god"), which we have to care for. Here Philo seems to go very far in calling it a θεός, though he is careful to qualify his statement. It is possible that he is encouraged to do so by an exegesis of Exod 7:1, where the LXX strikingly calls Moses "a god for Pharaoh." Nevertheless the actual number of texts in Philo in which the human intellect or rational part of the soul is called "divine" or "the divine element" is comparatively rare, which makes the current text all the more striking. For a full discussion with references to numerous texts see Runia *PT* 332–334, and the further elaboration at 1988, 64–66.

who ... bears it around as a divine image. Philo here again uses the striking verb ἀγαλματοφορέω, already discussed above at §18. As in §137, it is used here as an image for the body carrying the intellect just like a god in a sacred shrine. An excellent parallel is found at Cicero *Resp.* 1.59: "For the person who knows himself will recognize first that he has a divine element in himself and will regard his mind in himself as a kind of consecrated divine image (*simulacrum*)."

the same position ... The analogy between the macrocosm (God and the world) and the microcosm (the intellect in the human being) is probably Stoic in origin (cf. Cicero *Somn. Scip.* 26; Seneca *Ep.* 65.24), but does not have to be interpreted in an immanentist way (cf. above on §8). One is strongly reminded of the allegorical theme of Abraham's discovery of God, in which the train of thought goes in exactly the reverse direction, *Abr.* 74 (cf. also *Migr.* 192–194):

> For it cannot be that in yourself there is an intellect (νοῦς) appointed as your director (ἡγεμών) which the entire community of the body obeys and each of the senses follows, but the cosmos, the fairest and greatest and most perfect work of all ... is without a king who holds it together and directs it with justice. Do not be amazed that the king is invisible, for neither is the intellect in you visible ...

the Great director. ὁ μέγας ἡγεμών, the famous phrase used of Zeus in Plato's *Phaedrus* myth, 246e4. Apart from being used for the sun at §116, it is found nowhere else in Philo. Much more common is the expression "Great king," which we shall encounter in §71.

the human intellect in the human being. Cf. above on the motif from *Alc.* 133c, and also the comments on §66. Borgen (1997, 236), following Cohn (PCH 1.51), points out the similar thought in *Talmud Berachot* 10a: "Just as the Holy One, blessed be He, fills the whole world, so the soul fills the body. Just as the Holy One, blessed be He, sees but is not seen, so the soul sees but is not itself seen." The parallel is striking, and no doubt rests on the fact that it is a commonplace rather than on direct influence. It is to be agreed with Urbach 1987, 249, however, that there is a vast difference between Philo's and the rabbis' anthropology. Philo has undergone the strong influence of Hellenic intellectualization, as is apparent in the fact that he regards God as mind and sees the relation between God and humankind in terms of the powers of intellect. None of this is present in rabbinic thought. Urbach goes too far, however, when he states of the present passage with its depiction of the flight of the mind (*ibid.*): "This portrayal, which is nearer to that of Eros in Plato's *Phaedrus* than to the Midrash, is based *au fond* on the view of the body as a prison, a view that also pervades Philo's allegorical interpretations." This does not correspond to the nuanced depiction of the created human body in *Opif.* A further aspect of the anthropology pointed out by Borgen (1997, 236) is that in both Greek (Platonic and Stoic) and Jewish tradition (apocalyptic and rabbinic) the soul is associated with heaven and the body with earth. This forms an essential presupposition for the concept of the flight of the soul which is found in both traditions. See further on §70.

invisible. Cf. *Det.* 87 (in the continuation of the passage quoted above):

> The invisible Deity engraved on the invisible soul the markings of himself (τύποι), so that not even the region of the earth would be devoid of a divine image. Yet the archetype was so lacking in visible form that the image too was invisible, but having been marked in accordance with the model, it received thoughts that were no longer mortal but immortal.

Because of the context (exeg. Gen. 4:10) there is no comment on the relation between the mind and the body in which it is housed, as here in *Opif.*

yet its own nature is unclear. The two analogies between God and the human mind are meant to reinforce the thesis that it is in respect of his intellect that the human being is created in the divine image. At the same time the second analogy introduces the motif of the mind's flight. Just as the nature of the heaven is unclear (cf. §§54–55 and our comments ad loc.) so the nature of the mind is essentially unknowable; cf. esp. *Somn.* 1.30–32 (on which see Mansfeld 1990, 3117–21), *Mut.* 10, *Leg.* 1.91. The last two texts include the explicit analogy with God's unknown nature. On these sceptical texts and the role of scepticism in Philo's thought see further Nikiprowetzky 1977, 186.

(2b) *By means of the arts and sciences.* Philo's encomium of the powers of the intellect begins with the natural habitat of humans on earth, to which is added exploration of the sea. For the latter see also §114. "Arts and sciences" refers in the first place to the science of navigation, but also to the theoretical sciences of geography, meteorology etc. Philo also intends a contrast with "philosophy," which comes into play when one goes beyond the physical world, i.e. in §70.

all of them highways. I.e. busy routes used by many people.

over land and sea. The soul's journey is first structured by means of the four elements, thereafter by the distinction between the two realms of physical and intelligible reality.

investigating. Philo's choice of verb (διερευνώμενος) indicates that he has in mind a famous Platonic passage on the supreme value of the contemplative (or investigative) life at *Theat.* 173c–174b; see further *Spec.* 2.44–45 and Méasson 1986, 379.

§70. *Next it is lifted on high.* The words καὶ πάλιν πτηνὸς ἀρθείς would have been sufficient for Philo's readers to recognize that he was going to avail himself of the *topos* of the "flight of the soul (or mind)." This motif is best-known from Plato's myth in the *Phdr.* 246d–249d, in which the soul is depicted as having wings, so that it is borne aloft to the vault of heaven and joins Zeus with his heavenly chariot and the other gods in heaven. On the soul's wings which bear it aloft when they are properly nourished by wisdom see esp. 246d-e. But the motif is much more widespread. It is based on the notion that the body is heavy and stuck to the earth, whereas the soul or mind or spirit can elevate itself, not only to investigate the heavens, but also to actually be present there. Long before modern technology made it possible, human beings dreamt of being able to observe the world from great heights, enabling them to place earthly events in a proper cosmic perspective. (Little did they imagine that air travel would become for the most part a profoundly boring experience!) As Festugière 1949, 442 rightly points out, the motif comes in two distinct forms (though in practice these are not always easily distinguishable). It can depict the fate of the soul after death when it leaves the body behind (as meant by Plato's myth which assumes the process of reincarnation, cf. also the famous dream of Scipio in Cicero *Resp.* 6.10–26). It can also take place while one is still alive in the body, from which the soul temporarily dissociates itself. This is clearly what Philo assumes in our passage.

There are many comparable Philonic passages; e.g. in the Exposition of the Law *Spec.* 1.37–40, 207; 2.44–46; 3.1–6 (the famous autobiographical passage); *Praem.* 30. The motif is hinted at when describing the nation of Israel "who sees God" in *Legat.* 5. In the Allegorical commentary it is used to allegorize the birds in Gen 15:9–11 at *Her.* 126–128, 230–241 (cf. also 68–70); many parallel texts cited by Harl PAPM 15.119. In all these texts Philo consistently uses a distinctive terminology, much of which is derived from the *Phaedrus* myth and its exegesis. Some examples will be pointed out in our further comments. Note, however, that all these passages have their distinctive features, usually determined by the context. For example, at *Spec.* 1.37–40 Philo does not mention the noetic cosmos as he does here, but passes straight from heaven to God (cf. also *QE* 2.40 and *Det.* 87–89, discussed below in Exegetical parallels).

For discussion of the motif in Philo see Borgen 1993 (with copious references to further literature); 1997, 235–242; on the wider background, including Judaism and early Christianity also Segal 1980; Himmelfarb 1993; general surveys in the *RAC* articles of Courcelle 1972; Colpe 1991); on the Greek background Jones 1926; Boyancé 1963b; Theiler 1965, 484–485 (the latter two scholars argue persuasively that Philo reads the *Phaedrus* with the help of an exegetical tradition, but it seems to me pointless to try to attribute it to one particular philosopher such as Posidonius or Antiochus). The single best parallel to this passage is found in the 2nd cent. rhetor Maximus Tyrius in his speech *Who is God according to Plato, Diss.* 11.9–10 (the passage is too long to quote in its entirety, I have selected the most important parts):

> But the Divine itself cannot be seen by the eye or spoken of by the tongue or touched by the flesh or heard by the ear; it is only the noblest and purest and most intelligent and subtlest and most venerable aspect of the soul that can see it in virtue of their similarity ... By bringing to bear an upright, vigorous soul, by fixing its gaze firmly on that pure light and not falling prey to vertigo (σκοτοδινιῶν), nor sinking back towards the earth ... and entrusting its guidance to true Reason and vigorous Love ... as the soul advances thither and distances itself from things below, the clear radiance of what lies ahead of it, stage by stage, serves as a prelude to God's true nature. As it advances, it hears of God's nature; as it ascends, it sees it. The end of the journey is not the heavens nor the heavenly bodies. For though these are indeed things of wondrous beauty ... yet must we go beyond even these and emerge beyond the heavens (ὑπερκύψαι), into the region of true Reality and the peace which reigns there ... (translation Trapp).

Völker 1938, 188 argues: "Philo makes use of these views [i.e. of the flight of the soul], but they never meant more to him than images and literary reminiscences. Spiritually he stood far from them." This certainly cannot be maintained for the present passage, which is deliberately formulated in a crucial anthropological context.

the ether. Philo means the substance out of which the heavenly bodies are made (instead of fire which might be difficult for the soul to pass through!). Here and elsewhere (e.g. *Plant.* 3), Philo reflects Platonist efforts to absorb Aristotle's fifth element in a four-element cosmology. See further Dillon 1977, 170, and for Platonist vacillation between a four and a five element cosmology Dörrie and Baltes *DPA* vol. 5, §148.

after being carried around. The verb συμπεριπολέω occurs in Philo only in the context of passages on the ascent of the soul: it is also found at *Spec.* 1.37, 2.45, 3.1; *Praem.* 121.

in the dances. See the comment at §54 and esp. the monograph of Miller 1986.

the laws of perfect music. A veiled reference to the Pythagorean theory of the harmony of the spheres. See also §126. The music is perfect because it is produced by the motions of the heavenly bodies which are assumed, in accordance with the cosmology of the *Timaeus*, to be mathematically perfect.

following the guidance of its love of wisdom. In the *Phaedrus* myth the gods follow Zeus (246e6) and so does the soul who wishes to and is capable of doing so (247a6). Philo does not hesitate to take over the Platonic motif of *erôs*, which impels the soul towards truth and the divine, i.e. philosophy as the love and pursuit of wisdom. Cf. also *Symp.* 210–211 and the quote from Maximus cited above.

it peers beyond. The verb ὑπερκύπτω is difficult to translate. Literally it means "bend forward over," e.g. when one gets to the edge of a wall, lifts one's head above it and catches view of what is beyond. Cf. *Phdr.* 249c1–4: "This is recollection of those things which the soul saw when it journeyed with the god and, looking down at what we now say to be reality, gazed up at (ἀνακύψας) what is true being." Plato means that the charioteer, i.e. the rational part of the soul, can lift his head up and just catch sight of what is beyond the heavens (ἀνακύπτω means approximately the same as ὑπερκύπτω but from the perspective below). Philo replaces it with the other verb because he is primarily interested in the view "outwards," i.e. of the intelligible realm. The verb ὑπερκύπτω is a favourite one in "ascent" contexts; see *Praem.* 30; *Leg.* 3.100; *Fug.* 164; *Legat.* 5. The same verb is used for the final transcending move in the passage from Maximus quoted above.

on the intelligible realm. The phrase νοητὴ οὐσία recalls the noetic cosmos introduced in §16, whose location was explained in §§17–24, but here the context is epistemological and anthropological rather than directly connected with creation. In the *Phaedrus* myth, as just noted, the souls travelling with the gods contemplate τὰ ἔξω τοῦ οὐρανοῦ (what lies outside the heaven, 247c2), which is also called the ὑπερουράνιος τόπος (place beyond the heaven, 247c3). This is clearly a spatial metaphor for contemplation of the world of ideas which is beyond space and time, and was interpreted as such by later Platonists. In this way the intelligible cosmos can become a world that lies beyond the physical cosmos, only to be approached by the mind. See, in addition to our comments on §§16–20, the texts collected in Baltes *DPA* vol. 5, §131, the analysis in Runia 1999b, and for important developments in patristic thought Armstrong in Armstrong and Markus 1960, 16–29.

The ascent to the intelligible realm is thus the second stage in the ascent. For excellent parallels in "ascent" contexts see *Praem.* 37; *Mut.* 179–180 (with striking allusions to the *Phaedrus*); *QG* 4.138. In the text of Maximus cited above the words "emerge into the region of true Reality" also allude to this intelligible realms of the ideas (τὸν ἀληθῆ τόπον, combining *Phdr.* 247c3 and 248b6).

§71. **the models and forms ...** We recall the role of the intelligible world as model in §16. But, as I explain in Runia (1999b, 168), the intelligible world can also be separated from its role in creation and regarded as a higher world of ideas, to be contemplated or even to be inhabited as a kind of mystical home.

possessed by a sober drunkenness. The beauty of the transcendent realm is so overwhelming that the intellect loses all sense of itself and becomes inspired. Philo uses here one of his most famous phrases, describing a kind of intellectual or religious ecstasy; cf. also *Fug.* 166; *Prob.* 13 etc. In his monograph devoted to the subject Lewy (1929) argued that it was an original invention of Philo himself, but Chadwick (1967, 150) and Winston (*PA* 358) are not persuaded, both citing the allusion to the theme in the epigram on Cleopatra's ring (*Anth. Pal.* 9.352).

it becomes enthused like the Corybants. The verb is ἐνθουσιάω, literally "have a god (θεός) inside one." The image is taken from the followers of the Greek god Dionysus, Phrygian priests called Corybants, who work themselves into a frenzy with their whirling dances. See further Miller 1986, 74–76. The same image is used in *Contempl.* 11–12 of the Therapeutae, who pass beyond the visible sun and long to have a vision of God as Being.

Filled with another longing. Now, however, the Platonic theme of *erôs* receives a further rather unexpected development. Unlike in Maximus, where God and the intelligible world are not clearly distinguished, Philo regards the intelligible realm as a stage in the ascent which the mind aspires to leave behind. This is possible because God is the creator of this realm too; (cf. §§16–20, the model as the divine Logos; *Abr.* 88, God maker and ruler of both worlds; *Praem.* 37–38, the noetic cosmos directed by its charioteer).

the utmost vault of the intelligibles. Another obvious allusion to the *Phaedrus* myth, 247a8–b1: "when the gods go to their feasting and banquet, they advance to the very top of the vault that supports the heaven." But in a striking example of free adaptation, Philo has transferred the image from the physical heaven to the higher level of the intelligible world.

it thinks it is heading. The verb δοκεῖ here no doubt indicates subjective experience: the intellect gets carried away in its enthusiasm and forgets its limitations. Perhaps one might interpret the quest in terms of the distinction between God's existence and essence often used by Philo elsewhere (on which see further the comment on §170). The mind, through its contemplation of physical and intelligible reality, is convinced of the existence of God as supreme cause, but now it tries to grasp God's essence, a quest that is bound to fail, as even Moses discovered (*Spec.* 1.41–44).

the Great king himself. In classical Greek culture the Great king was the King of Persia, regarded as an omnipotent oriental despot quite different to the rulers in the fractious Greek world of small cities. His role was later taken over by Alexander (cf. §18) and the Roman emperors. The image is frequently used by Philo to convey his monarchic conception of God; cf. also §88; *Decal.* 61; *Spec.* 1.18, king of kings; *Agr.* 78; *QE* 2.44 etc. The extended image of the Great king, transcendent and hidden but exerting influence throughout the cosmos, at Ps.-Aristotle *Mund.* 6, 398a11–b6, is justly famous. But it is important to note that it misses the higher level of the intelligible world. See further my comments at *PT* 168, where I also discuss Plato's usage of the image and the subsequent development by his later followers.

overwhelmed by the brightness. The same Platonic term μαρμαρυγαί is used as in §6, but now in an theological and anthropological context. The mind aspires to contemplate God as he really is, but this cannot be accommodated to human nature. By implication, therefore, the ascent ends in a kind of failure. The resemblance of the image to its original here reaches its limit. If human beings could truly see God, they would no longer be "after the image" but equal to him. Although Philo shares the tendency to apophatic theology with the Platonist tradition, he places more emphasis on the overwhelming power of God which requires tempering when approached by human thought. See further my remarks at Runia 2001a, 297–299, and also the comments above on §23. Later in the Exposition the theme is further elaborated, when a description is given of Jacob's ascent as Israel (he who sees God), *Praem.* 37–40:

> For an incorporeal beam purer than ether suddenly flashed over him and disclosed the intelligible world led by its charioteer. That charioteer, irradiated by a circle of undiluted light, was difficult to discern or to divine, for the eye was enfeebled by the sparkling lights (μαρμαρυγαί). Yet in spite of the abundant light that flooded it, it held its own in its extraordinary yearning to behold the vision. The Father and Savior, perceiving his genuine longing and desire, felt pity, and lending strength to the penetration of his sight did not grudge him a vision of himself, to the extent that it was possible for created and mortal nature to contain it. Yet it was not a vision showing what he is, but only that he is ... For to God alone is it permitted to comprehend himself." (translation Winston).

Compare also the quest of Moses ascending the mountain in *Spec.* 1.40–50. These texts go beyond the present passage because epistemological deficiency is met with divine grace.

suffers from vertigo. The verb σκοτοδινιάω combines two aspects: the mind grows dizzy and things become dark (σκότος) as it were before its eyes; cf. what happens to Jacob in the quote above (though the verb is not used). The same rare verb occurs, we recall, in the text in Maximus of Tyre cited above. Plato himself uses it for the experience of confronting difficulties in dialectic; cf. *Theat.* 155c10; *Soph.* 264c11; *Laws* 892e7.

(3) *as an extra indication.* Philo's explanation of the additional words in Gen 1:26 — Moses never says anything without a purpose, cf. *Leg.* 3.147 — is surprisingly flat, especially when we consider that the term "likeness" here is ὁμοίωσις, the key word in the Platonist formulation of the end (τέλος) of human life (based on *Theat.* 176b1, cited at *Fug.* 63), which Philo exploits to a considerable extent elsewhere; see further the comment on §144. Compare, for example, the dynamic interpretation of Clement *Strom.* 2.131.5, who argues that "according to the image" indicates what the human being receives at birth, whereas "according to the likeness" represents the perfection that he can achieve during his life. More examples of the interpretation of the distinction at Alexandre *CLG* 187–188.

an accurate and clearly marked casting. Yet again we encounter the metaphor of seal and mark (cf. the comment on §69). "Casting" here translates ἐκμαγεῖον, not the indistinct receptacle of Plato *Tim.* 50c2, but the imprint made in a soft material like wax by a seal or mould. This can be clearly seen in *Fug.* 12, *Aet.* 15; see further my discussion in *PT* 163, 286. The same term is also used in §146.

Parallel exegesis

Gen. 1:26–27 is one of the texts most frequently cited or alluded to in Philo's works. *BPS* records no less than 63 instances. However, although there are many parallels for the main themes of the passage — the analogy between God and human mind, and the "ascent of the mind or soul" —, the only text which is a significant parallel for §§69–71 is *Det.* 79–90 which has been partially cited above. In *Det.* 87–89 there is also an ascent passage, in which the mind passes beyond the limit of the universe and tries to comprehend God (but not the noetic cosmos). The difference between the passages is that in *Det.* the exegesis is compounded with motifs inspired by Gen. 2:7. In *Opif.* the two texts are kept separate, as we shall see in Ch. 18.

Nachleben

Two 4th century Christian authors make extensive and detailed use of our passage, which they must have consulted in the original.

Didymus of Alexandria in his *Comm. Gen.* 54.13–58.2 cites Gen 1:26–28 and then devotes a number of pages to the human being who is described as being created in the text. On three points he follows Philo. (a) The human being according to the image is not stated in relation to the composite of body and soul, "for God does not have human shape" (56.16, a direct quotation of §69), but in respect of the interior human being, which is the *nous* or soul (cf. 55.3). (b) The term image is explained in terms of the metaphor of the seal and its markings; cf. 57.22–28. (c) A little further on Philo's explanation of "after the likeness" in §71 is paraphrased (58.18–22). Note, however, that Didymus emphasizes much more than Philo the role of the mind to *rule* over the animals, which is promptly allegorized in the Origenian tradition (60.15–61.11). See further my more detailed analysis in Runia 1998, 336–342.

Ambrose of Milan, in the second of his *Letters* which draw extensively on *Opif.*, gives an extensive unacknowledged paraphrase of the entire passage: *Ep.* 43 = 29.14–15 Faller. The bishop takes over and expands somewhat Philo's exegesis in terms of the human *nous* (he uses the Greek word), though the anti-anthropomorphic argument is left out. He also paraphrases the ascent of the soul, but profoundly Christianizes its latter stages. After travelling through the elements to the heavens,

> by means of a greater desire (cf. §71!) the intellect lifts itself to the very bosom of the Father, where dwells the only-begotten Son of God who relates the secrets of God and those things that are later to be revealed "from face to face" (cf. 1 Cor. 13:12). Now, however, to those worthy to receive them he outlines "partly as in a riddle" (the same text) and at the same time from his spirit and his face he pours forth a splendour of light in the manner of a torrent (cf. §71 again!) ...

The noetic world in Philo's ascent of the mind is thus wholly converted into the words of the Logos as God's son.

A third Church Father who should be mentioned is Gregory of Nyssa. In his treatise *Opif. hom.* he makes extensive use of themes from our treatise (for a specific case see below Ch. 14 on §§77–83). Influence of the current passage can be seen in §11 (the unknowability of both the divine and the human intellect) and §16 (humankind is created "in the image" through his rational part; see esp. PG 44.181B–C), Gregory's division into rational and irrational, however, is closer to *Fug.* 68–72. See also below on §134.

In the case of Clement *Strom.* 2.102.6 and Calcidius §55 usage of our text is possible, but cannot be definitely established; see the respective discussions in Van den Hoek 1988, 184 and Runia *PEC* 283.

In more general terms Philo's basic approach to Gen 1:26–27 as the foundational biblical text for anthropological doctrine was massively influential, especially in terms of the identification of humankind's intellectual powers as the specific aspect in which it stands in an image relation to God. But specific lines of influence are not so easy to trace. For a number of passages in which the "image" relation between God and humankind is denied for the body, see the passages cited by Riedweg 1994, 486, in his note on Ps.-Justin, *Coh.* 34.1 (note also Origen *Sel. Gen.* 12.96), and the full discussion in Alexandre *CLG* 175–188. We return to this theme below in Ch. 18 on §§134–135, where we adduce Origen *Hom. Gen.* 1.13, which may also draw on §69.

Further reading: Radice *FM* 266–272; Méasson 1986, 369–390 (very good on the Greek background); Miller 1986, 56–80 (but beware of his translation, which is a fanciful reinterpretation of the Greek); Borgen 1993; 1997, 235–240 (on the ascent motif); Kugel *TB*, 80–82 (more on the exegetical background and Jewish interpretations of the image relation).

Chapter Thirteen
Why was the human being not created by God alone?
(§§72–76)

Analysis/General comments

The following detail of the biblical text of Gen 1:26–27 to which Philo directs his attention is the remarkable plural form of the hortatory subjunctive ποιήσωμεν (let us make). In the case of all the other days Moses simply writes ἐποίησε (God made, cf. vv. 1, 7, 16, 21, 25), as he also does subsequently in v. 27. It is quite understandable that this plural has puzzled and intrigued exegetes throughout the ages. Of Rabbi Jonathan (beginning 3rd cent.) it is recorded (*Gen. Rab.* 8.8):

> When Moses was engaged in the writing of the Law, he had to write the works of each day. When he came to the verse, "And God said: 'Let us make man'," he said: "Sovereign of all, why do you provide the heretics with an argument?" God replied: "Write! Whoever wishes to err, let him err!" (translation Freedman & Simon)

This is not Philo's approach. He thinks there must be a very good reason for this unexpected reading, and gives a striking exegesis of the passage, which in its turn has received much attention from scholars.

(1) Philo commences his discussion by first introducing the difficulty which the exegete confronts and citing the text in which it occurs. The problem is that God in his omnipotence did not need any assistance for the earlier works (cf. §23), so why should he need it now for the creation of humankind? Philo will not vouch for the truth of his explanation, but is prepared to give a reasonable conjecture (§72).

(2) First it is necessary to look at the differences between the various living beings that are created. Philo presents a tripartition. The first group, consisting of plants and animals, have no reason, so cannot be regarded as doing good or evil. A second group, the heavenly beings superior to humans, do possess reason, but carry out no evil deeds. There is, however, a third "mixed" group, which has reason, but can incline to either good or evil. This group of course consists of human beings (§73).

(3) This division can now be applied to the problem under discussion. It was appropriate for God to make the first two groups on his own, but for the third group this was only appropriate for the better

part of its make-up. The plural thus reveals that God enlists collaborators, so that he is only credited with the good actions that humans perform, while the other actions can be assigned to his subordinates. After all, God cannot be the cause of evil (§§74–75).

(4) Philo appends a very brief comment on the words "male and female" in Gen 1:27. These refer to the most proximate species which are present in the genus, even though the individual humans have not yet appeared. Despite what the biblical text might seem to say, the human being, or rather his intellect, is still here envisaged at a pre-sexual stage (§76).

The main thrust of Philo's solution is theological and philosophical, involving the theme of theodicy. God as creator is in no way responsible for evil. The thought is surely biblical, and is also strongly defended by the rabbis; see for example the texts cited by Winston 1986, 105. Philo differs, however, because he introduces philosophical considerations, and this is largely due to the influence of Plato.

In the myth of Er the prophet pronounces to the souls who are about to choose their lot (*Resp.* 617e4–5): "The blame is for him who chooses; God is blameless." In the *Timaeus* this thought recurs, but it is combined with cosmological considerations. When the demiurge has finished creating the cosmos as a whole and the heavenly bodies, he addresses the so-called "young gods in a famous speech" (41a-d) and instructs them to create the remaining mortal genera of living beings. These he himself cannot create, for then they would be immortal. Of the whole human being, therefore, the demiurge only creates the rational soul. After it has been created, it is given instructions which it must obey, so that God cannot be held responsible for its evil deeds (42d2–4). The soul's irrational part and the body, on the other hand, are made by the demiurge's subordinates. Philo's solution is clearly indebted to the *Timaeus* in general terms. But when we look at points of detail, there are important differences: (a) In Plato the demiurge *delegates* a large part of the creative task to his helpers and then retires (42e5–6); in Philo God *calls in the assistance* of helpers for the limited task of creating humankind. (b) In Plato God creates the rational soul, his subordinates the irrational soul and the body; in Philo it is by no means clear exactly what is made by whom; there are certainly no grounds for concluding that God did not make the human body (though he does not do so in this context, since the subject focused on is the intellect, cf. §69). There is a consensus on this point between my position in *PT* 246, Tobin's in *CM* 41 and Pearson's in 1984, 324 (all written independently of each other). Winston (1986, 109) disagrees, arguing on the basis of *Spec.*

1.329 that God did not create anything corporeal. But this is not relevant to the point at issue. Even if God creates through the intermediation of the Logos (a consideration that is not expressly brought forward in *Opif.*), he still creates the mortal genera on the fifth and sixth days himself, as well as the human body in Gen 2:7. (c) In Plato the identity of the helpers is quite clear; they are the planetary gods. In Philo their identity remains rather obscure. But there are no grounds for thinking that Philo follows Plato literally and identifies them with the planetary gods, as suggested by Dillon 1977, 247. (d) In Plato the reason given for the division of labour concerns the issue of immortality; in Philo the problem is the origin and responsibility for moral evil. Radice (*FM* 275), citing A. M. Mazzanti, usefully distinguishes between ontological and ethical dualism. The two motivations are clearly related, but not exactly the same. The reason for all these differences is that Philo is expounding the thought of Moses and stays rather close to the problem and text at hand.

It is important to note that there are four other passages in which Philo makes use of the same basic theme: *Conf.* 168–183; *Fug.* 68–72; *Mut.* 30–32; *QG* 1.54. Two of these have as their starting-point other LXX texts with puzzling plurals, Gen 3:22 and 11:7 (the fourth and first respectively). These texts are largely in agreement with the present passage, although there are various discrepancies on points of detail. For further detailed discussion of these texts and of §§72–75 in particular see Runia *PT* 242–249 (particularly in relation to the *Timaeus*) and Winston 1986, who disagrees with my interpretation on a number of points.

Finally we note that scholars have argued that in this passage Philo shows proto-Gnostic tendencies. For example, Fossum (1985, 208) writes:

> When Philo's disquisitions on man receiving his base and material soul from God's agents are disrobed of their Platonic dress and transferred to a less sophisticated setting, it becomes palpable that they are expositions saying that the angels were the creators of the material body, which was the source of evil according to the popular opinion in the Hellenistic world.

Such views involve a misreading of our text. There can be no question of a substantial part of creation being attributed to malevolent powers or angels such as in the Gnostic myth. As we saw, Philo strongly asserts the goodness of creation and its creator. See further my comments at *PT* 249, with references to other scholars (note esp. Chadwick 1967, 145). A sound discussion of the role of Gen 1:26–27 and 2:7 in Philo compared with the Gnostic movement is found in Pearson 1984.

Detailed comments

(1) §72. *to raise the difficulty.* We have here a typical example of the exegetical method of the *quaestio*, in which difficulties (*aporiai*) are raised in relation to the biblical text under discussion. A number of scholars have argued that this is the fundamental method underlying Philo's exegetical commentaries, not only the *Quaestiones* (where it is obvious), but also the Allegorical Commentary, and even on occasion in the Exposition of the Law, as here. See Nikiprowetzky 1983, 5, 67–69; Borgen 1997, 80–101 (our passage is analysed at 82–84). Another clear example is found in §77.

as if to a plurality. It seems as if Philo is going to introduce a counter-factual situation, but this turns out not to be the case. There will be a plurality involved.

as saying these words. Of course God speaks continually during the creation account. But here he might be speaking to others, and this brings the account close to the *Timaeus*, as noted above in our General comments.

not be in need. God's absolute autonomy and self-sufficiency is a basic principle of Philo's theology; cf. *Spec.* 1.177; *Leg.* 3.181; *Cher.* 44; *Conf.* 175 (in similar context); *QG* 4.188; and the systematic comments of Wolfson 1947, 1.203. See also the remarks above on God and the heavenly bodies, §46.

any collaborator. That God created the cosmos alone has already been affirmed with a rhetorical flourish above at §23.

tiny and perishable creature. It is striking that Philo shifts his exegesis to the human being as a mortal creature, i.e. composite of body and soul, not just a mind as in §§69–71.

only God knows. Just like the rabbi cited at the beginning of the chapter, Philo here seems to assume that not Moses but only God knows the deepest meaning of scripture. Normally, however, he credits more autonomy to Moses as divinely inspired author, as has been demonstrated by Burkhardt 1988. See further the discussion on §5.

convincing and reasonable. Once again the language of academic scepticism is applied to the task of exegesis; cf. our comments on §45, where exactly the same terms are used.

a likely conjecture. The expression εἰκὼς στοχασμός (singular or plural) is often found in Philo; cf. §157; *Jos.* 7, 104, 143; *Decal.* 18 (also a *quaestio* context); *Aet.* 2 etc. As can be seen very clearly in §132, what is aimed at (the basic meaning of στοχάζομαι) is the truth, but one cannot be certain that it is attained. In *Decal.* 18 a similar contrast is made between "true reasons" known only to God and likely conjectures put forward by the exegete. The terms belong to the language of Academic scepticism, as *Somn.* 1.23 and *Ebr.* 167 show (the latter in the passage introducing the tropes of Aenesidemus); cf. also the brief comments of Theiler 1971, 28.

(2) §73 *Of the creatures that exist, some share ...* Philo sets out the ontological premiss of his argument by using the method of *diaeresis*

(division) so loved by the Greek philosophers. It is also required for the follower of Moses, as Philo affirms in his exegesis of Lev 11:4 at *Agr.* 134–142. At 139–140 some excellent examples of division are given, including one on the various kinds of beings; see further Früchtel 1968 41–45; on the method itself, which goes back to Plato and the Old Academy, see Mansfeld 1992, 326–331. The schema can be set out as follows:

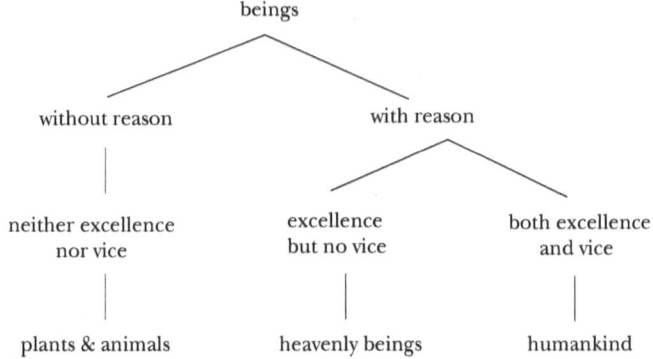

The assumption behind the schema is a hierarchy of beings based on cognitive functions; cf. the famous example with which Aristotle begins his *Metaphysics*, A 1, 981a27–b27. A certain level of cognitive development is prerequisite for moral behaviour. The present passage has been taken up in *SVF* 3.372 for no good reason. It is sufficiently general to be subscribed to by Stoics, Platonists and Aristotelians.

excluded from intellect and reason. Whether irrational animals have reason or not is the main theme of Philo's philosophical dialogue *De animalibus* (see the editions of Terian 1981 and PAPM 36), in which Philo defends the view that they do not against his nephew Alexander. Arnaldez ad loc. prefers the variant reading οὐ κέκτηται (have not gained possession of), but PCW's preference for ἐκτέτμηται is amply justified by parallels at *Spec.* 1.66, 330; *Leg.* 3.251; *Migr.* 67, 200.

living beings with intelligence. Some early Greek philosophers such as Anaxagoras and Democritus regarded the heavenly bodies as masses of solid matter, but from Plato and Aristotle onwards it was generally accepted that they were living beings whose superior intelligence could be deduced from their perfect movements. Their cognitive functions are thus superior to those of humans. Cf. *Plant.* 7; *Somn.* 1.135; and esp. *Gig.* 8: "For the stars are souls divine and without blemish throughout, and therefore as each of them is mind in its purest form, they move in the manner most akin to mind, the circle." On Philo's view of the heavenly bodies see the informative summary at Winston 1985a, 33. See also the monograph devoted to the theme of the life of the stars in Origen, Scott 1991 (63–77 on Philo).

creatures of a mixed nature. This group is mixed, not because it combines features from the other two groups, as one might at first think, but because it displays the opposed moral traits outlined. See further the comments on "intermediate *phronêsis*" at §154. Of course here Philo is primarily interested in human beings, but the formulation is such that there could be other members of this group. In *Gig.* 16 (exeg. Gen 6:2) he argues that evil can also be perpetrated by angels or demons, if these are taken to be incorporeal souls. See also the comment on §144.

wisdom and foolishness ... Philo simply lists the standard list of the four cardinal virtues and their opposites (but there is no actual standard list of cardinal vices, because strictly speaking, at least if we follow the Aristotelian doctrine of the golden mean, each virtue can have more than one opposite).

goodness and wickedness. These are the key terms in Philo's argument: ἀρετή, indicating a sound moral disposition and κακία, its opposite. "Goodness" and (moral) "excellence" are often better translations for *aretê* than "virtue."

(3) §74. *the virtuous beings.* "Virtuous" translates σπουδαῖα, a predominantly Stoic term describing a good moral disposition.

their family relationship. On the theme of family-relationship or kinship (συγγένεια) see the comments on §144.

indifferent beings. The technical term ἀδιάφορα, as commonly used by the Stoa to indicate what is neither good nor evil. Cf. L&S §58.

the better kind mixed in with them ... I understand the somewhat unclear formulation (kind translates ἰδέα, literally "form") to refer to the mixture of goodness and vice as outlined in §73. Both here and at *Conf.* 179 Philo declines to interpret the division of labour in terms of a division of parts of the soul. He does do this, however, in *Fug.* 69, where God forms the rational part, his powers the subordinate (i.e. irrational) part. One might ask where the tendency to evil actually comes from, the mind or the irrational part of the soul. Winston (1986, 108) rightly concludes

> When Philo wished to give an account of the human tendency to vice, he could do so from two different vantage points. He could either emphasize the irrational part of the soul, which provides both the material and the occasion for the vicious actions initiated by man's reason, or else he could focus his attention on the rational soul which energizes the irrational faculties in the first place and then falls into error when it allows itself to be overcome by irrational sense-perceptions and emotions.

The first vantage point, we might add, is more Platonic in emphasis, the second more Stoic.

§75. *the enlistment of others.* As noted in our analysis above, Philo declines to specify who the collaborators actually are. All he says is that they are subordinate to God as creator. In *Conf.* 171–174 it is implied that there are three possibilities: God's powers, the heavenly bodies or the angels. In *Fug.* 69 he says that God "converses with his powers." When it is obvious that Philo is being reticent, it seems pointless for the commentator to speculate about which group he might mean.

human being acts rightly. The verb κατορθοῦντος alludes to the Stoic doctrine of acts that are in accordance with right reason (κατορθώματα), i.e. performed by the wise person through the exercise of *logos* in conformity with nature. See further L&S §59 and esp. texts K–M.

assigned to God's account. In the sense that God, by creating humankind, made it possible for humans to exhibit sound moral behaviour.

the Father is blameless of evil in his offspring. Philo adapts Plato's words at *Tim.* 42d2–4: "After having decreed all these ordinances to them [the human souls], so that he would not be blamed for the evil that each of them would do in the future, he sowed some of them on earth ..." The term ἀναίτιος is the same that is also used at *Resp.* 617e5 (see the General comments above).

(4) §76. ***Most excellently.*** The same formulation as in §69. See our comment ad loc.

called the genus human being. Philo ignores the article in the Greek text, whereas at *Fug.* 72 he uses it for a vital distinction between the human being "mixed with sense-perception" (without the article, i.e. Gen 1:26) and the "true human being" who is "purest *nous*" (with the article, i.e. Gen 1:27).

he separates its species. The same process of division noted above in the comment on §73, but now in a creational context. Compare the famous section on the Logos cutter in *Her.* 133–236 where the division into male and female is mentioned at §§139 and 164. In the latter text Philo also cites Gen 1:27, pointing out (as he does not do here) that Moses uses "him" for the genus and "them" for the species of male and female.

the most proximate of the species. Philo uses the Aristotelian terminology of genus and species but with an intent adapted to the requirements of the Platonic doctrine of ideas. In Aristotelian nominalism universal terms can be used at different levels, e.g. I can say: "Black Beauty is a horse" or "Black Beauty is a mare," where "horse" is the genus and "mare" is the species. In Platonic realism, however, the species are *contained within* the genus. Thus the idea "living being" contains as it were the ideas of specific animals such as horse or human, but in an unspecified form. Thus if one knows what a living being is, one also knows that it occurs in both a male and a female variety. This is what Philo means when he says that the species are present in the genus. More sophisticated forms of this genus and species relation are developed in the allegorical explanations of generic and specific virtue in *Leg.* 1. Cf. Jastram 1991, but this aspect of Philo's thought has not yet been fully explored. (A slightly different exegesis of our text is given in *Leg.* 2.13, where Philo speaks of the generic human being containing the male and female genus rather than as species.) I cannot agree, therefore, with Tobin (*CM* 115), when he argues that the genus/species relation must be interpreted in terms of the distinction between the ideal and sensible worlds. Philo explicitly says that "the individuals had not yet taken shape," i.e. Adam and Eve as created humans. This does not happen until Gen 2:7 and is described in §§134–135. We note too that Philo's presentation here has nothing to do with a conception that the first human was androgyne, as suggested by Cohn at PCH 1.53n.; Urbach 1987, 229; and others.

The human being, identified primarily with his intellect (cf. §69) is thus still at a pre-sexual stage, despite the biblical words "male and female." Sexuality comes into play at a later stage; see §§134 and 152. In the first of these passages Philo refers back to Gen 1:27 and argues that "male and female" really means "neither male nor female" in the sense of "not yet male or female." See further our comment on §134.

Parallel exegesis

The important parallel passages in which Philo discusses the plural in Gen 1:26 (and also 3:22, 11:7) have been already been cited and referred to in our discussions above: see *Conf.* 168–183; *Fug.* 68–72; *Mut.* 30–32; *QG* 1.54. It is possible that this repetition of the same motif is indicative of an exegetical tradition, as supposed by Tobin (*CM* 38–40), but the connection with an anti-anthropological tendency which he postulates is not convincing.

For the final comment in §76 we noted above the parallel discussion in *Her.* 164, where there is no indication that the text speaks about ideas rather than concrete individuals.

Nachleben

The question of the plural in Gen 1:26 exercised the minds of numerous exegetes before and after Philo, and many of them come up with the idea that God is talking to collaborators. See the presentation of the evidence in Alexandre *CLG* 170–173 and Kugel *TB*, 51–52, 79–80. Both scholars emphasize that Philo stands somewhat apart on account of the Platonic motifs that he incorporates in his explanation. I have not found any texts where direct influence of Philo's passage may be detected. Both Didymus and Ambrose, for example, ignore it completely.

At *C. Ap.* 2.192 Josephus writes:

> We see his [God's] works: light, heaven, earth, sun, waters, the births of living beings, the sprouting of crops. These God created not with hands, not with toil, not requiring any collaborators (οὔ τινων συνεργασομένων ἐπιδεηθείς), but when he wished it, all things came into being immediately (εὐθύς) in all their beauty.

As Thackeray LCL ad loc. and Alexandre (*CLG* 170) have noted, the language here is so close to Philo §72 that it is quite possible that Josephus is polemicizing against him. Moreover the qualification "immediately" recalls §13. As noted at Runia *PT* 248 n., there is a vague similarity between Philo's emphasis on theodicy and the interpretation of the plural of Gen 1:26 attributed to the 4th cent. Rabbi Berekiah at *Gen. Rab.* 8.4. Dependence on Philo is most unlikely.

With regard to §76 I cannot agree with Alexandre *CLG* 197 that Gregory of Nyssa continues Philo's line of thought at *Opif. hom.* §§16–17, and esp. PG 44.189C–D. Gregory thinks that God adds sexual differentiation in anticipation of human fall into sin. Philo's approach here is purely philosophical.

Further reading. Radice *FM* 273–275; Runia *PT* 242–249; Winston 1986; Borgen 1997, 82–85; Pearson 1984, 322–324 (in relation to Gnosticism).

Chapter Fourteen
Why was the human being created last of all? (§§77–88)

Analysis/General comments

The following section of the treatise begins with another question directed at the Mosaic account: why does it record the human being as coming into existence last of all? Four answers are given, all of which are apparently regarded as mutually complementary (though the last is probably regarded as the most important, see the comment on §83). In §87 Philo returns to the original question and adds a final remark. This proves that the passage §§77–88 forms a unity. It should be noted, however, that the fourth answer is expanded at greater length, and includes in §84 an allusion to a part of the biblical text that has not yet been mentioned, Gen 1:28. This final section from §83 to §88 thus introduces an aspect of humankind's place in the cosmos, namely his sovereignty over the earth, that has not yet been given attention and which will recur later on in the treatise.

According to Borgen (1995, 372, 377, and 1997, 85), the exegetical question posed is prompted by the unexpected order and rank of the Pentateuchal account. I cannot agree with this interpretation. The passage continues the emphasis that we see throughout the entire treatise on the rational and didactic nature of the Mosaic account. Even though all things were created simultaneously (§13), the order in which their creation is recounted tells us much about creation and its contents. This present chapter is plainly a continuation of the discussion in §§65–68, where Philo proves that the creational succession in the animal realm makes excellent sense. See further our comments in Ch. 11. But, as Radice (*FM* 276) rightly remarks, the perspective in the two accounts is not the same. In the former passage humankind is examined as part of the natural realm. Here its creation is examined from the perspective of the entire cosmos, and the emphasis is strongly anthropocentric and teleological. We turn now to an analysis of Philo's argument.

(1) First the exegetical question is raised. Philo appeals to the scriptural account to verify that humankind is created last, but apart from that does not elucidate the question further. It is apparently regarded as self-explanatory (§77a).

(2) The first answer is that, because God has given the human being a special place in creation — only he has been made in God's image and is thus related to him through his possession of

rationality —, he wanted everything to be in readiness for him, both for life and for the good life. For the former an abundant supply of necessities was furnished, for the latter the marvellous spectacle of the heavens. The answer is elaborately illustrated with the image of a banquet and a theatrical contest (§§77b–78).

(3) The second answer draws an ethical lesson from the account. There is a connection between the human condition on earth and the state of humankind's moral life. If the human race were to live virtuously, there would be an abundance of goods, just as there was in the beginning. But since it has succumbed to passion and vice, it has been punished and lives in conditions of scarcity. If improvement were to occur, God might reward the human race by restoring abundance (§§79–81).

(4) The third answer is similar to the first. God thought there should be a kind of harmony between the beginning and the end of creation. The beginning was the heaven, the end was the human being. These are linked because the human being, though mortal, in a sense resembles the heaven (§82).

(5) The final reason has to do with humankind's dominant position in the earthly realm. (a) The human being had to appear last, so that he could instil astonishment in the animals over which he was to rule, and they would worship him and become tame and subservient (§83).

(b) God thus pronounced him king over the earthly realm and the creatures that inhabit it (though not over the heavenly beings) (§84a).

(c) For proof of this sovereignty one need only look at how animals are subservient to very ordinary human beings and do exactly what they are commanded (§§84b–86).

(d) Much more could be said by way of illustration, but the examples given are enough (§87).

(6) A final point is that humankind's final position should not be taken as indicating inferior rank. This can be shown by the example of reinsmen and pilots, whose place is at the back but control the entire movement. Thus the human being was established like a governor for the Great king (§88).

Once again it is a challenge to separate the various strands of Philo's thought in this section. Although the exegetical *quaestio* is raised by the biblical account, in the first three answers Greek philosophical thought is dominant. As we have seen in previous chapters, the attempt to find a rationale for the order of the creation account is influenced by exegesis of Plato's *Timaeus*. The influence of *Timaeus* exegesis is particularly apparent in the formulation of the third answer. The anthropocentric and teleological view of humankind's place in the cosmos also has strong Stoic roots. For the Stoa the cosmos exists primarily for the purpose of its rational inhabitants, i.e. gods and humans. But this emphasis is also mixed with ideas from the Platonic tradition, especially in the continuing emphasis on the role of contemplation of the heavens. It is in strong opposition to the views of the Epicurean tradition, as set out in Lucretius 5.925–987, in which humans gradually emerged from a primitive and endangered existence. The philosophical anthropocentrism of the Stoic and Platonic traditions could easily be combined with the strong biblical emphasis on the central place of humankind in God's creational dispensation.

The moral and didactic emphasis in the second answer is also a mixed bag. There is a clear relation to central themes of Philonic allegory, in which the soul is exhorted to control its passions and live virtuously and moderately. These, as is well known, have a strong philosophical bias. But these themes are combined, in a not very coherent way, with thoughts on the decline of human life from an earlier, more blessed age. Philo will pick up these themes again in §§140–150 and 167–170 where we shall discuss them at greater length.

In a valuable contribution Borgen (1995) has emphasized the biblical and Jewish aspects of Philo's account (see also 1997, 225–235). This is evident in the question raised of the biblical text and the image of the banquet in the first answer. Both have important rabbinic parallels, which point to Jewish traditions held in common with Philo. The Jewish background comes specially to the fore in the fourth answer on humankind's role in holding sway over the animal realm, based on the injunction in Gen 1:28. The human being is appointed king over the animals and God even delegates to him some of his authority over creation, so that the human being becomes his representative as "viceroy." See further Borgen 1995, 375–379. For a detailed analysis of the entire passage §§77–88 and its main themes the lengthy article by Jobling (1977) is warmly recommended. It should be borne in mind, however, that he treats the exegesis of Gen 1:28 as it is found in the entire corpus (see below Exegetical parallels) and not just in *Opif.*

Finally three brief comments on the formal aspects of Philo's presentation. Firstly, we note that this chapter is a classic example of how a question is put to an aspect of the biblical text and multiple answers to the question are given. In §77 Philo makes quite clear that he is indebted to anterior traditions of exegesis. On this method see further the Introduction, §4 (b) & (c). Secondly, it is very striking that the entire chapter contains almost no reference to the biblical text. Only in §84 is there an allusion to Ps. 8:7 and a very indirect reference to Gen. 1:28. Thirdly, we observe that Philo's style becomes very expansive in this section. We have tried to capture something of his fluency and verbosity in our translation. It is plain that he had an extraordinary command of the stylistic and rhetorical possibilities of the Greek language. On the wealth of Philo's vocabulary in general see Leopold 1983, in *Opif.* Cohn 1889, xli–l; on his style in general Conley 1997.

Detailed comments

(1) §77. **You might inquire ...** Again a typical Philonic formulation of an exegetical *quaestio*. See the comment above, and also our remarks on §72.

the final item. As we shall see in §89, the cosmos is completed in six days.

after all the others. The phrase ἐπὶ πᾶσι recalls §65 and indicates a climax (see the comment ad loc.), but τοῖς ἄλλοις has been added. Its reference is vague: it could refer to the creatures of the fifth and sixth days, or to all that has been created so far; cf. §83. We retain the ambiguity in our translation.

(2) **those who have made a profounder study of the laws ...** This phrase, together with the parenthetical remark in §26, are the clearest indications in our treatise that Philo, in presenting his exegesis, draws on anterior traditions. It is possible, by analysing his various references to such exegetes, to gain some idea of what these traditions were and how he stands in relation to them. This research has been carried out rather speculatively by Bousset (1915) and more thoroughly by Hay (1979–80, this passage cited at 42). See further Introduction §4(c) and §7(a).

kinship to himself. See above §74 and our further comments at §144. Philo builds here on the results of his exegesis in the three previous chapters.

he also did not begrudge him ... The creator shows specifically to humankind the same lack of envy that he showed to the cosmos as a whole; cf. §21 and the reference there to the Platonic background.

he made everything ready in advance. This solution amounts to an affirmation that the cosmos has been given its structure for the benefit of humankind, the strongest possible form of anthropocentric thought. It is even suggested that the heavenly bodies were made earlier so that humans could contemplate them, as was already implied in the earlier account of the fourth day at §§54–55 (see the comments ad loc.). Philo does, however, emphasize in §84 that there is no human dominion over the heavenly realm.

Such anthropocentric teleology is, as we have already seen, strongly present in the *Timaeus* (see the commentary on Ch. 10). A further example is found at 77a–c, where it is argued that the botanical world was created so that humans would have food. But Plato also recognizes the limits of this perspective. In a famous passage at *Laws* 903c he affirms that the cosmos was not made for humankind, but humankind for the cosmos. A more explicit anthropocentrism is found in Stoic thought. An elaborate statement of this view is found in Cotta's speech in Cicero *Nat. d.* 2.131–167. Some relevant passages are:

> §154. The cosmos itself was created for the sake of gods and humans, and the things that it contains were provided and contrived for the enjoyment of humans. For the cosmos is as it were the common dwelling-place of gods and humans ..., for they alone have the use of reason and live by justice and law ... (cf. also §133)
> §155. Again the revolutions of the sun and moon and other heavenly bodies, although also contributing to the maintenance of the structure of the cosmos, nevertheless also afford a spectacle for humans to behold; for there is no sight of which it is more impossible to grow weary ...
> §156. Then the earth, teeming with grain and vegetables of various kinds, which she pours forth in lavish abundance — does she appear to give birth to this produce for the sake of the wild beasts or for the sake of humans? What shall I say of the vines and olives, whose bounteous and delightful fruits do not concern the lower animals at all? In fact the animals are entirely ignorant of the arts of sowing and reaping ... All these products are both enjoyed and cultivated by men. (LCL translation, modified)

We note that the Stoa joins together gods and humans as rational creatures; on such texts see further Schofield 1991, 64–92 (and see further the comment on §144). Philo's emphasis is even more on humans, on account of the sequence of the creational account. The influence of Stoic anthropocentrism is strong in the dialogue *De providentia*; see esp. 2.83–110 and the remarks of Hadas-Lebel PAPM 35.83–87. On Philo's anthropocentrism and Greek antecedents see further the discussion in Jobling 1977, 52–61. He rightly remarks on p. 58 that Cicero's statement in *Nat. d.* 2.155 cited above is a compromise between anthropocentrism and cosmocentrism, and that the same tendency is present in Philo. (But one caveat. The view tentatively put forward on p. 53 that Stoic anthropocentrism is somehow unhellenic and might have been influenced by Semitic thought, advocated above all by M. Pohlenz, has lost all scholarly support. Moreover an attempt to distinguish between the various stages of the Stoic school is also tenuous. Anthropocentrism in various degrees was part of school doctrine during its entire existence.)

for life and for the good life. This distinction is essential for an understanding of Philo's argument, both in this paragraph and the next. For life at the biological level of the *body* food is required, the consumption of which gives enjoyment. Food in the form of plants is promised to humankind by God at Gen 1:29. The good life can be attained at the higher level of the *mind*. The same distinction is found in various forms throughout Philo's writings; cf. *Congr.* 33 (good life unspecified); *Decal.* 17 (good life through the Law), *Spec.* 1.339 (philosophy); *Spec.* 2.229

(education); *QE* 2.18 (good life through freedom from passion and health). See also the remark on the senses in §53 and the comment ad loc.

give enjoyment. Compare the same emphasis on enjoyment in the passages from Cicero quoted above. The lower form of sensual enjoyment is meant. The context elicits a mild attitude from Philo, who is usually very severe on any tendencies to a life of sensuality, as will become very clear towards the end of the treatise; see Ch. 23.

contemplation of the heavenly realm. Repetition of the Platonic theme of contemplation leading to philosophy, already used above in §54. See our extensive remarks there.

to spring up. The metaphor of the plant springing up out of the ground is very common in Philo; cf. my remarks at *PT* 324, where both biblical and Platonic backgrounds are indicated.

§78. *those who give a banquet.* The image of the banquet picks up what is "required for life" in §77, the image of the athletic or dramatic contests what is "required for the good life." Compare §54, where the two images are *not* separated. Philo uses this image repeatedly in differing contexts throughout his works; cf. the list at Nikiprowetzky 1977, 32 n. 110. The image has both Greek (cf. esp. Plato *Phdr.* 247e) and biblical roots. More specifically, Borgen (1995, 378), building on Cohn's note at PCH 1.54, has shown that a significant number of rabbinic texts use the image in the very same context as Philo. For example, *Tosefta Sanhedrin* 8.7 asks why the human being was created last and one of the answers is:

> Another matter: So that he might enter the banquet at once. They have made a parable: to what is the matter comparable. To a king who built a palace and dedicated it and prepared a meal and [only] afterwards invited the guests. And so Scripture says, "The wisest of women has built her a house" (Prov. 9:1). This refers to the King of the king of kings, blessed be He, who built his world in seven days by wisdom. "She has hewn out her seven pillars" (Prov. 9:1) — these are the seven days of creation. "She has killed her beasts and mixed her wine" (Prov. 9:2) — These are the oceans, rivers, wastes, and all the other things which the world needs ... (8.9, translation Neusner, as quoted by Borgen)

It is possible that the same midrashic tradition lies behind both this text and that of Philo (for further less explicit parallels see Borgen ibid.). Borgen appeals to verbal parallels, but these to my mind are not as strong as he thinks. But it is important to realize that the banquet is only the lesser half of Philo's double image. The spectacle of the heavens gives the good life. Philo once again adopts a Greek philosophical perspective, with its emphasis on the contemplative life.

those who organize athletic or dramatic contests. Philo appeals to a feature of Greco-Roman civic life. It was the duty of civic councillors and government officials to organize athletic and cultural contests at their own expense. For Philo's evidence on this practice cf. Harris 1976, 75–80. Sly 1996, 153 notes that by Philo's time, under the Romans, athletics had become a spectator sport. A horrific example involving the torture of Jews is described in *Flacc.* 85. At *Prov.* 2.100 (= 2.46 LCL) Philo uses the example of a gymnasiarch to illustrate the lavishness of Providence.

a most sacred theatre. Philo decides that the image of the theatre suits his purpose better than that of an athletic contest. The universe is compared to a theatre because it offers a marvellous spectacle. Compare *Gig.* 31, where Philo states that "souls who are free from flesh and body spend their days in the theatre of the universe, and without anyone hindering them enjoy sights and sounds divine, which they have desired with love (ἔρως) insatiable." As Winston and Dillon note in their commentary, 1983, 251, the image is not Platonic, but is consistent with Platonic themes in the *Phaedrus* and other dialogues. On the sight of the heavens as a grand spectacle cf. also Cicero *Nat. d.* 2.140, 155. Note that this motif is *not* the same as the much more common "all the world's a stage" (Shakespeare).

for his use and enjoyment. See the comment on §42.

absolutely stunning ... revealing the most wonderful motions ... Philo's description of the marvellous sight of the movements of the heavenly bodies repeats themes presented earlier in §54. The language becomes exceedingly baroque. As so often, he resorts to the superlative in order to describe the excellence and beauty of creation. The effect is heightened even further by a rather bombastic repetition of the adjective καταπληκτι-κωτάτας. For somewhat similar language see *Spec.* 1.321–322 on the wondrous sights and words of the virtuous person, who is compared with the bounty of nature.

the original and true and paradigmatic science of music. Plato emphasizes that the sciences of astronomy and music are closely related in his account of the four sciences preparatory to philosophy in *Resp.* 530e. The science of music studies harmonic proportions rather than actual sounds.

a most indispensable and useful art. Compare §126 on the lyre which emulates the harmonies of the planets.

(3) §79. **to mention a second.** Philo's argument can be reduced to the following steps:
1. When humans were created, they received all the requirements for the good life.
2. But nowadays life is harsh and resources are scarce.
3. This is due to moral degeneracy, for which humans are punished.
4. If humans were to improve their life, God might reward them and bring back the good things of life.

The assumption that life at first was simple yet in every respect perfect presupposes both the biblical conception of paradise and the myth of the Golden age, both of which will play an important role in Philo's account of Adam; see Ch. 19.

The argument is somewhat confusing. It seems in §79 that the scarcity of goods is the result of moral decline, i.e. if humans were to moderate their passions, there should be enough to go around. But then suddenly in §80 it appears that the scarcity of goods occurs as a punishment. Since God can remedy the situation if he wishes (§82), the implication is that the punishment occurs through divine intervention. The same thought is found at the end of the treatise in §§167–169. The theme of reward and punishment is prominent in the treatise (see Introduction §5e & g), as indeed in the entire Exposition of the Law; cf. Borgen 1997, 65–76.

to teach ... a lesson. The second reason is overtly didactic. It aims to teach a moral lesson. Compare the theological lessons drawn at the end of the work, §172.

all but shouting aloud. A favourite phrase of Philo's; cf. *Mos.* 1.69; *Spec.* 2.11; *Virt.* 147; *Congr.* 154; *Fug.* 84, 196; *Mut.* 56.

unreasoning pleasures ... Philo's description of the passions takes up themes from the *Timaeus* (note especially "that bad advisor fear," an allusion to 69d2) and from Stoic ethical theory (note the four primary passions pleasure, desire, grief and fear). See further my detailed analysis at *PT* 300–301.

as battle stations in the soul. According to LSJ the verb ἐπιτειχίζω means to "build a fort or stronghold on the frontier of an enemy's country to serve as basis for operations against him," i.e. these vices become established in the soul and attack its well-being from within. The metaphor is very common in Philo; cf. *Spec.* 4.5; *Praem.* 25; *Conf.* 54; *Somn.* 2.276 (in all cases used of the passions). The overriding metaphor of war in the soul is made explicit in §81.

§80. *the necessities of life are difficult to obtain.* This will be the result of the expulsion from the Garden of Eden in §§167–169. Philo, whose family probably owned landed estates in Egypt (cf. Fuks 1951), was well aware that agriculture in the ancient world was a risk-fraught business, easily upset by unusual climatic conditions or human interference through war and social conflict.

channel the streams of springs and rivers. Although Philo's descriptions are as usual very general, this phrase may reflect conditions in the Nile delta, with which Philo will have been familiar. See also the previous comment.

§81. *the war in the soul.* See the comment above on §79. The conception of conflict in the soul does have some Jewish roots (cf. James 4:1), but in Philo's case it is primarily derived from Platonic psychology. It is thus natural for him to use the metaphor of war in this context and he does so habitually. In *Leg.* 3.115–117, for example, in order to expound Gen 3:14, he sets out the Platonic theory of the tripartition of the soul and at the same time makes ample use of military metaphors:

> If therefore, O understanding, you seek the location which pleasure has received as its portion, do not look for the place in the head, where the reasoning faculty resides, for you will certainly not find it there, since reason is in conflict with passion and cannot remain in the same place with it. When reason prevails, pleasure is gone; when pleasure conquers, reason is an exile. But look for it in the chest and the belly ... Nothing has prevented the mind from abandoning the intelligible concerns which are proper to it and giving itself up to what is inferior. This happens whenever

war prevails in the soul, for then reason, which is in us not as an aggressive but as a peaceful element, must necessarily become a prisoner of war (§§116–117).

Another example is the allegory of the war against the Amalekites in terms of the fight against passion at *Leg.* 3.186–187.

God, who is a lover of virtue ... Exactly the same three epithets φιλάρετος, φιλόκαλος and φιλάνθρωπος are used of Moses in *Virt.* 175, cited below in the comment on §128.

well-disposed to humankind. Philo very often conveys the biblical doctrine of God's love for humankind with the term φιλανθρωπία; cf. *Plant.* 92; *Prov.* 2.15; *Mos.* 1.198 etc. In this humans should emulate God; cf. *Spec.* 4.73–74. On this virtue, which gains in importance during the Hellenistic period, see Winston 1984, 391–400; on its application to God Söding 1996, 327–330.

will cause the good things of life to be supplied ... For Philo it is part and parcel of the doctrine of divine providence that God intervenes directly in human life. The general principle was stated at the outset in §10, and is emphatically repeated in §171. But it is not necessary to think of miracles here. God can act through nature, as was the case when humankind first came into existence.

to bring what does not yet exist at all into existence. If God is able to create the entire cosmos from scratch, then he can obviously intervene to create bountiful provisions for human beings. This is a fine example of how the phrase "does not yet exist" (τὰ μὴ ὄντα) does not necessarily imply the doctrine of *creatio ex nihilo*. The contrast here is obviously between the practice of farmers who use seeds to grow new plants and the creative work of God who made the botanical world on the third day. He *may* have done this from pre-existent unformed matter. See further Excursus 2 in Ch. 4.

(4) §82. **the beginning and end of creation.** The third reason is similar to the first, but concentrates on the formal aspects of the account. The assumption is that the ἀρχή and the τέλος of the creation account contain its most important parts. The explanation takes themes and phraseology from the *Timaeus*, but adapts them for its own purposes. At *Tim.* 27a5–6 Plato writes that Timaeus should take on the task of speaking about the nature of the universe, "beginning with the genesis of the cosmos and ending with the nature of man." Philo adapts this by substituting the heaven for the cosmos. Philo's double phrase "the former ... the latter ..." is a deliberate adaptation of the description of the cosmos and demiurge at 29a5–6; see *PT* 86, 118. On this "language of excellence" see the comment above on §9.

Very similar to our text here is Philo's summary of the creation account towards the end of the Exposition of the Law, at *Praem.* 1:

> The entire creation account has been recorded excellently and in accordance with its divine subject, taking its commencement from the coming

into being of heaven and ending with the construction of humankind, for the former is the most perfect of immortal beings, the latter of mortal creatures. Weaving together immortal and mortal elements in the process of becoming, the maker fashioned the cosmos, the one group having come into being in order to rule, the other group in order to be subjects and come into existence in the future.

The resemblance to our passage would be even greater if the emendation ὁ μὲν γὰρ ἀφθάρτων τελειότατος, ὁ δὲ θνητῶν ἄριστος is accepted, as I have suggested at *PT* 118.

heaven. Which heaven is meant? If Philo is consistent, he must mean the firmament created on the second day, since in §29 the heaven of Gen. 1:1 was declared to be incorporeal.

miniature heaven. The expression reminds us, of course, of the famous depiction of the human being as microcosm. First attributed to Democritus, it is endemic to the *Timaeus* and much ancient and medieval cosmological and anthropological thought; cf. the overview of Gatzemeier 1980; in Philo see *Post.* 58; *Her.* 155; *Mos.* 2.135; *Prov.* 1.40; Harl PAPM 15.70; *PT* 466. But here we have a comparison of the human being with heaven, which is not the same. Once again an adaptation of an idea from the *Timaeus* may be suspected, namely the parallelism that Plato draws between the revolutions of the heavens and the circuits of the human mind in 47a–c and repeated in 90c–d. See further *PT* 276–278 and the comment below. There are no direct parallels for the expression βραχὺς οὐρανός in Philo (or anywhere else in Greek literature, to my knowledge). The qualifying phrase indicates that it is a daring expression. The closest parallel is found at *Her.* 88, prompted by exegesis of Gen 15:5 (cf. also 233): "For God wishes to picture the soul of the wise person as the counterpart of heaven (ἀντίμιμον οὐρανοῦ), or if we may speak hyperbolically, an earthly heaven containing in it, as in the ether, pure natures, ordered movements, harmonious dances, divine revolutions, supremely star-like and dazzling beams of excellences." But it should be noted that Philo here speaks of the soul in the human being, not the human being as such.

carries around in himself ... as images. Once again we encounter the remarkable verb ἀγαλματοφορέω, as at §18 and §69; see the comments there.

numerous star-like beings. The idea from the *Timaeus* cited above, here slightly adapted so that the contents of the human mind are compared with stars. See, as well as the texts cited in the note above, *Leg.* 3.40; *Virt.* 1; and my full discussion of the motif in *PT* 276–278.

taking the form of arts and sciences and noble theories. The Greek is difficult to construe. If the star-like beings are thoughts in the mind, then the sciences and theories will be the subject-matter of those thoughts, as I have translated. It is difficult to understand why Philo speaks of them in the dative.

the mortal and the immortal. Again we note (cf. §72) that Philo's exegesis assumes the human being as a mortal creature, composite of body and soul.

(5a) §83. *Last of all*. Philo yet again uses the expression ἐπὶ πᾶσι; see the comments on §65 and §77. It might just mean "finally" here, but taken as a whole the sentence seems to indicate that this fourth and last reason is — fittingly, given the context! — regarded as the most important of all.

stated. I.e. by the exegetes introduced in §77.

instil astonishment in them ... As Cohn (PCH 1.57), Jobling (1977, 66), and Borgen (1995, 375) rightly point out, Philo here alludes to Jewish Adam speculation, based on the Genesis text, but elaborated far beyond it; see Ginzberg 1909-38, 1.59-62, 5.78-84. Most of these themes are derived from Gen 2-3, and reappear below at §§135-148.

would worship him. Kugel (*TB*, 123) cites the *Cave of treasures* 2.22 (a late source, but probably containing early material): "God gave him [Adam] dominion over all the other creatures ... and they worshipped him and they were subservient to him." The text goes on to claim that this order was the reason that Satan and his allies apostasized from God! In *Pirqe Rabbi Eliezer* 11, cited by Borgen 1995, 375, Adam reproves the animals for worshipping him and commands them to prostrate themselves before God. These texts are rather different in emphasis from Philo.

their natural director. The same term ἡγεμών used so emphatically of God and the human *nous* in §69. Philo uses its cognate ἡγεμονία again in §87.

those which had the wildest natures. The implication is that at first wild animals were no problem for human beings. Later, however, their existence became a problem for those defending divine providence (cf. *Prov.* 2.91-92, 103-106). But in the following section Philo shifts his glance to the contemporary situation.

(5b) §84. *by means of a pronouncement.* This is a very oblique reference to the divine injunction in Gen 1:28: "Increase and multiply and fill the earth and subdue it and rule over the fishes of the sea ..." The appointment of the first human being as king is derived from the final verb. As Jobling (1977, 51) acutely observes, however, the biblical text refers to dominion by verbs in the imperative, but Philo's paraphrase converts this to the past indicative and expresses dominion primarily through nouns (the office of ruler, the function of rule), i.e. a dynamic expression has been replaced by a static one. The cultural imperative contained in the divine pronouncement, which has been so influential in western thought, is thus reduced to an ontological situation. See also the remarks of Cohen 1989, 72-76, who observes that Philo shows virtually no interest in the command to reproduce, but also does not read the verse "as a license to exploit the physical world" (73).

king of all the creatures. Very similar is the midrash in *Pesiqta Rabbati*, Suppl. 21 (cited by Cohn PCH 1.58; Borgen 1995, 373): "And God had in mind to appoint him ruler over his world, and king over all of his creatures, as he said: I am the King of the upper world and man is the king of the lower world."

all the creatures in the sub-lunary realm ... Philo's language reflects the customary categories of Greek cosmology, as we saw earlier in §§62–68.

excluding the creatures in heaven. These are not even mentioned in the biblical text. Philo includes them not only because of the scheme of the four elements, but also because he is much more aware of the intermediate ontological status of humankind in the cosmos as a whole. Above humans stand the heavenly bodies and the angels or *daimones* (cf. *Gig.* 6–18). Similarly Jewish texts are much concerned about the relation of Adam to the angels, who are nowhere mentioned in Genesis until 3:24 (the Cherubim); see Ginzberg 1909–38, 52–54; Kugel *TB*, 74–77, 122–124.

obtained a portion that is more divine. Cf. above §73.

he subjected to his rule. Philo's phrase here (πάντα ὑπέταττεν αὐτῷ) alludes to the famous words in Ps. 8:7: "You have established him over the works of your hands, you have subjected all things (πάντα ὑπέταξας) under his feet, sheep and all oxen, and also the beasts of the field, the birds of the air and the fish of the sea." The verb used earlier, καθίστη, also recalls the Psalmist's κατέστησας. Philo refers very rarely to the Psalms; *BPS* 89–90 records 39 examples, but does not include this text. For Philo's use of the Psalms, see now my article, 2001b; this text is discussed at 109, 116. Remarkably the later translators of the Hebrew Bible into Greek, Theodotion and Aquila (who post-date Philo) replace the LXX κατακυριεύσατε αὐτῆς [γῆν] with ὑποτάξατε αὐτήν.

(5c) *our experience.* Philo appeals to τὰ φαινόμενα, i.e. what we observe through our senses in our present life in the world. The examples are all taken from animals that have been domesticated by humankind. Wild animals are left out of the account. See the note above on §83. One might compare Cotta's account of the subordination of domestic animals to humankind at Cicero *Nat. d.* 2.158–160, but the argument is slightly different. These have been furnished by Providence for human use, i.e. more in line with Philo's first argument in §§77–79.

stand in awe of him. Perhaps Gen 9:1–2 has contributed to this depiction. This text repeats the injunction to humankind in Gen 1:28, but adds "the fear and the dread of you shall be on every beast of the earth ..." The two texts are combined in Sir 17:1–4. See also below on Parallel exegesis.

like slaves before their master. Cf. *Deus* 47 and the paraphrase of Gen 1:28 in Theophilus of Antioch, *Ad Aut.* 2:18 (often thought to have been influenced by Hellenistic–Jewish exegesis, if not by Philo himself; see Grant 1988, 157–159, Runia *PEC* 111): "When he had made him and blessed him so that he would increase and fill the earth, he subordinated all other beings to him as subjects and slaves." Here too the influence of Ps. 8:7 is felt (ὑπέταξεν αὐτῷ ... πάντα).

§86. *he moves at a swift pace.* Cf. Cicero *Nat. d.* 2.151: "We also tame the four-footed animals to carry us on their backs, their swiftness and strength bestowing strength and swiftness on ourselves."

(5d) §87. *Much more could be said.* We have no reason to dispute this! Philo seems occasionally to be aware of the extent of his verbosity.

no creature has gained its freedom. This might seem a gross rhetorical exaggeration. Yet even in Philo's day the increasing influence of human civilization could be detected on the habitat of wild animals. And in the light of the situation today, when we need to create special reserves so that tigers and rhinoceros do not succumb to extinction in the wild, Philo's words are entirely appropriate.

(6) *not created last of all.* Compare the common English phrase "last but not least." We might also adduce the account in Plato's *Timaeus*, which, after humankind has been fully discussed, briefly touches on the remaining living beings, descending until it reaches the limit of stupidity, fish and oysters (92b–c). On the differences in sequence between the Mosaic and the Platonic account see the General comment above in Ch. 11.

§88. *charioteers and pilots.* Two of the most common images for leadership and directive skill in Philo; see our comments above on §46. The comparison here, however, is only moderately successful, because it focuses on physical position rather than rank. An appeal to the biblical example of King David, youngest of the sons of Jesse, might have been better (but astonishingly Philo refers to David only once, at *Conf.* 149). Another possibility was Joseph. But Philo prefers more general examples which appeal to a more general audience Moreover the images chosen, though banal, can be put to good use for describing the role of humans in earthly affairs.

so to speak, the best of all those sailing. Philo is aware that the analogy would not work if we take into account that the ship could be carrying high dignitaries.

taking on the care ... like a governor ... The final words of the chapter are of great interest and in fact add two extra points not so far mentioned. "Care" translates ἐπιμέλεια, a term very frequently used by Philo and other writers for the exercise of providence; cf. the cognate verb at §9 and §171; *Abr.* 70; *Ebr.* 199. The same word is used for the care that the soul should take for the body at Plato, *Phdr.* 246e6. Humankind thus not only profits from the fact that the plant and animal worlds have been created for its benefit, but also has a responsibility towards them. One can even speak of a kind of delegated responsibility. Just as God cares for humans, so humans must care for what is below them in rank. Moreover the human being is designated the ὕπαρχος, literally "subordinate ruler" or viceroy, of God the Great king (on this title cf. our note at §71). The same title is used of the first human at §148. At *Agr.* 51 and *Somn.* 1.242, however, it is used of the Logos; at *Spec.* 1.14, 19 of the stars. The background of the conception of the human being as God's viceroy on earth must be biblical and Jewish. Compare the power and authority claimed by or given to Christ as the second Adam in heaven (!) and on earth in Matt 28:18, Eph

1:20–22. The theme of kingship is not found, however, in Jewish paraphrases of the creation of humankind in *Jubilees* 2:13–16, Sir 17:1–12, Wis 9:1–6, even though they all refer to humankind's dominion over the animal world.

after all the others. This translation of ἐφ' ἅπασιν is almost mandatory, since the images of the charioteer and the pilot explicitly state that they follow after their charges. Sequence once again has ontological significance.

Parallel exegesis

At *Praem.* 9 Philo alludes back to the same theme as in our passage, summarizing the first and the fourth answer (but the emphasis falls on the former). In *QG* 2.56, Gen 1:28 is quoted in an abbreviated form and it is pointed out that the repetition of the injunction makes Noah into the first representative of the second genesis of humankind. The same theme is found at *Mos.* 2.65.

The passage at *Agr.* 8 is of interest, because it shows how easily Philo could convert the theme of human dominion over the plants into a fertile allegorical theme (plants are selected for attention here and not animals because Noah is a farmer of crops). For about another ten texts which have covert references to the theme of the human being as lord over the earthly realm see Jobling 1977, 51. The text is more common than my remark at *PT* 472 n. 372 suggests, but the thesis that Philo devotes much less attention to human sovereignty over creation than the theme of human intellectual ability (which is not even present in Gen 1) is to my mind still quite defensible, *pace* Borgen 1997, 225.

Nachleben

As has been noted in our detailed comments, there are a number of texts in rabbinic literature in which the question is posed why humankind was created last. It would be risky to assert that the rabbis took this theme over from Philo, since there is almost no evidence that they read him (except Rabbi Hoshai'a, on whom see Ch. 4). This might mean that the *quaestio* was already a common exegetical tradition by Philo's time. See further Introduction §7(a) on Philo's relation to Jewish traditions outside Alexandria and Hellenistic Judaism. The same uncertainty applies to the parallel in Theophilus noted above on §85.

In four 4th century Christian authors, however, there can be little doubt that Philo was directly or indirectly utilized.
(1) Didymus *Com. Gen.* 60.2–10 briefly explains the dominion of humankind in terms very similar to §§84–85: a single lad or weak man can lead an entire flock. We also find the same allusion to Ps. 8:7. For the most part, however, Didymus follows his predecessor Origen in explaining the domination of humankind over the animals in allegorical terms.

(2) The question posed by Philo at §77 is the main theme of a long letter of Ambrose to Orontianus, *Ep.* 43 = 29 Faller, to which we have already referred in the *Nachleben* in Ch. 12. Ambrose regards it as legitimate to use the resources of human reason to speculate why humankind was created last. But he omits to tell his correspondent that his main resource in giving his answer is the work of an Alexandrian Jew. The entire letter is virtually a Christianizing paraphrase of §§77–88, to which in the middle §§69–71 has been added. Unfortunately space forbids us to follow in detail how creatively Ambrose combines Philo's ideas with all manner of references to the New Testament. For example, the banquet in §78 is aligned with Jesus' parable in Matt. 22:2–14, the athletic contest with "the good fight" in 2 Tim. 4:7, while the reward of the fruits of the earth for humans is life, the reward of the heavenly bodies is hope of eternal life. No detailed analysis has so far been made of this extensive Ambrosian adaptation, but the main borrowings are indicated in the apparatus to Faller's edition, 1968, 195–207.

(3) More briefly, at the beginning of his *Opif. hom.* §2, Gregory of Nyssa also discusses the question why humankind appeared last in creation. Two themes are picked up and loosely adapted: (a) from §§77–78 that the world was ready for humankind as a banquet and that it is a source of wonder (the borrowings are more extensive than indicated by Cohn in his apparatus); (b) from §83 that the human being was to appear as king, and the ruler should not precede his subjects.

(4) Even more briefly the late 4th cent. bishop Nemesius in his *De natura hominis* §1, 4.24–5.5 Morani states that Moses introduced the human being last of all not only because everything had been created for his use, but also because he was a binding element between the visible and the intelligible realm. The first reason summarizes §§77–81, the second is not drawn from our passage, but occurs below at §§134–135 (see *Nachleben* Ch. 18). Nothing in Nemesius' report could not have been derived from Gregory (who wrote his work slightly earlier), but since he does not appear to use the treatise elsewhere, direct use of Philo is perhaps more likely; see further the discussion in my *PEC* 262–263.

Further reading: Radice *FM* 275–279; Borgen 1995; 1997, 225–235; Jobling 1977.

Chapter Fifteen
The seventh day: excursus on the Hebdomad (§§89–128)

Analysis/General comments

Philo has now reached the end of Genesis 1, in which the works of the six days have been recounted. Only the seventh day remains, on which God the creator ceases from his creative activity (Gen 2:2–3). This feature of the creation account is wholly ignored by Philo (unlike at *Leg.* 1.5–7, 16). Instead he concentrates on the statement that God blessed and hallowed the seventh day (Gen 2:3), which he interprets to mean that God honoured this day as the birthday of the entire cosmos (§89). This encourages him to launch into an extremely long eulogy of the hebdomad as special cosmic number, a continuation and climax of the arithmology that is such a prominent feature of the treatise. As was the case for the discussion of the tetrad at §§47–52, the presentation takes the form of an excursus which is only superficially connected with the remainder of the treatise (§§90–128).

What strikes the reader above all is the sheer length of this excursus. It amounts to 40 sections out of 172 (= 23%) or 288 lines out of 1214 (= 24%) for the entire treatise. It is difficult not to conclude that it is disproportionately long. And it is tempting to draw the further conclusion that Philo has been self-indulgent and lost control over his material. But caution is required here. It is clear that the great length of the section is intimately connected with the function of arithmology in Philo's exegesis and is moreover influenced by the special role of the number seven in both Jewish and Greek tradition. See further our observations on the role of number in the Introduction §7.

The entire excursus forms a unity, and so should not be divided into smaller sections. We will thus treat it in its entirety as a single long chapter. The structure of the excursus is not without its difficulties. I have treated this question in a more detailed analysis, Runia 2000, in which I differ from the structure discerned by Radice *FM* 281, and before him Robbins 1921, 109. The results of this analysis will be assumed in what follows. My analysis is based primarily on the signposts that Philo himself gives in the course of the excursus. Unfortunately these are not always as clear and systematically organized as one might wish. In my view the main body of the treatment of the hebdomad clearly divides into two main parts. After some introductory words (§§89–90 = I), in the first main part (§§91–

110 = II) those features of the hebdomad are outlined which relate to some form of mathematical doctrine (mainly arithmetical, but also with reference to geometry, stereometry and music). In Philo's terminology these features are primarily noetic or intelligible, i.e. they have chiefly to do with objects in the realm of thought, but this does not preclude them from being related to and illustrated by some phenomena in the physical world (e.g. the moon and the ages of humankind). In the second part (§§111–127 = III) Philo relates those features of the hebdomad that are present in the sense-perceptible world as groups of seven things or periods of seven units of time, beginning with the heavens (§§111–116), then proceeding to the human being (§§117–125), and ending with the sciences as practised by humans (§§126–127). This second main part of the excursus has a much more straightforward structure. Towards the end Philo appears to realize that he has to bring his long excursus to a close. The treatment becomes less detailed, and some features of the hebdomad are presented by means of lists. Concluding the excursus, he returns to the role of Moses and recounts the celebration of the Sabbath as enjoined in the tables of the Law (§128 = IV).

Preliminary to the detailed commentary, I shall outline very compactly the structure and contents of the chapter, based on the structural analysis which we have just given, followed by some brief comments on Philo's sources for its contents and the role of Judaism in this part of the work.

Structure and contents

   Part I Introductory section
   (1) When the cosmos had been completed in accordance with the hexad, God proceeded to honour the seventh day and called it holy, because it is a festival for the entire universe, the birthday of the cosmos (§89).
   (2) It is perhaps not possible to celebrate the nature of the seven in an adequate way, but nevertheless we should make the attempt. These introductory remarks are an almost exact repetition of what Philo says when embarking on the exegesis of the creation account at §5. They indicate how seriously he takes the task of presenting his arithmological lore (§90).
   Part II Mathematical features of the hebdomad
   (3) Philo commences the detailed discussion of the seven by pointing out that in arithmetical terms it is found in two forms, within the decad and outside the decad (§91).

(4) The second of these is discussed first. The seventh number by multiplication from the unit always yields both a square and a cube, and so symbolizes both incorporeal and corporeal being (§§92–94).

(5a) Secondly, the seven inside the decad contains the numbers that make the various harmonic ratios. (§§95–96).

(5b) The seven also produces the right-angle, which in the area of geometry is the source of every shape and quality (§97).

(5c) The seven in the area of stereometry is the basis of both the two-dimensional surface and the three-dimensional body (§98).

(6a) Of all the numbers of the decad the seven is the only one that is neither product nor factor. For this reason it has been likened to Victory (i.e. Athena), but also by the Pythagoreans to the Director of the universe (§§99–100).

(6b) The seven also demonstrates its power in the sense-perceptible realm, as witnessed by the four phases of the moon which each last seven days (§101).

(7a) The seven is called the "completion-bringer" because it brings all things to completion. This is first illustrated in the area of stereometry. Every body has three dimensions and four limits, adding up to seven (§102).

(7b) This feature of the seven is also illustrated by the stages of life of human beings. The schema of ten stages each consisting of seven years is based on the elegaic poem of Solon, which Philo proceeds to quote in full. A second schema is supplied by the doctor Hippocrates, who posits seven stages of life, as witnessed by a prose quotation from his works (§§103–105).

(7c) The third "completion-bringing" feature of the seven which Philo records returns to the combination of arithmetic, geometry and stereometry. The seventh number is both a square and a cube, illustrating the equalities of the surface in the square and the solid in the cube (§106).

(8) The seven is also the most harmonious number, the source of the table which contains not only the basic musical harmonies, but also the three kinds of proportion: arithmetical, geometrical and harmonic. These are explained in arithmetical terms, with special attention paid to the harmonic progression (§§107–110).

Part III Features of the seven in the physical realm

(9) In his long account of the features of the seven Philo now explicitly makes the transition from the incorporeal realm to visible reality. The nature of the seven extends also to heaven and earth, for every part of the cosmos is a lover of the number seven (§111).

(10) He starts with the heavens where the seven occurs in the case of:

(a) the seven circles of heaven (§112);
(b) the planets, which exert such an influence on earthly matters (§113);
(c) the constellation of the Great Bear, so useful for sailors (§114);
(d) the constellation of the Pleiades, so important for farmers (§115);
(e) the equinoxes, which fall in the seventh month and are a time for festivals (§116).

(11) From the heavens the influence of the seven also extends to human nature, as illustrated by a large number of features:
(a) the seven parts of the irrational soul (§117);
(b) the seven external and internal parts of the body (§118);
(c) the seven parts of the head (§119);
(d) the seven visible qualities (§120);
(e) the seven modulations of the voice (§121);
(f) the seven basic movements (§122);
(g) the seven secretions (§123);
(h) in seven days, according to Hippocrates, the seed is fixed and flesh is formed (§124a);
(i) in women the menstrual flow lasts seven days (§124b);
(j) moreover seventh-month foetuses are viable, whereas those of eight months are not (§124c);
(k) illnesses of the human body reach their crisis on the seventh day (§125).

(12) In the area of the human sciences the power of the seven also extends its influence, as illustrated by:
(a) the science of music, where we encounter the seven-stringed lyre (§126a);
(b) the science of grammar, with its seven vowels (§126b).

(13) The reverence due the seven is also indicated by its name, which is etymologically linked to the words for venerability and dignity. This emerges even more clearly in Latin than in Greek (§127).

Part IV Conclusion

(14) Not only Greek and foreign thinkers have honoured the seven. Moses too recognizes its importance, especially in the institution of the seventh holy day (Sabbath), on which his followers carry out no work but devote themselves to the improvement of their character and the examination of their consciences (§128).

The chief difficulties in the structure of the passage are found in Part II (§§91–110), the sequence of which seems at first sight rather haphazard. See the detailed comments for discussion of how Philo's train of thought, which is often rather associative, can be recovered (and for more details see my article cited above). Not all untidy elements, however, can be explained away.

Sources of and parallels for Philo's material

As we have discovered in the other arithmological passages in *Opif.*, it is plain that Philo has made extensive use of existing collections of arithmological material which draw on the Pythagorean tradition of number symbolism. This dependence is even more apparent in the present excursus because it is so much more extensive than the other passages. Virtually all the material he presents can be found elsewhere, often in a large number of sources. Even though Philo is one of the earliest authors who uses this material, it is not likely that he played a decisive role in its development. In using this material, he probably drew on his own collection of material assembled in the lost treatise *On numbers*. On Philo's use of arithmology in general and his lost treatise we refer the reader once again to the Introduction §6.

Important parallel discussions on the hebdomad are found in a large number of Greco-Roman and patristic writings. The following, presented in approximate chronological order, are the most important (an asterisk means I will refer to this text below by the name of the author only):

Ps.-Hippocrates, *On the Sevens* §1–11 (on the text see the comments in §105);

Varro at Aulus Gellius*, *Attic Nights* 3.10 (we cite the LCL edition of Rolfe);

Nicomachus of Gerasa, cited by Ps.-Iamblichus* *Theology of Arithmetic* 56–71;

Theon of Smyrna*, *Exposition* 103–104;

Clement of Alexandria, *Stromateis* 6.139–145;

Censorinus, *On the Birthday* 7, 11–14;

Anatolius*, *On the first ten numbers* 35–38, partly cited by Ps.-Iamblichus *Theology of Arithmetic* 54–56;

Calcidius*, *Commentary on the Timaeus* ch. 35–37;

Macrobius*, *Commentary on the Dream of Scipio* 1.6.5–83;

Martianus Capella*, *On arithmetic* 266–268;

Favonius Eclogius*, *Disputation on the Dream of Scipio*, 7–10 (also derived from Varro);

John Lydus*, *On the months* 2.12 (and cf. 3.9);

Isidore of Seville*, *Book of scriptural numbers* 34–47.

For further details, including editions used and existing translations, see the list of works given in the Introduction §6. The treatment of the seven in these sources that stands closest to Philo is found in

Anatolius. Because of the inaccessibility of this text, I have given a complete translation below in Excursus 3.

Detailed references to this parallel material are given by Staehle (1931, 34–50; note, however, that he is not in every respect reliable; references should be carefully checked). We shall not be exhaustive in our cross-references, giving only the most important and/or accessible parallels. We shall also list parallel passages in Philo's own works at the appropriate places. It will not be possible to give an exhaustive discussion of all source problems associated with Philo's presentation. In Excursus 1 we give a further discussion of §100 and the relation of Philo's text to the evidence in John Lydus. In Excursus 2 we draw together some conclusions, based on our findings in the detailed comments, on Philo's use of arithmological sources. Special attention once again has to be given to the parallel passages in John Lydus.

A modern author on number symbolism has devoted an entire chapter to numerous examples of the importance of the number seven in a huge variety of cultural contexts; see Schimmel 1993, 127–155. She states that this number has fascinated humankind since time immemorial and gives a full list of examples. Her treatment is somewhat unsatisfactory, however, in that she does not indicate what the common element is in all the material she has collected. At least part of the fascination is caused, it seems to me, by the fact that it is the highest prime within the decad (cf. §99).

The hebdomad and Judaism

The link between the creation account, the Sabbath, and the number seven is not original to Philo, but was already made by Philo's Alexandrian predecessor Aristobulus (date ± 150 B.C.E.). I cite frg. 5 as found in Eusebius *Praep. Ev.* 13.12.11–13:

> Now, as for what is shown plainly in our code of laws, namely, that God ceased working on the seventh day, this does not, as some suppose, substantiate the view that God no longer does anything, but rather means that once he had ceased the arrangement of his works, that they were thus arranged for all time ... Our law code has clearly shown us that the seventh day is an inherent law of nature that serves as a symbol of the sevenfold principle established all around us through which we have knowledge of things both human and divine. And indeed all the world comprising all animal and plant life as well revolves through periods of seven; but that the seventh day is called the Sabbath means that it is a day of rest. Homer and Hesiod, who took their information from our books, plainly show that the seventh day is holy ... (quotations follow from Hesiod, Homer and Linus) (translation Holladay 1983–96, 183–189)

The same text is absorbed by Clement in his discussion of the fourth commandment at *Strom.* 6.137–144. See further the discussions of Walter 1964, 166–171, Hengel 1974, 1.166–169, Holladay 1983–1996, 3.176–195 and his commentary. Walter convincingly refutes the view commonly held in the 19th century that this text of Aristobulus is a forgery based on Philo's works, and postulates that it is an early witness for a form of Jewish Pythagoreanism. We thus have a significant illustration of how Philo's treatise continues a long tradition of Alexandrian biblical exegesis. Indeed it has recently been argued by Mansfeld 1989 that in the Greek tradition the Ps.-Hippocratic text on the hebdomad may well be a Jewish pseudepigraphon; see the detailed notes on §105.

In his important analysis of Philo's excursus (in the broader context of an account of the number seven in all the writings of Philo), Moehring 1995, 155, points out that it contains only three passages of unmistakably Jewish content, namely the introductory passage §89, the reference to national festivals at §116, and the concluding passage on Moses and the Sabbath in §128. On other hand, he continues, the excursus contains various quotations of Greek authors and allusions to Greek institutions which form an integral part of the whole. The implication is that Judaism takes a backseat in the entire passage (cf. n. 46 "even in this perfunctory bow to Moses"). I disagree with this view. Even though in the illustratory material on the seven almost no reference is made to Jewish themes, Philo's Judaism is clearly the motivating force for the whole, as is indicated by the fact that the excursus is framed by the two biblical passages. One might profitably compare Philo's five philosophical treatises, which superficially look just like works of Greek philosophy and contain many references to blatantly "pagan" Greek religious and literary motifs. Yet analysis shows that the motivating force behind these works is unmistakably Jewish, as shown for example in the opening section of *Aet.* (§§1–20), with its climactic reference to Moses (§19), and the closing passage of *Prob.* (§160).

Detailed comments

Part I Introduction
(1) §89. **the entire cosmos had been completed.** The biblical text in Gen 2:1 speaks of "the heaven and the earth and their entire adornment (κόσμος)." Except in the late books originally written in Greek the LXX does not use the term κόσμος in the sense of universe or world, but does use it in the sense of adornment applied to its parts, as here (cf. also Deut 4:19).

There is an important divergence between the LXX and the Hebrew Bible in Gen 2:2. According to the former God completed his works on the *sixth* day, according to the latter on the *seventh*. The Samaritan Pentateuch, *Jubilees* 2:16, the *Vetus Latina* and the *Peshitta* all have the same reading as the LXX. It is thus difficult to determine whether the Masoretic text represents the original reading. Certainly the logic of the LXX version is clearer. If God ended his work on the sixth day, it is clear that he does nothing on the seventh. If he ended it on the seventh day, it is always possible that he still had some work to do on that day. On the text see further Alexandre *CLG* 214–216; on the problems of interpretation Kugel *TB*, 52–53.

the perfect number six. This was explained at the outset of the treatise in §13. As was noted in our comments on §9 and §13, τέλειος means both perfect and complete, so Philo's text makes a direct link between the completion of the universe (ἐτελειώθη paraphrases the biblical συνετελέσθησαν) and the six as perfect number.

praising it. God's praise of the seventh day (not in the biblical text, where he "blesses" it) anticipates the praise of the hebdomad in the arithmological excursus.

festival ... of the universe. Philo means the Sabbath, but the day itself is not mentioned until the end of the excursus (§128), while its Hebrew name (hellenized as σάββατον) is avoided altogether. The Sabbath is not a local festival because its institution is related to the creation of the entire universe. In Philo's account of the Jewish feasts in *Spec.* 2, the Sabbath ranks second after the feast of every day and is discussed at length in §§56–139. On the Sabbath in Philo see further below on §128. In Philo's day the conception of a week as a pattern of seven days regulating social life was unknown outside the Jewish community, although from about the 1st century B.C.E. onwards there was a tendency to associate seven consecutive days with the names of the planets. The introduction of the week in society as a whole is connected with the Christianization of the Roman Empire. The week with Sunday as day of rest was instituted by the Emperor Constantine in 321 C.E. See further the curious little book on the origin of the week by F. H. Colson (1926), the translator of Philo in the LCL series.

universal. The Greek term πάνδημος means literally "belonging to the entire people." Philo uses it for national Jewish festivals at *Spec.* 2.149; *Flacc.* 116. But here the import is wider still. The Sabbath applies to all people, because all descend from the first humans created by God, who gave this day a special place in the event of creation. A little anachronistically one might translate "public holiday" (cf. Winston *PA* 85, "general holiday").

birthday of the cosmos. The same phrase is used of the Sabbath at *Mos.* 1.207; 2.210; *Spec.* 1.170; 2.59, 2.70. As Colson (LCL) observes in a note on the first of these texts, Philo must have noticed that the Sabbath is nowhere mentioned until the incident of the Manna in Exod 16, and so concluded that by that time people had lost count and had to be reminded which day it was. It must be suspected that non-Jewish readers of Philo's treatise found the notion of a weekly celebration of the cosmos' birthday rather strange. For example, the fascinating little work *On the birthday* by the 3rd century Roman writer Censorinus, the contents of which largely go back to Varro in the 1st cent. B.C.E., discusses the larger cosmic aspects of time (cf. §§16, 18), but has no notion of anything resembling a cosmic birthday. The only example of this notion that I have found outside Philo is in a fragment of Eusebius, PG 24.697, who mentions the creation account, but relates the actual phrase to Easter.

(2) §90. *nature of the seven*. Throughout the account Philo speaks of the "nature" (φύσις, cf. §§91, 95, 102, 111), "being" (οὐσία, cf. §98), and the "power" (δύναμις, cf. §§96, 101, 103, 126) of the hebdomad. One might be tempted to read into this terminology a distinction between essential nature and effect, but the distinction does not really work (note esp. "nature" at §111). It is best to treat all three as virtual synonyms.

give sufficient praise. Just as God praised the hebdomad (§89, with reference to Gen 2:3), so the faithful exegete must do the same. The verb here is in fact ὑμνῆσαι, "to sing a hymn to." Philo's long excursus amounts to a prose hymn in honour of the number seven.

we should keep our peace. As noted in the analysis above, Philo's language here is almost identical to §5, where he admits his inadequacy in giving a proper explanation of the Mosaic creation account (the words οὐ μὴν ... διὰ τοῦθ' ἡσυχαστέον, ἀλλ' ἐπιτολμητέον are in fact identical in both texts, while ἱκανῶς ἂν ὑμνῆσαι δύναιτο is almost the same as ἀξίως ἂν ὑμνῆσαι δύναιτο in §4). The parallelism is presumably deliberate. The task of presenting an adequate encomium of the hebdomad is a comparable challenge to giving exegesis of the entire creation account. But Moehring interestingly suggests that Philo may also have had another motive for his declaration (1995, 154): "Whenever Philo introduces a topic with a preliminary statement about its richness, importance, and difficulties, the reader is warned to expect a large amount of diverse materials collected from different sources." As a generalization this statement may be too daring, but it certainly is to the point in the present context. Philo has a mass of material, and now has to present it in an organized and illuminating manner.

Part II Mathematical features of the hebdomad

(3) §91. *spoken of in two ways*. Without any further introduction Philo commences with the arithmetical features of the seven, first indicating the two different kinds of operations that one can carry out with this number.

Pythagorean arithmology is basically concerned with the first ten numbers only. Comprehensive accounts of these numbers, such as we find in Theon, Anatolius and Ps.-Iamblichus, stop at the decad, but do sometimes refer to higher numbers when required for their explanations.

In the study of the Bible, however, much larger numbers are encountered, e.g. the 12 tribes and 70 elders of Israel, the 300 cubits of Noah's ark, and so on. For this reason Philo's arithmology is not confined to the first ten numbers. Staehle assumed in his dissertation that Philo's *On numbers* proceeded beyond the decad. This is certainly the case for a biblical arithmological compendium such as that of Isidore of Seville. See further the Introduction §6.

(4) §92. *should be ... investigated.* Both here and in §90, Philo uses the construction with the verbal adjective indicating necessity or obligation, which, as was noted in connection with §52, is so common in the treatise. It is an important device for structuring the entire excursus (cf. also §§95, 97, 99, 101). This statement sets up his programme for the next five capita. He first deals with the second kind of arithmetical feature (§§92–94), followed by the first (§§95–98). But see also the comment on §95.

both a cube and a square. In algebraic terms (unknown to the Greeks), $n^6 = n^2 \cdot n^3$, so it must always be both a square and a cube (it becomes the 7th number because the multiplication starts not from n, but from 1, which is multiplied by n to produce the second number). As was noted at §51, Pythagorean number theory envisaged numbers spatially. A number such as 4 thus forms a square and a number such as 8 forms a cube. On such "figured numbers" see further Heath 1931, 43–46 and the remarks of J. Sesiano at Paramelle 1984, 205–209. Philo's knowledge of arithmetic has been studied in depth by Robbins 1931, who concludes (346): "Philo was no mathematician, in the professional sense, and made no contributions ... to the mathematical sciences. He displays, however, extensive knowledge of the current arithmetic." This feature of the hebdomad is also given by Anatolius 35.14–21, who is cited at Ps.-Iamblichus 54.13–55.1. For illustration Anatolius uses exactly the same numbers that we find in §93, but does not make the link to two kinds of being.

both incorporeal and corporeal being. It might be thought puzzling that a surface should symbolize incorporeal being (usually this is related to the monad, implicitly by Philo at §15; see the comment ad loc.). It does so because, although it can belong to a body, strictly speaking it cannot on its own form a body on account of its lack of depth. Philo had already explained this in more detail in his excursus on the four at §49 (and illustrated it with the game of nuts in §50). Arithmological symbolism is of course infinitely flexible, and there are many points of contact between the features of the numbers 1, 3, 4, 7, and 10. See also on §98 below.

§93. *the numbers just mentioned.* I. e. in the introductory statement in §91. These examples use the smallest numbers available for purposes of illustration. Unlike in Anatolius, Philo does not spell them out in full. The two sequences of seven numbers are: 1, 2, 4, 8, 16, 32, 64; 1, 3, 9, 27, 81, 243, 729. In each case the final number is both a square and a cube: $64 = 8^2 = 4^3$; $729 = 27^2 = 9^3$. 64 is the smallest number that is both a square and a cube.

§94. *And invariably.* Since the seventh number generated is n^6, the same process can be started all over again for any given sequence that has already been generated. The sequence is thus now n^6, n^7, n^8, n^9, n^{10}, n^{11}, n^{12}, and the final number n^{12} is both $(n^6)^2$ and $(n^4)^3$. This process can be repeated *ad infinitum*, since the following seventh power (by inclusive reckoning) will always be divisible by two and three, e.g. n^{18}, n^{24} etc. The sequence used by Philo for illustration is 32, 64, 128, 256, 512, 1024, 2048, 4096. The final number 4096 is 2^{12}, i.e. $2^6 = 64^2$ and $2^4 = 16^3$. The number cubed now falls outside the actual sequence. (This sequence happens to be the same that produces kilobytes in modern computer science: one kilobyte = 1024 bits.) It should be noted that no other arithmological text has this further development.

has a side of 64. Here is a clear example of the spatialization of numbers in ancient arithmetic, as noted above in §92.

(5a) §95. *the other kind of the seven.* The two kinds have already been introduced in §91. It is best to take the section now introduced as extending to §98, though strictly speaking the feature discussed in §§99–100 also illustrates this kind of seven as well. Philo first discusses the musical, then the geometrical and stereometrical features of the seven. But in each case the arithmetical characteristics provide the foundation. In this way three of the four mathematical disciplines contained in the *enkyklios paideia* have been touched on, but exclusively in arithmological terms. Philo tells us in a famous passage at *Congr.* 74–80 that he first learnt the preliminary disciplines of the *enkyklios paideia* before moving on to philosophy and wisdom. On this subject see the monograph of Mendelson (1982), who rightly points out that to draw a distinction between arithmetic and arithmology runs the risk of anachronism (13), but does not treat the links that arithmology also has with music and geometry. On Philo's knowledge of arithmetic see the note on §92.

one, two and four. The relation between numbers and harmony has already been explained in relation to the four at §48. Here the three is lacking, so only two of the four basic harmonies can be produced. The same item is found in Proclus, *Comm. Tim.* 2.197.29–31. At Anatolius 35.24 we read: "The seven is said to be the number of the first concord, namely 4 to 3, and of the geometrical analogy 1, 2, 4." It looks like Philo may have applied the second group of numbers rather than the first to the musical doctrine. He returns to the subject at §107. See also the next note.

yoked pairs. The word ζυγάδην (literally "in a yoked manner") is extremely rare, found only in Philo, John Lydus (who may be dependent on him), and once in the *Souda*, a Byzantine dictionary. The division of the seven into the paired numbers $1 + 6$, $2 + 5$, $3 + 4$ is also found in Macrobius 1.6.6–7, 18, 23, 45, who uses them to organize a large part of his account. Except in John Lydus I have not found a parallel for the linking of the three yoked pairs to musical intervals which Philo sets out in §96 (Macrobius 1.6.43 is only partially similar).

§96. *relationship ... is highly musical.* Normally Pythagorean musical theory focuses on the harmonies of the octave and within the octave, as in the example from Macrobius just cited. The following intervals which Philo gives fall outside the usual discussions of harmony, and appear to be determined by the arithmological context rather than by musical theory itself.

six-fold ratio. I.e. it produces an interval of two octaves and a quint. Macrobius 2.1.24 states that the double octave is the limit for the human voice and the human ear, but that the range of celestial harmony goes to four octaves and a half (based on *Tim.* 35–36). Theon 52.8 stops at a double octave and a fourth.

as we shall demonstrate ... The cross-reference is rather unclear. I take Philo to be anticipating his discussion of harmony later at §§107–110. There, however, he does not discuss intervals greater than the octave. Müller (1841, 302), the only commentator to comment on this reference, thinks it is to the lost *On numbers*; but see the comment on §52.

ratio five to two. I.e. it produces a harmony of the octave and approximately a third. Philo mentions the octave because this harmony is close by.

ratio four to three. This is the only one of the three ratios discussed here that corresponds to one of the standard intervals explained in §48 and repeated at §107.

(5b) §97. *another of its beauties.* Philo now moves on to features of the hebdomad in the area of geometry.

a most sacred object of knowledge. Presented in these bald terms, i.e. not connected to any biblical material, this expression is probably a vestige of the original Pythagorean context of arithmology, in which features of numbers were taken over from early Greek cults and also systematically related to diverse divinities. Numbers could even be regarded as divine in their own right. See further the remarks of Moehring 1995, 146–150.

The right-angle triangle ... Lengths of three and four units, if joined together and then connected by a third length, must produce a right-angled triangle between them, as demonstrated in Pythagoras' famous theorem. The same feature is given in Anatolius 35.27–36.2 (also quoted at Ps.-Iamblichus 55.7–8), who calls the triangle thus produced "prototypical," but does not explain why this is the case. Arithmology can use the features of the right-angled triangle in various ways when explaining the Bible. (a) It can emphasize the $3 + 4 = 7$ aspect, as here. Or (b) it can dwell on the fact that $3 + 4 + 5 = 12$, as at *Spec.* 2.177 (the zodiac). Or (c) it can focus on the fact that $3^2 + 4^2 + 5^2 = 50$, as Philo points out at *Contempl.* 65 and *Spec.* 2.177 in relation to Pentecost; *Mos.* 2.80 and *QE* 2.93, 50 columns of the temple; *QG* 2.5, width of Noah's ark; *QG* 4.27, Abraham's 50 righteous men at Gen 18:24. At *QG* 4.8 the right-angled triangle is associated with the triad for obvious reasons (exegesis of three measures of flour, Gen 18:6).

the starting-point of the qualities. Because Philo twice in subsequent sentences speaks of the ἀρχή of *shapes and* qualities, one must suspect that two words, <σχημάτων καί>, have fallen out of the text here. In this context it is natural to think first of the role of the right-angled triangles in the structure of the elementary bodies in Plato's *Timaeus* (cf. Runia *PT* 292). For Plato the right-angle triangle is the basis of order and structure in bodily reality, and is thus partly instrumental in producing order out of disorder (cf. 30a, 53a–b). But the triangles presupposed in the *Timaeus* are quite different to the standard triangle here. The fundamental idea in our passage is the Pythagorean contrast between the One and the many. There can only be one right-angle, but every kind of acute or obtuse angle. Until the right-angle is produced, there can only be inequality and randomness.

irregularity, disorder and inequality. We recall the features of unformed matter as described at §22.

remains unaltered and never changes ... Characteristics reminiscent of the monad and of the divine, as will soon be emphasized at §100.

may be reasonably considered ... Once again an optative is used to express a logical conclusion; see the comment on §25. Philo's reasoning here takes the form of a syllogism.

(5c) §98. *another aspect.* The doctrine of the three dimensions involving the point (no dimension, one number), line (1 dimension, at least 2 numbers), surface (2 dimensions, at least 3 numbers) and solid (3 dimensions, at least 4 numbers), has already been outlined at §49 and was also briefly referred to at §92. It is further utilized at §§102 and 106. It can be connected with the numbers 1, 2, 3, 4, 7 and 10. This item is also found at Anatolius 35.21–24 (repeated at Ps.-Iamblichus 55.2–4) and in a modified form at Macrobius 1.6.35 (cited below).

the starting-point of geometry and stereometry. Cf. Gellius 1.20 (probably going back to Varro): "Of the figures which the geometers call shapes (σχήματα) there are two kinds, plane and solid." Philo probably intends geometry to refer here to "plane geometry," stereometry to "solid geometry." Theon regularly distinguishes the two, and so has five mathematical sciences instead of four: cf. *Expos.* 10.8, 15.13, 17.18. Note that this final sentence summarizes §98 only.

incorporeal and bodily reality. Philo's doctrine is paralleled (albeit not very exactly) by Macrobius 1.6.35: " ... all bodies are either mathematical, the products of geometry, or such as are perceptible to sight or touch. The former possess three stages of development: the line grows out of the point, the surface out of the line, and the solid out of the surface; the latter, because of the adhesive qualities in the four elements, harmoniously grow together into firm bodily substances." Macrobius separates mathematical and physical reality much more clearly than Philo does. See also above on §92.

(6a) §99. *sacred.* See above on §97.

it possesses a special feature. On ἐξαίρετος see the Commentary above on §16. The term λόγος is rather unclear in the context. It could also be rendered "value" (cf. Winston *PA* 85). Other translators suggest "position": cf. Kraus Reggiani and J. Cohn ad loc., but it is doubtful whether the word can have this meaning. This feature can be compactly summarized as "the seven is neither factor nor product" (cf. Moehring 1995, 156). It is also mentioned by Philo at *Leg.* 1.15; *QG* 2.12; and by almost all the other arithmological sources, e.g. Anatolius 35.5–6, Nicomachus at Ps.-Iamblichus 58.23–59.1; Theon 103.2–16; Macrobius 1.6.10–11.

§100. *liken this number to motherless and maidenly Victory* ... It was standard Pythagorean practice to identify numbers with various divinities of the Greek pantheon, and also use the features of numbers to explain various epithets that belonged to these gods. See, for example, the analysis of the epithets found in Nicomachus as cited by Ps.-Iamblichus in Delatte (1915, 139–164, complete list of epithets on 163–164). In Greek theology Victory (Νίκη) can be a separate goddess, but just as often it is an epithet associated with members of the Olympic pantheon, and most often with the martial goddess Athena. Even though the name Athena is not mentioned, the identification is made perfectly clear by the additional clause, which refers to the myth that Athena appeared full-grown and in full armour out of the head of Zeus. The phrase "according to the account" (λόγος ἔχει plus infinitive, very common in Philo), indicates that he will not vouch for the truth of the mythical story and so effectively dissociates himself from it. He does, however, mention the name of Zeus, the only time he does this in an exegetical treatise (but numerous examples in the philosophical and historical treatises).

The comparison or identification of the hebdomad with the goddess (though never explicitly named) is found in no less than 10 Philonic passages, listed at Moehring 1995, 156. The chief epithets referred to by Philo in these passages are "motherless" (ἀμήτωρ, in all texts except *Contempl.* 65) and "always-maidenly" (ἀειπάρθενος, cf. *Leg.* 1.15; *Mos.* 2.210 etc.). The reference to Athena is found in various arithmological texts; cf. Theon 103.3; Nicomachus at Ps.-Iamblichus 71.3, other refs. at Staehle 1931, 36 n. The epithets used by Philo are less common, but are found at Anatolius 35.7; Proclus *Comm. Tim.* 2.203.6. Clement *Strom.* 6.140.1 describes the seven as "motherless and sterile."

the other philosophers ... but the Pythagoreans ... Philo distinguishes between two groups of arithmological interpreters. The former, who are left anonymous, compare the hebdomad to Athena. The latter, who are identified with the Pythagoreans, compare it to "the director of the universe." Towards the end of the chapter a quote from the early Pythagorean writer Philolaus (about 470–400 B.C.E.) is cited in favour of this distinction (= 44B20 D-K, text also printed and translated in Huffmann 1993, 335–336).

Comparison with parallel texts makes Philo's distinction very problematic. For example Anatolius 35.6–8 opens his account of the hebdomad as follows: "The seven is the only number within the ten which neither generates nor is generated by any other number except the one. For this reason it is also called by the Pythagoreans 'maiden without a mother'." And Theon 103.4, after giving the same doctrine, concludes: "For this reason it was also called Athena by the Pythagoreans, being neither from a mother or itself a mother." Philo's distinction runs counter to these texts. In the parallel passage at *Leg.* 1.15 he himself attributes the comparison of the hebdomad with the "ever-maidenly and motherless (goddess)" to the mythicizing Pythagoreans. Even more problems are generated when we compare a very similar passage in Lydus *Mens.* 2.12, 33.8–34.3, where the final quote is not attributed to Philolaus but to "the rhetor from Tarentum" or a certain "Onetor from Tarentum" (depending on which manuscript reading one prefers). These issues are too complicated to discuss in the commentary, and will be further discussed in Excursus 1 at the end of the chapter.

Generation involves change. There are two textual issues here. Cohn prints γένεσις (genesis), but given the context and the close textual parallel in John Lydus (see Staehle 1931, 37) the conjecture γέννησις is justified. Cohn does add the supplementary words καὶ τὸ γεννῶν (both that which generates) proposed by Markland in the 18th century. This change is plainly mandatory.

the very ancient Ruler and Director. Who is meant by this description? It may be expected the Pythagoreans had Zeus in mind, and this is certainly what Philo's ancient readers would have assumed (it is also assumed by Staehle 1931, 37; Moehring 1995, 159). But in the parallel passage in Lydus (see Excursus 1) he is identified with Apollo and this identification is demonstrated by an etymology and an Orphic quote. At the same time we may be certain that Philo has in mind here an identification of this figure with God the supreme being and creator, who is recognized by all peoples (*Spec.* 2.165) and as sovereign ruler must be One (see also *Conf.* 170, where God is described in exactly the same terms as here, ἄρχων καὶ ἡγεμών, and this is illustrated by a quote from Homer, *Iliad* 2.204).

the seven would fittingly be called an image. Philo assumes here, but because of the context does not make explicit, the special relationship between the monad and the hebdomad. This feature is found in a few arithmological texts (e.g. Macrobius 1.6.10–11; Ps.-Iamblichus 72.7–9, but listed under the eight!). It is much more common in Philo's writings, and this can only be on account of his Jewish background. See the many passages listed and discussed in Nikiprowetzky 1996 (1977), 193; Moehring 1995, 159–164.

As we noted above, in the arithmological literature the numbers are identified with various deities or their epithets. Here the hebdomad is presented as the image (εἰκών) of God or Zeus. Such terminology is unusual. It is for example entirely missing in the Nicomachean material in

Ps.-Iamblichus, which is our most copious source for relations between gods and numbers. But cf. Proclus *Comm. Tim.* 1.151.16, where the monad and the hebdomad are both regarded as image (εἰκών) of Athena.

There exists the Director and Ruler of all things. Szymanski (1981, 117) correctly points out that if we take this phrase as the subject of the sentence, it is given seven epithets. This may be deliberate. But it is not enough to prove that Philo's information on Philolaus is authentic, as he wishes.

(6b) §101. *In the realm of intellect ... but in the realm of sense-perception* ... This sentence give rise to two major difficulties. Firstly, what kind of transition does Philo intend here and what is the relation to the similar kind of transition found in §111? Secondly, how is the lacuna in the Greek text to be filled? Earlier scholars, notably Radice *FM* 281 and by implication Staehle 1931, 40, have argued that this passage marks the main transition of the excursus from a presentation of the arithmology of the intelligible world to that of the sense-perceptible world. I have argued elsewhere (2000, 165–167), that this view is incorrect, because the transition they have in mind in fact occurs at §111. Philo is still working with the framework of a basically arithmetical presentation, which he began at §91. With his antithesis here he wishes to make a contrast between the monadic hebdomad discussed in §§99–100 and the "completive" or "perfective" hebdomad which also plays a role in nature, as illustrated by the phases of the moon. Arithmetically this contrast is reminiscent of the distinction between the role of the hebdomad inside and outside the decad, as introduced at the outset in §91.

a great and most essential power. I have translated συνεκτικωτάτην with "most essential" because that seems to be the meaning that Philo always gives the term elsewhere (cf. §§8, 162 and 19 other instances, all except one in the superlative). It is also possible that the word means more concretely "most connective," i.e. referring to the function of the seven in linking up the heavenly and earthly realm (see further the discussion of the text in Nicomachus below). The exact meaning of the sentence is obscured by the lacuna.

by which ... As noted by Mangey ad loc., the second part of the sentence, as transmitted in the manuscripts, is ungrammatical. "By which" (ἐν οἷς) is masculine or neuter plural in the majority of mss., so it cannot be taken with "power" which is feminine singular. But there is no point in accepting the variant reading ἧς or emending to ᾗ (as suggested by Mangey), because then the final phrase about the moon hangs in the air. In his two editions Cohn printed three asterisks in order to indicate the lacuna, but in his apparatus at PCW 1.34 he suggests the supplement "in the motions of the planets" (<πλανήτων κινήσεσιν>). This suggestion has been favourably received by subsequent editors and translators. Clearly they have been attracted by the contrast it introduces between the immobile nature of the monadic hebdomad and the mobile aspect of the hebdomad in the visible realm. We should observe, however, that this is not precisely the contrast that Philo has in mind, which is between immobility and impassibility on the one hand and completive force on the other. The presence of the seven in the heavens allows things to be completed on earth. This emerges clearly from the parallel passages in *Leg.* 1.8 and *Spec.* 2.57. Strictly speaking it is not the motions of the planets which are relevant but their hebdomadic nature or disposition (cf. §113). Moreover, on the basis of the parallels in *Leg.* 1.8 and *Spec.* 2.57, one might wish to add to the planets the other prominent examples of seven in the heavens, the Great Bear and the constellation of the Pleiades. The supplement would then become: "in the seven planets and the Great Bear and the choir of the Pleiades" (<πλάνησι ἑπτὰ καὶ ἄρκτῳ καὶ πλείαδι>, or perhaps, comparing §115, <...τῶν πλειάδων χόρῳ>). This suggestion has at least two advantages in comparison with Cohn's proposal. Firstly, it coheres slightly better with the following phrase "by which all things on earth are able to improve," since not only the growth supplied by the planets, but also the guidance given by the Great Bear and the constellation of the Pleiades, contribute to the improvement of life on earth (cf. §§113–115). Secondly, the lacuna can be more easily explained through the supposition that an entire line fell out of the text at some stage (approximately 30–40 characters in a papyrus text). I have included this conjecture in the text of my translation.

in the revolutions of the moon ... The phases of the moon make up 28 = 4 x 7. But 28 has two other noteworthy arithmological features. It is the sum of the first seven numbers $(1 + 2 + 3 + 4 + 5 + 6 + 7 = 28)$, and it is also the second perfect number after 6 (cf. §13), i.e. it is formed by the sum of its factors $(1 + 2 + 4 + 7 + 14 = 28)$. The doctrine of the four phases of the moon related to the perfect number 28 is found in most of the main arithmological texts: cf. Varro at Gellius 3.10.6; Anatolius 35.12–14, Theon 103.19–104.1, Ps.-Iamblichus 54.11–13 (abridged from Anatolius); 59.5–60.2 (= Nicomachus); Macrobius 1.6.48; Clement *Strom.* 1.143.1–2. It is worth comparing the Greek of the passages in Anatolius and in Philo; words held in common are printed in bold (for a translation of Anatolius' text see Excursus 3):

Anatolius 35.11–12	Philo §101
ἀπὸ μονάδος συντεθεὶς ὁ ζ΄ ἀριθμὸς ποιεῖ **τὸν κη΄ τέλειον καὶ τοῖς ἑαυτοῦ μέρεσιν ἰσούμενον. ἡμέραι σελήνης** κη΄ καθ' ἑβδομάδας **συμπληρωθεῖσαι.**	**ἀπὸ μονάδος συντεθεὶς** ἑξῆς **ὁ ἑπτὰ ἀριθμὸς** γεννᾷ **τὸν ὀκτὼ καὶ εἴκοσι τέλειον καὶ τοῖς αὐτοῦ μέρεσιν ἰσούμενον·** ὁ δὲ γεννηθεὶς ἀριθμὸς ἀποκαταστατικός ἐστι **σελήνης,** ἀφ' οὗ ἤρξατο σχήματος λαμβάνειν αὔξησιν αἰσθητῶς, εἰς ἐκεῖνο κατὰ μείωσιν ἀνακαμπτούσης· αὔξεται μὲν γὰρ ἀπὸ τῆς πρώτης μηνοειδοῦς ἐπιλάμψεως ἄχρι διχοτόμου **ἡμέραις** ἑπτά, εἶθ' ἑτέραις τοσαύταις πλησιφαὴς γίνεται καὶ πάλιν ὑποστρέφει διαυλοδρομοῦσα τὴν αὐτὴν ὁδόν, ἀπὸ μὲν τῆς πλησιφαοῦς ἐπὶ τὴν διχότομον ἑπτὰ πάλιν **ἡμέραις,** εἶτ' ἀπὸ ταύτης ἐπὶ τὴν μηνοειδῆ ταῖς ἴσαις· ἐξ ὧν ὁ λεχθεὶς ἀριθμὸς **συμπεπλήρωται.**

We see that the first sentence is virtually identical in both texts. Thereafter Philo appears to have fleshed out the telegrammatic description of the four phrases of the moon as we find it in Anatolius. The parallel strongly suggests that Philo may have used an arithmological source very similar to Anatolius, which he expanded by means of his customary florid language. The parallel passage in Nicomachus is also very interesting. It is somewhat fuller and emphasizes not only the completive role of the seven, but also the connective role that the moon plays between heaven and earth because of its intermediate position.

follows the same route. The same imagery from the racing track that we saw earlier. See §113 and the comment on §44.

the ... number ... is completed. The verb indicating completion or fulfilment makes a natural transition to the next theme in §102.

(7a) §102. *the completion-bringer.* The Greek term is τελέσφορος. I have translated it rather literally to bring out its full force. It is another of the epithets that the hebdomad has received in the Pythagorean arithmological tradition, similar to Τύχη (Chance), Καιρός (Right time) etc. The epithet is found at Anatolius 35.24; Ps.-Iamblichus 55.6 (from Anatolius); cf. 64.22 and 87.15 (in the latter text it is applied to the nine). The epithet and the related verb are used primarily to indicate the bringing to fruition of living things (cf. §§59, 113 with reference to the planets), and especially of babies, who are viable in the seventh and the ninth month of pregnancy (cf. below §124). Philo deviates from these texts by also applying the term to a combination of arithmetic and stereometry, both here and in §106. The section in between (§§103–105) does focus on human life. It cannot be denied that Philo's composition in this section is untidy.

all bodies with instrumental force. The basic meaning of the term ὀργανικός is "instrumental." Philo applies it to the animal or human body in the sense that it is equipped with parts that allow it (or rather the soul) to move and act (cf. §103; *Leg.* 1.4; *Ebr.* 111 etc.). In this text the term appears to receive a broader application. If any body is to be able to effectuate movement, it must have three dimensions and four limits.

three dimensions ... Similar stereometrical doctrines are also found at §§49 (in connection with the four), 98, 106. For parallels in the sources see above on §98.

the ideas of the first numbers. Dillon (1977, 159) claims: "That the ideas are to be viewed as numbers becomes clear from a number of passages, e.g. *Opif.* 102." I agree with Radice *FM* 286 that "ideas" should *not* be taken in the technical Platonic sense here (cf. also my comments at *PT* 480 on Krämer 1964, 273).

one, two, three and four. We recognize here again the Pythagorean doctrine of the *tetraktys*; see further the note on §47. For the association of the first four numbers and the decad with solid body see also *Decal.* 24–26. The flexible arithmologist can thus associate solidity with three numbers: four, seven and ten.

three intervals. Note that the same word διάστασις means both dimension and interval, the common notion being extension.

(7b) §103. ***the stages of life of human beings.*** Philo now illustrates the telesphoric (i.e. completion-bringing) power of the hebdomad with the theme of the ages of life, as illustrated by Solon's poem. This at least focuses on biological phenomena, but it is still not the same as the theme of the viability of babies, which is found in connection with the epithet in other arithmological texts (see the comment on §102).

The idea that human life has a fixed set of stages, each with its own particular features and developments is a common theme in Philo. See for example *Ios.* 127–129; *Cher.* 115; *Her.* 294–299; *Congr.* 82; *QG* 4.152; *Aet.* 58. In the parallel passage at *Leg.* 1.10 only three periods of seven years are given, with a palpably Stoic colouring. See further the note of Alexandre at PAPM 16.160. But there are also many texts in which Philo attempts to transcend the natural ages of humankind though the conception of a "spiritual maturity," and this theme is further developed in patristic thought; cf. Gnilka 1972, 76–87 and passim. The theme reappears famously in the *Confessions* of Augustine; cf. Starnes 1990, 27 n. 38. In the present arithmological context Philo presents two schemas. The first, consisting of 10 stages of seven years each, is based on Solon's poem. The second, attributed to Hippocrates, postulates seven stages of life, and requires some juggling in order to be fitted into the standard lifetime of seventy years. For further arithmological use of the theme see the discussion of parallel texts in the comments on §104.

During the first period of seven years ... Philo first gives a brief summary of the ten stages. Each stage is described by means of a nominal phrase (the verbs in the translation have all been added). Only in the case of the tenth stage does he expand just a little. The summary is clearly based on the poem of Solon which he proceeds to quote, but it would be going too far to call it a paraphrase. We note some of the more striking deviations:

(a) In the second stage Philo focuses on the young man's ability to reproduce. This is not found in Solon's much more general phrase, but finds parallels in a passage such as *Leg.* 1.10 and in other arithmological accounts, e.g. at Theon 104.6; see further Mansfeld 1971, 172.

(b) Solon takes the seventh and eighth stages together, whereas Philo sees the eighth as a further perfectioning of the seventh.

(c) Solon sees a cessation of reckless deeds in the sixth period. Philo converts this into a diminution of passion in the ninth period, which he regards much more positively than Solon does: Solon sees a weakening of the powers, Philo the attainment of serenity. The abatement of sexual passion in old age is a common theme in the ancient world; cf. the anecdote about Sophocles told by Cephalus at the beginning of Plato *Resp.* 329c.

perfection ... the end of life ... The terms τελείωσις (eighth stage) and τέλος (tenth stage) recall the theme of the hebdomad as τελέσφορος, "completion-bringer," as introduced in §102.

§104. *Solon, the lawgiver of the Athenians.* Solon (c. 640 – c. 560) gained enduring fame on account of his reform of Athenian society at the beginning of the 6th century, embodied in the Solonian legislation (see also the comment on §1). He was also a distinguished poet, who placed his poetic talent primarily in the service of his political goals. In later tradition Solon became one of the seven sages. Philo also mentions Solon as legislator at *Spec.* 3.22 and *Prob.* 47. Half a line from another poem is anonymously cited at *Virt.* 162.

the following elegaic verses. Philo often quotes lines of poetry in his writings (a complete list is given by Theiler at PCH 7.398). This is the longest quote to be found in his works. It consists of nine elegaic couplets (a hexameter followed by a pentameter). In the translation I have retained the conventional form of the couplets, but without making any attempt to render them metrically.

There are numerous editions of Solon's poems. The poem quoted by Philo is no. 27 in the edition of West (1992^2, 2.155–157, translation in West 1993, 80), no. 23 in the edition of Gentili and Prato (1988, 115–117). It is important to bear in mind that the editors of Solon have to try to determine the original form of the poem, based on all the preserved sources, whereas the task of Philo's editor is to publish the text such as it was written down by Philo. West's text differs from that of Cohn in five respects, Gentili and Prato only in two. I have translated Cohn's text, except for a small change in line 7, which hardly affects the sense (see the note to the translation).

Solon's poem is also cited by Anatolius 37.2–22 (with almost exactly the same text; note that both have the corrupt ἐν ἑβδομάδεσ(σ)ιν) and Clement *Strom.* 6.144.4–6 (text differs somewhat from Philo). Censorinus, who derives his arithmological information from Varro, alludes to the poem and paraphrases its contents at 14.7. These are the only three other arithmological texts which refer to the poem. Others, e.g. Nicomachus at Ps.-Iamblichus 65.3–67.2; Theon 104.5–9; Macrobius 1.6.69–76, include material on the ages of life (but usually concentrate on the first three to five stages), without reference to the Solonian material. See further Mansfeld 1971, 161–174 and my further comments on Philo's sources in Excursus 2. It seems that Clement did not derive his material from Philo, but probably from his predecessor Aristobulus: see Walter 1964, 169; Van den Hoek 1988, 204. On Ambrose's paraphrase of the poem, based on Philo, see below *Nachleben.*

God has made complete ... in completion of due measure ... Solon's poem twice uses the verb τελέω, at lines 3 and 17. This will have encouraged Philo to include this material with reference to the epithet τελέσφορος.

§105. *But the doctor Hippocrates.* Hippocrates of Cos (c. 460 – c. 370), the father of ancient medicine, is another famous name that Philo can invoke in support of the importance and excellence of the hebdomad. Philo refers to him rarely: apart from the further reference at §124, where he is glowingly described as "the authority on what happens in nature," he is only cited at *Contempl.* 16 for the famous aphorism "life is short but art is long" (also referred to anonymously at *Somn.* 1.10). For a general presentation of Hippocrates and the Hippocratean tradition see Jouanna 1999.

The Hippocratean division of the stages of life is clearly based on that of Solon, but it has been adapted to the seven Greek expressions for a male person from baby to old man (all of these are single words in Greek). This results in the grouping together of Solon's fifth, sixth and seventh and last two stages respectively, leaving seven distinct periods of human life. For a different set of Greek terms see *Ios.* 127 (five of the seven correspond).

child, boy, youth ... As in the case of Solon, Philo first gives a brief summary of the doctrine, before quoting the original source verbatim. But this time it is more difficult to do this elegantly. The exact repetition of the seven terms for a man's life within three lines is stylistically rather awkward.

He writes as follows. The Hippocratean quote is taken from a work entitled *On the sevens* (*De hebdomadibus*) §6: text at Littré 1839–1861, 8.636; Roscher 1913, 9; West 1971, 369 (to my knowledge no English translation is available). This pseudonymous work is composite: §§1–11 form an arithmological treatise, showing the structural unity of the cosmos and the human being, with a strong emphasis on the role of the hebdomad; §§12–53 is a treatise on fevers and acute diseases in general. Only the first five chapters (up to the first "old man" in Philo's quote) are extant in the original Greek. For the remainder we are dependent on Latin and Arabic translations. Philo has partly normalized the archaizing text into standard Atticistic Greek. He also changes καλέομεν (we call) into καλέουσι (they call); the first person form is retained in Anatolius' paraphrase.

Philo is the first direct witness to this Ps.-Hippocratean work (though it was probably known to Varro). There has been much discussion of its date and origin. In a detailed study of the first eleven chapters, Mansfeld (1971) argued for a very late date, between 60 and 30 B.C.E., on the grounds that it was influenced by Posidonius and pneumatic medicine (see his conclusions at 299–231). But he was unable to find a *Sitz im Leben* for the emphasis on the number seven. As noted above, he has more recently suggested (1989, 185) that it was written by an Alexandrian Jewish author. This of course would bring the work within Philo's cultural ambience. But it also encourages a slightly earlier dating because of the evidence in Clement (from Aristobulus), which was not taken into proper account in his monograph. West (1971, 383–385), on the other hand, argues for a much earlier dating to the late 5th century for the basic treatise, which was then later given a "heptadistic modelling," perhaps in the 4th century (for which he appeals to the Aristotelian passage cited below on §111). Jouanna 1999, 413, however, concludes that an early date is not justified on the basis of the Greek fragments. All in all it seems safer to connect the work with the Pythagorean revival in the 2nd and 1st cent.

B.C.E. than the earlier period. The Ps.-Hippocratean passage is paraphrased by Anatolius 37.23–38.5 and Censorinus 14.3 (derived from Varro). Mansfeld (1971, 162) argues that the order in Philo and Anatolius (Solon, then Hippocrates) probably corresponds to the source, and not the reverse, as we find in Censorinus. See further Excursus 2 on Philo's sources.

the expulsion of teeth. This remark suggests that the original author drew on Solon's poem. It is confirmed by the mention of the appearance of the beard, which uses the very rare Greek noun λάχνωσις, the verbal equivalent of which is found in Solon (line 6, λαχνοῦται).

(7c) §106. *Another feature ...* For his final illustration of the "completion-bringing" power of the seven Philo returns to the realm of arithmetic combined with geometry and stereometry. The feature in fact repeats what Philo has already outlined at §92, but here it is not brought in connection with the distinction between incorporeal and corporeal reality. For parallels in other sources see the comments on the earlier passage. There are no parallels for the connection that Philo here makes with the epithet τελέσφορος.

is truly a completion-bringer. Why, we may well ask, does this feature of the seven illustrate the epithet? Philo does not make this at all clear. Presumably the third number in the process of doubling "completes" the square, the fourth the cube, and the seventh the number that is both a square and a cube. This idea is far removed from the use of the epithet in other sources. See the comment on §102.

both kinds of equality. Equality is meant here in the sense of having sides of equal length, or if we think in terms of pebbles of beads (as the Pythagoreans did), units spatially distributed in an equidistant fashion.

(8) §107. *so to speak harmonious in the highest degree.* Philo rounds off his presentation of the mathematical features of the hebdomad by explaining its role in musical theory. This discussion had already been anticipated in §96: see our comment ad loc. Why does Philo qualify the attribute with the words "so to speak"? Probably because the seven on its own is not harmonious, but rather the numbers it contains and/or produces.

in a sense source of the fairest table. The four numbers 6, 8, 9, 12 can be used to produce the three basic harmonies of the octave, quint and quart. They also form the lowest set of numbers that can produce the three chief proportions. Philo uses two technical terms to describe this set of numbers, διάγραμμα and πλινθίον. The latter term literally means "brick" or "tile." The same term (= *laterculus* in Latin) is used in other arithmological texts. See esp. *QG* 3.38, where Philo dwells on the fact that the number 80 = 35 + 45: both 35 and 45 are "brick numbers," i.e. they include all the proportions (in the latter case 6, 9, 12, 18). See also *QG* 4.27, where the same term is used, and Staehle 1931, 66. It would seem that the term originates from the fact that the final number of the series has the form a^2b, i.e. $12 = 2^2.3$, $18 = 3^2.2$. On these sets of numbers see the exposition of Philo's contemporary Nicomachus, *Intro. arith.* 2.29, who calls them (§1): "the most perfect proportion ... which is most useful for all progress in music and in the theory of the nature of the universe" (translation D'Ooge).

Why does Philo again qualify his affirmation, this time with the phrase "in a sense"? Because, I suspect, he would have to admit that the relationship between the hebdomad and this set of numbers is not very direct, being formed by the fact that they add up to 35 and 7 x 5 = 35 (and additionally that 6 + 8 = 14, which is 7 x 2, while 9 + 12 = 21, which is 7 x 3). See the convincing note of Arnaldez at PAPM 1.216.

a ratio of a one plus a third. On the harmonies involved and parallel passages, see our comments on §§48 and 96.

§108. *all the proportions.* The term is ἀναλογία, which strictly speaking applies only to geometrical proportion (*as* a is to b, *so* c is to d). But both Philo and Nicomachus use the term to refer to all three kinds of proportions. On these in Philo see Robbins 1931, 356–358, and on the ancient theory Nicomachus, *Intro. arith.* 2.22–29. Note that in each of these sequences there are one or more intermediate numbers which mediate between the two end numbers (cf. the "middle term" in §110). It is by no means obvious that Philo should connect the doctrine of the three kinds of proportion to the number seven. The other arithmological sources all connect it to the number six (as the first number in the series): cf. Anatolius 34.19–35.2; Ps.-Iamblichus 43.9–17, 47.1–10 (including the harmonic accords); Theon 102.7–18; Martianus Capella 265.22–266.5. This may also explain his diffidence when introducing the feature at the beginning of §107.

The arithmetical ... In modern notation: for two numbers a and c, there is an intermediate number such that b – a = c – b; e.g. 6, 9, 12, since 9 – 6 = 12 – 9. See also the definition at *Decal.* 21 in a catalogue of virtues of the number ten.

The geometrical ... In modern notation: four numbers are in an analogical relation such that b/a = d/c; e.g. 8/6 = 12/9. There are thus two intermediates between the end terms. At *Tim.* 31c Plato uses this characteristic of geometrical proportion to establish the three-dimensionality of body; cf. Runia *PT* 176–178.

one plus a third. I.e. the ratio used to produce the quart among the musical accords.

The harmonic ... This form of proportion receives its name on account of its important role in music. Plato uses it, together with the arithmetic proportion, to construct the harmonic structure of the world-soul at *Tim.* 36a. See further the exposition of Nicomachus at *Intro. arith.* 2.25–26. Philo's explanation of how one can recognize a harmonic proportion in §§109–110 resembles Nicomachus' formulations in 2.25, 131.19–21 and 132.22–133.2.

§109. *The first* ... In modern notation: for three numbers a b c, when a > b > c, a harmonic proportion occurs when a/c = a–b/b–c; i.e. in Philo's example, 12/6 = 12–8/8–6 = 4/2. Philo's explanation and the example used are similar to Nicomachus 2.25, 131.19–132.10, though the formulation is rather different.

§110. *The other test* ... In modern notation: for three numbers a b c, when a > b > c, a harmonic proportion occurs when b = c + c/n and a = b + a/n; i.e. in Philo's example, 8 = 6 + 6/3 (a third of the lowest term), 12 = 8 + 12/3 (a third of the highest term). As Nicomachus explains at 2.25.3, the difference between arithmetic and geometric proportion is that in the former the difference between the mean and the two end terms is the same fraction of the mean but a different fraction of the end terms (e.g. in the case of 6, 9, 12, we have 3/9 = 1/3 for the mean term but 3/6 and 3/12 for the end terms), whereas in the latter the differences between the mean term and the end terms are the same fraction of the end terms, but a different fraction of the mean term (e.g. in the case of 6, 8, 12 we have 2/6 and 4/12 = 1/3 for the end terms, but 2/8 and 4/8 for the mean term). On Philo's exposition here see further the discussion of Robbins 1931, 357, who adduces the parallel explanation in Nicomachus.

Part III Features of the seven in the physical realm
(9) §111. *table or "brick"*. See the comment above on §107.
All these features ... As argued above in our analysis of the chapter's structure, this section (and not the seemingly similar remark at §101) marks the transition between the two major divisions of the excursus.

in the incorporeal realm and the objects of intellect. In Philo's terminology here incorporeal and noetic features of the seven refer to those aspects which are primarily mathematical and only secondarily instantiated in physical things. Most of the features discussed so far are directly related to one or more of the mathematical sciences, with arithmetic naturally playing a dominant role. The sections on the moon and the ages of humankind are not so easy to fit into this characterization, but here too arithmetical calculation still plays a role (e.g. 4 x 7 = 28, 10 x 7 = 70). From now on, Philo will only discuss various illustrations of the fact that there are groups of seven things in nature. No arithmetic is required or used. The entire section §§111–127 is closely paralleled in the "sister-passage" *Leg.* 1.8–14, which only refers to arithmetical doctrines briefly at the end in §15.

to the whole of visible reality. The Pythagoreans were very fond of pointing out how prominent the number seven was in all manner of features of nature, and many of these features have found their way into the arithmological literature (and also into a work such as Ps.-Hippocrates *On the sevens*). We shall note important parallels for the individual items. Such observations were already dismissed by Aristotle as being completely trivial; see his remark at *Metaph.* N 6, 1093a13–16, where he uses some of the same examples that we find in Philo (seven vowels, seven strings on the lyre, the Pleiades, new set of teeth at seven years).

heaven and earth. The combination is extra relevant in the case of Philo's treatise, which takes its starting-point from Gen 1:1.

philhebdomadic. The Greek word is φιλέβδομος, literally "lover or friend of the seven." Philo is very fond of such compounds, which have found their way into English in words such as philanthropic, philhellene etc. Numerous examples in Borgen, Fuglseth and Skarsten 2000, 353–354. My literal translation wishes to emphasize that it is an extremely rare term. The only extant examples are found here and in the related arithmological texts: Anatolius 36.25, πάντα φιλέβδομα (all things love the seven), also cited by Ps.-Iamblichus 55.12. At *Leg.* 1.8 Philo paraphrases as χαίρει δὲ ἡ φύσις ἑβδομάδι (nature takes delight in the seven). This remarkable conjunction must be related to Philo's use of source material. See further Excursus 2.

love and desire. Compare the very similar language used for wisdom and the task of exegesis at §5.

(10a) §112. *the heaven.* The first five examples are taken from the heavens, starting with the largest case, the vast circles of the sky. We should note, however, that Philo makes no attempt to make a sharp separation between heaven and earth. Instead he emphasizes the manner in which the heavenly hebdomads affect life on earth.

seven circles. The first five are the circles marking the zones of the earth projected onto the heaven in the geocentric hypothesis. This extrapolation is useful for explaining why not every part of the starry sky is visible from a particular location on earth. There is no exact parallel for this piece of arithmological lore. Anatolius 33.17 and Ps.-Iamblichus 32.21 include the five circles of heaven under the pentad. Varro at Gellius 3.10.3, mentions seven heavenly circles, but includes among them the two poles. Martianus Capella 267.12; Favonius 7.30; and Isidore 45 only mention seven heavenly circles without further specification.

The horizon. This is very likely Philo's own addition. Müller (1841, 325) cites a partial parallel at Macrobius 1.15.16, but this is not found in an arithmological context. As we noted above at §101, it is likely that for many of the features in his account Philo had only a brief list before him, which he expanded to a greater or lesser degree.

(10b) §113. *the planets.* The seven planets — Mercury, Venus, Mars, Jupiter, Saturn, plus the sun and the moon — naturally have a fixed place in virtually all the hebdomadic catalogues. See Varro at Gellius 3.10.2; Anatolius 36.2; Theon 104.13; Macrobius 1.6.47; Clement *Strom.* 1.143.1; and a full list at Staehle 1931, 41. Other Philonic parallels are found in arithmological contexts at *Leg.* 1.8; *Spec.* 2.57; *Decal.* 102–104; *QE* 2.78 (exeg. Exod 25:37a).

that army that forms a counterweight. In the dominant Platonic-Aristotelian cosmology of Philo's time, the motion of the fixed stars in one direction is balanced by the motion of the seven planets in the other. Philo regularly alludes to Plato's circles of the same and the different to explain this phenomenon; cf. *Tim.* 36c–d and my detailed comments at *PT* 208–213. The same image is also used at *Leg.* 1.8.

a very close affinity. A dominant feature of Philo's worldview is the separation of the heavenly and the earthly realm. But this separation is certainly not absolute. What happens in the heavens affects what happens on earth. Philo here uses the technical term συμπάθεια, literally "experiencing or undergoing together with." The term has a Stoic origin; cf. *SVF* 2.475, 532, and the note of Pease on Cicero *Nat. d.* 2.19. The divine *pneuma* pervades, orders and connects all things together. It has often been regarded as especially prominent in the thought of Posidonius, but the evidence for this is too thin to be convincing; cf. Kidd 1972–1988, 2.423. A lucid account of the role of the doctrine in ancient science and philosophy is found in Pyle 1995 149–153 (he notes the intrinsic though often denied connection with astrology). The notion of cosmic sympathy is very common in Philo; cf. further §117; *Abr.* 69; *Leg.* 1.8 (the moon!); *Migr.* 178–180 (attributed to both the Chaldeans and Moses) etc.; it is particularly important for an understanding of *Prov.* 2; cf. the discussion by Hadas-Lebel in PAPM 35.87.

the annual seasons. It is important to note that Philo interprets συμπάθεια between heaven and earth in a very specific way in this passage: the planets, presumably by means of their motions, affect the earth's atmosphere and produce the seasons. As is made clear in an excellent parallel passage at *Spec.* 1.16, already cited above in our comments on §58, he is thinking primarily of the sun and the moon, but also the planets play a role (note the presence of the term συμπάθεια in this text as well). Cf. also "the changes in the atmosphere" mentioned in *Leg.* 1.8. For the role of the moon, aside from *Leg.* 1.8, see also §101 and the long discussion of Nicomachus at Ps.-Iamblichus 59.5–60.20 (συμπάθεια at 60.19).

The doctrine that the planets (i.e. other than the sun and moon) affect the air and bring about the seasons is not found in extant authors prior to Philo. See the detailed study by Röhr 1928, 270 (cited by Mansfeld 1971, 140–146, who also cites Philo's near contemporary Pliny, *Nat.* 2.33, 105, 116). Note also Sextus Empiricus *Adv. Phys.* 1.79: " ... in accordance with certain risings and settings of the heavenly bodies alterations in the surrounding atmosphere and all varieties of change in the air take place, sometimes for the better, but sometimes fraught with pestilence" (LCL translation; passage cited by Cohn 1889, 79).

numerous changes. The choice of weather types is not arbitrary, but moves from calm to extremely violent weather. In modern terms they represent four different positions of the barometer, from extreme high pressure to extreme low pressure. Contrast the arrangement of the four kinds of weather in pairs at §58, in connection with weather signs. In *Georg.* 1.356–423 Virgil discusses signs of wind and rain, followed by fine weather, i.e. the opposite sequence to Philo.

the alternation of low and high tides. Philo now in effect moves from the air to the domain of water. In other arithmological collections the role of moon in causing the tides (well-known by this time, cf. Strabo *Geography* 3.5.8 = Posidonius F217 E.-K.) is emphasized in connection with the seven: cf. Nicomachus at Ps.-Iamblichus 60.6–18, Macrobius 1.6.61. Philo does not mention the moon specifically, because the seven planets in their totality are the focus of attention. At *Somn.* 2.121 he tells a most curious story about "Germans" (probably living in what is now the Netherlands) who try to repel the onrushing flood-tide with their weapons and thus deserve to be accused of godlessness because they oppose unfettered parts of nature; on this text see Lührmann 1991.

all things on earth. Philo now turns to change and growth on the earth. This recalls the subject of §§40–44.

bring them to completion. The verb here corresponds to the epithet τελέσφορος explained earlier in §§102–106.

to run the full cycle. On the imagery see the comment on §101.

(10c) §114. *The Great Bear.* This example of the influence of the hebdomad is also found in Varro at Gellius 3.10.2; Anatolius 36.4; Clement *Strom.* 1.143.1; and in Philo himself at *Spec.* 2.57; *Leg.* 1.8. The Great Bear is the most prominent constellation in the northern sky. Even in our times of massive light-pollution it can easily be seen, but its seven stars look more like a saucepan than an animal. Its importance for navigation lies in the fact that it never sets, as emphasized by Aratus *Phaen.* 48; Cicero *Nat. d.* 2.105.

which they call the sailors' escort. Despite Philo's formulation I have found no parallels for this expression in Greek literature.

an incredible task which goes beyond human nature. The hyperbole is explained by the fact that the natural place of human kind is on land. Philo may be thinking in his description of human achievement of the famous Sophoclean chorus at *Antigone* 332–375, and esp. the opening words: "Many things are formidable, and none more formidable than man! He crosses the gray sea beneath the winter wind, passing beneath the surges that surround him ..." (translation Lloyd-Jones LCL). The biblical equivalent is Ps. 8. Further texts which admire human ability to use the sea for communication at §147; *Spec.* 1.335 (allegorically "the champions of mind"!), 4.155–156. The role of the stars for navigation is not stressed earlier at §58, but cf. *Spec.* 1.91: "Who could have opened and shown to the voyager his path through the seas and all the expanses of the deep, had not the stars as they wheel and revolve in their courses done their work."

most God-beloved. Cf. *Somn.* 1.108, where humankind is most God-beloved because it has been endowed with *logos*, i.e. reason and speech.

(10d) §115. *the starry choir of the Pleiades.* The same example is found in Varro at Gellius 3.10.2; Anatolius 36.7; Clement *Strom.* 1.143.1; and at *Spec.* 2.57. For the importance of this constellation see esp. Hesiod *Op.* 383–384: "Begin the harvest when the Pleiades, daughters of Atlas, rise, begin the ploughing when they set." Cf. also Aratus *Phaen.* 256–267:

... they are individually faint to observe. Seven in number they are in the lore of men, although there are only six apparent to the eye ... All alike they are small and faint, but they are famous in their movements at morning and evening, and Zeus is the cause, in that he authorized them to mark the beginnings of summer and winter and the onset of ploughing time. (translation Kidd 1997, 91–93)

made complete by the seven. This may be a reference to the fact that only six of the stars are visible; see the previous note.

The risings and settings. As indicated in the two poetic quotes cited above, the risings and the settings of the Pleiades were extensively used to mark the seasons of the year and the times for carrying out agricultural activities. Philo explains this usage, probably with the passage of Hesiod quoted above in mind. The Pleiades had two so-called risings and settings per year. (1) At about April 1st there was the evening setting, i.e. when they could no longer be seen on account of the movement of the sun in the zodiac. (2) After 45 days the morning rising followed, i.e. they became visible again just before sunrise. (3) After another six months they were so far ahead of the sun that they could be seen all night, so when they rose for the last time, this was called the evening rising (about October 3rd). (4) About 40 days later came the day on which they were seen to set just before morning, which was the morning setting. See further Kidd 1997, 279, to whom I am indebted for the above explanation. Hesiod has in mind the growth of winter wheat, and so connects the morning rising (about May 15th) with the harvest and the morning setting with the ploughing of the fields (about November 15th). Philo probably has the same schema in mind (the spring harvest is mentioned in §116).

When they are about to rise ... when they have risen. It is not entirely clear whether this means two separate periods of the year or that the same period is meant, i.e. the morning rising at about May 15th when the harvest of wheat takes place. It is possible that the former description refers to the period of 45 days after the evening rising, when the Pleiades are invisible and the farmers wait for their reappearance in order to begin the harvest.

(10e) §116. *The great ruler over the day, the sun.* Philo's use of the expression ὁ μέγας ἡγεμών of the sun is unique in his *œuvre*. It may be influenced by the biblical text at Gen 1:16 (cf. §57). Usually "great ruler" and similar expressions refer to God, as in §69; see the comment ad loc.

two equinoxes. The equinoxes fall each time in the seventh month by inclusive reckoning. The same example is found in Anatolius 36.7 and Theon 104.14; Macrobius 1.6.57 mentions both solstices and equinoxes; Varro at Gellius 3.10.2 only solstices.

the largest and most popular public festivals. Although the Greeks also had important festivals at the time of the equinoxes, there can be no doubt, as Moehring (1995, 154) has remarked, that Philo is especially thinking here of the Jewish festivals, and so introduces a specifically Jewish element into the material he has drawn from his arithmological sources. A subtle connection is thus also made with the festival of the Sabbath which was, we recall, the pretext for the excursus in the first place; see above §89. For the festival of the unleavened bread at the spring equinox see *Spec.* 2.150–152; for the festival of the tabernacles at the autumn equinox see *Spec.* 2.204. In his exegesis of Exod 12:2, "this month is the first of the year" at *QE* 1.1, Philo gives an extensive account of the equinoxes and their relative importance. The spring equinox obtains first place because it was then that the cosmos was created.

(11a) §117. **things on earth.** Philo now moves from heaven to earth, and more particularly from the macrocosmic to the microcosmic perspective. The remaining examples all have to do with the human being. We note that, as at §§101 and 111, Philo continues to use transitional passages to organize his account. This does not occur systematically in the parallel arithmological texts. See further Excursus 2.

through a natural affinity. The term συμπάθεια again, as in §113; see our comment there. Note that there is no question of the heavenly bodies exerting influence on humans here. Philo wants to say no more than that the seven occurs both in the heavens and in the case of humans.

our soul. The same example is only found at Anatolius 36.8–10 (very similar) and Nicomachus at Ps.-Iamblichus 65.15–18 (not so close). The latter author's addition "according to many philosophers" is an indication that this doctrine is not universally shared in the philosophical tradition (see the next note). Philo repeats this item in his list at *Leg.* 1.11, and also at *QG* 2.12.

divided sevenfold. Philo's psychology here draws on Stoic doctrine (this text is referred to at *SVF* 2.833). Unlike Plato, the Academy and Aristotle, who make a basic division into rational and irrational parts of the soul, the early Stoa had a unitary conception of the soul, in which the directive part (ἡγεμονικόν) was aided by seven *non*-rational parts. Elsewhere Philo accommodates this Stoic division to the rational–irrational schema and speaks of the irrational part or parts, e.g. at *Leg.* 1.11, *Her.* 232. In our text this is avoided, but it is difficult to tell whether this is deliberate. On Philo and the Stoic conception of the soul see Reydams-Schils 1999, 157–165, who argues that Philo conflates the Stoic and the Platonic-Aristotelian positions (but does not discuss this text). On Philo's various psychological schemas see Runia *PT* 301–305, Radice *FM* 290–291 (both with copious references) and the judicious remarks of Dillon 1977, 174.

in puppet shows. The same image is used in a (Stoicizing) psychological context at *Abr.* 73; *Fug.* 46; *QG* 1.24 (Greek text at PAPM 33.47); cf. also *QG* 3.48 (PLCL 12.247). The image has its origin at Plato *Laws* 644d; cf. Billings 1919, 101.

manipulated by the ruling element ... Philo rightly indicates that in Stoic psychology the ἡγεμονικόν is very much in charge. The passions only occur when the mind goes astray. The orthodox Stoics (but not Posidonius) reject the conflict model propagated by Plato and Aristotle. See also the comment on §81.

(11b) §118. *Those that are visible* ... After the soul comes the body, as at *Leg.* 1.11–12. The list of external parts is paralleled at Anatolius 36.10–11; Nicomachus at Ps.-Iamblichus 68.1–2; Macrobius 1.6.80 (all with slight variations on Philo's scheme); Martianus Capella 374.11 (exactly the same as Philo). In *Leg.* 1.12 the list differs: "the parts of the body are ... : head, neck, chest, hands, belly, underbelly, feet."

The parts within. The same item is found at Anatolius 36.11–12; Nicomachus at Ps.-Iamblichus 67.18–20; Theon 104.15–16; Calcidius §37; Macrobius 1.6.77 etc. Philo's list is identical with that in Anatolius (and is repeated in *Leg.* 1.12); in all the other cases the tongue replaces the stomach. Note that the lungs are considered a single part: the term is in the singular.

internal organs. In Greek σπλάγχνα, i.e. those internal parts which during sacrifices were reserved to be eaten by the sacrificers at the beginning of the feast (LSJ). Ps.-Iamblichus and Macrobius also call them the dark parts. They are not to be confused with the entrails, which include the bowels (these are included in a separate list at Macrobius 1.6.77).

(11c) §119. *the most directive part of the living being, the head.* The same term as in §117, but now used in the superlative. In his catalogue at *Leg.* 1.12 Philo presents the same item, but attributes the parts to the *face*, which is given the same epithet ἡγεμονικώτατον (cf. also *Spec.* 4.123, exeg. Gen 2:7). Cf. *Tim.* 44d5–6, where Plato calls the head "that which is most divine and rules over all our (bodily) parts." The same arithmological item is found at Anatolius 36.14–15; Nicomachus at Ps.-Iamblichus 68.2–3; Theon 104.14–15; Martianus Capella 374.13, etc. The version at Clement *Strom.* 6.144.2 does not stand in very close relation to Philo; for its mention of the senses compare Calcidius §37.

seven highly essential parts. It is a little strange that, in contrast to the parallel passages noted above (and also *Leg.* 1.12), Philo does not emphasize that we are dealing here with seven *orifices*. One wonders whether the word πόροις has fallen out of the mss.; cf. the text in Anatolius 36.14: κεφαλὴ χρῆται πόροις ζ' ...

as Plato has said ... This is an erudite literary allusion to Plato *Tim.* 75d5–e5:

> Those who gave the body its structure equipped our mouth with teeth and tongue and lips for the sake of what is necessary and what is best, constructing it as an entrance for what is necessary and an exit for what is best. For all that enters it necessarily gives sustenance to the body, but the stream of speech that flows out in service to the intelligence is the fairest and best of all streams.

As Colson already pointed out (PLCL 1.95), Philo alters Plato's contrast from necessary versus best to mortal versus immortal. See further my analyses at *PT* 317; 1996, 265. Philo also makes the same allusion in a different context at *QE* 2.118 (exeg. Exod 28:28). To my knowledge there are no parallels in extant Greco-Roman literature. He also alludes on various occasions elsewhere to the phrase "the stream of speech"; see the references cited by Petit at PAPM 28.145 on *Prob.* 13.

Mansfeld has argued (1971, 192, 201) that the allusion may be taken over from Posidonius via the arithmological literature. It is true that the *Timaeus* is used in this literature, esp. in relation to the seven numbers of the psychogony at 35a–c. Philo does the same in a fragment discovered by A. Terian, which probably derives from his book *On numbers*; see Terian 1984, 175 and my discussion with further references at *PT* 202–204 (where I argue that Philo deliberately omits this item in *Opif.* because there is no room for a world-soul in a Mosaic cosmogony). Since none of the arithmological texts contain this allusion, but Philo does use it elsewhere, it seems likely that he himself added it as part of his literary embellishment of the (presumably) rather dry arithmological lists, such as we find in Anatolius, which were his chief sources.

speech. The Greek term is λόγοι, which can be rendered words, arguments, reasonings etc. Elsewhere Philo often takes over the Stoic distinction between λόγος προφορικός (literally "(speech) borne forth") and λόγος ἐνδιάθετος (literally "(thought) placed inside"); cf. *Mos.* 2.127 and the note of Winston and Dillon 1983, 264 on *Gig.* 52. Here the former is meant, but it is based on the latter and thus makes the life of reason possible.

(11d) §120. *Objects discriminated ... by sight.* The same rather interesting list is found at Anatolius 36.15–16 and (taken over from him) Ps.-Iamblichus 55.9–10, but nowhere else. This and the following two sections on modulations of voice (§121) and motions (§122) are kept very short. We may surmise that Philo was starting to realize that his excursus was becoming too long, but that he still wanted to round off his treatment in such a way that the ubiquitous prominence of the hebdomad had been fully demonstrated. Müller (1841, 336) aptly refers to Aristotle, *Sens.* 1, 437a4–9, but the correspondence is only partial.

the best of the senses, sight. See the comment above on the same expression at §53.

(11e) §121. *the modulations of the voice.* This list too is a rarity in the arithmological literature: it is found, apart from at *Leg.* 1.14, only in Anatolius 36.17–18 and, derived from him, in a shortened version, Ps.-Iamblichus 55.13.

acute, grave, circumflex. The modulations listed by Philo combine pitch, aspiration and quantity, and amount to a list of the features of Greek pronunciation. The first three are the accented tones in Greek speech and writing (the Greek language originally had tonal rather than stress accents). The fourth and fifth refer to the beginnings of words: if a word is aspirated, it begins with a rough breathing, pronounced like our h; if a word is unaspirated, it begins with a vowel or a diphthong, which in Greek writing is marked by a smooth breathing. The sixth and seventh refer to the length of vowels and syllables in Greek, which are important above all in poetic composition. See further the note of Cherniss (LCL) on Plutarch *Mor.* 1047B, who notes that Philo's combination of features is also found in section on pronunciation in the *Scholia in Dionysii Thracis artem grammaticam* 131.25–30 Hilgard. The seven items given by Philo are also the same as the first seven of a list of ten diacritical signs given in the *Supplementa artis Dionysianae vetusta* 105.1–106.1 Uhlig.

This feature would surely have been better placed in a list of grammatical features, such as Philo will briefly give at §126. This is in fact the category under which exactly the same list is presented at *Leg.* 1.14, where the term τάσις (pitch) is used rather than μεταβολή (change or modulation) found here.

(11f) §122. *seven motions.* The same item is found at Anatolius 36.17 and Ps.-Iamblichus 55.10–11 based on him; Calcidius 121; Macrobius 1.6.81. Philo also mentions it at *Leg.* 1.12 (where he distinguishes six "instrumental" and one circular motion), but a few pages earlier he had cited the six straight motions in honour of the six (*Leg.* 1.4, exeg. Gen 1:2). This too is found in the arithmological literature, e.g. at Martianus Capella 370.20. The doctrine of the bodily motions is taken from Plato: seven at *Tim.* 34a, six at 43b. See also in non-arithmological contexts *Ebr.* 111 and *Conf.* 139 (in both cases only six), and further my discussion at *PT* 198.

a display of dancing. Elsewhere Philo's comments on dancing have a disapproving tone; cf. *Ebr.* 35 (when the senses run riot), *Legat.* 42 (the disgraceful behaviour of the emperor Gaius).

(11g) §123. *It is also said ...* Literally "they say too." Perhaps an indication on Philo's part that he is using material drawn from a source.

the secretions of the body. Apart from the parallel passage at *Leg.* 1.13, there are no other references to this feature in the arithmological literature (Staehle's reference, 1931, 49, to Martianus Capella is mistaken). On the other hand Macrobius in his section on the parts of the body has four items that Philo does not cover: seven organs dealing with food and air, seven tissues of the body, seven parts of the arm and the leg.

discharges ... one at the back. Compare the curious exegesis of the side door of the ark at *QG* 2.6, to which Augustine took great exception; see *C. Faust.* 12.39 discussed at Runia *PEC* 322.

which is very much a part of nature. Literally "the very natural emission." It is worth noting that according to some ancient theorists women also emitted seed; see Van der Horst 1990.

(11h) §124. *Hippocrates.* On the "father of medicine" and the description given here see the comment on §105.

fixing of the seed and the formation of flesh. Philo now turns to questions of conception, gynaecology and embryology, which were commonly associated with the hebdomad in the arithmological tradition. For example, Macrobius introduces his long discussion of such issues (1.6.62–70) as follows: "Seven is the number by which man is conceived, developed in the womb, is born, lives and is sustained, and passing through all the stages of life attains old age; his whole life is regulated by it." See also the collection of material at Theon 104.1–5; Nicomachus at Ps.-Iamblichus 61.2–63.5, etc. Both Macrobius and Nicomachus refer to a passage in Hippocrates in which empirical evidence is given for the formation of the embryo at seven days. Due to his (not very fortunate) decision to introduce the theme of the ages of the human being earlier at §§103–105, Philo has separated this theme from the rest of human development.

Philo here paraphrases part of the opening words of the Ps.Hippocratean treatise *On the sevens* (cited above in connection with §105), §1: "The entire form of the cosmos and each of the parts it contains are adorned in this way. It is necessary to have the form of the seven and boundaries of seven days for the fixing of the human seed and for the formation of the human person and for the determination of illnesses and whatever decays in the body." See the text (only preserved, apart from Philo's paraphrase, in Latin and Arabic translations) at Littré 1839–1860, 8.634; Roscher 1913, 1; West 1971, 369.

Parallels for this item are scarce. An indirect reference to the same text is found in Varro cited by Gellius at 3.10.7 (and similarly Macrobius 1.6.63). More interesting is the only other reference, in the late 4th cent. C.E. author Favonius Eclogius, who writes (9.22): "Hippocrates of Cos, that distinguished examiner of nature, states in the books which he calls *On the sevens*, that this number is present when bodies are formed. For the seed that is poured forth and received in the mother's womb is changed into blood on the seventh day ..." Favonius' description of Hippocrates as *naturae scrutator egregius* is so close to Philo's that we must suspect a common source (since it is most unlikely that he would have been acquainted with our treatise). The connection almost certainly runs via Varro to an earlier arithmological work; cf. Grilli 1979, 203.

(11i) *the menstrual flow*. This item is not so common in other arithmological authors. Aside from the mention at *Leg.* 1.13, there are also references to it at Ps.-Iamblichus 61.2–4; Macrobius 1.6.62. See further below §132 for another reference to the female menstrual cycle.

(11j) *fetus in the womb*. The conviction that at seven months the fetus is fully formed and able to survive when born is extremely common in the arithmological literature. See Varro at Gellius 3.10.8; Anatolius 35.25–26; Theon 104.1–2; Nicomachus at Ps.-Iamblichus 62.20–63.5 etc. It is the first item of examples of the seven in the earthly realm in Philo's parallel list at *Leg.* 1.9. Anatolius connects this item with the fact that the hebdomad is also called τελέσφορος, an epithet which Philo uses rather differently; see above on §102.

in a highly paradoxical fact. The claim that seven-month-old foetuses can survive, whereas this is generally not the case for eighth-month-old ones is also found in the other arithmological writings, e.g. Nicomachus at Ps.-Iamblichus 63.1–5: "That the hebdomad is particularly responsible for viability is shown by the fact that even seven-month children are, thanks to it, no less likely to survive that nine-month ones, while eight-month children, which occur between both, perish from natural necessity" (transl. Waterfield). It was observed in the ancient world that babies can be born at different times of their development, and that some survive, while others do not. From the 5th century B.C.E. onwards it was generally agreed that a fetus had to be seven months old to survive. See the chapter in the doxographer Aëtius, *Plac.* 5.18, entitled "Why are seven-month-olds viable" (Diels *DG* 427, Ps.-Plutarch *Mor.* 907F–908C). A treatise in the Hippocratic corpus entitled "On the eight-month-olds" explains why these do not survive. There is a difficult period of growth for the embryo in the eighth month, and when this is combined with the rigours of parturition, viability is not possible. This double problem does not occur for seven-, nine- and ten-month-olds, and so they can survive. See further Jouanna 1999, 270, 386, who notes the contribution of arithmological factors. Aristotle agrees with this view on eight-month-olds as far as Greek women are concerned, but not for Egyptian women, who bear children more easily; see *Hist. an.* 9.4, 584a36–b14. In the present context, of course, Philo is not at all interested in scientific explanations, and prefers to stress the unexpected nature of this empirical fact (as he thinks).

(11k) §125. *Serious illnesses* ... This item too is very common in the arithmological literature: see Varro at Gellius 3.10.14; Anatolius 35.27; Theon 104.9; Nicomachus at Ps.-Iamblichus 68.12–15 (who also mentions fevers); Macrobius 1.6.81; Clement *Strom.* 1.145.1 etc. The same item is also found in the list at *Leg.* 1.13.

the bad mixing of our powers. Philo here takes over the principle of ancient medicine — dominant from Alcmaeon and Hippocrates onwards — that health is the result of the proper mixture or balance (εὐκρασία) of the various powers of the body, and especially of the four basic fluids or humours. The opposite occurs when the mixture or balance is bad (δυσκρασία, the term used here), i.e. one of the powers becomes dominant at the expense of the others. See Philips 1973, 48–52; Longrigg 1993, 52–53. For Philo's views on the source of health and disease, both physical and psychic, see the material collected by Gross 1930, 50–63.

are ... resolved. The Greek verb διακρίνονται implicitly refers to the noun κρίσις. Cf. *Leg.* 1.13 where the seventh day is called κριτικωτάτη. The term does not just indicate the serious nature of the illness, but has a more technical intent, i.e. it refers to the decisive stage in an illness, and so can also refer — as Philo intends here — to the fact that the fate of the person is *decided* on a particular day (κρίνειν means "judge," "determine," "decide"). To give an example, before antibiotics were discovered, the fate of a patient suffering from pneumonia became clear on the tenth day. The association with the seventh day is also derived from the Hippocratic tradition; see the quote from *On the sevens* cited at §124, and texts cited by Jouanna 1999, 338–341.

(12a) §126. *the best of the sciences*. Philo now makes a transition to the human sciences or arts (ἐπιστῆμαι). These are to be contrasted to the earlier examples which belonged to the realm of nature. Although the examples can be paralleled elsewhere, as we shall see, Philo is the only author to make a separate section out of them. In the other writings they are simply part of a longer list. He does the same at *Leg*. 1.14-15, where he deals with the same pair of sciences (there called τέχναι), but adds to grammar the item on the seven sounds which in *Opif*. was presented earlier at §121.

The seven-stringed lyre. This item is only found elsewhere (aside from *Leg*. 1.14) at Anatolius 36.19-22 and Clement *Strom*. 6.144.1. The poetic quote from Terpander, which both authors cite in order to illustrate this feature, is missing in Philo. The lyre was the chief instrument used for the accompaniment of song and poetry in ancient Greece. Its purported inventor was Terpander (c. 675 B.C.E.), whose lyre had seven strings. Later musicians added more strings, but the seven-stringed lyre remained normative, at least in the literary tradition. See (Ps.-)Plutarch *Mus*. §30, *Mor*. 1141C; Barker 1984-89, 1.236. Philo is fond of the example of the harmony of the lyre and uses it often in allegorical contexts, e.g. at *Cher*. 111; *Post*. 88, 108; *Deus* 24; *Plant*. 167, etc.

in the entire instrumental production of music. The phrase τῆς κατὰ μουσικὴν ὀργανοποιίας ἁπάσης is not entirely clear. Elsewhere Philo consistently uses the uncommon word ὀργανοποιία with φωνή (voice), i.e. the articulated production of sound through the instrument of the voice; cf. *Spec*. 1.147; 4.49; *Mos*. 1.84; 2.127, 196, 239. I have adapted this meaning for the case of music.

renowned harmonies. The Greek phrase here is not entirely clear. The adjective ἐλλόγιμος might be taken to mean harmonious or concordant (it contains the root *logos* meaning ratio). But usually the word means "distinguished" or "renowned." Are the harmonies renowned because of the analogy with the motions of planets (see next note)? A preferable alternative is offered by the parallel passage at *Leg*. 1.14. There the lyre is the best of instruments because the enharmonic genus of melodies is played on it, and this genus is the most venerable (cf. Aristoxenus *Elem. harm*. 19, who calls this genus "the highest;" cf. Barker 1984-89, 2.139).

in the choral dance of the planets. An obvious reference to the Pythagorean doctrine of the harmony of the spheres, as well as a reminder of the seven planets encountered earlier at §§101 and 117. See the comment on §54.

(12b) *the elements*. In early Greek grammar the terms στοιχεῖα (elements) and γράμματα (letters) were both used for the letters of the alphabet. No systematic distinction was yet made between sounds and the signs used to represent them. Other texts where Philo speaks of στοιχεῖα as letters are found at *Agr*. 137 ("the letters of sound written down"); *Her*. 210, 282 etc. The term γράμματα is used for letters less often, but see for example *Mut*. 63, where he says that letters, whether vowels or consonants, were not a gift of God but the work of Adam. In the introductory grammar of Dionysius Thrax Ch. 6 is entitled Περὶ στοιχείου and deals with the 24 letters/sounds. This feature of the hebdomad is also found at Anatolius 36.19 and (based on him) Ps.Iamblichus 55.12; Calcidius 121; Macrobius 1.6.70 etc.

the vowels. In Greek the five standard vowels of written English exist in both a long and short form, but not every one has its own letter. As Dionysius §6 explains, Greek has two long vowels (η, ω), two short vowels (ε, ο), and three "dichronic" vowels, i.e. which can be both long and short (α, ι, υ), making seven vowels in total.

named in conformity with their nature. See below on §127.

sound of their own accord. Dionysius Thrax *Ars gramm.* §6 gives a similar definition: φωνήεντα δὲ λέγεται, ὅτι φωνὴν ἀφ' ἑαυτῶν ἀποτελεῖ.

semi-vowels ... voiceless consonants. Philo ignores the division into vowels and consonants, and immediately gives a further division of consonants. Dionysius §6 divides these two groups as follows: the semi-vowels are the liquids, nasals and sibilants — ζ, ξ, χ, λ, μ, ν, ρ, σ; the voice-less consonants are the rest, i.e. the three groups of labials, dentals, and palatals in their plosive, voiced and aspirated forms — π, β, φ, τ, δ, θ, κ, γ, χ (note that the modern category "voiced" differs from Philo's division). For an arithmological use of the 24 letters of the entire alphabet see *QG* 2.5 (PLCLSup 1.74).

(13) §127. *those who ... conferred names on things.* Although etymology is a part of grammar (cf. Dionysius Thrax *Ars gramm.* 1), in my analysis I have argued that Philo does not continue his section on grammar here, but makes a transition to a brief concluding section on the name given to the number seven. If it were a continuation of grammar there should be a list of seven things once again, which is not the case. On etymology and the giving of names, see the discussion on §148. Philo assumes here a correspondence between the name and the thing in the sense that the name is related to other similar-sounding root words. On the term ἔτυμος, used here and in §126, see the comment on §36. When used of words it means "true to the nature it signifies." I have had to paraphrase this in my translation.

seven (hepta). As LSJ in its lemma on ἕπτα informs us, the relation that Philo envisages between this word and the root of σέβομαι (I revere) and σεμνός (venerable) is entirely fanciful (but the last two words *are* related). For more detail see the etymological dictionary of Chantraine, 1968–80, 362–363. The same etymology is found in two other texts: Nicomachus at Ps.Iamblichus 57.13–16: "The Pythagoreans say that the seven is not similar to other numbers and that it is deserving of reverence (σεβασμός), and indeed they call it septad (σεπτάς), as Prorus the Pythagorean also records in his *On the Hebdomad*;" Macrobius 1.6.45: "this number is now called *heptas* ..., but the ancients used to call it *septas*, the Greek word testifying to the veneration owing to the number." Once again the idea is not original to Philo.

the letter S. Unlike Greek, Latin retains the s at the beginning of the word which is part of the original Indo-European root word; cf. *saptá* in Sanskrit, *sibun* in Gothic etc. Compare how French replaces an s at the beginning of a word with an é, as in école (school), étonnant (stunning) etc.

Part IV Conclusion

(14) §128. ***All this and even more.*** Philo at long last brings his excursus to a close with a piece of ring composition. It began with Moses and now ends with him. But he cannot resist telling his reader that even more could be said. With its 305 lines of text, Philo's account of the hebdomad is not even the longest we still possess (both the account in the *Theologoumena arithmeticae* and in Macrobius are longer). There are indeed more features of the hebdomad that he could have added. But within the context of this treatise the excursus is more than long enough.

the highest honours in nature. The Pythagoreans, and Philo in their wake, were of course quite wrong about this. Although mathematics is the most powerful tool we know for the description and understanding of the natural world, numbers themselves do not have a privileged placed in nature. This can be seen from the fact that the so-called constants in physics, the most fundamental numbers that exist in the natural realm, are not integers at all (for example Planck's constant in quantum-theory is $6.624*10^{-27}$). Or compare the number of days that the earth takes to travel around the sun (= 365.2422). In certain cases, of course, integers are unavoidable, e.g. the number of planets (you cannot have half a planet). But here too there happen to be nine rather than seven, and no one today would read any significance into that number.

Greeks and foreigners. The only time in our treatise that Philo uses the division of all peoples — endemic in Greek literature — into the categories of those who are Greek and those who are not. Elsewhere he uses it about 15 times (cf. *Abr.* 136, 267; *Spec.* 2.165; *Ebr.* 193; *Conf.* 6; *Mut.* 36; *Prob.* 98 etc.). Two observations are worth making. Firstly, since the distinction is primarily based on language, it is a moot point in which category Philo would have placed himself. The Egyptians certainly were barbarians (cf. *Mos.* 2.19), but Alexandria is *ad Aegyptum*, not *in Aegypto*, i.e. still thought of as part of the Greek world. Though a Jew, Philo may well have regarded himself in the terms of this division as a "Greek." This would not have applied to Moses, who spoke and wrote in Hebrew or Chaldean (cf. *Mos.* 2.27). Secondly, βαάρβαρος is not necessarily a pejorative term. Platonists such as Numenius in the 2nd century had a great admiration for the achievements of barbarian wisdom. See further Baltes 1999, and also the comments on §8.

the science of mathematics. Philo retains the idea that arithmology belongs primarily to the realm of mathematics, and particularly arithmetic.

This fits in better with the first major part of the excursus (up to §116) than the second.

But it has been especially honoured. Philo's formulation is subtle. The hebdomad is honoured (τιμᾶται) by the Greeks and foreigners, but it has been especially honoured (ἐκτετίμηται) by Moses. The use of the intensified verb shows a difference of degree. Moreover the change of tense from present to past may not be innocent. See the comment at §131 and the reference to Pilhofer 1990, who notes that in such passages it is assumed that Moses is chronologically prior, and thus deserving of greater respect.

that lover of excellence. Philo uses the epithet φιλάρετος elsewhere of Moses only at *Mut.* 113 (as allegorical figure) and *Virt.* 175. The latter text is an instructive parallel: "The most holy Moses, as lover of excellence and lover of goodness (φιλόκαλος) and especially lover of his fellow human beings (φιλάνθρωπος), exhorts all people everywhere to pursue piety and justice, offering to those who repent the great prize of victory that they become members of the best of societies ..." In other words, by obeying the Law, the Jews will live a life of excellence or virtue, and will receive as their reward the good life. The same line of thought is summarized in the final words of *Contempl.*; see my article, 1997b. See further the comments on §§79 and 81.

to keep the seventh day holy. Philo's formulation here recalls the words of the Decalogue, Exod 20:8 and Deut 5:12.

practising philosophy. As Nikiprowetzky has shown in a magisterial chapter in his monograph on Philo, in many Philonic texts "philosophy" means above all the study and practice of the Law. This does not mean that philosophy in the sense of Greek philosophy or philosophy as we know it are entirely irrelevant, for in studying the Law, the reader can also take into account his philosophical knowledge, as Philo did himself. But it is not the primary meaning. See Nikiprowetzky 1977, 97–116. In subsequent patristic texts φιλοσοφία often means "living the Christian life." The connection with earlier Greek philosophy lies in the originally Stoic notion, taken over in Platonism, that philosophy is "the art of life;" cf. Plutarch *Mor.* 613B; Görgemanns 1993, 620; and the monograph of Malingrey, 1961 on the evolution of the term *philosophia*.

Various texts in Philo refer to the practice of studying the Law on the Sabbath in the synagogue. See esp. *Mos.* 2.215–216:

> Especially on the seventh day it was customary to pursue the study of wisdom (φιλοσοφεῖν), with the leader expounding and instructing on what one should do and not do, while those listening made progress in goodness and improvement in their character and life. And even up to now the Jews every seventh day practise their ancestral philosophy, devoting that time to the acquisition of knowledge and contemplation of the truths of nature. For what else are our places of prayer in the cities than schools of practical insight and courage and self-control and justice, and also of piety and holiness and the whole of moral excellence, by which duties to God and human beings are discerned and performed.

See also *Decal.* 98–100; *Spec.* 2.62–64; *Hypoth.* 7.10–14; and the comments of Nikiprowetzky 1977, 42, 177–180. Important parallel passages for Philo's view of Sabbath observance are to be found at *Decal.* 98–101; *Spec.* 2.61–64; both in the context of an exposition of the fourth commandment. In both texts he makes a distinction between the "practical way of life" performed on the six days of the week and the "life of contemplation" practised on the Sabbath. If applied to our text, the latter must be broad enough to include ethical questions. On Philo's views of the sabbath see further Weiss 1991; Döring 1999, 315–383.

examination of their conscience. The conscience (συνειδός) for Philo is an internal monitor which accompanies the person in all his thoughts and actions, examining and judging them in the light of reason and the commandments of the Law (for Philo there is no absolute distinction between these two sources of ethics). Sometimes he also calls the conscience the ἔλεγχος, using the Socratic term for refutation. The idea of the conscience is present in germ in Plato and Aristotle, but was explicitly developed during the Hellenistic period. It is difficult to know how original Philo was in his presentation on account of the bad state of our evidence concerning philosophy in the period 150 B.C.E. to 50 C.E. See the studies of Nikiprowetzky 1967 and Wallis 1975, who examine all the relevant passages and conclude that Philo's originality probably lay in his combination of Jewish and Greek ideas. Wallis (29) notes that the image of a judge or a law court occurs in several texts, e.g. in the parallel passage at *Decal.* 98 in which Philo also refers to the conscience:

> [the Jews] ... should also consider whether any offence against purity has been committed in the preceding days, and exact from themselves in the council chamber of the soul, with the laws as their fellow-assessors and fellow-examiners, a strict account of what they have said or done in order to correct what has been neglected and to take precaution against any repetition of wrong-doing.

deliberate ... involuntary acts. The classic distinction between voluntary and involuntary action (cf. Aristotle *Nic. Eth.* 3.1, 1109b30–34), which Philo exploits, for example, in his exegesis of the six Levitical cities of refuge at *Fug.* 86–94.

EXCURSUS ONE
On John Lydus and the interpretation of §100

We return to the question of the interpretation of §100, especially in relation to the additional evidence supplied by John Lydus. As we shall discuss at length in the following Excursus, at various points the text of John Lydus' discussion of the hebdomad is so close to Philo's that they cannot be independent of each other. For this particular paragraph I place the two texts side by side. Words italicized are identical in both texts; for the sake of the comparison my translation of Philo differs slightly from my rendering in the main body of the translation:

SEVENTH DAY: EXCURSUS ON THE HEBDOMAD   299

Philo, *Opif.* 100

The seven *alone*, as I said, *has the nature neither to generate or be generated.* For this reason the rest of the philosophers liken this number to *motherless* Victory and to the Maiden, who according to the account appeared out of the head of Zeus, but *the Pythagoreans* liken it *to the Director of the universe. That which neither generates nor is generated* remains *unchanged.* For *genation involves change,* since <both that which generates and> that which is generated cannot do without change, *in the one case so that it can generate, in the other case so that it can be generated.* That which *alone* is neither changing nor changed is the very ancient Ruler and Director, of whom the seven would fittingly be called an image. As witness for my account there is Philolaus *when he states: "For there is the Director and Ruler of all things, God who is one, always existent, abiding, unchanged, himself identical to himself* and differing from all others."

John Lydus, *Mens.* 2.12, 33.8–34.3

The Pythagoreans dedicate the seventh day *to the Director of the universe,* that is the One, and Orpheus is their witness when he says: "The seventh (day), which the accomplisher from afar king Apollo loves." We said earlier (2.3, 21.18) that the one was called in a mystical fashion Apollo because he is apart from the many (ἄποθεν τῶν πολλῶν), that is, he is *alone.* Rightly, therefore, Philolaus has called the number seven "*motherless,*" for it *alone has the nature neither to generate or be generated. That which neither generates nor is generated is unchanged.* For *generation involves change, in the one case so that it can generate, in the other case so that it can be generated.* Of such a nature is the god, as the rhetor* from Tarentum himself indicates. *He states as follows: "There is God the Director and Ruler of all things, who is one, the always existent god, abiding, unchanged, himself identical to himself."*

* alternative reading: Onetor

It is clear that in Lydus the argument proceeds by three stages. (a) The Pythagoreans dedicate the seventh day (i.e. Saturday) to the Director of the universe, who is identified with the One and Apollo. (On the vital connection between the seven and the one see the note in the commentary.) (b) Philolaus calls the hebdomad "motherless," because of the arithmological feature that it is neither factor nor product. (c) The god (i.e. Apollo?) has such an unchanging nature too, as is shown by a poetic quote from "the rhetor from Tarentum" (or Onetor). Philo's focus is different. He begins with the number seven and briefly indicates the arithmological feature in question. Then he makes the distinction between the two groups noted above. The comparison of the seven with the director of the universe is attributed to the Pythagoreans, while the poetic quote at the end is attributed to Philolaus.

C. A. Huffmann, the most recent editor of the fragments of Philolaus, has made a thorough analysis of the two passages (1993, 334–339). He accepts the view of Robbins (1921, 99–112) and Boyancé (1963a, 91–95) against Staehle (1931, 16), that Philo and Lydus both use the same arithmological source (though in the case of Lydus it may have been reworked) and that Lydus is not directly dependent on Philo. This use of the common source explains the verbal parallels. The ascription of the epithet "motherless" to the hebdomad by Philolaus is likely to be genuine, because it is supported by an apparent fragment of Aristotle in Alexander of Aphrodisias (frg. 203 Rose = *Comm. Metaph.* 39.3; note, however, that this text speaks only of the Pythagoreans, not Philolaus, as do the arithmological texts cited above). Huffmann is also convinced that Philo is incorrect in ascribing the final quote to Philolaus. He takes over the view of Thesleff 1965, 138, supported by Burkert 1972, 249, that we should accept the alternative manuscript reading in Lydus ονητωρ instead of ο ρητωρ, i.e. that the author of the lines is a certain Onetor of Tarentum. Aside from the fact that it is the *lectio difficilior*, at least two arguments can be given in favour of this reading. Though Philolaus in some sources is said to hail from Tarentum, nowhere else is he called a rhetor. Moreover a scholion on Proclus' *Commentary on the Republic*, published at 2.378 Kroll, cites an author with this name who wrote at least five books on *Arithmetical analogy*, in which he discusses the view of Pythagoras that seven and ninth month old babies are viable, while eight-month-old babies are not (cf. §124).

On the basis of these observations Huffmann concludes that "it is possible to make sense of the very confused passage in Philo" (338). Unlike Lydus, Philo misread his original source. The implication that the Pythagoreans did not liken the seven to Athena is incorrect. Huffmann points to Aristotle for this, but in fact the arithmological sources offer better evidence. He suggests that Philo's text of the source which he shares with Lydus had the alternative reading "the rhetor from Tarentum." Philo must have assumed that this referred to Philolaus, who had been mentioned earlier in the passage. He may then have thought that, if this was Philolaus' description of the Director of the universe associated with the hebdomad, then he and his school could not have equated it with Athena, which led to the distinction he makes between the two groups.

Huffmann's interpretation has an attractive explanatory force, but only on condition that one agrees with his earlier observations. We should point out, however, that he makes at least one mistake. When discussing the first part of Lydus' text he first states (338): "It is important to note that nothing here suggests the identification of the leader of the universe and the hebdomad." A little further on he continues: "Philo does not say with Lydus that the Pythagoreans *dedicated* the number 7 to the leader of the universe but that they *likened* it to the leader of the universe rather than to Athena" (his emphasis). But Lydus' text reads τὴν ἑβδόμην, which must refer to the seventh day, not the hebdomad. This is determined by the context, which is a discussion of the seven days of the week with a strong admixture of arithmological material. Lydus cannot have found the dedication of the hebdomad to the "Director of the universe" in his original source, and it is quite well possible that he based his statement on Philo, to which he then added the quote from the Orphic hymn missing in the Philonic account. If, however, we accept the reading Onetor, then it must be conceded that Lydus could not have derived his information from Philo. But the arguments for this reading, though strong, are not entirely conclusive.

EXCURSUS TWO
Further discussion on Philo's use of sources

On the basis of the material that we have collected in our commentary on Philo's excursus on the hebdomad, it is possible to draw some modest conclusions on his use of arithmological source-material.

Firstly, it will be convenient to sum up our evidence in the following table. It consists of the 34 separate features of the hebdomad which Philo has collected and indicates the parallels that can be found in four sets of writings:
(1) Philo's own extensive parallel section at *Leg.* 1.8–15 (on which see further under exegetical parallels);
(2) the five most important arithmological parallel sources;
(3) the parallel items in Clement of Alexandria (on which see further in the section on the *Nachleben*);
(4) the parallel passages in John Lydus (on which see further below).

KEY H = Hebdomad; PL = Philo, *Leg.* 1.8–15; V = Varro in Gellius (or Censorinus or Favonius); N = Nicomachus in Ps.-Iamblichus; Th = Theon of Smyrna; A = Anatolius; M = Macrobius; C = Clement of Alexandria; JL = John Lydus
    x   = good parallel
   (x) = weaker parallel
   •   = parallel under another number

§	item	PL	V	N	Th	A	M	C	JL
§92	H both square and cube					x			
§95	H and musical harmony					(x)	(x)		x
§97	H and right-angled triangle					x			
§98	H and geometry/stereometry					x	(x)		
§99	H neither factor nor product	x		x	x	x			x
§100	H maidenly, like Athena	x		x	x	x	x	x	x
§100	H image of Director of universe								(x)
§101	H in phases of the moon	x	x	x	x	x	x	x	
§102	seven bodily dimensions & limits*					x	x		
§103	H in the ages of human life	x	x	x	x	x	x		
§104	ages of man: Solon's poem		x			x		x	
§105	ages of man: Hippocrates' quote		x			x			
§107	H and the three proportions			•	•	•			
§111	all things philhebdomadic	(x)				x			
§112	seven heavenly circles		(x)	•		•			x
§113	seven planets	x	x		x	x	x	x	
§114	seven stars in the Great Bear	x	x			x		x	
§115	seven stars in the Pleiades		x			x		x	
§116	equinoxes in the seventh month		(x)		x	x	(x)		
§117	seven non-rational parts of the soul	x		(x)		x			x

§	Topic	C1	C2	C3	C4	C5	C6	C7	C8
§118	seven external parts of the body	(x)		x		x	x		
§118	seven internal parts of the body	x		x	x	x	x		
§119	seven parts of the head	x		x	x	x		x	
§120	seven objects of sight					x			x
§121	seven modulations of the voice	x				x			x
§122	seven motions of the body	x				x	x		x
§123	seven secretions of the body	x							
§124	Hippocrates on conception	x	(x)				(x)		
§124	menstrual flow lasts seven days	x	x			x			
§124	foetuses viable at seven months			x	x	x	x		x
§125	crisis in illnesses on seventh day	x	x	x	x	x	x	x	
§126	seven strings of the lyre in music	x				x		x	
§126	seven vowels in grammar					x	x		x
§127	etymology of seven			x			x		

* but not epithet τελέσφορος

The results of this table are highly illuminating and allow the following conclusions.

(1) Philo's lack of originality is clearly demonstrated by the fact that almost all his arithmological items can be paralleled in other writings which are almost certainly independent of his treatise. The only item which has no parallel at all outside Philo is the seven secretions of the body (which is repeated at *Leg.* 1.13). The connection he sees between the hebdomad and the Director of the universe is elsewhere only found in John Lydus (who, as we shall see, may not be independent of Philo).

(2) In general the parallels for the arithmetical material that predominates in §§92–110 are less good than for the parallels in the area of cosmology and anthropology in §§111–127 (and §§103–105).

(3) By far the best parallel source is the chapter on the hebdomad in the third cent. C.E. writer Anatolius. 29 of Philo's 34 items are found in his collection, of which only three are not reasonably exact. We noted on a number of occasions that even Anatolius' wording was very similar to that of Philo; see our comments on §§92, 101, 104, 111, 117. Moreover Anatolius is the only other source which contains most of the arithmetical parallels that abound in Philo (those in Macrobius are mostly not very exact). Like Philo, he mixes up the two different kinds of arithmological material to some extent (esp. in the interposition at 35.26–27). Because of the importance of this parallel text and the lack of an accessible text or translation, I have appended a translation of his section on the hebdomad in Excursus 3.

The briefest perusal of Anatolius, however, shows that his work has a quite different character than Philo's excursus. It is no more than a bald list of material. It lacks the many introductory and transitional passages found in Philo, notably at §§91, 101, 111 and 117. In the commentary I put forward the suggestion more than once that Philo's excursus may be an expanded version of material found in a list such as we find in

Anatolius. See for example the passages set out in parallel in the comments on §101. This procedure seems very likely. There is, however, one further problem that has not yet been fully discussed, namely the evidence in John Lydus.

(4) As we noted in the previous Excursus, the evidence of the early Byzantine writer John Lydus (490 – ± 565) in relation to Philo's arithmological passages has led to scholarly controversy. In his antiquarian work *On the months*, Lydus collected a large amount of material on the weeks and months of the year, including much arithmological material. A comparison of all the arithmological passages in Philo's *Opif.* and Lydus' work shows that there are fifteen cases in which we are certainly dealing with shared material. The passages are given in the following list (the relevant passages are set out in parallel columns by Staehle (1931), to whom we give the reference):

*1. *Opif.* 13   JL 32.4, 8–14: hexad as most generative number = Staehle no. 33a, 34a, 35a
 2. *Opif.* 15   JL 21.3–6 (and cf. 23.13): first day not "first" but one = St. 3b
 3. *Opif.* 47   JL 30.15–16: tetrad as source of the decad = St. 23a
*4. *Opif.* 51   JL 30.8–15: tetrad as square number = St. 22
 5. *Opif.* 62   JL 31.12–14: pentad as related to sense-perception = St. 32a
*6. *Opif.* 95–96 JL 34.9–15: hebdomad and musical harmony = St. 46
*7. *Opif.* 100   JL 33.8–9, 33.16–34.3, 34.14–15: hebdomad compared to Athena and the Director of the universe = St. 43a, 44a
*8. *Opif.* 111   JL 34.16–17: hebdomad's influence extends to the visible realm = St. 50b
*9. *Opif.* 112   JL 34.17–20: the seven circles of heaven = St. 51a
*10. *Opif.* 117 JL 34.21 – 35.2: the seven non-rational parts of the soul = St. 63a
 11. *Opif.* 120 JL 35.2–5: the seven things objects of sight = St. 66
 12. *Opif.* 121 JL 35.9–11: the seven modulations of the voice = St. 67a
 13. *Opif.* 122 JL 35.18–20: the seven motions of the body = St. 68a
*14. *Opif.* 124 JL 35.11–13: seven-month children viable = St. 61a
*15. *Opif.* 126 JL 35.20 – 36.5: the seven vowels = St. 73a.

The nine passages marked by an asterisk reveal an extensive word-for-word parallelism which prove beyond all doubt that the two texts are directly related to each other. (The parallels are not limited to *Opif.* only; in ten other Philonic texts from *QG* 2–4 and *Spec.* 2 we find the same kind of parallelism.) A full discussion of this problem and the controversies to which it has given rise cannot be undertaken in this context. Suffice it here to say that there are three possible explanations. (1) Philo and Lydus have both copied out virtually verbatim the same source, which explains the verbal identities. (2) Lydus has copied out passages from Philo, which he has mixed with other source-material. (3) Lydus has made excerpts from Philo's lost book *On numbers*, on the (unproved) assumption that there was extensive verbal parallelism between it and Philo's account in *Opif.*

Now if we were to accept that Lydus read Onetor in his source for item no. 7 in the above list (cited and discussed at length above in Excursus 1), then we would have to accept that he and Lydus both used versions of the same source. It is pretty clear that Philo read "the rhetor," so Lydus could not have derived the name from him, and he would not have made up the name himself. But this reading is not certain. On the other hand the passages verbally parallel to Philo in Lydus contain various peculiarities which to my mind are best explained as being taken over from Philo. For example, Lydus has exactly the same seven heavenly circles as Philo, an idiosyncratic list found nowhere else in this form. And how likely is that the distinction between "day one" and first day (no. 2 above) would also have been found in a pagan source wholly independent of the LXX text?

My inclination, therefore, is to conclude that Lydus drew directly on Philo's excursus in *Opif.* If this is the case, then there is no need to assume that Philo copied word for word another source, which was also used five centuries later by Lydus. In this case he may have used a brief list such as we find in Anatolius, which he expanded in his inimitable fashion.

EXCURSUS THREE
A translation of Anatolius' chapter on the Hebdomad

The brief compendium entitled Anatolius *On the ten and the numbers within it* is found in a single very late 15th century manuscript. Its author was probably the Aristotelian philosopher who later in life became a Christian bishop; see Eusebius *Hist. Eccl.* 7.32 and a full collection of evidence at Goulet 1989–2000, 1.179–183. Remarkably, in a quote preserved at Eusebius 7.32.16, the bishop refers to Philo in connection with the date of Easter, on which see Runia *PEC* 232. The text has been published by J. Heiberg together with a translation by P. Tannery; see Heiberg 1900. The extracts from the work found in Ps.Iamblichus have a superior text, but are not as complete as the text published by Heiberg. This text is the basis of the following translation. As in our translation of Philo we translate ἑβδομάς with "the seven." Numbers in brackets indicate page and line numbers in Heiberg:

On the seven

(35.6) The seven is the only number within the ten which neither generates nor is generated by any other number except the one. For this reason it is also called by the Pythagoreans "maiden without a mother." But of the other numbers with the ten the 4 is generated by the two and multiplied by itself generates (10) the 8, the 9 is generated by the 3 but itself does not generate, while the 3 and the 5 generate, the former producing the 6 and the 9, the latter the 10. When added up from the monad the 7 produces the 28, a perfect number which is equal to its own parts. The days of the moon are 28 and are completed in accordance with the sevens. The 7 numbers from the unit when multiplied in a double ratio produce the first number that is both a square and (15) a cube, 64: 1, 2, 4, 8, 16, 32, 64. The 7 numbers from the unit when multiplied in a triple ratio produce both a square and a cube, 729, the square of 27, the cube of 9, as follows: 1, 3, 9, 27, 81, 243, 729. And always the 7 numbers when multiplied produces a similar result: starting from the 64, the 7 numbers when multiplied in the double ratio (20) produce the cube of 16. In addition the seven, since it consists of the [three] dimensions and the four limits, reveals body and what is instrumental. The limits are point, line, surface, solidity; the dimensions are length, breadth, depth. The 7 is said to be the number of the first concord through the ratio of 4 to 3, and also of the geometrical proportion (25) [through] 1, 2, 4. It is also called the "completion-bringer," for the seven-month-old [foetuses] are viable. In the case of diseases the seven is indicative [of the crisis]. In the case of the prototypical (36.1) right-angled triangle the 7 contains the sides surrounding the right angle, for of these sides the one is 3, the other 4. There are 7 planets. Of the moon itself there are 7 appearances, twice the sickle, twice the half-moon, twice the gibbous, one the full moon. The Bear has seven stars. Heraclitus (5) says [frg. 126a D-K]: "In accordance with the ordering of the seasons the seven is brought together in the case of the moon, but it is separated in the case of the Bears, for a sign of undying memory." The Pleiades have seven stars. The equinoxes and the solstices occur every seven months. The soul apart from its leading part is divided into 7, into 5 senses and the organ of speech and the reproductive part. The complete parts of the body are seven: head, neck, (10) chest, two feet, two hands. The internal organs are seven: stomach, heart, lungs, liver, spleen, two kidneys. Herophilus says [frg. 100b Von Staden] that the intestines of a human being are 21 cubits long, which is three sevens. The head has 7 orifices: two eyes, two ears, two nostrils, the mouth. We see 7 things: body, extension, shape, size, (15) colour, motion, rest. The modulations of the voice are 7: acute, grave, circumflex, rough, smooth, long, short. The motions are 7: up, down, forwards, backwards, to the right, to the left, in a circle. The vowels are 7: *a e ê i o u ô*. The lyre has seven strings. Terpander says about the (20) lyre: "But we, rejecting the song with four tones, shall sound forth new hymns on the seven-stringed phorminx." Plato composes the soul in the *Timaeus* out of seven numbers. The straits mostly change their current seven times a day. (25) All things are philhebdomadic. Moreover, the ages of life from childhood to old age are 7: child, boy (ἔφηβος) (37.1), youth, young man, man, older man, old man. And through periods of seven years we advance from childhood to boyhood, from boyhood to youth and to the subsequent ages of life. Solon speaks about these: *there follow the 9 couplets of his poem as found in Philo §104.* Hippocrates says: there are 7 seasons, which we call ages of life: child, boy (παῖς), youth, young man, man, older man, old man: *there follows the rest of the quote as found in Philo §105.*

Parallel exegesis

By far the most important passage for this chapter is found in the parallel section in the Allegorical commentary (which begins its exegesis with Gen 2:1) at *Leg.* 1.8–15. As has been noted in the course of our commentary above, almost the entire contents of this second account are to be found in the longer excursus in *Opif.* (see the table in Excursus 2). But it must not be seen as a summary of the *Opif.* account. There are two major differences. Firstly, the *Leg.* passage corresponds for the most part to *Opif.* 111–127, i.e. it contains almost none of the arithmetical and geometrical contents of §§91–110, with the exception of the concluding remarks in §15. Secondly, the account of the ages of life in §§9–10 differs markedly from what we find in §§103–105, proceeding only to the third period of 7 years and containing different themes on human development which can be paralleled in Nicomachus and Macrobius (see Mansfeld 1971, 181 n.). There are also some minor differences: (1) in the list of the parts of the body at §12, see above on §118; (2) in the placement of the section on sounds; cf. above on §121; (3) in the explicit identification of the monad and the hebdomad at §15, which is only hinted at in §101.

Two other texts which relate the hebdomad to the Sabbath on the basis of the creation account and give some arithmological material are *Decal.* 101–105 (fourth commandment) and *Post.* 64–65 (which cites Gen 2:2 and 2:4, but gives an interpretation which is incompatible with his views in *Opif.*).

The second account of the Sabbath in the Exposition of the Law at *Spec.* 2.56–59 also includes an arithmological section. This passage contains some material that is not explicitly found in our excursus: (1) the hebdomad is ἀνδρειότατος (most courageous) and ἀλκιμώτατος (hardiest) of the numbers; (2) it is called καιρός (right time), cf. Nicomachus at Ps.Iamblichus 59.4; 70.24; 71.3; (3) Moses calls it συντέλεια (perfection) and παντέλεια (all-completion); (4) it is the light of the six, revealing what the six has produced (cf. *Leg.* 1.18, and the comments on §14).

There are eight other texts in which the hebdomad is called motherless or virginal, listed in Moehring 1995, 156: *Decal.* 102; *Spec.* 2.56; *Praem.* 153; *Mos.* 2.210; *Her.* 170, 216; *Contempl.* 65; *QG* 2.12.

Nachleben

Although Philo was regarded as an authority in the area of arithmology (cf. the comment of Didymus cited in Runia *PEC* 201), the use of our lengthy excursus in the patristic period appears to have been fairly limited. The following three instances can be mentioned.

(1) Basil of Caesarea (?), *Hom. creat. hom.* 2.8, in expounding Gen 2:2, asserts that the biblical text contains the germs of arithmetic, but that he himself will concentrate on examples of the hebdomad found in scripture. The one arithmological example which he cites may have been derived from *Opif.* 99 (though it is a well-known feature of the seven and the term στείρωσις (deprivation) attributed to the seven is not found in Philo). See further Runia *PEC* 240–241.

(2) In *Ep.* 44 PL (= *Ep.* 31 Faller) Ambrose turns at §3 to Gen 2:2 which he cites. From here on until §15 he makes use of no less than 12 passages from Philo's excursus. The fullest treatment is given to the passage on the ages of man in §§103–105: see §§12–13, where a complete paraphrase is given of Solon's poem. Just like Censorinus (see above on §105), Ambrose first mentions Hippocrates and then Solon. See further the extracts listed by Cohn at CW 1.xc–xci and the full text with *apparatus fontium* in Faller 1968, 217–224. As is usual in Ambrose, the heavy indebtedness to Philo is not acknowledged.

(3) Jerome twice makes explicit reference to Philo's account of the ages of man in his *Comm. Amos* 3.6 and his *Dial. c. Pelag.* 3.6. See the texts at Radice and Runia (1999, 410, 414), and a brief discussion at *PEC* 315, where I claim that the reference to Philo must be based on Jerome's own reading (though the possibility that he derived it from Ambrose should not be entirely excluded).

There are extensive thematic parallels between Philo's excursus and Clement's passage on the fourth commandment at *Strom.* 6.137–144. As noted in Excursus 2, however, the actual wording of the material is not very similar. This encourages the conclusion, already anticipated in our note at §104, that this arithmological material (including Solon's poem) is not taken directly from Philo but derives from another branch of the arithmological tradition. A good candidate then would be Philo's Alexandrian predecessor Aristobulus. For more details see the discussion at Van den Hoek 1988, 201–205.

On the ten passages in John Lydus which reveal extensive parallelism with *Opif.* and may have been directly copied from it, see our discussions above in Excursuses 1 and 2.

The number seven is of course ubiquitous in later Jewish writings. See for example Ginzberg's note, 1909–38, 5.9. These observations relate either to biblical material or to observations on the role of seven in nature such as Philo presents in §§111–117. The kind of arithmetical speculation that we find in §§90–110 is absent. In this connection it is fascinating to observe that *Midrash Tadsche* 6, a work which we already had cause to mention in connection with §§29–31 and §45, has also taken over various items of arithmological content from §§114–123. Since the text is very inaccessible, I shall cite the passage in which Philonic material is taken over (as indicated in brackets) in a literal English translation based on the Hebrew text at Jellinek 1855, 168–169 (cf. also the German translation, Wünsche 1910, 96–97). It has been prepared with the assistance of Folker Siegert (Münster):

> There are seven stars which the sun and moon see, and there are seven stars which they do not see. That is: the seven stars of the one which is called Kesil (Orion) and the seven stars of the Pleiades. (As for) the Pleiades, at the time when they set the land is ploughed for sowing, and when they rise it is harvested (§115). There are seven parts in the human being: head, throat, belly, two hands, two feet (§118). There are seven statures: child, boy, youth, young man, man, older man, old man (§105). There are seven holes in the human head: two eyes, two ears, two nostrils, and the mouth (§119). And further there are seven things inside the human being and they are called like (?) this: gullet and heart and lungs and spleen and liver and two kidneys (§118). Further seven days of menstruation (§124) and seven origins for waters: it comes from the eyes and from the mouth and from the feet at the back and at the front and the ejaculation and the sweat of the whole body (§123). Further there are seven directions: of above and below, of front and back, of right and left, and of around (cf. §122). [Cf. also the theme of the seven creations on "Day one," discussed in Ch. 6 *Nachleben*.]

I agree with Epstein 1890, 88 (who discovered the correspondence) and J. Cohn at PCH 1.68 that the author must have been indebted to Philo. Ginzberg's counter-argument in the note cited above is unconvincing. The origin and authorship of this work are uncertain. Its name is derived from the Hebrew text of Gen 1:11 with which it commences. It is placed in the mouth of the Tannaite Rabbi Pinchas ben Yair (c. 200 C.E.), but this must be false. The author is also acquainted with the *Book of Jubilees* and has knowledge of rabbinic esoteric doctrines. Epstein argued that it was the work of Mosheh ha-Darshan, an 11th century rabbi from Southern France. G. Scholem also locates the work in this area, as reported in Strack and Stemberger 1991, 376. If more certainty could be gained about its origin, we would obtain valuable information on the dissemination of Philo in the Middle Ages.

Further reading: Radice *FM* 279–293; Moehring 1995; Robbins 1921 (on the arithmological tradition); Runia 2000.

Chapter Sixteen
A summarizing reflection (§§129–130)

Analysis/General comments

Though the account of the seven days of creation has reached its conclusion, the creation account as a whole is by no means yet finished. Most importantly the creation of the first man and woman has yet to occur. Since the treatise describes events up to the end of Ch. 3 of Genesis, it is clear that for Philo too the creation account has not yet ended (see the introductory chapter on the title). Philo, we must bear in mind, regards the creation account as a unified whole. He does not show the slightest inclination to follow the methods of modern critical biblical scholarship and interpret it as a composite whole, i.e. consisting of two or more earlier and wholly independent accounts which have been merged together. This is shown by the fact that he now proceeds to quote Gen 2:4–5a in full. He thus combines what represents, according to the generally accepted source analysis of the Genesis account, the final part of the Priestly account and the opening part of the Yahwist account respectively. In doing so, he is faithful to the LXX text. Modern translations, in contrast, split up Gen 2:4 and start a new paragraph with the words: "In the day that the Lord God made the earth and the heavens ..." (On this source analysis see further Westermann 1984, 6–18, and for the history of scholarship Houtman 1994.) The problems of the text are further complicated by the fact that the LXX mistranslates the Hebrew word "not yet" with "before." Philo had in front of him a very puzzling text.

In the present chapter Philo gives an absolutely minimal interpretation of the passage. Two brief points are raised. The remaining aspects of the text are ignored.

(1) After introducing and citing the biblical text, he draws attention to one aspect only, namely that the text clearly confirms his earlier interpretation (given in the exegesis of "day one", §§16–35), in which he emphasized that prior to the creation of the world in its present physical appearance, there first took place the creation of the conceptual forms of all its contents (see above Ch. 4, 6–7). This conclusion is surely based on the word "before" in the text, though Philo does not state this explicitly (§129).

(2) But this conclusion may give rise to a question. Why does Moses now only mention a few items, namely first the heaven and the earth and then green of the field and grass? The reason has to

do with the lawgiver's love of brevity. He mentions just one or two things by way of example, but the existence of ideas of all physical things can be extrapolated from them. Without these ideas nature could not bring to completion the physical world such as we encounter it in our experience. Exegetically, the effect of Philo's interpretation is striking. The mention of the botanical world in Gen 2:5 is entirely cut off from the appearance of the "spring from the earth" in Gen 2:6 (cited in §131). The Mosaic account is thus atomized (§130).

Because of its strategic location as a transitional passage between the interpretation of the two parts of the creation account, this text has attracted a good deal of scholarly attention. Two interpretations of the passage are to be rejected.
(a) In his analysis of Philo's various interpretations of the creation account Nikiprowetzky claimed (1996 [1965], 61) that Philo understood the Genesis account to be making a new start at Gen 2:4, so that the remainder of the account is a *recapitulation* of what had previously been presented under the guise of the scheme of the seven days. This recapitulation is not, however, a mere reduplication of what had happened earlier. According to Nikiprowetzky the events of creation are now presented from a new and different angle. This solution cannot, however, solve all the problems involved. We mention here only the fact that the participle ἐπιλογζόμενος cannot mean "recapitulating." For further aspects of Nikiprowetzky's interpretation see my critique in *PT* 553–554.
(b) Tobin (*CM* 123–124, see also 170–171) argues that this passage offers a different demarcation between the creation of the intelligible world and that of the sense-perceptible world than was furnished in the exegesis of §§16–88. The division is now between the sixth and the seventh day. The divergence is caused by the fact that the interpretation is derived from a different exegetical tradition, and is closely related to what we find in *Leg.* 2.11–13 and *QG* 1.2, 19 (see below Parallel exegesis). He bolsters his interpretation by reading κατὰ γένος instead of κατὰ μέρος in §130. As will emerge in our detailed comments, we reject his proposal.

My interpretation of the passage is that Philo sees in the biblical words a reflection on the creation account as it has so far been presented. The interpretation of a noetic phase (or component) in creation is confirmed by Moses' explicit words. It is surprising, however, that the "day on which" in the quoted text is not explicitly identified with "day one" of creation (as does occur in *Post.* 65). The reason for this, I surmise, is that Philo sees the account of the seven days as of limited, i.e. primarily arithmological and didactic, value. To introduce the scheme here again would only complicate matters unnecessarily. From this point onwards in the exegesis the scheme of the seven days is no longer directly referred to.

Detailed comments

(1) §129. **Reflecting on his account of the creation ...** There can be no doubt that the formula at Genesis 2:4 is meant to conclude the account of the seven days. (It recurs at 5:1 and is part of the emphasis on the generations (γενέσεις, Hebrew *tôledôt*) in the entire book; cf. Harl 1986, 32; Alexandre *CLG* 225. "Account of creation" here is κοσμοποιία, on which see the comment on §3. The participle ἐπιλογίζομενος can mean either "concluding" or "reflecting upon". The latter meaning is clearly intended in *Abr.* 75; *Leg.* 1.62; 3.99. I now think (*pace PT* 554), in agreement with Arnaldez and Kraus Reggiani against Whitaker, that this is what Philo means here. A different interpretation is found in *Post.* 64–65: "Moses himself makes this clear when he states in the epilogue (ἐπιλόγῳ) of the creation account ... [Gen 2:2–3 is cited]. Then he adds (ἐπιλέγει) ... [Gen 2:4 is cited up to the word "earth"]. The word ἐπιλέγει of course differs from what we find in the text here. As noted in the General comments, I interpret him to mean that he is giving a reflection on the account of creation as presented *so far*. In the parallel passage at *QG* 1.1 (Greek text at Petit PAPM 33.41) ἐπιλογίζομενος is again used but not explained.

This is the book of the genesis ... The biblical quote is a precise rendition of the LXX text. We note that Philo makes no attempt to explain what book the text is speaking about (unlike in *QG* 1.1).

when it occurred. The Greek text has a singular ὅτε ἐγένετο. I have translated with the singular, since that is how Philo appears to take it in *QG* 1.1, assuming the subject to be γένεσις. It could be taken as a plural if a neuter plural subject such as ταῦτα (i.e. heaven and earth) is assumed.

incorporeal and intelligible ideas. These two epithets ἀσώματος and νοητός were prominent when Philo first introduced his theory of the intelligible exemplars of creation forming the noetic cosmos in (or as) the divine Logos in §16.

the seals of the completed products. For "seals" see §§25 and 34 and the general comments on Philo's use of this metaphor at §§16 and 18. For "completed products" cf. §28.

before ... In the biblical text the preposition πρό is used (here paraphrased with πρίν). Used as a prefix in the verbs προλαβών and προεξετύπου it was prominent in Philo's account of "day one". See our comment at §16, where we note that the precedence meant is ontological. As Nikiprowetzky (1996 [1965], 62), rightly observes, Philo regards the biblical text here as confirming his interpretation of "day one" in terms of the creation of intelligible models for the rest of the creational process. It is the LXX text that makes such an interpretation possible. The Hebrew text says there was *no* green of the field on the earth before the fresh water sprang up, whereas the LXX speaks about "*all* the green of the field," and this phrase can only be taken as object with the verb "made." It is worth placing yourself in Philo's shoes and asking how you would interpret this passage!

in the nature of things. A remarkably general and vague phrase, especially when we recall that the ideas have their location in the divine Logos!

not visible. It seems obvious that it was not visible because it had not yet risen up. But Philo from his philosophical perspective converts it into ontological non-visibility! Compare the earth that is invisible in Gen 1:2, cited in §29.

(2) §130. *anterior forms and measures.* This is the task of measurement carried out by the Logos (with the help of the ideas), as indicated in §23 (see the comment ad loc.). Cf. the polemical passage at *Spec.* 1.327: "Some state that the incorporeal ideas are but an empty name devoid of true substance, thereby destroying the most essential being in the things that exist, which is the archetypal model of all qualities of being, according to which each thing has been given form and measured."

pre-existed. The verb προϋπῆρχε starts with the same prefix *pro* that occurs as preposition in the biblical text.

given form. The verb εἰδοποιέω occurs elsewhere in Philo only at *Spec.* 1.48 and 1.327 (cited above).

gone through the partial things all together. I think that the reading of a good number of mss., εἰ μὴ τὰ κατὰ μέρος ἀθρόα πάντα, gives a defensible reading, and thus makes the conjecture of Cohn unnecessary (though not necessarily misguided). The contrast is between each thing individually (cf. first words of §130) and everything taken together (cf. "the nature of the whole of reality"). Moses just mentions a few things, but they are enough to indicate what applies to the whole; cf. §29, where the seven most important components of the intelligible cosmos are picked out on the basis of Gen 1:1–3. Cf. also the passage at *Leg.* 3.145 cited below. Cohn's conjecture yields the reading "even if he has not gone through everything individually <but> together," which has basically the same meaning. It has been accepted by all recent translators, including Winston *PA* 101. Cohn might have appealed to *Aet.* 92: "If the flame is wholly and entirely extinguished, then it is necessary that the light (αὐγήν) also be destroyed not partially (κατὰ μέρος) but totally (ἀλλ' ἀθρόαν)." The conjecture is rejected by Tobin, who accepts the reading εἰ μὴ τὰ κατὰ γένος ἀθρόα πάντα found in a single good ms. He argues (*CM*, 123 n. 61): "Philo is arguing from the exemplary to the general and not from the general to the particular." But Philo does not intend a contrast between generic ideas (cf. the κατὰ γένος statements in scripture) and individual things. Tobin is too keen to harmonize our text with *Leg.* 2.13.

brevity of speech. At *Spec.* 4.96 Moses is praised for being a "lover of concision" (φιλοσύντομος). An even better parallel is found at *Leg.* 3.145:

> We should not fail to notice that Moses, when he rejects the belly ... in effect rejects the other passions too. The lawgiver uses one portion (ἀπὸ μέρους ἑνός) to give a clear presentation of the whole (τὸ σύμπαν), and having mentioned the most essential matter, virtually goes through the rest on which he has been silent.

A little further on (§147) we are told that Moses never uses a single expression pointlessly. This is an important assumption for the exegete, who thus claims licence to read major doctrines into brief statements.

which brings ... to completion. A perhaps surprisingly "immanent" expression (cf. the comment on "nature of things" in §129). But it should be borne in mind that "nature" in Philo often represents the immanent working of the divine Logos, or can even be shorthand for God himself; cf. our comments on §§43 and 66 above.

without an incorporeal model. This recalls God's cogitation in §16.

Parallel exegesis

In three other passages Philo interprets the same verses. In *QG* 1.2 the exegesis is exactly the same as here, i.e. in terms of incorporeal ideas. *Post.* 64–65 notes that heaven and earth were created on the first day (*sic!*), and thus concludes that what is created on the seventh day (in this verse apparently) is referred back to the first day. Nothing is said about whether the contents of the days are intelligible or sense-perceptible. In *Leg.* 1.19–25 a detailed allegorical explanation of the verses is given in terms of the Logos, the archetypal mind and its contents.

Nachleben

One would expect Philo's solution to the problem to have exercised some appeal, at least in the Alexandrian tradition. But none of his Alexandrian successors were interested in this text, to judge by the thorough indices of the *Biblia Patristica*. The same problem was raised by both Latin translations of the Old Testament. Alexandre (*CLG* 229) points to the solution given by Augustine in *Gen. litt.* 5.4.7, namely that "green of the field" and the grass existed in the earth as causes or reasons in the manner of seeds, but this is only vaguely similar to Philo's exegesis.

As noted in the analysis, the problematic aspect of the text is caused by a mistranslation of the Hebrew in the LXX. No Jewish material resembling Philo's interpretation is thus to be expected outside the Hellenistic-Jewish tradition. The verse is ignored by Josephus in his extremely brief paraphrase of the creation account.

Further reading: Radice *FM* 293–295 (with a good survey of various interpretations), Runia *PT* 553–555; Tobin *CM* 122–124; Nikiprowetzky 1996 (1965) 61–63 (but see my criticisms above).

Chapter Seventeen
The separation of the fresh from the salt water (§§131–133)

Analysis/General comments

After skipping the last two phrases of Gen 2:5, Philo continues his exegesis of the creation account by quoting the short verse Gen 2:6 in its entirety. It is part of a logical sequence of thought, he emphasizes, but without explaining why. The reason will become clear in §136: God uses the moistened earth in the form of clay for the creation of the first human being in Gen 2:7. The passage can be divided into three parts.

(1) Having quoted the verse, Philo first favourably compares Moses with what "other philosophers" have said on the subject. There is a slight jump in the train of thought here. In fact, as becomes clear at the beginning of §132 where Philo speaks of an "explanation," he implicitly assumes an exegetical *quaestio* (on this method see above on §72), namely the problem why Moses separates off the fresh water from the salt water. As we already saw in §§38–39, this separation took place on the third day. The other philosophers do not make this distinction as clearly as Moses does, which naturally redounds to his credit. The first explanation has in fact already been given in the exegesis of the third day (to which Philo cross-refers). Fresh water had to be mixed with the earth in order to hold it together like a glue. Otherwise it would fall apart, as Philo no doubt had observed whenever he left the Nile Delta and entered the sands of the Egyptian desert (§131).

(2) A second reason for the separation is that moisture is necessary for the growth of living things, whether animals or plants. In the former case seed is always moist, in the latter case moisture is required so that plants can sprout. A further comparison is made with the birth of human beings, for which the moist menstrual flow of the mother is required as material substance (§132).

(3) This comparison encourages Philo to develop further the idea of the analogy between earth and mother, which he had already briefly mentioned (with a slightly different slant) in §38. Just as mothers have breasts providing food for their infants, so the earth has rivers and springs for making things grow and providing drink for living beings. In fact the earth herself is a mother, as is shown by a reference to her ancient name Demeter and by an erudite allusion to a passage in Plato (§133).

As in the previous chapter, Philo's exegesis in this passage is again rather "atomistic." He cites and explains the biblical text, but apart from the minimal cross-reference to the earlier passage, no attempt has been made to integrate the explanations into the more general account of creation. What precisely is the logical train of the thought claimed at the outset (§131), i.e. the relation of this description to what was described in the account of the seven days? Are the two accounts describing the same "event"? And if so, why does Moses, who loves brevity (§130), repeat it? Moreover, it has to be said that the passage is rather rhetorical and that Philo hardly enters very penetratingly into the problems that the text raises. This can be shown by a comparison with his exegesis at *QG* 1.3 and *Fug.* 179, where he does ask questions such as how was it possible to water the entire earth with a single spring and, more generally, whether one should read the passage literally or allegorically (see Parallel exegesis). Such differences furnish important clues to what Philo is aiming to achieve in this particular treatise; see further Introduction §4(b). On the other hand the passage is an excellent illustration of Philo's broad learning and literary talents, as will become clear in the detailed comments.

Detailed comments

(1) §131. *succession of thought ... series.* The two terms (ἀκολουθία, εἱρμός) are the same as have already been used in both §§28 and 65. Here they are used for the sequence of events in the narrative. Although according to §28 the entire creational event happened simultaneously, the order in which separate events are recounted has a philosophical message. The same applies here, except that Philo does not make clear what the significance is.

he next states. Gen 2:5 is quoted in its entirety and with full accuracy. For reasons that defy exact explanation the section Gen 2:4–7 is cited almost completely but given very brief explanations; see Introduction §4(a).

Other philosophers. This is the only explicit comparison of Moses with other philosophers in the treatise, although it is implied in §§1–2 and 128. Naturally Moses is presented as being superior in his insight, a fixed theme of Philo's apologetics. A very interesting aspect of this passage is that a little later on these philosophers are in passing described as coming "after" Moses. The implication is that Moses is superior because he is older, the so-called *presbyteron kreitton* motif ("what is older is superior"). The same is implied at *Her.* 214 (Heraclitus); *QG* 3.16 (Aristotle and the Peripatetics, Pythagoras); *QG* 4.167; *Aet.* 19. See further the excellent discussion of Pilhofer 1990, 173–187, who on our passage affirms (184): "Here no actual proof of the antiquity motif is given, but the result of such proofs is assumed."

one element of the four. In earliest Greek philosophy the physical world was explained in terms of the fundamental contraries hot–cold and wet–dry. From Empedocles (c. 450 B.C.E.) onwards the doctrine of the four elements became standard, certainly with regard to the sublunary realm. It is fundamental to the physics and cosmology of Plato (e.g. in the *Timaeus*), Aristotle and the Stoics (but not for atomist theories). A complicating factor is formed by the heavenly realm. The ether out of which it is composed can be regarded as a form of fire or a separate element. See further the comment on §70.

from which the cosmos was created. The verb (ἐδημιουργήθη) indicates that for "the philosophers" Philo probably has Plato foremost in mind, but the Stoics too in their accounts of the cosmic cycle rely on the doctrine of the four elements.

a fourth part of the entirety of things. As we noted in Ch. 5, there is often some ambiguity in the treatise as to whether Philo means elements in the sense of the fundamental corporeal components of reality (physics) or to indicate the various regions of the cosmos (cosmology). Here the cosmological aspect prevails. Water in the form of the Great sea or Ocean forms one of the four great regions, concentrically arranged in the sequence earth–water–air–fire (or ether). Cf. Pliny's description of the cosmos in *Nat.* 2.10–11 and Lucretius' account of the evolution of the cosmos in 5.195–325.

the Ocean. The Ocean was known from the time of Homer and Hesiod onwards as the great expanse of water surrounding the known inhabited world (so by implication Moses is older than the poets, who by this time were also regarded by many as distinguished philosophers, cf. *Aet.* 17). See for example the detailed description of the Ocean in Ps.Aristotle *Mund.* 3, 393a16–b19.

not of the (element) water. I.e. of the element as cosmological region.

the earth would be held together. Philo's description of sweet water and its conglutinative role repeats what he has already said in §38. On the philosophical and scientific background see the comment ad loc.

for the reason mentioned earlier. I.e. in §38. The term αἰτία, used here and at the beginning of §132, is somewhat ambiguous. It can mean "cause" or "explanation." Here the first meaning might be preferable (i.e. moisture as cause), but in §132 the second seems required (because it aims at the truth).

held together and continue to exist. Here a purely physical explanation is given. The terms found here (συνέχω, διαμένω, a little earlier δεσμός, bond) are elsewhere often used by Philo to depict the activity of the divine Logos. At *PT* 179 I have described this as the "tendency to theologize the theme of the bonding of the elements." Cf. for example *Her.* 23, 188 (Logos as "glue" and "bond"); *Fug.* 122; and also the further discussion at *PT* 238–241.

partly through the force of the unificatory spirit. Philo recognizes that moisture is not the only physical factor holding earth together. In the case of rocks for example, there is no water present, so they must be held together by another force. The broader context of the doctrine Philo has in mind is given at *Deus* 35 (cf. also *Leg.* 2.22):

> Among the various kinds of bodies, the Creator has bound some by means of cohesion (ἕξις), others by growth (φύσις), others by soul, and others yet by rational soul. Thus, in stones and timber that has been detached from its organic growth, he made cohesion a truly powerful bond. The latter is a spirit (πνεῦμα) returning to itself; for it begins to extend itself from the centre of the body to its boundaries, and when it has reached the outermost surface it bends back on its course till it arrives at the very place from which it first set out (translation Winston).

This theory is indebted to the Stoics (= *SVF* 2.458, cf. also 455, 457, 716). The activity of the *pneuma* (a mixture of fire and air) produces tension in the matter and gives it its unifying structure and form. See further Sambursky 1959, 1–11 and Hahm 1977, 165–166.

(2) §132. *one explanation.* I.e. for the implicit exegetical *quaestio* as to why Moses separates the sweet from the briny water.

aims at the truth. For the epistemological use of στοχάζω see the comment on §72.

without moist substance. Philo's second explanation is of course a scientific platitude (though none the less true for that). One is reminded of Aristotle's speculation on why the first philosopher Thales concluded that the ἀρχή of all things was water, *Metaph.* A 3, 983b21–28: "Presumably he derived this assumption from seeing that the nutriment of everything is moist ... and also from the fact that the seeds of everything have a moist nature ..." Cf. some reflections on seed and nutriment at *Aet.* 98:

> Nothing that exists is brought to completion from seed alone apart from its appropriate food. Seed is like a beginning, and a beginning on its own does not come to fruition. For neither should you suppose that the ear of wheat grows only from the seed sown in the field by farmers. A great deal is contributed to its growth by the double nutriment from the earth, both moist and dry. In the womb too the foetuses cannot be brought to life from the seed only, but also require food flowing in from outside, which the pregnant mother supplies.

the menstrual flow. Already mentioned in a different context at §124.

bodily substance of foetuses. Effectively this is the view of Aristotle as set out in *Gen. an.* 2.3–4. The male sperm provides the form and structure of the embryo, the female womb, or more specifically the residue of its menses supplies the matter. For accounts of this theory see Balme 1990; Dean-Jones 1994, 184–193. For a more general account of theories of conception in antiquity see Van der Horst 1990, who includes examples of Jewish appropriation of Aristotelian views, e.g. *b. Ketuboth* 10b: "It has been taught in the name of rabbi Meir: every woman who has abundant (menstrual) blood has many children." See further *QG* 3.47 (the same Aristotelian theory); *Spec.* 3.32–33 (longer passage on menstruation, seed and conception, prompted by the injunction at Lev 18:19). Sly 1990, 86–89, on the basis of *Fug.* 188–194 concludes that a blood taboo lurks beneath the surface of Philo's thought. But here the tone is studiously neutral.

(3) §133. **What I now shall state.** Cf. the same conceit in §38. As I note in my comments there, the theme of the earth as mother is better suited to the context here, where a spring is said to flow from the earth and water its face.

Nature. Cf. our comment on the mention of nature as creative force in §130.

breasts like fountains. Prompted by the mention of a spring or fountain in the biblical text, Gen 2:6.

the earth too is a mother. The same theme at §38; *Plant.* 15; and at some length at *Aet.* 57–66, where Philo expands the argument of the Peripatetic Critolaus that humans have always existed and refutes with much rhetorical passion the mythical idea that the first humans were "earth-born," i.e. sprung full-grown from the earth. This leads him to deny that the earth has breasts at §66, a fine example of how the context can determine the direction of Philo's argumentation. The proof is: "But no river, no spring in the inhabited world has ever been recorded as running milk instead of water"! In his eschatological vision at *Praem.* 153–166, Philo describes how the earth will recover from the desolation brought upon her by her wicked inhabitants. Cf. esp. §158: "Then like a fond mother she will pity her sons and daughters whom she has lost ... Young once more, she will be fruitful and bear a blameless generation ..." But note that Philo has changed earth (γῆ) to land (χώρα), i.e. the land of Israel. Both words are feminine.

Demeter. The etymology of Demeter, goddess of the fruits of the earth and especially corn, is derived from δα or δη (perhaps Doric Greek for γῆ, earth) and μήτηρ (mother). The same etymology is implied at *Decal.* 54 and *Contempl.* 3. The etymology is very widespread in Greek and Roman literature; cf. Diodorus Siculus 1.12.4 (quoting an Orphic verse, frg. 302 Kern); Sextus Empiricus *Adv. Phys.* 1.189; Cicero *Nat. d.* 2.67, and the learned note of Pease ad loc.

as Plato has said. An erudite literary allusion to *Menexenus* 237e–238a, part of the speech of Pericles on the Athenians killed in battle:

> There is a great proof for this claim, that she brought forth our common ancestors, namely that she has provided the means of support for her offspring. For as a woman proves her motherhood by giving milk to her young ones — and she who has no fountain of milk is not a mother — so did this our land prove that she is the mother of men ... And these are truer proofs in a country than in a woman, for the woman in her conception and giving birth imitates the earth, and not the earth the woman. (translation Jowett modified)

As I have shown in my analysis (1997, 265–266), Philo adheres rather closely to Plato's words in 238a4–5, retaining for the most part the original word order. There is a less direct allusion to *Menex.* 238a7 in a similar context at *Aet.* 63. An exact parallel to Philo's allusion occurs in Plutarch *Mor.* 638A.

The race of poets. As explicitly indicated, Philo gives three poetic epithets for the earth. The least common is the first, παμμήτωρ (all-mother); cf. Aeschylus, *Prom.* 90; *Orphica* frg. 168.27 Kern; *Anth. Gr.* 7.461. For the second adjective καρποφόρος (fruit- or crop-bearing) I have found only one pre-Philonic poetic text which uses it of the earth, *Orac. Sibyl.* Prol. 97, p. 5 Geffcken. But it is used of Demeter at Aristophanes *Ran.* 385 (cited by Radice *FM* 296), of ploughed fields by Pindar *Pyth.* 4.6, *Nem.* 6.9 (cited by Müller 1841, 355); in prose the phrase "the crop-bearing earth" is very common, e.g. at *Her.* 32; Clement *Strom.* 1.9.1, etc. The epithet πανδώρα (giver of all), is used of the earth at Aristophanes, *Aves* 971.

'giver of all' (Pandora). Cf. *Aet.* 63 in a similar context: "And therefore it seems to me that the poets did not go amiss in giving her [the earth] the name Pandora, because she gives all things that bring benefit and pleasurable enjoyment to all beings that share in life."

with flowing rivers and springs like breasts. See the note above on parallel passages in Philo and esp. *Aet.* 66. A rather similar passage is found in *1 Clem.* 20:10: "Ever-flowing fountains, fashioned for enjoyment and health, provide without fail breasts for human beings in order to live." By means of a complicated argument using the techniques of *Quellenforschung* Jaeger (1959) argued that the parallels between Clement of Rome and Philo *Aet.* 63; *Opif.* 38 and 133 were to be explained through a common origin in a lost tragic fragment exploited by the Peripatetic Critolaus. The hypothesis is too speculative to convince; cf. Runia *PEC* 88; Lona 1998, 264. See also the comment on §168.

Parallel exegesis

Philo gives exegesis of the text Gen 2:6 in five other passages, which reveal a wide variety of exegetical approaches. The closest to our passage is a reference at *QG* 2.67 in connection with Gen 9:20: just as God made fountains of drinkable water flow forth, so he gives wheat and barley for human nourishment. *QG* 1.3, specifically focusing on this text, also gives a literal exegesis. Philo asks how a spring can water the entire earth and offers various possible answers. A comment is also made on the word "face," which is taken to represent the fruit-bearing part of the earth. A very interesting passage is found at *Fug.* 177–182, when Philo discusses the various meanings of the word "spring" in the Pentateuch. We are told (177) that "those unversed in allegory and the nature which likes to hide itself" compare the spring with the Nile, a literal approach which Philo in this allegorical context sets aside (on this text see Goulet 1987, 43, 99). Allegorical explanations of the text in terms of the mind and the senses are found in *Fug.* 181–182; *Leg.* 1.28–29. But at *Post.* 127, prompted by the etymology of Seth as ποτισμός (watering), the interpretation is given in terms of the Logos of God watering the virtues and is linked with Gen 2:10.

Nachleben

Philo's exegesis of the text as a kind of repetition of the separation of the waters on the third day appears to have found very little echo in the Fathers. Alexandre (*CLG* 232) notes a similar exegesis in Theodoret *QG* 22, PG 80.119C; the words νοτίς and ἰκμάς could go back to Philo, either directly or indirectly (both are found in §38, the former recurs in §131). Elsewhere some of his other interpretations are preferred; cf. Alexandre *CLG* 231–233; Runia *PEC* 265; Romeny 1997, 187–192. The link with the third day of creation is not made in the extensive rabbinic exegesis of the verse in *Gen. Rab.* 13.9–17 (but the Hebrew was taken to read "mist," not "spring"). On the parallelism with Clement of Rome see the note on §133. As I note in *PEC* 88–89, a common Hellenistic-Jewish background is to be assumed.

Further reading: Radice *FM* 295–296 (cursory).

Chapter Eighteen
Creation of the first human being from the earth (§§134–135)

Analysis/General comments

Following the lead of the biblical text, Philo now reaches the description of the second creation of the human being in Gen 2:7, who is this time formed out of clay from the earth and inbreathed with the divine spirit. As we noted earlier (see General comments Ch. 16), Philo regards the Mosaic creation account as a unified whole, so he cannot avoid the question how this creation is related to the earlier one in Gen 1:27, and his commentator too cannot avoid asking how exactly he sees this relation. The chapter proceeds in two steps.

(1) The biblical text of Gen 2:7 is quoted literally, though without its final phrase. Philo then first observes that there is a vast difference between the human being formed now and the one that came into being earlier. He demonstrates this by listing for each one five opposed characteristics, as can be seen in the following table (cf. Runia *PT* 336, Tobin *CM* 109):

human being after the image (Gen 1:27)	**moulded human being** (Gen 2:7)
object of thought	object of sense-perception
kind of idea or genus or seal	participating in quality
incorporeal	composed of body and soul
neither male nor female	either man or woman
by nature immortal	by nature mortal

Unfortunately Philo does not explain in any detail what exactly he means by this set of contrasts. This has led to the divergences of interpretation which we shall discuss below (§134).

(2) Instead Philo continues with an explanation of what the text in this passage describes. The individual human being whose creation is described here is a composite creature, because his body is moulded from clay. His soul, however, is not taken from anything that has come into being, but is inbreathed from the divine spirit (*pneuma*). This composite nature makes the human being into a borderline creature, sharing both in mortality and immortality, the former associated with the body, the latter with the soul. What comes together, must sooner or later come apart. For this reason human mortality is inevitable. But the higher part will remain. As we shall see below (see *Nachleben*), Philo's anthropological conception of the human being as a borderline creature will prove to be influential in patristic thought (§135).

Philo is far too brief and dogmatic in this passage, and its interpretation has given rise to numerous controversies in the scholarly literature. We focus on four issues.

(1) In the exegesis of Gen 2:7 in the *Legum Allegoriae*, Philo translates the distinction between the two human beings into that between a "heavenly" and an "earthly" human being (1.31–32). Most commentators conflate these two accounts, which is understandable enough on account of the contrast above between immortality and mortality. But, strictly speaking, the description "heavenly" is absent in our text and is not so easily placed in the left column of the table. Because *Leg.* belongs to a different exegetical series than *Opif.*, we do not take this further distinction into account (it is also absent in the *Quaestiones*).

(2) How many human beings are referred to in this passage? Some commentators regard the "plasmatic" human being in §134 as not the same as the "pneumatic" human being in §135; e.g. Baer 1970, 29, who argues that the man after the image is the generic heavenly man, the man now moulded is the generic earthly man, while the individual man in §135 is the first empirical man; Radice *FM* 296 who affirms that both men represent the individualization of the idea of humankind, but the "plasmatic" man is the translation into the sensible realm of the Idea-body (i.e. man as corporeal realization), whereas the "pneumatic" man is the individualization of the man after the image inasmuch as he represents the rational part of man. I believe that a reasonable interpretation of the passage can be given if the two are identified, i.e. the composition of body and soul in the list in §134 is explained by the composite nature explained in §135. The distinction introduced by Baer 1970, 31 between irrational soul in §134 and rational soul in §135 is also to be rejected.

(3) But what difference exactly does Philo envisage between the two human beings in §134, and how does the exegesis here relate to the explanation of Gen 1:27 in terms of the *nous* in §69–71? Certainly, the terminology that is used here of the "human being after the image" (νοητός, ἰδέα, σφραγίς) is reminiscent of that which we find used of the ideas in "day one" (§§16–35). Many commentators have concluded that Philo refers to the "Idea of humankind" in the technical sense, i.e. the single intelligible model for the diversity of "empirical" human beings; cf. Nikiprowetzky 1996 (1965) 65; Winston 1985a, 25; 1998, 53. But this introduces a strange anomaly into the creation account. Why are the other ideas created on "day one," but the Idea of humankind on the sixth day? A solution that is radically opposed to this view was put forward by Baer 1970, 30. He argues

that the human being created after the image can be interpreted as the rational *nous* in empirical man rather than the Idea of man in the technical sense. Such an interpretation has the advantage of removing any contradiction with §§69–71. At *PT* 336–338 I followed this line of interpretation, but with the modification that a simple equation between the *nous* created in Gen 1:27 and the divine part of the composite empirical human being created in Gen 2:7 should not be attempted. Rather the former is an idealization, i.e. the "true human being" such as he should and can be when the cares of the body and earthly life have entirely fallen away (cf. *Gig.* 33). A third line of interpretation represents a kind of compromise position. Tobin (*CM* 126) argues that there is a shift between §76, where Philo still thinks of an Idea as paradigm, and §134 in which the human being after the image becomes a real figure, to be identified with the "heavenly human being" of *Leg.* 1.31–32 (note that Tobin's two stages are not required if §76 is read as referring to generic humankind, as we argued in the comment ad loc.). Cf. also Dillon 1977, 176, who argues that this "'true' Man" (his capital letter) may be identified with the intellect, but is also a transcendent archetype in the intelligible world, and will become personalized in the archetypal *Anthropos* of the *Hermetica* (e.g. *Poim.* 12–15).

It seems to me that there are certain indications that Philo is not here thinking of an Idea of humankind in the technical sense. He speaks of "a kind of idea" (ἰδέα τις) and does not emphasize its paradigmatic role (as *is* done in §130). This is quite different from the way that, for example, Alcinous speaks of the idea of one human being as model for countless human beings (*Did.* 12.1). A further consideration is the interpretation of Gen 1:27 at §25, which does not make sense in terms of an Idea of humankind (in the argument the human being is placed parallel to the sense-perceptible cosmos). Nevertheless it must be conceded that his use here of the term σφραγίς (seal) is difficult, since that is usually a technical term for the relation between model and copy. The interpreter will be on safest ground if he interprets "the human being after the image" as the "ideal" person, i.e. an idealization of human nature in terms of the intellect. This admittedly leaves the question of the relation to the Idea of humankind and the intellect or rational soul of empirical humankind somewhat up in the air. We can put the blame on Philo for this lack of clarity. It is fascinating to observe that the same divergences of interpretation are already present in patristic references to this passage; see below *Nachleben*.

(4) How is the inbreathing of the divine *pneuma* in Gen 2:7 to be related to the image relation in terms of the intellect in Gen 1:26–

27? It is clear that both are interpreted in terms of human rationality, seen in accordance with Greek philosophy as the specific trait that distinguishes humans from other creatures; cf. our General comments in Ch. 12 and Ch. 14. In many texts Philo tends to reconcile the two accounts to a large degree; cf. *Spec.* 1.171; *Virt.* 203–205; *Det.* 80–86; *Plant.* 18–20; *Her.* 56. In *Mut.* 223 Philo indicates that theologically he has a preference for the Platonizing image-relation rather than the Stoicizing part-whole relation. But both have a biblical foundation. See further *PT* 335, 472; Tobin *CM* 87–101. It would be mistake, however, simply to identify the *nous* in §69 with the "invisible" in §135. Not only does the distinction between the generic and the individual have to be added, but the former state is what the latter must aspire to attain.

Detailed comments

(1) §134. *After this he says.* Philo cites Gen 2:7 literally, but leaves out the final phrase "and the human being became a living soul."

taking clay. The participle λαβών is found in only one manuscript of the LXX, where it precedes the noun, whereas it follows it in Philo. It is also found in readings of the Vetus Latina. As Alexandre (*CLG* 236) notes, many patristic texts include also it; the variants are given in Wevers 1974, 84. Exactly the same phrase is found in Josephus' paraphrase at *Ant.* 1.34: ἔπλασεν ὁ θεὸς τὸν ἄνθρωπον χοῦν ἀπὸ τῆς γῆς λαβών. The fact that Philo appears to include it at *Leg.* 1.31, and also refers to it in his paraphrases in §§135 and 137 strongly suggests that it was present in his LXX text. But the issue is complicated by the fact that not all mss. contain the participle both here and in *Leg.* 1.31, so that various kinds of contamination are possible. See now the discussion of Royse 2000, 15–16, who argues against the view of Katz 1950, 9 and Howard 1973, 207–208 that Philo might be following an "aberrant" LXX text.

this text too. I.e. in addition to what the biblical text tells us in Gen 1:26–27 and in 2:4–6.

who has been moulded now. The Greek verb πλάσσω means to form or mould (in my translation I use the latter rendering), and is primarily used of an artisan who works in soft material substances such as wax or clay (cf. the English "plastic"). The word is thus very suitable to indicate the formation of the human body. Philo frequently uses the phrase "moulded from the earth" (διαπλασθεὶς ἐκ γῆς) to refer specifically to the first human being; cf. §140; *Plant.* 34; *Congr.* 90; *QG* 2.66, etc. (and also, without biblical warrant, of Eve at §153 and *Post.* 33). On the extensive use of the word to indicate the creation of Adam in Hellenistic-Jewish and patristic literature see Alexandre *CLG* 233–235.

came into being. Philo uses the verb γίγνομαι (come into being) rather that ποιέω (make) which is used in the biblical text at Gen 1:26–27. He does the same at *Leg.* 1.31, where a distinction is also made between πλάσμα (moulded thing) and γέννημα (thing that is born). Presumably he thinks the verb "make" might obscure the distinction which he has in mind, because it can be taken to mean "manufacture."

participates in quality. The term use here is ποιότης. It refers to accidental properties necessarily possessed by things that are sense-perceptible and corporeal. cf. §§22, 57, 97, 131 etc. At §141 Philo speaks of "powers and qualities of both body and soul." God, in contrast, is ἄποιος, "without quality." On the technical philosophical aspects and their theological application see further Wolfson 1947, 2.101–110.

consists of body and soul. In various texts Philo uses this phrase to define what the human being is: cf. *Spec.* 2.64; *Cher.* 113; *Sacr.* 126; *Ebr.* 69; *Conf.* 62 (in contrast to the Logos). But the most interesting text is *Gig.* 33, in which Philo gives an exegesis of the Hebraism in Lev 18:6:

> Saying the word not once but twice, human being human being (ἄνθρωπος ἄνθρωπος), is an indication that he means not the person of body and soul, but the person devoted to excellence. For he is indeed the true human being, of whom one of the ancients [the cynic Diogenes] spoke when he lit a lantern in the middle of the day and told inquirers that he was looking for a human being.

He may well have the distinction between the two human beings in Gen 1:26–27 and 2:7 in mind. In texts such as *Her.* 231; *Fug.* 71; *Somn.* 1.215; *Congr.* 97; *Plant.* 42; *Prob.* 111, the notion of the "true man" points to the role of the intellect (see also §68 and the comment ad loc.).

is either man or woman. I.e. anticipating the creation of Eve; cf. §151.

is a kind of idea or genus or seal. See the remarks above in the General comments on whether this should be taken to indicate a Platonic idea in the technical sense of the term. "Genus" recalls §76. See next note.

neither male nor female. The terms ἄρρεν and θῆλυ are derived from Gen 1:27, where the human beings are said to be created "male and female." It would seem to be an exegetical sleight of hand now to conclude that the human being after the image was *neither* male nor female! According to Tobin (*CM* 109–100) the reasoning (which he attributes to Philo's predecessors) proceeds in three steps: (1) the human being moulded in 2:7 is explicitly composite, but the one in 1:26–27 is not, i.e. he is a unitary being; (2) but then it would improbable that he was both male and female, i.e. an androgyne; (3) therefore the words should be taken to mean that he is *neither* male nor female. Another interpretation could be to make the link with the earlier exegesis in §76 and argue that the human being after the image was generic and thus neither male nor female in the sense that he (or it) was *not yet* male or female. See the comment ad loc.

(2) §135. **the sense-perceptible and individual human being.** The term αἰσθητός (sense-perceptible) picks up the moulded human being as portrayed in §134. ἐπὶ μέρους (individual) may also be an explication of

"partaking in quality," since qualitative features allow individualization to be realized. Adam's descendants possess qualities of soul and body that share less and less in his original excellence, as we shall learn in §141.

is composed of. Because the moulded human being is σύνθετος (composite), he will ultimately dissolve into his component parts. This is what constitutes his mortality.

the Craftsman. Fossum (1985, 207) tendentiously argues that Philo intends an opposition between the Craftsman (τεχνίτης) and the Father and Director in the following line, i.e. the maker of the body is inferior (and is equivalent to angels in traditions less influenced by philosophy). There *is* a distinction, but it is not one of person, but rather of function: the Craftsman fashions the body, the Father "inbreathes" it with life and mind.

the divine spirit. Philo translates the biblical expression "breath of life" (πνοὴ ζωῆς) into the philosophical and scientific term *pneuma*; on the distinction and its background in the Hebrew Bible cf. Alexandre *CLG* 239–241. As we have already seen, in both Aristotelian and Stoic psychology this concept plays a central role. In Aristotle it is the special material that enables soul to use body as its instrument and bring about movement; see the comment on §30. In the Stoa *pneuma* is the divine active principle that structures matter at various levels and is manifest in human beings as logos; see the comment on §131 and further discussion in L&S §47; Hahm 1977, 156–174. In Plato and Platonism, however, the term *pneuma* almost never occurs in the context of human psychology (when it does, it is usually under the influence of later developments, e.g. in the Ps.-Platonic *Axiochus* 370c; Diogenes Laertius 3.67; in a text such as Justin *Dial.* 6.2 the influence of the Genesis account is probably already felt, cf. Van Winden 1971, 105). Philo thus has to ask himself what Moses can intend with the term and how it relates to the *nous* which was central to the interpretation of Gen 1:26–27 in §§69–71. In various texts in which Gen 2:7 is explained, Philo interprets it to mean that God places a divine fragment (ἀπόσπασμα) of himself within the human being; see further on §146 (where we also discuss earlier Hellenistic-Jewish material). At the same time he shows a strong tendency to reconcile Stoic *pneuma* and Platonizing *nous*. For an important text in this regard we can refer back to *Det.* 83, quoted above in connection with §69 (cf. also §§86–87; *Plant.* 18–20). It is clear that Philo is keen to avoid any suggestion of Stoic materialistic psychology and shows a preference for Platonist views without being able to reject the biblically grounded notion of *pneuma* altogether. See further my comments at *PT* 325–329 and a detailed examination of all relevant texts in Tobin *CM* 77–101, read in terms of his hypothesis of evolving exegetical traditions. The concept of *pneuma* is also highly important in Philo's thought for other reasons as well. It suggests the notion of a *spiritual* life as opposed to the life of the *flesh* (cf. the exegesis of Gen 6:3 in *Gig.* 19–33 and the remarks of Harl PAPM 15.109–111), and also the notion of prophetic inspiration (cf. *Spec.* 4.49, Levison 1995). For broader treatment of the theme of *pneuma* in Philo see the monographs of Weaver 1973, Isaacs 1976.

has emigrated here. Literally "has established a colony," suggesting that God is in heaven and the human being receives a portion of his spirit here on earth; cf. *Her.* 283; *Virt.* 217; but qualified in *Plant.* 18.

from that blessed and flourishing nature. The terms are μακάριος and εὐδαίμων. The former is biblical (e.g. in the Beatitudes, Matt 5:3–11), the latter is taken from Greek philosophy, where from Plato and Aristotle onwards it is the chief term for describing someone who has a flourishing life or a life of well-being. That Philo should use these terms of God, a practice which *never* occurs in the Bible, is a further indication of the strong influence of Greek philosophy on this thought. See further §§150, 172 and my full analysis of the theme of *eudaimonia* in Philo in Runia (forthcoming). Similar statements connecting human spirit with divine blessedness and perfection are found at §146; *Spec.* 4.123; *Det.* 90.

for the assistance of our kind. This addition fits in well with the theme of divine providence which is so prominent in the treatise as a whole; cf. esp. §172. Was Philo thinking of the Greek god Prometheus when he wrote these lines? The link is made some centuries later by Porphyry *Ad Gaurum* 11 = Stern *GLAJJ* §466; Rinaldi 1989, §42. Alexandre (*CLG* 234) pertinently adduces the famous 3rd cent. Roman sarcophagus in which Prometheus models the first man and Minerva breathes the soul of life into him. The term "kind" (γένος) can also mean "species" or "race". The latter meaning is in the present context, of course, not an option.

stands on the borderline. Because of his composite nature the human being shares in both the features of the higher immortal and imperishable realm and the lower realm of mortality and flux. He is on the borderline and can share in both. During his earthly life he is largely stuck with his feet on the ground, but his intellect or spirit is free to roam and aspire to what is higher (cf. §§69–71). On separation from the body his immortal soul can rejoin the heavenly realm (e.g. Moses at *Mos.* 2.288). Philo expresses this existential situation with the term μεθόριος. The term occasionally occurs in an anthropological context in Platonist authors (Maximus Tyrius *Or.* 10.9; Plotinus *Enn.* 4.4.3.11; Plutarch *Mor.* 416C, used of demons situated between gods and humans). It is extremely common in Philo, who uses it for the intermediate position of human beings in general or in particular cases such as the high priest or the wise person: cf. *Decal.* 107 (parents); *Spec.* 1.116 (high priest); *Virt.* 9; *Her.* 45, 205 (the Logos, cf. *Fug.* 101); *Mut.* 45; *Somn.* 1.188 (high priest); 2.230, 234. See further the study of Mazzanti 1978. From Philo it passes into the patristic tradition. See below *Nachleben*.

the mind. The Greek term here is διάνοια, often also translated "understanding." It is a slightly more general term, closer to *logos* than to *nous* (which we consistently try to translate with "intellect").

Parallel exegesis

Gen 2:7 is one of the biblical texts that Philo cites or alludes to most frequently in his writings. *BPS* lists no less than 77 examples outside *Opif.* The specific theme of the difference between the two human beings is also discussed in *Leg.* 1.31–32; *QG* 1.4, 1.8; 2.56 (in this last text the "moulded human being" is said to have been moulded into an earthly statue on the seventh day). It is worth noting that in the parallel passage at *Leg.* 1.31–42 in the context of the Allegorical Commentary Philo asks much more detailed questions of the text, such as why does God breathe into the face (briefly alluded to at §139, also posed at *QG* 1.5) and why does he speak of breath (πνοή) rather than spirit. The comparison reveals the rather general nature of much of the exegesis in *Opif.* Other important discussions of the text and the consequences for human anthropology are found at *Spec.* 4.123; *Det.* 80–86; *Plant.* 18–20. The allusions are much less common in the Exposition of the Law than in the other two Commentaries (but note *Virt.* 203).

Nachleben

Two themes from this Philonic passage had a significant impact on patristic literature.

(1) The distinction between "the human being after the image" and "the moulded human being" is picked up by Origen. At *Hom. Gen.* 1.13 we read:

> To be sure, this human being, whom he says was made after the image of God, we should not understand to be corporeal. For the shape of the body does not contain the image of God, and the corporeal human being is not said to be made but moulded (*plasmatus*), as is written in what follows. For he says: "And God moulded the human being, that is he shaped it, out of clay from the earth." But he who has been made after the image of God is our interior person, invisible and incorporeal and uncorrupted and immortal. For in such characteristics the image of God can be rightly be understood. For if anyone should think that he who was made after the image and similitude of God was corporeal, he would seem to infer that God himself was corporeal and of human form, but to think this concerning God is manifestly impious.

The basic antithesis seems to depend on Philo. Moreover the final sentence may involve a recollection of §69. Similar passages are found in *Hom. Jer.* 1.13; *Comm. Cant.* Prol. 63.31 Baehrens; further discussion at Van den Hoek 2000a, 66. In Calcidius §278 and Ps.-Justin *Coh. ad Graecos* 30.3, however, we find a different approach. The distinction between the two human beings is explained in terms of the difference between the idea as model and the corporeal product fashioned from the earth as image. In the latter text it is argued that Plato derived this notion from Moses. Further discussion in Runia *PEC* 187, 286 and Riedweg 1994, 461–463. See also *Nachleben* above in Ch. 4. It is fascinating to observe that the modern controversy on whether the "human being after the image" is an idea or an intellect is already anticipated in these patristic texts.

(2) The Philonic theme of the human being as borderline figure (μεθόριος) is taken over in the writings of Gregory of Nyssa, as was pointed out by Daniélou 1967, 338, cf. 1961 and 1970, 116–132 (but he exaggerates its importance). See esp. *Hom. Cant.* 11, 333.13 Langerbeck; *Vita Macrinae* PG 46.972A. Its role is more significant in Nemesius' treatise *De natura hominis*, where it is used three times in the first pages in describing human nature: 2.24; 5.9; 6.6 Morani). We cite the final passage:

> The Hebrews affirm that man was originally born neither wholly mortal nor immortal, but on the borderline of both natures, so that if he follows the inclinations of bodily passions, he will also encounter bodily vicissitudes, but if he gives priority to the noble realm of the soul, he will be deemed worthy of immortality.

The parallelism with §135 is patent (set out in parallel columns at Runia *PEC* 263). Jaeger (1914, 141) argued that Nemesius meant by "Hebrews" a direct reference to Philo. This is doubtful. In *PEC* 264 I suggested that Nemesius may have taken over the Philonic material from Origen's *Commentary on Genesis*. But since the term scarcely occurs in his remains, and certainly not in an anthropological context, this too is perhaps not so likely. It is possible that Nemesius read Philo, but he never refers to him by name.

In a recent article Sterling (1999a, 9) has pointed out that in the Hellenistic-Jewish apocalyptic work *2 Enoch* the following lines are very reminiscent of Philo's interpretation of Gen 2:7 (30.10 [J]):

> From invisible and visible substance I created man.
> From both his natures come both death and life.

Because this work contains three more motifs that seem parallel to themes in *Opif.*, Sterling plausibly suggests that its author may have come from Egypt and been acquainted with Philo's work.

As noted above in the comments on §134, Josephus' paraphrase of Gen 2:7 is strongly reminiscent of Philo's language. The cited passage continues: καὶ πνεῦμα ἐνῆκεν αὐτῷ καὶ ψυχήν (and he instilled breath into him and soul). Once again the presentation is too concise to allow Philonic influence to be proven.

Further reading: Radice *FM* 296–300; Runia *PT* 325–340; Tobin *CM* 77–101; Baer 1970, 20–35; Mazzanti 1978 (on the theme of the double creation); Kugel *TB* 80, 108 (Jewish exegetical parallels).

Chapter Nineteen
The excellence of the first human being (§§136–147)

Analysis/General comments

After the brief section on the creation of the first human being consisting of body and soul, Philo now continues with a rather extended reflection on what the consequences of this creation are, in the first place for that first human being, and in the second place for us, i.e. Philo and his readers, who are that man's distant descendants. Structurally the chapter seems a little untidy. At §145 Philo seems to round off his description of the first human being and turn to his descendants. But these have already been discussed in §§141–142. It is best to interpret the chapter in terms of an A–B–A–B structure, with the A-sections concentrating on the first human being and the B-sections on his relation to later humans. The chapter thus divides into four parts. (Because the next section, §148, involves a return to the biblical text, I have kept it separate and regarded it as beginning a following chapter. But one could also treat §§136–150 as a whole. See further our analysis in Ch. 20.)

(1a) The first human being born from the earth was truly excellent both in body and soul and superior to his descendants (§136a).

(1b) First the excellence of his body is demonstrated by means of three arguments: (i) the material that he was made from must have been pure because the earth had just been formed, i.e. it had had no time yet to become polluted or worn out; (ii) God would have taken the purest material available for the task; (iii) God, as excellent designer, must have given the body excellent proportions and other beautiful traits. As Philo implies at the beginning of §138, the three arguments are not of equal value, but rather of ascending importance: the first is materialistic, the second is teleological, the third theological (reiterating the fundamental goodness of God established in §21) (§§136b–138).

(1c) The excellence of the first human's soul is established by an appeal to the divine Logos, of which he is a copy. The model-copy relation is effectuated by the divine inbreathing into the face. Philo first draws two conclusions from this exegetical detail. (i) The face is the location of the senses, which thus form the link between soul and body. (ii) But reason, the king located in the ruling part of the human being, requires the senses so that it can interact with the world of experience. (iii) The strongest argument, however, for the excellence of the human soul is that the model, i.e. the divine Logos, is transcendently splendid, so that its copy must be splendid also. Analogously to the section on the body, there is a movement in the argument from physiological to psychological to theological considerations. The final argument, however, is not so easy to relate to the role of the Logos as location of the ideas (cf. §24) (§139).

(2a) Philo now extends the result of the argument so far by applying it to other subsequent humans, including us now. The first human being was far superior because his maker was superior. He was created directly by God, whereas we have our origin in other human beings. The first human being was created as his very peak, whereas we have since degenerated (§140).

(2b) The process is illustrated by two analogies. (i) One can compare what happens in the arts: copies are always inferior to the originals. (ii) The same is illustrated by the magnet: the further the iron rings are from the source of the attraction, the weaker is the force that connects them to the origin. Both images (and also the earlier comparison with a living being at its peak) can be criticized (see the detailed comments). But the message is clear enough. Not only did the chicken precede the egg, but we are a shadow of what humankind was when it was first created (§141).

(3a) But Philo is not yet finished with his description of the first human being. Implicitly he responds to the observation that this person could not be a social animal because he was completely alone, and he could also not take advantage of any achievements of human civilization, since there were none. In fact, however, his place of residence was the cosmos as a whole, in which he could live in peace without fear, since he had been given dominion over earthly affairs (as already expounded in §§83–88) (§142).

(3b) But if one lives in a city, one also has to live according to a law or a constitution. For the first human being this was the right reason of nature (*orthos logos*) or, better, the divine law called *thesmos* (ordinance) (§143a).

(3c) But this cosmic city must have had citizens before the first human being. Who then are his fellow-citizens? These must be divine beings, some with bodies such as the stars and some without (probably the angels are meant) (§§143b–144a).

(3d) Such circumstances and such company must have allowed the first human being to live a life of complete well-being (*eudaimonia*). This was possible because he was related to God the Director of the universe through the manner of his creation, and so could direct all his actions towards him. But being related to God is not enough. One has to recognize that the goal of life (*telos*) is assimilation to God, and that this goal can only be reached through the practice of the (moral) excellences (*aretai*) (§144b).

(4a) But what of the first human's descendants? These do share in his original form, albeit rather faintly. For this relation Philo uses the term *sungeneia*, exactly the same term used above for the relation of the first human being to God (§145).

(4b) But what does this "family relationship" consist of? With regard to the mind (or rational soul), it involves being related to the Logos (§146a).

(4c) With regard to the body, it is expressed in the fact that human beings are related to the entire cosmos. Philo explains this in two different ways. (i) Firstly, through the four elements which the creator took in order to fabricate the compound of the body. (ii) Secondly, through the fact that humans are — in differing ways — at home in the four elements. The four situations are very briefly illustrated. In the case of the heaven Philo returns to the theme of sight earlier set out in §54 and esp. §70 (§§146b–147).

From its starting-point in the biblical account, this chapter develops a large number of anthropological, cosmological and theological themes, which will be further elucidated in the detailed comments. But first we make five general observations.

(a) In this passage Philo gives a very positive evaluation of the human body. Indeed, in contrast to §§69–71, he places more emphasis on it than on the excellence of soul and mind. Partly, of course, this is determined by the exegetical context. Nevertheless it is very striking in the light of Philo's frequent inclination to a platonizing devaluation of the corporeal. The roots of this view lie primarily, I would argue, in the Bible and its continuation in Jewish thought. But it should not be overlooked that Plato too was by no means always negative about the body. Indeed, if read properly, the *Timaeus* gives a very positive portrayal; cf. esp. 87c–89c and my remarks at *PT* 321. Moreover we should note that the terms in which Philo expresses this bodily excellence in §138 are more Greek than Jewish. For a balanced view of Philo's view of the body compared to rabbinic thought see Winston 1998.

(b) Although humankind as it is now found has degenerated considerably when compared with its first ancestor, it is still related to him. That means it shares his family relationship with both God and the cosmos. It also means that the life of that first human can still represent an ideal that is to some degree at least attainable for human beings.

(c) Philo expresses that ideal in general terms with the theme of well-being (*eudaimonia*), which is fundamental to Greek ethical thought (see esp. §144). Except for the brief reference to the nature of God in §135, it occurs here for the first time, but will become more and more prominent, reaching a climax in the work's final sentence. The conception of humans being "citizens of the cosmos" also represents an ideal, because it means they can lead a life in complete harmony with the cosmos and its law of reason. This returns to the theme first outlined at the very beginning of the treatise (§§1–3). The conception of cosmic law and the citizenship of the world is strongly indebted to Stoic philosophy, but had become by Philo's time a widespread and popular philosophical theme by no means confined to the Stoic school. See further the detailed comments on §143.

(d) It is striking that in our treatise Philo never uses the biblical name Adam (it should not be included in the text at §149, see our note there), and that it occurs nowhere else in the entire Exposition of Law. Elsewhere he is called the earth-born or the first human being (cf. *Abr.* 12, 56; *Virt.* 199, 203). In many respects he is more a type than a real person. For an illuminating general account of Philo's treatment of Adam see Levison 1988, who emphasizes the predominance of Greek philosophical conceptuality in the portrait, setting it apart from the other Jewish sources which he analyzes. He concludes (88): "Most details and general tendencies in Philo's portrait of the first man are his own and should not be amalgamated with other early Jewish interpretations into a hypothetical 'Adam tradition'." Much depends on what and whom Philo is compared with. It may be assumed, I believe, that a Greek reader of Philo's treatise would find it peculiarly Jewish.

(e) In his account of the story of Adam and Eve, the first human beings in biblical and Jewish tradition, Philo can hardly avoid touching on various themes related to the origins of humankind. We note, for example, the observation that there was not as yet any kind of housing (§142). A tension may be observed between a presentation as *history*, i.e. an account of the life of early mankind, and a presentation in terms of *actualization* and *idealization*, i.e. seeing Adam and Eve as types of human beings. The latter view predominates and, when taken to its furthest conclusion, leads to allegory, such as we find in §§157–165. With regard to the former, it seems that in this treatise and subsequent parts of the Exposition of the Law, Philo shows little interest in those aspects of the account which have to do with the origins of human culture and civilization. The biblical doctrine of the Garden of Eden encourages him to paint a rosy picture of the initial conditions of human life, as already hinted at in §§77–88. (There is an obvious parallel in the Greek myth of the Golden age or the Age of Kronos, when nature supplied what humans needed and they lived a simple but happy life; see the comment on §142.) Philo exploits this theme chiefly for moral and religious purposes. It is applied to the human situation as it is for the contemporary reader.

Detailed comments

(1a) §136. *who was born from the earth.* Philo's use of the term γηγενής with specific reference to the first human being is noteworthy. Cf. *Abr.* 12, 56, *Spec.* 2.160 (plural of the first generations); *Virt.* 199, 203; *Praem.* 9. Compare the words put in the mouth of Solomon at Wis 7:1: "I too ... am a mortal human being the same as all the rest, a descendant from the earth-born (γηγενής) first-moulded man (πρωτόπλαστος)." The latter term, a direct reference to the human being created in Gen 2:7, is found in Philo only at *QG* 1.32 (PAPM 33.51); *QE* 2.46 (33.268). By using the term γηγενής Philo invites comparison with the theme of the "earth-born" in Greek mythology and ethnography, in which it always occurs in the plural; cf. Plato *Pol.* 269b2; Aristotle *Pol.* 1269b2; Sextus Empiricus *Adv. Phys.* 1.28 (attributed to younger Stoics); Diodorus Siculus 1.26.7, etc. Philo cites the arguments of Critolaus against this conception of the origin of humans at *Aet.* 66–68. Paul describes Adam in 1 Cor. 15:47 as ὁ πρῶτος ἄνθρωπος ἐκ γῆς χοϊκός (the first human being, from the earth, of clay); for a detailed comparison of Paul's and Philo's descriptions see the discussion of E. Schweizer in *TDNT* 9.474–477.

the original ancestor. The term is ἀρχεγέτης, also used of the first human being at §§79, 142; *Mut.* 64; *Spec.* 4.123; of Noah as second Adam at *Abr.* 46; of Abraham at *Abr.* 276 etc.

of our entire kind. The word γένος can also mean "race," e.g. in the case of Abraham as ancestor of the Jewish race at *QG* frg. 17 (PAPM 33.228). But in this treatise the perspective is universal. Contrast *Jubilees* 2.19, where Israel is chosen from the Seventh day of creation onwards.

most excellent. The word ἄριστος has already been used of God in §21, heaven in §§27 and 36, and of the human being as crown of creation in §82. Here it is used to describe a specific individual. On the language of excellence in the treatise see the comments on §§9 and 82.

a noble person. Here too Philo's terminology is revealing. The term is καλὸς καὶ ἀγαθός, literally "beautiful and good," the standard term in classical Greek for a man with all the qualities of birth, character and appearance that one should admire. The connotations of the term were often aristocratic (cf. Dover 1974, 41–45).

(1b) *the great body of water which was named sea.* Cf. §§39 and 131.

the material ... easy to work with. Clearly an implicit analogy is made with the work of the potter or sculptor. The better the clay, the better the product. "Material" here is ὕλη, already possessing certain qualities, not like the οὐσία in §§8–9. Philo would have liked the 19th century Protestant hymn (loosely based on Jeremiah 18): "Have thine own way, Lord! Have thine own way! / Thou art the potter, I am the clay./ Mold me and make me, after thy will, / While I am waiting, yielded and still."

§137. *took clay.* Philo repeats the participle which he included in the citation of the biblical text. See on §134.

with the utmost care. Whittaker (PLCL 1.109) translates the phrase μετὰ τῆς ἀνωτάτω σπουδῆς "as rapidly as possible" and takes them to indicate what God did not do. The words can bear this meaning, but the word order tells in favour of my translation, which I share with the other translators.

a home or holy temple. The imagery emphasizes the high value that Philo attaches to the body in this context. See our remarks in the General Comments. To my knowledge this is the only text in Philo where the body is called a temple. For the head as dwelling-place or temple for the mind cf. *QG* 1.5 (perhaps alluding to Plato *Tim.* 44a1); *QE* 2.51, 100. More common is the depiction of the soul as a shrine or temple for the indwelling of God; cf. *Somn.* 1.149, 215; and Paul at 1 Cor. 3:16; 6:19; 2 Cor. 3:16.

carry around as the most god-like of images. The fourth and final time in the treatise that we encounter the *verbum Philonicum* ἀγαλματοφορέω cf. §§18, 69, 82 and comments ad loc.

the creator also excelled in knowledge. The words ἀγαθὸς ἦν recall Plato's solemn pronouncement at *Tim.* 29e1, already alluded to in §21. But here God's goodness is further specified in terms of his competence as creator. Cf. the praise of the first human being at *Virt.* 203: "In terms of noble birth he should be compared with no other mortal, for with divine hands he was shaped into a statue with the figure of a human body through the sculptor's skill at its very peak, while in the case of his soul ..."

symmetry. The description of the beauty of the human body in terms of proportion and symmetry is very Greek. Both Plato (cf. *Tim.* 87c–d; *Phil.* 64e) and the Stoa understand physical beauty in such terms. An excellent parallel is the Stoic viewpoint at Cicero *Tusc. Disp.* 4.31: "In the case of the body a certain suitable shape of the limbs combined with a certain charm of colouring is called beauty." Plotinus argues against this view in his treatise *On beauty* (*Enn.* 1.6), and wants to replace symmetry with sublimity (ἀγλαία) as the chief characteristic of beauty. Similar accounts of physical beauty are found at *Mos.* 2.140; *QG* 4.99 (included by Von Arnim as *SVF* 3.592). Joseph's physical beauty is praised at *Ios.* 40, 269. But Philo is negative about such beauty at *Spec.* 4.89 and *QG* 4.99, because even harlots can possess it! One might contrast the Jewish portrayal of Adam as a body of immense size; cf. Kugel *TB*, 82–84. True to the biblical text *Gen. Rab.* 14, giving exegesis of Gen 2:7, says nothing about the beauty of Adam; he is in fact inferior to Abraham (§6.2).

a beauty of flesh, a beauty of colour. As we just saw, this is part of the definition of physical beauty. This is exactly what a human sculptor cannot give his work of art (though we should bear in mind that ancient statues were painted).

embellish it. This is a *hapax legomenon*, i.e. the only instance of the verb ἀνθογραφέω, literally "paint with the bright colours of flowers," preserved in ancient Greek literature. It is typical of the "flowery" language that Philo can sometimes use.

(1c) §139. **God used no other model.** A very clear illustration of how Philo tends to reconcile and coalesce the two creation accounts, as was discussed at length in Ch. 18. The notion of a model is extraneous to the account in Gen 2:7 on which the present passage concentrates. Perhaps the words "it is probable" refer to this exegetical move. But ἔοικε can also be translated as "it is fitting," which would mean that Philo *assumes* rather than postulates the coalescence of the two texts.

as I said. Unless Philo's memory plays tricks on him, this must refer to §25, because the Logos was not mentioned at all in the exegesis of Gen 1:26–27 in §§69–88. See also the next comment.

its likeness and representation. These terms, ἀπεικόνισμα and μίμημα are exactly those used of the relation of the Logos as location of the Ideas and as model for the human being and the cosmos in §§16 and 25, making the cross-reference to §25 probable. The word τούτου is tricky. It refers to the Logos rather than to God, so should we translate it by "its" or "his"? If we do not want to personalize the Logos too much, as Philo declines to do in this treatise, we should perhaps opt for the former.

into the face. See Exegetical parallels in Ch. 18.

reason ... as king in the directive part. Philo must assume here, given the exegetical context, that the ἡγεμονικόν is located in the head. It may seem obvious that the head should be the location of the mind, but in the context of ancient psychology this was by no means the case. In Philo's time there was an unresolved controversy between followers of Aristotle and the Stoa, who regarded the heart as the location of the directive part, and followers of Plato, who placed it in the head. Philo tends to follow the Platonic line, but at *Spec.* 1.213 and *Sacr.* 136 he states that the Mosaic view is unclear. See further *PT* 267, and also the next comment.

for the ruling part to be flanked with bodyguards. In Philo there are a number of texts in which the mind is described as a king or even the Great king who resides in palace or acropolis with the senses as his bodyguards (*Spec.* 3.111; 4.123; *Somn.* 1.32) and more texts where it is described as the directive part. These texts are collected at *PT* 306–307. The passage at *Spec.* 4.123 is an extremely close parallel to our text (and also to §§144–146):

> The essence of that [rational] soul is divine *pneuma*, and this is certainly the view of Moses, who in the creation account states that in the case of the first human being and ancestor of our kind God inbreathed the breath of life into the most lordly part of the body, the face, where the senses are stationed as bodyguards of the intellect like those of the Great king. It is clear that what was breathed in was ethereal *pneuma* or what is superior, if

such there be, to ethereal *pneuma*, an effulgence (ἀπαύγασμα) of the blessed and thrice-blessed nature.

Similar imagery is found in many authors from Cicero onwards. Its origin is clearly exegesis of Plato *Tim*. 70a, but it has not proved possible to trace further intermediate sources. See the large number of parallels collected at *PT* 306–307 and supplemented by Mansfeld 1990, 3105.

on its own. The senses are vitally important for human beings because they form a double link: in the first place between body and soul, since sense-perception is a faculty of the soul, but it requires bodily organs in order to function; in the second place between the world of mind and the outside world, since without the senses the mind would find itself in total isolation.

The Logos of God is even superior. The general intention of this final sentence is clear enough: the divine Logos is superior to beauty of any kind. But the exact meaning is difficult to determine. This is particularly the case if we bear in mind that according to §§24–25, the Logos is identical with the noetic cosmos and thus must contain beauty as one of its ideas. It is possible that we shall have to be content with the view that Philo is being rhetorical rather than philosophical here. But in the comments below we make a number of suggestions in order to "rescue" the passage philosophically.

to the beauty. The text as transmitted reads "beauty itself," but this is doubtful for two reasons. Firstly, the expression αὐτὸ κάλλος is strange. It is found nowhere else in Philo, who usually speaks of αὐτὸ τὸ καλόν, e.g. in §8. Secondly, it is awkward to speak of "beauty itself which is beauty in nature," if this is understood in Platonizing terms, since the beauty in nature participates in beauty itself and is not to be equated with it. We thus propose to read [αὐ]τοῦ κάλλους. It is, however, perhaps possible to take "nature" here as the "nature of things," i.e. both in the sense-perceptible and the noetic realm. The Logos would then give beauty its place in both realms.

if the truth be told. One of Philo's favourite expressions, occurring no less than 34 times in his works (including §82). It often breaks up a phrase, as here, and is regularly used to introduce a bold or a hyperbolic expression.

is itself beauty's pre-eminent adornment. The reading ἐκπρεπέστατον found in some of the manuscripts is almost certainly to be preferred to εὐπρεπέστατον read by PCW. It occurs in the superlative five times elsewhere in Philo (*Post.* 92; *Plant.* 65; *Congr.* 124; *Abr.* 94; *Mos.* 2.111; in the first three cases associated with κάλλος), whereas the superlative form read by PCW is found nowhere else in Philo. The thought expressed seems to be something like this. In the case of a beautiful flower we can say that it possesses beauty or is adorned with beauty, but there may be other things that are even more beautiful. In the case of the divine Logos, however, we cannot say that it possesses beauty or is adorned by beauty, because there is nothing more beautiful than it is. Its nature is such that it exemplifies beauty in its highest manifestation. Philosophically the problem remains that the Logos exemplifies beauty and thus would seem in a sense to be subordinate to it, which, as we noted above, cannot be reconciled with the theological metaphysics of §§24–25. In the light of this difficulty we should consider whether it might not be possible to find another referent for the final word ἐκείνου (of that), namely God in the phrase 'the Logos of God'. It is neither theologically nor philosophically objectionable to call the Logos 'God's pre-eminent adornment'. There would also be a kind of play on the notion that the Logos is himself a cosmos, i.e. to be identified with the noetic cosmos. But it has to be admitted that it is much more natural to take ἐκείνου to refer to the nearest available noun, namely κάλλος (beauty). This is the way that all translators and commentators have interpreted the phrase hitherto. But they were insufficiently sensitive to the theological and philosophical problems posed by the passage.

(2a) §140. *He surpassed all those living now* ... Later in the Exposition of the Law Philo uses the same argumentation to illustrate the excellence of nobility of birth. See the entire passage *Virt.* 203–205, which is too long to quote. It is a kind of summary of *Opif.* 137–152, ending with the same theme, exchange of *eudaimonia* for *kakodaimonia*; see further the comment on §152.

for our origin is from other human beings ... Cf. *Virt.* 204: "for his [Adam's] father was no mortal, but the everlasting God, whose image he in a sense became with respect to the intellect as director in the soul (cf. §69) ..." Elsewhere in the Exposition, however, when expounding the fifth commandment, Philo argues that human reproduction emulates the creator. See *Spec.* 2.225 (cf. *Decal.* 107): "Parents stand in between the divine and the human, and share in both: of the human obviously because they both have been born and will perish, of the divine because they have given birth and brought non-being into existence. What God is for the cosmos, this parents are for their children ..."

just as that which is at its peak ... Philo compares the degeneration of humanity with the decline of a living thing past its prime. But the comparison is flawed. The biological succession of living things can degenerate in certain circumstances, e.g. genetic exhaustion, but this is exceptional. Genetic variation usually ensures that a new generation is different but not systematically inferior, while various kinds of genetic selection can lead to improvement.

(2b) §141. *the arts of sculpture and painting.* Philo assumes here the Platonic and Aristotelian theory of art as imitation, on which see Verdenius 1949; Kardaun 1983. His attitude towards art can be severe when he thinks of its relation to idolatry; cf. *Gig.* 59, with an obvious allusion to Plato's driving out the artists from the ideal *politeia*. Here the reference is fairly neutral. It is inherent in the theory of mimesis that copies are inferior to the original; cf. *Plant.* 26–27, comparing Moses and

Bezalel. If the aim of art is to produce a likeness (an assumption that since the Romantic period has generally been rejected), then a copy of a copy will always be inferior to the original, since the original is not used as model (compare Roman copies of Greek statues). Nowadays a comparison with a photocopier might be more to the point: photocopies are always deficient compared with the original, and a photocopy of a photocopy is worse again. But even this comparison is flawed in the present context, since human reproduction can in no way be compared to artistic representation. The relation between parents and child is not that between model and copy, but rather one might say that the child is a variation on the form of its parents. Even without knowledge of modern genetic theory, Philo might have realized this by reflecting on the Aristotelian theory of form and matter (on which see the comments on §67 and §132). It would be more correct for him to say, as he does at *Decal.* 111, that humans imitate God by producing children; see the comment on §140.

the magnetic stone. According to Pliny *Nat.* 36.127 it received the name from its discoverer Magnes. Philo also uses the image at *Praem.* 58 (of Abraham attracted to the vision of God) and *Gig.* 44 (of the attraction of pleasure). The image here focuses on the weakening of attraction, perhaps inspired by two famous examples, Plato *Ion* 536a (the weakening of poetic inspiration), and (implicitly) Ps.-Aristotle *Mund.* 6, 397b28–30 (on God's *dynamis*). In the light of our remarks above, it hardly needs to be said that Philo's image is inappropriate for this context.

are held less and less tightly. The verb χαλινόω means "bridle" or "restrain." An adverb seems required. I have suggested ἧττον because of the similar usage a few lines earlier.

fainter and fainter. As will appear in §145, the adjective ἀμυδρός can be used to indicate that the markings of a stamp become ever more faint or dim, and thus more difficult to recognize. Cf. *Deus* 43, where the same term is used when forgetfulness smoothens the stamp of the memory in the mind.

(3a) §142. *the only real citizen of the cosmos.* The first human being, through being created and living alone in the cosmos, fulfils the ideal of being κοσμοπολίτης, as Philo has outlined at the very outset of the treatise in §3. On the term and the ideal it represents see the comment ad loc. The word μόνος (alone) has a prescriptive force; cf. LSJ II 4 "expressing rhetorically pre-eminence in an action or quality."

For the ideal of cosmopolitanism Philo is indebted to Stoicism. Cf. the Stoic definition of the city given by Clement *Strom.* 6.172 (= *SVF* 3.327):

> The Stoics say that the universe is in the proper sense a city, but that those here on earth are not ... For a city or a people is something morally good, an organization or group of men administered by law which exhibits refinement (translation Schofield).

The doctrine of the cosmos as the true city was widely held by thinkers of Philo's time and a little later, such as Seneca, Dio Chrysostom, Epictetus etc. (and also earlier by Cicero, cf. *Leg.* 1.23). In a famous passage Plutarch attributed it retrospectively to Zeno and Alexander the Great (*Alex. virt.* 329A–B). On the theory and its place in the development of Stoic philosophy see Schofield 1991, 57–103. Philo adapts the theory to the singular situation of Genesis 2, namely that there is but a single human being, who is as yet entirely uncorrupted in his excellence.

with complete safety. The first man can live in full security, not only because he is master of the animal realm, but also because he does not have to fear the most savage of all animals, the humanbeing himself. Philo's phrase is perhaps an implicit reference to the preoccupation of philosophers such as Epicurus with the problem of security. If life in primeval times was brutish and violent, humans were necessarily in constant fear of their safety. For this reason they needed to make a social contract as the foundation of civil society. It is improbable that this contract can extend to all humankind, i.e. true cosmopolitanism is unattainable. See Epicurus *KD* 6–7, 14, 28, 31–40 (esp. 39); Lucretius 5.1011–27. Philo rejects the naturalistic basis of this theory of the origin of society. Instead he implicitly adapts the opposed current of thinking in the ancient world, namely that in earlier times there was a "golden age," before civilization and its discontents began; cf. Hesiod, *Op.* 109–201, playfully adapted by Plato *Politicus* 271e–272b. For surveys of Greek and Roman theories on the origin of human culture see Guthrie 1957; Winston *PA* 339; Heckel 1999. Guthrie rightly argues (69) that the two opposed theoretical tendencies of "idealized primitivism" and "progressivism" are not absolute and can even be combined. On the Jewish side there is much suggestive material on the origin of culture in Genesis, but it did not apparently lead to systematic reflection; see Ginzberg 1909–38, vols. 1 and 5; Kugel *TB*, 173–181 on the role of Enoch.

trained or compelled. As in §§83–88 there is an implicit division between domesticated and wild animals.

unassailably. Elsewhere — e.g. *Abr.* 4; *Spec.* 2.44; *Mos.* 2.1 — the adverb ἀνεπιλήπτως has a moral force, i.e. "unblameworthily," but here it should be taken more literally. *Spec.* 2.42–48 is an interesting complement to our present passage. For Philo human violence is always the result of the absence of virtue, as expressed through injustice and the pursuit of pleasure. The wise seek to live "a life of peace without conflict" (§44), focused on contemplation, as is fitting for true "cosmopolitans" (§45).

(3b) §143. **made use of the constitution.** Here too we are strongly reminded of §3, where Philo draws a strict parallel between the law observed by human beings and the law of the cosmos, which is the law of nature. The difference between the two passages is that in the former the law for human beings implicitly referred to is the Law of Moses, whereas here that Law is strictly speaking irrelevant. The first human being can be compared to the patriarchs and Moses himself, who were "living laws" (*Abr.* 5, *Mos.* 1.162), i.e. they needed no instruction to follow the law of nature. See the comments on §3 and Excursus 1 on Law, cosmos and nature in Ch. 1.

the right reason of nature. The expression ὁ τῆς φύσεως ὀρθὸς λόγος is somewhat unusual. To my knowledge it is only found in Philo, who uses it no less than seven times: *Ios.* 31 (particular laws of cities contrasted with the law of nature); *Mos.* 1.48 (source of *aretai*); *Spec.* 1.191; *Virt.* 127; *Prob.* 62 (note also §46); *QE* 2.3 (Greek frg. at Petit PAPM 33.241). In Stoic philosophy *orthos logos* is the usual term for the reason inherent in humans beings, through whose guidance, if followed, right action is achieved. "Of nature" is added to emphasize that it is not confined to humans, but pervades the whole of the reality, so that a correspondence can exist between human action and universal law. The close affinity of Philo's conceptuality here with Stoic thought can be shown through a comparison with the Zenonian definition of the goal of life recorded at Diogenes Laertius 7.88 cited above in Excursus 1 to Ch. 1. But Philo would not say that the Law of nature was identical to God, though he might be prepared to identify it with his Logos. Von Arnim includes part of §§142-143 as *SVF* 3.337.

'ordinance', a divine law. In §§61 and 171 Philo places the terms νόμος and θεσμός parallel to each other. Here he makes a clear distinction, θεσμός being described as a νόμος θεῖος. Though θεσμός is clearly derived from the root of τίθημι, "I place" or "I set," there may be an attempt at a play on words here, or even a (playful) etymology, as suggested by Alexandre PAPM 16.190 on *Congr.* 120. The reversal of the words νόμος and θεῖος in ms. G is maybe due to recognition of this attempt. As Colson LCL 9.509 and Petit PAPM 28.143 (both commenting on *Prob.* 3) point out, Philo regards a *thesmos* as a higher law because it is laid down and instituted by God. At *Congr.* 120 the Decalogue is described as *thesmoi*, the chief headings of an endless number of special laws (*nomoi*). Stephanus (*TLG* 5.340) cites the explanation of θεσμοί as θεῖοι νόμοι in the lexicon of Hesychius, but does not exploit the Philonic evidence. LSJ ad loc. is less helpful, only stating that θεσμός is "especially used of divine laws."

(3c) *must have had citizens.* Philo answers the implicit objection that it is absurd to speak of a city and a constitution when there was only a single human being. Cf. *Post.* 49-51, where in response to the biblical account that Cain builds a city (Gen 4:17) it is argued that this is impossible on his own and the text is allegorized.

citizens of the great city. They are μεγαλοπολῖται, i.e. citizens of the cosmos as μεγαλόπολις. See above on §19.

greatest and most complete. Once again the language of excellence (two of the four superlatives are used of the cosmos by Plato in *Tim.* 92c7-9).

§144. *the rational and divine natures.* As already stated in §§73 and 84, in the hierarchy of living beings some creatures have a higher status than humankind. In §73 only the heavenly bodies are explicitly mentioned. Here the group of creatures superior to humankind is divided into two groups, those without and those with a body. The former are incorporeal rational natures, to be identified in Philo's Jewish perspective with angels. See further the comments on §§73 and 84. What characterizes these higher creatures is their excellence and faultless behaviour, making them ideal fellow-citizens for the first human being in the cosmic city. For the notion that the cosmos is a mega-city having both divine and human beings as its citizens, Philo again draws on the Stoa. See for example Arius Didymus at Eusebius *Praep. Ev.* 15.15.3 (frg. 29 Diels):

> They [the Stoics] call the cosmos the residence of gods and humans, or that which consists of gods and humans and what has come into existence on their account. Just as a city is described both as a residence and as a composite whole consisting of its inhabitants together with the citizens, so the cosmos is like a city consisting of gods and humans, the gods holding power, while the humans are subordinate. They form together a community because they share in reason, which is the natural law.

In *Mor.* 1065F and 1076F Plutarch ridicules this doctrine in his polemics against Chrysippus. See also the comment on §77.

intelligible beings. In the sense that they can only be observed by the intellect, not in the sense that they belong to the intelligible cosmos.

(3d) *in undiluted well-being.* For the first time in the treatise Philo uses the key philosophical term εὐδαιμονία (εὐδαίμων is used of God in §135, see the comment ad loc.). The term is best translated as "well-being" rather than "happiness" because it represents an objective state based on certain criteria rather than a subjective feeling. It is intrinsically connected with the concept of the good life (in Latin it is translated as *beata vita*), representing the life that it to be aimed for by human beings within the limits of their humanity and mortality. As Aristotle affirms at the start of his *Nicomachean Ethics* (1.4, 1095a17–22), all agree on the term *eudaimonia* for the good life, but there is much dispute on what it precisely constitutes. In Hellenistic and Imperial philosophy the interpretation of *eudaimonia* in terms of a particular goal (*telos*) of life was one of the key doctrines that differentiated the various schools of thought (a famous list is given by Clement at *Strom.* 2.126–133). In this paragraph Philo alludes to two well-known formulations of the *telos* and adds a biblical formulation of his own. See further the discussion at Völker 1938, 340–350 (on this passage 346); *PT* 344–345.

closely related. The relationship between God and humankind is one of συγγένεια, i.e. a family relationship (literally sharing the same *genos*). Here Philo elucidates the relationship through the inbreathing of the divine *pneuma* as recorded in Gen 2:7. In §77 it was through the possession of a rational nature; in §146 it will be through the mind (in relation to the divine Logos). See also *Decal.* 134; *Spec.* 4.14; *Praem.* 163; *Plant.* 18; *QE* 2.29 etc. In Greek philosophy the term is habitually used to indicate the relationship between the human and the divine in its various manifestations, e.g. the heaven (Plato *Tim.* 47b8, 90c8), the ideas (*Resp.* 490b4), the Logos (Cleanthes, *Hymn to Zeus* 1.4) etc. For a detailed analysis see the monograph of Des Places 1964, though unfortunately Philo is almost totally ignored. For the theme in Philo see further Alexandre PAPM 16.228; Runia *PT* 341; Graffigna 1994.

to be pleasing. The formula εἰς ἀρέσκειαν can be taken as expressing the *telos* of human life in terms of biblical spirituality. Philo takes his cue from the statements about the patriarchs that they were pleasing to God (Enoch in Gen 5:24, cf. *Abr.* 17; *Mut.* 34; Noah in Gen 6:9, *Abr.* 35; Abraham in Gen 17:1, *Mut.* 39). Of the three chief patriarchs Philo states at *Praem.* 24 that "they pressed forward to the same goal of life (*telos*), to be well pleasing to the Maker and Father of the universe" (cf. also *Abr.* 130, 235; *Somn.* 1.66). See the brief remarks on this theme at Alexandre PAPM 16.158, 212 on *Congr.* 80, 156; other important texts at *Spec.* 1.176, 300, 317; *Fug.* 88 etc.

in whose footsteps he followed ... As Theiler (1965, 488 and 1971, 34) points out, in the remainder of the paragraph Philo alludes to both the Pythagorean (and Homeric) and Platonist formulations of the *telos*, as becomes clear from the following passage in Stobaeus which probably goes back to Eudorus of Alexandria (*Ecl.* 2.49.8–18, Mazzarelli frg. 25):

> Socrates and Plato agree with Pythagoras that the goal of life (τέλος) is assimilation to God (ὁμοίωσις θεῷ). Plato articulated it more clearly by adding "to the extent possible" (*Theat.* 176b1), and it is possible only through practical wisdom (φρόνησις), that is, living according to excellence (ἀρετή). In God resides the capacity to create the cosmos and to administer it, but in the wise person establishment and regulation of a way of life are present. Homer hints at this [*telos*] when he says (*Odyssey* 5.193): "proceed in the footsteps of God," while Pythagoras after him says: "follow God." Clearly by "God" he means not the visible god who advances [i.e. the cosmos], but the intelligible god who is harmonic cause of the good cosmic order [text somewhat dubious].

An important Philonic parallel is *Migr.* 128 (exeg. Gen 12:4, cf. also §131):

> This is the goal of life praised by those who philosophize best, living in accordance with nature. This occurs when the intellect enters on the path of excellence, proceeds in the footsteps of right reason and follows God, recalling his injunctions and securing them all at all times and everywhere in both deeds and words.

At *Abr.* 60; *Decal.* 100; and *Praem.* 98, Philo also makes a clear connection between this formulation of the *telos* and Jewish observance of the Law; see the comments of Nikiprowetzky 1977, 127–128.

are permitted to approach him. Only those souls who have been purified from sin and idolatry may draw near to God. In order to do this they must turn away from their previous practices, which can only take place if they recognize God's existence, hearken to his call, and aspire to becoming like him. The classic example for Philo is Abraham, cf. *Abr.* 87–88.

assimilation to God. As the climax Philo cites the Platonist formulation of the *telos*, derived — as we saw in the quote above — primarily from *Theat.* 176b1, but also related to texts such as *Resp.* 500c5, 613b1; *Tim.*

90c8. It is given a prominent place in all relevant Middle Platonist texts (e.g. Alcinous *Did.* 2, 28; Plutarch *Mor.* 550D; *Anon. Theat. Comm.* 7.19 etc.) and is eagerly taken over by the Church fathers; see esp. Clement *Strom.* 2.100.3, the discussion at Lilla 1971, 106–112, and the monographic study of Merki 1952. Philo cites the chief Platonic source passage at *Fug.* 63 and refers to the doctrine frequently in his works; cf. §151; *Abr.* 87; *Decal.* 101; *Virt.* 168; *Deus* 48; *QG* 2.62, etc. Scholarly discussions at Runia *PT* 342–343 (with further references), Belletti 1982, Helleman 1990. For some reason Philo prefers the word with the prepositional prefix ἐξομοίωσις, only using the simple noun ὁμοίωσις when quoting Gen 1:26 and the Platonic *Theaetetus* passage.

The entire final sentence of §144 is a fine example of Philo's philosophical erudition placed in service of the exposition of scripture.

(4a) §145. ***Our description*** ... With this sentence Philo appears to round off the passage §§136–144, but see the remarks on the structure of the chapter in the General comments above.

it falls far short of the truth. Another disclaimer by the modest exegete, to be added to those at §§5, 72 and 90.

the marks of the family relationship. The imagery of the seal or mould is now used to explain how the original qualities of the first human being are passed on to his descendants but become less and less clear; cf. §141.

§146. ***What does this family relationship consist of?*** The same term συγγένεια, used of the relationship between God and the first human being in §144, is now used of the latter's relationship to his descendants. In contrast to the discussion of the first human's excellence in §§137–140, Philo first gives the soul a very brief treatment and then turns quickly to the body.

(4b) ***his mind.*** The term here is διάνοια, the same as in §135; see the comment ad loc.

is akin. The verb here is ᾠκείωται, from οἰκειόω, to make one's own, become familiar with. As Lévy 1998, has shown, Philo rejects the Stoic doctrine of *oikeiosis*, in which the human being appropriates his own nature (see further on §161) in favour of a doctrine of becoming God's own, in which the term οἰκείωσις differs little from (ἐξ)ομοίωσις. A fine parallel to the present passage is *Somn.* 2.231 on the high priest as Logos: "If therefore he then does not become a man (cf. Lev 16:17), clearly he also is not God, but God's minister, assimilated (οἰκειούμενος) through his mortal aspect to creation, through his immortal aspect to the uncreated One." Cf. also *Cher.* 18; *Post.* 135; *Plant.* 55 (nearly all examples in the Allegorical Commentary).

to the divine Logos. As the final words of the Eudoran text cited above on §144 reveal, for the doctrine of *homoiosis/oikeiosis*, it is important to determine to whom (or to which god) one is assimilated. Cf. also Alcinous *Did.* 28.3: "The goal of life would thus be consistent with its first principle, namely to be assimilated to God, obviously to the heavenly god, not — by

Zeus — to the super-celestial god, who does not possess excellence, but is superior to it." Here Philo privileges the divine Logos as that aspect of the divine to which humankind is akin though his mind. Cf. §139, but Philo doubtless also has the double εἰκών theory in mind; cf. Tobin *CM* 28, 31. A fascinating parallel is found in an exegesis of Gen 9:6 given in *QG* 2.62 (Greek text at Petit PAPM 33.116):

> For nothing mortal can be modelled on the highest Father of the universe, but only on the second God, who is his Logos. For it was necessary that the rational stamp in the human soul be imprinted by the divine Logos, since the God who is anterior to the Logos is superior to all rational natures. It is not permitted for any created being to be assimilated to the God beyond the Logos who is established in a most excellent and exceptional form.

This text is unique in Philo because it explicitly speaks of a "second God." It is possible that this is the result of Christian tampering with the text, as tentatively suggested by Harl (PAPM 15.159). Be that as it may, in the present context Philo is occupied with articulating the relationship that exists between God the creator and humankind, not the gulf between humankind and God in his transcendent state.

a casting or fragment or effulgence. Philo uses three terms in order to describe the relationship of *oikeiosis* between God and humankind. (1) For ἐκμαγεῖον (casting) see above on §71; this term is chosen to express the εἰκών relation of Gen 1:26–27. (2) "Fragment" renders ἀπόσπασμα, literally "a piece drawn off." It is a Stoic term, used to express the whole-part relation between the divine *pneuma* in its totality and the part located within the human being; cf. Diogenes Laertius 7.143 = *SVF* 2.633. Philo finds the term useful for describing the relation between the divine *pneuma* and what is inbreathed in the human being in Gen 2:7; cf. esp. *Det.* 90, "how is it likely that the human intellect which is so small, contained in the small mass of brain or heart, should be able to contain the great size of heaven and universe, if it were not an inseparable fragment of that divine and flourishing soul." On Philo's somewhat problematic use of the term and his difficulty in shaking off a materialistic psychology, see Harl PAPM 15.91 and Tobin *CM* 84–91. The term is not further used in the Exposition of the Law. (3) "Effulgence" renders ἀπαύγασμα, derived from the term αὐγή (beam of light). The term has the advantage of being less materialistic, since light can illumine at a distance. Philo also uses it in an anthropological context at *Spec.* 4.123 when alluding to Gen 2:7 (cited above on §139). The same term is used of Sophia in Wisdom 7:26 and of Christ in Hebr. 1:3; see further Winston 1979, 186; Tobin *CM* 85.

The three terms are placed in parallel. Philo chooses not to distinguish between them because the context does not require an exposition of psychology (this has already been done, albeit summarily at §135). I cannot agree with Tobin (*CM* 85 n. 77), that the third term reinterprets the second. Elsewhere, in an important statement at *Mut.* 223, Philo clearly expresses a preference for the term ἐκμαγεῖον above ἀπόσπασμα; see further Runia *PT* 472.

of the blessed nature. On God's blessed nature see above on §135.

(4c) *each of the elements.* In §§135–136, following the biblical text, Philo stated that the human body was moulded from clay, i.e. a mixture of earth and (sweet) water. Here he reverts to the predominant doctrine in Greek philosophy and science that the body consists of a compound of each of the four elements. For a collection of texts on the composition of the body see Gross 1930, 10–13 and Runia *PT* 259–260. The same doctrine is also found in Jewish sources: cf. the note of J. Cohn at PCH 1.79 and *Nachleben* below.

entirely sufficient material. I.e. for the task at hand. Nothing else was required. Exactly the same terms are used for the creation of the entire cosmos at *Prov.* 2.50.

§147. *in all the elements.* I.e. the regions of the earth and cosmos where each of the elements predominates. See the comments on §131.

most congenial and familiar. The Greek terms οἰκειοτάτοις καὶ συγγενεστάτοις recall the themes of *sungeneia* and *oikeiosis* used for the relation between God and the soul. This is no doubt deliberate. A parallel relation exists between the human body and the cosmos as its physical environment.

a being of the earth ... Philo uses four single words here, χερσαῖος ἔνυδρος πτηνός οὐράνιος. The first three were already used of the living beings created on the fifth (and sixth) day in §§62–64, and much of the remaining language in this passage is similar to what we find there. All four terms are used by Plato at *Tim.* 39e6–40a2 to describe the four genera of animals which correspond to the four regions of the cosmos (cf. Runia *PT* 227). Using his rhetorical talent, Philo now applies them to the human being. It is impossible to find corresponding single words in English.

through sight. Brief return to the theme already developed at considerable length in §§53–54, 78.

sight, the most directive of the senses. Sight gives leadership to the soul because it draws its attention to observed phenomena, either for good or for ill; cf. *Mos.* 2.211 (how one should *not* observe the Sabbath); *Spec.* 3.195.

Parallel exegesis

Philo does not expound a specific biblical text in this chapter, so there are no exact exegetical parallels. As was observed in the comments above on §140, however, the passage at *Virt.* 203–204 is a kind of summary of our passage, while §205 summarizes §§151–170.

Nachleben

The influence of this rather general Philonic passage does not appear to have been very great, but we can note the following texts.

(1) As I noted at *PEC* 173, a papyrus fragment of Origen, probably from his lost Genesis commentary, emphasizes the excellence of the first man,

both in body and in soul, but the reason he gives for the difference between him and us departs from Philo, namely that his descendants received the composition of their body not from God "but from the intercourse and passion and desire of a father and mother." This sounds almost gnostic in its negative attitude, but we might compare Philo's ambiguous attitude to sex in §152. In *Hom. Gen.* 1.13 Origen emphasizes only the excellence of the human being created in the image, not of his bodily component. In his *De opificio hominis* Gregory of Nyssa is less negative. The human body is well made, but primarily as instrument for the rational soul (§8.8). Both soul and body are excellently made so that human beings can exercise royalty (§4). But Gregory is not interested in the difference between the first man and humans now.

(2) In *Ep.* 45 (= 34 Faller) Ambrose freely adapts various passages from the final part of *Opif.* on the subject of paradise, on how human beings have fallen into sin and what lessons the story has for us now. From the present chapter he takes over the following themes:
(i) 45.11: the face as place of the senses, cf. §139;
(ii) 45.13: the first man lapsed so easily, even though he was made from virginal earth, cf. §§136–137;
(iii) 45.14: the image of the magnet developed at considerable length to show the decline of humanity, cf. §141;
(iv) 45.16: even more than the sage who has the world as his fatherland, the first man must have been an inhabitant of the world and a κοσμοπολίτης, cf. §142 (Ambrose includes the Greek term in his text).

In the final paragraph of *Ep.* 43 (= 29 Faller), §19, Ambrose freely adapts from §147 the theme that the human being, created last of all creation (cf. Ch. 14), can dwell in all the various elements. We note that in Ambrose's text he does not contemplate the heavenly bodies, but converses with the angels.

(3) Finally we briefly note some interesting convergences between our Philonic passage and a number of prayers preserved in the late 4th century Christian compilation *The Apostolic Constitutions,* which are thought to go back to the Hellenistic-Jewish synagogue. See esp. 7.34.6, 8.9.8, 8.12.35–40; Greek text in Metzger *SC* 336, English translation in Charlesworth *OTP* 2.679, 689, 692. Themes shared are the human being as κοσμοπολίτης; the body formed from the four elements; receiving an implanted law, and so on. Direct Philonic influence is less likely than a shared Hellenistic-Jewish background. But the date of these Prayers could be quite late; see the remarks of Fiensy at Charlesworth *OTP* 2.673.

Further reading: Radice *FM* 300–305; Levison 1988, 69–75; Runia *PT* 340–346 (on the various ethical themes).

Chapter Twenty
The giving of names (§§148–150)

Analysis/General comments

The next theme that Philo expounds is the imposition of names recorded in Gen 2:19–20. This involves a considerable jump in his handling of the biblical text, since the last verse cited was Gen 2:7 in §134. Indeed the whole of §§134–147 can be regarded as an extended exegesis of that verse. In the meantime in Gen 2:8–17 the biblical text has introduced the theme of paradise, which Philo chooses to postpone until after the creation of Eve in 2:21–25 (as he points out by implication in §153). In a rather dexterous move the theme of the naming of the animals is joined up with the previous passage by taking it as a further demonstration of the excellence of the first human being. It thus becomes the final illustration of Adam's splendour before the creation of woman and the beginning of his fall.

As noted in our comments on the previous chapter, §§148–150 follow on directly from §§136–147 and could be taken together with that passage as a single chapter. I have chosen to keep this section separate because it introduces a new lemma from the biblical text. The brief discussion is best analyzed in two main parts, each answering an exegetical question (compare the three questions at *QG* 1.20–22). The final sentence rounds off the entire account of human life as it was before the descent into wickedness and misfortune.

(1) Moses' ascription of the imposition of names to the first human being is excellent. But why was this a suitable task for that first man? Firstly, he needed to have the wisdom and insight to give the appropriate names. This he had received from God. Secondly, he possessed the authority as lord over the animals, and so it was fitting for him to call them by name (§148).

(2) But why does scripture state that God led the animals to the first man in order to see what names he would impose? This does not indicate a lack of knowledge on God's part. Rather, he had created humankind as a "self-mover," so this task was a test which gave him the opportunity to show what he was capable of. The first human being could do such a good job because his rational nature was still uncorrupted and the impressions he received were very exact. For this reason the names hit the mark exactly (§§149–150a).

(3) The first human being thus attained the very limit of human well-being (§150b).

THE GIVING OF NAMES 349

The origin of the words we use for things and of language in general was a much discussed topic in Greek philosophy from the sophists onwards. Though Philo can hardly avoid referring to the topic briefly, he declines to expatiate on it at length, as he does do in the parallel passages at *Leg.* 2.15 and *QG* 1.20. He takes over the idea from the Pythagorean and Platonist tradition that the imposition of names is the task of a wise person, but remains virtually silent on what this means for the status of words, e.g. whether they are natural or conventional, and so on (see the comments on §148). This is because he is fully focused on the theme of the spiritual and moral excellence of the first human being, as summarized in the final sentence of §150. Questions relating to the philosophy of language are set aside (in contrast to *Leg.* 2.15). For an excellent account of Philo's views on the origin of language see Winston 1991, 109–119; see also Dawson 1992, 84–90, but the connection he makes between Adamic and Mosaic language goes beyond the texts.

Detailed comments

(1) §148. ***Most excellently.*** Compare the similar expressions of Mosaic excellence at the beginning of exegeses in §§69 and 76.

the imposition of names. Philo's expression τὴν θέσιν τῶν ὀνομάτων betrays the fact that he knows it to be a standard philosophical theme. It goes back at least to Plato's famous dialogue on the status of names, the *Cratylus*, cf. 397c1, 401c10; taken over at Alcinous *Did.* 6.10; also Cicero *Tusc.* 1.62 qui primus omnibus rebus imposuit nomina; Proclus *Comm. Crat.* 16.2, ὁ τὰ ὀνόματα τοῖς πράγμασι θέμενος, etc. Origen *C. Cels.* 1.24 gives a useful doxographical overview of the ancient controversy on the status of names:

> ... a profound and obscure question is raised by this subject, that concerning the nature of names. The problem is whether, as Aristotle thinks, names were given by arbitrary determination; or, as the Stoics hold, by nature, the first utterances being imitations of the things described and becoming their names (in accordance with which they introduce certain etymological principles); or whether, as Epicurus teaches (his view not being the same as that held by the Stoics), names were given by nature, the first men having burst out with certain sounds descriptive of the objects (translation Chadwick).

Philo follows the position attributed by the Platonists to Plato on the basis of the *Cratylus*. Names are not natural (φύσει), as argued by the Stoics, but conventional (θέσει) in the sense that they are imposed by a wise person who has insight into the nature of things. As Alcinous *Did.* 6.10 states: "the best name-giver is he who signalizes through a name the nature of the thing." This Platonic theory does not necessarily imply that there is but a single original name-giver. In the present context Philo ascribes this achievement to the first human being. It is moreover strongly implied that he imposed all the names, not just those of the animals (this interpretation is explicitly defended at *QG* 1.22). At §127, however, such name-givers were referred to anonymously in the plural, which corresponds to the more usual view in Greek discussions (cf. also §133 and *Mos.* 2.130). Earlier in the treatise the naming of various parts of created reality as described in the Genesis account is frequently referred to: see §§12, 29, 36–37, 39, 57 and comments ad loc.

Early rabbinic texts speak of Adam's wisdom in being able to name all the animals (and also recognize his own name and that of God). Later texts add that he received prophetic powers. See references at Ginzberg 1909–38, 1.61, 5.83. For further Philonic texts on the origin and status of names (apart from those listed in the exegetical parallels below) see *Cher.* 56; *Agr.* 1–2 (Moses); *QG* 4.146 (Isaac).

That person was wise ... Philo has praised the excellence of the first human being's rational soul in a general way at §139, but now this intelligence is given a specific application.

a self-taught and self-instructed wisdom. The first human being is αὐτομαθής and αὐτοδίδακτος in the sense that he did not learn his wisdom from human teachers, but obtained it directly from God (who is compared to a teacher in §149). The same epithets are habitually used of Isaac, the symbol of *physis*, "natural" or innate wisdom and knowledge; cf. texts cited at PLCL 10.326.

through divine beneficence. On a surprisingly large number of occasions in this part of the work there is a discrepancy between the text transmitted by ms. M and the remainder of the mss. tradition. Cohn very often chooses for M because he judges the reading to be superior. Here I think he is mistaken. M reads χέρσι θείαις, "by divine hands," but this is only relevant for the body, not for the mind, which was inbreathed (cf. §139). The first human receives his innate wisdom through divine grace, χάρισι θείαις, not human learning. The reading of the majority of the mss. is to be preferred.

he was king ... Return to the theme of §§83–88 and repetition of various themes already outlined at some length there.

subordinate to himself but as ruler over all other creatures. Cf. the final words of §88. In both cases the vital term is ὕπαρχος, literally "subordinate ruler."

the race has become feeble. Recalling the theme of generic decline in §§141–142, 145. The adjective ἐξίτηλος is often used of the faded colours of paintings (cf. *Post.* 113) or of foodstuffs that have lost their flavour.

torch ... of rule and authority. The metaphor of the relay race in which a torch is passed on from hand to hand; often used elsewhere by Philo, esp. in the context of biological succession; cf. *Gig.* 25; *Ebr.* 212; *Her.* 37, 311; Harl PAPM 15.51; Harris 1976, 81–82.

(2) §149. *to the human being.* The text in Cohn reads "to Adam," which brings the paraphrase closer to the biblical text in Gen 2:19. But we have here another case where the editor has chosen for M against all the other mss. Since in the remainder of the treatise, and indeed in the entire Exposition of the Law, Philo never uses Adam's biblical name, it is not likely that he did so here (note that it is not part of a biblical quotation). As noted in the General comments on Ch. 19, for Philo the first man is more a type than a historical personage, and for this reason he does not receive a name (the same applies to the first woman, Eve, as well). In the creation account itself the first man is not called Adam until Gen 2:16, as Philo himself observes in *Leg.* 1.90.

not because he was in any doubt. To interpret God's move in terms of an uncertainty as to what was going to happen would be to commit the error of anthropomorphism. Unlike human beings God is omniscient. This aspect receives more attention in the *quaestio* at *QG* 1.21, on which see Exegetical parallels. (Tobin *CM* 37 speculatively sees the origin of the exegesis in "anti-anthropomorphic interpretations" of the Genesis account.) Note the very similar question at *QG* 1.55, in the answer to which Philo devotes some lines to the problem of anthropomorphic language about God. At *Det.* 57–60 he reflects on whether God can be said to ask a question (as occurs at Gen 4:9). The answer is that strictly speaking God cannot ask what he does not know, since he knows everything, but it is possible to put forward a question without asking or inquiring. The aim is "that the soul who will give the answers [in this case Cain] may be convicted by itself on the basis of its good or bad answers" (§59).

freedom of movement. Literally with a nature that is αὐτοκίνητος, i.e. self-moved. This is the only time that Philo uses this term, which in modern Greek has become the word for a car.

would have no share in wickedness. The same motif as at §§73–75. See the comments ad loc.

as a teacher tests a pupil. God is the teacher *par excellence*; cf. *Spec.* 1.41–42; *Mos.* 1.80, 2.190; *Sacr.* 7, 65, 79; *Plant.* 52; *Her.* 19; *Mut.* 216; *QG* 4.208, etc. The adaptation of the Greek *paideia* motif within the framework of the biblical tradition was to become the chief theme of Origen's theology; cf. the famous study of Koch 1932.

to demonstrate. Mangey's emendation from πρός τι (M) or προσέτι to πρὸς ἔνδειξιν is bold, but yields excellent Philonic Greek. Cohn was right to take it over. Philo often uses the expression, and it occurs in the parallel passage at *QG* 1.21 (Greek text PAPM 33.46).

would reveal ... the individual characteristics. Names are thus not arbitrary conventions, as Aristotle thought (see the comment on §148), but tell us something important about the thing or person in question. For this reason it is informative to inquire into the etymologies of words.

§150. *the rational nature ... was still uncorrupted.* Repetition of the theme of §140.

not a single weakness or disease or passion. I.e. before the events about to be described in §§151–170.

he took in wholly unblemished impressions. Philo takes over here the famous Stoic doctrine of the καταληπτικὴ φαντασία as criterion of truth. Certain impressions made by material objects on the mind are so clear that, if assented to, they give direct access to truth. See further L&S §40.

of things material and immaterial. The phrase τῶν σωμάτων καὶ πραγμάτων literally means "of bodies and things"; cf. Whitaker's translation (LCL) "bodies and objects." Philo very often uses the phrase, and two learned notes have been devoted to it: see Harl PAPM 15.330 and Winston and Dillon 1983, 298. According to Harl the expression intends to indicate "the whole of reality, material and immaterial." Winston and Dillon think a contrast is meant, which can take on different forms depending on the context. For our passage they think of a contrast between animate and inanimate objects. But the use of σώματα to indicate an "animate object" is not persuasive. In my translation I follow the interpretation of Harl.

their natures were pronounced and understood. One might have expected the two verbs λεχθῆναι and νοηθῆναι to be placed in reverse order, since logically insight (*noêsis*) into the nature of things precedes the expression in language (*logos*). But Philo wants to emphasize that in the case of the first human being both occurred at the same time.

(3) ***In this way.*** This sentence summarizes the entire section on the first human being, §§134–150. See also the comment on §170a.

the very limit of human well-being. The climactic term is *eudaimonia*, on which see the General comments in Ch. 19, and the detailed comment on §144. Its position here is very deliberate. It represents the summit of what can be achieved in human life. In §§151–152 the turn to *kakodaimonia* takes place, but in the final words of the treatise the aspiration to *eudaimonia* returns. See the comments on §172.

Parallel exegesis

Philo expounds the biblical lemma Gen 2:19–20 in both his other Commentaries: in the Allegorical Commentary at *Leg.* 2.14–18, and in the *Quaestiones* at *QG* 1.20–22. Comparison with the treatment in *Opif.* is instructive. In both other texts Philo dwells longer on the theory of names and refers explicitly to thinkers who are preoccupied with the question. Two of the three questions posed in *QG* are implicitly present in *Opif.* At *Leg.* 2.16–18 an ἠθικὸς λόγος (i.e. moral allegory) is given which involves greater philosophical complexity than would be suitable for *Opif.* (note esp. the linguistic analysis of what τί (what) can mean in Gen 2:19).

The only other passage in which direct exegesis of the text is given is at *Mut.* 63, in the context of a discussion of changed biblical names, where it suits Philo to point out that not God but the wise person assigned names.

Nachleben

The theme of the giving of the names is occasionally referred to in patristic texts (cf. Eusebius *Praep. Ev.* 11.6.8, who links Plato, Moses and Adam; Alexandre *CLG* 281), but the specific influence of Philo seems to be lacking. Unfortunately this part of Didymus' *Genesis Commentary* has been lost.

Further reading: Radice *FM* 305–306; Tobin *CM* 37–38; Winston 1991.

Chapter Twenty-one
Woman appears on the scene (§§151–152)

Analysis/General comments

Directly after the naming of the animals, the biblical text goes on to describe the creation of woman in Gen 2:21–25. But Philo pays practically no attention to this further creational act, referring to it only in a subordinate clause. Instead he imposes on the narrative his own structure, using the crucial terms *eudaimonia* (well-being) and *kakodaimonia* (misfortune). From here up to §170 he will record how humankind rejects the life of bliss, and dwells at some length on the moral lesson that the episode teaches.

The present chapter serves to introduce woman into the narrative and also to focus attention on the chief cause of human decline into misery. The line of thought follows three brief stages.
(a) An introductory passage on how humankind had to suffer misfortune and that the starting-point of this reversal for the first human being was woman (§151a).
(b) A brief summary of the first man's solitary life hitherto (§151b).
(c) An account of man's reaction to the creation of woman. He welcomes her and is welcomed in return. Their interaction leads to love and the desire for union. A further step is desire for physical pleasure, which alas is the fatal starting-point for rejection of the law and misery (§§151c–152).

The interpretation of this passage, though central to Philo's purpose in writing the entire treatise, is rather difficult. The blame can be put firmly at Philo's doorstep. The treatment is too short (as was the case in §§134–135), forcing the reader to resort to speculative interpretation.

(1) Why is the creation of woman reduced to a single subordinate clause? The fact, for example, that woman is created to be man's helper and companion is not mentioned at all. By way of contrast, in the *Quaestiones* 8 sections are devoted to the creation of woman. It cannot be the case that Philo is put off by the "mythical" aspect of the narrative (Adam's rib), for in the case of the snake this is accepted and explained (§§157–166). It seems as if Philo is disinclined to write the straightforward words "and then God created woman."

(2) The interpretation of the creation of woman as the turning point in the fortunes of humankind involves a drastic adaptation of the biblical narrative. The entire account of the idyllic life in

paradise has so far been set aside. As we shall see, the role of the trees and the nature of the first sin will be readjusted as well. A problem raised by Philo's reading is the status of man's life when he was still alone. Philo appears to imply that his life was better because it emulated God's unicity better (and we recall the positive interpretation of his solitary existence in §§143–144). The next step is to conclude that it would have been better if woman had not been brought into existence. But why then did God create woman? The obvious answer is that human beings are not like God, and that sexuality is required for the survival and perpetuation of the species. This answer can only be found in Philo's text through extrapolation.

(3) The statement that "woman becomes for him the starting-point of a blameworthy life" (§151) certainly does not sound very flattering for one half of the human race. This passage can rightly be regarded as a chief witness for Philo's negative attitude towards women. But the passage does have to be read carefully and exactly. Philo does not say that sexual desire is the beginning of all evil. Sexual desire is fine if directed towards procreation. But it can easily lead to the desire for physical pleasure, and that is what causes human downfall. Philo's views have often been not properly understood. We discuss scholarly interpretations of Philo's attitude to women, particularly in relation to this particular passage, in an Excursus at the end of the chapter.

(4) There can be no doubt that Philo's presentation of the creation of woman and its consequences for man is strongly influenced by Plato and especially his handling of the topic in the *Timaeus*. Similarities are the fact that woman appears on the scene after man and that her arrival means the beginning of love (ἔρως), which leads to the birth of children (*Tim.* 91a–d). Philo also alludes in §152 to Plato's playful theory on the origins of love put forward by the comic poet Aristophanes in the *Symposium*. But Philo's connection of *erôs* with physical pleasure and the descent into wickedness represents a severer view than we find in Plato. Indeed, when looked at in detail, Philo's attitude to sexuality bears little resemblance to that of Plato. See further our detailed comments on §152 and in the Excursus.

Detailed comments

(a) §151. ***nothing is stable.*** We can compare the world of flux so vividly described in the purple passage at *Ios.* 126–143, though there nothing is said about vicissitudes in the moral realm. The same is said of the soul at *Gig.* 28–29 on the basis of Gen 6:3:

> Therefore the divine spirit can remain in the soul for a time, but not abide there ... And why should we wonder at this? For of nothing else is there

> secure and firm possession, since human affairs incline in opposite directions and swing to both extremes as in a balance and are subject to continual change. But the greatest cause of lack of understanding is the flesh and kinship (οἰκείωσις) to the flesh ...

The generalizing tone of these statements is striking. Philo does not give the impression of regarding the descent into wickedness as a "fall from grace," i.e. a single event which might not have happened, but rather as a structural feature of the world of becoming.

had to enjoy. Though Philo is not noted for his humour, this might be light-hearted touch. One could better do without the enjoyment that leads to such a unmitigated disaster.

the starting-point. Compare the pronouncement of Ben Sirach 25:24: "From a woman comes the starting-point of sin (ἀρχὴ ἁμαρτίας), and because of her we all die." See further *Nachleben*. On the question of mortality see below on §152.

woman. The translation follows the Greek, in which the word is placed at the very end of the sentence for climactic effect. So far the female sex has been mentioned twice. At §76 we read that the female species was present in the genus, but had not yet taken individual shape (based on Gen 1:27). In §134 Philo stated that the "moulded human being," in contrast to the "human being after the image," is either a man or a woman. Now at last it is time for woman to appear on the scene.

(b) **he resembled God and the cosmos in his solitariness.** A remarkable formulation of the *homoiôsis* doctrine, on which see our comments on §144. In *PT* 342 I suggested that Philo has applied the relation of unicity that Plato draws between model and cosmos at *Tim.* 30c–31b (note 31b1 κατὰ τὴν μόνωσιν, the same words as here) to the relation between God, the cosmos, and the first human being. But the comparison goes deeper. Solitariness also represents an ethical, or perhaps even a mystical, ideal. We may compare Abraham's emigration to the desert (*Abr.* 87):

> He alone ... thought that the most pleasant life was one without association with the multitude. And this is quite natural, for those who seek and yearn for God love the solitude (μόνωσις) that is dear to him, and in this way hasten first of all to become like his blessed and fortunate nature.

See further texts at Völker 1938, 326 and Merki 1952, 40–41. One might even compare the famous mystical formula taken over by Plotinus from Numenius, with which the *Enneads* end: φυγὴ μόνου πρὸς μόνον (flight of alone to the alone, *Enn.* 6.9.11.51). Van den Hoek 2000b, 65–66, goes even further and suspects that one of Philo's prime speculative concerns is hovering in the background here, namely the concept of unity and diversity, inspired by Platonic thought. Cf. also *QG* 1.15 on Gen 2:16; *Somn.* 2.70–72; and our comments on §154. But there is an essential difference between an ethical/mystical and a cosmological/anthropological perspective. Does Philo really mean to say that it would have been better had woman not been created? As noted in the General comments above, it seems likely to me that Philo is blending the two perspectives somewhat here. Despite his musings, somewhat reminiscent of a crusty old bachelor, he is realistic enough to accept that sexuality is an intrinsic part of human nature. In its brief account of the creation of Adam, Wis 10:1 stresses that he was "created alone"; cf. Winston 1979, 213, who gives rabbinic parallels.

the delineations of both natures. The term is χαρακτῆρες, already used earlier at §§6, 18, 69. It is not entirely clear if Philo here only refers to the matter of unicity, or that the markings have a broader connotation. The use of the plural and the following remark suggests the latter.

but as many as a mortal constitution could contain. A variation of a characteristic Philonic formula indicating the limitations of human nature, above all in the area of knowledge. Cf. esp. *Spec.* 1.43–44, cited above on §21; *Abr.* 203; *Praem.* 39; *Her.* 33; *Mut.* 15.

(c) *But when woman too was moulded.* As noted above in the General comments, Philo skips the details of the creation of woman from Adam's rib. The verb ἐπλάσθη (cf. §153 διαπλασθείσης), not used in Gen 2:21-25, has the effect of relating the creation of woman to the fundamental anthropological text of Gen 2:7.

he observed a sisterly form ... Cf. on this text Winston 1998, 56: "Philo's description of Adam's initial counter with Eve is clearly idyllic and touchingly romantic. It highlights the feelings of love and fellowship and the couple's hope of future offspring." We note too that the emphasis is above all on bodily or physical appearance. This is illustrative of the fact that for Philo the differences between male and female relate primarily to the body, but in two different ways: (1) the patent physical and biological differences between the two sexes; (2) the fact (as he sees it) that the female nature (i.e. primarily her soul) is more affected by bodily and physical matters than the male. The second difference is the foundation for the allegory of man as mind and woman as sense-perception.

§152. *modestly responded to his greeting.* The adverb translates the expression μετ' αἰδοῦς. As Sly (1990, 205–206) notes, Philo habitually applies the term αἰδώς (modesty or self-respect, but not in this context shame) to female behaviour of which he approves (cf. *Spec.* 3.25, 176; *Contempl.* 33, etc.; the opposite at *Spec.* 3.51). She further argues that the addition is gratuitous and that Philo is implying here that woman greets man as her master. She thus suggests a translation "appropriately" or "as a woman ought" (cf. also Van den Hoek 2000b, 72, who detects here "priggish overtones"). I would suggest that Philo is importing into the scene what he regards as ideal womanly behaviour, and this involves an appropriately modest response to the man's overture.

The love that ensues. The term here is ἔρως, erotic love. It supervenes as result of physical proximity and attraction.

the two separate halves of a single living being. A rather obvious allusion to Plato's celebrated account of the origins of physical love at *Symp.* 189–193. Originally there were three kinds of human beings: males, females and hermaphrodites, each round in shape with two heads, four arms and four legs. When their behaviour became too bold, Zeus split them into two halves, and since then they are continually trying to find the half from which they were separated (the theory accounts for both heterosexual and homosexual behaviour, but Philo is not interested in the latter). The god who can help bring this about is Eros, and he should not be withstood. Verbal allusions are: ἔρως ... συναγωγῶν, cf. 191d1–2 (and also *Tim.* 91d1); τμήματα, cf. 191d6, e3, 6. For Philo the allusion is an attractive way of expressing the powerful attraction that love brings about. In a different context, however, at *Contempl.* 63, he is scathing about "mythical fictions concerning double-bodied persons who originally attached to each other by unifying forces," and states that the disciples of Moses have nothing but contempt for such presentations.

in order to produce a being similar to themselves. Here Philo departs from the *Symposium* account, which for obvious reasons does not emphasize the aspect of reproduction, but comes closer to the *Timaeus* (cf. esp. 91d).

This desire also gave rise to bodily pleasure. So far Philo has given a wholly positive account of the relation between the sexes. This is in full agreement with his views on sexual relations elsewhere. As Baer (1970, 94–95) and Gaca (1996) have shown, Philo consistently defends the view that sexual relations should only be undertaken within marriage for the purpose of procreation. Gaca argues that this view has a Pythagorean background and is imposed by Philo on the text of the Pentateuch, which is less strict. Philo's views are probably stricter than those of Plato. Though Plato personally appears to have been in favour of sublimating sexual desire (in so-called Platonic love), in his *Laws* he allows unrestricted sexual relations within marriage (841d-e; cf. Winston 1998, 58). Of course we do not know what Philo's more personal attitude was, since we do not even know whether he was married. Philo's views are certainly stricter than those of the rabbis, who prescribe that the husband should respect his wife's sexual desires; cf. Winston 1998, 59. Since, therefore, the first man and woman are to be regarded as husband and wife, Philo is happy to grant them love and desire for sexual relations leading to the birth of children. The problem is that this desire (πόθος) can easily be perverted into desire for pleasure, i.e. sexual gratification. That, for Philo, is the starting-point of wickedness and a life of misery. He thus agrees with Augustine that desire (and not violence) is the root of all evil. In the present protological context, he reduces such desire to desire for sexual gratification. A broader discussion of desire is given in the context of the tenth commandment at *Spec.* 4.78–132. For further analysis, including a discussion of scholarly views on this passage, see the Excursus below.

life of immortality. Influenced as we all are by the Pauline and Augustinian reading of the Creation story, it is easy to misread the passage and conclude that humankind falls from grace and receives mortality as punishment. Philo, however, explicitly links up mortality with pleasure, and not with sexual relations as such. If human beings are immortal in both soul and body, there is no need for reproduction. But Philo assumes that there were sexual relations before the descent into wickedness. So he must take immortality here in a more restricted sense, i.e. a spiritual condition. Compare, for example the final words of book I of *De specialibus legibus*:

> We the ... disciples of Moses ... consider knowledge of God to be the goal of well-being (τέλος εὐδαιμονίας) and also age-long life, just as the Law too says that all those that cleave unto God live (cf. Deut 4:4), laying down a doctrine that is necessary and philosophical, for truly those who are godless in their souls die, whereas those who have taken up their rank in the service of the true God live an age-long life (345).

This theme returns at §156; see also *Leg.* 1.105–108 (on the punishment threatened in Gen 2:17) and the extended analysis of the entire theme of the life and death of the soul in Zeller 1995. Kugel *TB* 127 notes a similar ambiguity in Ben Sirach at 17:1-2 and 25:24: Adam receives mortality as a punishment, even though he had always been intended for mortality.

they exchange ... A very similar formulation in the "summary" of Genesis 2-3 at *Virt.* 205, but only (note well!) applied to the man: because he chose evil instead of good, "it was quite reasonable that he exchanged an immortal life for a mortal life and, forfeiting his blessed and fortunate state, quickly converted to an arduous and unfortunate (κακοδαίμονα) existence."

well-being ... misfortune. As noted in our General comments at the beginning of the chapter, the concepts of εὐδαιμονία and κακοδαιμονία — wholly foreign to the Bible — are used by Philo to impose his own structure on the biblical narrative. The opposition returns at §156. Exactly the same interpretation of the paradise story is given in these terms at *Leg.* 3.52 (cf. also *Plant.* 37).

EXCURSUS
Philo's attitude towards women and sexuality

In recent years a lot of scholarly attention has been focused on Philo's attitude to women and sexuality. There can be no doubt that his writings contain a considerable number of passages in which the male is placed higher than the female and the female is the object of pejorative or disparaging remarks. These texts are collected and thoroughly analysed by Baer in a pioneering study, 1970. One of the monograph's great virtues is that these pronouncements are carefully linked with Philo's exegetical and allegorical concerns. For a collection of negative remarks see esp. 40–44. But what do they mean for Philo's attitude to women?

Some scholars have gone all the way and accused Philo not only of misogyny, but also of being the origin of systematic misogyny in the Western tradition. Two outspoken champions of this view have been Gilaberti Barberà 1990 and Boyarin 1993, 77–83. Both emphasize the influence of Platonism. Boyarin distinguishes sharply between Hellenistic Judaism, influenced by dualist, spiritualist and anti-corporeal ways of thinking (77 n.1), and later rabbinic Judaism, which represents a strong reaction against that kind of thinking and rejoices in sexuality within the confines of marriage (on this antithesis see further our remarks below on *Nachleben*). A similar interpretation is given by Wegner 1991. She does note, however, that Philo assigns woman a positive role in procreation, and so suggests (50–51) that "Philo's true attitude to women was one of ambivalence — perhaps even cognitive dissonance — rather than the misogyny that seems to inform most of his theoretical statements about the female."

In her important monograph on Philo's perception of women, 1990, Dorothy Sly attempts to go beyond the research of Baer and determine what Philo's attitude to women was, not as a category of thought but as real human beings of flesh and (menstrual) blood. This involves searching Philo's writings for answers to questions which she is convinced that he himself never asked (219). For Sly Philo is not a misogynist (cf. 58). The crucial element in his attitude to women is control. Lust is seen as a feature of womanhood, whereas sexual control is man's responsibility. In this context Sly discusses our passage (109):

> There is little doubt that ... Philo sees the "fall" as sexual ... In *Op.* 152 he states explicitly that sexual desire is the cause: when Adam and Eve see one another, *eros* intervenes, sets up desire, and begets "bodily pleasure, that pleasure for the sake of which men bring on themselves the life of mortality and wretchedness in lieu of that of immortality and bliss." Several other passages imply that it was sexual desire that caused Adam's sin ... There is no doubt then that uncontrolled womanhood is the occasion for the first sin of man.

A comparison of Sly's paraphrase and quote with the original reveals that she has somewhat tendentiously coalesced the text in such a way that Philo's implicit distinction between legitimate desire (for sex in order to procreate) and illegitimate desire (for pleasure) is obscured. For Philo only the latter has pernicious results. (I myself made exactly the same mistake at *PT* 346 when I spoke of "Philo's extreme view in §152 that sexual desire is the ἀδικημάτων καὶ παρανοημάτων ἀρχή which converts man's life from immortality and bliss to mortality and misery.") Furthermore, in the context of her book and its explicit distinction between man's and woman's role in sex, it was unwise for Sly to take over the LCL translation "men bring on themselves," since the third person verb clearly refers to the first man and the first woman. They descended into misery together.

By far the most nuanced discussion of our passage from the viewpoint of Philo's attitude to women and sexuality is found in a recent article of David Winston on Philo and rabbis on sex and the body, 1998, written in response to Boyarin's study. Winston's disputes the view that the fall of humankind is inherent in the creation of woman. He notes (56) that "it is explicitly stated that it was not their tender desire for one another in itself, but rather the bodily pleasure which it naturally begot, that became the source of potential wrongs and lawless deeds." Winston also argues against the viewpoint that woman has for Philo a secondary ontological status because he has been influenced by the Platonic presentation of woman being created later than man (i.e. in the *Timaeus*). The narrative in Genesis has mythical status. But why does Philo introduce a comparison between man's idealized existence before the creation of woman and his compromised life thereafter? Winston finds this a difficult question and suggests (57) that "Philo is doing his best to give the story of Adam's fall some sort of non-allegorical meaning" and so "sees in it an expression of the limited intellectual scope that God has in his mysterious wisdom imposed on the human creature." Although Winston regards it as undeniable that Philo is strongly androcentric and that misogynist sentiments underlie some of his statements on women, he nevertheless thinks it would be a mistake to see his views and those of the rabbis as radically divergent. Both share a fundamentally positive attitude to the sexual act. Where they disagree is chiefly in the matter of sex divorced from procreation, but even there the rabbis' views are not without some ambiguity. It is a gross over-simplification to conclude that Philo, Hellenistic Judaism and Christianity are fatally tainted with Platonic views on body-soul dualism, whereas rabbinic Judaism develops biblical views entirely unaffected by Greek philosophy (cf. 59).

Parallel exegesis

Gen 2:21–25 are extensively interpreted in *Leg.* 2.19–70 and *QG* 1.24–30. The former passage is confined to allegorical exposition. The latter contains a good deal of literal exegesis, but with virtually no thematic correspondence with *Opif.* The reason for this is clear. In *Opif.* 151–152 Philo scarcely touches on woman's creation and in fact anticipates later developments. The exegesis in *QG* adheres much closer to the biblical text. Other brief references are found at *Cher.* 60; *Post.* 33; *Her.* 257.

Nachleben

Boyarin (1993, 81), commenting on *Opif.* 151–152, argues that "Philo had an overwhelming effect on the formation of early Christian thought. It is in Hellenized Judaism such as Philo's that the origins of Europe's Eve are to be found." See also Baudry 1996, who regards the text of Sirach 25:24 as the starting-point of the tradition. As Kugel *TB* 100–102 notes, many Jewish texts too "blame it on the woman." Not all of these are influenced by Greek thought. Through 1 Tim. 2: 13–14 this view was taken up in the Christian tradition and became authoritative.

I have not found any examples of the direct influence of Philo's amalgam of specific themes here, i.e. sexual desire, pleasure, the end of the good life and the beginning of misery and wretchedness.

Further reading: Radice *FM* 306–307; Baer 1970, 36–37; Winston 1998, 56–57; Kugel *TB* 100–102.

Chapter Twenty-two
Events in the garden of delights and their interpretation
(§§153–156)

Analysis/General comments

In order to explain humankind's fall from grace and descent into death and mortality Philo has to return to the section of the creation account which he has so far passed over, the story of the installation of the first human beings in paradise. He makes this quite clear by paraphrasing Gen 2:8 in §153 and relating it to the subsequent formation of woman which he has already described in §151. The passage up to §154 thus covers Gen 2:8–17 (albeit very selectively). But in §155 Philo already looks forward to the fall from grace of the first humans in paradise, and the explanation of what happens in §156 is based — again very selectively — on Gen 3:1–7.

The passage has a narrative structure (there are no specific exegetical questions) and can be divided into three parts.

(1a) The garden of delights planted by God cannot be compared to gardens in our own experience, because the trees planted in it are quite different to trees in the botanical world. They are plants with soul and mind, bearing fruit in the form of virtues (§153).

(1b) A symbolic interpretation of this garden must be given. The garden of delights itself represents the ruling part of the soul, while the two chief trees represent reverence for God and intermediate practical wisdom (§154).

(2) Having planted the garden, i.e. established these trees as boundaries or markers in the soul, God watched to see which way it would incline. When he saw that it disregarded the claims of piety and inclined to criminality, he expelled it from the garden with no hope of return (§155).

(3) But the reason for these events still has to be outlined, and this involves the story of the snake, who seduces the woman into eating the highly attractive fruit and sharing it with her husband. This deed converted them from innocence to deviousness, for they chose mortality and misfortune instead of excellence and well-being. God was displeased and fixed appropriate punishments. These will be outlined in §§167–170a, after the deeper meaning of the incident with the snake has been explained in Ch. 23 (§156).

As will have become clear in the analysis just given, in this passage Philo combines somewhat indecisively narrative and allegorical interpretation. He begins by mentioning the man and the woman, then relates the story of the creation of the garden. This has to be understood symbolically. In explaining what it means in §155, he speaks of the soul only, and it is the soul which receives punishment in the form of expulsion. But when he continues with the story of the snake, the woman and the man return and it is they who are punished. Then in the following chapter the allegory of soul returns in full force. This vacillation justifies the conclusion which we reached earlier (see Ch. 19) that, in spite of Philo's claim that he is recounting the beginning of the cosmos, the first human and his wife tends to be presented more as types than as real persons.

It is moreover clear that Philo is not interested in giving a full and detailed account of the events in paradise. He only picks out those details that he needs to explain the fundamental choice of the way of life that the first human beings confronted. The references to the biblical account are scanty and often insufficiently clear. For example, it is not explicitly stated that the first humans are exhorted to eat from the one tree (the tree of Life) as well as all the others in the garden, but are prohibited from eating from the other one (the tree of the Knowledge of good and evil). Nevertheless the description only makes sense if the choice between well-being and misfortune, life and death, is coupled with the choice between the two trees. The virtue of θεοσέβεια (reverence for God) is opposed to φρόνησις μέση (intermediate practical insight). But what exactly does this opposition mean? Philo does not explain it very clearly. Indeed one keeps on getting the impression that he is dependent on an anterior exegetical tradition (also partly preserved in the Allegorical Commentary), which he does not feel he has to expound at any length. *Theosebeia* means being directed towards God and contemplation of the cosmos which he made, i.e. the life led by the solitary first human being before woman appeared on the scene (§151). Intermediate *phronêsis* is linked with knowledge of good and evil. It means that one turns one's hand to every kind of activity, with the risk that in the world of practical action one may choose for evil rather than good. And this is in fact what happens. See the detailed comments on §155. This distinction finds its chief philosophical inspiration in a distinction between wisdom and practical insight found in some Peripatetic and Platonist authors, but is overlaid with central themes from Jewish thought. The difficulty noted in the previous chapter remains: is the reversal of human fortune something which unfortunately happened in the beginning, or is it simply part and parcel of human existence? In spite of the protological context of the account, the latter seems nearer to what Philo intends.

In my interpretation of this passage I have been greatly aided by the lengthy and very impressive article of Marguerite Harl on Philo's interpretation of the two trees of paradise (1962), which has received less scholarly attention (apart from French scholars) than it deserves. It should be noted, however, that the events in paradise are far more extensively discussed in the Allegorical Commentary (esp. in *Leg.* I–II and *Plant.*) and in the *Quaestiones*; see further Exegetical parallels below. Harl naturally bases her interpretation on all available texts. Our task differs. We must base our interpretation primarily on what is stated in the text being commented on. I also believe that Harl, under the twin influence of Völker and Festugière, somewhat overestimates the influence of Jewish piety and correspondingly underestimates the influence of Greek philosophy in her reading of the passage. Further discussion of relevant anterior exegetical traditions is found in Tobin *CM* 143–145; Goulet 1987, 106–113.

Detailed comments

(1a) §153. *his solitary life*. As explained in §151. The term μονήρης recalls the solitary cells (μοναστήρια) of the Therapeutae (*Contempl.* 25, 30), which encouraged Eusebius to interpret them as proto-Christian monks. They did, however, have a restricted communal life, for example in the Pentecost banquet (§§40–82).

it is related. On the phrase λόγος ἔχει see above §100. Here it concerns a biblical account, so that a sceptical attitude cannot be meant. But the account does require proper interpretation, as explained in §154.

a garden of delights. The biblical term παράδεισος is often translated pleasure-garden, but in the light of §§157–166 this rendering is best avoided. The word is originally Persian. It was first used by Xenophon in his descriptions of Persia, and passes into *koine* Greek; cf. LSJ s. v., BAGD 614.

which bears no resemblance ... Almost exactly the same phrase is used when introducing the garden at *Plant.* 36 cited below.

For these have timber ... Compare the earlier no less florid description of the botanical world at §§40–42. In §40 we find the same division into domesticated and wild trees. See the comment there on ὕλη meaning "timber."

luxurious living. Philo is often very critical of luxury, e.g. a few lines later in §158, but here the description is neutral.

possess soul and reason. Whether plants in fact possessed soul was a matter of dispute in Greek philosophy. Plato *Tim.* 77b affirmed that they do, but in the Stoic scheme presented by Philo at *Deus* 35–40 they are assigned φύσις rather than ψυχή (see the comment on §62; cf. also *Anim.*

78, 94 and Terian's notes ad loc.). Philo of course here means soul in the sense of a moral agent possessing *aretai*, excellences or virtues.

bearing fruit in the form of the virtues ... Although at first sight it seems that Philo is speaking in general terms, I agree with Harl (1962, 334) that his description should be related first to the garden as a whole (i.e. the *aretai*) and then to the two specific trees of Gen 2:9.

neutral understanding and keenness of mind. The two excellences are σύνεσις and ἀγχίνοια. The adjective describing the former is unclear in the mss.: some record ἀδιάφθορος (uncorrupted), others ἀδιάφορος (indifferent, neutral). Clearly the latter is the *lectio difficilior*, and thus to be preferred if other arguments for preference are about equal. I agree with Harl (1962, 339) that the latter should be adopted. Both virtues clearly relate to the tree of Knowledge of good and evil, as the allusion to Gen 2:9 makes clear. See also on intermediate *phronêsis* in §154. In §154 Philo again calls the second tree "of *sunesis*," though there is no textual warrant for this in the LXX. It is not only a handy abbreviated form of reference, but also replaces the very awkward phrase in the LXX text (on which see the comments on §154).

what is good and what is evil. τὰ καλὰ καὶ τὰ αἰσχρά, corresponding to the καλόν and πονηρόν in Gen 2:9. Literally one might translate "what is noble and what is disgraceful," but we opt for the more usual rendering.

life without disease and indestructibility. This is a clear reference to the tree of life. The parallel passage at *Plant.* 36 is fuller, and should be cited at some length:

> We must therefore turn to the method of allegory dear to men of (spiritual) vision. Indeed the oracles offer us in the clearest way starting-points (ἀφορμαί) for its application. For they tell us that in the garden of delights there were trees which bear no resemblance to those in our experience, but are trees of Life (ζωή), of Immortality (ἀθανασία), of Knowledge (εἴδησις), of Comprehension (κατάληψις), of Understanding (σύνεσις), of Conception (φαντασία) of good and evil. These would not be plants in earthly soil, but are necessarily plants of the rational soul (λογικὴ ψυχή), namely its path to virtue with as goal life and immortality, whereas its path to wickedness is flight from these and death. Therefore we should understand that God in his graciousness plants in the soul as it were a paradise of virtues and the actions carried out in accordance with them, a garden which leads the soul to perfect well-being (εὐδαιμονία).

This passage gives essentially the same interpretation as in *Opif.*

(1b) §154. **These themes ... are philosophized.** Philo now turns to an interpretation of what the garden means. I have translated "philosophize" here rather literally so as to preserve Philo's rather characteristic use of the verb, denoting not philosophy in the more technical sense, but a presentation in terms of the deeper (allegorical) meaning of scripture, in which of course use is made of technical philosophical concepts. The "philosophizing" is done in the first instance by Moses, and then by his disciples as interpreters; cf. *Decal.* 121; *Conf.* 1; *Her.* 257; *Fug.* 68, 77, 120, etc. See also on §128.

symbolically rather than in the proper sense of the words. The antithesis between συμβολικῶς and κυρίως is also found at *Spec.* 1.205 and *Her.* 296. κυρίως here is a synonym of the more common ῥητῶς. "Proper" thus means in the literal sense of the words, where a tree is simply a plant. By "symbolically" is meant that a particular term with an "ordinary" meaning in fact stands for something else with a deeper meaning (50 examples of the adverb in Philo, also used at §164). Originally a *symbolon* was a token or a sign of an agreement, e.g. two halves of a knuckle-bone or a sherd (Plato uses it at *Symp.* 191d of the two halves of the original double human being; see on §152). From here the usage was transferred to mystery cults and in time became a standard term in allegorical interpretation. See further S. Meier-Oeser in *HWPh* 10 (1998), 710. On "symbol" in Philo see also Conley 1987, 62–63.

have ever appeared on earth ... he hints at. Very interesting light is shed on this text by the parallel passage in *Plant.* 36, which we cited above in the comments on §153. The fact that in the garden trees are found that bear no resemblance to our own experience is taken to provide an ἀφορμή (starting-point, pretext) for the application of the allegorical method. The same thought is expressed by the verb αἰνίττεται (hints at) in the following line, which is used to describe the same process ("signifies" in the LCL translation is not strong enough). On these technical terms in allegorical theory see Pépin 1967, 161–167; the former term appears to be quite rare; it is not cited in this sense in LSJ.

Philo thus rejects a literal reading of this text, at least to the extent that it is taken to mean that there were really trees of the excellences planted in it. The interpreter is thus forced by its very strangeness to read it symbolically (the same will occur at §157). Pépin in the article just cited gives a full list of such passages. They are comparatively rare. Philo's usual view is that the biblical text should be read both literally and allegorically, but that the latter interpretation is more profound. This is his normal procedure, notably in the *Quaestiones*, which are entirely built upon the method of double exegesis.

the ruling part of the soul. The same interpretation is found at *Plant.* 37 cited above, where paradise is interpreted as "plants of the reasonable soul." Somewhat different are the interpretations in *Leg.* 1.43, "earthly virtue as copy of heavenly virtue;" *Conf.* 6, "garden of heavenly virtues;" *QG* 1.6, "wisdom or knowledge of the divine and human and their causes." The main difference is that δόξαι (opinions) in our text is far more neutral than "virtues" or "wisdom." Similarly in *Plant.* 37 the reasonable soul can follow the path leading to life or the path leading to death. The differences in interpretation of the garden and its trees reflects a diversity of Alexandrian exegetical traditions anterior to Philo, as can be clearly seen in *QG* 1.6–11. See also the General comments above.

tree of life ... reverence for God. At *Leg.* 1.59 the tree of life is generic virtue; at 3.52 wisdom; at *Migr.* 37 "goodness flanked by the particular excellences and the deeds done in accordance with them." At *QG* 1.10 a host of possible interpretations is given, including physical ones such as the earth and the sun (overview at Goulet 1987, 512). But Philo gives pride of place (i.e. the final view) to the same view that we find in our text. The formulation betrays that it is traditional (cf. Hay 1979–80, 43): "But worthy and excellent men say that the tree of life is the best of the virtues in man, namely piety, through which pre-eminently the mind becomes immortal." Marcus (PLCLSup 1.7) suggests a retranslation εὐσέβεια here, whereas our text reads θεοσέβεια. But there is virtually no difference between the two terms. In the next paragraph we read εὐσέβεια καὶ ὁσιότης, the same combination with which Philo ends the treatise at §172. At *Congr.* 130 *theosebeia* is called the "perfect good;" at *Fug.* 150 the "finest possession;" cf. also *Abr.* 114; *Spec.* 4.134; *Virt.* 186. *Eusebeia* is called the "highest and greatest of the excellences" at *Abr.* 60; cf. also *Decal.* 52; 119, *Spec.* 4.135; *Mut.* 76 etc. On its central role in Philo see Sterling (forthcoming). It is important to observe that for Philo reverence for God is not just a religious attitude, but also means a theoretical orientation towards God, as was made clear in §71 (cf. also §§151 and 172). Cleaving unto God means seeing and knowing God; cf. *Spec.* 1.345 cited in the comments on §152. As Harl (1962, 354) notes, *theosebeia* can be closely linked with *aretê*, *sophia* and *theôria* (cf. also Wolfson 1947, 2.213). It is this orientation that allowed the first human being to become like God, a state which he is now going to lose.

which makes known ... There is a textual difficulty here. Most mss. read γνωστικοῦ, but M has ὁριστικοῦ. In his first edition Cohn retained γνωστικοῦ, but in PCW he took over Wendland's suggestion γνωριστικοῦ, no doubt inspired by the use of the verb γνωρίζειν in §§153 and 156. The reading of the mss. is defensible if it is taken as based on the awkward phrase τὸ ξύλον τοῦ εἰδέναι γνωστὸν καλοῦ καὶ πονηροῦ in Gen. 2:9 (for translation see Introduction §4a). γνωστικός can have an active sense "for knowing;" cf. LSJ s.v. In *Leg.* 1.60 the biblical phrase is paraphrased with the verb γίνωσκειν. Harl 1962, 336 is tempted by ὁριστικοῦ, "capable of defining," but does not decide definitely in its favour.

intermediate practical insight. This term, φρόνησις μέση, is the key to the entire passage, but unfortunately Philo does not make very clear what he means by it. We start with the exegetical parallels. In *QG* 1.11 the second tree is "φρόνησις, the science of knowing, through which good and beautiful things and bad and ugly things are distinguished" (cf. also 2.87). In *Somn.* 2.70 it is the "twin tree" which, when touched by Adam, brings death because "he honours the dyad before the monad, that which has come into being before the maker" (cf. §7). It seems, then, that the second tree is primarily identified with φρόνησις. This virtue is not just equivalent to *sophia* — this would efface the difference between the two trees —, but is what allows one to determine and thus know what to do in the concrete situation involving action.

The background of these doctrines in Greek philosophy is rich and complex. As Lilla (1971, 72–74) has clearly shown, in the Platonic and

Aristotelian tradition which flow together into Middle Platonism there is a double track. On the one hand *phronêsis* is practically identified with *sophia* and related to both the theoretical and the practical sphere; this is found in Plato, Xenocrates, and is taken over by Alcinous at *Did.* 2.2 153.5–7 and Clement *Strom.* 6.154.4. Aristotle, however, distinguishes between the two, reserving *phronêsis* for the practical sphere, cf. *Nic. Eth.* 6.7, 1141a8–21; Arius Didymus at Stobaeus *Ecl.* 2.145.19–21. The distinction is taken over by Plutarch *Mor.* 443E–F (the entire passage, too long to quote, is illuminating as background for Philo's thought here). This is the view presupposed by Philo in our passage. An excellent parallel is found at *Praem.* 81 (exeg. Deut 30:11–14):

> If our words correspond with our decisions, and our deeds with our words, and these reciprocate each other, bound together by the indissoluble bonds of harmony, well-being (εὐδαιμονία) prevails, and this is wisdom (σοφία) devoid of all falsehood and practical insight (φρόνησις), the former for the service of God, the latter for the regulation of human life.

On *phronêsis* in Philo see further Völker 1938, 212 and Wolfson 1947, 2.212.

But why is *phronêsis* called "intermediate"? Clearly *not* because it is intermediate between two vices, as in the Aristotelian doctrine of virtue as the mean (against Arnaldez PAPM 1.245n.). It is in the first place intermediate because it gives insight into both what is good and evil, so that the practitioner of excellence can choose the better path. Harl (1962, 347–349 and 364) rightly points to the parallel exegesis at *Plant.* 45:

> It was to be expected there that God should place in paradise the intermediate intellect (τὸν μέσον νοῦν), which is exposed to forces drawing it in opposite directions and is moved to a discrimination between them, so that, impelled to choice or avoidance, if it welcomes the better, it gains immortality and fame, if it welcomes the worse, it discovers reprehensible death.

Phronêsis is thus not infallible; it is possible to make the wrong choice. This neutrality fits in well with the reading ἀδιάφορος which we adopted as description for σύνεσις in §153; see the comments above. We note too that "intermediate" comes close here to the "mixed nature" of humans in §§73–74. A similar interpretation is found in Theophilus *Ad Aut.* 2.24: "the human being had come into existence as a intermediate figure (μέσος), being neither wholly mortal nor completely immortal, but receptive of both conditions" (cf. also 2.27). See further the comments on πανουργία in §155.

(2) §155. *these boundaries in the soul.* Although Philo is far from clear on the point (partly because he fails to refer to Gen 2:17), these two boundaries must be identified with the two trees, and *not* with the good and the evil between which the soul has to discriminate. The tree of knowledge of good and evil is forbidden, we must conclude, because there is a risk. Practising intermediate *phronêsis* can lead to the wrong choice,

and thus to evil and death, the wrong branch of the "twin tree." But this development was inevitable, it seems (cf. the first words of §151).

it would incline. The metaphor of the balance, which is very common in Philo. Cf. *Her.* 46 (human life is mixed, oscillating between good and evil) and the comments of Harl PAPM 15.117.

cunning. As Harl (1962, 341) rightly points out, πανουργία is not quite the same as κακουργία (wickedness), though it does have a pejorative sense. It means that one is prepared to do anything and everything to achieve one's goals. I am at a loss to find a really good English equivalent. One might also consider "unscrupulousness" or "deviousness." It should be noted that the snake is called φρονιμώτατος in Gen 3:1. This could be linked to the μέση φρόνησις in §154, but Philo does not make this move. In *Leg.* 2.107 it is allegorically linked with pleasure, which is described as πανουργότατον because it is so cunning and inventive in finding arts and materials that pander to it.

having little regard. Cf. *Virt.* 205: "he spurned what was good and fine and true."

piety and holiness. See our comments above on §154.

he banished it. This is the only time Philo explicitly mentions the expulsion from the garden. In §§167–170 it is not included among the punishments, though it is implied by the fact that the lavish supply of goods is discontinued.

the reason for the deception. It is tempting to translate ἀπάτη with "mistake" or "error" (cf. Arnaldez PAPM 1.247), but the word does not carry that meaning. Philo, it seems, anticipates on his account in §156 (the related verb is used by Eve in Gen 3:12 when she says "the snake deceived me, and I ate").

not to be passed over in silence. A similar formula is found in §6, where it introduces a preliminary comment. Here it introduces the next stage of the exegesis. First the literal explanation is given (§156), followed by the rather lengthy allegorical explanation (§§157–166).

(3) §156. *could project a human voice.* Philo appears to accept the literal meaning, though it is rather ambiguously undercut at the beginning of §157; see the comments there. In *QG* 1.32 he defends it as a matter of course: "it is likely that in the beginning of the world's creation the other animals were not without a share in speech, but that man excelled in voice, being more clear and distinct" (translation Marcus, slightly modified)." Compare *Jubilees* 3.28 (and also Josephus *Ant.* 1.41): "On that day [of the expulsion] the mouth of all the beasts and cattle and birds ... was stopped from speaking because all of them used to speak with one another with one speech and one language."

highly attractive to behold. Loosely based on Gen 3:6. The LXX uses three adjectival phrases for the tree, Philo the same number to describe the fruit. They correspond, but not exactly, as the following table shows:

LXX	Philo
– good (καλόν) for eating	– highly attractive (πάγκαλον) to behold
– pleasing for the eyes to see	– most pleasant to taste
– beautiful (ὡραῖον) for knowing	– extremely advantageous for enabling one to discern what is good and what is evil

Philo's second phrase clearly anticipates the allegorical explanation in §§157–166.

Without further reflection ... The word ἀνεξετάστως is the same as used in the famous pronouncement of Socrates in *Apol.* 38a5 that "the unexamined life is not worth living for the human being."

an unstable and unsettled conviction. I.e. the mental state opposite to the stability of the (rational) mind that is fixed on God; cf. *Virt.* 216; *Praem.* 30; *Post.* 22–32; *Somn.* 2.221–229; *QG* 3.1; and the note of Alexandre at PAPM 16.241. Because the mind under the influence of pleasure is impulsive, it does not stop to examine its situation with the use of reason.

changed them ... The verb is μετέβαλεν, exactly the same form as in §8. But there the context was ontological and involved a change from worse to better. Here the context is ethical, and the change goes in the reverse direction. Cf. *Virt.* 205: "he effortlessly changed (ῥᾶστα μετέβαλεν) to a laborious and unfortunate life." As Harl (1962, 348 and PAPM 16.148) notes, verbs with *meta* indicating change are highly significant in Philo. Cf. for example μετάνοια (repentance) and μετανάστασις (migration elsewhere). According to Farandos 1976, 177, 202 the latter concept is the clue to Philo's entire thought!

from innocence and simplicity of character. Repeated below at §170. Harl (1962, 345) interprets this in terms of the innocence of a child, who as yet has no knowledge of good and evil (i.e. no original sin!), adducing the interpretation of Adam's and Eve's nudity in Gen 2:25 at *Leg.* 2.53 (cf. also *QG* 1.30). This is also the interpretation given by Theophilus in *Ad Aut.* 2.25, where it is remarkable to see that exactly the same combination of words ἐν ἁπλότητι καὶ ἀκακίᾳ is found. But at *Leg.* 2.54–64 Philo gives three interpretations of "nudity": (a) beyond passion, like Moses; (b) descent into foolishness, like the drunken Noah; (c) neutral, as yet not participating in virtue or wickedness. For Adam and Eve he opts for the third view (2.64). But in our text this is problematic, since the ideal is the state of the first human being as described in §§137–150, and that was hardly infantile. I think Philo means here genuine virtue and goodness, not naiveté. See also on §170a.

cunning. πανουργία again; see on §155.

The Father. A striking instance of Philo's use of this epithet for God. It is associated especially with the doctrine of providence, as made plain in §10. God is concerned with the cosmos and with the humans who live in it. But this doctrine for Philo is essentially double-edged, involving beneficence and grace, but also punishment if the divine commands are neglected or contravened. On the "dialectic of reward and punishment" in Philo see Mendelson 1997.

deserving to give rise to anger. But it should not be thought that God's anger is like a human passion, as Philo carefully explains in *Deus* 51–69. Such language is used deliberately by Moses for purposes of instruction and admonition (§52).

the fruits of an age-long life of well-being. This repeats the fundamental antithesis set out in §152. Additional is the contrast between enduring life and ephemeral temporality. This is probably under the influence once again of the allegorical interpretation we are about to hear. Pleasure indulges in the gratification of the moment without thinking of the long-term effect. But the antithesis may go deeper. The βίος (life) associated with well-being is structured, stable, possessing unity; temporality (χρόνος) associated with misfortune is a sequence of happenings, without stability or a unifying pattern. The term μακραίων (age-long) contains the word αἰών, which is particularly associated with the entirety of life; see *Spec.* 1.345 (cited in the comments on §152); Keizer 1999, 241–243.

Parallel exegesis

As noted in the General comments, the biblical text underlying the narrative in this passage is expounded at much greater length in both the Allegorical Commentary (*Leg.* 1.43–108; 2.71–108; the part of *Leg.* dealing with Gen 3:2–7 is missing) and in *QG* 1.6–16, 32–40. Other important passages that offer insight into the interpretation of the trees in paradise are *Plant.* 32–45, *Leg.* 3.52, 107; *Migr.* 37; *Somn.* 2.70; *QG* 2.12. We have made frequent reference to these texts in our comments above.

Nachleben

Direct usage is made of our passage by Ambrose *Ep.* 45 = 34.7–8, which is a summarizing paraphrase of §154. All four identifications are taken over: the garden with the ruling part of the soul filled with opinions; the tree of Life with piety; the tree of knowledge of good and evil with humankind's unique knowledge of good and evil (cf. also §74); and the other plants with the virtues (cf. also *De paradiso* 1.6–2.7, but the correspondences are less direct). *Ep.* 45.9 is based on §155: note the contrast between *astutia*, "cunning" = πανουργία, and *prudentia*, "wisdom" = φρόνησις, while *inclinaretur* recalls ῥέπουσαν. But the reference to God's omniscience linked up with Gen 2:16–17 is added by Ambrose.

Direct consultation may also be surmised behind Josephus' very compact description of paradise at *AJ* 1.37: note (a) the postponement of the description of paradise until after the creation of woman (also found in *Jubilees* 3); (b) the diversity of plants (cf. §153); (c) the identification of the second tree with *phronêsis* (§154), though the qualification "intermediate" is not used.

See further the exegetical traditions collected by Alexandre *CLM* 250–257. The significant parallels in Theophilus *Ad Aut.* 2.24–27 on human simplicity and the intermediate position between mortality and immortality have been cited in the comments on §§154–155. On this text see further Martín 1989, 43–47, who concludes that there is direct Philonic influence; but it is also possible that there is a common Jewish background, as suggested by Grant 1988, 157. A fine distant echo of Philo's exegesis, both in *Opif.* and *Leg.* is found in Augustine *Civ.* 13.21.

Further reading: Radice *FM* 307 (very little); Harl 1962, on which see General comments above; on relevant exegetical traditions Tobin *CM* 143–145 and Goulet 1987, 106–113.

Chapter Twenty-three
Interpretation of the snake (§§157–166)

Analysis/General comments

The tragic events in the garden described in Gen 3:1–8, briefly outlined in §156, need to be explained at a deeper level. The entire passage follows the method of allegorical exegesis. Philo does not return to the first man and woman (whether as real people or as character types) until §167. Analysis of the passage reveals that it corresponds to a succession of three exegetical *quaestiones*, which in fact are virtually identical to the questions posed and answered in *QG* 1.31–33.

(1a) Introductory: the contents of the narrative with the snake patently invite the reader to practise the allegorical method (§157a).

(1b) The first question implicitly posed is: what does the snake represent? Philo first presents a hypothesis and the grounds on which it is put forward: the snake is a symbol of pleasure, because of (i) its physical characteristics; (ii) its food; (iii) and the fact that it has poison in its teeth (§157b).

(1c) Proof of the hypothesis is now given by demonstrating that each of these grounds apply to the lover of pleasure (φιλήδονος). (i) Just like the snake, the lover of pleasure is weighed down and stays close to the ground. (ii) Like the snake, he feeds on earthly food, rejecting the heavenly food of wisdom. Gluttonously he indulges in wine and rich food, which leads to the stimulation of the appetite for food and drink, as well as rousing sexual lust. (iii) He carries poison in his teeth, because these are the servants of an insatiable appetite, the effect of which is deadly for a human being (§§158–159).

(2a) But why is the snake said to project a human voice? The hypothesis is put forward that pleasure has numerous human defenders who argue on its behalf (§160).

(2b) Proof of the hypothesis can be seen first in the argument that pleasure is an essential concomitant in the physical process by which births take place. And when the baby is born it shows an instinctive affinity for pleasure (the Epicurean doctrine of *oikeiôsis*) (§161).

(2c) A second argument is that all animals, but especially human beings, regard pleasure as their goal, not only in food and sex, but also in the delights of sight and sound (§§162–63).

(2d) Additional proof can be found in the symbolism of the insect called the "snake-fighter," which Moses allows to be eaten in his food laws. Unlike the snake, it jumps away from the earth. It symbolises self-control, which welcomes the simple austere life and is the exact opposite of pleasure (§§163–164).

(3a) Why, then, does pleasure first entice the woman, and through her, the man? This can be well understood if the hypothesis is accepted that man represents intellect and woman sense-perception, with pleasure working through the senses to deceive the mind (§165a).

(b) As proof we see that the senses are all seduced by what pleasure offers them. These gifts are presented to the mind and he immediately succumbs, with the result that he becomes enslaved. Another image that can be used is that of the prostitute who uses pimps to solicit a lover. As a quick foray into epistemology shows, the mind needs the senses for its information, and this is precisely what pleasure exploits (§§165b–166).

Although the role of allegory in the treatise as a whole is limited, we receive a partial compensation in this passage, which in fact amounts to a classic example of the allegorical method. The following features should be noted.
(a) As we saw earlier (§154), the allegorical method is not arbitrary, but is prompted by peculiarities of the text. Vocal snakes are odd, but not mythical. They invite the reader to interpret at a deeper level.
(b) The exegesis proceeds through questions posed at the text, whether explicit or implicit (note that the implicit question §160 is explicitly stated in §163). On the method of the *quaestio* see the comments on §72.
(c) The symbolism proposed also should not be arbitrary, but should be fitting (cf. "quite fittingly" in §157, "quite suitably and appropriately" in §165). This occurs through the explication of the *tertium comparationis*, i.e. the symbol A represents what it symbolizes, B, because of similarities C_1, C_2 etc. The method is very well illustrated by the three ways (C) in which a snake (A) resembles the lover of pleasure (B) in §§157–159.
(d) An allegory can also be expanded and given further proof by appealing to other texts. In the present passage Philo does this at §163, when he invokes the example of the "snake-fighter" from Leviticus 11:22. This procedure, in which exegesis of the primary text is illustrated and deepened by secondary exegesis, is the chief cause of the incredible complexity of the Allegorical Commentary, as may be seen §§163–164 is compared with *Leg.* 2.77–106 (the

method is scarcely used in the *Quaestiones*). See further my detailed analysis of this procedure in Runia 1984 and 1987, and also the remarks in Introduction §4(a).

There is, however, an important difference between the allegory of the snake as presented in §§157–159 and in §§165–166. In the former Philo concentrates not on an analysis of pleasure itself, but rather of the "pleasure-lover." In the latter he introduces the more complex allegory of Adam as intellect, Eve as sense-perception and the snake as pleasure. This allows for a more sophisticated analysis of the events in the garden. The end result, however, is not so very different, since the mind seduced by pleasure via the senses effectively becomes a "pleasure-lover," albeit a more passive version than the active pleasure-seeker in §§158–159.

Philo's handling of the theme of pleasure in this chapter is also very typical of his use of philosophical concepts in the exegetical process. As Le Boulluec has recently shown in an excellent analysis (1998), Philo's thoughts on the subject are complex, and not without a certain subtlety when read in the context of his exegesis. In the current passage we must distinguish between a number of different strands. It is plain that the basic attitude towards pleasure is negative. The snake is hardly a positive symbol, and the destructive effect of pleasure has already been made plain in §152. We recognize the popular platonizing theme of pleasure associated with the body, the earth, the passions of stomach and groin, and so on. It goes back to *Tim.* 69d1 ("pleasure, the greatest lure of evil") and other texts; cf. Runia *PT* 300. The rather verbose depictions of the "pleasure-lover" being attracted by all manner of delicacies recall the exhortatory language of the Stoic-Cynic diatribe; see the comments on §158. But the imagery of the prostitute in §166 recalls to mind the famous debate between pleasure as prostitute and virtue as modest maiden in *Sacr.* 21–33, which goes back to Prodicus as recorded by Xenophon and was greatly admired by the Stoics. The conception of ἡδονή as a passion (πάθος) in §§163 and 166 is Stoic, as is the explanation in epistemological terms at §166. The most surprising part of Philo's depiction of pleasure, however, is found in §§161–163, where he draws on the Epicurean doctrine of pleasure as instinctive to living beings and the goal for human life. As Carlos Lévy has shown in his recent analysis (2000, 127–130), Philo's summary gives valuable information on the theory which has been ignored by students of Epicureanism. We should note, however, that he is very careful to place the theory in the mouth of the advocates of pleasure, to whom he himself most definitely does not belong. Elsewhere he is prepared to admit that pleasure can play a neutral or even a positive role in human life (cf. *Leg.* 2.17), and there is also the theme of pleasure being raised to the higher level of joy (χαρά), which is no longer a πάθος (passion) but an εὐπάθεια (good feeling). There is no place, however, for such themes in *Opif.* In spite of the encomium of §§161–163, pleasure plays a negative role in the allegory of the events in the garden.

Philo's allegory of intellect, sensation and the passion of pleasure has become notorious, especially in feminist critiques of its ideology. Its emphasis on rationality shows him in his most Hellenic frame of mind. The interpretation is set out in much more detail in the *Legum allegoriae*, and an informative summary is found at *Agr.* 94–101. Jewish and early Christian interpretations of the snake as Satan or the devil (cf. Kugel *TB* 98–100, 121–125) are quite remote. Philo's allegory did, however, exert a limited influence on early Christian exegesis; see *Nachleben*.

Detailed comments

(1a) §157. **not the fabrications of myth.** As was already indicated in the first lines of the treatise (§1), Philo strongly dissociates scripture from myth. The former represents truth, the latter falsehood. Cf. esp. *Conf.* 2–15, where he polemicizes against those who compare the account of the Tower of Babel with myths found in Homer. The difficulty is that Philo sometimes tries to have it both ways. He also wants to take over the Greek practice of basing allegory on the unacceptability or strangeness of the literal meaning. Indeed he sometimes goes so far as to call a biblical presentation "mythical." This is said of the creation of woman at *Leg.* 2.19, and Philo goes close to saying it of the snake at *Agr.* 96: "Described in this way, these matters resemble apparitions and marvels, a serpent projecting a human voice and using sophistic arguments on a completely innocent character and deceiving a woman with seductive persuasion." On the other hand, he wants to claim absolute truth for scripture, also in the literal sense. See further the comments of Pépin 1967, 139–150 and Tobin *CM* 160–161. The latter scholar correctly points out that in the present passage Philo is careful not to identify any specific aspect of the story as mythical (161):

> Philo does not really want to reject the literal interpretation of the fall found in *Opif.* 151–152 ... At the same time he needs some reason, some "opportunity" (ἀφορμή) offered by the text, which would enable him to move to the allegorical level. So, instead of seizing on the notion of the talking serpent, he simply rejects in very general terms any literal interpretation of Gen 3:1 which would involve a "mythical fiction."

It must be said, however, that Philo is not fully consistent in his approach to myth. In other passages he affirms that myth can have a paedeutic purpose. See further the important articles of Kamesar (1997, 1998).

the race of poets and sophists rejoice. Two separate categories of Greek educators; cf. Winter 1999, 77. On Homer see the previous comment.

character types ... As Hanson (1959, 40) and Radice (*FM* 307) point out, in his brief description of allegory Philo uses three central technical terms: τύπος, "general character type or figure revealed and illustrated by the allegory"; ἀλληγορία, "saying one thing by means of another"; ὑπόνοια, "hidden underlying meaning discovered by the allegorist." On the final term see further Conley 1987, 63–64

(1b) *follow a reasonable conjecture.* The claim of reasonable and stochastic (i.e. not infallible) exegesis, was already made at §§46 and 72.

suitable. The allegorical exegesis has to "fit" or "suit," as will now be demonstrated. Cf. §165 "quite suitably and appropriately" and the General comments above.

legless creature. The theme of orientation to earth rather than heaven connected with the source of food is taken from *Tim.* 92a2–7 (ἄποδα in 92a7 recurs in Philo's ἄπουν). For Plato reptiles represent very stupid earthly reincarnated humans, which comes very close to being a moral allegory. For a full discussion with other parallels in Philo see Runia *PT* 349. Philo uses this theme to give a symbolic explanation of the food laws at *Spec.* 4.113: "By reptiles he hints at those who devote themselves to their stomachs. By the four-legged and many-footed he hints at those who are wicked slaves not of one passion, desire, but of them all ..."

clumps of earth as food. Philo's argument is plainly based on the biblical text at Gen 3:14. The conviction that snakes eat dust or earth as food appears to belong more to the biblical and Jewish tradition (cf. also Isa 65:25; Mic 7:17) than to Greek views. It is taken over by the church fathers; cf. Alexandre *CLM* 313.

(1c) §158. *the lover of pleasure.* φιλήδονος is a post-classical word which became popular about the time of Philo, e.g. Plutarch *Mor.* 6B. Philo uses it quite often in his allegorical treatises, but seldom in the Exposition of the Law (only elsewhere at *Ios.* 153; *Spec.* 3.113; 4.112). The hedonist is one who regards pleasure as the goal of life (cf. §162), in opposition to the moralist, who aims at excellence or virtue. Philo regards the latter as reconcilable with biblical thought, but not the former.

can he raise his head. Implicit here is the widespread *topos* of the difference between human beings with erect stature and animals who lower their heads to the ground; cf. Plato *Tim.* 90a, 91e; Cicero *Nat. d.* 2.140 and Pease's note ad loc.; Runia *PT* 324, 346. In other words, the lover of pleasure is a bestial type.

lack of self-control. See below on §164.

throws him forward and trips him up. In the translation I have retained the order of the verbs, though a reverse order seems to make more sense. Philo often expresses one idea through two verbs.

He does not feed on the heavenly food ... The principle is that there are two kinds of food: heavenly and spiritual, earthly and bodily. The orientation of the soul is revealed by the choice which it makes: would you rather listen to a lecture or sermon, or go to a fancy restaurant? Philo associates heavenly food above all with the manna of Exod 16:4; "behold I rain upon you bread out of heaven." See esp. *Leg.* 3.161–178 and the monograph of Borgen 1965.

wisdom. For the numerous Philonic texts which connect wisdom with nourishment and interpret it as heavenly food see Sandelin 1986, 89–90.

indulgence in wine ... Here begins the rather florid description of how the lover of pleasure flings himself at the offerings of food and drink. Many passages in Philo fulminate against indulgence in this area, no doubt based at least partly on his own experience in Alexandrian high society. Cf. *Ios.* 151–156; *Ebr.* 210–222; *Somn.* 2.48–51, 155–168 (on Pharaoh's baker and butler); *Agr.* 23–25; *Spec.* 1.174; 4.113; *Prob.* 31, 156; *Contempl.* 53–56, etc. These themes are plausibly connected by Wendland (1895, 18–24) to the Stoic-Cynic genre of the diatribe, found esp. in the writings of Musonius; cf. also Van Geytenbeek 1962, esp. 96–110.

love of delicacies and gluttony. I.e. qualitative and quantitative overindulgence in the area of food. The three categories, the "boozer," the epicure, and the glutton are stock sub-types of the ἀκόλαστος, the uncontrolled person. For philosophical discussions of the problem of the right attitude to food and drink see Seneca *Ep.* 18 and 83; Epictetus *Diatr.* 3.26.

enslaved. There are no good grounds for excising the participle ἀνδραποδίζουσαι found in all the mss. It adds the aspect of addiction. Cf. *Sacr.* 26.

ugly head. The adjective εἰδεχθής is elsewhere used by Philo mainly of prostitutes (*Leg.* 3.62; *Aet.* 58; *Prov.* 2.27), but also of the seven ugly cows in Pharaoh's dream (*Jos.* 101, 107). A sexual connotation is out of place here (it does occur in §166). But the heads of Breughelian gluttons are ugly enough. On the curiosity of the glutton see also *Contempl.* 53. But Philo may be thinking of the movement of the head of a snake.

§159. ***carries poison in his teeth.*** A more literal approach is found in *Agr.* 97, "longing to cause death by poisonous and painless (?) bites." The allegory explains why the bites cause death, but is rather forced.

deadly by nature. Cf. *Spec.* 4.100: "For gluttony begets indigestion, which is the starting-point and source of diseases and infirmities." Students of English history will recall the notorious death of bad King John caused by the excessive eating of peaches and beer.

(2a) §160. ***to project a human voice.*** Philo now moves to the second *quaestio* (made explicit in §163). Exactly the same words φωνὴν προΐεσθαι are found at §156; *Agr.* 96; cf. also *QG* 1.32.

pleasure makes use of countless defenders and champions. The hypothesis is that the snake's human voice (A) symbolizes pleasure's human advocates (B) because they both give eloquent expression to the importance of pleasure in human life (C). On the method of symbolism in allegory see the General Comments above. In the well-known allegory of those who are banished from the holy congregation in *Spec.* 1.327–345, we encounter "champions of the mind" and "champions of the senses." Being in favour of a human faculty or capacity can virtually become a religious (or idolatrous) attitude, because it conflicts with the loyalty towards God.

go so far as to teach ... The use of the verb τολμάω, often translated "dare," to express assertion can be fairly neutral, but in the present context it certainly has a negative ring. Philo reports the arguments in defence of pleasure without subscribing to them himself. As we shall see, both arguments have an Epicurean background.

the power of pleasure. This applies above all to the first argument in support of pleasure, namely its central role in reproduction, birth, and life from a baby's first breath onwards. In §162 a second consideration focusing on pleasure as goal is introduced.

(2b) §161. *The offspring naturally first feel an affinity*. The use of the term οἰκειοῦσθαι will have revealed to Philo's learned reader that he is making use of the famous Epicurean doctrine of *oikeiôsis*, not to be confused with the Stoic argument which uses the same concept (on which see §146). When a human being is born, it shows the natural inclination to seek out what is pleasant and avoid what is painful, because the former is "proper" or "appropriate" (οἰκεῖος) to him or her, while the latter is "alien" (ἀλλότριος). This is the so-called "cradle argument," used to prove that "pleasure" is the *telos*. It was hotly contested by the Stoa, who affirmed that the goal was ἀρετή. See further the detailed analysis of both arguments by Brunschwig 1986.

Parallels for the argument here are found at Sextus Empiricus, *Adv. Eth.* 96, *Pyr.* 3.194; Cicero *Fin.* 2.31 etc.; see Usener 1887, 274–275 (but he missed the Philonic passage). Lévy (2000, 127–130) argues that Philo supplies information missing in the other accounts, allowing us to take seriously Sextus' attribution to "Epicureans" rather than Epicurus himself. The detail about the baby reacting to the cold air is a response to Sceptic (or possibly Stoic) arguments in the Hellenistic discussion.

(2c) §162. *they say*. This introduces the following argument. Philo is careful to remind the reader that he is reproducing the arguments of others.

pleasure as its most necessary and essential goal. For pleasure as the Epicurean *telos*, cf. Diogenes Laertius 10.137; Cicero *Fin.* 2.7; Origen *Cels.* 3.80 etc. At *Nic. Eth.* 1.4, 1095b15 Aristotle regards the conception of pleasure as *telos* as a significant ethical option usually followed by ordinary people. Contrast *Leg.* 2.17, where pleasure is said to be necessary for life, but not more than that. It is the worthless person (ὁ φαῦλος) who treats it as the perfect good.

sights and sounds. A significant addition to the scope of pleasure, to be treated in more detail in §§165–166. All the senses are involved, including the higher ones, sight and hearing. Philo would not be in disagreement here. After all, in the encomium of sight in §54 sight is said to "instill unspeakable delight and pleasure in the soul." But pleasure is not the chief goal of contemplation.

ears and eyes. Again the order is reversed (cf. §158), but this time deliberately as a chiastic construction.

(2d) §163. ***passion.*** As noted above on §79, pleasure is one of the four standard Stoic πάθη (passions). For the Platonist Alcinous pleasure and pain are the primary passions, desire and fear are secondary because they are more complex; see *Did.* 32.2. Although Philo often refers to the theory of the four passions, it appears that for him pleasure and desire are more dangerous than fear and cowardice. In the present context pleasure is the passion *par excellence.* See also the comments on §152.

highly native and akin. οἰκειότατον καὶ συγγενέστατον, the same combination as in §147 (on human habitat). But the themes of *oikeiôsis* and *sungeneia* in §146 are in strong contrast to the assertion here.

in the detailed laws too. Philo divides the Laws of Moses into the generic laws, i.e. the Decalogue, and the detailed or partial laws, i.e. the rest of the code. The expression for the latter used here, οἱ κατὰ μέρος νόμοι, is also found at *Congr.* 120; *Spec.* 1.12. These laws are expounded in the four books of *De specialibus legibus*. According to Cohen 1995, 72–85, Philo and the later rabbis probably share a common midrashic tradition. Kugel *TB* 639–640 is more reticent on this point.

the animals which should be offered as food. I have translated the verb προσφέρεσθαι rather literally here, because I suspect that Philo intends a parallel with the offering of pleasure by the senses to the mind in §165 (the same verb, but in the active voice). A detailed exposition of the Mosaic food laws is given later in the Exposition of the Law, at *Spec.* 4.100–118 in the explanation of the special laws linked to the Tenth commandment. The purpose of these injunctions is in the first place to prevent gluttony and encourage self-control. But the distinction between the various animals also gives rise to various important symbolic meanings, as in the case of the "snake-fighter."

the animal named the snake-fighter. In order to reinforce his interpretation of the symbolism of the snake, Philo recalls its opposite, the "snake-fighter." This insect, the ὀφιομάχης, is listed among the edible animals in the food laws at Lev 11:22, where it belongs to the category "flying creeping things, which have legs above their feet." Some kind of locust or cricket seems to be meant, but Philo finds the triple combination of its unusual name, its propensity for leaping from the ground and the fact that it may be eaten eminently suitable for his symbolic allegory. It symbolizes ἐγκράτεια (self-control), for it fights against pleasure (i.e. the snake), leaps away from earthly things, and is thus pronounced edible by the lawgiver. The same exegesis is found at *Leg.* 1.105–108; cf. also *Her.* 239 (soaring on high to achieve immortality), *QG* 2.57 (the wider class of insects symbolizes the good emotional state of joy as against the passion of pleasure).

lack of self-control and pleasure. ἡδονή is here linked with ἀκρασία (often translated "incontinence," also used in §158), the state of mind examined in depth by Aristotle *Nic. Eth.* Book 7, in which one acts against one's better judgment, e.g. by smoking a cigarette in full awareness that it is bad for one's health.

Self-control especially welcomes simplicity ... Of Philo's numerous texts in praise of *enkrateia* we might single out *Contempl.* 34, where it is asserted that this excellence lays the foundation for the austere life of the Therapeutae. Very similar language at *Mos.* 2.185 (symbolism of the nut). See further Völker 1938, 130–135.

harsher than death. How pleasure, which seems so soft and attractive, can in fact be harsh is explained in §167. At *Leg.* 1.105–108, giving exegesis of Gen 2:17, Philo explains that there is a death of the soul which is different and worse than the natural death of the body, occurring when the soul is entombed in all manner of passion and wickedness. So we might interpret the expression here, which seems somewhat hyperbolic, as meaning that pleasure brings about a living death worse than physical death. See also the comments on §152.

(3a) §165. *Pleasure does not dare*. Philo now turns to the *quaestio* why the snake approaches the woman rather than the man. Cf. *QG* 1.33, which poses the same question. Given the imagery used by Philo, it seems best to treat pleasure as a feminine subject in the following sections. In order to understand the allegory that Philo is about to unfold, it is important to observe that the words used for mind by Philo, νοῦς and λογισμός, are masculine, while the words for perception (αἴσθησις) and pleasure (ἡδονή) — are feminine. As Mattila 1996, 114 rightly notes, however, the word for snake in Greek is masculine. Philo circumvents the problem by speaking of pleasure only.

quite suitably and appropriately. See above on §157.

for in us the intellect has the role of the man ... The famous allegorical scheme which dominates *Legum allegoriae*. The entire account of Gen 2–3 is interpreted in terms of this scheme. For a detailed analysis see Goulet 1987, 93–156, who tries to recover from it a pre-Philonic and purely philosophical allegorical tradition. It is quite well possible that Gen 1 was also interpreted in this way, but has been lost; cf. Goulet 136–139 and Tobin 2000. Since Baer's monograph (1970), there has been much discussion about whether this scheme is sexist. Certainly, in order to explain the scheme, Philo makes many comments (esp. in *QG*) which are uncomplimentary to women, for example at *QG* 1.33: "and woman is more accustomed to be deceived than man ... the judgment of woman is more feminine, and because of softness she easily gives way and is taken in by plausible falsehoods which resemble the truth." This allegory can be seen as illustrating the ideological association of masculinity and rationality that has permeated western culture, as Lloyd (1984) has analysed well. Moreover, through Philo's influence, the allegorical scheme passed into patristic thought; see *Nachleben*. In Philo's defence it may be pointed out that it is no more than a scheme. It does not divide humanity up into two groups, for as he states here explicitly, the allegory applies to us all (I see no reason to assume that Philo is writing for men only). "Male" and "female" represent a kind of psychological imagery that can help explain the workings of the soul. The schematic nature of the allegory is lost if one regards Eve as "the archetypal female," as Sly (1990, 109) does. For Philo Eve is the embodiment of archetypal female characteristics. For a sensitive exposition of Philo's "gender-based hierarchy" see Mattila 1996, who concludes (128) that the role of wisdom and nature (both feminine) show that even for Philo "the power of this ideological device had its limits."

(3b) *Each of the senses.* We recall the pleasure given by sights and sounds in §162. The sense of touch is not included because it does not work with a specific organ, and so does not work so well with the epistemological scheme set out in §166.

in the manner of female servants. Unwittingly the wife has been split up into and replaced by a group of servants!

they offer them. On the verb here see §163.

taking persuasion along as their advocate. Cf. the champions of pleasure in §§161–163.

He is immediately ensnared. The imagery of pleasure as a lure or snare is derived from Plato *Tim.* 69d1, and is very common in Philo. Cf. in the parallel passage *Agr.* 103: "for there is not a single thing that does not yield to the snare of pleasure, and is caught and dragged along in her highly complicated nets, from which it costs a lot of trouble to escape." See further Runia *PT* 300. The same image is also used in §166.

ruler ... subject, slave ... lord ... The rhetorical antithesis of opposites disjoined by the preposition ἀντί greatly beloved by Philo; cf. *Cher.* 75; *Sacr.* 88; *Post.* 145; *Plant.* 98; *Her.* 77; *Congr.* 93; *Flacc.* 37, etc.

§166. *like a shameless prostitute.* Pleasure is compared with a prostitute in the famous passage at *Sacr.* 21, based on the dialogue between virtue and vice attributed to Prodicus by Xenophon *Mem.* 2.1.21–34. It is a fine example of the diatribe style. The same comparison is found in the parallel passage at *Leg.* 3.62.

help her lure him. The image of the angler catching a fish with a hook.

They convey the external appearances inside. Elaboration of a basically Stoic epistemological scheme, as indicated by various technical terms (external appearances = φανέντα, characteristics = τύποι, impressions = φαντασίαι, comprehend = καταλαμβάνω); see further our comment on §150 and L&S §40. On the image of impressions in wax see the comment on §18. This passage is included by Von Arnim as *SVF* 2.57.

the passion that corresponds to them. Which πάθος does Philo have in mind here? Cohn 1889, 84 adduces as parallel Aëtius *Plac.* 4.12 at Ps.-Plutarch *Mor.* 900E (= *SVF* 2.54):

> Whenever we see something white through sight, there is an affection (πάθος) which has been engendered through vision in the soul; and it is this affection which allows us to say that there is a white object which moves us. The same happens in the case of touch and smell.

If we apply this parallel, then the *pathos* Philo is speaking about corresponds to the five senses. This would mean that he uses *pathos* in a different sense from what we read in §163. The adjective ὅμοιον supports this interpretation. I do not, however, think it is completely impossible that in this context Philo means the various kinds of pleasure associated with the diverse senses, as explained in §165. A few lines later *pathos* again must refer to pleasure (§167). To preserve the ambiguity I have translated *pathos* by passion in all three cases.

not being able on its own to do this. This was already stated at §139, as Philo himself points out with his cross-reference.

Parallel exegesis

In the *Legum Allegoriae* Gen 3:1a is extensively commented on in 2.71–108. Philo dwells at length on other snakes in the Pentateuch, some of whom have a positive symbolism (esp. the bronze snake of Num 21:8). Unfortunately the part dealing with Gen 3:1b–7 has been lost. The entire passage is treated at *QG* 1.31–41, the first three sections of which run parallel with our passage. A further important parallel is *Agr.* 94–101, where reflection on the text Gen 49:17 (Dan as snake on the road) leads Philo to give a kind of summary of the entire symbolism of the snake (note esp. the statement on the allegorical method in §§96–97). A link between the snake who moves on its belly and the food laws in Lev 11:42 is made at *Leg.* 3.139. This is all grist to Philo's allegorical mill. See also *Her.* 238–239 on earthbound and flying reptiles.

Nachleben

Philo's allegory of the snake as symbol of pleasure, combined with the interpretation of Adam as mind and Eve as sense-perception, did not enjoy a great popularity in patristic exegesis, which on the whole — and with the strong encouragement of the apostle Paul — was quite content to explain the literal meaning. But two 4th cent. exegetes take it over very explicitly.

In *Comm. Gen.* 95.19–21 Didymus writes: "There too we allegorize the order in accordance to what we said before. Pleasure, who is the snake, first was present in sense-perception, which we called the woman, then she herself ministers to the mind, who has also been called the man." The cross-reference shows that Didymus must have introduced the Philonic allegory in his exegesis of Gen 3:1–6, which unfortunately is missing in the papyrus. See also references to the allegory at 82.23–83.1; 83.20; 95.13–14. We may be sure that Didymus read Philo directly. But was he encouraged in taking over this exegesis by the example of his great Alexandrian precedessor Origen? Unfortunately at *Cels.* 4.39, responding to Celsus' contemptuous comments on the snake, Origen says that it is not the time to explain the story about the snake and the paradise of God. We do not know whether he referred to the Philonic allegory in his extremely detailed Genesis commentary (13 books on the first four chapters!). It is partly found, however, in Origen's predecessor Clement, who at *Protr.* 111.1 allegorizes the snake in terms of pleasure, but links it with the first human being's succumbing to desire (cf. §152).

In *Ep.* 45 = 34.10 Ambrose continues his borrowings from *Opif.* with a section on the symbolism of the snake, who represents pleasure (*delectatio*). The proofs are taken from §§157–159: he moves on his stomach, he eats earthly food, he has poison in his teeth, which are the instruments of disaster for the glutton. He refers to the broader allegory in his exegetical treatise on paradise, in a text which cites Philo, albeit anonymously (*De paradiso* 2.11; the Greek terms are contained in the Latin text):

> For one of our predecessors has recorded that the transgression was committed by the man through pleasure and sense-perception, taking the form of the snake as the symbol of pleasure, establishing the sense-perception of the mind and intellect, which the Greeks call αἴσθησις as symbolized by the woman. When sense-perception is deceived, according to the story, she claimed the mind as transgressor, whom the Greeks call νοῦς. Rightly therefore in Greek νοῦς is symbolized by the man, αἴσθησις by the woman. Hence some exegetes also interpret Adam as earthly νοῦς.

The final sentence refers to the more detailed allegory in *Leg.* 1.90. As Savon (1977, 1.50) points out, Ambrose takes up this allegory in order to placate readers who are scandalized by the idea that the devil was present in paradise. Philo represents an entirely different tradition, which in this particular context can prove useful.

Despite an extensive search I have found no patristic use of the theme of the "snake-fighter."

Further reading: Radice *FM* 307–310; Baer 1970, 38–44; Mattila 1996, 112–120 (on the allegorical scheme of mind and sensation); Sly 1990, 91–110 (on Eve); Levy 2000, 127–130 (on the defence of pleasure).

Chapter Twenty-four
The consequences of wickedness (§§167–170a)

Analysis/General comments

After the section on the symbolic meaning of the snake and other features of the events in paradise, Philo returns to a literal exposition and now recounts the punishments that the first man and woman received on account of their transgression. The first sentence of §167 neatly illustrates how the allegorical and literal interpretations dovetail together. The first human beings succumb to illicit pleasure, which corresponds to the symbolism of the snake deceiving the mind via the senses. This brief section rounds off Philo's treatment of the events in paradise and of the creation account of Genesis 1–3 as a whole. The passage can be divided into four brief sections. A rather general narrative style predominates. The exegetical questions posed in the parallel section in *QG* are much more specific.

(1a) The punishments that ensued from giving in to pleasure were soon experienced (note that the fact that God prescribes these punishments is glossed over). (i) First the two punishments received by the woman are set out: pain on account of her children, and subjection to her husband. (ii) Then the punishment inflicted on the man is outlined, i.e. the toil and sweat required in order to procure the necessities of life. This section is based on Gen 3:16–19, but the punishment of the snake is omitted (§167).

(1b) A contrast is drawn between the heavens, which remained unchanged because wickedness has no place there (cf. §73 once again), and the earth, which would have continued to yield abundance, were it not that evil now flourishes and the fountains of God's grace have to be checked. Implicit here is the question why the earth's bounty was changed into scarcity (cf. the curse on the earth in Gen 3:17, which is also glossed over). God could not allow wickedness to flourish (§168).

(1c) But the extent of the punishment could have been a lot worse, were it not for God's mercy. The human race was not wiped out, as it deserved to be, but now does have to work for its food and livelihood, a fact which places a curb on its wickedness (§169).

(2) A final sentence summarizes the entire account of the events in paradise as expounded in §§151–169 (§170a).

Although, as been noted above, the punishments outlined by Philo are based on the biblical account in Gen 3, they are placed within a theological and moral framework which assumes fundamental doctrines in Philonic thought. In fact the main themes of our passage have already been outlined in considerable detail in §§79–81, where Philo argued that human beings were created last in the creation in order to teach them a moral lesson. That passage is in one sense fuller than this one because it also contemplates a scenario of hope, i.e. what God will do if humans improve their ways. This aspect is missing here, presumably because it is soon to be illustrated by the lives of the patriarchs. On the background of the passage here we note the following points.

(1) The twin themes of the punishment inflicted by God and God's mercy are inseparably connected to the doctrine of the divine powers, even though they are not explicitly mentioned in this passage. The two names of He who IS are God and Lord, the former expressing his creative power (cf. §21), the latter his royal or authoritative power. Under these two powers others can be subsumed: under the former the power of mercy, under the latter the power of retribution. For these schemes see, for example, *Fug.* 95; *QE* 2.68; and the comments above at §21; further discussion of the Jewish background in Wolfson 1947, 1.224; Urbach 1987, 448–461; Dahl and Segal 1978; Winston 1984, 21–22. Just as creation takes precedence over rule, so God's mercy is stronger than his desire for justice; see esp. the meditation on Ps. 100:1: "I will sing to you of mercy and judgment" at *Deus* 73–76; further reflections at *Praem.* 163; *Migr.* 122; *Her.* 272 etc.

(2) As was made quite clear in Ch. 13, it is theologically axiomatic that God cannot be the cause of real evil. Yet divine punishment does occur, as our passage makes quite plain. Philo has two ways of evading the problem. Retributive punishment can be assigned to the powers, who act as God's lieutenants (cf. *Decal.* 176–178, and recall §§73–75). Alternatively, it can be affirmed that the punishment handed out is not really an evil, but has an educational purpose (cf. the long discussion at *Congr.* 157–180, with a reference to Adam and Eve at §171, and our comments above at §149). This is the line of thought that is followed in our passage. The lack of spontaneous goods from the earth teaches humankind not to be lazy or overindulgent.

(3) The drift of Philo's thought might be taken to be: once humans start to be virtuous again, evils will disappear, on the assumption that the worst evils are done by humans to each other, through injustice and violence. But comparison with §§79–81 shows

that this solution is unlikely. There it is envisaged that God will intervene in nature and supply bountiful food again. Implicit is the doctrine of providence, allowing direct divine intervention in nature. On this argument see the critical comments at §79.

(4) Surprisingly, after the heavy emphasis that the subject received in §§151–156, Philo does not dwell on the aspect of mortality and death, except to say that the human race was not wiped out completely. Note, however, that the punishment does not involve the *introduction* of mortality; see the comments on §152.

Detailed comments

(1a) §167. *The consequences of pleasure.* The opening sentence of the passage announces its main theme. The term τὰ ἐπίχειρα is often translated "wages," which is its first meaning. But Philo usually uses it for the consequences of bad behaviour; cf. *Somn.* 2.85; *Mos.* 1.139; *Praem.* 142, 171. The famous Pauline expression, Rom 6:23, is different: τὰ ὀψώνια τῆς ἁμαρτίας θάνατος.

slaves of a passion. Baer (1970, 38) rightly takes this to refer above all to sexual passion, adducing *Leg.* 2.74; *Spec.* 1.9; *QG* 3.48. This interpretation coheres well with §152.

(i) *the griefs that occurred successively* ... A creative extrapolation of Gen 3:16, which mentions childbirth only. One is reminded of Mary, who "kept all these things, pondering them in her heart" (Luke 2:19).

the loss of freedom and the absolute mastery. This is directly based on the biblical text Gen 3:16. Compare the immensely influential Pauline text in 1 Tim 2:11–15, with its injunction of female submission based on the events in paradise; see Clark Kroeger 1992, with a brief discussion of Philo at 146–148.

(ii) *obtained toil and hardships.* Compare the more elaborate description in §80. Here Philo adheres more closely to Gen 3:17–19. See further on §169.

(1b) §168. *after they had once been commanded to do so.* Cf. above §§55–57. In Gen 1:18 there is no actual command to the sun and moon, as there is for example to the earth in 1:11. But it is certainly implicit. On the commands of the Genesis account see the comment on §13.

wickedness has been exiled far away from the borders of heaven. As the parallel in *Leg.* 1.61 shows, the phrase is a distant development of Plato *Phdr.* 247a, "for envy stands at a far remove from the divine choir;" see further Runia *PT* 136. The distinction between the Aristotelian supra- and sub-lunary worlds is here given a moral twist.

ever-flowing fountains of God's grace. We recall the image of springs like mother's breasts at §133 and the close parallel at 1 Clem 20:10. But here it is used metaphorically of divine grace. For the expression frequent parallels can be found in Philo, cf. *Virt.* 79; *Cher.* 123, etc., but also outside his writings, e.g. at Cicero *Nat. d.* 2.79; *Orac. Sib.* 4.15, etc. For a full investigation of the metaphor see Zeller 1990, 40, and, in much more detail 1993, where he concludes (94): "The metaphor is quickly used by Greek writers, especially in poetic texts. A theological application is first found in Philo. A concrete starting-point for his usage can hardly be determined any more."

wickedness. A much fuller account of such wickedness is given in §§79–80.

to flourish at the expense of the virtues. For a transitive use of the verb παρευημερεῖν, cf. *Abr.* 67. The same verb is used of the vices in §80. It is a veritable *verbum Philonicum.* Of the 30 instances yielded by the TLG (two should not be counted, since they are doublets of Basil), 21 are in Philo (and two in Philonic extracts in Eusebius!). Only one is in an author earlier than or contemporary with Philo, namely Diodorus Siculus 20.79. Basil's use of the term in his sermon on fasting (PG 32.188A) seems influenced by Philo's passage here: fasting is surpassed by pleasure and results in a far greater lack of food as punishment.

(1c) §169. ***If the human race ...*** In our General comments above we already referred to *Deus* 73–76, where Philo reflects on Gen 6:7–8 and the subject of divine mercy. Noah was excluded from the punishment of the flood because "he found grace with God." The difference here is that there are no exceptions to the general wickedness, since the only two living humans both succumb.

ingratitude. The obverse of the doctrine of grace. God is gracious and the appropriate response of human beings is to show thankfulness. For an excellent passage illustrating this view see *Spec.* 1.209–211 on the symbolism of the division of the animal in the holocaust offering; see also Zeller 1990, 54–59. But as the history of humankind and of the people of Israel in the Pentateuch show, this response is very often not forthcoming. For this reason Israel has received the task of becoming the race of suppliants, beseeching God to show mercy to the nation and the entire human race. For this crucial Philonic doctrine, which builds on fundamental biblical themes, see Nikiprowetzky 1963; Harl PAPM 15.132–150; Zeller 1990, 59–61.

laziness and over-indulgence. This suggests the corrective and paideutic nature of God's punishment. See the General comments above. As Theiler (1971, 35) has pointed out, Philo's thought here can be profitably compared with the famous passage of Virgil *Georg.* 1.118–146, ending with the lines: *labor omnia vicit | improbus et duris urgens in rebus egestas* (insatiable toil took over the whole of (human) existence, and when things are tough, lack prevails). Jupiter makes life tough, so that laziness will not be prevalent and humans will be forced to develop their skills. The differences outweigh the similarities. Philo does not emphasize the concept of progress. His moralism is much more pronounced, and is imbedded in a much weightier theological framework. See also the General comments at Ch. 19.

(2) §170. *Such was the life ...* This concluding sentence summarizes the entire passage §§151–170. "Life" here refers not so much to conditions of living as to the status of the first persons' lives in terms of *eudaimonia* and *kakodaimonia*, as introduced in §§151–152. The sentence should thus be contrasted with the final sentence of §150, which summarizes §§134–150. See also the comments on §150.

innocence and simplicity. The same combination of terms as in §156.

from which one should abstain. The textual question discussed in the notes to the translation has further interpretative connotations. Harl 1962, 344 adduces the words excised by Cohn in favour of his interpretation of the first human being's "pre-moral" existence. She takes ὧν to refer to both κακία and ἀρετή, i.e. human beings should refrain from *all* personal activity in the area of morality, leaving this up to God, who ordains what should be done. See our comments on §156, where we reject this view. God wants humans to exercise ἀρετή actively, as §§144 and 156 show. If the excised words are to be retained, then ὧν should refer to evil only. Since a plural antecedent is required, we prefer the reading κακίας, at the cost of an imbalance between plural deeds of wrong-doing and excellence in the singular.

Cohn (1889, lix) notes the excellent emendation suggested by Hanssen (1888), but does not include it in his later edition: τοιοῦτος μὲν ὁ βίος τῶν ἐν ἀρχῇ μὲν ἀκακίᾳ καὶ ἁπλότητι χρωμένων, αὖθις δὲ κακίᾳ ἀντ' ἀρετῆς, προτιμώντων ὧν ἄξιον ἀπέχεσθαι (such was the life of those who in the beginning enjoyed innocence and simplicity, but then (took to) wickedness instead of virtue, giving preference to those things from which one should abstain). The language of the emendation is perfectly Philonic (for αὖθις δέ in a temporal sense see *Mos.* 150; *Legat.* 326). It is also more fluent than Cohn's text. The only argument against it is that Philo nearly always uses προτιμάω with both the accusative and the genitive, as retained by Cohn.

Parallel exegesis

Gen 3:16–19 are expounded at great length in book 3 of *Legum allegoriae*, and more compactly in *QG* 1.49–51. Note the explanation of the description of paradise as τρυφή (delight, Gen 3:23) at *QG* 1.56:

> For in truth a life of wisdom is a delight of spacious joy and an enjoyment most suitable to the rational soul. But a life without wisdom is harsh and terrible. For it has been completely deceived by pleasures, which are followed by pain, both in the beginning and at the end. (translation Marcus PLCLSup)

The distinction between pleasure (i.e. a *pathos*) and joy (i.e. a *eupatheia*) is crucial for Philo, but is not emphasized in *Opif*. Cf. also the summary of the story of the events in paradise at *Virt.* 203–205, where a "life of toil" (§205) parallels our passage.

Nachleben

Didymus' literal reading of Gen 3:16–19 at *Comm. Gen.* 101.11–24 shows similarities to Philo's treatment here, esp. in his expansion of the pains and griefs of the woman beyond childbirth to matters of upbringing. Unlike in Philo, however, these cares are shared by her husband.

On a possible reminiscence of §168 in a sermon by Basil on fasting, see the comment above.

Further reading: Radice *FM* 301; Zeller 1990, 54–55.

Chapter Twenty-five
Moses teaches five vital lessons (§§170b–172)

Analysis/General comments

Wholly in the manner of a Greek σύγγραμμα (prose treatise), Philo concludes his work with a summary of its main message. It is a short passage, written in a strikingly didactic style. Not only are the conclusions compactly presented in the form of five lessons, but each one is also uniformly formulated. The final long period is climactically phrased in order to provide a fitting end for the entire work. The structure of the passage can thus be divided into three parts.

(1) An introductory sentence stating that Moses above all teaches us five lessons (§170).

(2) A list of five doctrines, each presented in a similar way. First the ordinal number is given, followed by a brief propositional formulation in each case introduced by ὅτι (that), and concluded by a slightly longer motivation, introduced the first three times by διά (on account of), then by ἐπειδή (since) and in the final case by γάρ (for).

(a) First, (he teaches) that God exists, on account of the atheists;
(b) Second, that God is one, on account of the polytheists;
(c) Third, that the cosmos is created, on account of the proponents of its eternity;
(d) Fourth, that the cosmos is one, for theological and cosmological reasons;
(e) Fifth, that there is divine providence, as decreed by the laws of nature (§§170–171).

(3) The final sentence spells out what it means for the reader to subscribe to these doctrines. If thoroughly imprinted on the soul, they will ensure a blessed and fortunate life. The five doctrines are then summarized once again in a formulation that is slightly more theocentric than the original presentation (§172).

As the above analysis clearly shows, Philo has done all he could when writing this concluding passage to ensure that his readers remembered its salient points. Whether he obtained success in the case of his ancient readers we cannot know (its *Nachwirkung* was limited; see *Nachleben*). Modern readers have certainly been struck by this text. In fact it is one of the most famous passages in the entire Philonic corpus, appearing in numerous anthologies and introductory works, as well as in important discussions of Philo's thought as a whole.

Goodenough (1962 [1940], 37) called it "the first creed in history." In his systematic presentation of Philo's thought, Wolfson (1947, 1.164–199) largely based his "eight principles constituting the essential principles of the religion of scripture" on this summary. More recently Mendelson (1988, 29) has interpreted these principles as "keys to Philo's concept of orthodoxy," regarding them as "a kind of touchstone, a lowest common denominator of religious belief, which Philo would have regarded as essential for the preservation of Jewish identity." For Amir (1987, 229) they also represent a "*Summa* des Glaubens*,*" though he would not wish to identify them with the "centre" of scriptural thought.

It is first necessary, however, to examine the passage in its original context. As we have seen, it is a concluding summary of the treatise. Its contents should therefore be carefully examined to see to what extent they really do refer back to earlier material and summarize it. We shall be very attentive to this aspect in our detailed comments below. The five conclusions can be related to the treatise as a whole as follows (cf. Radice *FM* 312):

(1) God's existence is the fundamental assumption of the entire treatise, as can be seen at the very outset in §§7–12.
(2) God's unicity is for the most part assumed rather than explicitly stated. But we note the denial of any being beside God in §23 and a reference to his aloneness in §151.
(3) The creation of the cosmos by God is introduced in §§7–9 and seen as the fundamental doctrine of the creation account, for example in Gen 1:1 cited in §26.
(4) The unicity of the cosmos is nowhere argued for, until in the concluding passage itself, but is briefly referred to in §151.
(5) The working of divine providence is introduced in §§9–11 and assumed in the remainder of the treatise, above all in the final part.

It may be concluded, therefore, that the summary does cover a number of vital themes and presuppositions of the treatise, but that there is also much that falls outside its scope. One might mention the creator's goodness (§21) and the cosmos' perfection (§§9, 14, 36). Moreover not a single word is devoted to the features of arithmology and anthropology which are so prominent in the treatise. The single reference to laws of nature also does not correspond to the importance of the theme in the treatise.

A further examination of the five doctrines reveals that they have a strong philosophical slant. Four of the five belong to the absolutely standard philosophical questions of Philo's time, as can be seen if we compare them with a passage such as *Ebr.* 199, which gives a doxographical summary of such questions, or with the standard doxographical manual of Aëtius (God's existence 1.7, the cosmos' createdness 2.4, its unity 1.5, 2.1, providence 2.3; see also the comments on §54). The one question that is not found in these sources is that of God's unicity. But Philo formulates the conclusion in such a way that it closely resembles Platonic and Aristotelian doctrine. Indeed many philosophers in Philo's time would have agreed that God was one, though not in a manner that would have elicited his full agreement (for further discussions on pagan monotheism see Kenney 1986, Frede 1999). Goodenough (1962, 38) was quite right to remark that much in our passage represents standard Platonic-Pythagorean doctrine, and that many gentile readers would have been in general agreement. We note too that the influence of Plato's *Timaeus*, which was so strong in the first part of the work, reappears, as witnessed by allusions to three further passages of that work dealing with the unicity of the cosmos.

At the same time, however, it is apparent that the passage has a strong polemical edge. For four of the five doctrines (only the last is an exception) Philo refers in a rather sharp tone of voice to thinkers who hold opposed views. It is not difficult, as many scholars have done, to fill in names of Greek philosophers whom Philo might have had in mind. But just as the reference to other thinkers in §§7–12 is general (see our interpretation in Ch. 2), so here Philo envisages kinds of thinking rather than specific philosophers. This can be seen from a passage at *Conf.* 114, where the builders of the tower of Babel espouse "arguments of impiety and godlessness" which correspond to three of the opposed doctrines in our passage, and also from the five kinds of thinking banished from the holy congregation in *Spec.* 1.319–343.

But the five doctrines are not just a matter of theory. They also impinge on human life — this applies esp. to the fifth doctrine on divine providence —, which compensates for the lack of reference to anthropology in the conclusion. A further application is given in the final sentence. By subscribing to them, the reader will be characterized by the doctrines of piety and will obtain a blessed life. Given the correspondence of terminology, it may be assumed that this life will resemble the life of excellence and immortality enjoyed by the first human being before his transgression. This means that piety and holiness are given a doctrinal component. Sound theology is part of worshipping God. This view is consistent with the important conclusion to Book 1 of *Spec.* (cited in our comments on §152), in which knowledge of God is said to the goal of well-being. The doctrines summarized here frequently turn up in the accounts of the patriarchs and various allegories of the soul in quest of God (some examples will be given in the detailed comments).

What then is the precise status of these five lessons of piety and holiness? Although they are taught by Moses, i.e. are revealed, they are not (*pace* Goodenough) a creed or articles of faith in which one must believe before one can belong to Judaism. Rather, it seems to me, they represent the fundamental or preliminary doctrines (*dogmata*) of which one must be intellectually convinced in order to embark on an understanding of the scriptures that embrace both the Mosaic legislation and the wider Jewish tradition. Without these convictions there is no point in reading further in the Exposition of the Law, for they are presupposed in the accounts of the patriarchs and the explanation of the divine commandments. The threshold is not very daunting. The doctrines can even be accepted on the basis of rational considerations. In Philo's view Judaism is in its fundamental aspects a reasonable religion. Radice (*FM* 313) is right in pointing out that other vital aspects of Philo's thought prominent in *Opif.*, such as the doctrines of the Logos, the divine Powers and the double creation of humankind, can easily be subsumed under these five doctrines. Yet their absence is surely deliberate. The five doctrines are preliminary in that they will ultimately lead the reader to the centre of Mosaic thought. But, as Amir rightly saw, they do not represent that centre themselves. This can be seen by comparing them to the quest of Israel described later in *Praem.* 40–46. Nevertheless, as we point out in the *Nachleben*, this passage is important evidence for the process which will lead to Christian dogmatic theology. Gregory Sterling has suggested to me that, because the fit of the five doctrines with the rest of *Opif.* is not so close, they may have a pre-Philonic origin. This is possible, but the strong philosophical emphasis makes it likely in my view that Philo decisively contributed to their formulation.

Because the passage is so rich and can be related to so many central themes and passages in Philo's works, we shall have to be restrictive in the parallels we cite in the Detailed comments. As already indicated above, we place particular emphasis on the relation of this concluding passage to the contents of the treatise as a whole.

Detailed comments

(1) §170b. **the creation account which we have discussed.** This recalls the introductory passage §§4–6, where Philo announces his exegetical intentions.

he teaches. Mangey ad loc. thought the name Moses should be introduced into the text, but the conjecture was rightly rejected by Cohn.

If a verb has an unspecified subject in Philo, we have to supply either God or Moses. Here it is quite clear that the latter is meant. On Moses as teacher and founder of a *hairesis*, see Runia 1999a, 127–135.

(2a) *the divinity is and exists.* Philo here joins together two verbs to express God's existence, ἔστι καὶ ὑπάρχει. In the rest of the sentence the latter is picked up by the noun ὕπαρξις, the former by the infinitive μηδ' ὅλως εἶναι. In the summary in §172 the same two verbs are again joined together. Two more instances of this conjunction are found in the corpus, both in theological contexts: *Spec.* 1.41; *Post.* 168. The two verbs do not mean exactly the same: *hyparchein* indicates "being there," i.e. having a real existence (cf. the contrast between really existing and being called or regarded as such in *Det.* 160, *Congr.* 80; or being a shadow in *Flacc.* 164); *einai* denotes having being in a fuller sense so that one is a real entity. It is easy to see how the difference leads Philo to distinguish between God's existence (ὕπαρξις) and his essence (οὐσία) in passages such as *Spec.* 1.35–36, 41; *Post.* 169; *Somn.* 2.231. For a discussion of this terminology in Philo see Glucker 1994, 19–20, who points out that Philo is the first extant writer to use the noun ὕπαρξις and suggests it may have been his invention. Frick (1999, 2) also supports this interpretation in terms of the distinction between existence and essence. Contrary to these readings, I incline to the view that in the present text we have a *hendiadys*, i.e. Philo is saying the same thing twice in order to give it more emphasis. That a distinction between essence and existence cannot be meant is strongly suggested by the two texts cited above, *Spec.* 1.41 and *Post.* 168, where both verbs are used of God's existence (as cause) which can be known, as opposed to his essence which is beyond human knowledge. The LCL translation, which imports the aspect of eternity, is seriously misleading. I have preferred not to follow Winston's rendering "is and subsists," because the latter term suggests the verb ὑφίστημι (and the noun ὑπόστασις). The question of knowledge of God's essence is lightly touched upon in §§71 and 151; see our comments there. But there is no discussion of natural theology or argument from design in the treatise. The fact of God's existence is assumed.

on account of the godless. In order to situate his opponents in relation to his own doctrine, Philo makes use of part of the basic *diaeresis* frequently found in discussions of philosophical theology. See for example the presentation at the very beginning of Cicero's *De natura deorum* (1.2):

> As regards the present subject most thinkers have affirmed that the gods exist, which is the most likely view and to which we are led through the guidance of nature, but Protagoras said he was in doubt, while Diagoras of Melos and Theodorus of Cyrene thought none existed at all.

A similar *diaeresis* is found at Sextus Empiricus *Adv. phys.* 1.50, couched in the language of scepticism (note that unlike Cicero he speaks of God in the singular). For further discussion of this diaeresis see Runia 1996b, 550–553 (and in connection with providence 564–565). At *Praem.* 40 Philo reproduces the standard *diaeresis* with various elaborations. Here, however, he deviates from the scheme by using the atheists to cover both agnostics and outright deniers of God's existence. The original and the revised scheme can be compared as follows:

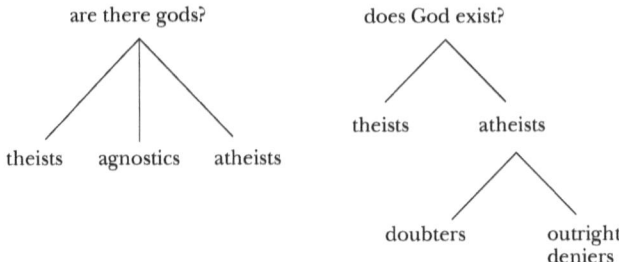

There can be little doubt that Philo's Judaism is the inspiration behind this adaptation. Atheism for him is a failure to recognize God, and the agnostic can certainly be charged on this account. According to *Spec.* 1.330 atheism is the worst of evil deeds. Philo associates it esp. with Egypt; cf. *Mos.* 2.193–196. The archetypal biblical atheist is Pharaoh, who says "I do not know the Lord" (Exod 5:2); cf. *Ebr.* 19; Earp at PLCL 10.399. The doctrine is attributed to the Babel-builders in *Conf.* 114. In the background Hebrew Bible texts such as Ps. 13:1 (LXX) on the fool who says in his heart, "there is no God" also play a role. To my knowledge there is no scholarly treatment of Philo's views on atheism.

some of whom are in doubt. Philo may have in mind Protagoras (mentioned by Cicero) or the sceptics. As was noted above in the comments on §§69 and 72, he himself is sympathetic to a kind of scepticism, but this certainly does not entail doubt about the existence of God (it is not accidental that in a list of disputed topics at *Ebr.* 199 the question of God's existence is not mentioned).

incline in two directions. The verb ἐπαμφοτερίζω refers to the metaphor of the balance (cf. *Praem.* 64), precisely the image used by the sceptics to express the equal weight of arguments leading to withholding of assent (ἐποχή). See the definition of Pyrrhonian scepticism at Sextus Empiricus *Hyp.* 1.8. Exactly the same language is used for the agnostic position at *Praem.* 40.

he does not exist at all. The parallels at *Praem.* 40 (μηδ' ὅλως εἶναι, the same as here); Cicero *Nat. d.* 1.3 (nullos esse omnino); and Aëtius 1.7 at Ps.-Plutarch *Mor.* 880D (καθόλου μὴ εἶναι), point to a standard formulation that Philo has taken over.

is only said to exist. What we would now call a virtual existence.

by people who overshadow the truth with mythical fictions. I am convinced that Wolfson (1947, 1.167) is quite correct in seeing here a reference to one of the most famous of the ancient atheists, Critias (c. 460–403), an older relative of Plato and a member of the infamous Athenian junta of the Thirty. In his play the *Sisyphus* he introduces a character who explains the origin of the belief in God (recorded in some 40 lines of verse preserved by Sextus Empiricus *Adv. Phys.* 1.54, cf. 88B25 D-K). At first anarchy prevailed in human interaction, but then the rule of law was introduced. Evils deeds, however, were still done in secret. The problem was solved by a clever man, who invented the concept of an eternally flourishing and omniscient God living in the heavens. Fear of this God would constrain humankind to obey the law in all circumstances. Philo's formulation alludes in particular to the following verses (24–26): "by speaking such words he introduced the pleasantest of doctrines, concealing the truth with a false account." The same view is also alluded to in a parallel text on atheists at *Spec.* 1.330:

> Those who conceal the existence of God assert that, though he does not exist, he is said to do so for the benefit of human beings, who would refrain from wrongdoing on account of fear of him who, it was supposed, was present everywhere and watched all things with eyes that never sleep.

If this interpretation is correct, then "the truth" in Philo's text denotes the atheist position that God actually does not exist, but is only said to do so in mythical, i.e. false, reports. This is not only quite different from the mythical fictions spoken about in §157, but also from Philo's usual language, in which "truth" refers to monotheism and "myth" to the false gods of polytheism! On Critias see further Guthrie 1969, 298–304, and on all aspects of ancient atheism the fundamental research of M. Winiarczyk. It should be noted that as an intellectual view atheism was a minority position throughout antiquity, and certainly in the time of Philo it would have met with very few supporters. But naturally there will have been numerous people who acted as if God or the gods did not exist.

(2b) §171. **God is one.** There are quite a few texts in which Philo asserts, in accordance with the first commandment, the unique nature of God: cf. *Spec.* 1.30; *Leg.* 2.1–2; *Somn.* 1.229; Wolfson 1947, 1.171–172. In *Opif.* this doctrine is alluded to at §23 (where it is not in conflict with the doctrine of the Logos!) and §151. But Amir (1978, 13), is right to warn us not to assume too easily that Philo conforms to the standard view of Jewish monotheism. For example it is remarkable that he never refers to the Shema (Deut 6:4); on this question see Mendelson 1994, 166. At *Decal.* 51 and *Spec.* 1.12 he refers to the first commandment as being concerned with God's sole rule (μοναρχία), as is also implied in our text when he describes the opponents he has in mind (see below). See also the comments at §27 on the description of the heavenly beings as "gods whose appearance is perceived by the senses."

the polytheistic opinion. In conformity with Hellenistic Jewish practice (e.g. Wis 13–14) extensive polemical accounts are given of pagan polytheism and concomitant idolatry in *Decal.* 52–81 and *Spec.* 1.21–29. As the eminent historian of European religion, Prof. B. Gladigow, once pointed out to me in conversation, the concept of polytheism is in fact first found in Philo. In *Virt.* 214–215 Abraham, founder of the Jewish nation, migrates from the πολύθεος δόξα (same expression as here) to discovery of the one God; cf. also *Decal.* 65; *Virt.* 221; *Praem.* 162; *Ebr.* 110

(linked with atheism), etc. In *Opif.* the question of polytheism is indirectly raised at §7 in the attack against those who give the cosmos too much reverence; cf. *Decal.* 66, where Philo says that this offence is less than the worship of idols.

they transfer ... from earth to heaven. On earth there are many rulers and much disorder (though a political system of monarchic hierarchy can exist, as in the Roman empire); in heaven there is perfectly ordered movement set in motion by the supreme God. God himself, of course, is beyond the heavens; cf. §§70–71. This is the theme of *monarchia* noted above. See esp. *Conf.* 170:

> Now it must be affirmed first of all that no existent subsists as equal in honour to God, but there is one ruler and director and king, by whom alone it is right that all things are administered and directed. For the lines "the rule of many lords is not a good thing; let there be one Lord, one King" (Homer *Iliad* 2.204–205) could not more justly be said of cities and humankind than of the cosmos and God. Since it is one, it is necessary that its maker and father and master too should also be one.

The same Homeric quote is used by Aristotle of his hierarchical cosmology in the final line of *Metaph.* Λ (§10, 1076a4). In *Opif.* we recall esp. the contrast made by Philo in §11 between God's providential rule and the power-vacuum (ἀναρχία) that can exist in a city. See the comments ad loc.

rule by the mob. The term is ὀχλοκρατία, the opposite in Philo's view to his political ideal of δημοκρατία; see the exposition of these terms of political theory at Barraclough 1984, 520–529. Philo speaks not only as a upper-class Roman citizen, but also as a Jew who experienced the turmoil of the anti-Jewish riots of 38 C.E. (or of threats of similar action; we cannot know when *Opif.* was written, but *Spec.* 3.1–6 suggests it was in the second half of the thirties; see Introduction §1). A very similar thought is repeated in *Decal.* 155 in connection with the first commandment (ὀλιγαρχία is added). Confusing earth and heaven is the great mistake of the Egyptians, and leads to atheism (*Mos.* 2.193–195).

(2c) **the cosmos has come into existence.** The cosmos is γενητός, the conclusion of Philo's preliminary remarks at §§7–12, to which he here refers.

ungenerated and eternal. The words ἀγένητος καὶ ἀίδιος repeat the formulation of §7, which we interpreted to be primarily a reference to the Chaldean way of thinking. But it can also be taken to refer to Aristotle and Platonists. See the comments at §7.

attributing no superiority to God. Cf. §7 again. If the cosmos is eternal, then it has the same temporal status as God, and so can be identified with him (the mistake of the Chaldeans). The phrase can also be interpreted as "attributing no further activity to God," referring to the charge of ἀπραξία (idleness) in §7, but this seems to me linguistically less likely.

(2d) **the cosmos too is one.** The fourth lesson comes as somewhat of a surprise, because it is nowhere argued for in the treatise (in §35 the noetic cosmos is one, but nothing is said about the sense-perceptible cosmos modelled on it), and is only briefly mentioned at §151 (the first human being was alone, just like God and the cosmos are). Elsewhere there are frequent texts in Philo declaring that the cosmos is one and connecting it with God's oneness; cf. *Spec.* 3.189; *Conf.* 170 (cited above); *Migr.* 180 (view shared with the Chaldeans), etc. The question of whether the cosmos was one or whether within the single universe there were many *kosmoi* was a standard theme in Greek philosophy. See for example the doxographical treatment in Aëtius *Plac.* 2.1. Philo refers to a part of this standard schema at *Aet.* 8; see further Pépin 1964, 72–78. The majority of schools in Philo's time — Platonists, Peripatetics, Stoics — supported the position of unicity, though not all on the same grounds. As Wolfson (1947, 1.181) points out, Philo significantly deviates from Jewish tradition, which emphasizes divine omnipotence through a doctrine of a vast (but not infinite) number of worlds; for more details see Ginzberg 1909–38, 5.12–13.

since. Unlike in the case of the first three lessons, Philo here gives arguments in its favour, perhaps in recognition of the fact that he is introducing a new element. Three arguments are briefly given, one from the viewpoint of the creator, the other two from the viewpoint of the material used (we recall the "activating cause" and the "passive object" of §8).

the creator is one as well. I.e. combining the second and third lessons (the latter in its theistic variant, as summarized in §172).

he has made his product similar to himself in respect of its unicity. An adaptation of Plato's famous but controversial argument at *Tim.* 31a–b, where he deduces the unicity of the cosmos from the unicity of the model. The phrase κατὰ τὴν μόνωσιν used by Philo is found literally at 31b1, while the participle ἐξομοιώσας recalls rather distantly ἀφωμοιωμένον at 31a8. But God's making the cosmos like himself also recalls (though not verbally) the statement at 29e7 that the demiurge "wished to make all things as similar to himself as possible." We recall too the theme of (ἐξ)ὁμοίωσις used in §§146 and 151, but here it moves from God to creation, not the other way around. As I note in my discussion of this text at *PT* 175, Plato's dialectical argument has been revised in accordance with the doctrine that the noetic cosmos is equivalent to God's thoughts or his Logos. This allows the model to be identified with the demiurge, so that a *homoiôsis* relation can be postulated between creator and product. This is patently a Middle Platonist development: see for example Plutarch's formulations at *Mor.* 1014B, 1015B (though it is not used in connection with the unicity of the cosmos).

expending all the available material. Cohn reads τῇ ὕλῃ with M, while all other mss. have τῇ οὐσίᾳ. Since Philo very clearly uses *ousia* for the pre-existent matter in §21, whereas *hylê* is not used in that sense in the treatise, I doubt whether he is right. But little hangs on the issue. On the term *ousia* see our comments at §21.

The important parallel passage for our text is *Prov.* 2.50–51, where Philo argues against Alexander that God, being superior to human craftsman, must have been able to calculate the precise amount of material required for the job (both οὐσία and ὕλη are used; the Greek text is preserved in Eusebius *Praep. Ev.* 7.21). It should be noted that the context of this argument is dialectical and it is not evidence in favour of *creatio ex nihilo*. We have here the technological metaphor for creation *in optima forma* (cf. my remarks at *PT* 183).

not have been a complete whole. Philo's mention of the cosmos as a whole leads to a further argument. We have here a distant echo of Plato's argument at *Tim.* 32c–33a that the cosmos is perfect, complete and unassailable because it is made of complete parts, i.e. the total amount of the four elements. Note esp. 33a2: "[it is] one because nothing had remained from which another such entity could originate." Philo's argument is more dialectical than physical. Since the parts are complete, so must be the whole. But the argument is unclear, since it is not explained what these parts are. Are the four elements meant? Or the regions of the universe? Philo could be thinking of the argument that God would not have left anything incomplete, because that might mean debris dangerous for the cosmos (cf. *Aet.* 21, Mendelson 1988, 44–46). But if so, he does not make this clear either.

There are those who suppose. As in the case of the atheists, Philo again uses a *diaeresis*. On the question of the number of worlds there are three options: either one, or infinite, or — the option in between — multiple. But if examples of this problem in Greek philosophy are consulted, e.g. at Aëtius *Plac.* 2.1, we see that they always work with a dichotomy (taken over by Philo at *Abr.* 162; *Spec.* 3.189). The inspiration here is no doubt again Plato's *Timaeus*, where at 31a2 he poses the question, "have we then spoken rightly of one heaven (= cosmos), or would it be more correct to speak of many or an infinite number?", and at 55d2 (in the passage to which Philo will now allude), where he toys with the idea of five *kosmoi*. The only other Greek example of multiple *kosmoi* that I know is Petron of Himera who according to Plutarch *Mor.* 422B-D postulated 183 *kosmoi* arranged in a triangle. It seems to me quite improbable that he is aiming his polemic against the Jewish thinkers cited by Wolfson (1947, 1.181) or their predecessors.

boundless ... boundlessly ignorant. A well-nigh untranslatable play on the word ἄπειρος taken over from Plato, *Tim.* 55c7–d1. The term can mean both unlimited (from *a-peras*) and inexperienced (from *a-peira*). Plato is making a contemptuous reference here to the atomist view of infinite worlds, propagated esp. by Democritus. In Philo's time this had been expanded to include Epicurus. The two philosophers are grouped together at *Aet.* 8, where Philo loosely speaks of "many worlds."

(2e) **God also takes thought for the cosmos.** The fifth lesson repeats the substance of §§9–10. The question whether there is divine providence and whether it extends to the earthly realm is another standard topic in the Greek philosophy of Philo's time. See for example the *diaeresis* at Sextus Empiricus *Hyp.* 3.9: "He who affirms that God exists, states either that he takes thought for the things in the cosmos or he does not, and if he does take thought, he does so either for all or for some." Further discussion at Runia 1996b, 564–565. This is the only lesson where Philo does not specifically mention opponents of his view. But he does certainly have particular persons in mind, e.g. philosophers such as Epicurus and possibly also Aristotle. And he will also be thinking of opinions of biblical figures such as the Babel-builders (*Conf.* 114), Pharaoh (*Ebr.* 19; *QG* 4.87), the evil generation of Noah (*Praem.* 23), and even also of his nephew Alexander, to judge by the dialogue *Prov.* 2. The question of divine providence is a crucial assumption for the final part of *Opif.*, once the creation of humankind has taken place. God is very concerned with the response of humans to his grace, and either rewards or punishes them correspondingly; cf. esp. §§155, 167–170a.

by the laws and ordinances of nature. In §10 Philo used the relationship between a father and his offspring as an analogy in the philosophical context of the doctrine of creation. Here the caring relationship between parents and children is regarded as fixed by natural law. Cf. *Praem.* 42, where those who determine the existence of God from the order of the cosmos by means of natural theology also conclude that "there must be providence, for it is a law of nature that the maker should take care for what has been made." On the difference between law and ordinance see §143.

(3) §172. **not so much with his hearing.** In spite of the encomium of sight in §54, Philo here privileges the sense of hearing for the task of listening to the lessons of scripture, but immediately overtrumps it with the philosophical conception of thinking. This is interesting against the background of the famous distinction of Boman (1960) between the two paradigms of Hellenist visuality and biblical hearing (as in the Shema).

imprinted. The imagery of marking and imprinting yet again (cf. §18 etc.). But here a religious dimension is added to the epistemological image. Philo is expressing in Greek philosophical terms the injunction of Deut 6: 6: "the words which I enjoin upon you today, shall be in your heart and *in your soul* (LXX, my emphasis)." Close parallels in *Spec.* 1.30, 59. We note that the final word of the treatise is "marked" (χαραχθείς). The tone is evangelical. The reader must imprint these truths on his mind, and he does so because he has read Philo's treatise.

namely that ... We now get a summary of the summary, with various verbal equivalents in §§170–171, but with two interesting changes.

he who truly exists. The famous name of God revealed in Exod 3:14, ἐγώ εἰμι ὁ ὤν (I am who IS), has so far not been used in the treatise. The next clear example in the Exposition is at *Abr.* 121, where it is called God's proper name.

he made the cosmos ... The third and fourth lessons are now summarized in a theocentric form: the cosmos has come into being because God has created it; it is one because God has made it one.

a blessed life of well-being. Philo reverts to the theme of *eudaimonia* which is so prominent in the final part of the treatise. See the comments on §§144, 150. On the two terms μακάριος and εὐδαίμων see also §135. But here the concept is applied not to a distant primal figure (however generalized he might be) but to the reader himself.

The treatise thus reaches its climax with a return to the theme of *eudaimonia*. This is a technique that Philo practises at a number of strategic points elsewhere. In the Exposition of the Law we note *Spec.* 1.335 and *Virt.* 50 (end of a sub-section). Elsewhere *Post.* 185; *Ebr.* 224; *Somn.* 1.256; and most strikingly *Contempl.* 90 (which ends with the words ἐπ' αὐτὴν ἀκρότητα φθάνον εὐδαιμονίας, attaining to the very summit of felicity). This remarkable collection of climactic passages formed the starting point of my inaugural lecture in Leiden (1993) in which I observed that many other ancient works share this feature, e.g. Xenophon *Mem.* 4.8.11; Plato *Gorg.* 527c–e; *Resp.* 354c, 621c; Aristotle *Nic. Eth.* 10.6–8; Ps.-Aristotle *Mund.* 7, 401b23–29; Cicero *Tusc.* 5.119–120; Seneca *Ep.* 124; Diogenes Laertius 10.138; Plotinus 6.9.11; Augustine *Civ.* 22.30; see also Runia 1997b, 14–15 on *Contempl.* 90. We have to do here with a topos in which two kinds of climax, literary and ethical, both covered by the single term *telos*, come together.

doctrines. A distinction is intended between δόξα (opinion), as used of the polytheists in §171 (cf. also *Spec.* 1.328) and δόγμα (doctrine), as used here of the five lessons (cf. also *Spec.* 1.345). Philo's usage is not absolute, however, for at *Post.* 51 he speaks of Cain's δόγμα.

piety and holiness. The same combination of terms as at §155; cf. also *Decal.* 110; *Spec.* 1.54, 186, 2.63, 3.127, 4.135; *Mos.* 2.216; *Plant.* 35, etc. On the importance of these religious virtues see our comments at §154. It should be noted that all mss. except M have θειότητος instead of ὁσιότητος. Given the fact that the former word only occurs once in Philo, at *Det.* 86 and is used of God himself, and in the light of all the texts just cited, Cohn was clearly right in opting for the reading of M.

The final section of *Opif.* can be profitably compared with a passage in the *Letter of Aristeas*, §§234–235:

> The king ... asked the tenth guest [of the Seventy], "what is the highest form of glory." He said, "Honouring God. This is not done with gifts or sacrifices, but with purity of heart and with the devout conviction that all things are constructed by God and administered according to his will. And this is also your continual disposition, as all people can observe from your actions in part and present." With a loud voice the king saluted them all, while the others present, but especially the philosophers, joined in the approval, for these people far surpassed them in both their conduct and their discourse, because they took their starting-point from God.

The Jewish piety held in common can easily be recognized, but Philo's approach is much more intellectual.

Exegetical parallels

There is no exegesis in this chapter, so there are also no parallels. For other Philonic passages with similar contents, see the General comments.

Nachleben

No definite *Nachwirkung* of the final section of *Opif.* can be determined. Rather similar is a passage in Theophilus, *Ad Aut.* 3.9:

> We too confess God, but only one, the founder and maker and demiurge of this entire cosmos. We know that everything is governed by providential care, but by Him alone. We have learned a holy law, but we have as legislator the real God, who teaches us to practise justice and piety and beneficence.

As has been noted by Grant (1988, 167) and by myself (*PEC* 114), the parallelism in terms of content is really quite striking. But the literary resemblances, both in structure and vocabulary, are not strong. It is certainly safer to suppose a common Judaeo-Hellenistic background. Similar but less close is the *regula fidei* at Origen *Princ. praef.* 4. In Runia 1995, 12–13 I argue that this Philonic passage is an important piece of evidence for the process which will lead to the rise of Christian dogmatism.

Further reading. Radice *FM* 310–313; Goodenough 1962 (1940), 37–38; Wolfson 1947, 1.164–165, 171–181; Mendelson 1988, 29–49.

BIBLIOGRAPHY

1. Philo of Alexandria

(a) Editions and Translations of *Opif.*

Turnebus, A. 1552. *Philonis Iudaei in libros Mosis, de mundi opificio, historicos, de legibus; eiusdem libri singulares.* Paris: Adrianus Turnebus. Pages 1–27 (*editio princeps*).

Mangey, T. 1742. *Philonis Judaei opera quae reperiri potuerunt omnia.* 2 volumes. London: William Humphrey. Volume 1, pages 1–42.

Yonge, C. D. 1854–55. *The Works of Philo Judaeus, the Contemporary of Josephus, translated from the Greek*, 4 volumes. London: Bohn. Reprinted in a single volume, Peabody Mass.: Hendrickson, 1993. Pages 3–24 of the Reprint.

Cohn, L. 1889. *Philonis Alexandrini libellus de opificio mundi*, Breslauer philologische Abhandlungen 4.4. Breslau: Guilelmus Koebner Pages 1–67.

Cohn, L. 1896. In L. Cohn, P. Wendland, and S. Reiter, *Philonis Alexandrini opera quae supersunt*, 6 volumes. Berlin: George Reimer, 1896–1915; reprinted Berlin: De Gruyter, 1962. Volume 1, pages 1–60. (= PCW)

Cohn, J. 1909. In L. Cohn, I. Heinemann, and W. Theiler, *Philo von Alexandria: die Werke in deutscher Übersetzung.* 7 volumes. Breslau: Marcus Verlag 1909–38 (6 volumes), Berlin: De Gruyter 1964 (vol. 7). Volume 1, pages 25–89 (= PCH).

Whitaker, G. H. 1929. In F. H. Colson, G. H. Whitaker (and R. Marcus), *Philo in Ten Volumes (and Two Supplementary Volumes)*, Loeb Classical Library. London and Cambridge Mass.: Heinemann, 1929–62. Volume 1, pages 6–137 (= PLCL).

Arnaldez, R. 1961. *Philon d'Alexandrie De opificio mundi.* Les œuvres de Philon d'Alexandrie. Edited by R. Arnaldez, J. Pouilloux, and C. Mondésert. Volume 1. Paris: Éditions du CERF (= PAPM).

Kraus Reggiani, C. 1987. In R. Radice and G. Reale, *Filone di Alessandria. La Filosofia Mosaica.* Milan: Rusconi. Pages 47–94.

Van Winden, J. C. M. 1996. "De schepping van de wereld volgens Mozes." Unpublished Dutch translation.

(b) Commentaries on *Opif.*

Müller, J. G. 1841. *Des Juden Philo Buch von der Weltschöpfung.* Berlin: G. Reimer.

Radice, R. 1987. "Commentario a La creazione del mondo". In R. Radice and G. Reale, *La filosofia mosaica.* Milan: Rusconi. Pages 231–313 (= FM).

(c) Other Philonic texts

Aucher, J. B. 1826. *Philonis Iudaei Paralipomena armena. Libri vidilicet quatuor in Genesin, Libri duo in Exodum. Sermo unus de Sampsone. Alter de Jona. Tertius de tribus angelis Abraamo apparentibus.* Venice: Typis Coenobii PP Armenorum.

Petit, F. 1973. *L'ancienne version latine des Questions sur la Genèse de Philon d'Alexandrie, volume I édition critique, volume II Commentaire*, 2 volumes. TU 113–114. Berlin: Akademie Verlag.

Petit, F. 1978. *Quaestiones Fragmenta Graeca.* Les œuvres de Philon d'Alexandrie 33. Paris: Éditions du CERF.

(d) Anthology

Winston, D. 1981. *Philo of Alexandria: The Contemplative Life, The Giants and Selections*, The Classics of Western Spirituality. New York and Toronto: Paulist Press (= *PA*).

(e) Lexica and Indices

Leisegang, I. 1926–30. "Indices ad Philonis Alexandrini opera." In *Philonis opera quae supersunt*, volumes 7–8. Berlin: G. Reimer.
Earp, J. W. 1962. "Indices to volumes I–X." In F. H. Colson and G. H. Whitaker, *Philo in Ten Volumes*, Loeb Classical Library. London and Cambridge Mass.: Heinemann, 1929–62. Volume 10, pages 189–520.
Theiler, W. 1964. Sachweiser zu Philo. Pages 386–411 in *Philo von Alexandria: die Werke in deutscher Übersetzung*. Edited by L. Cohn et al. Volume 7. Berlin: De Gruyter.
Mayer, G. 1974. *Index Philoneus*. Berlin: De Gruyter.
Biblia Patristica Supplément: Philon d'Alexandrie. Paris: Éditions du CNRS, 1982.
Thesaurus Linguae Graecae CD-ROM 1999. University of California at Irvine. Version E.
Borgen, P., Fuglseth, K., and Skarsten, R. 2000. *The Philo Index: A Complete Greek Word Index to the Writings of Philo of Alexandria*. Grand Rapids: Eerdmans, 2nd edition.

(f) Bibliographies

Goodhart, H. L. and Goodenough, E. R. 1938. "A General Bibliography of Philo Judaeus." Pages 125–321 in E. R. Goodenough, *The Politics of Philo Judaeus: Practice and Theory*. New Haven: Yale University Press (= G-G).
Radice, R. and Runia, D. T. 1988. *Philo of Alexandria: an Annotated Bibliography 1937–1986*. VChr.S 8. Leiden: Brill, 2nd edition 1992 (= R-R).
Runia, D. T. 2000. *Philo of Alexandria: an Annotated Bibliography 1987–96*. VChr.S 57. Leiden: Brill (continued in *The Studia Philonica Annual*) (= RRS).

2. *Other ancient texts*

Only texts that are not so well known or not very accessible are listed. Other texts are cited in accordance with the Loeb Classical Library or standard editions. See also the listing in L. Berkowitz and K. A. Squitier, *Thesaurus Linguae Graecae: Canon of Greek Authors and Works*, New York: Oxford University Press, 1990³. Texts pertaining to Philo's arithmological excursuses are separately listed in the Introduction §6 and Ch. 15, General comments.

Achilles
    E. Maass, *Commentariorum in Aratum reliquiae*. Berlin: Weidmann, 1898, 1958².
Aëtius the doxographer
    H. Diels, *Doxographi Graeci*, Berlin: De Gruyter, 1965⁴ (first published 1879), pages 267–444 (= DG).
    See also Ps.Plutarch, Stobaeus.
Alcinous
    J. Whittaker and P. Louis, *Alcinoos Enseignement des doctrines de Platon*. Paris: Les Belles Lettres, 1990.

Ambrose
  O. Faller, *Sancti Ambrosii Opera Pars X Epistulae et Acta, tomus I Epistularum libri I–VI*, CSEL 82.1. Vienna: Hoelder-Pichler-Tempsky, 1968.
Anonymous Theatetus Commentary
  Corpus dei Papiri Greci e Latini. Volume 3, pages 227–562. Edited by G. Bastianini and D. Sedley. Florence: Olschki Editore, 1995.
Aristotle
  V. Rose, *Aristoteles qui ferebantur librorum fragmenta* Stuttgart: Teubner, 1967 (first published Leipzig 1886).
Atticus
  E. des Places, *Atticus: Fragments*. Paris: Les Belles Lettres, 1977.
Calcidius
  J. H. Waszink, *Timaeus a Calcidio translatus commentarioque instructus*, Plato Latinus 4. London: Warburg Institute; Leiden: Brill, 1962, 1975^2.
Cicero
  Pease, A. S. 1955–58. *M. Tulli Ciceronis De natura deorum*. 2 vols. Cambridge Mass.: Harvard University Press.
Cornutus
  C. Lang, *Cornuti Theologiae graecae compendium*. Leipzig: Teubner, 1881.
Corpus Hermeticum
  A.-J. Festugière and A. D. Nock, *Corpus Hermeticum*, 4 vols. Paris: Les Belles Lettres, 1946-54.
  B. P. Copenhaver, *Hermetica*. Cambridge University Press, 1992.
Didymus of Alexandria
  P. Nautin, *Didyme L'Aveugle Sur la Genèse*, 2 volumes. SC 233, 244. Paris: Éditions du CERF, 1976–78.
Dionysius Thrax
  G. Uhlig, *Ars Grammatica*, Grammatici Graeci I.1. Hildesheim: Olms 1965 (first published in 1883).
  A. Hilgard, *Scholia in Dionysii Thracis Artem Grammaticam*, Grammatici Graeci I.3. Hildesheim: Olms 1979 (first published in 1901).
Epicurus
  H. Usener, *Epicurea*. Leipzig: Teubner, 1887. Reprinted Stuttgart 1966.
Eudorus
  C. Mazzerelli, Raccolta e interpretazione delle testimonianze e dei frammenti del medioplatonico Eudoro di Alessandria. *Rivista di Filosofia Neoscolastica* 77, 1985:197–209, 535–555.
Favonius Eclogius
  A. Holder, *Favonius Eclogius Disputatio de somno Scipionis*. Leipzig: Teubner, 1901.
Genesis Catena
  F. Petit, *La Chaîne sur la Genèse: Édition intégrale,* 4 volumes. Louvain: Peeters, 1992–97.
Gregory of Nyssa
  Apologia in Hexaemeron: G. H. Forbes, *S. P. N. Gregorii Nysseni quae supersunt omnia tomus I*. Burntisland 1855, pages 1–95.
  De opificio hominis: ibid. pages 96–319.
Johannes Lydus
  R. Wuensch, *Ioannis Laurentii Lydi liber de mensibus*. Leipzig: Teubner, 1898.
Maximus Tyrius
  M. B. Trapp, *Maximus Tyrius Dissertationes*. Leipzig and Stuttgart: Teubner, 1994.
  M. B. Trapp, *Maximus of Tyre: the Philosophical Orations*. Oxford: Clarendon Press, 1997.

Nemesius
  M. Morani, *Nemesii Emeseni de natura hominis*, Leipzig: Teubner, 1987.
Nicomachus of Gerasa
  R. Hoche, *Nicomachi Geraseni Pythagorei Introductionis arithmeticae libri II*. Leipzig: Teubner, 1866.
  M. L. D'Ooge, F. E. Robbins, and L. C. Karpinski, *Nichomachus of Gerasa Introduction to Arithmetic*. New York–London: The Macmillan Company, 1926.
Numenius
  E. des Places, *Numénios: Fragments*. Paris: Les Belles Lettres, 1973.
Origen
  H. de Lubac and L. Doutreleau, *Origène Homélies sur la Genèse*, SC 7b. Paris: Éditions du CERF, 1958.
Orphica
  O. Kern, *Orphicorum fragmenta*. Berlin: Weidmann, 1922.
Posidonius
  L. Edelstein and I. G. Kidd, *Posidonius: the Fragments*. Cambridge University Press, 1972.
Pseudepigrapha
  J. H Charlesworth, *The Old Testament Pseudepigrapha: vol. 1 Apocalyptic Literature and Testaments, vol. 2 Expansions of the 'Old Testament' and Legends, Wisdom and Philosophical Literature, Prayers, Psalms, and Odes, Fragments of Lost Judeo-Hellenistic Works*. London: Darton, Longman & Todd, 1983–85 (= *OTP*).
Pseudo-Justin
  Cohortatio ad Graecos: see §3 below, Riedweg 1994.
Pseudo-Plutarch
  J. Mau, *Plutarchi Moralia*, vol. 5.2.1. Leipzig: Teubner 1971.
  G. Lachenaud, *Plutarque Œuvres morales Tome XII^2: Opinions des Philosophes*. Paris: Les Belles Lettres, 1993.
Rabbinica
  Midrash Rabbah, translated by H. Freedman and M. Simon. 10 volumes. London: The Soncino Press, 1939.
  J. Neusner, 1985. *Genesis Rabbah: The Judaic Commentary on Genesis. A New American Translation*. 3 volumes. Atlanta: Scholars Press.
Septuaginta
  J. W. Wevers, *Genesis*. Septuaginta Vetus Testamentum Graecum 1. Göttingen: Vandenhoeck & Ruprecht, 1974.
Stoa
  J. von Arnim, *Stoicorum Veterum Fragmenta*, 4 volumes. Stuttgart: Teubner, 1978 (first published 1903–24) (= *SVF*).
Stobaeus
  C. Wachsmuth and O. Hense, *Ioannis Stobaei Anthologium*, 5 volumes. Berlin: Weidmann, 1974 (first published 1884–1912).
Theophilus of Alexandria
  R. M. Grant, *Theophilus of Antioch Ad Autolycum*, Oxford Early Christian Texts. Oxford University Press, 1970.
Xenocrates
  M. Isnardi Parente, *Senocrate–Ermodoro frammenti*, La scuola di Platone 3. Naples: Bibliopolis, 1982.

3. Modern scholarly literature

Alexander, L. 1993. *The Preface to Luke's Gospel: Literary Convention and Social Context in Luke 1.1–4 and Acts 1.1*. SNTSMS 78. Cambridge University Press.

Alexander, P. J. 1977. A Neglected Palimpsest of Philo Judaeus: Preliminary Remarks *Editorum in Usum*. Pages 1–14 in *Studia Codicologica*. TU 124. Berlin: Akademie Verlag.
Alexandre Jr., Manuel. 1999. *Rhetorical Argumentation in Philo of Alexandria*. BJS 322. Studia Philonica Monographs 2. Atlanta: Scholars Press.
Alexandre, Monique. 1967. *De congressu eruditionis gratia*. Les œuvres de Philon d'Alexandrie 16. Paris: Éditions du CERF.
——. 1988. *Le commencement du livre Genèse I–V: la version grecque de la Septante et sa réception*. Christianisme Antique 3. Paris: Beauchesne. (= *CLG*)
——. 1997. 'Du grec au latin: Les titres des œuvres de Philon d'Alexandrie'. Pages 255–286 in *Titres et articulations du texte dans les œuvres antiques: actes du Colloque International de Chantilly 13–15 décembre 1994*, edited by J.-C. Fredouille *et al*. Collection des Études Augustiniennes 152. Paris: Institut des Études Augustiniennes.
Amir, Y. 1978. Die Begegnung des biblischen und des philosophischen Monotheismus als Grundthema des jüdischen Hellenismus. *Evangelische Theologie* 38:2–19.
——. 1987. Die "Mitte der Schrift" aus der Sicht des hellenistischen Judentums. Pages 217–236 in *Mitte der Schrift? ein jüdisch-christliches Gespräch: Texte der Berner Symposions von 6–12. Januar 1985*. Edited by M. Klopferstein. Judaica et Christiana 11. Bern and Frankfurt: P. Lang.
Armstrong, A. H. and Markus, R. 1960. *Christian Faith and Greek Philosophy*. London: Darton, Longman & Todd.
Aucher, J. B. 1826. See above §1(d).
Baer, R. A. 1970. *Philo's Use of the Categories Male and Female*, ALGHJ 3. Leiden: Brill.
Balme, D. 1990. "Ἄνθρωπος ἄνθρωπον γεννᾷ: Human is generated by Human. Pages 20–31 in *The Human Embryo: Aristotle and the Arabic and European Traditions*. Edited by G.R. Duncan. Exeter: University of Exeter Press.
Baltes, M. 1976–78. *Die Weltentstehung des platonischen Timaios nach den antiken Interpreten*. 2 volumes. Philosophia Antiqua 30, 35. Leiden: Brill.
——. 1999. Der Platonismus und die Weisheit der Barbaren. Pages 115–138 in *Traditions of Platonism: Essays in Honour of John Dillon*. Edited by J. J. Cleary. Aldershot etc.: Ashgate.
——. See also Dörrie and Baltes 1987–.
Barker, A. 1984–89. *Greek Musical Writings*. 2 volumes. Cambridge University Press.
Barnes, J. 1997. Roman Aristotle. Pages 1–69 in *Philosophia Togata II*. Edited by M. Griffin and J. Barnes. Oxford: Clarendon Press.
Barraclough, R. 1984. Philo's Politics: Roman Rule and Hellenistic Judaism. Pages 417–553 in *Hellenistisches Judentum in römischer zeit: Philon und Josephus*. Edited by W. Haase. Aufstieg und Niedergang der römischen Welt II Principat vol. 21.1. Berlin–New York: De Gruyter.
Barthélemy, D. 1967. Est-ce Hoshaya Rabba qui censura le "Commentaire Allégorique"? A partir des retouches faites aux citations bibliques, étude sur la tradition textuelle du Commentaire Allégorique de Philon. Pages 45–78 in *Philon d'Alexandrie. Lyon 11–15 Septembre 1966: colloques nationaux du Centre National de la Recherche Scientifique*. Paris: Éditions du CNRS.
Baudry, G.-H. 1996. La responsibilité d'Ève dans la chute: analyse d'une tradition. *Mélanges de Science Religieuse* 53:293–320.
Belletti, B. 1982. La dottrina dell'assimilazione a Dio in Filone di Alessandria. *Rivista di Filosofia Neoscolastica* 74:419–440.
——. 1987. La creazione delle idei e dell'uomo nel trattato *De opificio mundi* di Filone Alessandrino. *Humanitas (Brescia)* 42:273–279.
Berkowitz, L. and Squitier, K. A. 1990³. *Thesaurus Linguae Graecae: Canon of Greek Authors and Works*. New York: Oxford University Press.

Bickerman, E. J. 1988. *The Jews in the Greek Age*. Cambridge Mass.: Harvard University Press.
Billings, T. H. 1919. *The Platonism of Philo Judaeus*. Diss. Chicago: University of Chicago Press.
Blass, F. and Debrunner, A. 1961. *A Greek Grammar of the New Testament and Other Early Christian Literature*. Chicago: University of Chicago Press.
Boman, T. 1960. *Hebrew Thought Compared with Greek*. London: SCM Press. ET of German edition, 1954².
Borgen, P. 1965. *Bread from Heaven: an Exegetical Study of the Concept of Manna in the Gospel of John and the Writings of Philo*. NT.S 10. Leiden: Brill. Reprinted in 1981.
———. 1993. Heavenly Ascent in Philo: an Examination of Selected Passages. Pages 246–268 in *The Pseudepigrapha and Early Biblical Interpretation*. Edited by J. H. Charlesworth and C. A. Evans. JSP.SS 14. Sheffield University Press.
———. 1995. Man's Sovereignty over Animals and Nature according to Philo of Alexandria. Pages 369–389 in *Texts and Contexts: Biblical Texts in their Textual and Situational Contexts: Essays in Honor of Lars Hartman*. Edited by T. Fornberg and D. Hellholm. Oslo and Boston: Scandinavian University Press.
———. 1996. Philo of Alexandria – a Systematic Philosopher or an Eclectic Editor? *Symbolae Osloenses* 71:115–134.
———. 1997. *Philo of Alexandria: an Exegete for his Time*. NovTSup 86. Leiden: Brill.
Borgen, P., Fuglseth, K. and Skarsten, R. 2000². *The Philo Index: A Complete Greek Word Index to the Writings of Philo of Alexandria*. Grand Rapids: Eerdmans.
Bormann, K. 1955. *Die Ideen- und Logoslehre Philons von Alexandrien: eine Auseinandersetzung mit H. A. Wolfson*. Inaug. diss. Köln.
Bos, A. P. 1998. Philo of Alexandria: A Platonist in the Image and Likeness of Aristotle. *SPhA* 10:66–86.
Bousset, W. 1915. *Jüdisch-christlicher Schulbetrieb in Alexandria und Rom: literarische Untersuchungen zu Philo und Clemens von Alexandria, Justin und Irenäus*. FRLANT N.S. 6. Göttingen: Vandenhoeck & Ruprecht.
Boyancé, P. 1963a. Études Philoniennes. *REG* 76:64–110.
———. 1963b. Sur l'exégèse hellénistique du *Phèdre* (*Phèdre* p. 246 c). Pages 45–53 in *Miscellanea di studi alessandrini in memoria di A. Rostagni*. Turin: Bottega d'Erasmo.
———. 1974. Le Dieu très haut chez Philon. Pages 139–149 in *Mélanges d'histoire de religions offerts à H. C. Puech*. Paris: Presses Universitaires de France.
Boyarin, D. 1993. *Carnal Israel: Reading Sex in Talmudic Culture*. Berkeley: University of California Press.
Bréhier, E. 1908, 1950³. *Les idées philosophiques et religieuses de Philon d'Alexandrie*. Paris: Vrin.
Brunschwig, J. 1986. The Cradle Argument in Epicureanism and Stoicism. Pages 113–144 in *The Norms of Nature: Studies in Hellenistic Ethics*. Edited by M. Schofield and G. Striker. Cambridge–Paris: Cambridge Univ Press; Editions de la Maisons des Sciences de l'homme. Reprinted in Brunschwig 1995, pages 69–112.
———. 1995. *Études sur les philosophies hellénistiques: Epicurisme, stoïcisme, scepticisme*. Paris: Presses Universitaires de France.
Burkhardt, H. 1988. *Die Inspiration heiliger Schriften bei Philo von Alexandrien*. Giessen and Basel: Brunnen Verlag.
Carmichael, C. M. 1996. *The Story of Creation: its Origin and its Interpretation in Philo and the Fourth Gospel*. Ithaca: Cornell University Press.
Chadwick, H. 1967. Philo and the Beginnings of Christian Thought. Pages 137–192 in *The Cambridge History of Later Greek and Early Medieval Philosophy*. Edited by A. H. Armstrong. Cambridge University Press.

Chantraine, P. 1968–1980. *Dictionnaire etymologique de la langue grecque: histoire des mots.* 4 fascicles. Paris: Klincksieck.
Charlesworth, J. H. 1983–85. See above §2.
Clark Kroeger, R. and C. 1992. *I Suffer not a Woman: Rethinking 1 Timothy 2:11–15 in Light of Ancient Evidence.* Grand Rapids: Eerdmans.
Cohen, J. 1989. *"Be Fertile and Increase, Fill the Earth and Master It": the Ancient and Medieval Career of a Biblical Text.* Ithaca–London: Cornell University Press.
Cohen, N. G. 1987. The Jewish dimension of Philo's Judaism: an elucidation of *de Spec. Leg.* IV 132–150. *JJS* 38:165–186.
———. 1995. *Philo Judaeus: his Universe of Discourse.* Beiträge zur Erforschung des Alten Testaments und des Antiken Judentums 24. Frankfurt etc.: P. Lang.
———. 1997. The Names of the Separate Books of the Pentateuch in Philo's Writings. Pages 54–78 in *Wisdom and Logos: Studies in Jewish Thought in Honor of David Winston [= SPhA 9 (1997)].* Edited by D. T. Runia and G. E. Sterling. BJS 312. Atlanta: Scholars Press.
Cohn, L. 1889. See above §1(a).
———. 1899. Einteilung und Chronologie der Schriften Philos. *Philologus* Supplbd. 7:385–437.
Colpe, C. 1991. Art. "Himmelfahrt". Pages 213–219 in *RAC* 15. Stuttgart: Anton Hiersemann.
Colson, F. H. 1926. *The Week.* Cambridge University Press.
Conley, T. M. 1987. *Philo's Rhetoric: Studies in Style, Composition and Exegesis.* Berkeley: Center for Hermeneutical Studies.
———. 1997. Philo of Alexandria. Pages 695–713 in *A Handbook of Classical Rhetoric in the Hellenistic Period 330 B. C. – A. D. 400.* Edited by S. E. Porter. Leiden etc.: Brill.
Courcelle, P. 1972. Art. "Flügel (Flug) der Seele". Pages 29–66 in *RAC* 14. Stuttgart: Anton Hiersemann.
Dahl, N. A. and Segal, A. F. 1978. Philo and the Rabbis on the Names of God. *JSJ* 9:1–28.
Daniel-Nataf, S., ed. 1986. *Philo of Alexandria: Writings, vol. 1, Historical writings, Apologetical writings [Hebrew].* Jerusalem: Mosad Byalik.
———. ed. 1991. *Philo of Alexandria: Writings, vol. 2, Exposition of the Law, Part One [Hebrew].* Jerusalem: Mosad Byalik.
Daniélou, J. 1961. La notion de confins (*methorios*) chez Grégoire de Nysse. *RechScRel* 49:161–187.
———. 1967. Philon et Grégoire de Nysse. Pages 333–345 in *Philon d'Alexandrie. Lyon 11–15 Septembre 1966: colloques nationaux du Centre National de la Recherche Scientifique.* Paris: Éditions du CNRS.
———. 1970. *L'être et le temps chez Grégoire de Nysse.* Leiden: Brill.
Dawson, J. D. 1992. *Allegorical Readers and Cultural Revision in Ancient Alexandria.* Berkeley: University of California Press.
Dean-Jones, L. A. 1994. *Women's Bodies in Classical Greek Science.* Oxford: Clarendon Press.
Delatte, A. 1915. *Études sur la littérature pythagoricienne.* Bibliothèque de l'École des hautes Études 215. Paris: Libraire Champion.
Diels, H. 1879, 1976⁴. *Doxographi Graeci.* Berlin: De Gruyter.
Dillon, J. 1977. *The Middle Platonists: a Study of Platonism 80 B. C. to A.D. 220:* . London: Duckworth. Revised edition with a new afterword, 1996.
———. 1990. Review of Reale and Radice, *La filosofia mosaica. SPhA* 2:177–182.
———. 1993. *Alcinous: The Handbook of Platonism.* Oxford: Clarendon Press.
———. 1995. Reclaiming the Heritage of Moses: Philo's Confrontation with Greek Philosophy. *SPhA* 7:108–123.
Dodd, C. H. 1935, 1964³. *The Bible and the Greeks.* London: Hodder & Stoughton.

Döring, L. 1999. *Schabbat. Sabbathalacha und -praxis im antiken Judentum und Urchristentum.* TSAJ 78. Tübingen: Mohr Siebeck.
Dörrie, H. 1970. Der König: ein platonisches Schlüsselwort, von Plotin mit neuen Sinn erfüllt. *Revue Internationale de Philosophie* 24:217–235. Reprinted in 1976, pages 390–405.
———. 1976. *Platonica minora.* Studia et testimonia antiqua 8. Munich: Wilhelm Fink Verlag.
Dörrie, H. and Baltes M. 1987– . *Der Platonismus in der Antike.* 5 volumes so far. Stuttgart–Bad Cannstadt: Frommann & Holzboog (= *DPA*).
Dorandi, T. 2000. *Le stylet et la tablette: dans le secret des auteurs antiques.* Paris: Les Belles Lettres.
Dover, K. J. 1974. *Greek Popular Morality in the Time of Plato and Aristotle.* Oxford: Blackwell.
Drummond, J. 1888. *Philo Judaeus, or The Jewish–Alexandrian Philosophy in its Development and Completion.* 2 volumes. London. Reprinted 1969, Amsterdam: Philo Press.
Effe, B. 1970. *Studien zur Kosmologie und Theologie der Aristotelischen Schrift „Über die Philosophie".* Zetemata 50. Munich: Beck.
Epstein, A. 1890. Le Livre des Jubilés, Philon et le Midrasch Tadsché. *REJ* 21:80–97.
Faller, O. 1968. See above §2 Ambrose.
Farandos, G. D. 1976. *Kosmos und Logos nach Philon von Alexandria.* Elementa 4. Amsterdam: Rodopi.
Feldman, L. H. 2000. *Flavius Josephus Translation and Commentary,* vol. 3 *Judean Antiquities Books 1–4.* Leiden etc.: Brill.
Festugière, A. J. 1949, 1981[2]. *La révélation d'Hermès trismégiste, vol. 2 Le dieu cosmique.* Paris: Les Belles Lettres.
Fossum, J. 1985. Gen. 1,26 and 2,7 in Judaism, Samaritanism, and Gnosticism. *JSJ* 16:202–239.
Frede, M. 1999. Monotheism and Pagan Philosophy in Later Antiquity. Pages 41–68 in P. Athanassiadi and M. Frede, *Pagan Monotheism in Late Antiquity.* Oxford: Clarendon Press.
Freedman, H. and Simon M. 1939, 1951[3]. See above §2.
Freudenthal, G. 1995. *Aristotle's Theory of Material Substance: Heat and Pneuma, Form and Soul.* Oxford: Clarendon Press.
Frick, P. 1999. *Divine Providence in Philo of Alexandria,* TSAJ 77. Tübingen: Mohr Siebeck.
Früchtel, U. 1968. *Die kosmologischen Vorstellungen bei Philo von Alexandrien: ein Beitrag zur Geschichte der Genesisexegese.* ALGHJ 2. Leiden: Brill.
Fuks, A. 1951. Notes on the Archive of Nicanor. *JJP* 5:207–216. Reprinted in idem, 1984. *Social Conflict in Ancient Greece.* Jerusalem: Magnes Press; Leiden: Brill, pages 312–321.
Gaca, K. L. 1996. Philo's Principles of Sexual Conduct and their Influence on Christian Platonist Sexual Principles. *SPhA* 8:21–39.
Gatzemeier, M. 1980. Art. "Makrokosmos/Mikrokosmos". Volume 5, pages 640–649 in *HWPh.* Darmstadt: Wissenschaftliche Buchgesellschaft.
Geljon, A. C. 2000. *Moses as Example: the Philonic Background of Gregory of Nyssa's De vita Moysis.* Diss. Leiden.
Gentili, B. and Prato, C., eds. 1988. *Poetarum elegiacorum testimonia et fragmenta.* 2 volumes. Leipzig: Teubner.
Geytenbeek, A. C. van. 1962. *Musonius Rufus and Greek Diatribe.* Wijsgerige Teksten en Studies 8. Assen: Van Gorcum.
Giblet, J. 1948. L'homme image de Dieu dans les commentaires littéraux de Philon d'Alexandrie. *Studia Hellenistica* 5:93–118.
Giet, S. 1949, 1968[2]. *Basile de Césarée Homélies sur l'Hexaéméron.* SC 26. Paris: Éditions du CERF.

Gilaberti Barberà, P. 1990. "... Però la dona ho esguerrà tot": El De opificio mundi de Filó d'Alexandria (LIII–LXI) o els fonaments grecs d'una fita en la història da la misogínia occidental. *Anuario de filologia: Studia Graeca et Latina* (Barcelona) 13:55–84.
Ginzberg, L. 1909–38, 1968[12]. *The Legends of the Jews.* 7 volumes. Philadelphia: Jewish Publication Society.
Girardet, K. M. 1995. Naturrecht und Naturgesetz: eine gerade Linie von Cicero zu Augustinus? *RhM* 138:266–298.
Glucker, J. 1994. The Origin of ὑπάρχω and ὕπαρξις as Philosophical Terms. Pages 1–23 in *Hyparxis e hypostasis nel neoplatonismo.* Edited by F. Romano and D. P. Taormina. Lessico Intellettuale Europeo 64. Firenze: L.S. Olschki.
Gnilka, C. 1972. *Aetas spiritalis: die Überwindung der natürlichen Altersstufen als Ideal frühchristlichen Lebens.* Theophaneia 28. Bonn: Peter Hanstein Verlag.
Goodenough, E. R. 1935. *By Light, Light.* New Haven: Yale University Press. Reprinted Amsterdam: Philo Press, 1969.
———. 1940, 1962[2]. *An Introduction to Philo Judaeus.* New Haven: Yale University Press. Second edition revised and amplified. Oxford: Blackwell.
Goodhart, H. L. and Goodenough, E.R. 1938. See above §1(e).
Gooding, D. and Nikiprowetzky, V. 1983. Philo's Bible in the *De gigantibus* and the *Quod Deus sit Immutabilis.* Pages 89–125 in *Two Treatises of Philo of Alexandria.* Edited by D. Winston and J. Dillon. BJS 25. Chico Calif.: Scholars Press.
Göransson, T. 1995. *Albinus, Alcinous, Arius Didymus.* Studia Graeca et Latina Gothoburgensia 61. Göteborg: Acta Universitatis Gothoburgensis.
Görgemanns, H. 1993. Art. Philosophie: A. Griechische Patristik. Volume 5, pages 5.616–623 in *HWPh.* Darmstadt: Wissenschaftliche Buchgesellschaft.
Goulet, R. 1987. *La philosophie de Moïse: essai de reconstruction d'un commentaire philosophique préphilonien du Pentateuque.* Histoire des doctrines de l'Antiquité classique 11. Paris: Vrin.
Goulet, R., ed. 1989–2000. *Dictionnaire des Philosophes Antiques,* 3 vols. so far. Paris: CNRS Éditions.
Graffigna, P. 1991. Un hapax di Filone d'Alessandria: ἀγαλματοφορεῖν. *Maia* 43:143–148.
———. 1994. Tra il doppio e l'unita: parentela (συγγένεια) tra uomo e Dio in Filone d'Alessandria. *Koinonia* 19:5–15.
Grant, R. M. 1988. *Greek Apologists of the Second Century.* Philadelphia: Westminster Press.
Grilli, A. 1979. Sul numero sette. Pages 1.203–219 in *Studi su Varrone sulla Retorica storiografica e poesia Latina. Scritti in onore di Benedetto Riposati.* 2 volumes. Rieti: Centro di studi varroniani, Milano: Universita catolica S. Cuore.
Gross, J. 1930. *Philons von Alexandrien Anschauungen über die Natur des Menschen.* Diss. Tübingen.
Grumach, E. I. 1939. Zur Quellenfrage von Philos *De Opificio Mundi* § 1–3. *MGWJ* 83:126–131.
Guthrie, W. K. C. 1957. *In the Beginning: Some Greek Views on the Origins of Life and the Early State of Man.* Ithaca: Cornell University Press.
———. 1969. *The Greek Enlightenment.* Volume 3 of *A History of Greek Philosophy.* Cambridge University Press.
Haas, C. 1996. *Alexandria in Late Antiquity: Topography and Social Conflict.* Baltimore: The Johns Hopkins University Press.
Hadas-Lebel, M. 1973. *Philon De Providentia.* Les œuvres de Philon d'Alexandrie 35. Paris: Éditions du CERF.
Hahm, D. E. 1977. *The Origins of Stoic Cosmology.* Ohio State University Press.
Hanson, R. P. C. 1959. *Allegory and Event: a Study of the Sources and Significance of Origen's Interpretation of Scripture.* London: SCM.

Hanssen, F. 1888. Miscellanea Graeca. *AJP* 9:457–463.
Harl, M. 1962. Adam et les deux arbres du Paradis (*Gen.* II–III) ou l'homme *milieu entre deux termes* (μέσος-μεθόριος) chez Philon d'Alexandrie: pour une histoire de la doctrine du libre-arbitre. *RecSR* 50:321–388.
———. 1966. *Philon Quis rerum divinarum heres sit.* Les œuvres de Philon d'Alexandrie 15. Paris: Éditions du CERF.
———. 1986. *La Bible d'Alexandrie. La Genèse: traduction du texte grec de la Septante, introduction et notes.* Paris: Éditions du CERF.
Harris, H. A. 1976. *Greek Athletics and the Jews.* Trivium Special Publications 3. Cardiff: University of Wales Press.
Hay, D. M. 1979–80. Philo's References to Other Allegorists. *SPh* 6:41–75.
———. 1991. References to Other Exegetes. Pages 81–97 in *Both Literal and Allegorical: Studies in Philo of Alexandria's Questions and Answers on Genesis and Exodus.* Edited by D. M. Hay. BJS 232. Atlanta: Scholars Press.
Heath, T. L. 1931. *A Manual of Greek Mathematics.* Oxford: Clarendon Press.
Heckel, H. 1999. Art. "Kulturentstehungstheorien". Volume 6, pages 908–914 in *Neue Pauly.* Stuttgart: J.G. Metzler.
Heiberg, J. 1901. Anatolius sur les dix premiers nombres. Pages 27–57 in *Annales Internationales d'histoire: Congrès de Paris 1900.* Paris: Librarie Armand Colin (includes a French translation by P. Tannery).
Helleman, W. E. 1990. Philo of Alexandria on Deification and Assimilation to God. *SPhA* 2:51–71.
Hengel, M. 1974. *Judaism and Hellenism: Studies in their Encounter in Palestine during the Early Hellenistic Period.* London: SCM Press.
Himmelfarb, M. 1993. *Ascent to Heaven in Jewish and Christian Apocalypses.* Oxford: Clarendon Press.
Hoek, A. van den. 1988. *Clement of Alexandria and his Use of Philo in the* Stromateis: *an Early Christian Reshaping of a Jewish Model.* VChr.S 3. Leiden: Brill.
———. 2000a. Philo and Origen: a Descriptive Catalogue of their Relationship. *SPhA* 12:44–121.
———. 2000b. Endowed with Reason or Glued to the Senses: Philo's Thoughts on Adam and Eve. Pages 63–75 in *The Creation of Man and Woman: Interpretations of the Biblical Narratives in Jewish and Christian Traditions.* Edited by G. P. Luttikhuizen. Themes in Biblical Narrative: Jewish and Christian Traditions 3. Leiden etc.: Brill.
Holladay, C. R. 1983–1996. *Fragments from Hellenistic Jewish Authors.* 4 volumes. Texts and Translations 20, 30, 39, 40. Chico, Calif.–Atlanta: Scholars Press.
Horovitz, J. 1900. *Untersuchungen über Philons und Platons Lehre von der Weltschöpfung.* Marburg: Elwert'sche Verlag-Buchhandlung.
Horsley, R. A. 1978. The Law of Nature in Philo and Cicero. *HThR* 71:35–59.
Horst, P. W. van der. 1990. Sarah's Seminal Emission. Hebrews 11:11 in the Light of Ancient Embryology. Pages 287–302 in *Greeks, Romans, and Christians: FS A. J. Malherbe.* Edited by D. L. Balch, E. Ferguson and W. A. Meeks. Minneapolis: Fortress. Reprinted in Van den Horst. 1998. Pages 187–220 .
———. 1993. "Thou shalt not Revile the Gods": the LXX Translation of Ex. 22:28 (27), its Background and Influence. *SPhA* 5: 1–8.
———. 1998[2]. *Hellenism–Judaism–Christianity: Essays on their Interaction.* Contributions to Biblical Exegesis and Theology 8. Leuven: Peeters.
Houtman, C. A. 1994. *Der Pentateuch : die Geschichte seiner Erforschung neben einer Auswertung.* Kampen: Kok Agora.
Howard, G. E. 1973. The "Aberrant" Text of Philo's Quotations Reconsidered. *HUCA* 44:197–209.
Huffmann, C. A. 1993. *Philolaus of Croton: Pythagorean and Presocratic.* Cambridge: Cambridge University Press.

Isaacs, M. E. 1976. *The Concept of Spirit: a Study of Pneuma in Hellenistic Judaism and its Bearing on the New Testament.* Heythrop Monographs 1. London: Heythrop College.
Jacobson, H. 1983. *The Exagoge of Ezechiel.* Cambridge University Press.
Jaeger, W. W. 1914. *Nemesios von Emesa: Quellenforschung zum Neuplatonismus und seinen Anfängen bei Poseidonios.* Berlin: Weidmann.
———. 1959. Echo eines unerkannten Tragikerfragments in Clemens' Brief an die Korinther. *RhM* 102:330–340.
Jastram, D. N. 1991. Philo's Concept of Generic Virtue. *SBLSP* 30:323–347.
Jellinek, A. 1855. *Bet ha-Midrasch, vol. 3.* Vienna. Third edition Jerusalem: Sifre Vahrman, 1967.
Jobling, D. 1977. "And have Dominion...": the Interpretation of Gen. 1, 28 in Philo Judaeus. *JSJ* 8:50–82.
Jones, R. M. 1926. Posidonius and the Flight of the Mind. *CPh* 21:97–113.
Jouanna, J. 1999. *Hippocrates: Medicine and Culture.* Baltimore: The John Hopkins University Press. English translation of French original: Paris, 1992.
Kamesar, A. 1998. Philo, the Presence of "Paideutic" Myth in the Pentateuch, and the "Principles" or Kephalaia of Mosaic Discourse. *SPhA* 10:34–65.
———. 1999. Review of P. Borgen, *Philo of Alexandria: an Exegete for his Time. JThS* 50: 753–758.
Kardaun, M. 1993. *Der Mimesisbegriff in der griechischen Antike.* Verh. d. Kon. Ned. Akad. v. Wetensch. Afd. Letterkunde NR 153. Amsterdam etc.: North-Holland.
Katz, P. 1950. *Philo's Bible: the Aberrant Text of Bible Quotations in Some Philonic Writings and its Place in the Textual History of the Greek Bible.* Cambridge University Press.
Keizer, H. M. 1999. *Life Time Entirety: A Study of ΑΙΩΝ in Greek Literature and Philosophy, the Septuagint and Philo.* Diss. Amsterdam.
Kenney, J. P. 1986. Monotheistic and Polytheistic Elements in Classical Mediterranean Spirituality. Pages 269–292 in *Classical Mediterranean Spirituality: Egyptian, Greek, Roman,* Edited by A. H. Armstrong, World Spirituality: an Encyclopedic History of the Religious Quest 15. New York: Crossroad.
Kidd, D. A., ed. 1997. *Aratus Phaenomena.* Cambridge Classical Texts and Commentaries 34. Cambridge University Press.
Kidd, I. G. 1972–1988. *Posidonius: the Fragments.* 2 volumes in 3. Cambridge Classical Texts and Commentaries 13–14. Cambridge University Press. (Volume 1 together with L. Edelstein).
Klein, F. N. 1962. *Die Lichtterminologie bei Philon von Alexandrien und in den hermetischen Schriften: Untersuchungen zur Struktur der religiösen Sprache der hellenistischen Mystik.* Leiden: Brill.
Knight, D. A. 1985. Cosmogony and Order in the Hebrew Tradition. Pages 133–157 in *Cosmogony and Ethical Order: New Studies in Comparative Ethics.* Edited by R. W. Lovin and F. E. Reynolds. Chicago University Press.
Koch, H. 1932. *Pronoia und Paideusis: Studien über Origenes und sein Verhältnis zum Platonismus.* Leipzig: De Gruyter.
Koester, H. 1968. ΝΟΜΟΣ ΦΥΣΕΩΣ: the Concept of Natural Law in Greek Thought. Pages 521–541 in *Religions in Antiquity: Essays in Memory of E. R. Goodenough.* Edited by J. Neusner. SHR 14. Leiden: Brill.
Krämer, H. J. 1964. *Der Ursprung der Geistmetaphysik: Untersuchungen zur Geschichte des Platonismus zwischen Platon und Plotin.* Amsterdam: Hakkert.
Kraus Reggiani, C. 1979. *Filone Alessandrino, De opificio mundi, De Abrahamo, De Josepho.* Biblioteca Athena 23. Rome: Edizioni dell'Ateneo & Bizzarri.
Kraus Reggiani, C., Radice, R. and Reale, G. 1987. *Filone di Alessandria: La filosofia Mosaica.* La creazione del mondo secondo Mosè (translated by C. Kraus Reggiani). Le allegorie delle Leggi (translated by R. Radice), prefaces, apparatus, and commentaries by R. Radice, introductory monograph by G. Reale and R. Radice. Milan: Rusconi.

Kugel, J. 1998. *Traditions of the Bible: a Guide to the Bible as it was at the Start of the Common Era.* Cambridge Mass.–London: Harvard University Press. (= *TB*)
Le Boulluec, A. 1981. *Clément d'Alexandrie: Les Stromates.* Stromate V. Volume 2. Commentaire, bibliographie et index. SC 279. Paris: Éditions du CERF.
——. 1998. La place des concepts philosophiques dans la réflexion de Philon sur le plaisir. Pages 129–152 in *Philon d'Alexandrie et le langage de la philosophie.* Edited by C. Lévy. Turnhout: Brepols.
Leopold, J. 1983. Philo's Vocabulary and Word Choice. Pages 137–140 in *Two Treatises of Philo of Alexandria: a Commentary on De Gigantibus and Quod Deus Sit Immutabilis.* Edited by D. Winston and J. Dillon. BJS 25. Chico: Scholars Press.
Levison, J. R. 1988. *Portraits of Adam in Early Judaism from Sirach to 2 Baruch.* JSP.MS 1. Sheffield University Press.
——. 1995. Inspiration and the Divine Spirit in the Writings of Philo Judaeus. *JSJ* 26:271–323.
Lévy, C. 1992. *Cicero Academicus: recherches sur les Académiques et sur la philosophie cicéronienne.* Collection de l'École Française de Rome 162. Rome: École Française de Rome.
——. 1998. Éthique de l'immanence, éthique de la transcendance: le problème de l'*oikeiôsis* chez Philon. Pages 153–164 in *Philon d'Alexandrie et le langage de la philosophie.* Edited by C. Lévy. Turnhout: Brepols.
——. 2000. Philon d'Alexandrie et l'épicurisme. Pages 122–136 in *Epikureismus in der späten Republik und der Kaiserzeit.* Edited by M. Erler. Philosophie der Antike 11. Stuttgart: Franz Steiner Verlag.
Lewy, H. 1929. *Sobria ebrietas: Untersuchungen zur Geschichte der antiken Mystik,* Beihefte zur Zeitschrift für die Neutestamentliche Wissenschaft 9. Gießen: Alfred Töpelmann.
Lilla, S. R. C. 1971. *Clement of Alexandria: a Study in Christian Platonism and Gnosticism.* Oxford Theological Monographs. Oxford University Press.
Littré, E. 1839–1861. *Œuvres complètes d'Hippocrate.* 10 volumes. Paris: Chez J.B. Baillière.
Lloyd, G. 1984. *The Man of Reason: "Male" and "Female" in Western Philosophy.* London: Methuen.
Lona, H. E. 1998. *Der erste Clemensbrief.* Kommentar zu den Apostolischen Vätern 2. Göttingen: Vandenhoeck & Ruprecht.
Long, A. A. 1974, 1986². *Hellenistic Philosophy.* London: Duckworth.
——. 1995. Art. "Skeptizismus (Antike)". Pages 938–950 in *HWPh* 9. Darmstadt: Wissenschaftliche Buchgesellschaft.
Long, A. A. and Sedley, D. N. 1987. *The Hellenistic Philosophers.* 2 volumes. Cambridge University Press. (= L&S)
Longrigg, J. 1993. *Greek Rational Medicine: Philosophy and Medicine from Alcmaeon to the Alexandrians.* London–New York: Routledge.
Lührmann, D. 1991. The Godlessness of Germans Living by the Sea according to Philo of Alexandria. Pages 57–63 in *The Future of Early Christianity: Essays in Honour of Helmut Koester.* Edited by B. A. Pearson et al. Minneapolis: Fortress.
Malingrey, A. M. 1961. *"Philosophia": étude d'un groupe de mots dans la littérature grecque des Présocratiques au IVe siècle après J.-C.* Paris: Klincksieck.
Mangey, T. 1742. See above §1(a).
Mansfeld, J. 1971. *The Pseudo-Hippocratic Tract* Περὶ ἑβδομάδων *ch. 1–11 and Greek Philosophy.* Philosophical Texts and Studies 20. Assen: Van Gorcum.
——. 1988. Philosophy in the Service of Scripture: Philo's Exegetical Strategies. Pages 70–102 in *The Question of "Eclecticism".* Edited by J. Dillon and A. A. Long. Berkeley: University of California Press. Reprinted in *Studies in Later Greek Philosophy and Gnosticism.* London: Variorum Reprints, 1989.
——. 1989. Review of J.-H. Kühn and U. Fleischer. *Index Hippocraticus, Mnemosyne* 42:182–186.

——. 1990. Doxography and Dialectic: the Sitz im Leben of the "Placita". Pages 3056–3229 in *Aufstieg und Niedergang der römischen Welt*. Edited by W. Haase and H. Temporini. II Principat vol. 36.4. Berlin and New York: De Gruyter.
——. 1992. *Heresiography in Context: Hippolytus' Elenchos as a Source for Greek Philosophy*. Philosophia Antiqua 56. Leiden: Brill.
Mansfeld, J. and Runia, D. T. 1996. *Aëtiana: The Method and Intellectual Context of a Doxographer*, Philosophia Antiqua 73. Leiden etc.: Brill.
Martín, J. P. 1986. La presencia de Filón en el Exámeron de Teófilo de Antioquía. *Salmaticensis* 33:147–177.
——. 1989. La antropologia de Filon y la de Teofilo de Antioquia: sus lecturas de Genesis 2–5. *Salmaticensis* 36:23–71.
——. 1996. El motor inmóvil de Aristóteles y el Dios de Filón. *Methexis. Revista Argentina de Filosofía Antigua* 9:84–98.
Mattila, S. L. 1996. Wisdom, Sense Perception, Nature and Philo's Gender Gradient. *HTR* 89:103–129.
May, G. 1994. *Creatio ex nihilo: the Doctrine of "Creation out of Nothing" in Early Christian Thought*. Edinburgh: T & T Clark. Translation of German edition: Berlin, 1978.
Mazzanti, A. M. 1978. L'aggettivo μεθόριος e la doppia creazione dell'uomo in Filone di Alessandria. Pages 25–42 in *La "doppia creazione" dell'uomo negli Alessandrini, nei Cappadoci e nella Gnosi*. Edited by U. Bianchi. Rome: Edizioni dell'Ateneo & Bizzarri.
Mazzerelli, C. 1985. Raccolta e interpretazione delle testimonianze e dei frammenti del medioplatonico Eudoro di Alessandria. *Rivista di Filosofia Neoscolastica* 77:197–209, 535–555.
Méasson, A. 1966. *Philon De sacrificiis Abelis et Caini*. Les œuvres de Philon d'Alexandrie 4. Paris: Éditions du CERF.
——. 1986. Du char ailé de Zeus à l'Arche d'Alliance: Images et mythes platoniciens chez Philon d'Alexandrie. Paris: Études Augustiniennes.
Mendelson, A. 1982. *Secular Education in Philo of Alexandria*. Monographs of the Hebrew Union College 7. Cincinnati: Hebrew Union College Press.
——. 1988. *Philo's Jewish Identity*. BJS 161. Atlanta: Scholars Press.
——. 1994. "Did Philo Say the Shema?" and Other Reflections on E. P. Sanders. *Judaism: Practice and Belief*. *SPhA* 6:160–170.
——. 1997. Philo's Dialectic of Reward and Punishment. Pages 104–125 in *Wisdom and Logos: Studies in Jewish Thought in Honor of David Winston [= SPhA 9 (1997)]*. Edited by D. T. Runia and G. E. Sterling. BJS 312. Atlanta: Scholars Press.
Merki, H. 1952. ΌΜΟΙΩΣΙΣ ΘΕΩΙ: *von der platonischen Angleichung an Gott zur Gottähnlichkeit bei Gregor von Nyssa*. Paradosis 7. Freiburg in der Schweiz: Paulusverlag.
Metzger, M., ed. 1985–87. *Les Constitutions Apostoliques*. 3 volumes. SC 320, 329, 336. Paris: Éditions du CERF.
Miller, J. 1986. *Measures of Wisdom: the Cosmic Dance in Classical and Christian Antiquity*. Toronto: University of Toronto Press.
Moehring, H. 1995. Arithmology as an Exegetical Tool in the Writings of Philo of Alexandria. Pages 141–176 in *The School of Moses: Studies in Philo and Hellenistic Religion in Memory of Horst R. Moehring*. Edited by J. P. Kenney. Brown Judaic Series 304 (= Studia Philonica Monograph Series 1). Atlanta: Scholars Press.
Morris, J. 1987. The Jewish philosopher Philo. Pages 809–889, Volume III.2 in *The History of the Jewish People in the Age of Jesus Christ (175 B.C. – A.D. 135)*. Edited by E. Schürer, G. Vermes et al. Edinburgh: T & T Clark.
Mühlenberg, E. 1966. *Die Unendlichkeit Gottes bei Gregor von Nyssa: Gregors Kritik am Gottesbegriff der klassischen Metaphysik*. Forschungen zur Kirchen- und Dogmengeschichte 16. Göttingen: Vandenhoeck & Ruprecht.

Müller, J. G. 1841. See above §1(b).
Niehoff, M. R. 1995. What's in a Name? Philo's Mystical Philosophy of Language. *Jewish Studies Quarterly* 2:220–252.
Nikiprowetzky, V. 1963. Les suppliants chez Philon d'Alexandrie. *REJ* 122:241–278. Reprinted in 1996, pages 11–44.
——. 1965. Problèmes du "récit de la création" chez Philon d'Alexandrie. *REJ* 124:271-306. Reprinted in 1996, pages 45–78.
——. 1967. La doctrine de l'élenchos chez Philon, ses résonances philosophiques et sa portée religieuse. Pages 255–273 in *Philon d'Alexandrie. Lyon 11–15 Septembre 1966: colloques nationaux du Centre National de la Recherche Scientifique.* Paris: Éditions du CNRS.
——. 1977. *Le commentaire de l'Écriture chez Philon d'Alexandrie: son caractère et sa portée; observations philologiques.* ALGHJ 11. Leiden: Brill.
——. 1977. ΣΤΕΙΡΑ, ΣΤΕΡΡΑ, ΠΟΛΛΗ et l'exégèse de I Sam. 2, 5 chez Philon d'Alexandrie. *Sileno* 3:149–185. Reprinted in 1996, pages 171–197.
——. 1989. Thèmes et traditions de la lumière chez Philon d'Alexandrie. *SPhA* 1:6–33.
——. 1996. *Études philoniennes.* Patrimoines Judaisme. Paris: Éditions du CERF.
Oden, R. A. 1992. Art. "Cosmogony, Cosmology". Volume 1, pages 1162–1171 in *The Anchor Bible Dictionary.* New York: Doubleday.
Paramelle, J. 1984. *Philon d'Alexandrie: Questions sur la Genèse II 1–7: texte grec, versions arménienne, parallèles latins.* Cahiers d'Orientalisme 3. Geneva: Patrick Cramer.
Pearson, B. A. 1984. Philo and Gnosticism. Pages 295–342 in *Hellenistisches Judentum in römischer Zeit: 1. Halbband, Philon.* Edited by W. Haase. Aufstieg und Niedergang des römischen Welt II Principat vol. 21.1. Berlin and New York: De Gruyter.
Pease, A. S. 1955–58. See above §2 Cicero.
Pépin, J. 1953. Recherches sur les sens et les origines de l'expression "Caelum caeli" dans le livre XII des *Confessions* de S. Augustin. *Archivum Latinitatis Medii Aevi [Bulletin du Cange]* 23:185–274, esp. 248–251, 259–274. Reprinted in Idem 1977. *"Ex Platonicorum persona:" études sur les lectures philosophiques de Saint Augustin.* Amsterdam: Hakkert. Pages 39–130.
——. 1958, 1976². *Mythe et allégorie: les origines grecques et les contestations judéo-chrétiennes.* Philosophie de l'Esprit. Paris: Éditions Montaignes.
——. 1964. *Théologie cosmique et théologie chrétienne (Ambroise, Exam. I 1, 1–4).* Paris: Presses Universitaires de France.
——. 1967. Remarques sur la théorie de l'exégèse allégorique chez Philon. Pages 131–167 in *Philon d'Alexandrie. Lyon 11–15 Septembre 1966: colloques nationaux du Centre National de la Recherche Scientifique.* Paris: Éditions du CNRS.
——. 1971. *Idées grecques sur l'homme et sur Dieu.* Paris: Les Belles Lettres.
——. 1986. Cosmic Piety. Pages 408–435 in *Classical Mediterranean Spirituality: Egyptian, Greek, Roman.* Edited by A. H. Armstrong. New York: Crossroad.
Petit, F. 1973. See above §1(c).
——. 1992–97. See above §2 under *Genesis Catena.*
Petit, M. 1974. *Quod omnis probus liber sit.* Les œuvres de Philon d'Alexandrie 28. Paris: Éditions du CERF.
Phillips, E. D. 1973. *Greek Medicine.* London: Thames & Hudson.
Pilhofer, P. 1990. *Presbyteron kreitton: Der Alterbeweis der jüdischen und christlichen Apologeten und seine Vorgeschichte.* WUNT 2.39. Tübingen: Mohr Siebeck.
Places, E. des. 1964. *Syngeneia: la parenté de l'homme avec Dieu d'Homère à la Patristique.* Études et commentaires 51. Paris: Klincksieck.
Pohlenz, M. 1916. Paul Wendland. *Neue Jahrbücher für das klassische Altertum* 19:57–75.

Popa, T. M. 1999. Functions of the *Typos* Imagery in Philo of Alexandria. *Ancient Philosophy* 19:1–12.
Pyle, A. 1995. *Atomism and its Critics: from Democritus to Newton*. Bristol: Thoemmes Press.
Radice, R. 1989. *Platonismo e creazionismo in Filone di Alessandria*. Pubblicazioni del Centro di Ricerche di Metafisica: sezione di Metafysica del Platonismo nel suo sviluppo storico e nella filosofia patristica. Studi e testi 7. Milan: Vita e Pensiero.
——. 1991. Observations on the Theory of the Ideas as the Thoughts of God in Philo of Alexandria. Pages 126–134 in *Heirs of the Septuagint. Philo, Hellenistic Judaism and Early Christianity: Festschrift for Earle Hilgert*. Edited by D. T. Runia, D. M. Hay and D. Winston. BJS 230 [= *SPhA* 3 (1991)]. Atlanta: Scholars Press.
——. 1994. *La filosofia di Aristobulo e i suoi nessi con il «De Mundo» attribuito ad Aristotele*. Pubblicazioni del Centro di Ricerche di Metafisica: Collana Temi metafisici e problemi del pensiero antico. Studi e Testi 33. Milan: Vita e Pensiero.
Radice, R. and Runia, D. T. 1999. Testimonia de Philone. Pages 365–445 in D. T. Runia, *Filone di Alessandria nella prima letteratura cristiana*. Milan: Vita e Pensiero.
Reale, G. 1979. Filone di Alessandria e la prima elaborazione filosofica della dottrina della creazione. Pages 247–287 in *Paradoxos politeia: studi patristici in onore di G. Lazzati*. Edited by R. Cantalamessa and L. F. Pizzolato. Milan: Vita e Pensiero.
Reydams-Schils, G. J. 1995. Stoicized Readings of Plato's *Timaeus* in Philo of Alexandria. *SPhA* 7:85–102.
——. 1999. *Demiurge and Providence: Stoic and Platonist Readings of Plato's "Timaeus"*. Monothéismes et Philosophie. Turnhout: Brepols.
Reynolds, L. D. and Wilson, N. G. 1968, 1974[2]. *Scribes and Scholars*. Oxford University Press.
Riedweg, C. 1994. *Ps.-Justin (Markell von Ankyra?) Ad Graecos de vera religione (bisher «Cohortatio ad Graecos»). Einleitung und Kommentar*. Schweizerische Beiträge zur Altertumswissenschaft 25. Basel: Reinhardt.
Rinaldi, G. 1989. *Biblia Gentium*. Rome: Liberia Sacre Scritture.
Robbins, F. E. 1912. *The Hexaemeral Literature: a Study of the Greek and Latin Commentaries on Genesis*. Chicago University Press.
——. 1920. Posidonius and the Sources of Pythagorean Arithmology. *CPh* 15:309–322.
——. 1921. The Tradition of Greek Arithmology. *CPh* 16:97–123.
——. 1931. Arithmetic in Philo Judaeus. *CPh* 26:345–361.
Röhr, J. 1928. Beiträge zur antiken Astrometereologie. *Philologus* 83:259–305.
Rösel, M. 1994. *Übersetzung als Vollendung der Auslegung: Studien zur Genesis-Septuaginta*. BZAW 223. Berlin and New York: De Gruyter.
Romeny, R. B. ter Haar. 1997. *A Syrian in Greek Dress: the Use of Greek, Hebrew, and Syriac Biblical Texts in Eusebius of Emesa's Commentary on Genesis*. Traditio Exegetica Graeca 6. Diss. Leiden, Leuven: Peeters.
Roscher, W. H., ed. 1913. *Die hippokratische Schrift von der Siebenzahl in ihrer vierfachen Überlieferung*. Studien zur Geschichte und Kultur des Altertums 6.3-4. Paderborn: F. Schoningh.
Royse, J. R. 1993. Reverse Indexes to Philonic texts in the Printed Florilegia and Collections of Fragments. *SPhA* 5:156–179.
——. 2000. The Text of Philo's *Legum Allegoriae*. *SPhA* 12:1–28.
——. 2001. Philo's Division of his Works into Books. *SPhA* 13:59–85.
Rudolph, K. 1987. *Gnosis: the Nature and History of Gnosticism*. San Francisco: Harper and Row.

Runia, D. T. 1981. Philo's *De aeternitate mundi:* The Problem of its Interpretation. *VChr* 35:105–151. Reprinted in Runia 1990.
———. 1984. The Structure of Philo's Allegorical Treatises. *VChr* 38:209–256. Reprinted in Runia 1990.
———. 1986². *Philo of Alexandria and the Timaeus of Plato.* Philosophia Antiqua 44 Leiden: Brill. (First edition diss. Amsterdam: VU Boekhandel 1983). (= *PT*).
———. 1987. Further Observations on the Structure of Philo's Allegorical Treatises. *VChr* 41:105–138. Reprinted in Runia 1990.
———. 1988. God and Man in Philo of Alexandria. *JTS* 39:48–75. Reprinted in Runia 1990.
———. 1989. Polis and Megalopolis: Philo and the Founding of Alexandria. *Mnemosyne* 42:398–412. Reprinted in Runia 1990.
———. 1990. *Exegesis and Philosophy: Studies on Philo of Alexandria.* London: Variorum Reprints.
———. 1991. Review of M. Marcovich, Athenagoras *Legatio pro Christianis* and Pseudo-Justinus *Cohortatio ad Graecos, De monarchia, Oratio ad Graecos. VChr* 45:398–403.
———. 1992a. The Language of Excellence in Plato's *Timaeus* and Later Platonism. Pages 11–37 in *Platonism in Late Antiquity.* Edited by S. Gersh and C. Kannengiesser. Christianity and Judaism in Antiquity 8. Notre Dame: University of Notre Dame Press.
———. 1992b. Verba Philonica, ΑΓΑΛΜΑΤΟΦΟΡΕΙΝ, and the Authenticity of the *De Resurrectione* Attributed to Athenagoras', *VChr* 46:313–327. Reprinted in Runia 1995.
———. 1993. *Bios eudaimoon.* Inaugural lecture. Leiden.
———. 1993. *Philo in Early Christian Literature: a Survey.* CRINT III 3. Assen: Van Gorcum; Minneapolis: Fortress Press (= *PEC*).
———. 1995. *Philo and Church Fathers: a Collection of Papers.* VChr.S 32. Leiden: Brill.
———. 1996a. Caesarea Maritima and the Survival of Hellenistic-Jewish Literature. Pages 476–95 in *Caesarea Maritima: a Retrospective after Two Millenia.* Edited by A. Raban and K. G. Holum. Documenta et Monumenta Orientis Antiqui 21. Leiden: Brill.
———. 1996b. Atheists in Aëtius: Text, Translation and Comments on *De placitis* 1.7.1–10. *Mnemosyne* 49:542–576.
———. 1997a. The Text of the Platonic Citations in Philo of Alexandria. Pages 261–291 in *Studies in Plato and the Platonic Tradition: Essays Presented to John Whittaker.* Edited by M. Joyal. Aldershot etc.: Ashgate.
———. 1997b. The Reward for Goodness: Philo, *De Vita Contemplativa* 90. Pages 3–18 in *Wisdom and Logos: Studies in Jewish Thought in Honor of David Winston [= SPhA 9 (1997)].* Edited by D. T. Runia and G. E. Sterling. BJS 312. Atlanta: Scholars Press.
———. 1998. L'exégèse philosophique et l'influence de la pensée philonienne dans la tradition patristique. Pages 327–348 in *Philon d'Alexandrie et le langage de la philosophie.* Edited by C. Lévy. Turnhout: Brepols.
———. 1999a. Philo of Alexandria and the Greek *Hairesis* - model. *VChr* 53:117–147.
———. 1999b. A Brief History of the Term *Kosmos Noētos* from Plato to Plotinus. Pages 151–172 in *Traditions of Platonism: Essays in Honour of John Dillon.* Edited by J. J. Cleary. Aldershot etc.: Ashgate.
———. 2000. Philo's Longest Arithmological Passage: *De opificio mundi* 89–128. Pages 155–174 in *De Jérusalem à Rome: mélanges offerts à Jean Riaud.* Edited by L. J. Bord and D. Hamidovic. Paris: Guethner.
———. 2001a. Philo of Alexandrian and the End of Hellenistic Theology. Pages 281–316 in *Traditions of Theology: Studies in Hellenistic Theology, its Background and Aftermath.* Edited by A. Laks and D. Frede. Philosophia Antiqua. Leiden: Brill.

———. 2001b. Philo's Use of the Psalms. Pages 102–121 in *In the Spirit of Faith. Studies on Philo and Early Christianity in Honour of David Hay*. Edited by D. T. Runia and G.E. Sterling. BJS [= *The Studia Philonica Annual* 13]. Atlanta: SBL Publications.
———. 2001c. Eudaimonism in Hellenistic-Jewish literature. Forthcoming in *Shem in the Tents of Japheth*. Edited by J. L. Kugel. Leiden: Brill.
Sambursky, S. 1959. *Physics of the Stoics*. London: Routledge & Paul.
Sandelin, K.-G. 1986. *Wisdom as Nourisher. A Study of an Old Testament Theme, its Development within Early Judaism and its Impact on Early Christianity*. Acta Academiae Aboensis Ser. A Humaniora 64.3. Åbo: Åbo Akademi.
Savon, H. 1977. *Saint Ambroise devant l'exégèse de Philon le Juif.* 2 volumes. Paris: Études Augustiniennes.
Scheil, V. 1893. Deux traités de Philo. *Mémoires publiés par les membres de la Mission Archéologique Française au Caire* 9.2:151–216.
Schimmel, A. 1993. *The Mystery of Numbers*. New York: Oxford University Press.
Schofield, M. 1991. *The Stoic Idea of the City*. Cambridge University Press.
Schubart, W. 1921^2, 1964^3. *Das Buch bei den Griechen und Römern*. Heidelberg: Lambert Schneider.
Scott, A. B. 1991. *Origen and the Life of the Stars*, Oxford Early Christian Studies. Oxford: Clarendon Press.
Schwabe, M. 1999. Philo, *De opificio mundi* § 15. Edited and translated from the Hebrew with an introductory note by Adam Kamesar. *SPhA* 11:104–112.
Segal, A. F. 1980. Heavenly Ascent in Hellenistic Judaism, Early Christianity and their Environment. Pages 1333–1394 in *Religion*. Aufstieg und Niedergang der römischen Welt II Principat vol. 23.2. Edited by W. Haase. Berlin–New York: De Gruyter.
———. 1987. Torah and *Nomos* in Recent Scholarly Discussion. Pages 131–146 in *The Other Judaisms of Late Antiquity*. Edited by Idem. BJS 127. Atlanta: Scholars Press.
Siegert, F. 1996. Early Jewish Interpretation in a Hellenistic Style. Pages 130–198 in *Hebrew Bible / Old Testament. The History of Its Interpretation*. Edited by M. Sæbø. Göttingen: Van den Hoeck & Ruprecht.
Sly, D. 1990. *Philo's Perception of Women*. BJS 209. Atlanta: Scholars Press.
———. 1995. *Philo's Alexandria*. London: Routledge.
Smyth, H. W. 1956^2. *Greek Grammar*. Revised by G. M. Messing. Cambridge Mass.: Harvard University Press.
Söding, T. 1996. „Gott ist Liebe": 1 Joh 4,8.16 als Spitzensatz Biblischer Theologie. Pages 306–357 in *Der lebendige Gott. Studien zur Theologie des Neuen Testaments: Festschrift für Wilhelm Thüsing zum 75. Geburtstag*. Edited by T. Söding. Neutestamentliche Abhandlungen NF 31. Münster: Aschendorff.
Sorabji, R. 1983. *Time, Creation and the Continuum*. London: Duckworth.
Spoerri, W. 1959. *Späthellenistische Berichte über Welt, Kultur und Götter*. Schweizerische Beiträge zur Altertumswissenschaft 9. Basel: Reinhardt.
Staehle, K. 1931. *Die Zahlenmystik bei Philon von Alexandreia*. Leipzig and Berlin: Teubner.
Stahl, W. H. and Johnson, R. 1971–1977. *Martianus Capella and the Seven Liberal Arts*. 2 volumes. New York: Columbia University Press.
Starnes, C. 1990. *Augustine's Confessions: a Guide to the Argument of Confessions I–IX*. Waterloo: Wilfred Laurier University Press.
Sterling, G. E. 1992. '*Creatio Temporalis, Aeterna, vel Continua?* an Analysis of the Thought of Philo of Alexandria', *SPhA* 4:15–41.
———. 1997. Prepositional Metaphysics in Jewish Wisdom: Speculation and Early Christological Hymns. Pages 219–238 in *Wisdom and Logos: Studies in Jewish Thought in Honor of David Winston [= SPhA 9 (1997)]*. Edited by D. T. Runia and G. E. Sterling. BJS 312. Atlanta: Scholars Press.

———. 1998. A Philosophy according to the Elements of the Cosmos: Colossian Christianity and Philo of Alexandria. Pages 349–373 in *Philon d'Alexandrie et le langage de la philosophie*, edited by C. Lévy. Turnhout: Brepols.

———. 1999a. Recherché or Representative? What is the Relationship between Philo's Treatises and Greek-speaking Judaism? *SPhA* 11:1–30.

———. 1999b. "The School of Sacred Laws": the Social Setting of Philo's Treatises. *VChr* 53:148–164.

———. Forthcoming. "The Queen of the Virtues": Εὐσέβεια in Philo of Alexandria. Paper presented at SBL meeting 1999.

Stern, M. 1974–84. *Greek and Latin Authors on Jews and Judaism*. 3 volumes. Jerusalem: Israel Academy of Arts and Sciences (= *GLAJJ*).

Strack, H. L. and Stemberger, G. 1991. *Introduction to the Talmud and Midrash*. Translated by M. Bockmuehl. Edinburgh: T & T Clark.

Szymanski, M. 1981. On the Authenticity of Philolaus' Fr. B 20. *Archiv der Geschichte der Philosophie* 63:115–117.

Tarrant, H. 1985. *Scepticism or Platonism? The Philosophy of the Fourth Academy*. Cambridge Classical Studies. Cambridge University Press.

Tcherikover, V. A. 1957. *Corpus papyrorum judaicarum*. In collaboration with A. Fuks. Volume 1. Cambridge Mass.: Harvard University Press.

Terian, A. 1981. *Philonis Alexandrini de Animalibus: the Armenian Text with an Introduction, Translation and Commentary*. Studies in Hellenistic Judaism: Supplements to Studia Philonica 1. Chico, CA: Scholars Press.

———. 1984. A Philonic Fragment on the Decad. Pages 173–182 in *Nourished with Peace: Studies in Hellenistic Judaism in Memory of Samuel Sandmel*. Edited by F. E. Greenspahn, E. Hilgert and B. L. Mack. Scholars Press Homage Series 9. Chico, CA: Scholars Press.

———. 1991. The Priority of the *Quaestiones* among Philo's Exegetical Commentaries. Pages 29–46 in *Both Literal and Allegorical: Studies in Philo of Alexandria's Questions and Answers on Genesis and Exodus*. Edited by D. M. Hay. BJS 232. Atlanta: Scholars Press.

———. 1992. *Quaestiones et Solutiones in Exodum I et II e versione armeniaca et fragmenta graeca*. Les œuvres de Philon d'Alexandrie 34c. Paris: Éditions du CERF.

———. 1997. Back to Creation: The Beginning of Philo's Third Grand Commentary. Pages 19–36 in *Wisdom and Logos: Studies in Jewish Thought in Honor of David Winston [= SPhA 9 (1997)]*. Edited by D. T. Runia and G. E. Sterling. BJS 312. Atlanta: Scholars Press.

Theiler, W. 1964. See above §1(e).

———. 1965. Philo von Alexandria und der Beginn des kaiserzeitlichen Platonismus. Pages 199–218 in *Parusia: Studien zur Philosophie Platons und zur Problemgeschichte des Platonismus; Festgabe für J. Hirschberger*. Edited by K. Flasch. Frankfurt: Minerva.

———. 1971. Philo von Alexandria und der hellenisierte *Timaeus*. Pages 25–35 in *Philomathes: studies and essays in the humanities in honour of Philip Merlan*. Edited by R. B. Palmer and R. G. Hamerton-Kelly. The Hague: Martinus Nijhoff.

———. 1982. *Poseidonios: die Fragmente*. 2 volumes. Texte und Kommentare 10. Berlin and New York: De Gruyter.

Thesleff, H. 1965. *The Pythagorean Texts of the Hellenistic Period*. Acta Academiae Aboensis A 30.1. Åbo: Åbo Akademi.

Tobin, T. H. 1983. *The Creation of Man: Philo and the History of Interpretation*. CBQ.MS 14. Washington: Catholic Biblical Association of America (= *CM*).

———. 1992. Article "Logos". Volume 4, pages 348–356 in *The Anchor Bible Dictionary*. New York: Doubleday.

———. 2000. The Beginning of Philo's *Legum Allegoriae*. *SPhA* 12:29–43.

Urbach, E. E. 1975, 1987³. *The Sages, their Concepts and Beliefs*. Translated from the Hebrew by I. Abrahams. 2 volumes. Jerusalem: Magnes Press; Cambridge Mass.: Harvard University Press.
Usener, H. 1887. *Epicurea*. Leipzig: Teubner. Reprinted Stuttgart 1966.
Verdenius, W. J. 1949. *Mimesis: Platos Doctrine of Artistic Imitation and its Meaning to us*. Philosophia Antiqua 3. Leiden: Brill.
Vlastos, G. 1975. *Plato's Universe*. Oxford: Clarendon Press.
Völker, W. 1938. *Fortschritt und Vollendung bei Philo von Alexandrien: eine Studie zur Geschichte der Frömmigkeit*. TU 49.1. Leipzig: J. C. Hinrichs Verlag.
Vogel, C. J. de. 1985. Platonism and Christianity: a Mere Antagonism or a Profound Common Ground? *VChr* 39:1–62.
Wächter, L. 1962. Der Einfluss platonischen Denkens auf rabbinische Schöpfungsspekulationen. *ZRGG* 14:36–56.
Wallis, R. T. 1975. *The Idea of Conscience in Philo of Alexandria*. CHSHMC 13. Berkeley. Also published in 1974–75 in *SPh* 3:27–40 (which we cite).
Walter, N. 1964. *Der Thoraausleger Aristobulos: Untersuchungen zu seinen Fragmenten und zu pseudepigraphischen Resten der jüdisch-hellenistischen Literatur*. Berlin: Akademie-Verlag.
Waterfield, R. 1988. *The Theology of Arithmetic*. Grand Rapids: Phanes Press.
Weaver, M. J. 1973. *Πνεῦμα in Philo of Alexandria*. Diss. Notre Dame.
Wegner, J. Romney. 1991. Philo's Portrayal of Women—Hebraic or Hellenic? In *"Women like this:" New Perspectives on Jewish Women in the Greco-Roman World*. Edited by A.-J. Levine. Early Judaism and its Literature 1. Atlanta: Scholars Press.
Weiss, H. 1991. Philo on the Sabbath. Pages 83–105 in *Heirs of the Septuagint. Philo, Hellenistic Judaism and Early Christianity: Festschrift for Earle Hilgert*. Edited by D. T. Runia, D. M. Hay and D. Winston. BJS 230. [= *SPhA* 3 (1991)]. Atlanta: Scholars Press.
Weiss, H. F. 1966. *Untersuchungen zur Kosmologie des hellenistischen und palästinischen Judentums*. TU 97. Berlin: Akademie Verlag.
Wellmann, M. 1901. *Die Fragmente der Sikelischen Ärtze Akron, Philostion und des Diokles von Karystos*. Berlin: Weidmann.
Wendland, P. 1890. Review of L. Cohn, *Philonis Alexandrini libellus De opificio mundi*. *Berliner Philologische Wochenschrift* 10:237–242.
———. 1895. Philo und die kynisch-stoische Diabribe. Pages 1–75 in P. Wendland and O. Kern, *Beiträge zur Geschichte der griechischen Philosophie und Religion*. Berlin: Georg Reimer.
West, M. L. 1971. The Cosmology of "Hippocrates," *De Hebdomadibus*. *CQ* NS 21:365–388.
———. ed. 1992². *Iambi et elegi graeci*. 2 volumes. Oxford: Clarendon Press.
———. ed. 1993. *Greek Lyric Poetry*. Oxford: Clarendon Press.
Westermann, C. 1984. *Genesis 1–11: a Commentary*. Minneapolis: Augsburg. Translation of German edition: Neukirchen-Vluyn, 1974.
Whittaker, J. 1996. The Terminology of the Rational Soul in the Writings of Philo of Alexandria. *SPhA* 8:1–20.
Winden, J. C. M. van. 1971. *An Early Christian Philosopher: Justin Martyr's Dialogue with Trypho Chapters One to Nine*. Philosophia Patrum 1. Leiden: Brill.
———. 1983. The World of Ideas in Philo of Alexandria: an Interpretation of *De opificio mundi* 24–25. *VChr* 37:209–217.
———. 1988. Art. Hexaemeron. *RAC* 14:1250–69. Stuttgart: Anton Hiersemann.
———. 1997. *Arche: a Collection of Patristic Studies*. Edited by J. den Boeft and D. T. Runia. VChr.S 41. Leiden: Brill.
Winston, D. 1979. *The Wisdom of Solomon*. The Anchor Bible. Garden City NY: Doubleday.
———. 1981. See above §1(d) (= *PA*).

———. 1984. Philo's Ethical Theory. Pages 372–416 in *Hellenistisches Judentum in römischer zeit: Philon und Josephus.* Edited by W. Haase. Aufstieg und Niedergang der römischen Welt II Principat vol. 21.1. Berlin and New York: De Gruyter.
———. 1985a. *Logos and Mystical Theology in Philo of Alexandria.* Cincinatti: Hebrew Union College Press.
———. 1985b. Review of T. Tobin, *The Creation of Man. JBL* 104:558–560.
———. 1986. Theodicy and Creation of Man in Philo of Alexandria. Pages 105–111 in *Hellenica et Judaica: hommage à Valentin Nikiprowetzky.* Edited by A. Caquot, M. Hadas-Lebel and J. Riaud. Leuven: Peeters.
———. 1989. Two Types of Mosaic Prophecy according to Philo. *JSP* 4:49-67.
———. 1990. Judaism and Hellenism: Hidden Tensions in Philo's Thought. *SPhA* 2:1–19.
———. 1991. Aspects of Philo's Linguistic Theory. Pages 109–125 in *Heirs of the Septuagint. Philo, Hellenistic Judaism and Early Christianity: Festschrift for Earle Hilgert.* Edited by D. T. Runia, D. M. Hay and D. Winston. BJS 230 [= *SPhA* 3 (1991)]. Atlanta: Scholars Press.
———. 1998. Philo and the Rabbis on Sex and the Body. *Poetics Today* 19:41–62.
Winter, B. W. 1997. *Philo and Paul among the Sophists.* SNTSMS 96. Cambridge University Press.
Wolfson, H. A. 1947, 1968[4]. *Philo: Foundations of Religious Philosophy in Judaism, Christianity and Islam.* 2 volumes. Cambridge, Mass.: Harvard University Press.
Wünsche, A. 1910. *Aus Israels Lehrhallen. Band V 2 Kleine Midrashim: Neue Pesikta und Midrasch Tadsche.* Leipzig: E. Pfeiffer.
Yarbro Collins, A. 1984. Numerical Symbolism in Jewish and Early Christian Apocalyptic Literature. Pages 1222–1287 in *Hellenistisches Judentum in römischer zeit: Philon und Josephus.* Edited by W. Haase. Aufstieg und Niedergang der römischen Welt II Principat vol. 21.2. Berlin and New York: De Gruyter.
Yonge, C. D. 1854–55, 1993. See above §1(a).
Zeller, D. 1990. *Charis bei Philon und Paulus.* Stuttgarter Bibelstudien 142. Stuttgart: Katholisches Bibelwerk.
———. 1993. Notiz zu den "immerfließenden Quellen der göttlichen Wohltaten." *SPhA* 5:93–94.
———. 1995. The Life and Death of the Soul in Philo of Alexandria: the Use and Origin of a Metaphor. *SPhA* 7:19–56.

INDICES

It should be noted that the first three sections of these indices do not contain all references, but only include those texts cited or discussed in some detail. Page numbers joined by a dash indicate a reference on each of the pages concerned, not necessarily a continuous discussion. For ancient names see both §§3 and 4; repetitions are avoided where possible.

1. Index of biblical passages cited

Genesis		19:24	192
1–3	10–14 and passim		
1:1	158	Deuteronomy	
1:3	168		
1:5	128	6:4	200
1:26–27	149–50, 223	30:15–20	25
1.28	255		
2:2	267	Psalms	
2:7	223	8:7–9	14, 256
2:8	144	100:1	386
8:22	209		
9:1–2	256	Isaiah	
		40:13	116
Exodus			
2:7	166	Wisdom	
3:14	119, 401	7:1	334
7:1	227	11:20	147
16:4	378		
20:11	126	1 Corinthians	
22:27	160	13:12	234
		15:47	334
Leviticus			
11:21–2	14, 380		

2. Index of Philonic texts cited

De opificio mundi		1.105–108	381
passim		2.11–3	220
		2.13	242
Legum allegoriae		2.14–8	352
1.2	158	3.116–7	252
1.2–6	129	3.139	383
1.8–15	283, 305	3.145	313
1.14	294		
1.18	166	*De cherubim*	
1.19–25	312	44	125
1.43	161	62	214

INDEX OF PHILONIC TEXTS CITED

De sacrificiis	
12	189
65	126

Quod deterius	
57–60	351
79–90	234
83	226
87	228
90	345

De posteritate Caini	
64–5	306, 311, 313

De gigantibus	
8	240
16	241
28–9	355
31	251
33	325

Quod deus immutabilis sit	
32	171
35	317
43	339
73–76	388

De agricultura	
8	258
94–101	383
96	376
103	382

De plantatione	
36	365–6
45	368
86	97
117	195
120–5	195
121–2	194
123	192
188	209

De confusione	
114	393
170	119, 274, 398
179	241

De migratione	
37	366
128	343
181	190
187	202
192–3	116

Quis heres	
32	181
53	217
88	254
115	184
164	243

De congressu	
149	112
143	218
197	217

De fuga	
12	148
69	241
72	242
177	319
178	97
179	315

De mutatione nominum	
4	200
63	352
223	324, 345
267	171

De somniis	
1.21–4	202
1.75	168
1.121	286
1.203–7	189
2.231	344
2.270	367

De Abrahamo	
1	120
2	2, 5
13	2, 5
13	195
69	112
74	227
87	356
88	139
156–64	201
162	204

De vita Moysis	
1.1	98
1.21–4	114
1.207	267
2.44	107
2.50–1	101
2.84	192
2.194	177
2.215–6	297

De decalogo

18	239
58	158
98	298
101–5	306
111	339

De specialibus legibus

1.13–14	190
1.16–9	208
1.19	160
1.28–31	102
1.43–4	147
1.66	159
1.91	206, 286
1.279	169
1.327	312
1.330	397
1.345	359
2.42–8	340
2.56–9	306
2.58	128
2.59	166
2.151	186
2.225	338
3.1–6	4
4.96	313
4.100	378
4.113	377
4.123	336

De virtutibus

175	253, 297
203–5	338, 346, 389
203	335
205	359

De praemiis

1–3	2, 100
1	253
3	5
9	258
37–40	233
42	118, 401
46	167
81	368

Quod probus

140	217

De vita contemplativa

1	99, 105
16	280
34	381

63	358
90	402

De aeternitate mundi

1–2	105
7–19	113
15	139
19	120
52	158
63	319
66	318
69	185
86	169
92	312
98	317

De providentia

passim	249
1.20	158
2.50–1	399
2.109	207

De animalbus

passim	240

Quaestiones in Genesim

1.1	311
1.2	313
1.3	315, 319
1.10	19, 367
1.11	367
1.19	220
1.20–2	352
1.32	369
1.33	381
1.55	145, 351
1.56	389
1.64	177, 218
2.18	160
2.47	186
2.56	258
2.62	345
2.66	186
2.67	319
3.1	112
3.3	200
3.33	190
3.38	281
4.57	177

Quaestiones in Exodum

1.1	186, 288
1.7	127
2.85	165

3. Index of ancient texts cited

(a) Greek and Roman texts

Aëtius the doxographer
Placita
4.12   382

Alcinous
Didaskalikos
6.10   349
9.1   147
12.1   150
28.3   344

Alexander of Aphrodisias
Commentary on Aristotle's Metaphysics
38.10–6   194

Anatolius
On the first ten numbers
32.3–6   193
35–7   304–6
35.11–2   276
35.6–8   274
39.6–8   192

Aratus
Phaenomena
256–67   287

Aristotle
De generatione animalium
2.2, 736a13–7   218
2.3, 736b27–9   219
De progressu animalium
15, 713a2–15   215
Metaphysics
A 3, 981b21–8   317
Nicomachean Ethics
1.4, 1095a17–22   342

Arius Didymus
ap. Eus. *Praep. Evang.*
11.23.6   150
15.15.3   342
15.15.4–5 107

Atticus
frg, 4   118

Cicero
On the Laws
1.18–9   107

2.16   102
2.23–4   107
On the Nature of the Gods
1.19   141
1.2   395
2.100   215
2.154–6   249
On the Republic
1.59   227
Tusculan disputations
4.13   335

Diodorus Siculus
Universal History
1.7.1   181

Diogenes Laertius
Lives of the Philosophers
7.153   176

Hesiod
Works and Days
383–4   286

Ps.-Hippocrates
On the Sevens
1   292

Ps.-Iamblichus
Theology of Arithmetic
29.1–12   193
50.8–10   127
57.13–6   295
86.3–5   192

Macrobius
Commentary on the Dream of Scipio
1.6.35   272
1.6.45   295
1.6.62–70   291

Maximus Tyrius
Dissertations
11.9–10   230

Nicomachus of Gerasa
Introduction to arithmetic
2.29.1   282

Ovid
Metamorphoses
1.72–5   215

Plato
Alcibiades major
133c   226
Menexenus
237c–238a   318
Phaedrus
247a   232
247c   104
249c   231
Republic
617e   237, 242
Timaeus
27a   253
27e–28b   119–20
28b–c   121
28c   114
29d–e   144
30a   145
31a   400
31a–b   399
33a   400
38b   158
40c–d   205
42d   242
47a–b   197
47a–c   201–3
48e–49a   137
55c–d   400
92a   377
44d   289
75d–e   289

Ps.-Plato
Epinomis
986c–d   207

Pliny
Natural History
2.166   182

Plutarch
On Isis and Osiris
369B   100

Posidonius
frg. F178   101

Proclus
Elements of Theology
134   136

Sextus Empiricus
Against the Logicians
1.94   195
Against the Physicians
1.79   285
Outlines of scepticism
3.9   400

Seneca
Letters to Lucilius
90.28   204
Natural Questions
2.1.4   182

Stobaeus
Eclogae
2.49.8–18   343

Theon of Smyrna
Exposition of Plato's doctrines
19.12   171
99.24–100.8   129
103.4   274

Vergil
Georgics
1.118–146   388

(b) Jewish texts

Aristobulus
frg. 5   126, 265

Cave of Treasures
2.22   255

2 Enoch
24.5   155
30.10   329

Genesis Rabbah
3.7   170
8.8   236

Josephus
Against Apion
2.192   243
Jewish Antiquities
1.18   108
1.26   103

INDEX OF ANCIENT TEXTS CITED 429

1.29	130	*Pesiqta Rabbati*	
1.37	371	Suppl. 21	255

Jubilees, Book of
2:2 135
3.28 369

Jesus ben Sirach
25:24 356

Letter of Aristeas
234–235 402

Talmud
Berachot
10a 227
Tosefta Sanhedrin
8.7 250

Midrash Tadsche
1 196
6 173, 307–8

(c) Christian texts

Ambrose
On paradise
2.11 384
Letters
43 = 29 259
43 = 29.14–5 234
43 = 29.19 347
44 = 31.3–15 306
45 = 34.7–9 371
45 = 34.10 384
45 = 34.11–6 347

Basil of Caesarea
Homilies on the Hexaemeron
1.1, 2A 109
2.3, 33B 123

Calcidius
Commentary on Plato's Timaeus
276 161

Catena in Genesim
84 196

Clement of Alexandria
Stromateis
2.131.5 233
5.93–4 153
5.93 130, 173
5.94 178
6.172 339

Didymus of Alexandria
Commentary on Genesis
34.25–7 130
40–1 209
54.13–58.2 234
60.2–10 258
95.19–21 383

101.11–24 390

Eusebius
Praeparation of the Gospel
8.12.22 3
8.12.22 96
11.24.7–12 173
11.30.1–3 210
11.6.19 178

Gregory of Nyssa
On the creation of humankind
2 259

Hippolytus
Refutation of the philosophers
1.19.1–2 152

Johannes Lydus
On the months
2.12, 33.8–34.3 299
4.64, 115.15–17 193

Nemesius
On the nature of humankind
1, 4.24–5.5 259
1, 6.6 329

Origen
Against Celsus
1.24 349
4.39 383
Commentary on John
1.114 154
Commentary on Matthew
frg. ad 25:30 173
Homilies on Genesis
1.2 178
1.31 328

Selecta in Genesim (PG 12)		2.13	178
27	130	2.15	195
97	154	2.18	256
		2.24	368
Theophilus of Antioch		2.25	370
To Autolyus		3.9	403
2.12	109		

4. Index of subjects and names

Abraham 209, 227, 334–5, 343
Academy, scepticism of 239
Achilles 176
Adam 324, 333, 335, 348, 350–1, 357, 386
   and animals 255
Adam speculation, Jewish 255
admiration 189
Aenesidemus 35, 239
Aeschylus 319
Aëtius the doxographer 115, 136, 158, 175, 202, 293, 393, 396, 399–400
ages of life 278
agnosticism 396
agriculture 206, 252
air 165, 170, 285
Alcinous 146, 151, 158, 190, 323, 344, 349, 368, 380
Alcmaeon 293
Alexander of Aphrodisias 28, 165, 299
Alexander the Great 140, 340
Alexander Philalethes 218
Alexandre, Monique 36
Alexandria 296, 378
   exegesis 19–20
   founding 140–1
   pogrom 119
Alexandrian Judaism 30
Allegorical Commentary 1, 3, 5
allegorical exegesis 373–6
allegorical interpretation 366
allegory 247, 333, 362–3
   and symbolism 378
   of the soul 24
alpha-privatives 117
Ambrose 37–8, 123, 130, 161, 221, 279
Amir, Y. 392
analogical argument 118
analogy 331
analysis of treatise's contents 8

Anatolius 28, 127, 129, 191–5, 214, 264–308 passim (and esp. 304–6)
Anaxagoras 175, 183, 240
Anaximander 106
androcentrism 23, 103, 361
androgyne 325
   first human as 243
angels 256, 342, 347
   of God 371
animals 211, 214
   bound to earth 377
   domesticated 256, 340
   genera of 346
   and reason 240
   subservient to humans 246
   wild 340
Anonymous Theaetetus Commentary 344
anthropocentrism 23, 180–1, 184, 197, 199, 204, 206, 211, 245, 247–8
anthropology, Mosaic 23
anthropomorphism 351
Anthropos 323
anti-anthropomorphism 223, 225
Antioch of Ascalon 34, 189, 229
apologetics 99, 119, 223, 335
Apollo 274
Apollodorus the Stoic 176
apophatic theology 233
Apostolic Constitutions 347
appropriation (*oikeiôsis*) 379
Aquila 256
Aratus 208, 286
Arcesilaus 189
Aristobulus 20, 29, 30, 101, 102, 125, 166, 225, 279–80, 307
Aristophanes 319, 355
Aristotle 34, 111, 113, 115, 119, 121–2, 127, 140–1, 148, 157, 159, 166, 176, 182–3, 185–6, 193–4, 200, 204, 213, 219, 227, 240, 283, 288–9, 293, 298–9, 316–7, 334, 336, 368, 380, 398, 401–02

INDEX OF SUBJECTS AND NAMES 431

on art 338
De Mundo see Ps.-Aristotle
fifth element 204, 230
and names 349, 351
nominalism 242
on pleasure 379
pneuma doctrine 326
Aristoxenus 294
arithmetic 188, 193–4
  and seven 261–308 passim
  arithmetic, Philo's knowledge of 269
arithmology see also number symbolism
arithmology 17, 26, 264
Arius Didymus 33, 368
Arius the Stoic see Arius Didymus
Armenian translators 38
Arnaldez, R. 42
Arrian 140
art, theory of 338
arts, the 254
assimilation to God 356
astrology 205, 285
astronomy 201, 203, 251
atheism 395–8
Athena 262, 273
athletics 170, 192
  see also under imagery
Atticus 140, 220
Augustine 38, 100, 130, 153, 157, 159, 161, 170, 202, 278, 291, 313, 358, 372, 402
Aulus Gellius 264, 276, 283, 286–7, 292–3
autonomy, human 190

Babel-builders 393, 396, 401
babies 293, 379
Baer, R. A. 43, 322–3, 359
barbarians 296
Barrow, J. 162
Barthélemy, D. 21
Basil 37, 123, 130, 186, 196, 209, 221, 306, 388, 390
Basilides 154
beauty 167, 337
  physical 335
becoming like God 233
beginning, and end 186
Bezalel 339
biblical text, citation of 14–16
bio-diversity 214
biology 35
birds 211, 215

body
  human 289, 332
  negative attitude towards 347
  and numbers 277
  as temple 335
bond 316
Borgen, P. 6, 31, 43, 245, 247
Bos, A. P. 34, 122
botanical world 180–91
botany 35, 184
boundaries, in the soul 368
Bousset, W. 19
Boyancé, P. 32–3
Boyarin, D. 359–60

Cain 341
Calcidius 28, 38, 235, 264, 289, 291, 328
Carneades 35, 189
causes, first 190
Censorinus 28, 264, 268, 279–80, 306
Chaldeans 111, 112
Chaldeanism 187, 190, 205, 398
Chance 277
chapters of treatise 8
Christ 345
  as second Adam 257
Chrysippus 158, 166, 217, 219, 342
Cicero 33, 100, 113, 118, 200, 208, 217, 225, 229, 256, 286, 318, 337, 340, 349, 379, 388, 396, 402
citizenship of first human 333
city
  constitution of 331, 341
  cosmos as 331
civilization, origins of 333
clay 335, 346
Cleanthes 208, 217, 342
Clement of Alexandria 37, 235, 264–308 passim, 342, 344, 384
Clement of Rome 319–20
Cleopatra 231
climate 205
Cohen, N. 31
Cohn, J. 41, 42
Cohn, L. 1, 38–41
collaborators, in work of creation 237
Colson, F. H. 42, 267
commands, divine 207
commentary, method of 45–6
conception, physical 291, 317
conscience 298
constitution, of city 331, 341
contemplation 197, 250

Cornutus 176
Corybants 231
cosmic religion 199, 201, 207–9
cosmocentrism 249
cosmogonic literature 180
cosmology 23, 316
  biblical versus Greek 174
  Greek 198–9, 256
cosmos
  citizens of 342
  as city 331, 342
  created 398
  creation of 392
  everlasting or created 113
  and God 110
  and human being 332
  and law 106–7
  noetic 22
  number of 400
  order of 201
  perfection 392
  unicity of 392, 398
  as whole 400
cradle arguments 379
creatio aeterna 157, 172
creatio ex nihilo 152, 159, 172, 253, 400
creatio simultanea 157
creation account, extent of 309
creation, and time 125
creation
  beginning of 246
  end of 246
  rationality of 199
  sequence of 160, 212, 257–8
  simultaneous 125, 218
creed 394
criminality 369–70
Critias the atheist 102, 189, 396–7
Critolaus 185, 319
culture, human 333, 340
Cynicism 375

daimones 256
dances 230
  of stars 201
dancing 291
darkness 163
David, King 257
day 170
Decalogue 341, 380
decline, of human life 247
Demeter 314, 318
Democritus 175, 240, 254, 400
demons 215

desire 358
diaeresis, method of 240, 395
dialectic 200
diatribe 375, 378, 382
Didymus 37, 154, 161, 196, 221, 306, 353
Diels, H. 38
Dillon, J. 32, 43
dimensions, three 272, 277
Dinocrates of Rhodes 140
Dio Chrysostom 204, 339
Diodorus Siculus 35, 141, 216, 318, 334, 388
Diogenes of Apollonia 218
Diogenes the Cynic 103
Diogenes Laertius 341, 402
Dionysius the Areopagite 201
Dionysius Thrax 295
Dionysus 231
diseases 293
DNA 184
doctrines, Mosaic 393–4
domination, human 255
Dörrie, H. 203
doxography 111, 113, 202, 399
dry land 179

earth 164, 179–80, 182, 215–6, 288, 309, 398
  and food 377
  and human beings 224
  as mother 182, 184, 314, 318
  and scarcity 385
earthly human being 322
Easter 268
Egypt 396
Egyptians 296
elements 172, 195, 215, 230, 316, 347
  and human body 346
  four 164, 256
embryo 218
embryology 291
emendations 39
Empedocles 182, 195, 316
end, and beginning 186
enjoyment 250
enkuklios paideia 270
Enoch 208, 343
Epictetus 339, 378
Epicureanism 34, 247, 373, 375, 379
Epicurus 165, 206, 225, 340, 349, 400–01
  doctrine of *oikeiôsis* 379
  on pleasure 379
Epinomis 189

INDEX OF SUBJECTS AND NAMES

epistemology 187, 352, 382
equality 281
equinoxes 287–8
erôs 230, 232
eternity 112, 120
   and time 171
ether 204, 230, 316
etymology 174, 175–7, 295, 341, 351
eudaimonia 25, 327, 331, 333, 338, 342, 352, 354, 389, 402
Eudorus 32, 177, 343
Euripides 189
Eusebius 3, 31, 36, 96, 123, 161, 268, 353, 388
Eve 333, 348, 351, 357, 361, 369, 382, 386
evil 24
   origin of 238
evolution 185
excellences 25
   see further virtues
exegesis
   method of 17–19, 239
   multiple 20
   reasonable 176, 377
   styles of 16
exegete
   limitations of 268
   modesty of 344
   Philo as 204
exegetical traditions 19–20, 223, 248, 364, 381
Exposition of the Law 2–4, 6
expulsion, from garden 369
eye 217
Ezechiel tragicus 30

fairness 194
familiarity, God and humanity 344–5
Favorinus Eclogius 264, 292
feasts 202
female 237
feminism 376
festivals 287
Festugière, A.-J. 208
fetuses 292–3, 317
fire 230
firmament 174, 175
fish 211
flesh, life of the 326
flight of the mind 222, 228–33
flux, world of 355
food 249
   earthly 377
   heavenly 377

Fossum, J. 238
France, Southern 308
fresh water 314
future 205

Garden of Eden 333, 362–84 passim
Genesis Rabbah 31, 131, 154, 178, 181, 243, 320, 335
gender, and allegory 381–2
Genesis, as title of book 110, 120
genus 185, 325
   and species 242
geometry 194, 261–2, 270–2, 277, 281
Germans 286
glue 182, 316
gluttony 378
Gnosticism 24, 190, 209, 238, 347
goal of human life 25, 342
God
   anger of 371
   assimilation to 343
   and assistance in creation 236
   autonomy of 239
   blessed nature of 327, 346
   and cosmos 110
   as creator 22, 144
   essence of 395
   and evil 23, 237, 386
   existence of 392, 395, 401
   as the Existent 115
   as Father 114, 370
   as first cause 190
   goodness of 23, 133, 146, 392
   and grace, divine 22, 25, 144, 146
   as Great king 232, 257
   and human being 332, 342
   and the ideas 116
   infinite 146
   lack of envy 145
   love for humanity 253
   mercy of 385–6
   monarchic rule 119, 397
   names of 137, 144, 386
   and nature 191, 219
   as Nous 116, 226
   omnipotence 191, 351
   rest 113
   second 345
   self-sufficiency of 239
   sole creator 146
   as teacher 351
   transcendence 22, 116, 142
   unicity of 355, 392, 397
   worship of 393
      see also monotheism

Golden age, myth of 251, 334
Goodenough, E. R. 19, 392
Goulet, R. 19
grace 133, 350, 387–8, 401
grammar 294–5
   Greek 291
grass 309
Great Bear 275, 286
Great king 232
   mind as 336
Great sea 316
Greeks 296
Gregory of Nyssa 37, 146, 162, , 221, 244, 329, 347, 178, 235
gynaecology 291

hairesis, Philo and Greek 32
happiness
   see *eudaimonia*
hardship 387
Harl, M. 36, 364
harmony, musical 192, 294
   and numbers 270–1
   of the spheres 201, 230
Hay, D. 19
head 289
health 293
hearing 200, 401
heaven 159, 174–5, 187, 204, 254, 284, 309, 398
   and number seven 263
   substance of 204
   without evil 177
heavenly bodies 187, 190, 197–8, 256, 341
   divine 160
   nature of 240
   and worship 112, 160
heavenly human being 322
hedonism 377
Heraclitus 106, 200, 305
Hermetica 323
Herodotus 200
Herophilus 305
Hesiod 165, 286–7, 340
Hesychius 162
hierarchy 185
   of being 341
   and gender 382
High priest 206
high society 378
Hippocrates 262, 278–81, 291–3, 306
Hippolytus 154
history 17, 24, 33
holiness 367, 369, 393

Homer 101–02, 119, 225, 274, 343, 376, 398
hope 25
Horovitz, J. 32, 148–9
human being 23–25 and passim
   and animals 348
   as body and soul 325
   borderline creature 326–7
   citizen of cosmos 333, 339
   and cosmos 332
   creation of 222–35, 321–9
   degeneration of 338
   double creation of 223
   erect 377
   excellence of first 24, 330
   first 330–53 passim
   and God 332, 342
   idea of 322
   ideal 323
   and Logos 330, 332
   and number seven 263
   resemblance to God 222
   second creation of 321–9 passim
   social aspects 331
   as viceroy 257
human body, composition of 346
human life, stages of 278–81

ideas, doctrine of 310, 342
   and Logos 336
   as God's thoughts 151–2
   as thoughts of God 139
idols, polemic against 112
imagery
   architect 140
   athletic contests 250
   athletic race 184–5
   balance 369, 396
   banquet 250
   charioteer 191, 257
   chariot-racing 192
   city 119, 133
   dramatic contests 250
   fountains 387
   king 140
   light 167–8
   lure 382
   magnet 331
   mark 103
   marking 401
   pilot 191, 257
   plants 250
   potter 335
   puppet-shows 288
   racing track 277

relay race 350
sculptor 335
seal 105, 107, 139, 141, 216, 226, 233, 311, 344
snare 382
springs 387
temple 204
theatre 250
war in the soul 252
wrestling 170
immortality 24–25, 238, 359
inceptive imperfect 160
incorporeal beings 342
infinity, divine 146
ingratitude, human 388
innocence 370, 389
instability 370
intellect 217, 219
    as god 226–7
    location 336
    and sight 200
    and soul 226
    unknowable 228
intellect, human
    and God 222
intelligible cosmos 132, 134, 136, 138, 143, 231, 309–10
    contents of 149, 163
intelligible realm, and numbers 261, 275, 283
introduction of treatise 98
Isaac 350
Isidore of Seville 28–29, 264
Israel 394
    as race of suppliants 388

Jerome 3, 38, 307
Jerusalem, temple 204
John Lydus 28, 38, 127, 131, 191, 194, 264–5, 274, 298–304, 307
Jobling, D. 43, 247
John of Damascus 38
Joseph 257, 335
Josephus 6, 30–1, 37, 101–2, 178, 183, 186, 209, 221, 324, 329, 369
joy 389
Jubilees 6, 166, 173, 181, 258, 267, 308, 334
Judaism, and excursus on seven 266
Julian 208
justice 194, 386
    see also fairness

kakodaimonia 338, 352, 354, 389
Kamesar, A. 136

Katz, P. 21
king, human being as 255
knowledge 200
    see also epistemology
knowledge, human
    limitations of 198, 206
Kraus Reggiani, C. 41, 42
Kronos, Age of 334
Kugel, J. 31

Laban 148
language of excellence 117, 253, 341
language 35, 41
    origin of 349
    Philo's 251
    and Torah 108
Latin 296
law 101–3, 106–7, 207, 331, 339
    cosmic 333
    higher 341
    of Moses 22, 106–7, 340
    of nature 21, 106–7, 340, 401
    observance of 34, 297
laziness 388
Le Boulluec, A. 375
legislators 100
Letter of Aristeas 30, 102
letters of alphabet 294–5
Levison, J. 333
Lévy, C. 43
life 389
    blessed 391, 393
    goal of 331, 342–3
    and the good life 249
    of well-being 371
light 163, 167–9, 197, 200
literary style 35
Logos 142–3, 336, 342
    and assimilation to God 344
    as bond 316
    and creation 22, 133–4, 149, 168
    cutter 242
    as divider 170
    doctrine of 394
    and God 168
    and human being 337–8
    and measurement 312
    as intermediate 225
love 105, 284, 354
lover of pleasure 375
Lucretius 35, 181, 247, 316, 340
luxury 364
Lycurgus 100
Lydus see John Lydus
lyre 294

Macrobius 228, 264–308 passim
magnet 339
male 237
male and female 127, 242, 325
    differences 357
man, as intellect 374
    see also human being
Mangey, T. 38, 275
Manicheism 170
manuscripts 3, 39, 350
Markland, J. 145, 274
Martianus Capella 28, 264, 282, 289, 291
material 335
mathematics 296
matter 116–7, 183, 399
    doctrine of 152–3
    origin of 152
    status of 145
Maximus Tyrius 230–3, 327
Mazzanti, A. M. 238
Méasson, A. 33
measurement
    and divine Logos 147
medicine, ancient 293
Mendelson, A. 392
menstruation 292, 317
metaphor
    biological 22, 119
    demiurgic, technical 22, 119
    see also imagery
microcosm, human being as 254
Middle Platonism
    Philo and 32–33 and passim
Midrash 250
Midrash Tadsche 37
mind see intellect
miracles 253
misogyny 359, 361
mixture 116
mob-rule 398
model
    and copy 137–8
    and creation of human being 336
Moehring, H. 26, 268
monotheism 393, 397
moon 204
moon 275, 286
mortality 24–25, 246, 254, 358, 387
Moses 1, 21 and passim
    antiquity of 316
    as author 239
    authority of 111
    education 114
    and *hairesis* 395
    inspiration 114
    love of brevity 310, 313
    and other philosophers 315
    as lawgiver 101
    as prophet 114
    praise of 169, 224, 314, 349
    superiority of 297, 315
    as teacher 395
Mosheh ha-Darshan 308
mother, earth as 314, 318
motions, of body 291
mouth 289
Müller, J. G. 41
music 230, 251, 261–2, 270, 281
Musonius Rufus 378
myth 102, 354, 397
    Greek 225
    and scripture 376

Nachleben 36 and passim
names, origin of 349
    see also naming
naming 129, 165, 175, 295, 348–53
    of animals 348–53
narrative 17
natural theology 191, 395
nature 106–7, 318
    and creation 219
    and God 219, 313
    and Logos 313
necessities of life 246, 252
Nemesius of Emesa 37
Neopyrrhonism 35
Netherlands 286
New Academy 189
Nicomachus of Gerasa 28, 193–4, 264–308 passim
Niehoff, M. 108
night 205
Nikiprowetzky, V. 42, 167, 310
Nile 319
Nile delta 252
Noah 334, 343, 388
noetic cosmos
    see intelligible cosmos
nous see intellect
number
    and creation 22
    and time 198
    importance of 198
number symbolism 25–29, 264–5
numbers
    one (monad) 128–9, 171, 272, 274
    two 174, 177, 194

three 180, 213
four 188, 191–5
five 211, 214
six 124, 126–8, 211, 267
seven 163, 166, 260–308 passim
ten 191, 268
  in Bible 269
  and gods 273
  figured 269
  significance of 296
  translation of terms for 94
Numenius 140, 146, 356
nutrition 317

Ocean 183, 316
Old Academy 193, 240, 288
On numbers, Philo's treatise 4, 27, 194, 264, 290, 303
Onetor of Tarentum 274, 299–300
optative 148
order 160, 175
  and number 126
organs, bodily 289
Origen 37, 130–1, 154, 161, 186, 209, 235, 240, 258, 328–9, 346, 379, 403
Orphic literature 319
Orphism 274
Ovid 35, 181

paideia 351
Pandora 319
paradise 251, 348, 355, 362–84 passim, 385, 389
paraphrase 15
Parmenides 100
passions 23–24, 252, 380
patriarchs 340, 343, 385
Pentateuch 30 and passim
  text of 20–21, 324
Peripatetics 399
Peshitta 267
Petron of Himera 400
Pharaoh 396, 401
philanthropy 253
Philo of Alexandria passim
Philo of Larisa 35
Philolaus 273–5, 299–300
philosophers 218
philosophy 197, 199, 203
  as art of life 297
  as interpretation of scripture 365
  and Law 297
  and Moses 114
physics 202

physiology, Greek 218
piety 367, 369, 393
  cosmic 208
  Jewish 402
pig 217
Pindar 319
planetary gods 238
planets 285
plants 179, 183, 214
  and soul 364
Plato
  Alcibiades major 217
  Cratylus 176, 178, 349
  Gorgias 402
  Laws 100–02, 249, 288
  Phaedrus 33, 136, 140, 169, 191, 201, 224, 250–1, 257, 387
  Phaedrus myth 227, 229–32
  Politicus 191, 334, 340
  Republic 33, 100, 102, 105, 128, 136, 140, 169, 177, 189, 200, 225, 251, 402
  Sophist 164
  Symposium 33, 141, 355, 357–8
  Theaetetus 141, 229, 343
  Timaeus 26, 32–3, 111, 113, 115, 117, 119, 125, 134–5, 138, 140, 145, 157, 164, 171, 176–7, 183, 189–90, 192, 197–9, 204, 206, 212, 215–6, 237, 246–7, 254, 257, 272, 282, 285, 290–1, 305, 316, 332, 335, 337, 342, 346, 355, 364, 375, 393
  anthropocentrism 249
  on art 338
  erôs theme 230, 232
  ideas 151
  image of cave 167
  image of sun 167
  and Moses 139, 144
  Platonic love 105
  psychology 252, 288–9
  realism 242
  and sun 105
  on sex and love 358
  on time 158
  theology 102
Platonism
  Philo and 32–33
  and sex 359–61
Platonists 398
pleasing to God 343
pleasure 24, 202, 354, 358, 373–82, 389
Pleiades 275, 283, 286–7
Pliny the Elder 35, 316, 339

Plotinus 148, 182, 189, 327, 335, 356, 402
plurality 116
Plutarch 119, 127–8, 143, 165, 204, 318, 327, 340, 342, 344, 377, 399–400
pneuma 219–20, 285, 317, 321, 323, 345
poetry 35, 279
poets 377
poison 378
polemics 393
political theory 398
polytheism 160, 397–8
Porphyry 191, 327
Posidonius 28, 34, 182, 219, 229, 280, 285–6, 288, 290
Powers
  divine 113, 143–4
  doctrine of 394
practical insight (*phronêsis*) 363, 367–8
prepositional metaphysics 139, 151
primitivism 340
principles, doctrine of 115–6, 152
Proclus 208, 270, 273, 275, 349
Procopius 196
procreation 355, 358
Prodicus 375, 382
progressivism 340
Prometheus 327
pronunciation, Greek 290
proportion, theory of 282
prostitute 382
Protagoras 396
proto-history 24
protreptic literature 102
providence 110, 117–8, 122, 207, 253, 256, 327, 370, 386, 392, 400
  and wild animals 255
Ps.-Aristotle *De mundo* 107, 122–3, 140, 176, 183, 208, 232, 316, 339, 402
Ps.-Hippocrates 264, 266, 280–1, 283, 292
Ps.-Iamblichus 28–29, 127, 129, 191–5, 214, 264–308 passim
Ps.-Justin 123, 154, 328
Ps.-Philo *Liber antiquitatum biblicarum* 6
Ps.-Vindicianus 218
Psalms 256
psychology 212, 288, 345
punishment 25, 246, 252, 358, 371, 385–9, 401

pupil 217
Pythagoras 100
Pythagoreanism 26, 272
  Jewish 265
Pythagoreans 201, 126–7, 191–5, 230, 261–308 passim, 343, 349, 358

quaestio method 7, 239, 247–8, 317, 373
Quaestiones 5
quality 325

Rabbi Berekiah 243
Rabbi Hoshai'a 37, 154
Rabbi Jonathan 236
Rabbi Meir 318
Rabbi Pinchas ben Yair 308
rabbinic texts 350
rabbis 31, 37, 209, 237, 258
  anthropology 227
  on sex 358–61
Radice, R. 41, 238 and passim
rationality 199, 207, 324
  and male 381
reason 336
Religion cosmique 112
reproduction 255, 379
reptiles 377
responsibility, human 257
revelation 187, 191
reverence for God 367, 369
reward 371, 401
rhetoric 35
right times 198
right-angled triangle 271–2
Robbins, F. E. 28
romanticism 357

Sabbath 113, 166, 261, 267, 288, 297–8, 306
safety 340
salt 217
salt water 314
Samaritan Pentateuch 267
Satan 376
scepticism 34, 189, 395–6
Schimmel, A. 29, 127, 129, 191, 214, 265,
Schwabe, M. 136
science 35
sciences 228, 254
  Greek 199
  and number seven 263, 294
scientists 218
Scipio, Dream of 229

sea 286, 334
seasons 195, 198, 285
secretions of the body 291
security 340
seed 218, 317
   women's 291
self-control 374, 380–1
semen 219–20
Seneca 147, 152, 180, 207, 227, 339, 378, 402
senses 289–90, 336–7, 346, 374, 379, 382
Septuagint 30 and passim
   Greek of 206
   language 214
   text of 324
sequence of creation 160, 257–8
seven days of creation 124–5, 310
Sextus Empiricus 191, 318, 334, 379, 395
sexual passion 387
sexuality 23–24, 243, 347, 355–61
Shema 200, 397
Sibylline oracles 388
Siegert, F. 307
sight 197, 200–02, 290, 332, 346, 379, 401
signs 198, 205–06, 285
simplicity (of virtue) 370
Sirach, Jesus ben 256, 258, 359
Sitz im Leben, of treatise 29–36
Sly, D. 43, 360
snake 354, 362, 369, 373–84
   story of 24
snake-fighter 373, 380, 384
sober drunkenness 231
solidity 176, 193
Solon 95, 100, 262, 278–81, 306
sophists 190, 349, 377
Sophocles 278
   Antigone 286
Souda 270
soul 214
   divisions of 288
   and intellect 217
   see also psychology
sources, for arithmology 301–4
sovereignty, of human being 245
space 170
Special laws 380
species 185
   perpetuation of 180
speech 289
spermatikoi logoi 184
spirit 163, 166

see also *pneuma*
spiritual life 326
spring 186
Staehle, K. 27, 265
stereometry 193, 261–2, 270, 272, 277, 281
Sterling, G. E. 394
Stoa 33–34, 106, 141, 165–6, 176, 183–4, 186, 213, 219, 241, 247, 288, 297, 316,-7, 333, 335–6, 341–2, 344, 352, 375, 379, 382, 399
   and anthropology 249
   ethical theory 252
   and origin of names 349
   and *pneuma* 326
   and principles 115
   and providence 118
Stoic-Cynic diatribe 375, 378
Strabo 141, 286
style, Philo's 248
summary 391
sun 169, 204, 287
Sunday 267
superlative 251
symbol 366
symbolic interpretation 362
symbolism 27, 374
   method of 378
symmetry 335
sympathy, cosmic 285
Synagogal prayers 30
synagogue 297

tabernacle 159
teleology 23, 180, 245, 247
telos 342–3
temple 159
   and body 335
   in Jerusalem 204
Terpander 294
tetraktys 191, 195, 277
text of treatise 38
   indirect tradition 39
Thales 317
Theiler, W. 32
theocentrism 199
theodicy 24, 237
Theodore of Mopsuestia 130, 320
Theodotion 256
Theon of Smyrna 28, 127, 177, 191, 264–308 and passim
Theophilus of Antioch 30, 37, 153, 173, 372
Theophrastus 115
Therapeutae 231, 364

three-dimensionality 176
tides 286
Timaeus Locrus 136, 177, 220
time 198, 206
　and cosmos 156
　and creation 22, 156
　and God 125
　infinite 206
　measures of 171, 206
title of work 96–7
Tobin, T. 19–20, 43, 223, 310, 323, 376
Torah 108
translation, method of 43–4
tree of life 365–6
truth 187, 352
　and certainty 189
　and exegesis 176
Turnebus, A. 1
typology 24, 333

unhappiness
　see *kakodaimonia*

variegation 189
Varro 28, 151, 264–308 passim
verba Philonica 103, 141–2, 213, 388
verbal adjectives 104, 194, 269
Vetus Latina 267, 324
Victory 273
Vienna codex 39, 96
violence 358
Virgil 285
virtue 297, 332, 388
　cardinal 241
　see also excellences
Vitruvius 140
voice 290
void 165, 170
Völker, W. 43

Walter, N. 265
water 316
　kinds of 182
weather 285
week 267
well-being
　see *eudaimonia*
Wendland, P. 39
Whitaker, G. H. 41
wickedness, human 351, 385
wild animals 255, 257
Winden, J. C. M. van 42, 149–50
wine 378
Winston, D. 42, 114, 172, 241, 360–1
wisdom 363, 367
　and first human being 350
　and nourishment 378
Wisdom of Solomon 30, 185, 221, 345, 357
wise person 349
Wolfson, H. A. 43, 171, 392
woman 23, 354–61
　Philo's attitude towards 359–61
　symbolizing sense-perception 374
wonder 111
worldview, Platonic-Aristotelian 175, 177, 185, 187, 201, 284
worship 189, 208

Xenocrates 220, 368
Xenophanes 225
Xenophon 364, 375, 382, 402

Yarbro Collins, A. 29

Zeller, D. 388
Zeno of Citium 100, 158, 340–1
Zeus 227, 229, 273–4
zoology 212–3

5. Index of Greek terms

ἀγαθός	10	αἴσθησις	381
ἀγαλματοφορέω	141, 227, 254, 335	αἰσθητικός	219
ἀγένητος	112, 398	αἰσθητός	325
ἀγχίνοια	365	αἰσχρός	365
ἄδηλος	206	αἰτία	316
ἀδιάφορος	241	αἰών	171, 371
ἀειπάρθενος	273	ἀκολουθία	160, 216, 315
ἀεροπόρος	215	ἀκρασία	380
ἀΐδιος	112, 398	ἀλληγορία	377
ἀϊδιότης	120, 185	ἀμήτωρ	273
αἰδώς	357	ἄμυδρος	339

INDEX OF GREEK TERMS

ἀνάγνως	113	δεσμός	316
ἀναλογία	282	δημιουργός	175
ἀναρχία	119	δημοκρατία	398
ἀναχέω	181	διάγραμμα	281
ἀνεξετάστως	370	διακοσμέω	183, 188
ἀνεπιλήπτως	340	διακρίνειν	293
ἀνήρ	103	διαμένω	316
ἀνθογραφέω	336	διάνοια	44, 327, 344
ἄνθρωπος	103	διάστασις	278
ἀόρατος	120, 164–65	δίαυλος	184
ἀχανές	165	διερευνώμενος	228
ἀπάτη	369	δικαιοσύνη	194
ἀπαύγασμα	345	δόγμα	402
ἀπεικόνισμα	336	δολιχεύειν	184
ἄπειρος	400	δολιχός	184
ἀπλανής	161	δόξα	366, 402
ἀπόσπασμα	326, 345	δραστήριον αἴτιον	115
ἀπραξία	113, 115	δύναμις	144, 219, 268
ἀρέσκεια	343	δυσκρασία	293
ἀρετή	25, 116, 241, 389		
ἄριστος	334	ἐγκράτεια	380
ἄρρεν	325	εἰδεχθής	378
ἀρτιοπέριττος	128	εἰδοποιέω	312
ἀρχέτυπος	139, 226	εἰκός	126, 189
ἀρχή	44, 103, 158, 186, 253	εἰκότως	176
		εἰκών	222, 225–26
ἀρχὴ γενέσεως	202	εἱρμός	160, 216, 315
ἀρχηγέτης	334	εἰς	206
ἄστρα	199	ἔκγονοι	190
ἀσώματος	311	ἐκμαγεῖον	233, 345
ἀτελής	184	ἐκπρεπέστατος	337
αὐγή	169	ἔλεγχος	298
αὐτοδίδακτος	350	ἐλλόγιμος	294
αὐτοκίνητος	351	ἐμμελής	201
αὐτομαθής	350	ἔμψυχος	214
ἄψυχος	214	ἑξαήμερος	125, 221
		ἐξαίρετος	135
βάρβαρος	296	ἐξίτηλος	350
βιβλίον	5	ἐξομοίωσις	344, 399
βίβλος	5	ἔνυδρος	214, 346
βίος	371	ἔοικε	336
βραχὺς οὐρανός	254	ἐπαμφοτερίζω	396
		ἐπαποδύομαι	170
γάρ	94, 127	ἐπὶ πᾶσι	216, 248, 255
γένεσις	94, 120, 144, 274	ἐπιλογιζόμενος	310, 311
γενητός	112, 398	ἐπιμέλεια	257
γέννησις	274	ἐπιστήμη	116, 200
γένος	185, 214, 327, 334	ἐπιτειχίζω	252
γηγενής	216, 334	ἐπίχειρα	387
γίνομαι	324	ἑπτά	295
γνωστικός	367	ἔρως	105, 251, 355, 357
γράμματα	294	ἔτυμος	295
γραφή	5	ἐτύμως	175
		εὐδαιμονία	25, 331, 342, 352, 359
δένδρον	183		

εὐδαίμων	327, 402		μακάριος	327, 402
εὐκρασία	293		μακραίων	371
εὔλογος	189		μαρμαρυγαί	105, 232
εὐπάθεια	389		μεγαλόπολις	142
εὐσέβεια	367		μεγαλοπολίτης	341
			μεθόριος	216, 327, 329
ζυγάδην	270		μεταβάλλω	370
ζῳοπλαστεῖν	213		μεταβολή	291
			μετανάστασις	370
ἡγεμονικώτατος	289		μετάνοια	370
ἡγεμών	225, 255		μίμημα	336
ἡδονή	380–81		μονήρης	364
ἡγεμονικόν	336		μόνος	339
ἥμερος	183		μόνωσις	128, 171, 356
θεοειδής	199		νηκτός	221
θεολογέω	121			
θεός	137		ξύλον	15, 183
θεοσέβεια	363, 367			
θεοφιλής	104		νοητός	311, 322
θεσμός	207, 331, 341		νοητὸς κόσμος	136, 138
θῆλυ	325		νομοθέτης	100
θρεπτικός	219		νόμος	207, 341
θύραθεν	219		νόμος φύσεως	107
			νοτίς	320
ἰδέα	322–23		νοῦς	44, 116, 222, 381
ἰκμάς	320			
			οἰκεῖος	380
καιρός	183, 206, 277, 306		οἰκειόω	344
κακία	241		οἰκείωσις	119, 344
κακοδαιμονία	359		ὁμοίωσις	233, 344
κακουργία	369		ὁμοίωσις θεῷ	343
κάλλος	337		ὁρατός	176
καλός	10, 167, 365		ὀργανικός	277
καλὸς καὶ κἀγαθός	334		ὀργανοποιία	294
καρπός	183		ὀρθὸς λόγος	331, 341
καρποφόρος	319		ὅρος	176
καρυατίζω	193		ὁσιότης	367
καταληπτικὴ φαντασία	352		οὐράνιος	346
κατορθόω	242		οὐρανός	176
κατόρθωσις	206		οὐσία	144–45, 202, 268
κίνησις	218		ὀχλοκρατία	398
κολοσσιαῖος	105			
κοσμοποιία	97, 103, 311		πάθος	380, 382, 389
κοσμοπολίτης	103, 339		παθητός	115
κόσμος	183, 199, 266		παμμήτωρ	319
κρίσις	293		παν-	169
κριτήριον	168		παναύγεια	169
κυρίως	366		πάνδημος	267
			πανδώρα	319
λάχνωσις	281		πανουργία	369
λογισμός	148, 381		παντέλεια	192
λόγος	5, 44, 273, 290		παράδεισος	364
λόγος ἔχει	273		παρευημερεῖν	388

INDEX OF GREEK TERMS

πέρας	175		σώματα	352
περιεργάζομαι	202			
πιθανός	189		τάξις	162, 216, 218
πλάσσω	324		τάσις	291
πλινθίον	281		τέλειος	94, 127, 267
πνεῦμα	166, 226		τελειόω	267
πνοή	166		τελέσφορος	277, 281
πνοὴ ζωῆς	326		τέλος	184, 186, 253, 342
πόθος	105, 358		τεχνίτης	142, 219, 326
ποικίλλω	184, 188		τέχνη	219
ποιότης	325		τολμάω	379
πράγματα	352		τόπος	140
πρό	311		τύπος	139, 226, 377
πρόλογος	98		τύχη	277
προοίμιον	98			
πρός	139		ὕλη	183
προσφέρω	380		ὑμνέω	268
προτιμάω	389		ὕπαρξις	395
πτηνός	215, 346		ὑπάρχειν	395
			ὕπαρχος	257, 350
σάββατον	267		ὑπερκύπτω	230
σέβομαι	295		ὑπερουράνιος τόπος	231
σεμνός	295		ὑπόνοια	377
σημεῖον	205		ὕστερος	189
σκοτοδινιᾶν	233			
σπέρμα	184, 218		φιλανθρωπία	253
σπλάγχνα	289		φιλάνθρωπος	253, 297
σπουδαῖος	241		φιλάρετος	253, 297
στερεός	176		φιλέβδομος	284
στερέωμα	175		φιλήδονος	373, 377
στοιχεῖον	181, 294		φιλόθεος	104
στοχαστής	189		φιλόκαλος	253, 297
συγγένεια	241, 342, 344		φιλοσοφία	200, 297
συγγενής	380		φρόνησις μέση	363, 367–68
σύγγραμμα	5, 391		φύσις	199, 218, 268
συμβολικῶς	366		φωστήρ	15, 205
συμπάθεια	285, 288		φωσφορεῖν	197
συμπεριπολέω	230			
συμπληρόω	128		χαλινόω	339
συνειδός	298		χάος	165
συνεκτικώτατος	114, 275		χαραχθείς	401
σύνεσις	365		χερσαῖος	215, 346
συνέχω	316		χορεία	201
σύνθετος	326		χρόνος	371
σύνταξις	5			
συντέλεια	306		ὁ ὤν	119
σφραγίς	139, 322–23			

www.ingramcontent.com/pod-product-compliance
Lightning Source LLC
Chambersburg PA
CBHW031701230426
43668CB00006B/69